ENCYCLOPEDIA *of* PERCUSSION

Garland Reference Library of the Humanities
(Vol. 947)

ENCYCLOPEDIA *of*
PERCUSSION

Edited by John H. Beck

Garland Publishing, Inc.
New York & London / 1995

Library of Congress Cataloging-in-Publication Data

Encyclopedia of percussion/ edited by John H. Beck.
p. cm.—(Garland Reference Library of the Humanities; vol. 947)
Includes bibliographical references and index.
ISBN 0-8240-4788-5 ISBN 0-8153-2894-X (Pbk.)
1. Percussion instruments—Dictionaries. I. Beck, John, 1933– . II. Series.
ML102.P4E5 1995
786.8'19'03—dc20 93-48846

Printed on acid-free, 250-year-life paper

Manufactured in the United States of America

Contents

Preface

The *Encyclopedia of Percussion* is an extensive guide to percussion, organized for research as well as general knowledge. This book is intended for those interested in percussion as it is defined in the Western tradition, but as much as space permits, it reaches out to the world at large. Focusing on idiophones and membranophones, it covers in detail the instruments of the standard orchestral battery. These include not only instruments whose usual sound is produced *percussively* (like snare drums and triangles), but those whose usual sound is produced *concussively* (like castanets and claves) or by *friction* (like the *cuíca* and the lion's roar). Because Western percussionists are often called upon to supply sound effects, it also covers relevant aerophones and chordophones.

The expertise of the contributors has been used to produce a wide-ranging list of percussion topics. The volume includes: (1) an alphabetical listing of percussion instruments and terms from various cultures of the world; (2) an extensive section of illustrations of percussion instruments; (3) twenty-eight articles covering topics from Basel drumming to the xylophone; (4) a list of symbols and a section on the range of mallet instruments; (5) a table of percussion instruments and terms in English, French, German, and Italian; and (6) a section of published writings on methods for percussion. This encyclopedia is, we hope, the most definitive source of percussion information available.

The bulk of the alphabetical listing was compiled by five contributors: Keith A. Aleo, John R. Beck, David Hagedorn, Elizabeth Hardcastle Radock, and Andrew Spencer. The authors were asked to provide definitions of relevant terms beginning with the letters of the alphabet assigned to them, taking into account the information available in several main sources: *Handbook of Percussion Instruments,* by Karl Peinkofer and Fritz Tannigel (Mainz: B. Schott's Söhne, 1969; English translation, London: Schott, 1976); *Musical Instruments: A Comprehensive Dictionary,* by Sibyl Marcuse (New York: Norton, 1975); *The Percussionist's Dictionary*, by Joseph Adato and George Judy (Melville, N.Y.: Belwin-Mills Publishing, 1984); *The World of Percussion,* by Emil Richards (Sherman Oaks, Calif.: Gwyn Publishing, 1972); and *The Dictionary of Percussion Terms As Found in the Symphonic Repertoire,* by Morris Arnold Lang and Larry Spivack (New York: Lang Percussion Co., 1977; revised editions, 1978 and 1988). Other bibliographic sources are listed in the articles. Transliterations are used for non-Western entries, such as terms in Arabic, Chinese, Sanskrit, etc.

Because of its uniqueness, *The Dictionary of Percussion Terms As Found in the Symphonic Repertoire* has been incorporated, with modifications and corrections, into the first section of the encyclopedia. Its "Symbols" and "Range of Mallet Instruments" sections comprise Appendix A of the present book. *The Dictionary* is used by permission of the authors.

Appendix B is an alphabetized list of percussion instruments and terms in English, French, German, and Italian. Its purpose is to provide an aid in identifying the most frequently used percussion instruments and terms in four of the major Western languages. Appendix C is a compilation of historically important books on percussion methods, many of which are out of print.

The illustrations section was organized by the editor with photographs taken by Laurie Beck Tarver. In putting together this section it was my intent to cover a wide spectrum of percussion instruments, ranging from the standard orchestral ones to the most unusual ethnic instruments or sound effects. To photograph all percussion instruments that are known worldwide would be a lifelong task and would cover many volumes. This representative overview, along with those photographs contained within the articles themselves, will give the reader an expanded visual image of percussion instruments. For more photographs, the reader can refer to the aforementioned research sources.

For the articles, contributors were asked to base them on their own expertise, with the aim that their essays would be used for research and general knowledge and should therefore include all pertinent information on the subject. Since they are authorities in their fields, the content of their sections was not changed; as a result, there are some differences in writing styles and in length from one article to another.

I acknowledge with gratitude all those who contributed to the *Encyclopedia of Percussion,* for without them my task would have been impossible. I am also extremely grateful to Garland Publishing for giving me the opportunity to be the book's editor. It is my hope that this work will become a viable source from which percussionists, scholars, and the general public may derive valuable information.

John H. Beck
Professor of Percussion
Eastman School of Music
November 1993

Contributors

Keith A. Aleo
Percussionist
Fort Lauderdale, Florida
Alphabetical Listing of Percussion Instruments and Terms (L, M)

John H. Beck
Professor of Percussion
Eastman School of Music
Rochester, New York
Percussion Ensembles

John R. Beck
Percussionist
Washington, D.C.
Alphabetical Listing of Percussion Instruments and Terms (D–K)

Edmund A. Bowles
Falls Church, Virginia
The Kettledrum

Robert B. Breithaupt
Professor of Percussion
Capital University
Grove City, Ohio
The Drum Set: A History; Drum Set Players; Vibraphone Players

William L. Cahn
Holcomb, New York
The Xylophone

George Carroll
Street, Maryland
The Rope-Tensioned Drum in America

Gary Cook
Professor of Percussion
University of Arizona at Tucson
Calfskin Heads: Their History and Manufacture

Leonard DiMuzio
Director of Artist Relations and Education
Avedis Zildjian Cymbal Company
Norwell, Massachusetts
Cymbals

Fred Fairchild
Professor of Percussion
University of Illinois
Urbana, Illinois
The Percussive Arts Society: An Historical Perspective

Eric A. Galm
Consultant—Brazilian music
Boston, Massachusetts
Brazil: Percussion Instruments

John K. Galm
Professor of Percussion and Music History
University of Colorado at Boulder
Brazil: Percussion Instruments

Norbert Goldberg
Latin Percussion Specialist
New York, New York
Latin-American Percussion; Latin Percussionists

Alfons Grieder
Munchenstein, Switzerland
The Basel Drum

David Hagedorn
Professor of Percussion
University of Wisconsin at Superior
Duluth, Wisconsin
Alphabetical Listing of Percussion Instruments and Terms (P)

Laurence D. Kaptain
Professor of Percussion
University of Missouri at Kansas City
The Marimba in Mexico and Related Areas

Lloyd S. McCausland
Vice President
Remo, Inc.
North Hollywood, California
The Plastic Drumhead: Its History and Development

Harrison Powley
Professor of Music
Brigham Young University
Provo, Utah
Janissary Music (Turkish Music)

Elizabeth Hardcastle Radock
Disney World Enterprises
Orlando, Florida
Alphabetical Listing of Percussion Instruments and Terms (Q–Z)

Michael Rosen
Professor of Percussion
Oberlin Conservatory of Music
Oberlin, Ohio
The Tambourin Provençal

Steven Schick
Professor of Percussion
University of California at San Diego
Multiple Percussion

Andrew Spencer
Director of Percussion Studies
Central Washington University
Ellenberg, Washington
Alphabetical Listing of Percussion Instruments and Terms (A, B, C, N, O, Q, R); The Bass Drum; Castanets; The Snare Drum; The Tambourine; The Triangle

James Strain
Professor of Percussion
Kansas State University
Manhattan, Kansas
Published Writings on Methods for Percussion

Jeffrey Thomas
Percussionist/Ethnomusicologist
Chicago, Illinois
Steel Band/Pan

Hal Trommer (deceased)
The Vibraphone, Vibraharp, and Vibes

Michael W. Udow
Professor of Percussion
University of Michigan
Ann Arbor, Michigan
Percussion and Dance

Norman Weinberg
Professor of Percussion
Del Mar College
Corpus Christi, Texas
Electronic Percussion

Amy White
Percussionist
Lake Jackson, Texas
Table of Percussion Instruments and Terms in English, French, German, and Italian

ILLUSTRATIONS OF PERCUSSION INSTRUMENTS

Laurie Beck Tarver
Photographer
Philadelphia, Pennsylvania

ASSISTANT EDITOR AND PROOFREADER

Eileen M. Mance
Rochester, New York

Abbreviations

c.	circa
comp.	compiled, compiler
ed.	edited, edition, editor
Eng	English
enl.	enlarged
Fr	French
Ger	German
Hung	Hungarian
illus.	illustration
It	Italian
L	Morris Arnold Lang and Larry Spivack. *The Dictionary of Percussion Terms As Found in the Symphonic Repertoire.* New York: Lang Percussion Co., 1977.
Lat	Latin
L/JG	*The Dictionary of Percussion Terms.* Rev. ed. with corrections by John Galm. New York: Lang Percussion Co., 1978.
L/WM	*The Dictionary of Percussion Terms.* Rev. ed. with additions by William Moersch. New York: Lang Percussion Co., 1988.
OE	Old English
Pol	Polish
Port	Portuguese
rev.	revised
rev. ed.	revised edition
Russ	Russian
Sp	Spanish

I.
Alphabetical Listing of Percussion Instruments and Terms

Alphabetical Listing of Percussion Instruments and Terms

Entries are alphabetized letter-by-letter, ignoring diacriticals. The abbreviation immediately following an entry (e.g., "Fr") indicates the language of the term if not English; (L) at the end of an entry refers to Morris Lang and Larry Spivack's *Dictionary of Percussion.* (See p. xi for a complete list of abbreviations.) Cross-references appear in boldface. The pitch system used has "c^1" as middle C; "c" is one octave below; and "c^2" an octave above (written pitch).

A BAMBAGIA (It), padded.

ABDÄMPFEN (Ger), dampen, mute.

ABWECHSELND (Ger), changeable, alternating.

ACCIAIO (It), steel.

ACCORDATO (It), tuned (to).

ACCORDÉ (Fr), tuned (to).

ACME SIREN WHISTLE, *see* **siren whistle.**

ACUTO (It), sharp, high, piercing.

À DEMI (Fr), at the middle.

À DEUX or À 2 (Fr), two (cymbals, crash cymbals). For example, in performances of Béla Bartók's *Music for Strings, Percussion and Celesta* (1936) by the New York Philharmonic, a pair of crash cymbals is held with the plates flat by one player and rolled on, with soft mallets, by a second. *A due* or *a 2* in Italian, *zu 2* in German. *See also* **frottez.** (L)

A.D.GR.TR. BEFESTIGT (Ger), abbrev. for *an der grossen Trommel befestigt.* (L)

A DUE or A 2 (It), *see* **à deux.**

ADUFE, Brazilian frame drum.

ADUFO, *see* **cuíca.**

AEOLIAN BELLS, small bells that are hung outside and strike one another when agitated by the wind. *See also* **wind chimes.**

AEOLIAN CRYSTALLOPHONE, glass wind chimes.

AEOLINE (Fr), wind machine.

AEOLOPHON (Ger), *see* **wind machine.** (L)

AEROPHONE, instrument whose tone is created by causing air to vibrate, e.g., the bull-roarer and bird whistle.

A FILO (Sp), at the edge.

AFOCHÊ, serrated Brazilian rattle. *See also* **cabasa.**

AFOXÊ, Brazilian instrument about 5 inches in diameter and consisting of a coconut shell with about 50 indented ridges. Sometimes called a *cabaça. See also* **afuxé**; "Brazil: Percussion Instruments," p. 153.

AFRICAN CLAY BONGOS, single-headed laced Moroccan drums that have clay shells and are played with the fingers.

AFRICAN GOBLET DRUM, *see* **talking drum.**

AFRICAN GOURD SISTRUM, instrument made from the forked section of a tree branch, one part with ten to fifteen disks strung on it, the other serving as a handle. *See also* **wasamba rattle.**

AFRICAN MARIMBA, an instrument from central Africa with sixteen bars suspended over gourd resonators. The resonators have small holes that are covered with vellum, which creates a buzzing sound when the bar is struck. Generally played from a sitting position.

AFRICAN RHYTHM WOOD BELL, central African instrument fashioned in the shape of a bell but with no sustaining tone. Jingles in the mouth of the instrument rattle when the bell is struck with a mallet.

AFRICAN SLIT DRUM, *see* **log drum.**

AFRICAN TALKING DRUM, *see* **talking drum.**

AFRICAN THUMB PIANO, *see* **mbira.**

AFRICAN TREE DRUM, *see* **log drum.**

AFRICAN XYLOPHONE, higher-pitched version of the African marimba.

AFRIKANISCHE HARFE (Ger), marimbula. (L)

AFRIKANISCHE SCHLITZTROMMEL (Ger), log drum. (L)

AFRO-BRAZILIAN DRUM, drum made from a hollowed tree trunk and covered with an animal skin head.

AFRO-BRAZILIAN METAL BELL, metal bell with a conical shape. Generally struck with a stick.

AFRO-BRAZILIAN MUSICAL BOW, wooden rod strung with a wire or gut cord and rubbed with a piece of wood or bone. *See also* **berimbau.**

AFUCHE, a cabasa-like instrument with metal beads strung around a textured metal cylinder. *See* Illus. 34, p. 133.

AFUXÉ, rattle like a cabasa but made from a coconut instead of a gourd. *See also* **afoxê.** (L/JG)

AGBE, African name for shekere.

AGITARE (It), shake, rub.

AGITÉ(E) (Fr), shaken, rubbed.

AGITÉES (L'UNE CONTRE L'AUTRE) (Fr), rubbed (one against the other, for cymbals).

AGITER, AGITEZ (Fr), shake, rub.

AGOGÔ, Afro-Brazilian double bell attached to a "u-shaped" metal rod. The bells are conical in shape, with an opening 2½ to 3 inches long and 1½ to 1¾ inches wide. Also called *ngonge*. *See also* "Brazil: Percussion Instruments," p. 153; Illus. 34, p. 133.

AGUDO (Sp), high.

AGUNG, bossed gong of the Philippines.

AHOGAR (Sp), dampen.

AIGU (Fr), high.

AIR-RAID SIREN, a rotating disk with a number of holes that interrupt the flow of air, thus creating ascending and descending glissandi. The disk is rotated electrically or by hand crank. Examples of its use may be found in Edgard Varèse's *Ionisation* (1931).

AIS (Ger), A-sharp.

À LA JANTE (Fr), on the rim.

ALARM BELL, fire alarm bell or ship's bell cast from heavy bronze. A leather strap pulls the clapper against the inner wall of the bell. Occasionally used in opera scenes, such as Giuseppe Verdi's *Don Carlos* (1867) and Modest Mussorgsky's *Boris Godounov* (1874, revolution scene).

ALARMGLOCKE (Ger), alarm bell.

ALBERO DI SONAGLI (It), bell tree, Turkish crescent.

AL CENTRO (It), at the center.

AL CERCHIO (It), on the hoop.

ALDABA (Sp), clapper.

ALIMBA, xylophone of Zaire. *See also* "The Xylophone," p. 347.

ALINDI, *see* **lukimbi**.

ALLA CAMPANA (It), on the dome or bell (of a cymbal).

ALLA META (It), at the middle or center.

ALLE (Ger), all.

ALLEIN (Ger), alone.

ALL'ESTREMITÀ (It), at the edge, rim.

ALL'ORDINARIO (It), in the usual manner, bells down.

AL MARGINE (It), at the rim, at the edge.

ALMGLOCKEN (Ger), pitched cowbells, Alpine herd bells. Generally of pot-bellied construction, these metal bells can be arranged from lowest to highest pitch to produce a range of two to two-and-a-half octaves. Uses in the orchestral literature include Gustav Mahler's Symphony No. 6 (1904), Anton Webern's *Five Pieces for Orchestra* (1913), and Olivier Messiaen's *Sept Haïkaï* (1963) and *Couleurs de la cité céleste* (1964). *See also* Illus. 18, p. 125.

À L'ORDINAIRE (Fr), as usually played, clashed.

ALPINE HERD BELLS, less common term for Almglocken.

ALTA (Sp), high.

ALTEZZA (It, Sp), pitch.

ALTO (It), high.

ALTO METALLOPHONE, bar percussion instrument developed for Carl Orff's *Schulwerk* (a music education system for the young). The bars can be lifted off the frame, making it possible to exchange notes and create different scales and combinations of notes. Even though this instrument was designed for music education, the quality of its sound is high enough to meet the demands of regular orchestra playing. The range is middle c up one octave and a half to a^2; it sounds as written and is struck with large hard felt beaters or mallets.

ALTO-SOPRANO METALLOPHONE, combination of the alto and soprano metallophone.

ALTO-SOPRANO XYLOPHONE, combination of alto and soprano xylophone.

ALTO XYLOPHONE, xylophone with a range of c^1 to a^2, sounding as written and played with small hard-felt sticks.

ALUMINOPHONE, keyboard percussion instrument with bars made from aluminum. It was popular as a substitute for the xylophone in early recordings.

ALUMINOPHONE DE EMILIO, three-octave micro-tonal instrument constructed by Emil Richards. The bars are made from cut metal conduit pipe. The bottom, middle, and upper octaves have thirty-nine, thirty-five, and twenty-nine tones respectively.

AMALÉ, name for ganzá in Bahia, Brazil.

AMBIRA, Ethiopian xylophone. Also called *mbila*. *See also* "The Xylophone," p. 347.

AMBOSS (Ger), anvil.

AMERICAN INDIAN TOM-TOM, general term used to describe single- and double-headed drums made from a hollowed log by Native Americans. While authentic Indian tom-toms are hard to come by, some instrument manufacturers are producing replicas of those. Used in Carlos Chávez's *Sinfonia India* (1935), Silvestre Revueltas's *Sensemayá* (1938), and Elliott Carter's *Pocahontas* (1939). *See* Illus. 38, p. 137.

AMPLIFIED VIBRAPHONE, vibraphone that is electronically enhanced by microphones or pickups placed on the individual bars. The signal can then be manipulated much like any other electrical instrument.

AM RAND (Ger), at the edge.

AM RANDE DER MEMBRANE (Ger), at the edge of the head, edge (rim).

AM RANDE DES FELLES (Ger), at the edge (rim) of the head; used in Béla Bartók's *Music for Strings, Percussion and Celesta* (1936). (L)

ANCIENT CYMBALS, hand bells without pitch. *See also* **crotales.**

ANDEAN JINGLE RATTLE, rattle from hollowed dried fruit that is filled with pebbles or dried seeds.

ANDERES BECKEN NEHMEN (Ger), take the other cymbal.

AN DER GROSSEN TROMMEL BEFESTIGT (Ger), mounted on the bass drum.

ANFANGSGRÜNDE (Ger), rudiments of snare drumming.

ANGEBUNDEN (Ger), dampened, fixed.

ANGEDEUTET (Ger), indefinite.

ANGELEGT (Ger), put on, laid on.

ANGKLUNG, bamboo instrument of Bali and Java consisting of cut bamboo tubes that are tuned in octaves. These tubes (usually two) are attached to a frame that allows them to be shaken, thus producing a pitched rattling sound. The range of the various anklungs can cover two octaves. Orchestral examples include Carl Orff's *Catulli carmina* (1943), *Weihnachtsspiel* (1960), and *Prometheus* (1968).

ANIMAL BELLS, single or multiple bells strung around the neck of an animal. Depending on the region, these bells may be made from various metals or plant life such as dried fruit husks or wood. *See also* **Alpine herd bells; cowbell; elephant bells.**

ANKLE BEADS, rattle worn by dancers around their ankles.

ANKLE BELLS, metal rattle worn by dancers around their ankles.

ANSCHLAGSTELLEN (Ger), beating spots.

ANTELOPE HORN RATTLE, rattle made by placing dried seeds in an antelope horn.

ANTIKES BECKEN (Ger), antique cymbal, crotale.

ANTIQUE CYMBALS, *see* **crotales.**

ANVIL, an actual anvil on occasion, but usually metal blocks or plates. The resulting sound of any device used for these parts must have a metallic ring and contain a predominance of high partials. Scoring for anvil may be found in Giuseppe Verdi's *Il Trovatore* (1853) and Richard Wagner's *Das Rheingold* (1869).

ANZAHL (Ger), number, variety.

ÄOLSGLOCKEN (Ger), aeolian bells.

À PEINE FRÔLÉ (Fr), barely touching.

À PEINE SENSIBLE (Fr), barely audible.

APITO DE SAMBA, Brazilian whistle originally made of wood but now of metal. *See also* "Brazil: Percussion Instruments," p. 153.

APORO, Congolese double bell constructed of sheet metal. The bells have no clappers and are hit with a wooden beater.

APPENA TOCCATA (It), barely touching.

ARABIAN HAND DRUM, handheld drum shaped like a goblet. *See also* **darabucca.**

ARABIAN TABLAS, small bowl-shaped drums that are throng-tensioned, with leather heads and indefinite pitch. *Timbales orientale* in French, *timpani orientali* in Italian.

ARABISCHE TROMMEL (Ger), Arabian hand drum. *See also* **darabucca.**

ARCHED TREE CHIMES, suspended brass tubes of different lengths. When suspended in a row, they create an arch with their bottom edges.

ARCHET (Fr), bow.

ARCHET DE CONTREBASS (Fr), bass bow.

ARCO (It), bow, play with a bow.

ARENAIUOLO (It), sandbox, maracas. (L)

ARMONICA, *see* **glass harmonica.**

ARMONICA DI VETRO (It), glass harmonica.

ARPA AFRICANA (It), marimbula.

ARPILENGO (It), xylophone.

ARRÊTER (Fr), stop.

ARRÊTER LE ROULEMENT (Fr), stop rolling; used, for example, in Pierre Boulez's *Pli selon pli* (1962). (L)

ARTILLERY SHELL GONG, device based on the long, sustained tone of an empty artillery shell, which was discovered by Emil Richards and Harry Partch. It sounds best when struck with a soft mallet.

AS (Ger), A-flat.

ASSEZ DUR (Fr), medium hard.

ASSEZ MOLLE (Fr), medium soft.

ASTA (It), rod, pole.

ATABAL (Sp), kettledrum.

ATABALOO (Sp), kettledrum. (L)

ATABAL TURQUÉS, Spanish term for Turkish drum.

ATABAQUE, Brazilian one-headed barrel-shaped drum that comes in three sizes, the largest being the *rum*, the middle being the *rompi*, and the *le* being the smallest. *See also* "Brazil: Percussion Instruments," p. 153.

ATABOR (Sp), tambourin provençal.

ATARIGANE, small Japanese bronze bell gong that is struck with a horn hammer on the inner rim; it is about 4 inches in diameter with a 1-inch flange. (L/WM)

ATRANATRA (ATRANATRANA), xylophone from southeastern Madagascar. *See also* "The Xylophone," p. 347.

ATUMPAN, West African drum, drum ensemble.

AU BORD (Fr), at the edge.

AU BORD DE LA MEMBRANE (Fr), at the edge of the head.

AU BORD DE LA PEAU (Fr), at the edge of the drumhead; used in Béla Bartók's *Music for Strings, Percussion and Celesta* (1936). (L)

AU CENTRE (Fr), at the center.

AUDUBON, bird call made from birchwood and metal. The metal sleeve is twisted around a metal cone, and the resulting friction produces chirps and squeaks.

AUF BEIDEN FELLEN (Ger), on both heads, sides.

AUF DAS FELL MIT DÜNNEN RUTEN (Ger), on the skin with thin sticks.

AUF DEM FELL (Ger), on the skin.

AUF DEM HOLZ GESCHLAGEN (Ger), struck on the wood.

AUF DEM HOLZRAND DES TROMMELS (Ger), on the shell (frame) of the drum.

AUF DEM RAND (Ger), on the rim.

AUF DEM REIFEN (Ger), on the hoop.

AUF DEN SAITEN (Ger), on the snares.

AUF DER KUPPEL (Ger), on the bell or cup (of a cymbal).

AUF DER MITTE (Ger), at the center.

AUF DER SEITE GEDREHT (Ger), laid on its side.

AUFGEHÄNGT (Ger), suspended.

AUFSCHLAGIDIOPHON (Ger), percussion idiophone.

AUFSCHLAGPLATTE (Ger), percussion plate.

AUFSTELLUNG DER 4 PAUKEN (Ger), set up four timpani.

AUFTAKT (Ger), upbeat.

AU MILIEU (Fr), in the center (of a drum), on the bell (of a cymbal).

AU MILIEU SUR LA PROTUBÉRANCE (Fr), on the bell (of a cymbal).

A UNA PELLE (It), single-headed.

À UNE PEAU (Fr), single-headed.

AU REBORD (Fr), on the hoop.

AUS FILZ (Ger), made of felt.

AUS GUMMI (Ger), made of rubber.

AUS HOLZ (Ger), made of wood.

AUS KAPOK (Ger), made of kapok.

AUS ROHR (Ger), made of cane.

AUS SCHWAMM (Ger), made of sponge.

AUSTÖNEN (Ger), let ring.

AUTO BRAKE DRUMS, *see* **brake drums**.

AUTO HORN, horn played by squeezing a bulb at one end, which forces air through a reed in the instrument, producing a honking sound. Used in George Gershwin's *An American in Paris* (1928). Also known as a *bulb horn, motor horn, taxi horn. See also* Illus. 33, p. 132. (L)

AUTOHUPE (Ger), auto horn, taxi horn.

AVANADDHA, general term for drums from India.

AVEC (Fr), with.

AVEC CORDES (Fr), with snares, snares on.

AVEC DEUX BAGUETTES SUR UNE CYMBALE (Fr), with the two sticks on a cymbal.

AVEC DEUX MAINS (Fr), with both hands.

AVEC LE BOIS (Fr), with the wood.

AVEC LE POUCE (Fr), with the thumb, thumb roll.

AVEC LES CORDES LÂCHES (Fr), with the snares loosened.

AVEC LES DOIGTS (Fr), with the fingers.

AVEC LES JOINTURES (Fr), with the knuckles.

AVEC LES MAINS (Fr), with the hands.

AVEC LES ONGLES (Fr), with the fingernails.

AVEC TIMBRES (Fr), with snares.

AVVOLTA, wound or covered (with).

AVVOLTA DI LANA (It), wound with wool.

AVVOLTA IN PELE (It), covered with leather.

AXATSE, rattle from Ghana, made from a dried calabash gourd covered with a web of beads. It is played by shaking and striking with the palm of the hand.

AYACAXTLI, Latin-American gourd rattle.

AZTEC MARACAS, metal diamond-shaped maracas from Mexico.

BABYLONIAN DRUM, very large pitched drum created for Benjamin Britten's *The Burning Fiery Furnace* (1966) (tuned to a D below the bass staff). (L)

BABY'S CRY, whistle that produces a sound like an infant's cry.

BABY'S RATTLE, toy rattle that produces a maraca-like or a jingling bell sound.

BACCHETTA(E) (It), stick(s).

BACCHETTA(E) A BAMBAGIA (It), padded stick(s).

BACCHETTA(E) A DUE CAPI (It), two-headed stick(s) (double stick[s]).

BACCHETTA(E) D'ACCIAIO (It), steel stick(s).

BACCHETTA(E) DI CANNA (It), rattan stick(s).

BACCHETTA(E) DI CAPOC (It), stick(s) with fiber head (knob).

BACCHETTA(E) DI FELTRO (It), felt stick(s), soft felt stick(s).

BACCHETTA(E) DI FELTRO DURO (It), hard felt stick(s).

BACCHETTA(E) DI FERRO (It), iron stick(s), hard leather stick(s).

BACCHETTA(E) DI GOMMA-ELASTICA (It), rubber (covered) stick(s).

BACCHETTA(E) DI GRAN CASSA (It), bass drum beaters.

BACCHETTA(E) DI LANA (It), wool-headed stick(s).

BACCHETTA(E) DI LEGNO (It), wood(en) stick(s).

BACCHETTA(E) DI METALLO (It), metal stick(s).

BACCHETTA(E) DI PELLE (It), leather stick(s).

BACCHETTA(E) DI PELLE CRUDA (It), rawhide stick(s).

BACCHETTA(E) DI SPUGNA (It), sponge-covered stick(s).

BACCHETTA(E) DI TAMBURO (It), drumstick(s).

BACCHETTA(E) DI TAMBURO MILITARE (It), snare drumstick(s).

BACCHETTA(E) DI TIMPANI (It), timpani stick(s).

BACCHETTA(E) DI TIMPANI A FELTRO (It), felt timpani stick(s).

BACCHETTA(E) DI TIMPANI A LEGNO (It), wooden timpani stick(s).

BACCHETTA(E) DI TIMPANI A PELLA CRUDA (It), rawhide timpani stick(s).

BACCHETTA(E) DI TIMPANI A SPUGNA (It), sponge timpani stick(s).

BACCHETTA(E) DI TIMPANI CON PALLADINE DI FELTRO DURO (It), hard felt timpani mallet(s).

BACCHETTA(E) DI TIMPANI MOLLE (It), soft timpani mallet(s).

BACCHETTA(E) DI TIMPANI MOLLE A FELTRO (It), soft felt timpani stick(s).

BACCHETTA(E) DI TIMPANI MOLTO MOLLE (It), very soft timpani stick(s).

BACCHETTA(E) DI TRIANGOLO (It), triangle beater(s).

BACCHETTA(E) DI XILOFONO (It), xylophone stick(s).

BACCHETTA(E) DURA(E) (It), hard stick(s).

BACCHETTA(E) FELPATA(E) (It), plush stick(s).

BACCHETTA(E) GROSSA(E) (It), thick stick(s).

BACCHETTA(E) LEGGIERA(E) (It), light stick(s).

BACCHETTA(E) MEDIA(E)-DURA(E) (It), medium hard stick(s).

BACCHETTA(E) MOLLE (It), soft stick(s).

BACCHETTA(E) MOLTO DURA(E) (It), very hard stick(s).

BACCHETTA(E) MORBIDE(A) (MOLLE) (It), soft stick(s).

BACCHETTA(E) ORDINARIA(E) (It), ordinary beater(s).

BACCHETTA(E) SOTTILE (It), thin stick(s).

BACCHETTE DI VETRO SOSPESE (It), glass wind chimes.

BACH. (It), abbrev. for *bacchetta.* (L)

BAG. (Fr), abbrev. for *baguette.* (L)

BAG. EP. (Fr), abbrev. for *baguette d'éponge.* (L)

BAGUETTE(S) (Fr), stick(s).

BAGUETTE(S) ASSEZ DURE(S) (Fr), medium hard stick(s).

BAGUETTE(S) D'ACIER (Fr), steel stick(s).

BAGUETTE(S) DE CAISSE CLAIRE (Fr), snare drumstick(s).

BAGUETTE(S) DE CUIR DUR (Fr), hard leather stick(s).

BAGUETTE(S) DE (EN) BOIS (Fr), wooden stick(s).

BAGUETTE(S) D'ÉPONGE (Fr), sponge-covered stick(s).

BAGUETTE(S) DE PELUCHE (Fr), plush stick(s).

BAGUETTE(S) DE TAMBOUR (Fr), drumstick(s).

BAGUETTE(S) DE TIMBALES (Fr), timpani stick(s).

BAGUETTE(S) DE TIMBALES DOUCE(S) (Fr), soft timpani stick(s).

BAGUETTE(S) DE TIMBALES EN BOIS (Fr), wooden timpani stick(s).

BAGUETTE(S) DE TIMBALES EN FEUTRE (Fr), felt timpani stick(s).

BAGUETTE(S) DE TIMBALES EN FEUTRE DOUCE(S) (Fr), soft felt timpani stick(s).

BAGUETTE(S) DE TIMBALES EN PEAU (Fr), rawhide timpani stick(s).

BAGUETTE(S) DE TIMBALES ÉPAISSE(S) (Fr), thick timpani stick(s).

BAGUETTE(S) DE TIMBALES TÊTE EN FEUTRE DUR (Fr), hard-felt timpani mallet(s).

BAGUETTE(S) DE TIMBALES TRÈS DOUCE(S) (Fr), very soft timpani stick(s).

BAGUETTE(S) DE TIMBALES TRÈS DURE(S) (Fr), very hard timpani stick(s).

BAGUETTE(S) DE TRIANGLE (Fr), triangle beater(s).

BAGUETTE(S) DE VERRE SUSPENDUE(S) (Fr), glass wind chime(s).

BAGUETTE(S) DE VIBRAPHONE (Fr), vibraphone mallet(s).

BAGUETTE(S) DE XYLOPHONE (Fr), xylophone stick(s).

BAGUETTE(S) DOUCE(S) (Fr), soft stick(s).

BAGUETTE(S) DURE(S) (Fr), hard stick(s).

BAGUETTE(S) EN CAOUTCHOUC (Fr), rubber (covered) stick(s).

BAGUETTE(S) EN CAPOC (Fr), stick(s) with fiber heads (knobs).

BAGUETTE(S) EN CUIR (Fr), leather stick(s).

BAGUETTE(S) EN (DE) METAL (Fr), metal stick(s).

BAGUETTE(S) EN ÉPONGE (Fr), sponge-covered stick(s).

BAGUETTE(S) EN FER (Fr), iron stick(s).

BAGUETTE(S) EN FEUTRE (Fr), felt stick(s).

BAGUETTE(S) EN FEUTRE DUR (Fr), hard felt stick(s).

BAGUETTE(S) EN LAINE (Fr), wool-headed stick(s).

BAGUETTE(S) EN PEAU (CUIR BRUT) (Fr), rawhide stick(s).

BAGUETTE(S) EN ROTIN (Fr), rattan stick(s).

BAGUETTE(S) ENTRECHOQUÉE(S) (Fr), concussion stick(s).

BAGUETTE(S) ÉPAISSE(S) (Fr), thick stick(s).

BAGUETTE(S) LÉGÈRE(S) (Fr), light stick(s).

BAGUETTE(S) MINCE(S) (Fr), thin stick(s).

BAGUETTE(S) MINCE(S) EN BOIS (Fr), thin wood stick(s).

BAGUETTE(S) NORMALE(S) (Fr), ordinary beater(s).

BAGUETTE(S) NORMALEMENT TENUE AU CENTRE DE LA PEAU (Fr), struck in the center of the head with the stick(s) held in the usual manner; used in Pierre Boulez's *Pli selon pli* (1962). (L)

BAGUETTE(S) ORDINAIRE(S), (return to) ordinary (regular) stick(s).

BAGUETTE(S) OUATEUSE(S) (Fr), padded stick(s).

BAGUETTE(S) (MAILLOCHE[S]) SUR CYMBALE(S) (Fr), stick(s) on cymbal(s).

BAGUETTE(S) TRÈS DURE(S) (Fr), very hard stick(s).

BAJIDOR, *see* **jedor**.

BAJO (Sp), low.

BAK, Korean wooden instrument consisting of six small hardwood bars (about 13½ inches by 2¼ inches) strung together at one end by a cord passing through two small holes. The instrument produces a very loud, fast series of claps by first fanning out the bars and then quickly pushing them together.

BALA, name in Mali and Guinea for xylophone.

BALAFO, BALAFON, West African xylophone that produces a buzzing sound. *See also* "The Xylophone," p. 347.

BALAI (Fr), wire brush.

BALAI MÉTALLIQUE (Fr), wire brush.

BAL. MÉTALL. (Fr), abbrev. for *balai métallique.* (L)

BAMBOLA, *see* **bamboula.**

BAMBOO BRUSH, brush made of split bamboo approximately two feet in length. Generally used to strike the bass drumhead and shell. *See also* **switch**.

BAMBOO CLAPPER, instruments often used as claves. However, the bamboo does not produce the penetrating sound of the rosewood claves and in general has a less-focused sound.

BAMBOO RATTLE, *see* **angklung**.

BAMBOO SCRAPER, bamboo güiro.

BAMBOO SHAKER, *see* **Brazilian bamboo shaker**.

BAMBOO SLIT LOGS, ancestor of the tubular woodblock and made from a section of bamboo that is closed at both ends and has a horizontal slit cut into the side. A handle at one end serves as another striking surface when the instrument is placed on the ground.

BAMBOO STRIPS, strips made from 20-inch lengths of bamboo bound together, or a single 16-inch piece of bamboo that is split into ten or twelve tongues for 12 inches of its length. The strips are struck against the shell of a bass drum or a thin wooden box. Orchestral examples include Gustav Mahler's Symphonies No. 2

(1895), No. 3 (1896), and No. 6 (1904), Richard Strauss's *Elektra* (1909), Edgard Varèse's *Intégrales* (1925), and Alban Berg's *Wozzeck* (1925) and *Lulu* (1937). *See also* **switch.**

BAMBOO TUBE, bamboo güiro.

BAMBOO WIND CHIMES, lengths of bamboo suspended in the air next to one another. Often used in twentieth-century compositions. Also known as *Japanese* or *wooden wind chimes.*

BAMBOU BRÉSILIEN (Fr), Brazilian bamboo shaker.

BAMBOULA, Latin-American hand drum made from a hollowed tree trunk. Also *bambola.*

BAMBOU SUSPENDU (Fr), bamboo wind chimes.

BAMBÙ BRASILIANO (It), Brazilian bamboo shaker.

BAMBÙ SOSPESO (It), suspended bamboo chimes.

BAMBUSRASPEL (Ger), bamboo scraper.

BAMBUSROHRE (Ger), bamboo wind chimes.

BAMBUSTROMMEL (Ger), boobam.

BĀMYĀ, generic name for the deeper of the pair of hand drums from India commonly known as *tablā.* The bāmyā, on the player's left, is played from a sitting position and requires considerable finger dexterity. Its metal shell is roughly hemispherical in shape and has a skin head mounted on it. The head has two pieces of skin that are attached to each other. Near the middle of the head is a circular patch of dark paste, which greatly affects the tuning and timbre of the drum. Further adjustment of the tuning is achieved by the heel of the performer's hand, which alters the pitch by pressing into the head while the fingers strike. *Bānyā* in Bengal; *bạyā* in north and central India. *See also* Illus. 39, p. 137.

BANDA DEI GIANNIZZERI (It), Janissary music.

BANDAIR, *see* **bendīr.**

BANDA TURCA (It), Janissary music.

BANGI, heavy Japanese board gong (about 12 by 18 by 1½ inches) suspended and played with a wooden hammer. (L/WM)

BĀNYĀ, *see* **bāmyā.**

BAQUETA(S) (Port, Sp), drumstick(s).

BARIL DE BOIS (Fr), wooden barrel.

BARIL DE SAKE (Fr), sake (wooden) barrel.

BARILE DI LEGNO (It), wooden barrel.

BARILE DI SAKE (It), sake (wooden) barrel.

BARKING DOG, smaller version of the lion's roar.

BARRA DI SOSPENSIONE CON I SONAGLI (It), bell tree, Turkish crescent. (L)

BARREL, Japanese wooden barrel used to make sake. The top of the barrel is struck with wooden mallets, producing a dark sound. Also known as *sake barrel, wooden barrel.*

BARREL DRUM, any drum having a barrel-like appearance. The diameter at the middle of the shell is greater than the diameter at the ends, and the shape is generally curved.

BARRES D'ACIER TREMPÉ (Fr), bars of tempered steel.

BARRIL (Port), barrel drum.

BASEL DRUM, a descendant of the typical side or snare drum; its name comes from the Swiss city of Basel. It is a rope-tensioned field drum about 16 inches in diameter and 16 inches in depth. *See also* "The Basel Drum," p. 145.

BASEL DRUMMING, drum style of Basel. *See also* "The Basel Drum," p. 145.

BASKETROMMEL (Ger), incorrect use of the term "baskische Trommel"; used in Bruno Maderna's *Quadrivium* (1969). (L)

BASKISCHE TROMMEL (Ger), tambourine, timbrel.

BASLER TROMMEL (Ger), Basel drum, parade drum.

BASS BOOM, largest and lowest-sounding type of bamboo tube used in the pan band. *See also* "The Steel Band/Pan," p. 297.

BASS CHIMES, chimes that extend the low end of a set of chimes.

BASS DE FLANDRES (Fr), bumbass.

BASS DRUM, an orchestral instrument ranging in diameter from 32 to 40 inches, with a shell depth of between 18 and 22 inches. It almost always is double-headed, with either calfskin or synthetic vellums, and it is often mounted on a stand. The bass drum is used to create a low, undefined pitch, and it is played with a wide variety of mallets. It was introduced into the western orchestra via the Turkish Janissary bands of the seventeenth and eighteenth centuries. The toe-operated pedal was invented in 1909 by W.F. Ludwig.

Well-known works that make prominent use of the bass drum include W.A. Mozart's *Die Entführung aus dem Serail* (1782), Gasparo Spontini's Overture to *La Vestale* (1807), Ludwig van Beethoven's Symphony No. 9 (1824), Piotr Ilyich Tchaikovsky's Symphony No. 4 (1878), Gustav Mahler's Symphonies No. 3 (1896) and No. 5 (1902), and Igor Stravinksy's *Le Sacre du printemps* (1913). *Grosse caisse* in French, *grosse Trommel* in German, *gran casa* in Italian, *bombo* in Spanish. *See also* "The Bass Drum," p. 151; "The Rope-Tensioned Drum in America," p. 281; Illus. 4, p. 118.

BASS DRUM PEDAL WITH CYMBAL, commonly used in the trap drums in the first third of the twentieth century. The bass drum pedal has a metal arm attached to its shaft that strikes a cymbal mounted on the drum's rim, so that the bass drum and the cymbal are struck at the same time. Orchestral uses include Darius Milhaud's *Le Création du monde* (1923) and Concerto for Percussion and Small Orchestra (1930). *See also* "The Drum Set: A History," p. 173.

BASS DRUM WITH CYMBAL ATTACHED, concert bass drum with a cymbal attached to the top by means of mounting hardware. The performer is expected to strike the bass drum with one hand while holding a cymbal in the other and crashing it against the mounted cymbal. This arrangement became popular in the Parisian opera orchestras of the nineteenth century. Eventually the two instruments were played by two performers, since the sound of both instruments suffered when played by only a single percussionist. Examples of use in the orchestral literature are Gustav Mahler's Symphony No. 1 (1888) and Igor Stravinsky's *Petrouchka* (1911). *See also* "The Drum Set: A History," p. 173; Illus. 5, p. 119.

BASS MARIMBA, instrument constructed much like the marimba, except that its range extends from C to c^3 for a four-octave instrument. Some instruments extend even further to F below the bass staff. Some one-octave instruments have a range from C to c. Due to the thin bars in the extreme low range, the bass marimba is usually played with very soft mallets. It sounds as written.

BASS METALLOPHONE, same as the alto metallophone, except that the range is from c up an octave and a half to f^1. It sounds as written and is struck with large hard-felt beaters, but the best sound is achieved with rubber-cored beaters wound with wool yarn. *See also* **lujon.**

BASSO (It), deep.

BASS TIMPANI, timpani 30 or more inches.

BASSXYLOPHON (Ger), bass xylophone.

BASS XYLOPHONE, very low-pitched xylophone with a range of c to a[1]. It sounds as written and is played with large hard-felt sticks.

BATA, Nigerian double-headed drum with laced heads and a conical or hourglass shell. This instrument is played with the hands and fingers.

BATÁ DRUM, Cuban drum with two heads. Conical or cylindrical, the drum often has bells attached to one head. Originally used in religious ceremonies. *See also* "Latin-American Percussion," p. 227.

BATÁ-KOTÓ, single-headed Cuban drum.

BATERÍA (Sp), percussion.

BATINTIN (Sp), gong.

BATINTÍN (Sp), nipple gong.

BÂTON FRAPPÉ (Fr), percussion stick.

BÂTON MINCE D'ACIER (Fr), thin metal stick.

BATSU, Japanese metal cymbals.

BATT. (It), abbrev. for *batteria.*

BATTACCHIO (It), clapper.

BATTANT (Fr), clapper.

BATTÉ (Fr), struck.

BATTENTE DI VIBRAFONO (It), vibraphone mallet.

BATTENTE PER IL TRIANGOLO (It), triangle beater.

BATTERE (It), strike.

BATTER HEAD, top head of a drum; the head that is usually struck. (L)

BATTERIA (It), timpani.

BATTERIE (Fr), timpani.

BATTRE (Fr), to strike.

BATTUTE DI TIMPANI (It), timpani sticks.

BATUTTO COLLA MANO (It), strike with the hand.

BAUMWOLLE (Ger), cotton.

BẠYĀ, *see* **bāmyā.**

BCK. (Ger), abbrev. for *Becken.* (L)

B.D., abbrev. for *bass drum.* (L)

BEANBAG, beanbag ashtray that produces a unique percussive sound when the finger strikes the metal cup.

BEAN CAN, any metal shaker with beans inside. *See also* **chocalho.**

BEATEN RATTLES, family of instruments that produce a rattling sound when struck by hand or with a mallet of some kind. This family includes the African gourd sistrum, spurs, pandereta brasileño, quijada (vibraslap), cabasa, anklung, and rattle drum.

BEATERS, *see* **mallets.**

BĘBEN (Polish), drum.

BECHERTROMMEL (Ger), goblet drum.

BECK. (Ger), abbrev. for *Becken.* (L)

BECKEN (Ger), cymbals.

BECKEN (AUF STÄNDER) (Ger), (suspended) cymbal(s).

BECKEN (FREI, FREIHÄNGEND) (Ger), (suspended) cymbal(s).

BECKEN (PAARWEISE) (Ger), crash (clash) cymbals.

BECKEN AN DER GROSSEN TROMMEL BEFESTIGT (Ger), cymbal(s) attached to the bass drum.

BECKEN ANGEBUNDEN (Ger), dampened, muffled cymbal(s); cymbal(s) attached to the bass drum.

BECKEN FREI MIT SCHLÄGEL (Ger), suspended cymbal with stick.

BECKEN GEWÖHNLICH (Ger), clash(ed) cymbal(s).

BECKEN MIT FUSSMASCHINE (Ger), hi-hat.

BECKEN MIT TELLERN (Ger), crash (clash) cymbals.

BECKEN NATÜRLICH (Ger), pair of cymbals. (L)

BECKENSCHLÄGEL (Ger), cymbal sticks.

BECKEN-TAMBOURINE (Ger), tambourine. (L)

BEDECKT (Ger), covered (with), mute on.

BEḌUG, large barrel drum used in the Javanese gamelan.

BEER-CAN MARACAS, metal maracas made from empty beer cans and filled with items including pebbles, buckshot, grain, beans, or shells.

BEFESTIGT (Ger), attached.

BEFFROI (Fr), alarm bell from a watchtower.

BEIDE (Ger), both.

BEIDES VON EINEM GESCHLAGEN, both (instruments) struck by one player.

BEINKLAPPER (Ger), bones, slapstick.

BELL(S), instrument containing a cup, sounding rim, or lip, and a silent top or crown, and generally made from cast bronze, but sometimes from steel, aluminum, or nickel. The bell probably originated in ancient Asia and from there spread throughout the world. The characteristic sound of the cast bell comes from its fundamental, prominent sounding tone an octave above the fundamental, and the higher overtones, which become audible in varying degrees as the sounding tone decays. The bell's unique sound makes it difficult to imitate on the concert stage. Chimes (tubular bells) and bell plates achieve a fairly accurate representation of the higher notes, but imitation of the lower notes still remains a problem. Examples of orchestral use of bells include Giuseppe Verdi's *Don Carlos* (1867), Modest Mussorgsky's *Boris Godounov* (1874, coronation scene), Paul Dukas's *The Sorcerer's Apprentice* (1897), Giacomo Puccini's *Tosca* (1900), Gustav Mahler's Symphony No. 6 (1904), Zoltán Kodály's *Háry János: Suite* (1927), Leoš Janáček's *From the House of the Dead* (1930), Carl Orff's *Carmina burana* (1937), Richard Strauss's *Friedenstag* (1938), and Leonard Bernstein's Overture to *Candide* (1956). *Cloche* in French, *Glocke* in German, *campana* in Italian, Spanish. *See* Illus. 14, p. 123.

BELL BAR, any single or group of orchestral bell bars.

BELL CHIMES, set of bells tuned to various pitches, with a range of one-and-a-half octaves; also a set of tubular bells. Bell chimes were used in the Bronze Age and were found in Europe and ancient China. The European bell chime can be traced to the ninth century, when it was called *cymbala*. Mechanized chimes were developed in the thirteenth century, and large chimes for church towers in the fourteenth, with hammers to strike the outside of the bells. The modern chime, made of metal tubes, is struck with a mallet. Also called *dinner bells*.

BELL CLAPPER, striker usually freely suspended from the inside of a bell, so positioned to strike the inside of the bell.

BELLED WOODEN SPOONS, pair of wooden spoons, which have small bells attached to the handles.

BELL LYRE (LYRA), marching glockenspiel made of unresonated aluminum bars. The bell lyre has both manuals on the same level (like a vibraphone). One end of the instrument is placed in a strap around the player's waist, while the other is supported by the player's arm, leaving only one arm free to strike the instrument. It is rarely used in contemporary marching ensembles. Also known as *lyra glockenspiel, metal harmonica*. *See also* **orchestra bells**.

BELL PIANO, special instrument constructed to substitute for the Grail bells in Richard Wagner's *Parsifal* (1882). The instrument contained four sets of strings tuned to C, G, A, and E, which were struck with large padded hammers. *See also* **parsifal bells**.

BELL PLATES, rectangular plates of bronze, aluminum, or steel that originated in ancient Asia. Their range runs from C to g^2, and they are suspended from racks by heavy ropes. They are struck with heavy felt beaters; harder beaters may be used to create a more penetrating, but less focused sound. Bell plates are often used as a substitute for distant cast bells. They have been scored in all types of music from the symphony orchestra and the chamber ensemble to the theater orchestra. Orchestral examples include Verdi's *Il Trovatore* (1853), Richard Strauss's *Also sprach Zarathustra* (1896), Giacomo Puccini's *Tosca* (1900), Arnold Schoenberg's *Die glückliche Hand* (1913), and Anton Webern's *Six Pieces for Orchestra* (1909/1920). Also known as *plate bells.*

BELL STRAP, Indian ankle bells.

BELL TREE, (1) a string of small bells strung on a rope or dowel in order of descending size; a glissando effect is produced when a metal rod is drawn down the length of the instrument thus striking each bell in turn. Also known as *Pakistan tree bells.* (2) Turkish crescent. *See also* **calottes**; **orugoru**; **Thailand tree bell**; Illus. 35, p. 134.

BELL WHEEL, *see* **horologium**.

BEMOL (Ger), B-flat.

BEMOLLE (It), B-flat.

BEN ACCORDATO (It), well-tuned.

BEND DRUM, *see* **talking drum**.

BENDĪR, north African frame drum with snares running underneath its single head to create a buzzing sound when struck. Also known as *bandair.*

BENGALA (Sp), cane.

BENÜTZT (Ger), used.

BENÜTZUNG (Ger), use.

BEN-ZASARA, *see* **bin-sasara**.

BERIMBAU (BERIMBAO), musical bow with an attached gourd (cabaça), the principal instrument, sometimes in groups of twos and threes, of the Brazilian *capoeira.* Also known as *berimbau (berimbao) de barriga* (berimbau of the belly), *birimbau, bucumbumba, goba, macungo, urucungo. See also* "Brazil: Percussion Instruments," p. 153.

BERÜHREN (Ger), touch, activate.

BESEN (Ger), brush.

BEZEICHNET IST (Ger), notated, designated.

BGS., abbrev. for *bongos.* (L)

BICCHIERI DI VETRO (It), musical glasses.

BICYCLE BELLS, ringing bells commonly found on children's bicycles. Usually operated by the thumb pushing a lever that activates the hammer to strike a small, high-pitched bell. Also called *crank bell.*

BIDONI (It), plastic garbage pails. (L)

BIEN ACCORDÉ (Fr), well-tuned.

BIG BEN, brass rods found inside clock that mark the quarter hours in a manner similar to the chime tones of Big Ben in London. The rods are mounted on one end to a wooden box for amplification. The four descending pitches are mi, re, do, and sol of any major key. Also called *clock chimes.*

BIG DRUM, bass drum. (L)

BIN-SASARA (BEN-ZASARA), Japanese instrument with a series of ninety small boards (about 2 inches wide by 6 inches long by 1¼ inches) strung together. A quick flick of the two handles produces a dry, short clacking sound, much like a short ratchet. Used by Carl Orff in his

Prometheus (1968). Also known as a *strung clapper*. (L/WM)

BIRCH BRANCHES, alternative for bamboo strips, switch.

BIRD WHISTLE, whistle in a wide variety of instruments (mostly areophones) that imitate bird calls. *See also* Illus. 36, p. 135.

BIRIMBAU, *see* **berimbau.**

BIS ZUR UNHÖRBARKEIT ABNEHMEN (Ger), fade to where the sound is almost inaudible; used, for example, in Gustav Mahler's Symphony No. 2 (1895). (L)

BLADDER AND STRINGS, *see* **bumbass.**

BLANDO (Sp), soft.

BLANDO MEDIANO (Sp), medium soft.

BLANK GUN, gun used for gunshot effects. Also known as a *starting gun.*

BLECHTROMMEL (Ger), steel drum.

BLOC CHINOIS (Fr), Korean block.

BLOCCO DI LEGNO (It), Chinese block, tone block, wood drum.

BLOCCO DI LEGNO COREANO (It), Korean block.

BLOC DE (EN) BOIS (Fr), Chinese block, tone block, wood drum.

BLOC DE BOIS CYLINDRIQUE (Fr), woodblock (cylindrical).

BLOC DE METAL (Fr), cowbell.

BLOC EN BOIS (Fr), woodblocks, wood drums.

BNG., abbrev. for *bongos.* (L)

BOARD CLAPPER, *see* **slapstick.**

BOAT WHISTLE, large wooden whistle that produces a sound resembling a ship's whistle.

BOI, Latin-American friction drum.

BOING GONGS, children's metal snow sleds in the shape of a saucer. These are suspended and produce a "boing" effect when struck.

BOIS (Fr), wood.

BOÎTE À (DE) CLOUS (Fr), literally, box of nails; in music, maracas.

BOMBO (Port, Sp), Brazilian bass drum, Cuban snare drum. *See also* **zabumba;** "Brazil: Percussion Instruments," p. 153; "Latin-American Percussion," p. 227.

BONANG, Javanese and Balanese gongs of distinct pitch. They do not have long, sustained tones but rather tones that are short in duration. The bonang is part of the gamelan from these areas and consists of the *bonang panembung* (lowest), *bonang barung* (medium), and *bonang panerus* (highest). The performer strikes the raised bosses of the gongs with padded mallets. Bonang gongs are traditionally suspended in a circular frame.

BONES, pairs of short (3 to 5 inches) wooden slats that are held in one hand between the thumb, fore-, and middle fingers. The bones strike each other when the wrist is turned quickly, producing a dry clacking sound. Often pairs of bones will be held in both hands by a single performer. They mean castanets in some Russian pieces. *See also* Illus. 33, p. 132.

BONGHI (It), bongos.

BONGO(S), a small pair of Latin-American hand drums. Their sizes are approximately 7½ inches for the large drum and 7¼ inches for the smaller one. Both drums are generally 5⅝ inches deep. The skin heads are tensioned tightly to produce a high, penetrating tone. As with most hand drums a wide variety of tones and pitches can be produced using various strokes and dampening techniques. However, the sound produced by these hand techniques without amplification is often not audible in large ensembles. In such instances percussionists may use sticks or mallets to achieve an appropriate balance, but they will thereby sacrifice the timbral variety of the hand strokes. Examples of scoring for the bongos may be found in Edgard Varèse's *Ionisation* (1931), Pierre Boulez's *Le Marteau sans maître* (1955), and Wolfgang Fortner's *In His Garden Don Perlimplín Loves Belisa* (1962). Also called *Cuban tom-toms. See also* "Latin-American Percussion," p. 227; Illus. 24, p. 127.

BONGO ORGANS, *see* **roto toms.**

BONGOS SURAIGUS (Fr), very short, high-pitched bongos. (L)

BONGO-TROMMELN (Ger), bongos.

BOOBAMS, long tubular drums with a single head and generally tuned in a chromatic scale with a range of one to two octaves (F–f[1]). The heads are made from skin or plastic and the shells from wood or plastic.

BORD (REBORD) (Fr), edge, rim.

BORDE (Sp), edge, rim.

BORDONES (Sp), snares.

BOSS, raised section in the center of a cymbal. Sometimes called the *cup* or *bell.* (L)

BOSUN'S PIPE, high-pitched whistle used by a ship's bosun before announcements. It is capable of at least two distinct pitches.

BOTTLE CAP JINGLES, sistrum made from a short stick with loosely mounted soda bottle caps.

BOTTLES, TUNED, *see* **tuned bottles.**

BOTTLE TREE, cut bottle tops suspended by their necks on a single piece of rope or twine. The bottles are struck with a soft beater.

BOURDON (Fr), Waldteufel.

BOUTEILLOPHON (Ger), tuned bottles.

BOUTEILLOPHONE (Fr), pop bottles, tuned bottles.

BOWLS, crystal bowls or wine goblets that are rubbed around the rim with a moistened finger causing the crystal to vibrate and produce a sustained tone; used in Joseph Schwantner's *. . . and the mountains rising nowhere* (1977) and David Maslanka's *A Child's Garden of Dreams* (1981). Also called *porcelain bowls.*

BOX OF NAILS, maracas.

BRAKE DRUM, actual brake drum taken from junked automobiles. It is capable of a multitude of sounds (unpitched) depending upon the type of beater and area struck, and it is often used as a substitute for the anvil. Brake drums can be scored in sets of three or more in varying sizes and pitches. Examples of scoring include Henry Cowell's Symphony No. 14 (1960), John Cage's *First Construction in Metal* (1939), and Cage and Lou Harrison's *Double Music* (1941). *See also* Illus. 35, p. 134.

BRASS WIND CHIMES, wind chimes made from small brass tubes. Often referred to as *metal wind chimes.*

BRAZILIAN BAMBOO SHAKER, hollow piece of bamboo that is filled with seeds or pellets and closed at both ends.

BRAZILIAN WOODEN BLOCKS, two wooden blocks, one of which is grooved, the other smooth; the smoothed one is scraped against the other, producing a rasping sound much like a güiro.

BRÈF (Fr), short.

BREMSTROMMELN VON AUTOS (Ger), brake drums. (L)

BRETTCHENKLAPPER (Ger), slapstick. (L)

BREVE (It), short.

BRONZE BELLS, *see* **bells.**

BRONZE PLATES, suspended metal plates about $^{3}/_{8}$ inch thick, sometimes with actual pitches. (L)

BRONZE SHEETS, *see* **thunder sheet.**

BROSSE (Fr), brush.

BROSSES EN FIL DE MÉTAL (Fr), wire brushes.

BRUIT DE SONNAILLES DES TROUPEAUX (Fr), cowbells.

BRUIT DE TÔLE (Fr), foil rattle.

BRUMMEISEN (Ger), Jew's harp.

BRUMMKREISEL (Ger), humming top.

BRUMMTOPF (Ger), friction drum.

BUBBOLO (It), jingles.

BUCKELGONG (Ger), button gong.

BUCUMBUMBA, *see* **berimbau.**

BUDDHA TEMPLE BELL, Japanese cup gong. *See also* **dobači.**

BULB HORN, *see* **auto horn.**

BULL-ROARER, long, thin piece of wood with a piece of twine attached at one end through a small hole. When whirled through the air in a circle the bull-roarer creates a roaring or howling sound to imitate a bull. The smaller the piece of wood, the higher the pitch. Originally from Africa and Australia, the bull roarer can be found in Europe, Central Asia, Indonesia, and the Americas. Also called *thunder stick.*

BUMBASS, one of the first instruments to be used by one-man bands. The bumbass is constructed from a pole of approximately seven feet in height, to the top of which are attached two cymbals. A number of sleigh bells are attached a couple of feet lower, which add to the jingling when the pole is struck against the ground. About two feet from the bottom is a small drum. This drum may be a simple hoop drum or may have a shell. A wire is strung from the top of the bumbass to a bridge located just below the drum. The bumbass is played by striking the wire and drum with a notched stick while stamping the base of the pole against the ground in a steady pulse. Generally used for centuries by street musicians, classical composers have also scored for it, including Milko Kelemen, in his *Composé* (1967). Also called *bladder and strings, devil's fiddle, one-man percussion band.*

BUMBO, *see* **zabumba.**

BURMA BELL, flat brass plate shaped like a pagoda, which emits a high, focused pitch when struck. It is suspended on a thin cord, and a vibrato is achieved when the bell is spun after being struck. Also known as *Burmese temple bell, kyeezee bell, kye tsi.*

BURMESE TEMPLE BELL, *see* **Burma bell.**

BUTTIBU (It), friction drum. (L)

BUTTON GONG, any gong with a raised boss in its center. They are almost always struck on the boss and produce a definite pitch. Also known as a *raised gong. Buckelgong* in German. *See also* **Java gong; nipple gong.**

BUZZ MARIMBA, marimba from Central America, specifically Guatemala. It has wooden resonators that have small holes covered with a thin vellum that buzzes when the bar is struck. It is descended from the African marimba and adapted to the European diatonic scale. *See also* **marimba grande; nabimba.**

CABAÇA (Port), another name for afoxê. *See also* **cabasa.**

CABAQUINHA, Latin-American frame drum with a distinctive square shell.

CABASA (CABAZA), generic term used for any rattle that consists of a hollow gourd covered with a net of beads or small shells. The instrument is then shaken or the net scraped across the surface of the gourd to produce a rasping sound. Metallic cabasas are generally referred to as *afuche*. The cabasa is generally thought to be of African origin. *Calebasse* in French, *Kalabasse* in German, *cabasa* in Italian, *cabaza, cabaça* in Spanish.

CABLE DRUM, chain-tuned kettledrum. *See also* "The Kettledrum," p. 201.

CACCAVELLA (It), friction drum. (L)

CADENAS (Sp), chains.

CADRE DU TAMBOUR (Fr), shell of the drum.

CAISSE, French term originally meaning the shell of a drum but now referring to the drum itself; snare drum.

CAISSE À TIMBRE (Fr), snare drum.

CAISSE CLAIRE (Fr), snare drum.

CAISSE PLATE (Fr), small, narrow snare drum. (L)

CAISSE ROULANTE (AVEC CORDES) (Fr), field drum, tenor drum.

CAISSE SOURDE (Fr), tenor drum.

CAI TRONG, large Vietnamese barrel drum.

CAI TRONG CAI, double-headed Vietnamese signal drum.

CAI TRONG COM, *see* **trong com.**

CAI TRONG CON, Vietnamese child's drum.

CAI TRONG GIANG, small, conical Vietnamese drum.

CAI TRONG KHAN, small Vietnamese barrel drum.

CAI TRONG MET, Vietnamese frame drum.

CAI TRONG VA, single-headed Vietnamese drum.

CAIXA (Port), snare drum.

CAIXA CLARA (Port), snare drum.

CAIXA DE RUFO (Port), tenor drum.

CAIXETA, Latin-American woodblock.

CAJA (Sp), (1) drum, shell; (2) South American-Indian tambourine with two heads that are laced together. Usually in a square form, but may be round.

CAJA MILITAR (Sp), snare drum.

CAJÓN HARMÓNICA, South American wooden marimba resonators. (L)

CALOTTES, small bells shaped like skullcaps. Dating from the Middle Ages, they are used, in larger sizes, as a substitute for church bells on the concert stage. *See also* **bell tree.**

CALUNG RENTENG, xylophone of western Java. *See also* "The Xylophone," p. 347.

CALYPSOTROMMEL (Ger), steel drum.

CAMEL BELLS, cylindrical metal bells suspended inside one another on a single string. Each string may have as many as ten individual bells of decreasing diameter. Occasionally numerous small camel bells of roughly the same size will be strung together. Also known as *Persian temple bells*. *See also* Illus. 32, p. 131.

CAMESA, see **kameso.**

CAMISÃO, large one-headed Brazilian frame drum played traditionally with a leather strap or whip; used by Heitor Villa-Lobos. *See also* "Brazil: Percussion Instruments," p. 153.

CAMLLI. (It), abbrev. for *campanelli*. (L)

CAMP. (It), abbrev. for *campanelli*. (L)

CAMPAINHA (Port), bell.

CAMPANA (It, Lat, Sp), bell.

CAMPANACCIO DI METALLO (It), cowbell.

CAMPANA D'ALLARME (It), alarm bell.

CAMPANA DA PREGHIERA (It), prayer bell.

CAMPANA DI LEGNO (It), temple block.

CAMPANA GRAVE (It), low bell, church bell, steeple bell. (L)

CAMPANA IN LASTRA DI METALLO (It), bell plate. (L)

CAMPANA TUBOLARA (It), chime.

CAMPANE DA PASTORE (It), cowbells.

CAMPANELLA (It), small bell.

CAMPANELLE (It), tubular bells.

CAMPANELLE BASSE (Fr), low bells.

CAMPANELLE DA MESSA (It), Sanctus bells.

CAMPANELLE DI VACCA (It), cowbells.

CAMPANELLI (It), glockenspiel.

CAMPANELLI A TASTIERA (It), keyboard glockenspiel.

CAMPANELLI GIAPONESE (It), Japanese metal bars.

CAMPANELLO D'ALLARME (It), ship's bell, storm bell.

CAMPANEO (Sp), chime.

CAMPANETTE (It), orchestra bells, glockenspiel.

CAMPANE TUBOLARI (It), tubular bells, chimes.

CAMPANI (It), chimes.

CAMPANILLA (Sp), hand bell.

CAMPAÑUELA (Sp), small bells.

CAÑA (Sp), cane.

CANA (Port), cane.

CANE SWITCH, thin length of cane used to strike the head of a bass drum, as in the Turkish Janissary bands. Used, for example, by Mozart in *Die Entführung aus dem Serail* (1782). *See also* **bass drum**; "Janissary Music," p. 195.

CANNA (It), cane, reed.

CANNE (Fr), cane, reed.

CANNONE (It), cannon.

CANNON SHOT, sound created by shooting a cannon, used in outdoor concerts, by hitting a large bass drum sharply in the center, or by shooting a blank pistol into an oil barrel. (L)

CANON (Fr), cannon.

CANUSAO, South American snare drum. (L)

CAOUTCHOUC (Fr), rubber.

CAPOC (Fr, It), kapok.

CAR., abbrev. for *carillon.*

CARACACHA, Brazilian bamboo scraper used by the Guato and Mura Indians.

CARACAXÀ, Brazilian name for *ganzá*, *reco-reco*, and *maraca*. Also called *caraxa.*

CAR HORN, *see* **auto horn.**

CARIGLIONE (It), carillon, chimes.

CARILLON, large cast bronze church bells usually housed in church steeples. They come in diatonic or chromatic sets and are played from a keyboard or some type of automatic mechanism. Means "chime" in French. *See also* **tubular bells.**

CARILLONS DE VERRE AIGU (Fr), glass wind chimes.

CARIMBO, Latin-American drum made from a hollowed tree trunk with a parchment head.

CARRACA (Sp), Latin-American ratchet.

CARRASQUIÑA, Andalusian xylophone. *See also* "The Xylophone," p. 347.

CARRILHÃO (Port), orchestra bells, carillon.

CARTA SABBIATA (It), sandpaper (block). (L)

CARTA VETRATA (It), sandpaper (block).

CAS., abbrev. for *castanets.* (L)

CASCABELES (Sp), small bells, jingles, sleigh bells.

CASCAVEL (Port), rattles, jingles. *See also* **cascabeles.**

CASSA (It), drum, shell.

CASSA CHIARA (It), snare drum.

CASSA DEL TAMBURO (It), shell of the drum.

CASSA DI LEGNO (It), woodblock.

CASSA DI METALLO (It), metal block, cowbell. (L)

CASSA GRANDE (It), bass drum.

CASSA RULLANTE (It), tenor drum.

CASSA SORDO (It), military drum, parade drum, deep drum.

CASSETTINA (It), woodblock.

CASSETTINA DI LEGNO (It), Chinese block, woodblock.

CAST., abbrev. for *castanets.* (L)

CASTAG. (Fr), abbrev. for *castagnettes.* (L)

CASTAGNETTA(E) (It), castanet(s).

CASTAGNETTE (Fr), castanet.

CASTAGNETTE(N) (Ger), castanet(s). Also *Kastagnetten.*

CASTAGNETTE DI FERRO (It), mounted finger cymbals.

CASTAGNETTES DE FER (Fr), mounted finger cymbals.

CASTAÑETA (Sp), castanet.

CASTANETS, pair of spoon-shaped hard wooden shells, held in the dancer's hand in Spanish music and mounted on hand paddles or a board in orchestral music. *See also* "Castanets," p. 167; Illus. 35, p. 134.

CASTANHETAS, Latin-American castanets.

CASTANHOLAS (Port), castanets.

CASTAÑUELAS (Sp), castanets.

CAST BELLS, church bells.

CATACÁ, Latin-American scraper.

CATENE (It), chains.

CATUBA (It), bass drum.

CAUCHO (Sp), rubber.

CAVALRY TIMPANI, *see* "The Kettledrum," p. 201.

CAXAMBO(U), large one-headed Brazilian drum made from a hollowed tree trunk, held between the knees and played with a small wooden mallet; used by Heitor Villa-Lobos. *See also* "Brazil: Percussion Instruments," p. 153.

CAXIXI, woven Brazilian basket rattle. It has traditionally been used by *berimbau* players, who hold the caxixi in the hand, which strikes the wire of the *berimbau* with a thin stick. The caxixi has a wooden base and a loop handle woven into the basket. *See* "Brazil: Percussion Instruments," p. 153; Illus. 34, p. 133.

C.B., abbrev. for *cowbell.* (L)

C.CH. (It), abbrev. for *cassa chiara.* (L)

C.CL. (Fr), abbrev. for *caisse claire.* (L)

CEL., abbrev. for *celesta.*

CELESTA, keyboard instrument that uses steel bars suspended over wooden resonators. The bars are then struck by padded hammers that are controlled by a keyboard. The instrument generally has a five-octave range and was invented in 1886 by Auguste Mustel of Paris. *See also* **keyboard glockenspiel.**

CEMB. (It), abbrev. for *cembalo.*

CEMBALO (It), (1) dulcimer, (2) an obsolete term for cymbal, (3) an ancient European frame drum.

CEMBALUM, *see* **cimbalom.**

CENCERRO (Sp), cowbell.

CENTRO (Fr, It), middle, center.

CEPPI CINESI (It), Chinese blocks.

CEPPI DI CARTA VETRATA (It), sandpaper blocks.

CERCHIO (It), hoop, rim.

CERCLE (Fr), hoop, rim.

CES (Ger), C-flat.

CEWHAN, crescent-shaped jingling stick rattle with bells used in Janissary music; became Jingling Johnnie in English. Also known as *chaghāna. See also* "Janissary Music," p. 195.

CHAC-CHAC, *see* **shak-shak.**

CHAGHĀNA, *see* **cewhan.**

CHAIN DRUM, *see* "The Kettledrum," p. 201.

CHAÎNES (Fr), chains.

CHAINS, iron chains that are rattled or struck. *Chaînes* in French, *Ketten* in German, *catene* in Italian, *cadenas* in Spanish.

CHAKRA, African circular wooden castanets. (L)

CHALPARA, Turkish cymbals.

CHAMBER BOWLS, large cut pyrex bowls that produce long sustained sounds, rich in overtones, when struck with a soft mallet. They were originally designed by California composer Harry Partch (1901–1976).

CHANG-CHEN, Tibetan gongs with definite pitches and a long sustaining sound.

CHANGGO, Korean double-headed hourglass drum.

CHANG KU, Chinese hourglass drum made from a bamboo tube and two snakeskin heads. The heads are tucked around metal hoops and tensioned by a central mechanism.

CHAP, hand cymbals from Thailand. The large bell can be used to create a suction that produces a "wa-wa" sound. Also known as *wa-wa cymbals, charp.*

CHAPA, (1) (Sp) castanet, (2) small Japanese cymbals.

CHÂPEAU CHINOIS (Fr), bell tree, Jingling Johnnie, Turkish crescent. *See also* "Janissary Music," p. 195.

CHARLESTON (Fr), hi-hat.

CHARLESTON BECKENMASCHINE (Ger), hi-hat. (L)

CHARLESTON CYMBALS, cymbals used on low-boy and early hi-hat. *See also* "The Drum Set: A History," p. 173.

CHARP, *see* **chap.**

CHATTPA, pair of small, deep bell Japanese crash cymbals, about 8 inches in diameter. Sometimes called *chapa.* (L/WM)

CHCL. (Port), abbrev. for *chocalho.* (L)

CHEESE BOX, originally the wooden boxes used to transport cream cheese, now replaced by a very low woodblock that is struck with a soft mallet; used in Leonard Bernstein's *Dybbuk Variations* (1975). (L)

CHEESE GRATER, kitchen implement that can be used as a scraper when a thin stick or fingers covered with thimbles are dragged across its surface.

CHIAPAN MARIMBA, Mexican xylophone that is table-like in design; the two major types are the *diatonic marimba sencilla* and the *chromatic marimba doble. See also* "The Marimba in Mexico and Related Areas," p. 239.

CHI. BLOKS., abbrev. for *Chinese blocks.* (L)

CHICKEN CLUCKER, sound-effect instrument consisting of a small, open wooden box with a sliding handle. When the handle is slid over the box, the opening is sealed off. Both the handle and the lip of the box are coated with rosin, thus increasing the friction when the handle is slid into place. This friction creates a sound similar to a chicken clucking.

CHICO (Sp), small.

CHIMES, instrument consisting of a series of cast brass tubes of decreasing length (5 feet, 2 inches to 6 inches), with a diameter from 1 to 2 inches. The individual chimes are tuned and arranged in a chromatic series with a range of one-and-a-half octaves (c^1-f^2). They sound as written. Often used as a substitute for church bells, chimes are frequently used in all forms of Western art music, along with a variety of beaters ranging from metal triangle beaters to yarn mallets. The most common are rawhide hammers, which produce a clear, crisp articulation in imitation of church bells. Chimes are used not only to create programmatic representations of church bells, but also to display their unique timbre in their own right. Examples of orchestral scoring include Paul Hindemith's *Symphonic Metamorphosis* (1943), Benjamin Britten's *The Turn of the Screw* (1954), Carl Orff's *Oedipus* (1959), Hans Werner Henze's *Elegy for Young Lovers* (1961), Pierre Boulez's *Pli selon pli* (1962), and Olivier Messiaen's *Sept Haïkaï* (1963). Also known as *tubular bells* (when used in the orchestra). *See also* Illus. 30, p. 130.

CHIMTA, two sticks with small jingles mounted on one side and joined at one end to create a tong. The jingles rest on the outside of the resulting angle created by the two sticks. The instrument is played by either bringing the sticks together or by shaking them. Also called *metal jingle sticks*.

CHINESCO (Sp), Jingling Johnnie.

CHINESE BLOCK(S), *see* **temple blocks; woodblock**.

CHINESE BONGO, small single-headed hand drum played by the leader of the orchestra. It is held in one hand, while the bones of the other hand's finger strike the head in various areas to produce different effects. Also known as *pang-ku*.

CHINESE CONFUCIAN BELLS, small bowl-shaped microtonal bells that range in diameter from 2 to 10 inches and may be grouped in sets of varying numbers. Their pitches comprise a microtonal division of the octave, and their range is two-and-a-quarter octaves. Also known as *Chinese tree bells*, *dharma bells*, *Nyma bells*.

CHINESE CRASH CYMBALS, Chinese-made crash cymbals used in Western rhythm bands.

CHINESE CRESCENT, Chinese pavilion, Jingling Johnnie.

CHINESE CUP GONGS, *see* **cup gongs**.

CHINESE CYMBAL, suspended cymbal with upturned edges and a timbre significantly lower and darker than the regular suspended cymbals. Examples of its use can be found in Carl Orff's *Prometheus* (1968), Darius Milhaud's Concerto for Percussion and Small Orchestra (1930), Edgard Varèse's *Ionisation* (1931), and John Cage's *First Construction in Metal* (1939). *See also* Illus. 21, p. 127.

CHINESE DRUM, generally a small wooden shell drum with thick animal skin heads tacked to the shell. It was popular in the North American pit orchestras in the first third of the twentieth century.

CHINESE HAND DRUM, *see* **Chinese paper drum**.

CHINESE PAPER DRUM, small two-headed rattle drum mounted on a small stick. Attached to opposite sides of the shell are two short strings, each with a small wooden ball at the end. When the drum is rotated back and forth the balls alternately strike the heads of the drum. Often used as a child's toy, this instrument is scored in Mauricio Kagel's *Match for Three Performers* (1965). Also known as *Chinese hand drum, Chinese rattle drum,* and *t'ao ku. See also* **paper drum**; Illus. 37, p. 136.

CHINESE PAVILION, another name for Chinese crescent, Jingling Johnnie, Turkish crescent.

CHINESE RATTLE DRUM, *see* **Chinese paper drum.**

CHINESE TEMPLE BLOCKS, hollowed spherical blocks with a mellower sound than the rectangular woodblocks. Temple blocks are delicate instruments and are most effective when played with soft mallets. *See also* **dragons' mouths; Korean temple blocks; temple blocks; wooden fish**; Illus. 23, p. 127.

CHINESE THUMB PIANO, similar to the African kalimba or mbira but with metal tongues set on a wooden board instead of a sounding board or calabash.

CHINESE TOM-TOM, similar to the Chinese drum but with a greater shell depth. In addition, small iron rings are attached to the side of the drum to produce a rattle when the instrument is struck. Usually painted with dragons and traditional designs, it was popular in the North American pit orchestras in the first third of the twentieth century and was the direct forerunner of the modern-day drum set tom-toms.

CHINESE TREE BELLS, *see* **Chinese Confucian bells.**

CHINESE WOODBLOCKS, *see* **temple blocks; woodblock.**

CHINESISCHE BECKEN (Ger), Chinese cymbals.

CHINESISCHE BLÖCKE (Ger), Chinese blocks.

CHINESISCHER GONG (Ger), Chinese gong.

CHINESISCHES TOM-TOM (Ger), Chinese tom-tom.

CHINESISCHES ZIMBEL (Ger), Chinese cymbal.

CHING, (1) pair of small cup-shaped cymbals from Thailand and Cambodia, connected by a rope approximately 6 to 9 inches in length and made from thick brass; (2) Chinese gong.

CH'ING, stone chimes used in Confucian temples and suspended from frames; they range from one to two feet in length. Also *qing. See also* **stone chimes.**

CHING-A-RING, thin metal tambourine that can be attached to the upshaft of a hi-hat stand. The jingles are activated as the shaft is moved up and down by the performer's foot.

CHINOIS(E) (Fr), Chinese.

CHOCALHO, Brazilian metal tube shaker, 12 to 14 inches in length and 2 to 3 inches in diameter, filled with stones or pellets. Also called *chocallo, tubo, xucalho de metal. See also* "Brazil: Percussion Instruments," p. 153.

CHOCALLO, *see* **chocalho.**

CHOKE, quickly mute; usually used on a cymbal part.

CHOKE CYMBALS, *see* **hi-hat.**

CHOW IRON, large piece of iron, often in the shape of a triangle, which is struck with a metal beater. Generally used to call workers in from the field for meals. Also called *giant triangle.*

CHROMATIC DRUM, timpani drum that can be tuned by some mechanical device.

CHROMATIC MARIMBA, marimba originating in Chiapas or Guatemala. *See also* "The Marimba in Mexico and Related Areas," p. 239.

CHROMATIC WOODBLOCKS, woodblocks tuned to a chromatic scale and arranged in the same manner as a xylophone keyboard.

CHRYSOGLOTTE, metal-barred instrument usually found in theater organs. (L)

CHUNG, clapperless Chinese bells that are struck on the outside edge. Also *Vietnamese bell.*

CHURCH BELL, tuned metal plate or bell, chimes.

CHURCH RATCHET, large ratchet used in some Catholic areas to call worshippers to church during holy week, when church bells may not be used. These may have influenced Beethoven in his scoring for *Wellington's Victory* (1813), and Carl Orff in *Die Bernauerin* (1947).

CIGOLIO (It), hissing sound.

CIMBALI ANTICHI (It), antique cymbals, Greek cymbals.

CIMBALINI (It), antique cymbals, Greek cymbals.

CÍMBALO (Sp), cymbal.

CIMBALO ANTIGUO (Sp), antique cymbal.

CIMBALOM, stringed instrument akin to the santur and used extensively in Eastern European countries; it is struck with padded mallets. Also *czimbalom.*

CIMBALOS CRAPULOSOS (Sp), crash cymbals.

CIMBALO SUSPENDIDO (Sp), suspended cymbal.

CIMBALO SUSPENSO (Sp), suspended cymbal.

CIMBALUM, *see* **cimbalom.**

CINELLEN (Ger), cymbals.

CINELLI (It), cymbals.

CINELLI DITO (It), finger cymbals. (L)

CINESE (It), Chinese.

CINGLANT (Fr), swishing.

CIRCOLARMENTE (Fr), circularly, around.

CIS (Ger), C-sharp.

CITHARE (Fr), zither.

CLACSON (It), auto horn.

CLAIR (Fr), high.

CLAPPER, (1) wood or metal striker hung from the inside of a bell; (2) instrument made of two or more dowels or boards that are struck together. The dowels are of wood or metal and are often hinged together at one end. Clappers appear in cultures throughout the world and are found in all sizes and shapes.

CLAQUEBOIS (Fr), xylophone.

CLAQUETTE (Fr), clapper, rattle.

CLASH CYMBALS, another name for crash cymbals.

CLAVES, two rosewood concussion sticks associated with Latin-American music. These sticks are generally no longer than 7 inches and have a diameter of 1 to 1½ inches. The name *clave* also refers to the ostinato rhythm and pulse that accompanies nearly all Latin-American dance music. *See also* "Latin-American Percussion," p. 227; Illus. 36, p. 135.

CLAVITYMPANUM, obsolete word for xylophone.

CLAY RATTLES, maracas or shakers made from a hollow clay container.

CLAY SHAKER BELLS, four small clay bells with clappers, which are found at the node and shaken. This instrument comes from Mexico.

CLIQUET (Fr), ratchet.

CLIQUETTE (Fr), board clappers, bones.

CLOCA, CLOCCA (Lat), bell of Irish origin.

CLOCHE (Fr), bell.

CLOCHE(S) À VACHE (Fr), cowbell(s).

CLOCHE DE VACHE (Fr), cowbell.

CLOCHE EN LAME DE MÉTAL (Fr), bell plate. (L)

CLOCHES (Fr), bells.

CLOCHES PLAQUES (Fr), bell plates. (L)

CLOCHES TUBULAIRES (Fr), tubular bells, chimes.

CLOCHETTE (Fr), small bell.

CLOCHETTES (Fr), orchestra bells.

CLOCHETTES À MAINS (Fr), hand bells. (L)

CLOCHETTES POUR LA MESSE (Fr), Sanctus bells.

CLOCK CHIMES, *see* **Big Ben**.

CLOG BOX, woodblock. (L)

CLOGS, wooden shoes; the soles are struck together, one held firmly with the hand cupped around the aperture (+ = close aperture, o = open aperture); used, for example, in Oliver Knussen's *Where the Wild Things Are* (1983). (L)

CLOPOT (Romanian), bell.

CLOUD CHAMBER BOWLS, glass percussion instruments devised by Harry Partch. *See also* "Multiple Percussion," p. 257.

CLV., abbrev. for *claves*. (L)

CMP. (It), abbrev. for *campana*.

CMPLI. (It), abbrev. for *campanelli*.

CMP.TUB. (It), abbrev. for *campane tubolari*. (L)

COCKOLO, cabasa. (L)

COCKTAIL DRUM, double-headed tom-tom with legs, to which is added a bass drum pedal and a suspended cymbal.

COCO, Brazilian woodblock constructed by cutting a coconut shell into halves, replaced by Chinese temple blocks in orchestral performances. *See also* "Brazil: Percussion Instruments," p. 153.

COCONUT SHELLS, two hollowed halves of a coconut shell that are alternately struck against a wooden board to simulate the sound of horses' hooves in a gallop or trot. Also known as *horsehooves, hoofbeats*. *See* Illus. 33, p. 132.

COG RATTLE, idiophone comprised of a cogwheel, an axle as a handle, and a tongue fixed to the frame. When turned, the tongue strikes the cogs of the wheel one after the other. It is a forerunner of the present-day ratchet.

COIL SPRING, suspension spring from an automobile, usually fitted with jingles. When suspended by a rope and struck with a hard beater, it produces a great array of high-pitched overtones. Also known as *wire coils*.

COL FERRO (It), with metal.

COLGRASS DRUM, drum with cardboard shells and small wing nuts for tuning; the immediate forerunner of the modern-day roto tom. Invented by the composer Michael Colgrass. (L)

COLLA MANO (It), with the hand.

COLLA MAZZETTA (It), with the soft beater.

COL LEGNO (It), with the wood.

COLLE NOCCE (It), with knuckles.

COLLE UNGHIE (It), with the fingernails.

COLOMBIAN JUNGLE DRUM, log drum with a hole in its center, capable of producing a variety of sounds when struck with a heavy beater.

COLPETE, COLPIRE AL ORDINARIO (It), strike normally.

COLPETE, COLPIRE CON (It), strike with.

COLPI (It), strokes.

COLPO CON (It), struck with.

COL POLLICE (It), with the thumb.

COL PUGNO (It), (hit) with the fist.

COME UNA CAMPANA (It), like a bell.

CON BACCH. DA TAMB. (It), abbrev. for *con bacchetta da tamburo.* (L)

CON BACCHETTA DA TAMBURO (It), with the drumstick.

CONCERT TOM-TOMS, single-headed drums of varying shell depth and diameter, usually arranged in ascending pitch. They have shell diameters ranging from 6 to 18 inches and are often in sets of four different sizes. *See* Illus. 8, p. 120.

CON CORDE (It), with snares, snares on.

CONCUSSION BLOCKS, used in the music for Chinese and Japanese theaters. The wooden blocks are slapped together to produce a crisp and very penetrating sound. The two blocks are slightly curved and must be struck together at a very exact angle to achieve the most pronounced sound.

CONCUSSION STICKS, any pair of short sticks that can be struck against each other or the ground.

CONCUSSION VESSELS, any two instruments, such as castanets, that are conical and struck together.

CON DUE BACCHETTE A PIATTO (It), with the two sticks on the cymbal.

CONGA, long single-headed Cuban barrel drum, in three general sizes: the *quinto* (9¼ inches in diameter), the *conga* (11¾ inches), and the *tumba* (12½ inches). The shell may be made of either wood or fiberglass. It is very common in South, Central, and North American popular music and has also been used in twentieth-century art music to a limited degree. *See also* " Latin-American Percussion," p. 227; Illus. 29, p. 129.

CONGA-TROMMEL (Ger), conga drum.

CONGO, two-headed drum used in Trinidad and Tobago, Haiti, and Jamaica. Similar to a *bata*.

CONICAL DRUM, any drum with one end larger in diameter than the other.

CON LE DITA (It), with the fingers.

CON LE MANI (It), with the hands.

CON LE SPAZZOLE (It), with (wire) brushes.

CON SORDINO (It), with the mute.

CONTRABASS MARIMBA, marimba with an extended low range that reaches to C_2.

CONTRE LE GENOU (Fr), against the knee.

CONTRO L'ALTRO (It), one against the other.

COOKING POT, *see* **water-phone**.

COPERTO(I) (It), covered, muffled.

COQUILLES NOIX (Fr), coconut shells.

COQUILLES NOIX DE COCO (Fr), horsehooves. (L)

COR D'AUTO (Fr), auto horn.

CORDE (It), snares.

CORDE DEL TAMBURO (LASCIARE) (It), (loosen) snares.

CORDE DI PIANOFORTE (PERCOSSE) (It), (strike) the piano strings.

CORDES (Fr), snares.

CORDES DU PIANO (FRAPPER) (Fr), (strike) the piano strings.

COREANI (It), temple blocks. (L)

CORNE D'APPEL (Fr), toy trumpet. (L)

CORNO DI AUTOMOBILE (It), auto horn.

CORNO DI VACCA (It), cow horn.

CORTO (It), short.

COUCOU (Fr), cuckoo call.

COUP(S) (Fr), stroke(s), shot(s).

COUP ANGLAIS, French style of drumming. *See also* "The Basel Drum," p. 145.

COUP DE BOUCHON (Fr), pop-gun shot. (L)

COUP DE CHARGE (Fr), French style of drumming. *See also* "The Basel Drum," p. 145.

COUP DE MARTEAU (Fr), hammer stroke.

COUP DE PISTOLET (Fr), pistol shot.

COUP DE REVOLVER (Fr), gunshot.

COUPES DE VERRE (Fr), tuned glasses.

COURT (Fr), short.

COUVERT (Fr), covered.

COWBELL, originally a bell hung around the necks of cattle in order to identify their location, now referring to a conical or rectangular bell without a clapper that is struck with a wooden stick. A number of different tones can be achieved by striking the instrument in different areas and by muffling with the hand. It is a staple of Latin and Central American popular music and to a large extent that of North America. A sizable number of twentieth-century art-music works employ this instrument. These include Edgard Varèse's *Ionisation* (1931) and Darius Milhaud's *La Création du monde* (1923). *Grelot de vache* in French, *Herdenglocken* in German, *campanella di vacca* in Italian, *cencerro* in Spanish. *See also* "Latin-American Percussion," p. 227; Illus. 46, p. 141.

COWHORN, instrument consisting of three straight brass tubes with conical bores, developed for Richard Wagner's *Der Ring des Nibelungen* (1876). *Ranz des vaches* in French, *Stierhorn* in German, *corno di vacca* in Italian.

CPC. (It), abbrev. for *campanacci*. (L)

C.R. (Fr), abbrev. for *caisse roulante* (L); (It), abbrev. for *cassa rullante*. (L)

CRANK BELL, *see* **bicycle bells.**

CRANKED RATCHET, *see* **ratchet.**

CRASH CYMBALS, in an orchestral setting, refers to a pair of cymbals that are handheld and struck together sharply. In a drum set context, the term (in the singular) refers to a smaller suspended cymbal of metal, which is quick to peak and has a moderate decay. It is suspended by a strap or rested on a stand and struck with either sticks or mallets. Also called *clash cymbals*.

CR.CYMB., abbrev. for *crash cymbals*. (L)

CRÉCELLE (Fr), ratchet.

CRESCENT, *see* **Turkish crescent.**

CRICKET CLICKERS, metal child's toy that is activated by the hand and produces a sound resembling the chirping of a cricket. *See* Illus. 33, p. 132.

CROT., abbrev. for *crotales*. (L)

CROTALES, small brass disks with thick centers and specific pitches and arranged in two chromatic octaves. The written range is c^1 to c^3, and they sound two octaves higher. Crotales are generally struck with hard plastic or brass mallets; however, two crotales of the same pitch may be struck together to produce a more pronounced tone. Examples of use in the orchestral literature include Hector Berlioz's *Roméo et Juliette* (1839), Claude Debussy's *Prélude à l'après-midi d'un faune* (1894), Maurice Ravel's *Alborado del gracioso* (1905), Igor Stravinsky's *Le Sacre du printemps* (1913) and *Les Noces* (1923), and Carl Orff's *Antigonae* (1949). Also known as *antique cymbals*. *See also* Illus. 15, p. 124.

CROTALI (It), crotales, finger cymbals.

CROTALOPHONE, chromatic set of crotales of at least one octave.

CROTALUM, medieval European term referring to small metal bells with or without clappers.

CROW CALL, bird whistle that imitates the call of a crow.

CRYSTALLOPHONE, tuned glasses, cups, or bowls made from crystal that produce a ringing tone when struck with light mallets or rubbed on the rims with the fingers. *See also* **glass harmonica; musical glasses.**

CRYSTALS, *see* **glass wind chimes.**

C.S. (Fr), abbrev. for *cymbale suspendue.* (L)

CSSE.CL. (Fr), abbrev. for *caisse claire.* (L)

CUBAN COWBELL, cowbell.

CUBAN STICKS, claves.

CUBAN TOM-TOMS, *see* **bongos.**

CUCKOO CALL, two-pitched whistle that imitates the chiming of a cuckoo clock.

CUCKOO SLIDE WHISTLE, two-tone whistle that has a slide used to produce glissandi. *See also* **slide whistle.**

CUCULO (It), cuckoo call.

CUERDAS (Sp), snares.

CUERNO DE AUTO (Sp), auto horn.

CUERNO DE VACA (Sp), cowhorn.

CUERO (Sp), leather.

CUÍCA, Brazilian friction drum played by rubbing a thin bamboo stick with a cloth. The drum has one head, 10 inches in diameter, and a 12-inch metal (formerly wooden) shell. The thin stick is mounted on the inside of the drum in the center of the head. Also called *puita, quica. See also* "Brazil: Percussion Instruments," p. 153.

CUIR (Fr), leather.

CUP BELLS, *see* **cup gongs.**

CUP GLASSES, *see* **musical glasses.**

CUP GONGS, cup-shaped bells that rest on cushions and are struck with leather mallets in the inside rim. These instruments generally produce a soft sustained sound. Also known as *Chinese cup gongs, cup bells, prayer bells. See also* **Buddha temple bell; dobači; temple cup bells.**

CUPOLA (It), bell or cup (of a cymbal).

CYCLONE WHISTLE, *see* **siren whistle.**

CYLINDRICAL DRUM, any drum whose shell is a cylinder.

CYLINDRICAL WOODBLOCK, tubular wooden blocks with two pitches. (L)

CYM., CYMB., abbrev. for *cymbal.* (L)

CYMBAL, *see* **cymbals.**

CYMBALA (Lat), plural of *cymbalum. See also* **bell chimes.**

CYMBAL BELLS, *see* **crotales.**

CYMBALE (Fr), cymbal.

CYMBALE CHINOISE (Fr), Chinese cymbal.

CYMBALE LIBRE (Fr), suspended cymbal.

CYMBALE LIBRE AVEC BAGUETTE (Fr), suspended cymbal with stick.

CYMBALES À 2 (Fr), crash cymbals, pair of cymbals, *see* **á 2.**

CYMBALES À L'ORDINAIRE (Fr), crash cymbals.

CYMBALES ANTIQUES (Fr), antique cymbals.

CYMBALES À PÉDALE (Fr), hi-hat.

CYMBALES CHOQUÉES (Fr), pair of cymbals (see Olivier Messiaen's *Turangalila-Symphonie* [1949]). (L)

CYMBALE SUSPENDUE (Fr), suspended cymbal.

CYMBALETTES (Fr), jingles.

CYMBALS, curved metal plates with a raised bell (or cup) in the center; they are played either in pairs and struck or suspended and struck with a stick. *Cymbales* in French, *Becken, Zimbeln* in German, *piatti* in Italian, *platillios* in Spanish. *See also* "Cymbals," p. 169; Illus. 12, p. 122.

CYMBALS IN HAND, crash cymbals. (L)

CYMBAL TONGS, mounted finger cymbals. *See also* **metal castanets**. (L)

CYMBAL TREE, series of cymbals each smaller than the previous one, strung on top of one another. The entire series can then be struck with a variety of beaters, or even a violin bow, to produce a glissando of cymbal timbres. Also *tree cymbal.*

CYMBALUM (Lat; pl. *cymbala*), (1) small bell in antiquity; (2) small bowl-shaped bell in the Middle Ages, used in plainsong.

CYTHARRA (It), zither.

CZIMBALON, *see* **cymbalum**.

DABACHI, *see* **dobači**.

DABOO, bowl-shaped drum used in an Afro-Caribbean ensemble during the East Indian festival Hosein. *See also* "Steel Band/Pan," p. 297.

D'ACCIAIO (It), (made) of steel.

D'ACIER (Fr), (made) of steel.

DA DAIKO, Japanese drum suspended in a frame or rested on a cylindrical stand and played with two beaters.

DAF, Turkish frame drum. Also *duff.*

DAHINĀ, right-hand drum of the tablā.

DAI BYOSHI, large (18 inches by 18 inches) Japanese double-headed barrel drum played with two beaters.

DAIKO, generic name for a Japanese drum.

DA'IRA, original generic name of round drums in Arab countries; since advent of Islam, means tambourine with jingles and pellet bells.

DĀIRA, frame drum with one head from India.

DAI-SHOKO, bronze Korean bell chime or gong suspended and struck with cloth-covered beaters.

DAK, large African wedding drum. *See also* **dhol; dholak**.

DAKA DE BELLO, African six-tone slit drum played with rubber mallets.

ḌAMARU, South Indian hourglass drum.

DÄMPFEN (Ger), dampen, choke.

DÄMPFER (Ger), mute.

DÄMPFER AB, WEG (Ger), mute off. Also *Dämpfung ab.*

DAMPHU, African tambourine. (L)

DANBOLIÑ, variation of **danbore**.

DANBORE, Basque drum. Also called *danboliñ, gatamore, gathanbore, katambore, katamore.* See also **atambor; tambourin**.

DANCE CASTANETS, two castanets played traditionally with finger tips while being suspended around the thumb.

DANCE DRUM, (1) frame drum used specifically for dance accompaniment; (2) snare drum used within a drum set.

DANS LA COULISSE (Fr), offstage; used in Igor Stravinsky's *Petrouchka* (1911). (L)

DAPHON, *see* **taphōn**.

DARABUCCA, single-headed Middle Eastern hand drum with a clay or metal goblet or hourglass-shaped body; also *darabuka, darbaka, darbukat, darbuka, derabūka, derbaka, derbeki, doumbek, dumbeg, dümbek, dunbak. See also* Illus. 39, p. 137.

DARABUKA, *see* **darabucca.**

DARABUKKA (Ger), darabucca.

DARBAKA, *see* **darabucca.**

DARBOUKKA (Fr), darabucca.

DARBUKA (Sp), darabucca.

DARBUKAT, *see* **darabucca.**

DAR CON (Sp), strike with.

DARMU, small hourglass-shaped Indian drum with bells attached by strings. It is played by rotating. *See also* **monkey drum.**

DAUL, DAULE, *see* **davul.**

DAUMEN (Ger), thumb (roll).

DAVUL, double-headed Janissary bass drum played with one stick and one switch. Also *dawūl. See also* "Janissary Music," p. 195.

D.B. (Fr), abbrev. for **de bois**. (L)

DE BOIS (Fr), (made) of wood.

DE COTON (Fr), (made) of cotton.

DÉCOUVERT (Fr), uncovered, muffler removed.

DEDO(S) (Sp), finger(s).

DEER FOOT RATTLE, deer's foot filled with seeds.

DEER HOOF RATTLE, deer's hoof filled with seeds.

DEERSKIN RATTLE, shaker made from deerskin and filled with seeds.

DE FER (Fr), (made) of iron.

DEJAR VIBRAR (Sp), let vibrate.

DE MÊME (Fr), the same.

DEMI (Fr), middle (literally, half).

DENSHO, *see* **hanshō.**

D'ÉPONGE (Fr), (made) of sponge, sponge sticks.

DERABŪKA, *see* **darabucca.**

DERBAKA, *see* **darabucca.**

DERBEKI, *see* **darabucca.**

DERBOUKA (Fr), darabucca.

DERBUKA (Ger), darabucca.

DERECHA (Sp), right.

DES (Ger), D-flat.

DE SONORITÉ POINTUE ET PERÇANTE (Fr), clear and piercing tone; used in Iannis Xenakis's *Pithoprakta* (1955–1956). (L)

DESTRA(O) (It), right.

DÉTIMBRÉE (Fr), without snares.

DEUTLICH (Ger), distinct.

DEUX EXÉCUTANTS (Fr), two players.

DEUX PLATEAUX (Fr), crash cymbals.

DEVIL'S FIDDLE, *see* **bumbass.**

DEVIL'S VIOLIN, *see* **bumbass.**

D.F. (Fr), abbrev. for *de fer.* (L)

DHARMA BELLS, two-and-a-quarter-octave set of microtonal bells played with soft beaters. Also known as *Chinese Confucian bells, Chinese tree bells.*

DHOL (Hindi); (1) double-headed string-tensioned conical Indian drum; *dhola* in Sanskrit and Bengali; (2) drum used in an Afro-Caribbean ensemble during the East Indian festival Hosein; (3) large African wedding drum. *See also* "Steel Band/Pan," p. 297.

ḌHOLAK, barrel-shaped drum of India with two heads, played with the hand and stick.

DHŌLAKA, small North Indian double-headed string-tensioned wooden drum.

DHOLKI, small dhōlaka. *See also* Illus. 39, p. 137.

DIABLE DE BOIS (Fr), Waldteufel.

DIABYOSHI, Japanese double-headed barrel drum, about 6 inches in diameter and 12 inches deep, with heads mounted on oversized hoops and rope-tensioned; played with bamboo switches. Also *shimedaiko, uta daiko* (L/WM)

DIAMOND MARIMBA, marimba customized by Harry Partch.

DIATONIC MARIMBA, *see* **Chiapan marimba.**

DIAVOLO DI BOSCO (It), Waldteufel.

DI CANNA (It), (made) of rattan, cane.

DICK (Ger), thick.

DICKE PAUKENSCHLÄGEL (Ger), thick timpani sticks.

DICKE SCHLÄGEL (Ger), thick sticks.

DI COTONE (It), (made) of cotton.

DI FELTRO (It), (made) of felt.

DI FERRO (It), (made) of iron.

DI GOMMA (It), (made) of rubber.

DI LANA (It), (made) of wool.

DI LEGNO (It), (made) of wood.

DIMBA, marimba of the Congo. *See also* "The Xylophone," p. 347.

DIMENSIONI (It), dimensions.

DINNER BELLS, *see* **bell chimes.**

DINNER CHIMES, metal bars, usually in groups of three, played with a soft hammer.

DI PELLE (It), (made) of leather.

DIS (Ger), D-sharp.

DISC BUZZER, wooden top that buzzes when spun.

DI SPUGNA (It), (made) of sponge.

DITA(I) (It), finger(s).

DITO POLLICE (It), thumb.

DITUMBA, goblet-shaped Congolese drum with feet; cylindrical or goblet-shaped drum of Zaire; *matumba, mutumbwe* in plural.

DOB (Hungarian), drum; *dobos* in plural.

DOBAČI, Japanese cup-shaped bell that rests on a small cushion and is played with rubber-covered wooden beaters. Also called *dabachi, Japanese temple bell, prayer bell. See also* **Buddha temple bell; cup gong; temple cup bell.**

DOBOS, plural of *dob.*

DOG'S BARK, small skin-covered cylindrical friction drum that imitates the sound of a dog's bark when rubbed. *See also* **lion's roar.**

DOIGT(S) (Fr), finger(s).

DOIRA, small, single-headed Eastern European drum.

DOKO, Japanese brass or copper gong, usually arranged in sets of three. (L/WM)

DŌLAK, small North Indian double-headed, string-tensioned wooden drum. *See also* **dhol.** (L)

DOMBAK, *see* **zarb.**

DOMED GONG, nipple gong with a raised center. Also called *button gong, Java gong.*

DONNERBLECH (Ger), thunder sheet. (L)

DONNERMASCHINE (Ger), thunder sheet. (L)

DONO, African hourglass-shaped drum with string-tensioned heads and played with a beater. When the strings are squeezed with the arm the drum changes pitch. Also *dondo, iya ilu, squeeze drum. See also* **talking drum**.

DOPPELKONUSTROMMEL (Ger), drum with a double conical shape whose center is larger than either end.

DORA, small Japanese brass nipple gong about 18 inches in diameter and 3 inches deep; it is played with a soft mallet. (L/WM)

DOUBLE BELL, two Afro-Cuban iron bells attached at the handle.

DOUBLE CONICAL DRUM, double-headed drum whose center is larger than either end.

DOUCE, DOUX (Fr), soft.

DOUMBEK, *see* **darabucca.**

DOVE CALL, bird call sounding like the "coo" of a dove.

DRAGONS' MOUTHS, hollowed-out round blocks of wood played with soft mallets, often in sets of five, and decorated to look like dragon heads. Also called *drum temple blocks, fish drums. See also* **Korean blocks; temple blocks; wooden fish**. *See* Illus. 23, p. 127.

DRAHTBÜRSTE (Ger), wire brush.

DRESDEN DRUM, type of timpani made in Dresden, Germany. *See also* "The Kettledrum," p. 201; Illus. 2, p. 117.

DRINKING GLASSES, resonant crystal glasses that are rubbed. *See also* **bowls; glass harmonica**. (L)

DROIT(E) (Fr), right.

DROMSLADE (Old Ger), drumbeat, drummer.

DRUM, membranophone of various sizes and shapes with a shell and a vibrating head or heads; struck with the hand(s), stick(s), or mallet(s). *See also* **bass drum; field drum; log drum; long drum; military drum; snare drum; tabor; tenor drum**.

DRUM GONG, large circular metal plate suspended and struck with soft beaters.

DRUM KIT, set of drums, usually bass drum, snare drum, tom-toms, hi-hat, and cymbals. *See also* "Electronic Percussion," p. 191.

DRUM SET, standard dance band set, played by one player and consisting of bass drum, snare drum, two or more tom-toms, hi-hat, and suspended cymbals. *See also* **dance drum; drum kit; trap set**; "The Drum Set: A History," p. 173; Illus. 47, p. 141.

DRUMSTICK WIND CHIMES, wooden drumsticks suspended and played by rattling them.

DRUM TEMPLE BLOCKS, *see* **Chinese temple blocks**.

DUCK CALL, small hollow wooden tube with a reed inside that sounds like a duck when blown. *See* Illus. 36, p. 135.

DUCK QUACK, small hollow wooden tube with a reed inside that sounds like a duck when blown.

DUE BACCHETTE (CON) (It), (hit with) both sticks.

DUE ESECUTORI (It), two players.

DUE PIATTI (It), two cymbals, crash cymbals.

DUFF, *see* **daf.**

DUGGI, North Indian drum, the lower of a pair of tabla.

DUHUL, *see* **davul**.

DULCIMER, stringed instrument played with hammers. *See also* **cimbalom**.

DULCITONE, keyboard with a range of up to four octaves that activates tuning forks. (L)

DUMBEG, *see* **darabucca.**

DÜMBEK, *see* **darabucca.**

DÜMBELEK, Turkish goblet drum with one head. *See also* **darabucca**.

DUMPF (Ger), muffled.

DUNBAK, *see* **darabucca**.

DUNDUN, large Nigerian kettledrum.

DÜNN (Ger), thin.

DÜNNE METALLSCHLÄGEL (Ger), thin metal sticks.

DÜNNE RUTEN (Ger), thin sticks.

DUR (Fr), hard.

DURCHREIBEN (Ger), rub throughout.

DURES ET SÈCHES (Fr), hard and dry; used in Igor Stravinsky's *Le Sacre du printemps* (1913). (L)

DURO (It, Sp), hard.

DURO MEDIANO (Sp), medium hard.

DU RU MALAWI, sixteen-note African marimba with buzzing membranes over the resonators, played with rubber mallets.

DUST PAN GONG, suspended metal dust pan struck with a soft mallet.

DZWON (Polish), bell.

EBENSO (Ger), in the same way.

ÉCHELETTE(S) (Fr), seventeenth-century xylophone. *See also* "The Xylophone," p. 347.

EFFECTS, diverse sounds used to imitate trains, boats, planes, wind, etc. Also *sound effects*. *See* Illus. 36, p. 135.

EFFETTO DI PIOGGIA (It), rain machine, surf effect. (L)

EINFACH (Ger), single.

EINFELLIG (Ger), single-headed.

EINFELLIGE GROSSE TROMMEL (Ger), single-headed bass drum.

EINFELLIGE TOM-TOMS (Ger), single-headed tom-toms.

EIN MANN (Ger), one man (player).

EINZELTÖNE KLINGEN LASSEN (Ger), let each tone fade away; used in Krzysztof Penderecki's *Capriccio* (1967) (L)

EISEN (Ger), iron.

EISENSCHLÄGEL (Ger), iron beater.

EJECUTANTE (Sp), player.

EKIRO, small, Japanese Kabuki bell with pellet rattle inside. (L/WM)

EKTARA, Indian gourd with a string passing through a skin covering the open end. Also called *spike lute*. *See also* **oop gopi**.

EKWE, African slit drum.

ELECTRIC ACOUSTIC BELLS, tuned metal rods that are struck using an electro-mechanical keyboard. A 1930s' instrument used to imitate the sound of low bells.

ELECTRIC CHIMES, *see* **electronic chimes**.

ELECTRONIC CARILLON, amplified keyboard glockenspiel.

ELECTRONIC CHIMES, chimes amplified by electronic pickup. Also called *electric chimes*.

ELECTRONIC MARIMBA, marimba amplified by electronic pickup.

ELECTRONIC PERCUSSION, instrument whose sound is produced electrically. *See also* "Electronic Percussion," p. 191.

ELECTRONIC TIMPANI, invention of B.F. Miessener consisting of thirteen amplified chromatic strings that are struck with timpani mallets.

ELECTRONIC VIBES, vibraphone amplified by electronic pickup.

ELEFANTENGLOCKE (Ger), elephant bell.

ELEPHANT BELLS, small spherical brass bells with clappers and with claw-like pointed prongs on the lower half. Also called *Sarna bells.*

ELK CALL, sound effect used to imitate an elk's call.

EN BOIS (Fr), (made) of wood.

EN CANNE (Fr), (made) of cane.

ENCLUME (Fr), anvil, metal block.

EN COPA (Sp), on the bell or cup.

EN CUIR (Fr), (made) of leather.

END STROKE COMBINATIONS, new drum strokes created by Basel drummers. *See also* "The Basel Drum," p. 145.

EN ÉPONGE (Fr), (made) of sponge.

EN FER (Fr), (made) of iron.

EN FEUTRE (Fr), (made) of felt.

ENGKOK, small Japanese cymbals used in the gamelan orchestra together with the kemong. Also *engkuk.*

ENGKUK, another name for *engkok.*

EN GOMME (Fr), (made) of rubber.

EN LAINE (Fr), (made) of wool.

EN ROTIN (Fr), (made) of rattan.

EN SECOUANT (Fr), shaking.

EN S'ÉLOGNANT (Fr), very remote, far away; used, for example, in Claude Debussy's *Nocturnes* (1909).

ENTSPANNT (Ger), loosened, relaxed.

ENVELOPPÉ EN FIL DE LAINE (Fr), yarn-covered.

EOLIFÓN (Sp), wind machine.

EOLIFONI (It), wind machine.

EOLIPHONE (Fr), wind machine.

ÉPAISSE (Fr), thick.

ÉPERONS (Fr), spurs (jingles).

ÉPONGE (Fr), sponge.

ES (Ger), E-flat.

ESECUTATO SULLA CASSA DEL TAMBURO COL MANICO DELLA MAZZA (It), played on the shelf (of the drum) with the handle of the stick.

ESECUTORE(I) (It), player(s).

ESQUILA (Sp), clapper bell, cowbell.

ESTACA (Sp), stick.

ESTREMITÀ (It), edge.

ETINGILI, Latin-American plucked idiophone, African sansa.

ÉTOUFFÉ (Fr), choked, dampened.

ÉTOUFFEZ (Fr), choke, dampen.

ETSUZUMI, generic name for Japanese double-headed hourglass drum. *See also* **ōtsuzumi.**

ÉXÉCUTANT(S) (Fr), player(s).

FA'AIL, pipe, whistle; from the root word *ili,* meaning "to blow."

FACIMBALON, Hungarian xylophone. *See also* "The Xylophone," p. 347.

FASSTROMMEL (Ger), barrel drum.

FELL (Ger), drumhead, skin.

FELL (STARK) ENTSPANNT (Ger), drumhead (very) relaxed.

FELPATO (It), felt. (L)

FELTRO (It), felt.

FENG LING, Chinese aeolian bells.

FER (Fr), iron, steel.

FERRINHO, FERRO, Brazilian triangle. *See also* "Brazil: Percussion Instruments," p. 153.

FERRO (It), iron.

FERRO DEL TRIANGOLO (It), triangle beater.

FEUTRE (Fr), felt.

FIBRA (Sp), fiber.

FIELD DRUM, deep two-headed drum, often with snares. (L) *See also* **military drum**. *See* Illus. 25, p. 128.

FIELTRO (Sp), felt.

FILZ (Ger), felt.

FILZ-PAUKENSCHLÄGEL (Ger), felt timpani sticks.

FILZSCHLÄGEL (Ger), felt stick(s).

FINE (Fr), thin; (It), end.

FINGER(N) (Ger), finger(s).

FINGERBECKEN (Ger), finger cymbals. Also *Fingerzimbeln.*

FINGER BELL, *see* **tap bell**.

FINGER CYMBALS, small non-pitched metal disks about 2 inches in diameter, played with the thumb and index finger. *See* Illus. 36, p. 135.

FIS (Ger), F-sharp.

FISCHIETTO A PALLINA (It), pea whistle.

FISCHIO (It), signal whistle. (L)

FISCHIO D'UCELLO (It), bird whistle. (L)

FISCHIO SIRENA (It), siren whistle. (L)

FISH DRUM, *see* **Chinese temple blocks; dragons' mouths**.

FISSATO (It), attached.

FIXÉ (Fr), attached.

FLAGELLO (It), slapstick.

FLAMMED COUP DE CHARGE, new stroke created by Basel drummers. *See also* "The Basel Drum," p. 145.

FLAQUES SONORES (Fr, It), poured water. (L)

FLASCHENKORKENKNALL (Ger), pop-gun shot.

FLASCHENSPIEL (Ger), tuned bottles.

FLAUTO A CULISSE (It), slide whistle.

FLESSATONO (It), flexatone. (L)

FLEX. (Fr), abbrev. for *flexatone.*

FLEXATON (Ger), flexatone.

FLEXATONE, small sheet of spring steel in a frame with wooden strikers mounted on either side. The player shakes the beater while bending the steel in order to change the pitch. (L) *See* Illus. 35, p. 134.

FLEXATRON, flexatone. (L)

FLÖTENUHR (Ger), musical clock.

FLÛTE À COULISSE (Fr), slide whistle; used in Krzysztof Penderecki's *De natura sonoris II* (1971) (L)

FOG HORN, three wooden pipes of different pitches blown together; usually low pitched (L).

FOGLIE DI RAME COL MANO (It), metal wind chimes (struck) with the hands. (L).

FOGLIO DI METALLO (It), foil rattle.

FOIL RATTLE, sheet of thin metal foil, thunder sheet. (L)

FOOT CYMBAL, *see* **hi-hat**.

FOOTED DRUM, any drum with its lower end carved to form a foot.

FORTÉ-CAMPANO, Parisian instrument from 1825 developed to imitate the sound of bells.

FORTSETZEND (Ger), continuing.

FOUET (Fr), whip, slapstick.

FOUETTER (Fr), strike, hit.

FR. (It), abbrev. for *frusta.*

FRAME DRUM, any drum whose depth is less than its diameter, usually having only one head; some have handles and/or jingles. *See also* **hand drum**. *See* Illus. 38, p. 137.

FRAME RATTLE, rattle with objects attached to the outside of a frame (i.e., tambourine).

FRAPPÉ (Fr), struck.

FRAPPÉ AVEC (Fr), struck with.

FRAPPER À LA MANIÈRE ORDINAIRE (Fr), strike normally.

FRAPPER À L'ORDINAIRE (Fr), strike in the usual way.

FRAPPER LA MEMBRANE (Fr), strike the head.

FREGARE (It), rub, brush.

FREI (Ger), literally, free; on a cymbal part, use suspended cymbal. *See also* **Becken frei**.

FREIHÄNG. (Ger), abbrev. for *freihängend.* (L)

FREIHÄNGEND (Ger), suspended (cymbal).

FREIHÄNGEND MIT SCHLÄGEL (Ger), suspended (cymbal) with stick.

FRH.M.SCHL. (Ger), abbrev. for *freihängend mit Schlägel.* (L)

FRICTION DRUM, membranophone whose sound is produced through friction; in the *cuíca*, a stick pierced through its head is rubbed; in the *lion's roar*, a piece of leather or canvas is pulled along a string coming out of the center of the skin. *See* Illus. 35, p. 134.

FRIGIDEIRA, small Brazilian frying pan played with a metal rod about 3/16 inches thick and 6 inches long, with a diameter of about 5 inches. *See also* "Brazil: Percussion Instruments," p. 153.

FRÔLÉE(S) (Fr), lightly touched, brushed, rubbed (e.g., cymbals) (Fr).

FRÔLER, FRÔLEZ (Fr), lightly touch, brush, rub (e.g., cymbals).

FRÔLER LA MEMBRANE AVEC LA POUCE (Fr), rub the skin with the thumb, thumb roll.

FROTTÉ(E), rubbed (together), brushed (e.g., cymbals).

FROTTER, FROTTEZ, rub (together), brush (e.g., cymbals).

FRS. (It), abbrev. for *frusta.* (L)

FRULLO, FRULLONE (It), bull roarer.

FRUSTA (It), slapstick, whip.

FUMABATA NGOMA, *see* **yuka**.

FURIN, Japanese cast temple bells. (L/WM)

FURITSUZUMI, very small Japanese double-headed drums mounted on a handle that is played by twirling, whereupon two beads strike the heads. (L/WM)

FUSSBECKEN (Ger), hi-hat.

FUSTA (Sp), slapstick, whip.

FUSTO (It), shell.

FUSTO IN GIUNCO (It), cane handle.

FÛT (Fr), shell.

G., abbrev. for *gong.* (L)

GABELBECKEN (Ger), cymbal tongs.

GAGAKU DRUM, double-headed Japanese frame drum with laced floating heads, played with two sticks.

GAKUDAIKO, double-headed Japanese hourglass drum approximately 5 inches in diameter and 12 inches deep, played with the hands. (L/WM)

GAMBANG, Javanese term for wood or metal trough xylophone or sometimes a gong, used in the gamelan orchestra and having sixteen to twenty-one bars. *See also* "The Xylophone," p. 347.

GAMELAN, Indonesian or Malaysian percussion orchestra consisting of drums, gongs, wood or metal xylophones, and sometimes a wind instrument or voice. *See also* "Percussion and Dance," p. 265.

GAMELAN GONG, nipple gong used in a gamelan orchestra.

GANDA, footed drum of Kenya, open at the bottom.

GANE, *see* **kane**.

GANGÁRIA, Latin-American cowbell.

GANZÁ, type of chocalho or metal shaker, with a 9-inch-long handle (2-inch diameter), attached to the shaker in a cylinder (3 inches wide and 7½ inches in diameter). *See also* "Brazil: Percussion Instruments," p. 153; Illus. 34, p. 133.

GARIGLIONE (It), carillon.

GATAMORE, *see* **danbore**.

GATHANBORE, *see* **danbore**.

GAUCHE (Fr), left.

G.C. (It), abbrev. for *gran cassa*. (L)

G.C. (Fr), abbrev. for *grosse caisse*. (L)

G.CAISSE. (Fr), abbrev. for *grosse caisse*. (L)

GEAR MACHINE, hand-cranked device used to imitate turning gears.

GEBETSGLOCKE (Ger), temple bell, cup gong. (L)

GEDÄMPFT (Ger), muted (when referring to timpani), muffled (when referring to snare or tenor drum); can also mean "without snares," mute on.

GEGENEINANDER GESCHLAGEN (Ger), hit one against the other.

GEGENSCHLAGBLÖCKE (Ger), concussion blocks. (L); hyōshigi.

GEGENSCHLAGGEFÄSSE (Ger), concussion vessels.

GEGENSCHLAGIDIOPHONE (Ger), concussion idiophone.

GEGENSCHLAGSTÄBE (Ger), concussion sticks. (L)

GEKRATZT (Ger), rasped.

GELÄUTE (Ger), ringing of bells, cowbell with a clapper.

GENDANG, Malaysian barrel drum.

GENDER, six- to thirteen-note metallophone used in the Javanese gamelan orchestra in Indonesia.

GENDER BARUNG, medium-sounding multi-octave metallophone, part of the Javanese gamelan orchestra.

GENDER PANEMBUNG, low-sounding single-octave Javanese metallophone; lower octave of the gender barung; part of the gamelan orchestra. Also called *slentem*.

GENDER PANERUS, high-sounding multi-octave Javanese metallophone; part of the gamelan orchestra.

GENOU (Fr), knee.

GEOPHONE, double-headed drum (24 inches by 7 inches) filled with lead pellets and rotated to imitate the sound of the sea.

GERIEBEN (Ger), rubbed, scraped.

GES (Ger), G-flat.

GESCHLAGEN (Ger), struck.

GESCHLOSSEN (Ger), closed.

GESPANNT (Ger), under tension.

GESTIMMT (Ger), tuned (to).

GESTOPFT (Ger), muffled, muted, stopped.

GESTRICHEN (Ger), rubbed.

GEWIRBEL (Ger), roll (of drums).

GEWIRBELT (Ger), rolled.

GEWÖHNLICH (Ger), literally, ordinarily; in a cymbal part, play with a pair of crash (clash) cymbals (bells down); play in the usual manner; mute off.

GEWÖHNLICHER KLÖPPER (Ger), ordinary beater.

GEWÖHNLICHER SCHLÄGEL (Ger), ordinary beater.

GEWÖHNLICH MIT TELLERN (Ger), crash cymbals; together (cymbals).

GEWÖHNLICH SCHLAGEN (Ger), strike normally.

GHANA, generic names for idiophones from the Indian subcontinent.

GHAṬA, South Asian percussion vessel or pot, pot drums, membranophones.

GHUNGHURA (Bengali), Indian ankle bells. Also *ghunghuru*, *ghuṅgrū*.

GHUNGHURA STICK, Indian ankle bells mounted on a stick.

GHUNGHURU, *see* **ghunghura**.

GHUṄGRŪ, *see* **ghunghura**.

GIANT TRIANGLE, large steel rod bent into a triangular shape, which is used for calling cowboys to dinner. *See also* **chow iron**

GIAV. (It), abbrev. for *Javanese*. (L)

GIAVANESE (It), Javanese.

GIGELIRA (It), xylophone.

GILIM GILIM, Brazilian bell tree.

GINEBRAS, xylophone from the Basque area dating from 1628; also Cuban single-row xylophone. *See also* "The Xylophone," p. 347.

GINOCCHIO (It), knee.

GIRARE (It), to turn.

GIS (Ger), G-sharp.

GITTERRASSEL (Ger), bamboo tubes that are suspended and shaken, angklung.

GLÄSER (Ger), glass harmonica.

GLÄSERSPIEL (Ger), tuned glasses.

GLASHARFE (Ger), glass harp.

GLASHARMONIKA (Ger), glass harmonica.

GLASPAPIER (Ger), sandpaper.

GLASS CHIMES, *see* **glass wind chimes**.

GLASS CHORD, *see* **glass harp**.

GLASSES, bowls. (L)

GLASS HARMONICA, thirty or forty glass bowls or cups that are rotated or rubbed, producing sound by finger friction; it was invented by Benjamin Franklin in 1761. *Armonica* in Italian. *See also* **glass harp**; **musical glasses**.

GLASS HARP, instrument consisting of forty-six glass bowls or cups and invented by Bruno Hoffmann around 1929. Also called *glass chord*. *See also* **glass harmonica**; **musical glasses**. (L)

GLASSPIEL (Ger), musical glasses.

GLASSTÄBCHEN (Ger), glass wind chimes. (L)

GLASSTÄBE (Ger), glass wind chimes.

GLASS WIND CHIMES, suspended pieces of thin glass activated by the wind or by being touched slightly. Also *glass chimes*. (L)

GLAS-WINDGLOCKEN (Ger), glass wind chimes.

GLCK., GLCKSPL. abbrev. for *glockenspiel.* (L)

GLEICH (Ger), quickly.

GLEICH ABDÄMPFEN (Ger), quickly mute, dampen.

GLISSANDO AVEC LE LEVER (Fr), pedal glissando.

GLISSANDO COLLA PEDALE (It), glissando with pedal.

GLISSANDO MIT PEDAL (Ger), glissando with pedal.

GLÖCKCHEN (Ger), tubular bells. (L)

GLÖCKCHENSPIEL (Ger), little bells.

GLOCKE (Ger), bell.

GLOCKEN (Ger), tubular bells.

GLOCKENARTIG (Ger), bell-like; used in Bedřich Smetana's "Vyšehrad" from *My Fatherland* (1874) (L)

GLOCKENPLATTEN (Ger), bell plates. (L)

GLOCKENRAD (Ger), bell wheel played by spinning, horologium.

GLOCKENSPIEL, originally a German term, now used in English, for orchestra bells. *See also* **bell lyre**; **celesta**; **song bells**. *See* Illus. 14, p. 123.

GLOCKENSPIEL À CLAVIER (Fr), keyboard glockenspiel.

GLOCKENSPIESE (Ger), form of Turkish crescent included as part of Janissary music. *See also* "Janissary Music," p. 000.

GLOCKENSTAB (Ger), bell bar. (L)

GLOCKSP., abbrev. for *glockenspiel.* (L)

GLSP., abbrev. for *glockenspiel.* (L)

GNZ., abbrev. for *ganzá.* (L)

GOBA, *see* **berimbau.**

GOBLET DRUM, single-headed Arabian drum shaped like a goblet. *Tambour en goblet* in French, *Bechertrommel* in German.

GOG, Central American Indian word for marimba.

GOHON, Central American Indian word for marimba.

GOMA (Sp), rubber.

GOMMA (It), rubber.

GOMMA ELASTICA (It), rubber.

GOMME (Fr), rubber.

GONG, circular metal percussion disk having a definite or indefinite pitch. It may be flat, curved, have a central boss, curved or flat edges, is hung vertically, and is hit in the center by a soft beater. It differs from a bell in that the vibrations at the center are greater than at the edges. *See also* **tam-tam**; Illus. 19, 41, p. 126, p. 138.

GONG AGENG, largest and lowest-pitched gong in a set of bossed gongs in a Javanese gamelan. It plays at the start of each cycle. Also *gong gede.*

GONG À MAMELON (Fr), nipple gong. (L)

GONG BASS DRUM, large single-headed bass drum often used in theaters in the nineteenth century.

GONG CHIME, graduated set of button gongs usually arranged in a semicircle.

GONG CINESI (It), nipple gong, pitched gong. (L)

GONG DRUM, single-headed frame drum. (L) *See also* **gong bass drum**.

GONG GEDE, *see* **gong ageng.**

GONG GIAPPONESE (It), nipple gong, pitched gong. (L)

GONG GIAVANESE (It), Javanese gong, nipple gong, pitched gong. (L)

GONGO (Sp, Port), gong.

GONGS OF KOREA, long ringing, distinctly pitched gongs from Korea.

GONGSTROMMEL (Ger), steel drum. (L)

GONG SUWAKAN, Javanese gamelan gong.

GOURD, GOURD SCRAPER, notched empty calabash or fruit gourd that is played by scraping. *See also* **güiro**.

GOURD DRUM, drum whose shell is a hollowed gourd.

GOURD PIANO, *see* **piano de cuia**.

GOURD RATTLE, vessel rattle made from a dried gourd that is filled with seeds or pebbles. Sometimes beads are hung on the outside of the gourd. *See also* **cabasa.**

GOURD WATER DRUM, empty calabash or fruit gourd filled with water or floated on water and struck.

GOURD XYLOPHONE, xylophone with resonators placed under each bar; the gourds are selected by size to amplify the sound of the various bars.

GOYOM, Guatemalan marimba.

GRACIDIO DI ANITRA (It), duck call.

GRAGÉ, Haitian gourd scraper similar to a güiro.

GRAMMOFONO (It), record player. *See also* **usignuolo**.

GRAN CASSA (It), bass drum.

GRAN CASSA A UNA PELLE (It), single-headed bass drum, gong drum.

GRAND(E) (Fr, It), large.

GRANDE CLOCHE (Fr), large church steeple bell. (L)

GRAND TAMBOUR (Fr), long drum.

GRAN TAMBURO (It), bass drum.

GRAN TAMBURO VECCHIO (It), long drum.

GRAVE (Fr), low (pitch), deep.

GR.C. (Fr), abbrev. for *grosse caisse.* (L)

GR.C. E PIATTI (It), abbrev. for *grosse caisse e piatti.* (L)

GREEK CYMBALS, small metal disks often tuned to exact pitches that are usually played in pairs. *See also* **ancient cymbals; crotales**. (L)

GREEK DRUM, single-headed Middle Eastern clay or metal goblet or hourglass-shaped drum. *See also* **darabucca.**

GREGGE (It), literally, flock; in music, cowbell.

GREL. (Fr), abbrev. for *grelots.* (L)

GRELOTS (Fr), pellet bells, sleigh bells, harness bells, jingles. (L)

GRELOTS DE VACHES (Fr), cowbells.

GRF. (It), abbrev. for *grammofono.* (L)

GRIDO DI CORNO (It), toy trumpet.

GRIFF (Ger), handle.

GRIFFKLAPPER (Ger), clapper with a handle, slapstick.

GRIJUTIANS, Mexican rattle.

GRILLET (Fr), pellet bells.

GRO., abbrev. for *güiro.* (L)

GROSS (Ger), great, large.

GROSSE CAISSE (Fr), bass drum.

GROSSE CAISSE À PIED AVEC CYMBALS (Fr), bass drum played with a foot pedal, to which is attached a cymbal and striker; used in Darius Milhaud's Concerto for Percussion and Small Orchestra (1930).

GROSSE CAISSE À UNE SEULE PEAU (Fr), single-headed bass drum, gong drum. (L)

GROSSE CAISSE AVEC PEDALE (Fr), bass drum played with a foot pedal, dance drum.

GROSSE PAUKE (Ger), large kettledrum.

GROSSE RUHRTROMMEL (Ger), large tenor drum. (L)

GROSSES HÄNGENDES BECKEN (Ger), large hanging or suspended cymbal.

GROSSES TAM-TAM (Ger), large, low sounding tam-tam.

GROSSE TIEFE HOLTZTROMMEL (Ger), large low-pitched slit drum.

GROSSE TROMMEL (Ger), bass drum.

GROSSE TROMMELSCHLÄGEL (Ger), bass drum beater.

GROSSE TROMMELSTOCK (Ger), bass drum beater.

GROUND DRUM, membrane attached to several poles, which are driven into the ground, the membrane beaten as a drum.

GR.TR. (Ger), abbrev. for *grosse Trommel.* (L)

GR.TRM. (Ger), abbrev. for *grosse Trommel.* (L)

GR. TROMMEL (Ger), abbrev. for *grosse Trommel.* (L)

GRZECHOTKA (Polish), clapper, rattle.

GUACHARACA, notched Colombian stick that is scraped.

GUACHE, Colombian bamboo rattle filled with beads or seeds.

GUAJEY, large Latin-American gourd rattle.

GUARARÁ, Brazilian metal shaker shaped like a tube.

GUERO, *see* **güiro.**

GUIMBARDE (Fr), Jew's harp. Also *trompe de Béarn.*

GÜIRA, Dominican metal scraper that is played with a stick like a güiro. *See also* "Latin-American Percussion," p. 227.

GÜIRO, large Latin-American gourd sounded by scraping a stick or wires over notches cut into the upper surface. *See also* "Latin-American Percussion," p. 227; Illus. 34, p. 133.

GÜIRO DE JOBÁ, Afro-Cuban water gourd or water calabash struck with sticks. Also *jícara de jobá.*

GUIRRO (It), güiro.

GUITCHARO, Latin-American gourd scraper. *See also* **güiro.**

GUIZO (Port), small bell; jingle, sleigh bell.

GUMMI (Ger), rubber.

GUMMISCHLÄGEL (Ger), rubber stick(s).

GUT GESTIMMT (GER), well-tuned.

HACKBRETT (Ger), dulcimer.

HAKU HAN, Japanese wood clappers.

HALBHART (Ger), half-hard.

HALBMOND (Ger), half-moon, Turkish crescent.

HALB ZUR MITTE (Ger), at the middle.

HÄMMERND (Ger), hammered, struck.

HAMMERS, metal, rawhide, or wood tools played by striking them on the ground or resonant box. *See also* **mallets.**

HAMMERSCHLAG (Ger), hammer stroke.

HAND BELLS, brass bells with a soft felt clapper tuned chromatically and shaken by the hands.

HAND-CRANKED LINGUAPHONE, music box with metal tongues that are plucked.

HAND CYMBALS, brass cymbals played in pairs.

HAND DRUM, type of drum played primarily with bare hands; often a narrow wooden shell with a single head, like a tambourine without jingles.

HANDGLOCKEN (Ger), hand bells.

HANDGLOCKENSPIEL (Ger), hand bells. (L)

HANDGRIFF (Ger), handle.

HAND HARMONIUM, reed squeeze box of India used for playing a drone. Also known as *śruti-peṭṭi*.

HANDLE BELL, brass bell with a handle. *See also* **hand bells**.

HANDLE CASTANETS, pair of castanets mounted on a handle.

HANDLE CLAPPER, any clapper mounted on a handle.

HANDRATSCHE (Ger), ratchet. (L)

HANDS, pair of hands clapped together.

HAND SCREW TIMPANI, sixteenth-century tension-design timpani with individual tuning rods.

HAND SNARE DRUM, single-headed frame drum with springs on the underside of the head, played with one stick.

HANDTROMMEL (Ger), hand drum, tambourine, bongo. (L)

HANFSCHLEGEL (Ger), yarn mallet.

HÄNGEND (Ger), suspended.

HÄNGENDE BAMBUSROHRE (Ger), wind chimes (wood).

HÄNGENDE BECKEN (Ger), suspended cymbals. (L)

HÄNGENDE GLASSTÄBE (Ger), glass wind chimes.

HANGING BOARD, oblong wooden percussion board struck with a hammer, used in the rites of the Greek Orthodox Church. Also *sēmantērion, simandron*.

HANGING DRUM, *see* **tsuridaiko**.

HANSHŌ, Japanese Buddhist bell struck on the edge. Also *densho, hansō*.

HARANG (Hung), bell.

HARMONICA, *see* **glass harmonica.**

HARMONICA DE BOIS (Fr), wooden harmonica, xylophone.

HARMONICA DE FRANKLIN (Fr), glass harmonica.

HARMONICA DE VERRE (Fr), glass harmonica.

HARMONICON, glass harmonica. *See also* **musical glasses**.

HARMONIKON (Ger), glass harmonica, harmonicon.

HARNESS BELLS, non-pitched metal bells that are shaken. *See also* **sleigh bells**.

HÁROMSZÖG (Hung), triangle.

HARPE DE VERRE (Fr), glass harmonica.

HART (Ger), hard.

HARTER FILZ (Ger), hard felt.

HART GESCHLAGEN (Ger), struck hard.

HARTLEDERSCHLÄGEL (Ger), hard leather sticks.

HAT, *see* **Turkish crescent**.

HATSU, 12-inch pair of Japanese cymbals with a large, central bell.

HAUT (Fr), high.

HAUTEUR (Fr), height, pitch.

HEERPAUKE (Ger), kettledrum (obs.).

HERD BELLS, clapper bells of different pitches hung around the neck of an animal.

HERD COWBELLS, non-pitched metal bells with a clapper inside that are hung around the neck of an animal; cowbells.

HERDENGLOCKE(N) (Ger), cowbell(s).

HERRO (Sp), iron.

HERUNTERSTIMMEN (Ger), lower to (a pitch).

HIER ETWAS ABDÄMPFEN (Ger), here somewhat muted.

HIGH-HAT, *see* **hi-hat.**

HIGH-HAT MACHINE (Ger), hi-hat.

HI-HAT, pair of small cymbals mounted on a vertical rod controlled by a foot-operated pedal. Also called *foot cymbals, high-hat, pedal cymbal, sock cymbals. See* "The Drum Set: A History," p. 173.

HIN, Burmese bronze bell with a wooden clapper, suspended from the backs of pack animals. *See also* **yak bells.**

HOCH (Ger), high (pitch or timbre).

HOCHET (Fr), rattle, jingle.

HÖHE (Ger), upper register, height.

HOJALATA DE TRUENO (Sp), thunder sheet

HOLMXYLOPHONE, cross-support xylophone of Asia and East Africa.

HOLZ (Ger), wood.

HOLZBLOCK (Ger), woodblock.

HOLZBLOCKTROMMEL (Ger), woodblock.

HOLZE PAUKENSCHLÄGEL (Ger), wood(en) timpani sticks.

HÖLZERNES GELÄCHTER (Ger), obsolete south German and Austrian word for xylophone. Also *hültze glechter.*

HOLZFASS (Ger), wooden barrel.

HOLZFIEDEL (Ger), xylophone.

HOLZ GESCHLAGEN, AUF DEM (Ger), (struck) on the wooden shell; in Gustav Mahler's Symphony No. 2 (1895), the switch is struck on the bass drum shell. (L)

HOLZHAMMER (Ger), wooden mallet.

HOLZHARMONIKA (Ger), xylophone.

HOLZKASTEN (Ger), woodblocks.

HOLZKLAPPER (Ger), slapstick (e.g., Gustav Mahler's Symphony No. 5 [1902]); whip. (L)

HOLZPLATTENTROMMEL (Ger), wooden-headed tom-tom, wood-plate drum

HOLZRAND (Ger), wooden shell.

HOLZRASPEL (Ger), wooden scraper, wooden scratcher

HOLZSCHLÄGEL (Ger), wooden stick(s).

HOLZSTABSPIEL (Ger), xylophone.

HOLZ-TOM-TOM (Ger), wooden-headed tom-tom. (L)

HOLZTON (Ger), woodblock. (L)

HOLZTROMMEL (Ger), wood or slit drum.

HOLZ-UND SCHLAGINSTRUMENT (Ger), xylophone. (L)

HOLZ-UND STROHINSTRUMENT (Ger), xylophone.

HOLZ-WINDGLOCKEN (Ger), wooden (bamboo) wind chimes. (L)

HOOF BEATS, *see* **coconut shells.**

HOROLOGIUM, medieval wheel, with small bells attached to its rim. Also called *bell wheel.*

HORSEHOOVES, *see* **coconut shells.**

HOSANNA, small carillon.

HOURGLASS DRUM, double-headed drum whose shell is thinner at the center than at either end.

HPÀ-SI, Burmese bronze drum.

HSIAO-KU, 2- to 3-inch Chinese skin-headed frame drum; also *xiaogu.*

HSING-ERH, Chinese cymbals.

HUEHUETL, Mexican single-headed cylindrical wooden drum with feet; originally any pre-Columbian clay or wood drum. (L)

HUFGETRAPPEL (Ger), hoof beats.

HÜLTZE GLECHTER (Ger), *see* **hölzernes Gelächter**.

HUMMING TOP, child's toy top filled with seeds that rattle when spun. *Toupie bourdonnante* in French, *Brummkreisel* in German, *trompo silbador* in Spanish.

HUPE (Ger), auto horn.

HYŌSHIGE (HYŌSHIGI), Japanese wooden clappers, about 1½ by 1½ by 8 inches, that are struck against a board or each other and played face to face. Sometimes called *Kabuki blocks, Kabuki clappers.*

IDIOPHONE, any instrument that produces sound by the vibration of its body when it is shaken, rubbed, or struck; e.g., bell, gong, chimes, cymbals, xylophone.

IDIOPHONE PAR ENTRECHOC (Fr), concussion idiophone.

IDIOPHONE PAR PERCUSSION (Fr), percussion idiophone.

IDIOPHONE PAR SÉCOUEMENT (Fr), shaken idiophone.

IGBIN, open-ended Nigerian drum with feet.

IMMER (Ger), always.

IMMER GEDÄMPFT (Ger), always muted.

INCUDINE (It), anvil.

IN DER FERNE (Ger), in the distance, offstage.

IN DER MITTE (Ger), for drums, means in the middle; for cymbals, means on the bell. (L)

IN DER MITTE AUF DER KUPPEL (Ger), on the bell of the cymbal. (L)

INDIAN BELLS, small brass bells with clappers. (L)

INDIAN BELL STRAP, small bells attached to leather straps worn on the ankles.

INDIAN CHIMES, small bells attached to leather straps worn on the ankles.

INDIAN DRUM, clay or wood drum made from the body of a hollow log, with one or two heads played with mallets that are hollow and filled with beads, pebbles, or seeds; the heads are usually held by thongs of animal skin. Used by Native Americans. *See also* **American Indian tom-tom**; Illus. 38, p. 137.

INDIANISCHER TROMMEL (Ger), Indian drum, American Indian tom-tom.

INDIAN JINGLES, metal disks mounted to wooden frames played by striking them together.

INDIAN TABLAS, *see* **tablā**.

INDISCHE SCHELLENBAND (Ger), Indian ankle bells.

IN HAND, cymbals; pair of cymbals (crash cymbals).

IN VERSCHIEDENER GRÖSSE (Ger), (use) different sizes (refers to *Rührtrommel*); used in Carl Orff's *Antigonae* (1949). (L)

IRON CHAINS, metal link chains shaken or thrown against the floor or metal plates.

IRON PIPES, lengths of iron pipe struck with hard beaters.

ISTRUMENTO D'ACCIAIO (It), glockenspiel. (L)

IZQUIERDA(O) (Sp), left.

JACKDAW, English friction drum with friction cord. *See also* **lion's roar.**

JALTARANG, Indian musical bowls of two to three octaves, made of porcelain or clay, that are played with thin wooden sticks and tuned by adding water. Also *tuned bowls.* (L)

JANISSARY MUSIC, music of the Turkish sultan's bodyguard (c. 1400–1826); the instrumental ensemble consisted of bass drums, cymbals, triangles, and Turkish crescents. *See also* "Janissary Music," p. 195.

JANISSARY SWITCH, beater for a Turkish marching drum.

JANITSCHARENMUSIK (Ger), Janissary music.

JĀNK, Turkish bell.

JANTE (Fr), rim, metal hub of a car wheel.

JAPANESE BARREL DRUM, *see* **odaiko.**

JAPANESE METAL BARS, cowbell-shaped metal bars suspended over resonators.

JAPANESE TEMPLE BELL, *see* **dobači.**

JAPANESE TREE BELL, metal bells suspended end to end that are played by rubbing them with a finger or hand as a glissando.

JAPANESE WOODBLOCK, small wood disk with three legs that is played with a small hammer.

JAPANESE WOOD CHIMES, bamboo wood chimes. (L)

JAPANESE WOODEN DRUM, resonating wooden drum shaped like a disk and standing on three short, wooden legs that are attached to the bottom. *See also* **mokubio.**

JAVA GONG, nipple gong. (L)

JAVANISCHER BUCKELGONG (Ger), nipple gong. (L)

JAWBONE, dried jawbone of an ass with teeth used in Afro-Cuban music; it is scraped or struck with the fist, allowing the teeth to rattle. *See also* **quijada; vibraslap.**

JAW'S HARP, *see* **Jew's harp.**

JAZZBESEN (Ger), wire brushes. (L)

JAZZ COWBELL, cowbell used with a drum set.

JAZZ CYMBAL, small thin crash cymbal used with a drum set.

JAZZ DRUMS, tom-toms used with a drum set.

JAZZO-FLÛTE (Fr), slide whistle. (L)

J. DE T. (Fr), abbrev. for *jeu de timbres.* (L)

JEDEN, JEDER (Ger), each.

JEDEN TON GLEICH ABDÄMPFEN (Ger), damp every note immediately; used in Gustav Mahler's Symphony No. 2 (1895). (L)

JEDOR, large Japanese single-headed conical drum. Also called *bajidor, jidor.*

JE DREI PAUKEN (Ger), each (player) uses three timpani.

JEU À TUBES (Fr), tubular bells. (L)

JEU CHROMATIQUE DE CENCERROS (Fr), chromatically tuned cowbells.

JEU DE CLOCHE (Fr), tubular bells. (L)

JEU DE CLOCHETTES (Fr), orchestra bells. (L)

JEU DE TIMBRES (Fr), glockenspiel.

JEU DE TIMBRES À CLAVIER (Fr), keyboard glockenspiel. (L)

JEW'S HARP, frame of metal or wood with a flexible tongue; the metal tongue is plucked while held between the teeth. Also *jaw's harp*. (L)

JHANJ, pair of small brass hand cymbals used in an Afro-Caribbean ensemble during the East Indian festival Hosein. *See also* "Steel Band/Pan," p. 297.

JHĀNJH, large Indian cymbals.

JHĀNJHĀNA, Indian metal maracas.

JÍCARA DE JOBÁ, another name for *güiro de jobá*.

JIDOR, *see* **jedor**.

JINGLE BELLS, *see* **sleigh bells**.

JINGLES, sleigh bells, sistrum. (L)

JINGLE STICK, metal jingles mounted on a stick.

JINGLING JOHNNIE, percussion stick with bells and jingles, a corruption of the Turkish *cewhan* or *chaghāna*, used in the Janissary military bands. *See also* "Janissary Music," p. 195.

JOUER AUSSI (Fr), play also.

JOUER INDEPENDAMMENT DU CHEF (Fr), play independent of the conductor's beat; used in Pierre Boulez's *Pli selon pli* (1962). (L)

JOUÉ SUR LE CADRE DU TAMBOUR AVEC LE MANCHE DE LA MAILLOCHE (Fr), played on the shell (of the drum) with handle of the stick.

JUEGO DE CAMPANAS (Sp), tubular bells. (L)

JUEGO DE TIMBRES (Sp), orchestra bells. (L)

JUG, liquid storage vessel that produces a low hum when air is blown across the opening.

JUNGLE WOOD DRUM, *see* **log drum**.

JUSQU'À SIGNE DU CHEF (Fr), play on the cue from the conductor; used in Pierre Boulez's *Pli selon pli* (1962). (L)

KA, single-headed barrel-shaped Cuban drum.

KABUKI CLAPPERS, KABUKI BLOCKS, *see* **hyōshigi**.

KABUKI DRUM, single-headed frame drum on a handle that is played with one stick in Japanese Kabuki theater. *See also* **pancake drum; uchiwadaiko.**

KADIMBA, lamellaphone of Zaire.

KAFFIR PIANO (HARP), European name for mbira.

KAJIREI, Japanese metal rattle with three bells attached to a handle. Also called *zichirei, rattle of Japan*.

KALANBA (KALANGBA), KALANGWA, Congolese xylophone. *See also* "The Xylophone," p. 347.

KALIMBA, metal or wooden strips attached to a resonating box that is plucked with the finger tips. *See also* **Chinese thumb piano; mbira; sansa; thumb piano.**

KALUBA RAIN FOREST, double-headed drum filled with water, whose pitch changes as the water moves back and forth.

KAMESA, South American shaker filled with shot or sand. Also *camesa*. (L)

KAMESO, African shaker similar to the kamesa.

KAMSALA, generic name for gongs in Marathi.

KAMSARA, generic name for gongs in Bengali.

KAMSYA, generic name for gongs in Sanskrit. Also *kansya*.

KANE, Japanese name for a gong or bell. Also *gane*.

KANONE(N) (Ger), cannon.

KANSYA, *see* **kamsya.**

KAPOK, cotton, wool felt.

KARATĀLI, circular wooden clappers with handles from India. *Kartāl* in Hindustani, Marathi, and Punjabi; *kartali* in Bengali. Also *kurtar*.

K'AR-RNGA, Tibetan gongs.

KARTAL, African cymbals.

KARTĀL, *see* **karatāli.**

KARTALI, *see* **karatāli.**

KAS, KĀSA, (1) Islamic finger cymbal; (2) large bowl-shaped cymbal; *kāsāt* in plural.

KĀSĀT, *see* **kas.**

KASAYI, 17-key Rhuandan likembe.

KASIK, Turkish castanets.

KASTAGNETTEN (Ger), castanets.

KASTAN'ETY (Russ), castanets.

KASTANIETY (Polish), castanets.

KATAMORE, *see* **danbore.**

KATTKO, Japanese double-headed barrel drum, about 6 inches in diameter and 12 inches deep, with heads mounted on oversized hoops and rope-tensioned. (L/WM)

KAUM HÖRBAR (Ger), almost inaudible; used in Anton Webern's Six Pieces, Op. 6 (1909/1920). (L)

KAUM VERNEHMBAR (Ger), hardly perceptible.

KAZOO, hollow metal or wooden tube with a buzzing membrane that is played by humming into the instrument. *See also* **membranophone; mirliton.**

KBD. XYL., abbrev. for *keyboard xylophone*. (L)

KEGELTROMMEL (Ger), conical drum.

KELCHGLÄSER (Ger), cup glasses, glass harmonica.

KELCHGLÄSER, AM RANDE MIT FINGER GERIEBEN (Ger), literally, cup glasses; in music, rub finger around the edge; bowls. (L)

KEMONG, (1) small Javanese cymbals used in the gamelan, together with the engkok; (2) Balinese gong.

KEMPLI, Balinese gong.

KEMPUL, 20-inch Javanese button gong in the mid-range of a set of gamelan gongs. (L)

KEMPUR, Balinese button gong suspended in a frame.

KEMPYANG, (1) Javanese double gong or two gongs played simultaneously; (2) small Javanese frame drum.

KENDANG, double-headed lace-tensioned conical drum from Java used in the gamelan orchestra.

KENDANG AWI, *see* **Kinchir.**

KENDANG GENDING, double-headed lace-tensioned barrel-shaped hand drum from Java, used in the gamelan orchestra.

KENDE, Liberian concussion idiophone of metal; also in West Africa and Zimbabwe.

KENONG, high-pitched Javanese button gong used in the gamelan orchestra.

KENTONGAN, Indonesian slit drum (3 to 6 feet long), made from bamboo or a tree trunk.

KERO, double-headed Japanese processional drum (6 by 6½ inches), which is played with two sticks and hung from the player's neck. (L)

KESSELGONG (Ger), kettle gong, button gong.

KESSELPAUKE(N) (Ger), timpano(i). (L)

KESSELTROMMEL, (1) old German term for timpani; (2) Balinese double-headed monkey drum that is played by rotating.

KETIPUNG, small drum used in the Javanese gamelan orchestra.

KETTEN (Ger), chains (iron).

KETTENRASSEL (Ger), iron chains. (L)

KETTLEDRUM, large single-headed drum consisting of a bowl-shaped shell and made of copper, aluminum, or fiberglass; it is played with two sticks. The modern kettledrum is made with a foot-tuning mechanism (pedal drum, pedal timpani). *Timbale* in French, *Pauke* in German, *timpano, timballo* in Italian, *timbal* in Spanish. The term *timpani* is often used to mean *kettledrums* in modern scores. *See also* "The Kettledrum," p. 201; Illus. 13, p. 123.

KETTLE GONG, Southeast Asian bronze gong of great antiquity, with very deep rims and a flat, ornamented surface.

KETUK, small button gong used in a gamelan orchestra.

KEYBOARD GLOCKENSPIEL, set of orchestra bells with a keyboard that activates wooden balls against the bars. Its range (written) sometimes extends three and a third octaves, from c^1 to e^4, which sounds a third higher than the top note on the piano; it is not produced in the United States today. (L) Also called *keyed glockenspiel, keyboard orchestra bells. See also* **celesta.**

KEYBOARD ORCHESTRA BELLS, *see* **keyboard glockenspiel.**

KEYBOARD XYLOPHONE, harpsichord-shaped xylophone of four octaves, whose keyboard activates wooden balls against the bars; used in Béla Bartók's *Bluebeard's Castle* (1911). (L)

KEY CHIMES, metal household or automobile keys suspended like a wind chime; key tree wind chimes.

KEYED GLOCKENSPIEL, *see* **keyboard glockenspiel; keyboard orchestra bells.**

KEYED XYLOPHONE, xylophone activated by a piano keyboard.

KEY TREE WIND CHIMES. *See* **key chimes.**

KHAKHĀNI, *see* **kūs.**

KHANJERI, African tambourine. (L)

KHARTAL, Indian jingle stick played by shaking with both hands.

KHOL, South Indian conical hand drum with lace tensioning that has two different-sized heads and is wider in the middle than at either end.

KHONG, Thai gong.

KHONG THOM, high-pitched set of Cambodian gongs.

KHONG TOCH, a low-pitched Cambodian gong set.

KHONG VONG LEK, high-pitched Thai gong chime.

KHONG VONG YAI, low-sounding Thai gong chime.

KIDIMBA, Congolese marimba. *See also* "The Xylophone," p. 347.

KIESELSTEIN (Ger), stone.

KIKÓRI, *see* **kindembo.**

KIN, (1) Japanese cup-shaped bronze bells that are struck or rubbed with a soft beater while resting on cushions; (2) African leg rattles made from cocoons; (3) Chinese gong; (4) Japanese cup gong about 6 to 18 inches in diameter, played with a leather-covered rod.

KINABAN, Philippine Jew's harp.

KINCHIR, pair of West Javanese stamping tubes, which are played together. Also *kendang awi*.

KINDEMBO, Afro-Cuban wrist maraca. Also *kikóri*.

KINDERLEIER, (Ger), toy hurdy gurdy. (L)

KINDERSPIELZEUGTROMMEL (Ger), toy drum.

KINGIRA, a one-stringed instrument with a calabash resonator. Also called *stick ektara*.

KIRCHENGLOCKEN (Ger), church bells, tubular chimes. (L)

KISKILLA, (1) small Basque clapper bell; (2) pellet bell. *See also* **esquila.**

KIYADA, Latin-American jawbone.

KLAPPER (Ger), clapper, slapstick.

KLAPPHOLZ (Ger), slapstick. (L)

KLAVIATURGLOCKENSPIEL (Ger), keyboard glockenspiel.

KLAVIATURXYLOPHON (Ger), keyboard xylophone.

KLAVIER (Ger), piano.

KLAVIERGLOCKENSPIEL (Ger), keyboard glockenspiel.

KLAVIERSAITEN GESCHLAGEN (AN DEN) (Ger), struck (on the) piano strings.

KLAVIERXYLOPHON (Ger), keyboard xylophone.

KLAXON, hand cranked automobile horn used during the 1920s and 1930s. Also *klaxon horn, machine claxon. See also* **ooga horn**.

KLAXON À MANIVELLE (Fr), automated klaxon horn. *See also* **klaxon**.

KLAXON HORN, *see* **klaxon**.

KL. BECK. (Ger), abbrev. for *kleine Becken*. (L)

KLEIN (Ger), small.

KLEINE GLOCKEN (Ger), small bells.

KLEINE MILITÄRTROMMEL (Ger), small military drum.

KLEINER HOLZSCHLÄGEL (Ger), small wood stick, thin wood stick.

KLEINER SCHLÄGEL (Ger), short (small) stick.

KLEINER SCHWARZKOPF (Ger), sponge head.

KLEINES HÄNGENDES BECKEN (Ger), small suspended cymbal.

KLEINES STÄBCHEN (Ger), thin stick.

KLEINES TAM-TAM (Ger), small tam-tam.

KLEINE TROMMEL (Ger), snare drum.

KLEINE TROMMEL-STOCKEN (Ger), snare drumsticks.

KLINGEN LASSEN (Ger), let vibrate, do not damp.

KLINGSTEINE (Ger), stones.

KLINGT (Ger), (it) sounds, rings.

KLINGT, WIE IN ALLEN WEITEREN FÄLLEN, EINE OCTAVE HÖHER (Ger), sounding, as in all other times, an octave higher; used in Gustav Mahler's Symphony No. 2 (1895). (L)

KLINGT OKTAVE HÖHER (Ger), sounding an octave higher; used in Alban Berg's *Wozzeck* (1925). (L)

KLINGT WIE NOTIERT (Ger), sounds as written; used in Alban Berg's *Wozzeck* (1925). (L)

KLINTING, Javanese Jingling Johnnie having bells suspended from a wheel attached to a pole, which is struck on the ground.

KLOCKA (Swedish), bell.

KLOK (Dutch), bell.

KLOKKA (Norwegian), bell.

KLOKKE (Danish), bell.

KLOKKENSPEL (Dutch), church bells, orchestra bells, carillon. (L)

KLONG, Thai drum.

KLÖPPEL (Ger), bell clapper, bass drumstick. (L)

KLÖPPER (Ger), drumsticks.

KL.TR. (Ger), abbrev. for *kleine Trommel.* (L)

KL. TR. IM ORCH. (Ger), abbrev. for *kleine Trommel im Orchestra.* (L)

KNALLFROSCH (Ger), rattle.

KNARRE (Ger), cog rattle played by spinning; ratchet.

KNICKY-KNACKERS, seventeenth-century English term for bones or clappers.

KNIE GESTRICHEN (AM) (Ger), struck (on the) knee.

KNIESCHLAG (Ger), strike on the knee.

KNITTING NEEDLES, used to create various effects on percussion instruments.

KNOCHENKLAPPER (Ger), bones, slapstick. (L)

KNUT (Russ), slapstick.

KO, double-headed Korean drum with a handle, which is played with mallets or the hands. Also called *Korean hand drum.*

KO CH'ING, Chinese musical stone suspended in a frame.

KO CHUNG, 12- to 24-note bell chime from China. *See also* **chung**.

KOCIOL (Polish), kettledrum.

KODAIKO, small double-headed Japanese processional drum played with two sticks. (L)

KOKIRIKO, Japanese instrument consisting of several pieces of wood strung together and played with a whipping motion.

KOKOSNUßSCHALEN (Ger), coconut shells.

KOLATKA (Polish), clapper or beater.

KOLOKOL (Russ), bell.

KOLOKÓL'CHIKI (Polish), glockenspiel.

KONCHIKI, heavy bronze Japanese bell gong, about 6 inches in diameter, with a 1-inch flange; played with a horn hammer. (L/WM)

KONG, Cambodian gong.

KONGA, Congolese drum. *See also* **conga**.

KONG WONG YAI, 16-note low-pitched Thai gong chime. Also called *Thailand gamelan gongs.*

KONUSTROMMEL (Ger), conical drum.

KONZERT-TROMMEL (Ger), snare drum. (L)

KOPF (Ger), head.

KOREAN BENDING GONG, spun brass gong with a thin center, whose pitch changes when struck. Also *Chinese opera gong.*

KOREAN BLOCKS, temple blocks. (L)

KOREAN HAND DRUM, *see* **ko**.

KOREAN MOKO, *see* **mokubio**.

KOREAN MULTIPLE WHIP, six small woodblocks suspended on a cord, which are pushed together.

KOREAN SQUEEZE DRUM, double-headed hourglass-shaped drum with laced heads whose pitch changes when the laces are squeezed. Also *chang go.*

KOREAN TEMPLE BLOCKS, hollowed wooden blocks often played in sets of five.

KORK (Ger), cork.

KÖS, kettledrums of Janissary music. *See also* "Janissary Music," p. 195.

KOTLY (Polish), kettledrums.

KOTSO, single-headed hourglass-shaped Sudanese drum.

KOTSUZUMI, small double-headed lace-tensioned hourglass-shaped Japanese "squeeze" drum (about 5 inches × 12 inches), played with the hands. *See also* **ōtsuzumi**. (L/WM)

KOU, *see* **ku**.

KREIS (Ger), around, circular.

KREISFORMIGE BEWEGUNG (Ger), turn, whirl.

KREMBALON (KREMBALA), ancient Greek clappers.

KROTALEN (Ger), antique cymbals, finger cymbals. (L)

KROTALON (pl. *krotala*), ancient Greek clapper, usually used in pairs.

KROUMA, ancient Greek clappers.

KROUPALON, ancient Greek wooden clapper. Also *krupalon*.

KROUPEZION, ancient Greek wooden clappers played with the foot. Also known as *kroupalon*.

KRUG (Ger), jug.

KRUPALON, *see* **kroupalon**.

KRYSTALLOPHONE (Ger), glass harmonica. *See also* **crystallophone**.

KSILOFON (Russ), xylophone.

KU, Chinese term for drum. Also *kou*.

KŪBA, Middle-Eastern hourglass-shaped drum.

KUBA-PAUKEN (Ger), timbales.

KUCKUCK-INSTRUMENT (Ger), cuckoo bird call.

KUCKUCKSPFEIFE (Ger), cuckoo bird call.

KUCKUCKSRUF (Ger), cuckoo bird call. (L)

KUHGLOCKE(N), (Ger), cowbell(s).

KUHGLOCKE(N) OHNE KLÖPPEL (Ger), cowbell(s) without clapper(s).

KUHSCHELLE (Ger), cowbell.

KUKEM, Coptic term meaning drum.

KUPPEL (Ger), bell or cup of a cymbal.

KÜRBIS (Ger), gourd.

KÜRBISRASPEL (Ger), güiro or gourd rattle (L); guaracha.

KURTAR, *see* **karatāli**.

KURZ (Ger), short.

KURZE HALTE (Ger), short stop.

KŪS, large Arabic drum. *Kūsāt* in plural. Also *khakhāni*.

KWENINGBA, KWENGWE, Congolese xylophone. Also *linz, linzi*. *See also* "The Xylophone," p. 347.

KYEEZEE, *see* **Burma bell**.

KYE TSI, *see* **Burma bell**.

KYMBALA, ancient Greek cymbals. *Kymbalon* in singular.

KYMBALI (Finnish), cymbals.

LAISSEZ LES CYMBALES COLLER (Fr), let the cymbals drop against each other. (L/1978)

LAISSEZ VIBRER (Fr), let vibrate.

LAISSEZ VIBRER DOUCEMENT EN EFFLEURANT À PEINE LES DEUX PLATEAUX (Fr), let vibrate gently by barely touching.

LALI, West Polynesian slit drum.

LAMA DI COLTELLO (It), knife blade.

LAME D'UN CANIF (Fr), knife blade.

LAMELLAPHONE, plucked idiophone, e.g., mbira.

LAME MUSICALE (Fr), musical saw.

LAMINA METALICA (Sp), thunder sheet.

LANA (It), wool.

LANDSKNECHTSTROMMEL (Ger), military snare drum, tabor (L); long drum.

LANG (Ger), long.

LANG GEHALTEN (Ger), held for a long time.

LASCIARE, LASCI VIBRARE (It), let vibrate.

LASCIARE LE CORDES DEL TAMBURO (It), loosen snares.

LASCIARE VIBRARE LEGGIERAMENTE APPENA TOCCATA (It), let vibrate gently by barely touching.

LASTRA (It), sheet, slab, steel plate.

LASTRA DEL TUONO (It), thunder sheet. (L)

LASTRA DI LATTA (It), literally, sheet of tinplate; in music, thunder sheet. (L)

LASTRA DI METALLO (It), metal plate.

LASTRA DI SASSO (It), stone disks, lithophone. (L)

LATEINAMERIKANISCHE TIMBALES (Ger), Latin-American timbales.

LATHES, wooden slats struck on leather pads, as in Edgard Varèse's *Déserts* (1954). (L)

LÁTIGO (Sp), slapstick.

LATIN-AMERICAN FOLK INSTRUMENTS, include the timbales (timpani), campañuela (small bells), the marimbula and sansa (plucked idiophones), the caixa (snare drum), the bombo (bass drum), the cuíca (friction drum), and the pandeiro (tambourine). *See also* "Brazil: Percussion Instruments," p. 153; "Latin-American Percussion," p. 227.

LATIN-AMERICAN TIMBALES, *see* **timbales**.

LAVA ROCKS, volcanic rocks held in each hand and struck together; used in Samoa, Hawaii, and Tahiti.

LEDER (Ger), leather.

LEDER BEZOGEN (Ger), leather covered.

LEDERSCHLÄGEL (Ger), leather sticks. (L)

LEERE FLASCHEN (Ger), empty bottles.

LÉGER (Fr), light.

LEGGIERO (It), light.

LEGNETTI (It), claves, Cuban sticks. (L)

LEGNI DI RUMBA (It), claves. (L)

LEGNO (It), wood, wood stick, woodblock; in Sergei Prokofiev's *Alexander Nevsky* (1939), the *legno* part calls for a solid block of wood without the resonating slit. (L)

LEGNOFONO, nineteenth-century Italian xylophone. *See also* "The Xylophone," p. 347.

LEGWEGWE, Congolese spherical woven rattle played by dancers and sometimes used as a children's toy.

LEICHT (BERÜHRT) (Ger), light, barely (touching).

LEICHTE SCHLÄGEL (Ger), light sticks.

LEISE (Ger), soft.

LERO-LERO (It), reco-reco, wooden scraper, scraper.

LEVER TIMPANI, timpani that are tuned with a lever or crank.

LIDS OF GARBAGE CANS, lids that are struck or banged together to produce different sounds.

LIÈGE (Fr), cork.

LIGHT BULB RATTLE, common light bulb that is covered with papier-mâché, then broken, creating a rattle.

LIGNEUM PSALTERIUM (Lat), xylophone.

LIKEMBE, non-specific term for a sansa in the East Congo, Ruanda, Urundi, and areas of Uganda. *See also* "The Xylophone," p. 347.

LIMBA (Romanian), bell clapper.

LING, Chinese bells struck with an inside clapper.

LINGUAPHONE, plucked idiophone.

LINKES FELL (Ger), left head on a two-headed drum.

LINKS (Ger), left.

LINZ, LINZI, *see* **kweningba.**

LION'S ROAR, friction drum made from a large wood, metal, or clay cylindrical shell, sometimes with a closed bottom. The open end has a thin, mounted skin head with a rope or gut string that protrudes from the center. It is played by pulling a piece of canvas or leather, which has been moistened or rosined, along the string away from the instrument. To achieve the true sound of a lion's roar, the shell of the instrument should be attached to a wooden base and have the volume of a 2½ gallon (10 liter) bucket. The instrument originated in Africa. Unlike a cuíca, it uses a string rather than a stick. A smaller version of the instrument is the dog's bark. *Tambour à cordes* in French, *Brummtopf, Löwengebrüll* in German, *rugghio di leone* in Italian, *tambor de fricciòn* in Spanish. *See also* **friction drum**; **jackdaw**; **string drum**; Illus. 35, p. 134.

LIP, bottom part of a bell also referred to as the rim.

LITHOPHON (Ger), lithophone.

LITHOPHONE, modern stone-bar instrument consisting of a set of perforated stone disks mounted on rubber-covered pegs and positioned on a frame as a piano keyboard. It is played with heavy glockenspiel mallets and has a clear and penetrating sound. Since the instrument is somewhat awkward to play, agility is limited.

LITOFONO (It), lithophone, *litófono* in Spanish. (L)

LOCHSIRENE (Ger), siren.

LOG DRUM, large form of the slit drum, traditionally a hollowed-out log up to 30 feet, positioned over a pit and stomped upon. It has a warm sonority with limited carrying power and is struck with toy super ball beaters, hard felt or rubber mallets. The traditional log drum can be found in the Americas, Asia, and the South Seas. The modern log drum is similar to the Mexican slit or wooden drum (teponaztli). Also known as *African tree drum, jungle wood drum, teponaztli, tuned log, wooden drum. Tambour de bois* in French, *tamburo di legno* in Italian, and *Holztrommel* in German. *See also* **slit drum.**

LONG (Fr), long.

LONG DRUM, drum in which the depth of the shell is greater than the diameter of the heads. Originally it was used with fifes by mercenary soldiers in the Middle Ages. The drum was 20 to 30 inches deep and 16 to 20 inches in diameter with a wooden shell, gut snares (across the bottom head), and calfskin heads. The modern version of the instrument is approximately the same size and stands on three adjustable legs. It has four to six gut snares across the bottom head and has a dark muffled sound. The long drum of Provence is called a *tambourin.* In parts other than the French-speaking areas, *tambourin* and *tambour de basque* refer to a *tambourine*. The long drum is also known as a *tabor* or *mercenary soldiers' drum*. *Landsknechtstrommel* in German. The parade drum is a smaller version. *See also* "The Rope-Tensioned Drum in America," p. 281.

LOO-JON, *see* **lujon.**

LOTOSFLÖTE (Ger), slide whistle (L); swanee piccolo.

LOTOS FLUTE, slide whistle.

LOTTERY WHEEL, metal scraper used to simulate a lottery wheel (*roue de la lotérie*) in Erik Satie's *Parade* (1917). The ratchet can be used as a substitute.

LOURD (Fr), heavy.

LOW-BOY, precursor to the modern hi-hat, 13 to 18 inches tall. *See also* "The Drum Set: A History," p. 173.

LÖWENGEBRÜLL (Ger), lion's roar.

LST. (It), abbrev. for *lastra.* (L)

LUJON, pitched American metallophone consisting of thin, rectangular pieces of spring steel fastened to the edges of a tall, rectangular wooden box made of teak or rosewood. The original lujon had six notes but now can have as many as thirteen. It has limited projection and is played with soft timpani mallets or yarn mallets. Also known as *bass metallophone, loo-jon, metal log drum.*

LUKIMBI, single-headed Congolese slit drum. Also called *alindi.*

LUN, type of sansa.

LUNGO (It), long.

LV. (Fr), abbrev. for *laissez vibrer.* (L)

LYRA GLOCKENSPIEL, *see* **bell lyre.**

MACCHINA DAL (A) VENTO (It), wind machine.

MACCHINA DA SCRIVERE (It), typewriter.

MACCHINA DI TUONO (It), thunder machine, thunder sheet. (L)

MACETA (Sp), Latin-American mallet.

MACH. À V. (Fr), abbrev. for *machine à vent.* (L)

MACHINE À ÉCRIRE (Fr), typewriter.

MACHINE À TONNERRE (Fr), thunder machine, thunder sheet.

MACHINE À VENT (Fr), wind machine.

MACHINE DRUM, kettledrum with a mechanical device that tunes all lugs simultaneously. *Maschinenpauke* in German. *See also* "The Kettledrum," p. 201.

MACILLO (Sp), (piano) hammer.

MACUNGO, *see* **berimbau.**

MĀDALĀ (Bengali, Sanskrit), Indian barrel drum.

MADERA (Sp), wood.

MADERA Y PAJA (Sp), straw xylophone.

MADIMBA, African xylophone with resonators. Also *midimba. See also* "The Xylophone," p. 347.

MAGLIO (It), heavy mallet. (L)

MAILLET (Fr), hammer.

MAILLOCHE (Fr), large mallet. Usually used for bass drum, e.g., Claude Debussy's *La Mer* (1905) and Igor Stravinsky's *L'Histoire du soldat* (1918).

MAILLOCHE DE BOIS (Fr), wood stick. (L)

MAILLOCHE DE GROSSE CAISSE (Fr), bass drum beater. (L)

MAILLOCHE DE TIMBALES (Fr), timpani stick. (L)

MAILLOCHE DOUBLE (Fr), two-headed stick (double stick).

MAIN DROITE (Fr), right hand.

MAIN GAUCHE (Fr), left hand.

MAJIMBA, Congolese name for madimba.

MAL ACCORDÉ (Fr), not tuned (L); out of tune.

MALIMBA, Congolese xylophone. *See also* "The Xylophone," p. 347.

MALLETS, generic term for sticks, beaters, hammers, etc. In a strict sense, the term "mallet" indicates a ball-shaped, eliptical, or disk-shaped head mounted on a handle. The head can be made from wood, metal, rubber, or synthetic materials with different degrees of softness or hardness, and the head may be covered or padded. The handle can be made from wood, cane, or other materials. *See also* "Range of Mallet Instruments," p. 367; Illus. 42, p. 139.

MAMA CRY, tube with a mouthpiece on one end and open on the other. When the player blows into the mouthpiece and palms the opposite end, a "mama cry" is the resulting sound. *See* Illus. 42, p. 000.

MAMBIRA, *see* **valimba.**

MAMEDAIKO, small Japanese double-headed barrel drum, about 6 inches in diameter and 2 inches deep, with nailed heads. (L/WM)

MAMELON (Fr), nipple gong. (L)

MANCHE (Fr), handle.

MANCHE EN JONC (Fr), cane handle.

MANDALA HARP, *see* **tambura.**

MANDIRĀ, small heavy cymbals from India, approximately 1½ inches in diameter. They have a cup and curved edges or no edges at all. The pitches of the two cymbals are always very close. Sometimes referred to as a *manjira* in Hindi, Hindustand, and Hindustani.

MANICO (It), handle.

MANIMBULA, *see* **marimbula.** (L)

MANJA, *see* **manza.**

MANJIRA, *see* **mandirā.**

MANO DERECHO (Sp), right hand.

MANO IZQUIERDO (Sp), left hand.

MANO SINIESTRO (It), left hand.

MANTSHOMANE, South African frame drum of the Thonga, with a laced goatskin or buckskin head and played with a stick.

MANUAL CYMBALS, in orchestral percussion parts, indicates a pair of cymbals struck together. *See* **crash cymbals.**

MANZA (MANJA), Congolese ten-bar arc xylophone; xylophone of Zaire. *See also* "The Xylophone," p. 347.

MAQUINA DE TRUENO (Sp), thunder sheet. (L); thunder machine.

MAQUINA DE VIENTO (Sp), wind machine.

MAR., abbrev. for *marimba* (L).

MARACA(S), originally a gourd rattle of the South American Indians. The modern version is usually used in pairs and is made of a hollowed-out gourd attached to a handle and filled with dried seeds or pebbles. The sound of the instrument is determined by the size of the head and type of fillings used. The instrument is traditionally shaken so the interior particles strike the interior walls of the head. Maracas have become a given in the percussion accompaniment of the Latin-American dances, in particular the rhumba. The Cuban maraca is sometimes in the shape of an hourglass or a cross. It can also be made of a güira (an oval-shaped gourd) and is sometimes played in sets of four or more. The Brazilian maraca, also known as *xere* or *adja* in Pernambuco, is made of two short cones joined at their widest ends. Also called *sonaja*. *See also* "Latin-American Percussion," p. 227; Illus. 34, p. 133.

MARACA DE MÉTAL (Fr), metal rattle (L); tin horn.

MARACA DI METALLO (It), metal rattle (L); tin horn.

MARACA STICKS, sticks, mallets, or beaters that have been hollowed out and filled with beads to produce a rattle effect when played on a drum surface.

MARACHE (It), maracas.

MARB., abbrev. for *marimba*. (L)

MARCHING MACHINE, instrument consisting of a frame with blocks of wood loosely attached with wire or string. The player holds the frame and stamps the blocks of wood on the ground or resonating box to simulate the sound of marching feet.

MARGE (Ger), shell (L); rim.

MARGINE (It), edge, rim.

MARIMB., abbrev. for *marimba*. (L)

MARIMBA, mellow-sounding xylophone with gourd or box resonators, probably derived from xylophones brought to Central America by African slaves from the seventeenth to the nineteenth centuries. It can have one or two rows of bars, and it is played with yarn or rubber mallets. *See also* "The Marimba in Mexico and Related Areas," p. 239; "The Xylophone," p. 347; Illus. 10, p. 121.

MARIMBA CON TECOMATES, diatonic marimba with gourd resonators. *See also* "The Marimba in Mexico and Related Areas," p. 239.

MARIMBA CUACHE, the smaller instrument of the marimba doble. Also called *marimba picolo, marimba requinta, marimba tenor*. *See also* "The Marimba in Mexico and Related Areas," p. 239.

MARIMBA DE ARCO, a marimba without legs, suspended from the performer's body on an arched bough. *See also* "The Marimba in Mexico and Related Areas," p. 239.

MARIMBA DOBLE (MARIMBA CUACHE), chromatic marimba ("double marimba"), consisting of two separate instruments, one slightly larger than the other. *See also* "The Marimba in Mexico and Related Areas," p. 239.

MARIMBAFONO (It), marimba (L); marimbaphone.

MARIMBA GONGS, *see* **metallophone.**

MARIMBA GRANDE, the larger instrument of the marimba doble. *See also* "The Marimba in Mexico and Related Areas," p. 239.

MARIMBAPHON (Ger), marimbaphone.

MARIMBAPHONE, metal marimba (metallophone) produced by J.C. Deagan, Inc., of Chicago about 1920. Also called *steel marimba*.

MARIMBA PICOLO, *see* **marimba cuache.**

MARIMBA REQUINTA, *see* **marimba cuache.**

MARIMBA SENCILLA, diatonic marimba ("simple marimba"). *See also* "The Marimba in Mexico and Related Areas," p. 239.

MARIMBA TENOR, *see* **marimba cuache.**

MARIMBA-XYLOPHONE, *see* **xylomarimba.**

MARIMBULA, Afro-Cuban linguaphone or large sansa. The instrument has an unspecified number of tunable strips of spring steel mounted over a resonator with a soundhole. The resonator is usually rectangular, but sometimes circular, with its longest side 17 inches. The instrument is played by plucking the strips of steel with the thumbs or fingers or slapping the resonator with the palm.

MARK TREE, series of small graduated brass tubes that are suspended from a length of wood. A high-pitched microtonal sound is produced when the player glisses up or down the tubes with fingers or a triangle beater. The instrument is usually mounted on a cymbal stand. Named after its creator, Mark Stevens. *See also* Illus. 16, p. 124.

MARTEAU (Fr), hammer.

MARTEAU SUR UNE PLANCHE (Fr), hammer on a board.

MARTELLI METALLICI (It), metal hammers. (L)

MARTELLO (It), hammer.

MARTELO (Port), hammer.

MARTILLO (Sp), hammer.

MART. S.U.P. (Fr), abbrev. for *marteau sur une planche.* (L)

MARUGA, vessel rattle of Afro-Cuban origin made from various shaped gourds or metal or wooden containers. The instrument is filled with hard objects such as seeds or small pebbles. Can be replaced by a chocalho or maracas.

MASCELLA D'ASINO (It), jawbone of an ass. (L)

MASCHINENPAUKE (Ger), machine drum.

MATRACA (Sp), rattle, clapper; Brazilian wooden blocks (two) about 4 to 6 inches long and 3 inches wide that are held in the hands and clapped together, used by Heitor Villa-Lobos. *See also* "Brazil: Percussion Instruments," p. 153.

MATTAUPHONE, instrument invented by Joseph Mattau in or by 1855, consisting of thirty-eight tuned, graduated glasses mounted in a rectangular box and played by rubbing moistened fingers around the rim of each glass. It was tuned by varying the amount of water in each glass.

MATUMBA, plural of ditumba.

MAULTROMMEL (Ger), Jew's harp.

MAZZA (It), drumstick.

MAZZETTA (It), bass drum beater, soft mallet, wooden hammer. (L)

M.B. (Ger), abbrev. for *mit Becken.* (L)

M.B.F., abbrev. for *marimbaphone.*

MBILA, another name for ambira; xylophone of southern and southeast Africa. *See also* "The Xylophone," p. 347.

MBIRA, Bantu name for a sansa with six to thirty keys attached to a resonating box that is plucked with the fingertips. Also called *African thumb piano, kalimba. See also* **marimbula.**

M.D. (Ger), abbrev. for *mit dem* (L); (It), abbrev. for *mano derecho.* (L)

MECHANIZED CLAXON, *see* **klaxon.**

MEDIA DURE (It), medium hard.

MEDIA MOLLE (It), medium soft.

MEDIO (It, Sp), middle

MEHRERE (Ger), several.

MEHRERE BECKEN MIT TELLERN (Ger), several pairs of crash cymbals.

MEHTER, Turkish military band. *See also* "Janissary Music," p. 195.

MELODICON WITH DRUMS, piano with a chromatic set of tuned tambourines. The tambourines are sounded simultaneously with the strings of the piano. Patented in 1847 in New York by Nunns and Fischer.

MELODIC TRIANGLE BEATERS, triangle beaters that are mounted by their nodes in a resonating box. Struck with two triangle beaters, they produce toy-like sounds.

MELODIKON, friction keyboard instrument. When pressing down a key, a corresponding tuning fork is activated by a rotating steel cone. Invented by P. Riffelsen of Copenhagen in about 1800.

MELODION, same as the melodikon, except the sound is produced by rounded metal bars. Invented in Emmirich in 1805 by Johann Christian Dietz, Sr. The instrument is 4 feet by 2 feet.

MELODY STEEL DRUM, *see* **steel drum**.

MEMBRANA (It, Sp), skin, drumhead.

MEMBRANE, skin, drumhead.

MEMBRANE EXTRÊMEMENT TENDUE (Fr), skin extremely tight.

MEMBRANOPHONE, instrument whose sound is produced by the vibration of a stretched membrane, whether it is struck (e.g., timpani, drums), rubbed or twisted, thereby producing friction (e.g., string drum, cuíca), or blown, producing sound waves (e.g., mirliton or kazoo).

MERCENARY SOLDIERS' DRUM, *see* **long drum**.

MESSERKLINGE (Ger), knife blade.

MESSKLINGELN (Ger), Sanctus bells.

METÁ (It), (hit) in the middle.

METAL BAR INSTRUMENTS, idiophones made from metal that are struck singly, e.g., bells, gongs, triangles, single cymbals.

METAL BLOCK, struck idiophones of indefinite pitch. Composers use this term to designate jazz cowbell or anvil.

METAL CABASA, modern version of the Latin cabasa or afuche, consisting of metal beads loosely wrapped around a serrated metal disk. The instrument can be played a number of ways, the most common is by resting the beads in one hand, while the other turns the instrument.

METAL CASTANETS, small cymbals approximately 2 inches in diameter that are used in pairs and struck only by the edges or by the underside of each cymbal. They are held with one cymbal in each hand or by attaching one cymbal to the thumb and one to the forefinger. When they are mounted, they are commonly known as *cymbal tongs* or *mounted metal castanets*.

METAL CLAPPER, clapper used in cast bells, whose size depends on the size of the bell.

METAL CONTAINER RATTLE, *see* **metal rattle**.

METAL CYLINDER CABASA, possible substitute for the cabasa, afoxê, and afochê.

METAL DISKS, round steel disks that are approximately 8 inches in diameter, $1^{3}/_{16}$ inches thick, and may weigh as much as 11 pounds. They are mounted or suspended and struck with metal beaters.

METAL DRUM, circular bronze plate with curved deep rims and a flat beating area that is ornamented. The instrument is suspended and played with felt or cloth mallets. Obsolete name for the *kettle gong*. *See also* **drum gong**; **tam-tam**.

METAL FOIL, instrument in the foil rattle category that produces rattling sounds when beaten or shaken.

METAL HAMMERS, light to medium duty hammers that are commonly used for anvils and metal plates, and sometimes for tubular chimes and bronze bells.

METAL HARMONICA, *see* **bell lyre**.

METAL-HEAD MALLETS, mallets with metal heads, sometimes used for crotales, but more commonly for glockenspiel (substituting for keyboard glockenspiel).

METAL JINGLE STICK, *see* **chimta**.

METALL., abbrev. for (Eng, Fr) *metallophone*, (Ger) *Metallophon*, (It) *metallofono*.

METALLBLOCK (Ger), metal block, anvil. (L)

METALLFOLIE (Ger), foil rattle. (L)

METALLGEFÄSSRASSEL (Ger), metal rattle, tin rattle, metal container rattle.

METALLHÄMMERCHEN (Ger), metal beaters. (L)

METALLINO, three-octave keyboard glockenspiel.

METALLKASTAGNETTEN (Ger), metal castanets.

METALLKASTEN (Ger), metal block, anvil.

METALLOFONO (It), metallophone.

METAL LOG DRUM, *see* **lujon.**

METALLOPHON (Ger), metallophone.

METALLOPHONE, tuned-bar percussion instrument in which the striking surface is made of some type of metal, i.e., vibraphone, chimes, orchestra bells. Metallophones were known to exist in China as early as the seventh century A.D., and in Indonesia in 900 A.D. In modern orchestral percussion, the vibraphone with motor off and the resonators open may serve as a metallophone. The playing technique and mallets are the same. A bass metallophone called the *lujon* was developed in the United States in the modern era. Also known as *marimba gong*. *Metallophone* in French, *Stabspiel* or *Stahlspiel* in German, *metallofono* in Italian. *See also* **alto**, **bass**, **soprano metallophone**.

METALLPLATTE (Ger), steel plate or metal disk.

METALLRASPEL (Ger), metal scraper, rasper.

METALL-SCHLÄGEL (Ger), metal beater.

METALLSTÄBCHEN (Ger), triangle beater.

METAL MARACAS, Mexican Aztec maracas; Indian metal rattles containing metal pellets, also known as *jhanjhana*.

METAL MARIMBA, description of the vibraphone in about 1924. *See also* "The Marimba in Mexico and Related Areas," p. 239.

METAL PLATES, metal plates used (along with tuned gongs) to add metallic timbre to a giant dulcimer built for the four grail bell sounds in Richard Wagner's *Parsifal* (1882). These plates were positioned in a large resonator barrel and struck. *See also* **bell plates**; Illus. 32, p. 131.

METAL RASP, metal sticks, tubes, or other vessels with a grooved or notched surface that is scraped to produce a scratching, scraping, or clattering sound; used to imitate the sound of a roulette wheel. Also, ratchet that has a metal cog and slats.

METAL RATTLE, container rattle or rattles originally used by the Indians of the South American Islands. It consists of two canister-shaped tin containers positioned on handles and filled with pebbles. The instrument produces a loud and metallic sound. Modern replicas may be made by mounting tin cans or metal spheres on handles and filling them with pebbles or metal pieces. Sometimes referred to as *metal container rattle*, *tin horn*, *tin rattle*.

METAL RODS, short rods made from metal and commonly used for striking the triangle. Sometimes the rod will have a cloth or leather-wound grip. Used, rarely, to play the glockenspiel, lujon, vibraphone, piano strings, single crotales, cymbals, tam-tam, animal bells (mounted), metal block, and scrapers.

METAL SCRAPER, metal container with etched grooves. The instrument is held in one hand while the other hand scrapes the grooved surface with a metal rod. *See also* **metal rasp**.

METAL SHAKER, cylindrical tube made from metal and filled with pebbles, shot, or seeds, played by shaking the tube back and forth. Also called *metal tube*, *metal tube shaker*. *See* Illus. 34, p. 133.

METAL TUBE, *see* **metal shaker**.

METAL TUBE SHAKER, *see* **metal shaker**.

METAL WIND CHIMES, pieces of metal that are suspended from a frame and hung in such a way that they strike against each other when the wind blows or the frame is shaken. Most often the metal pieces are tubular. *See* Illus. 32, p. 131.

MEXICAN BEAN, dried bean pod approximately 12 inches long with loose seeds inside that produce a rattling sound. Also called *pod shakers*. (L) *See also* **pod rattle**.

MEXICAN BONGOS, bongos that are smaller than the standard size bongos.

MEZZO (It), medium, middle; on a cymbal part it refers to the cup or bell of the cymbal.

MEZZO DURO (It), medium hard.

MEZZO PEDALE (It), half-pedaled; can refer to hi-hat.

MICROPHONE BEATERS, timpani sticks used for a light, accentuated sound. The sticks are made from soft merino wool felt wrapped on Tonkinese reed sticks.

MIDI, Musical Instrument Digital Interface. *See also* "The Drum Set: A History," p. 173; "Electronic Percussion," p. 191.

MIDIMBA, *see* **madimba**.

MILIEU (Fr), middle; on a cymbal part refers to cup or bell of the cymbal.

MILITÄRTROMMEL (Ger), military drum.

MILITARY DRUM, snare drum with a metal shell that is 9 to 12 inches in depth and 15 inches in diameter. The two heads are stretched by tensioning screws, and a snare release lever quietly activates and deactivates at least eight gut, plastic, or metal snares. Usually the drum is mounted on a stand so the player can move quickly to other instruments. It produces a crisp and dry sound. The term came about in 1837, with the invention of the tensioning-screw mechanism. *See also* **field drum; parade drum; tenor drum**. *See* Illus. 25, p. 128.

MILIT. DR., abbrev. for *military drum*. (L)

MILLWHEEL STROKE, new stroke created by Basel drummers. *See also* "The Basel Drum," p. 145.

MIRDANGAM, barrel-shaped classical drum from South India used primarily to accompany vocal and instrumental music and played with the hands and fingers. The heads have rims and are tensioned with leather straps. The right skin has a permanent application of black paste in the center of the head to give the drum its characteristic tone. The left skin is 1½ times larger than the right and is tuned an octave lower by temporarily applying a different type of paste to this skin. This paste is removed after the drum is used. The drum is tuned to the tonic of the music. It is the same as the khol but has a wooden shell. Also known as the *mṛdaṅgam*. *See also* "Percussion and Dance," p. 265.

MIRLITON, membrane that alters the sound of an instrument, such as producing a buzzing sound. The buzzing is used to amplify and color the tone, often adding a nasal tone. The device may or may not be attached to the instrument and can be made from parchment, onionskin, paper, spider-egg membrane, or other materials. Used, for example, to cover the tops of resonators in African xylophones.

MISSION BELL TREE, replica of the large California mission bells that were used in the Spanish missions in the seventeenth century. They are attached to a bamboo stand and shaken. Sometimes called *tree bells*.

MISURATO (It), measured.

MIT BECKEN (Ger), with cymbals.

MIT BEIDEN SCHLÄGELN (Ger), hit with both sticks at one time.

MIT DEM, DEN, DAS (Ger), with the, (hit) with.

MIT DEM FUSS SCHLIESSEN (Ger), close (hi-hat) with the foot.

MIT DEM GRIFF (Ger), (hit) with the handle of the stick.

MIT DEM HÄMMERCHEN GESCHLAGEN, KEINE KLAVIATUR (Ger), played (orchestra bells) with mallets, no keyboard. (L)

MIT DEM KNÖCHELN (Ger), with the knuckles.

MIT DEN FINGERN (Ger), with the fingers.

MIT DEN HÄNDEN (Ger), with the hands.

MIT DEN NÄGEL (Ger), with the fingernails.

MIT DER FAUST (Ger), with the fist.

MIT EINEM HOLZSTÄBCHEN AUF DEM HOLZRAND DER TROMMEL GESCHLAGEN (Ger), played on the shell (of the drum) with handle of the stick.

MIT GROSSER STEIGERUNG (Ger), with big crescendo; used in Anton Webern's *Passacaglia* (1908). (L)

MIT METALLSCHLÄGEL (Ger), with metal beater(s).

MIT MÜNZEN TRILLERN (Ger), roll with coins.

MIT SAITEN (Ger), with snares.

MIT SCHLÄGEL (Ger), with a stick, sticks.

MIT SCHNARREN (Ger), with snares.

MIT SCHNARRSAITEN (Ger), with snares, snares on.

MIT SCHWAMMSCHLÄGEL (Ger), with soft stick(s).

MITTE (Ger), middle.

MITTEL (Ger), middle, medium.

MITTELHART (Ger), medium hard.

MIT TELLERN (Ger), (with) crash cymbals.

MIT 2 SCHLÄGEN (Ger), hit with both sticks at one time.

MIT WEICHEN SCHLÄGEL AUF EINER SEITE ROLLEN (Ger), roll on one side with soft sticks.

MIT ZWEI SCHLÄGEL AUF BECKEN (Ger), with the two sticks on cymbal.

MIXTUR-TRAUTONIUM, electronic instrument capable of simulating different percussion instruments such as the musical saw and bells. Since 1955, this instrument has been used occasionally for the bell sounds in Richard Wagner's *Parsifal* (1882) for performances at Bayreuth.

MO, Burmese gong, Vietnamese slit drum.

MODERN TOM-TOMS, single or double-headed drums with cylindrical plywood shells of various sizes mounted on stands and manufactured in six different sizes from 10 to 18 inches in diameter and 8 to 24 inches in depth. They are not tuned to a definite pitch. Modern tom-toms originated from the jazz drum set, and they use the same playing techniques and patterns. Snare drumsticks are standard, but other beaters may be requested by certain composers. *See* Illus. 8, p. 120.

MODO ORDINARIO (It), in the usual way; in a cymbal part, use crash cymbals; can also mean to employ the sticks normally used on an instrument (L); together; also, mute off.

MOKKIN, Japanese xylophone used in traditional kabuki music. *See also* "The Xylophone," p. 347.

MOKO, Korean woodblock.

MOK THAT, MOKT'AK, wooden gong in the shape of a bell from Korea, struck with sticks and used in Buddhist rites.

MOKUBIO, small Japanese wooden drum used by Buddhist priests and similar in size to that of the Korean temple block. It is disk-shaped, with a circular opening at the bottom that becomes wider, conically, and it stands on three short wooden legs and is struck with hardwood beaters or xylophone mallets. The overall sound of the instrument is similar to that of a clave or xylophone bar. This instrument has been used in modern Japanese music, i.e., Yuzo Toyama's *Rhapsody for Orchestra* (1960). Also called *Chinese wooden drum. See also* **Japanese woodblock; Japanese wooden drum; moko; mo kugyo; mu-yü.**

MO KUGYO, Japanese temple blocks. (L/WM)

MOKUSHO, round Japanese woodblocks (about 4 to 7 inches in diameter and 2 to 3 inches deep) resting on short feet. (L/WM)

MOLLE (Fr, It), soft.

MOLTO (It), very.

MOLTO DURO (It), very hard.

MOLTO MOLLE (It), very soft.

MOLTO MORBIDO (It), very soft.

MONG-KHONG, pitched Thai gongs.

MONKEY DRUM, hourglass-shaped Indian drum with two heads that are rope-tensioned. When the drum is rotated with a wrist motion, the ends of the rope strike one or both of the heads. Also known as *rattle drum. See also* **darmu.**

MONTATI (It), mounted (castanets, cymbal, etc.).

MORBIDO (It), soft.

MORCEAU DE FIL DE FER (Fr), piece of metal wire; thin triangle beater; used, for example, in Igor Stravinsky's *Song of the Nightingale* (1919). (L)

MOSCOW BELL, immense bell, measuring 20 feet high, 23 feet, 4 inches in diameter and weighing almost 440,000 pounds. Cast in 1733, it is located in the Kremlin in Moscow. It has not sounded since 1811, when it was seriously damaged by fire.

MOT., abbrev. for *motor.*

MOTBEL, Old English bell.

MOTEUR (Fr), motor (on).

MOTOR HORN, *see* **auto horn.**

MOU (Fr), soft.

MOULIN STROKES, French style of drumming. *See also* "The Basel Drum," p. 145.

MOUNTED CASTANETS, castanets mounted on a flat surface and spring-tensioned.

MOUNTED FINGER CYMBALS, finger cymbals that are attached to tongs or mounted on a flat surface and spring-tensioned. Also known as *mounted metal castanets.*

MOUNTED METAL CASTANETS, *see* **mounted finger cymbals.**

MOUTH, part of a bell (church type) that is in between the outer sound bow and the edge.

MOUTH SIREN, metal cylinder approximately 2$^{3}/_{8}$ to 4 inches long with a mouthpiece on one end. The player blows a stream of air into the instrument, which causes an interior fan disk to rotate and produces a howling glissando effect. As the player blows harder the disk rotates faster and the pitch rises. If the air pressure is decreased gradually, the pitch will fall gradually to the instrument's lowest pitch. The mouth siren was used widely to accompany silent films and vaudeville, and it has now found a place in concert music. Examples include Darius Milhaud's *Les Choëphores* (1915) and *L'Homme et son désir* (1918), and Paul Hindemith's *Chamber Music No. 1* (1922). *See also* **siren whistle**; Illus. 36, p. 135.

MOYEN (Fr), medium (size), medium (pitch).

MṚDAṄGAM, *see* **mirdangam.**

M.S. (It), abbrev. for *mano siniestro.* (L)

MUFFLED DRUM, old military term requiring the player to cover the batter head with a cloth or disengage the snares. Today, most players disengage the snares when seeing this term, unless the composer specifically requests the head to be covered; the composers will simply mark *senza corde* or *snares off.*

MUFFLED STROKE, term used to describe a particular technique and/or sound on hand drums. A muffled stroke on bongos is executed when one hand is placed on the head, while the index finger of the other hand strikes the center of the head. On conga drums, this stroke is executed when one hand is placed on the head to dampen or tense it through pressure, while the other hand strikes the center. Composers often use a "t" symbol to designate it.

MULTIPLE PERCUSSION, two or more percussion instruments played by one person. *See also* "Multiple Percussion," pp. 257; Illus. 1, p. 117.

MULTIPLE WHIPS, several boards of wood or clappers that are struck together, either simultaneously or alternately.

MUSCHEL-WINDGLOCKEN (Ger), shell wind chimes. (L)

MUSICAL CUPS, graduated cups made from porcelain, metal, or other materials.

MUSICAL GLASSES, set of tuned drinking glasses struck with light beaters with wooden heads or rubbed with fingers dipped in powdered rosin or water. The pitch of the glasses can be lowered by adding water to them. By using glasses of different sizes it is possible to encompass an entire scale. Also known as *cup glasses, tuned glasses. See also* **crystallophone; glass harmonica.**

MUSICAL SAW, saw blade that is bowed with a bass or cello bow or struck with a soft mallet, to produce a whining and ethereal tone as the pitch is changed by bending the blade as it is being bowed or struck. It can also be fitted with an electronic pickup and is most often played by specialists who are rarely orchestral musicians. Sometimes the notated range goes beyond the instrument's capability, and a ondes Martenot or a Mixtur-Trautonium must be used as a substitute. An electric guitar played with a metal bar is also a suitable substitute.

MÚSICA TURCA (Sp), Janissary music.

MUSIC BOX, linguaphone with tuned metal teeth that are activated by a hand-cranked mechanism.

MUSIQUE TURQUE (Fr), Janissary music.

MUSSAMBA, Brazilian word for maraca.

MUTA (It), change; usually refers to changing of timpani pitch.

MUTUMBWE, another name for *ditumba.*

MU-YÜ, Chinese woodblock in the shape of a fish.

NABIMBA, marimba with small vellums placed across openings in the resonators. The resulting tone has a distinct buzzing quality whenever the bar is struck. This resonated mallet instrument was made in the United States in the early part of the twentieth century and differs from the American marimba in that it has vibrating membranes in the bass resonators. Also called *nadimba*. *See also* "The Xylophone," p. 347.

NACAIRE, French term for the Mid-Eastern ancestor of the modern kettledrum. Small clay, kettle-shaped drums were mounted on horseback to be played in processions and military maneuvers. *See also* **naqqārah**.

NÁCARA (Sp), kettledrum. *See also* **naqqārah**.

NACCHERA (It), kettledrum. *See also* **naqqārah**.

NACCHERA CILINDRICA (It), cylindrical woodblock. (L)

NACCHERE (It), castanets.

NACH (Ger), (change) to. (L)

NACHTIGALLENSCHLAG (Ger), nightingale.

NADIMBA, *see* **nabimba**.

NAFA, Samoan slit drum.

NĀGAṘĀ, Indian kettledrum that is bowl-shaped. It may be made of clay or copper and is used in temples or on the backs of elephants during processions. Related to the naqqārah.

NAGARIT, Ethiopian kettledrum related to the naqqārah.

NĀGHĀRĀ, Pakistani clay drums similar to kettledrums.

NA KA LA, Chinese version of the nāghārā. *See also* **naqqārah**.

NAKER, English for the Mid-Eastern ancestor of the modern kettledrum. Small clay, kettle-shaped drum mounted on horseback and played in processions and military maneuvers. Also *nakere*. *See also* **naqqārah.**

NAKERE, another name for *naker*.

NAKORNPANAM, Thai mouth organ. The reedy tones can be produced in clusters or individually through various fingerings.

NAKOVALNYA, Russian anvil.

NAQQĀRAH, small Mid-Islamic kettledrum brought to Turkey and then throughout Europe and India; it eventually evolved into the modern kettledrum. These small drums are made of metal or wood and have laced heads. They are often played from horse or camel back and beaten with a pair of sticks. Naqqārya is the modern Mid-Eastern descendant. *See also* "Janissary Music," p. 195.

NARUCO (It), wooden wind chimes.

NARUKO, Japanese bamboo wind chimes.

NAT., abbrev. for *natural*. (L)

NATURAL, in the usual way, natural. (L)

NATURALE (It), play in the usual way.

NATUREL (Fr), mute off.

NATURLEDER PAUKENSCHLÄGEL (Ger), rawhide timpani sticks.

NATURLEDER SCHLÄGEL (Ger), rawhide sticks.

NEBELHORN (Ger), fog horn.

NEL CENTRO (It), in the center.

NGLENGE, Nigerian xylophone. *See also* "The Xylophone," p. 347.

NGOMA, kettledrum of South Africa.

NGONGE, *see* **agogô**.

NIETENBECKEN (Ger), sizzle cymbal.

NIGHTINGALE, bird whistle that is made of a metal cylinder from which extends a narrow blowpipe. The cylinder is filled partially with water and produces bird-like sounds when air is passed through it by means of the blowpipe. This instrument resembles a small tobacco pipe.

NIMMT ZU (Ger), take, play. (L)

NIPPLE GONG, tuned gong with a round, raised boss in the center that is usually the portion that is struck. Found throughout Asia and often the instrument of choice when a composer calls for tuned gongs. *Buckelgong* in German. *See* Illus. 17, p. 125.

NISHOKO, small Japanese gong.

NOCCHE (It), knuckles.

NOCE DI COCCO (It), coconut shells, horse hooves.

NOIX DE COCO, (Fr), maracas.

NON VIBREZ (Fr), literally, no vibrato; (vibraphone) motor off. (L)

NOTCHED BONES, original form of scrapers. These ancient instruments consist of two animal bones that are rubbed against one another. One of the bones has notches cut into it and thus produces a rasping sound.

NUR BECKEN (Ger), cymbals only.

NYMA BELLS, *see* **Chinese Confucian bells.**

OBERTONKONTROLLE (Ger), tone control.

OCTAMARIMBA, keyboard percussion instrument similar to a regular marimba, except that each bar is split and the two halves are tuned in octaves. Special double-headed mallets are used, which strike each half of the bar simultaneously, thus producing each tone in octaves. Produced by the J.C. Deagan Company in limited quantity in the first half of the twentieth century. Also known as the *octave marimba. See also* "The Xylophone," p. 347.

OCTOBANS, generally numbering eight per set, these long narrow tom-toms have one head and produce a focused pitch when struck. They are used mostly as an addition to the drum set.

ŌDAIKO (Ō-DAIKO), Japanese double-headed ornamental barrel drum about 24 inches in diameter and 30 inches deep, with nailed heads; used by Carl Orff in *Prometheus* (1968). (L/WM)

ODER (Ger), or.

OFFENES PEDAL (Ger), open pedal.

OHNE (Ger), without.

OHNE DÄMPFER (Ger), without muffler.

OHNE KLÖPPEL (Ger), (bell) without clapper.

OHNE SCHELLEN (Ger), without jingles.

OHNE SCHNARREN (Ger), without snares.

OHNE SCHNARRSAITEN (Ger), without snares.

OIL CAN POPPERS, bottom of oil cans that are depressed to produce a low clicking sound much like a bass cricket call.

OIL DRUM, *see* **steel drum.**

OKEDO, Japanese double-headed barrel drum used in kabuki theater; it is about 8 inches in diameter and 18 inches deep and is rope-tensioned; the okedo is played either with the hands or sticks. (L/WM)

OKWA, African log drum.

ONCA, Latin-American friction drum.

ONDES MARTENOT, early electronic instrument developed in 1928, whose pitch and volume are controlled relative to the positioning of the performer's hand near a horizontal cord. Some models had a seven-octave keyboard.

ONE-MAN PERCUSSION BAND, *see* **bumbass.**

ON THE RIM, play on the rim of a snare or bass drum; more effective when played on a wooden rim. (L)

OOGA HORN, air horn activated by depressing a plunger; used on many automobiles in the 1930s. *See also* **klaxon horn**.

OOP GOPI, Indian instrument consisting of a wooden bucket cut in half. The halves are separated and joined by a stick or small board. Heads are attached to the open ends of each bucket half, and a string or cord is run between the heads. As the cord is plucked, it produces vibrations in the heads, thus creating a twanging sound. *See also* **ektara.**

ORCHESTRA BELLS, keyboard percussion instrument made of hard steel bars suspended on soft ropes and played with hard mallets made from brass, hard plastic, or hard rubber. The resulting high pitches are particularly clear and resonant. This instrument is probably a descendant of the bell lyre used in European military bands in the nineteenth century. Examples of use in the orchestral repertoire include Paul Dukas's *The Sorcerer's Apprentice* (1897), Claude Debussy's *La Mer* (1905), Igor Stravinsky's *Petrouchka* (1911), Ottorino Respighi's *Pines of Rome* (1924), and Zoltán Kodály's *Háry János: Suite* (1927). Also called *glockenspiel*. *See also* **keyboard glockenspiel**; Illus. 14, p. 123.

ORCHESTRAL CLAPPERS, *see* **slapstick**.

ORD. (It), abbrev. for *ordinario*. (L)

ORD., L' (Fr), abbrev. for *l'ordinaire*. (L)

ORDINAIRE, L' (Fr), *see* **ordinario**.

ORDINARIO (It), return to ordinary or customary way of playing.

ORGANO DI LEGNA (It), xylophone.

ORILLA (Sp), edge, rim.

ORLO (It), edge.

ORNAMENTAL BELLS, bells ranging in size from ¾ inch to 4 inches in diameter and consisting of a brass hemisphere that extends into six to ten claw-like prongs holding a small pellet in the bell. As the bell is shaken the pellet strikes the sides of the bell, producing a delicate ringing sound. These bells are Indian in origin. *See also* **elephant bell**.

ORUGORU, set of small Japanese metal bells without strikers and often mounted in sets of five. *See also* **bell tree**. (L/WM)

OSCILLARTO (It), vibrate, motor on (vibraphone).

ŌTSUZUMI, Japanese drum like the kotsuzumi but larger; it is similar to the kotsuzumi but tensioned higher and drier in sound. About 6 inches in diameter and 12 inches deep, it is played with paper thimbles over the fingers. Sometimes called *okawa*. (L/WM)

OUATEUSE (Fr), padded.

PAAR (Ger), pair.

PAARWEISE BECKEN (Ger), crash cymbals.

PADINGBWA, generic name in Zaire for a xylophone without resonators. *See also* "The Xylophone," p. 347.

PA FANG KU, Chinese frame drum.

PAHU, (1) East Polynesian membrane drums; (2) Maori slit drum.

PAIA (It), pair.

PAILLA (Sp), timbale shell.

PAIO DI PIATTI (It), pair of cymbals.

PAIRE DE CYMBALES (Fr), pair of crash cymbals.

PAK, Korean wooden clappers.

PAKISTAN TREE BELLS, *see* **bell tree.**

PALILLO (Sp), thin wooden stick.

PALLINA (It), head of a stick.

PALLINA DI FELTRO DURO (It), (stick with) hard felt head.

PALO (Sp), stick.

PALO BUFONESCO (Sp), slapstick. (L)

PALO DE BOMBO (Sp), bass drumstick.

PALO DE TAMBOR MILITAR (Sp), snare drumstick.

PALO ZUMBADOR (Sp), bull roarer.

PAN, Trinidad word for steel band.

PANCAKE DRUM, hand drum important to Buddhist music. Its single head is lapped over an iron hoop attached to a wooden handle. It is beaten with a stick, then shaken in the air. *See also* **kabuki drum; uchiwadaiko.**

PANDAIR, medieval Mozarabic tambourine. *See also* **bendīr.**

PANDEIRO (Port), tambourine-like instrument with a few jingles and a large head; also called *pandero. See also* "Brazil: Percussion Instruments," p. 153; Illus. 34, p. 133.

PANDERETA (Sp), tambourine.

PANDERETA BRASILEÑO, Brazilian instrument with two rows of tambourine jingles on a handle. (L)

PANDERETA BRASILIANO (It), pandereta brasileño.

PANDÉRÉTA BRÉSILIENNE (Fr), pandereta brasileño.

PANDERETE, (1) (Sp) tambourine; (2) Afro-Cuban hourglass drum, played horizontally and perched on the player's knees.

PANDERO (Sp), tambourine.

PANDERO GRANDE, South American tambourine without jingles.

PANDERO PEQUENO, South American tambourine with jingles.

PANDÉROS, several tuned frame drums of different sizes; used by Manuel de Falla in his marionette opera *El retablo de maese Pedro* (1923). Also used in the Corpus Christi processions in Cadiz, where the drums were in sizes up to 39 inches in diameter.

PANDORELLA (Sp), tambourine without a head.

PANG, Chinese slit drum.

PANG-KU, another name for Chinese bong.

PANG TSE, (1) Chinese percussion sticks; (2) a Chinese slit drum with a handle on the bottom.

PANHUEHUETL, Central American drum, originally played by the Aztecs; now a cylindrical drum with one head about 3 feet high, played in a vertical position. *See also* **huehuetl.**

PAN PIPES, tuned bamboo tubes stopped at the lower end and joined together to form a raft. The tubes, without finger holes, are blown across the top.

PAPEL DE LIJA (Sp), sandpaper blocks.

PAPER DRUM, Chinese two-headed frame drum with a handle, to which are attached small wooden or metal balls hanging from strings. The balls produce a rattling sound when they hit the drumheads. *See also* **Chinese paper drum;** Illus. 37, p. 136.

PAPIER DE VERRE (Fr), sand blocks, sandpaper.

PAPPE (Ger), pasteboard.

PARADE DRUM, snare drum with a wood, metal, or brass shell with calfskin heads, ranging from 10 × 14 inches to 12 × 16 inches. There are four to six gut strings that lie across the bottom head. The drum can either stand off the ground using the three adjustable legs or be mounted on a stand. *Basler Trommel* in German. *See also* **field drum**; **long drum**; Illus. 25, p. 128.

PARADETROMMEL (Ger), parade drum.

PARADIDDLE, snare-drum stroke with systematic alternation of single and double strokes, allowing rapid strokes while going from instrument to instrument.

PARAR (Sp), dampen.

PARCHE (Sp), skin, head.

PARSIFAL BELLS, name used to designate orchestra bells made by Deagan from 1918 to 1932. The uniqueness of these bells was that the set had resonators and its own folding stand. *See also* **bass chimes**.

PARSIFAL CHIMES, eight chimes that extend the lower range of a set of chimes—used by Richard Wagner in *Parsifal* (1882). Also known as *bass chimes*.

PAS DE CHEVAL (Fr), hoofbeats, horsehooves.

PASTEBOARD RATTLE, soft rattle made of a pasteboard head mounted on wooden handles.

PATAHA (Sanskrit), drum.

PATIO XYLOPHONE (QUARTER-TONE XYLOPHONE), instrument made by Emil Richards out of redwood scraps of his patio, tuned to quarter tones and, in some cases, smaller tones. It has no set pattern or scale.

PATMA, Burmese barrel drum.

PATOUILLE, seventeenth-century French term for xylophone.

PAT WAING, twenty-one tuned Burmese drums.

PAUKE(N) (Ger), timpano(i); kettledrum(s).

PAUKEN FORTSETZEND, DER (Ger), continuation of the timpani line; used in Alban Berg's *Wozzeck* (1925). (L)

PAUKENSCHLÄGEL (Ger), timpani stick(s).

PAUKENSCHLÄGEL MIT HARTFILTZKOPFEN (Ger), hard felt timpani stick(s).

PAUKISTEN (Ger), timpanist.

PAVILION, *see* **Turkish crescent**.

PAVILLON CHINOIS (Fr), Chinese pavilion, Jingling Johnnie.

P.C. (It), abbrev. for *piatto cinese*. (L)

PEAU (Fr), skin, head.

PEAU DE BATTERIE (Fr), batter head.

PEAU DE TAMBOUR (Fr), drumhead.

PEAU DE TIMBRE (Fr), snare head.

PEA WHISTLE, like a police whistle, with a small, light ball enclosed in the hollow space where the air vibrates.

PED., abbrev. for pedal.

PEDAL CYMBAL, (1) cymbal screwed to the rim of a bass drum played by a pedal, so that the bass drum and the cymbal can be struck simultaneously; (2) two cymbals mounted on a metal rod operated by a foot mechanism that brings the two cymbals together. *See also* **charleston**; **foot cymbal**; **hi-hat**; **sock cymbal**.

PEDAL DRUM, machine drum with a pedal that raises and lowers the pitch. *Timbale à pédale* in French, *Pedalpauke* in German, *timpani a pedali* in Italian. *See also* "The Drum Set: A History," p. 173.

PEDALE APERTO (It), pedal open (hi-hat). (L)

PEDALE CHIUSO (It), pedal closed (hi-hat). (L)

PEDALPAUKE (Ger), pedal drum.

PEDAL TIMPANI, *see* **timbales chromatiques**.

PEITSCHE (Ger), slapstick, whip.

PEITSCHEND (Ger), swishing.

PEITSCHENKNALL (Ger), slapstick, whip. (L)

PEKING, *see* **saron peking.**

PELLE (It), skin, head. (L)

PELLE, DI (It), (made) of leather.

PELLE BATTENTE (It), batter head. (L)

PELLE CORDIERA (It), snare head. (L)

PELLET BELL, vessel rattle containing pellets, pebbles, or other materials that rattle when shaken. They can be worn on the ankles or as bracelets around the neck and date from antiquity, probably coming from Asia. Examples include sleigh bells. *Grelots* in French, *Schelle* in German.

PENNY WHISTLE, small whistle often played by percussionists. *See also* **police whistle.**

PEQUENO (Sp), small.

PERCUOTERE (It), strike.

PERCUSSÃO (Port), percussion.

PERCUSSION, section of orchestra containing percussion instruments. *Batterie* in French, *Schlagzeug* in German, *batteria* in Italian, *batería* in Spanish.

PERCUSSION BEAM, wooden beam used as a percussion instrument, often put on the ground and drummed upon; used in various parts of the world such as Africa and Asia. *Schlagbalkan* in German.

PERCUSSION DISK, *see* **percussion plate.**

PERCUSSIONE (It), percussion. (L)

PERCUSSION IDIOPHONE, instrument whose sound is produced by being struck, either with a nonresonant body (e.g., the hand or a stick) or against a nonresonant object (e.g., human body or the ground).

PERCUSSION INSTRUMENTS, instruments that are sounded by being shaken or struck; they can be divided into two major groups, membranophones and idiophones, and further, those of definite pitch, such as the kettledrum, xylophone, chimes, glockenspiel, and celesta, and those of indefinite pitch, a group that includes the snare, tenor, and bass drum, the tambourine, the triangle, the gong, and the cymbals. *Instruments à percussion* in French, *Schlaginstrumente, Schlagzeug* in German, *percussione* in Italian, *percusión* in Spanish.

PERCUSSION PLATE, percussion plate that occurs singly or in sets and may be either a lithophone or a metallophone. *Disque sonore* in French, *Aufschlagplatte* in German. Also **percussion disk.**

PERCUSSION POT, open-mouthed clay pot or gourd that is either drummed upon with the hands or beaters. The mouth can be alternately opened and closed by hand or by a flat beater. *Schlagtopf* in German.

PERCUSSION REED, metal reed struck with a small felt hammer.

PERCUSSION STICK, single stick or set of sticks struck against a hard object or by another stick. *Bâton frappé* in French, *Schlagstab* in German.

PERCUSSION TUBE, percussion instrument in the form of a tube, e.g., slit drum, stamping tube. *Aufschlagrohre* in German.

PERKUSIE, PERKUSTE (Polish), percussion.

PERSIAN TAMBOURINE, large jingles on a six-pound frame drum, struck with the hand or a stick.

PERSIAN TEMPLE BELLS, *see* **camel bells.**

PESANTE (It), heavy.

PETIT(E) (Fr), small.

PETITE BAGUETTE EN BOIS (Fr), small wood stick.

PETITE BAGUETTES (Fr), short (small) sticks.

PETITE CAISSE CLAIRE (Fr), snare drum.

PETITE MAILLOCHES (Fr), short (small) sticks.

PETITE TIMBALE (Fr), piccolo timpani. (L)

PETIT TAMBOUR (Fr), small drum, snare drum. (L)

PETIT TAMBOUR SANS TIMBRES (Fr), piccolo drum without snares.

PFT., abbrev. for *pianoforte.* (L)

PHILIPPINE SHELL CHIMES, shell wind chimes. (L)

PHONG YEU CO, Vietnamese hourglass drum.

PHONOLITHES (Fr), stones.

PIANITO, Cuban designation for ginebras. *See also* "The Xylophone," p. 347.

PIANO (It), soft; abbreviation for *pianoforte.*

PIANO AFRICANO (Sp), marimba.

PIANO BASQUE (Fr), group of tambourines manipulated from a keyboard; invented by Paul-Joseph Sormani in Paris in 1841.

PIANO DE CUIA, Afro-Brazilian gourd rattle. Also called *gourd piano. See also* **cabasa**.

PIANOFORTE, stringed keyboard instrument that produces a tone when the performer strikes its keys. It was first used in orchestral music (in a non-solo role) as part of the percussion section in the twentieth century, and its percussive quality was exploited by composers such as Edgard Varèse (1883–1965) and Henry Cowell (1897–1965). *Piano* in French, Spanish, *Klavier* in German, *pianoforte* in Italian.

PIANO-STRING BELLS, giant dulcimer having string choirs of eight strings each, to be struck with large felt-padded hammers; developed for the Grail scene in Richard Wagner's *Parsifal* (1882).

PIATTI (It), cymbals.

PIATTI A DUE, PIATTI A 2 (It), crash (clash) cymbals. (L)

PIATTI ANTICHI (It), antique cymbals.

PIATTI A PEDALE (It), hi-hat cymbals. (L)

PIATTI CHARLESTON (It), hi-hat.

PIATTI CINESI (It), Chinese cymbals.

PIATTI OSCILLARTI (It), cymbals rubbed one against the other. (L)

PIATTI PICCOLI (It), small cymbals. (L)

PIATTI SOLI (It), cymbals played alone (no bass drum).

PIATTI SOSPESI (It), suspended cymbals.

PIATTO(I) (It), cymbal(s).

PIATTO CHIODAT (It), sizzle cymbal.

PIATTO CINESE (It), Chinese cymbal.

PIATTO COLLA MAZZA (It), stick on cymbal.

PIATTO CON PICCOLA SPAZZOLA DI FERRO (It), cymbal with small wire brush. (L)

PIATTO FISSATO (It), suspended cymbal.

PIATTO PICCADO SOSPESI (It), small suspended cymbal.

PIATTO SOSPESO (It), suspended cymbal.

PIATTO SOSPESO CON BACCHETTA (It), suspended cymbal with stick.

PIATTO UNITO ALLA GRAN CASSA (It), cymbal attached to bass drum.

PICCOLA BACCHETTA (It), thin, small stick.

PICCOLA BACCHETTA DI LEGNO (It), small wood stick, thin wood stick.

PICCOLA BACCHETTA DI METALLO (It), thin metal stick.

PICCOLE BACCHETTE (It), short (small), thin sticks.

PICCOLE MAZZETTE (It), short (small) sticks.

PICCOLO (It), small.

PICCOLO CASSA (It), small snare drum. (L)

PICCOLO SNARE DRUM, small snare drum approximately 3 inches by 13 inches. The sound is thinner in timbre and higher in pitch than any other snare drum.

PICCOLO TIMPANO (It), small kettledrum, under 20 inches, extending the high range of the normal timpani.

PICCOLO TIMPANO ORIENTALO (It), small oriental timpani.

PIEN TA KU, Chinese drum.

PIERRES (Fr), stones.

PIETRA SONORA (It), stones.

PIKKOLOTROMMEL (Ger), piccolo snare drum.

PIO, Brazilian imitation bird call used by Heitor Villa-Lobos. *See also* "Brazil: Percussion Instruments," p. 153.

PISTOLENSCHUSS (Ger), pistol shot.

PISTOLETTATA (It), pistol shot.

PISTOL SHOT, 9mm caliber, 6-chambered revolver loaded with blank cartridges.

PISTON FLUTE, another name for *slide whistle.*

PIUTA, Brazilian friction drum.

PK. (Ger), abbrev. for *Pauken.* (L)

PLACÉ À PLAT (Fr), laid on its side.

PLANCHA DE CAMPANA (Sp), bell plate.

PLANCHE (Fr), board.

PLANCHETTE RONFLANTE (Fr), bull roarer. (L)

PLAQUE (Fr), plate.

PLAQUE DE MÉTAL (Fr), steel plate.

PLAQUE DE TONNERRE (Fr), thunder sheet. (L)

PLAQUES ÉPAISSES (Fr), thick plates. (L)

PLASTIC MARIMBA, plastic piccolo boobams that sound like regular boobams but are more percussive.

PLAT, À (Fr), laid flat; cymbals or gong laid on a flat surface.

PLATEAUX (Fr), crash cymbals.

PLATEAUX, AVEC (Fr), (with) crash cymbals.

PLATE BELLS, *see* **bell plates**.

PLATES (TWO), crash cymbals. (L)

PLATILLO(S) (Sp), cymbal(s); crash cymbal(s).

PLATILLO CHINESECO (Sp), Chinese cymbal.

PLATILLO SUSPENDO (Sp), suspended cymbal.

PLATOS (Sp), crash cymbals.

PLATTENGLOCKE(N) (Ger), bell plate(s).

PLUCKED DRUM, bucket-like container with a membrane bottom to which a string is attached. The string is held with one hand and plucked with the other. *Tambour par pincement* in French, *Zupftrommel* in German.

PLUCKED IDIOPHONE, idiophone whose elastic tongues or lamellae are plucked with the fingers or mechanically. Commonly called *lamellaphone, linguaphone.* Examples are the sansa and Jew's harp.

PLÜSCHSCHLÄGEL (Ger), plush sticks.

PO, bronze Chinese cymbals up to 24 inches in diameter. Similar to the Korean tong pal and the Japanese batsu.

PO CHUNG, Chinese single bell.

POD RATTLE, dried bean pod (about 12 inches long) with seeds; it is shaken to produce a rattle sound. Also called *pod shaker. See also* **Mexican bean**; Illus. 35, p. 134.

POD SHAKER, *see* **pod rattle.**

PODVÉSHENNAYA TARELKA (Russ), suspended cymbal.

PO FU, Chinese barrel drum.

POGREMÚSHKA (Russ), rattle.

POING, LE (Fr), (with) the fist.

POLICE SIREN, *see* **siren.**

POLICE WHISTLE, device with a small, light ball that vibrates when the whistle is blown. (L) *See also* **pea whistle; penny whistle; referee's whistle**; Illus. 36, p. 135.

POLIZEIFLÖTE (Ger), police whistle.

POLLICE (It), thumb (roll).

POLYNESIAN SLIT DRUM, *see* **touette.**

PON THON, highly laquered goblet drum of Thailand made of a clay and plaster shell. A skin head is laced and tied down over a metal hoop. Played with the fingers or open hand.

P'O PAN, Chinese wooden clappers.

POP GUN, device that produces the sound of a cork popping out of a champagne bottle. (L) *See also* Illus. 33, p. 132.

PORCELAIN BOWLS, *see* **bowls.**

POSÉ À PLAT (Fr), laid flat, on its side.

POTATO CHIP OOP GOPI, hollow potato chip can with a single string through the plastic lid. The string is held with one hand and plucked with the other while the hand holding the string applies pressure.

POT DRUM, clay pot with a membrane over its mouth. Originating in Asia, West Africa, and Central Africa. *Pot tambour* in French, *Topftrommel* in German.

POT TAMBOUR (Fr), pot drum.

POUCE (Fr), thumb (roll).

P.P. (It), abbrev. for *piatti piccoli.* (L)

PRATO, PRATO DE BRONZE (Sp), South American cymbal. (L)

PRATO DE LOUCA, Brazilian dinner plate; used by Heitor Villa-Lobos. *See also* Brazil: Percussion Instruments," p. 153.

PRAYER BELLS, *see* **cup gongs, dobači.**

PRAYER STONES, pair of flat stones, 2 or 3 inches in diameter, made of lava rock. They are cupped in the hand and struck together. Also *Tibetan prayer stones.* (L)

PRENDETE L'ALTRO PIATTO (It), take the other cymbal.

PRENDRE, PRENEZ (Fr), change to, take.

PRENEZ L'AUTRE CYMBALE (Fr), take the other cymbal.

PREPARED PIANO, piano played with beaters on the inside; piano altered in some way, popularized by Henry Cowell and later by John Cage.

PRÈS DU REBORD (Fr), close to the rim.

PRESS ROLLS, snare drumsticks pressed into the drumhead during a roll, causing the beats to be indistinguishable.

PRISME DE PLUIE (Fr), rain machine, surf effect. (L)

PROFOND (Fr), low, deep.

PROFONDO (It), low, deep.

PROTUBÉRANCE (Fr), bell or cup of a cymbal. (L)

PROVANSAL'SKII BARABÁN (Russ), tabor.

PROVENZALISCHE TAMBURIN (Ger), tabor.

PROVENZALISCHE TROMMEL (Ger), tambourin provençal.

P.S. (It), abbrev. for *piatto sospeso.*

PSALTERIUM LIGNEUM (Lat), xylophone.

PTI. (It), abbrev. for *piatti.* (L)

PTTI. (It), abbrev. for *piatti.* (L)

PUILI-PUILI (PŪ'ILI), length of Hawaiian bamboo, with the bark stripped from the end to form a switch; it is shaken or struck against the body. (L) *See* Illus. 31, p. 130.

PUITA, friction drum of the Congo, with cylindrical body, laced membrane, and friction stick of palm rib, about 20 inches long. Also synonym of *cuíca*.

PULGAR (Sp), thumb (roll).

PULGARETES (Sp), castanets.

PULGARILLAS (Sp), castanets.

PYON CHONG, Korean bell chime.

PYON KYONG, Korean lithophone.

QING, *see* **ch'ing.**

QUAIL CALL, slide whistle into which short breaths of air are blown, producing a sound while pulling on the slide.

QUARTER-TONE XYLOPHONE, *see* **patio xylophone.**

QUARTO DURO (It), half-hard.

QUASI CANNONE (It), cannon-like (refers to bass drum). Orchestral examples include Giacomo Puccini's *Madama Butterfly* (1904). *See also* **cannon shot.**

QUERĒQUEXÉ, *see* **reco-reco.**

QUEUE (DE LA BAGUETTE) (Fr), tail, butt (of the stick).

QUICA, *see* **cuíca.**

QUIJADA (Sp), Latin-American rattle made from the lower jawbone of a mule or horse; replaced by the vibraslap. *See also* **jawbone;** "Latin-American Percussion," p. 227.

QUIJADA DEL BURRO, Cuban name for jawbone with bells. *See also* **quijada.**

QUINTO, smallest drum of the family of conga drums, approximately 11 inches wide. It is played with the hands. (L) *See* Illus. 29, p. 129.

RACLE (Fr), scraper.

RACLEUR (Fr), scraper.

RAFT ZITHER, zither made from individual lengths tied together in a fashion similar to a raft. The hollow cane is filled with pebbles that rattle when shaken. However, the usual form of playing is by plucking the individual tubes.

RAG. (It), abbrev. for *raganella.*

RAGANELLA (It), rattle, ratchet.

RAGGIUNGERE (It), to rejoin.

RAHMENRASSEL (Ger), frame rattle.

RAHMENTROMMEL (Ger), frame drum.

RAIL D'ACIER (Fr), steel bar.

RAIN MACHINE, generally a barrel made of wire mesh and wooden slats. The barrel is filled with pebbles or shot and supported horizontally on a spindle. When rotated, the pebbles strike the mesh to produce a sound remarkably similar to that of falling rain.

RAMMELAAR (Dutch), rattle.

RANĀT ĒK, high-pitched Thai xylophone. *See also* "The Xylophone," p. 347.

RANĀT THUM, low-pitched Thai xylophone.

RAND, AM (Ger), at the edge.

RAND UND FELL ZUGLEICH SCHLAGEN (Ger), rim shot.

RANZ DES VACHES (Fr), cow horn.

RAP., abbrev. for *rapid*; refers to vibraphone vibrato. (L)

RÂPÉ (Fr), rasped.

RÂPE (Fr), rasper.

RÂPE À FROMAGE (Fr), cheese grater; güiro in music. (L)

RÂPE DE BOIS (Fr), reco-reco, wooden scraper.

RÂPE DE MÉTAL (Fr), metal scraper.

RÂPE GUIRO (Fr), güiro. (L)

RASCH ABDÄMPFEN (Ger), quickly dampen, mute.

RASP, any scraped instrument with a notched surface. Sound is produced by scraping a stick across the notches. *See also* **güiro**. (L)

RASPA (It), scraper, güiro.

RASPADERO (Sp), scraper.

RASPA DI METALLO (It), metal scraper, rasp.

RASPADOR (Sp), scraper.

RASPADOR METAL (Sp), metal scraper, rasp.

RASPATO (It), rasped.

RASPEL (Ger), scraper, güiro.

RASPER, Latin-American scraped instrument. It is usually a hollowed calabash with notches. *See also* **güiro**.

RASPING STICK, *see* **güiro, rasper**.

RASSEL(N) (Ger), rattle(s), maracas.

RASSELTROMMEL (Ger), rattle drum.

RATCHET, instrument consisting of two wooden slats held in a frame that are meshed with a widely toothed gear. As the gear is rotated, the slats are stretched and released with a violent snapping sound. This instrument may be found in numerous cultures throughout the world. There are two types of ratchets, those in which the handle attached to the wooded gear is stationary and the frame and slats revolve, and those that are held by the frame and the gear is spun by means of a handle. Descendant of the cog rattle. Examples of the ratchet's use in western art music include Carl Orff's *Carmina burana* (1937), Leopold Mozart's *Toy Symphony* (1786), Richard Strauss's *Don Quixote* (1897) and *Der Rosenkavalier* (1911), Ottorino Respighi's *Pines of Rome* (1924), and the Mussorgsky-Ravel *Pictures at an Exhibition* (1922). *See also* Illus. 33, p. 132; Illus. 36, p. 135.

RATIO XYLOPHONE, seven-tone xylophone made up of twenty-one bamboo slabs, invented and tuned in seven equal divisions of the octave by the composer Harry Partch.

RATSCHE (Ger), cog rattle, ratchet.

RATTLE, any object made from different materials and in different forms that is hollow and filled with smaller objects that produce a sound when shaken.

RATTLE DRUM, *see* **darmu, monkey drum**.

RATTLE OF JAPAN, *see* **kajirei**.

REBORD (Fr), edge, rim.

REBUBE (Fr), Jew's harp (obs.).

RECHT (Ger), right.

RECHTES FELL (Ger), right head (refers to bass drum).

RECLAMO (Sp), bird whistle.

RECO DE VOMO, gourd made of a calabash with two tin bells tied underneath. Notches are carved on the neck producing a scraper effect when played. It was developed by Emil Richards.

RECO-RECO, a Brazilian wood or bamboo scraper or rasper. It is sometimes called a *querēquexé*. *See also* "Brazil: Percussion Instruments," p. 153.

RECTANGULAR WOODBLOCK, block in many different sizes that has a resonating chamber cut into each of its sides. It is struck by sticks or mallets and usually mounted. The size of the block determines the pitch with the smaller being higher pitched.

REDOBLANTE (Sp), tenor drum.

REDOBLE (Sp), roll.

REFEREE'S WHISTLE, *see* **police whistle.**

RÉGALE DE BOIS, sixteenth-century French word for xylophone.

RÉGALE DE PERCUSSION (Fr), xylophone.

REGENMASCHINE (Ger), rain machine, surf effect.

REGENPRISMA (Ger), rain machine, surf effect.

REI, a small Japanese bronze hand bell with a clapper used by Buddhists. (L/WM)

REIBEN (Ger), rub, brush.

REIBTROMMEL (Ger), string drum, lion's roar, friction drum.

REIFEN (Ger), rim, hoop.

REIHENKLAPPER (Ger), strung clapper, bin-sasara.

REIHENRASSEL (Ger), suspension rattle.

REIN STIMMEN (Ger), (play with) great clarity.

REPIQUE, two-headed Brazilian drum (12 inches wide and long). *See also* "Brazil: Percussion Instruments," p. 153.

REPOSING TIGER, ceremonial Chinese reco-reco.

REPRENEZ (Fr), play again.

REQUE-REQUE, *see* **reco-reco.**

RESONANZKASTENXYLOPHON (Ger), trough xylophone.

RESONATEURS (Fr), resonators.

RESONATOREN (Ger), resonators.

RESONATORS, stopped tubes that are placed under the tuned bars of keyboard percussion instruments. The length of the resonator corresponds to the pitch. The resonator thereby amplifies (resonates) the fundamental of the bar while somewhat reducing the length of its ring.

RESO-RESO (It), reco-reco.

RETINTIN (Sp), jingles.

RETOURNER (Fr), return to.

REVOLVER, actual pistol shot from a gun. The sound is made by firing blanks.

RG. (It), abbrev. for *raganella.* (L)

RGN. (It), abbrev. for *raganella.* (L)

RHOMBE (Fr), bull roarer.

RHOMBOS, antique Greek bull roarer.

RHUGGIO DI LEONE (It), lion's roar, string drum.

RHYTHM BRUSHES, old name for wire brushes. (L)

RHYTHM LOG DRUM, *see* **log drum; slit drum.**

RHYTHM LOGS, *see* **log drum; slit drum.**

RIBEBA (It), Jew's harp.

RICHIAMO DE UCCELLI (It), bird whistle. (L)

RICOPERTA DI LANA (It), yarn-wound.

RICOPERTA IN PELLE (It), leather-covered.

RICOPERTO (It), wound (with), covered (with).

RIDE CYMBAL, suspended cymbal used in drum sets. *See also* "The Drum Set: A History," p. 173.

RIGOLS, eighteenth-century English word for régale de bois.

RIM SHOT, loud sound produced by striking the rim and head at the same time with one stick, or placing the left stick with its tip on the head of the drum, the middle of the stick resting on the rim, and striking it with the right stick (L).

RIN, Japanese bronze cup gong, about 4 to 8 inches in diameter, played with thin wood or a metal rod. (L/WM)

RING CHIME, small circular polished brass alloy plate. The sound is made by placing the plate through the finger and striking it with a metal beater.

RINGING GONGS, series of twenty-two pitched, loud ringing gongs of Bali, Burma, Japan, Java, Korea, Thailand, and Tibet. They do not form an authentic scale but are just specific pitches that were collected by Emil Richards.

RINGING STONES, *see* **lithophone**.

RIQQ, modern Egyptian tambourine without snares.

RISONATORI (It), resonators.

RIVET CYMBAL, suspended cymbal with small holes drilled near the edge that are filled with small rivets. These rivets create a sizzling sound when the cymbal is struck. *See also* **cymbal; sizzle cymbal**.

RIVOLTELLA (It), pistol shot. *See also* **revolver**.

RNGA, two-headed Tibetan drum used in Buddhist rituals.

ROASTING PAN, *see* **water-phone**.

ROCK AND ROLL SHAKERS, stick with tambourine jingles attached in pairs.

ROCK AND ROLL SHAKER STICK, modern jingle stick used for rock and roll tambourine rhythm sounds. *See also* **jingle stick**.

ROCK GONG, slab of rock played like a drum in Africa, Asia, and Europe.

ROCK-SALT WIND CHIMES, pieces of natural rock salt suspended under a half of a coconut shell; they make sounds when shaken. Instrument from Samoa.

ROHR (Ger), rattan.

RÖHRENGLOCKE(N) (Ger), tubular bell(s), chimes.

RÖHRENGLOCKENSPIEL (Ger), tubular chimes.

RÖHRENHOLZTROMMEL (Ger), cylindrical or tubular woodblock(s).

RÖHRENTROMMEL (Ger), cylindrical drum.

ROHRSCHLÄGEL (Ger), cane sticks.

ROHRSTÄBCHEN (Ger), cane stick.

ROHRSTIEL (Ger), cane handle. (L)

ROLLIERTROMMEL (Ger), tenor drum.

ROLLSCHELLE (Ger), pellet bell.

ROLLSCHELLEN (Ger), sleigh bells, harness bells.

ROLLTROMMEL (Ger), tenor drum without snares.

ROL-MO, loud Tibetan cymbals used in Buddhist rituals.

ROMBO SONORE (It), bull roarer.

ROMMELPOT, friction drum of German, Dutch, and Flemish origin made of earthenware. *See also* **cuíca**.

RONCADOR, Latin-American friction drum. *See also* **friction drum**.

RONEAT EK, RONEAT THUM, Cambodian xylophones. *See also* "The Xylophone," p. 347.

ROPE-TENSIONED DRUM, drum kept under tension by a rope; common until the second part of the nineteenth century; examples include the snare drum and bass drum. *See also* "The Rope-Tensioned Drum," p. 281; Illus. 44, p. 140.

RORKLOKKE (Dutch), chimes. (L)

ROTA CAMPANARUM (Lat), bell wheel. *See also* **horologium.**

ROTARY-TUNED TIMPANI, timpani built in 1821 in Amsterdam in which the entire drum is mounted on a central spindle and rotated. This procedure constantly changes the beating spot on the drum.

ROTA TINTINNABULIS (Lat), horologium.

ROTO TOM, single-headed drum developed by Michael Colgrass and later the Remo Company. These drums are easily rotated, which increases (or decreases) the head tension and thus affects the pitch of the drum. Roto toms are often used for soprano timpani parts, as they share a similar timbre. *See also* Illus. 7, p. 120.

ROTO TOM ACCORDÉ MANUELLEMENT (Fr), hand-tuned roto tom.

ROTO TOM AFINADO A MANO (Sp), hand-tuned roto tom.

ROTO TOM AFINADO A PEDALE (Y TAMBIÉN A MANO) (Sp), pedal-tuned and hand-tuned roto tom.

ROTO TOM À PÉDALE (PEUT AUSSI ÊTRE ACCORDÉ MANUELLEMENT) (Fr), pedal-tuned and hand-tuned roto tom.

ROTO TOM HANGESTIMMT (Ger), hand-tuned roto tom.

ROTO TOM PEDALGESTIMMT UND HANDGESTIMMT, German pedal-tuned and hand-tuned roto tom. *See also* **roto tom.**

ROUE À CLOCHETTES (Fr), bell wheel.

ROUE DE LA LOTERIE (Fr), lottery wheel.

ROULÉ (Fr), roll(ed).

ROULÉ AVEC LES DOIGTS (Fr), thumb roll.

ROULEMENT (Fr), roll.

ROULEMENT AVEC DEUX BAGUETTES DE TIMBALE (Fr), roll with two timpani sticks.

ROULER SUR UN SEUL COTÉ AVEC DES BAGUETTES MOLLES (Fr), roll on one side with soft sticks.

ROULEZ (Fr), roll.

ROUND BELLS, varying sizes of bells made of bronze alloy or tin originating in Asia.

ROUTELLE (Fr), cog rattle.

ROW RATTLES, series of suspended small, hard objects attached to any type of frame, e.g., chains.

RUDE (Fr), sharp, penetrating.

RUFHORN (Ger), toy trumpet. (L)

RUGGITO DI LEONE (It), lion's roar.

RUGIR DE LEON (Sp), lion's roar. (L)

RUGISSEMENT DE LION (Fr), lion's roar.

RÜHRTROMMEL (Ger), tenor or field drum.

RÜHRTROMMEL (HOCH) (Ger), (high-pitched) tenor or field drum.

RÜHRTROMMEL (TIEF) (Ger), (low-pitched) tenor or field drum.

RÜHRTROMMEL OHNE SAITEN (Ger), field or tenor drum without snares.

RUKINZO, Urundi zebra-skin head drum. Also called *zebra hair skin drum.*

RULLARE (It), to roll.

RULLATO MOLTO UNIFORME (It), rolled very evenly.

RULLO (It), roll (of drum).

RULLO CON IL DITA (It), finger roll, thumb roll.

RULLO SOPRA UNO LATO COLLE BACCHETTE MOLLE (It), roll on one side with soft sticks.

RULLO SOPRA UNO PIATTO SOSPESO CON BACCHETTE (It), roll on suspended cymbal with sticks.

RUMBABIRNE (Ger), maracas. (L)

RUMBAHOLZ (Ger), claves. (L)

RUMBAKUGELN (Ger), maracas.

RUMMANAH, Thai drum.

RUTE (Ger), switch, stick. Also *Ruthe.*

RUTE REIBEN (Ger), to brush.

RUTHE, *see* **rute.**

SABLIER (Fr), sandbox, maracas.

SÄGE (Ger), musical saw.

SAITEN (Ger), snares.

SAITENFELL (Ger), snare head.

SAKE BARREL, *see* **wooden barrel.**

SAKEFASS (Ger), wooden or sake barrel.

SALĀSIL, Arabic for cymbals. Also *selāsil.*

SAMBA, small Nigerian frame drum.

SAMBA BATUCADA, street samba used for the large Carnaval parades in Brazil. *See also* "Brazil: Percussion Instruments," p. 153.

SAMPHOR, Cambodian drum. *See also* **taphōn.**

SANBOMBA (Sp), friction drum.

SANCTUS BELLS, three or four steel bells attached to cross bars and shaken.

SANDBLÖCKE (Ger), sand blocks.

SAND BLOCKS, two blocks of wood in varying sizes covered with varying thicknesses of sandpaper rubbed together to produce a sound. Also called *sandpaper blocks.*

SANDBOX, metal tube, usually in the form of a shaker, with sand in it. (L)

SANDBÜCHSE (Ger), sandbox, maracas.

SAND DRUM, small tunnel with sand bridge between its two openings that is beaten by player's hands.

SANDPAPER BLOCKS, *see* **sand blocks.**

SANDPAPIER-BLÖCKE (Ger), sandpaper blocks.

SANDRASSEL (Ger), sandbox.

SAND RATTLE, *see* **sandbox.**

SANDUHRTROMMEL (Ger), hourglass drum.

SANGNA, Cambodian drum in which the two heads are tuned in the interval of a perfect fifth.

SANJ (Arabic), cymbal, finger cymbal; *sunūj* in plural.

SANJE (SANZHE, SANZHI), xylophone of southeastern Africa. *See also* "The Xylophone," p. 347.

SANS (Fr), without.

SANSA, African linguaphone with metal tongues fitted to a board resonator of many different types. It is played by using the thumb nails on the free metal tongues. Also called an *African thumb piano. See also* **mbira.**

SANS SOURDINE (Fr), without muffler.

SANS TIMBRES (Fr), without snares.

SANS TINTEMENTS (Fr), without jingles.

SANTUR, shallow Persian trapezoid box with eighteen courses of metal strings, each having its own individual bridge. Tuning pegs are secured into the right wall of the resonator box and it is played by hitting the strings with felt or wood sticks.

SANÚJ, Egyptian finger cymbals.

SANZA, *see* **sansa**.

SAPO CUBANA, *see* **bamboo scraper**.

S.À.R. (Fr), abbrev. for *sifflet à roulette.* (L)

SARNA BELL, *see* **elephant bell**.

SARON, metallophone of Bali and Java with bronze bars mounted on top of a wooden trough resonator, carved to resemble a dragon; there are three types according to pitch; used in the gamelan orchestra.

SARON BARUNG, single-octave saron, highest of the three types of saron used in the Javanese gamelan orchestra.

SARON DEMUNG, lowest-pitched of the three types of saron used in the Javanese gamelan orchestra.

SARON PANERUS, *see* **saron peking**.

SARON PEKING, highest-pitched of the three types of saron used in the Javanese gamelan orchestra. Also called *saron panerus, peking.*

SARTÉNES, Latin-American/South American family of folk instruments that are basically tuned skillets or frying pans mounted on a wooden block played with rubber beaters.

SASARA, pair of Japanese slit bamboo tubes stuck together (about 1 inch in diameter and 18 inches long); similar to the switch. (L/WM)

SASSI (It), stones.

SAW BLADE BELLS, collection of saw blades mounted from lowest to highest pitch that, when struck, creates long, sustaining, high piercing sounds.

SAW BLADE GONGS, two large mounted saw blades that are struck with a metal beater or a soft mallet.

SBATTERE (It), shake.

SCACCIAPENSIERI (It), Jew's harp.

SCAMPANELLIO DA GREGGE (It), cowbells.

SCANDÉ (Fr), stressed.

SCHALLBECKEN (Ger), cymbals. (L)

SCHALLENGLÖCKCHEN (Ger), small Buddha temple bell.

SCHARF (Ger), sharp, piercing.

SCHARF ABREISSEN (Ger), cut off sharply.

SCHÄRFER GESPANNT (Ger), more sharply tensioned (on snares).

SCHELLE (Ger), bell, pellet bell.

SCHELLEN (Ger), sleigh bells.

SCHELLENBAUM (Ger), bell tree, Jingling Johnnie, Turkish crescent.

SCHELLENBÜNDEL (Ger), bunched sleigh bells.

SCHELLENRASSEL (Ger), jingles.

SCHELLENREIF (Ger), bell hoop or a tambourine without a head.

SCHELLENTAMBURIN (Ger), tambourine.

SCHELLENTROMMEL (Ger), hand drum, tambourine.

SCHIFFSGLOCKE (Ger), ship's bell.

SCHIRRHOLZ (Ger), bull roarer.

SCHLAFF GESPANNT (Ger), loosened tension (on snares).

SCHLAGBALKEN (Ger), percussion beam.

SCHLAGBECKEN (Ger), crash cymbals.

SCHLAGBRETT (Ger), wooden board.

SCHLÄGE (Ger), strokes.

SCHLÄGEL (Ger), drumstick. Also *Schlegel.*

SCHLÄGEL AUF DEN BECKEN (Ger), stick on cymbal.

SCHLÄGEL MIT DEM KOPF AUS KAPOK (Ger), sticks with fiber head (knob).

SCHLAGEN (Ger), strike.

SCHLÄGER (Ger), drummer.

SCHLAGFELL (Ger), batter head.

SCHLAGIDIOPHON (Ger), struck idiophone.

SCHLAGINSTRUMENTE (Ger), percussion instruments.

SCHLAGRASSEL (Ger), jawbone, vibraslap.

SCHLAGSTAB (Ger), claves, percussion stick. (L)

SCHLAGTOPF (Ger), percussion pot.

SCHLAGZEUG (Ger), drum set or drums, timpani, percussion.

SCHLEGEL (Ger), mallet(s), drumstick(s). Also *Schlägel.*

SCHLEGEL FÜR GROSSE TROMMEL (Ger), bass drum beater. (L)

SCHLEGELKOPF (Ger), head of a stick.

SCHLITTELROHR (Ger), metal tube shaker.

SCHLITTEN-SCHELLEN (Ger), set of tuned sleigh bells; used, for example, in W.A. Mozart's *German Dances* K. 605 (1791). (L)

SCHLITZTROMMEL (Ger), slit or log drum.

SCHMIRGELBLOCK (Ger), sand block. (L)

SCHNARRE(N) (Ger), rattle(s), ratchet(s).

SCHNARRSAITE(N) (Ger), snare(s).

SCHNELL ABDÄMPFEN (Ger), quickly dampen.

SCHNURRASSEL (Ger), strung rattle.

SCHOTENRASSEL (Ger), Mexican bean.

SCHRAPER (Ger), scraper.

SCHREIBMASCHINE (Ger), typewriter.

SCHÜTTELIDIOPHON (Ger), shaken idiophone.

SCHÜTTELN (Ger), shake.

SCHÜTTELROHR (Ger), shaker, metal tube shaker, chocalho.

SCHWAMM-PAUKENSCHLÄGEL (Ger), sponge timpani sticks.

SCHWAMMSCH. (Ger), abbrev. for *Schwammschlägel.* (L)

SCHWAMMSCHLÄGEL (Ger), sponge-headed stick(s), soft stick(s).

SCHWER (Ger), heavy, hard.

SCHWIRRHOLZ (Ger), bull roarer.

SCHWIRRSCHEIBE (Ger), disc buzzer.

SCIE MUSICALE (Fr), musical saw.

SCOPERTO (It), muffler off.

SCORDATE (It), without snares, out of tune.

SCOVOLO DI FIL DI FERRO (It), wire brushes.

SCRAPED IDIOPHONE, *see* **scraper.**

SCRAPER, solid or hollowed-out body of wood, bone, shell, gourd, or other material that is notched on its surface and scraped with a stick. *See also* Illus. 34, p. 133.

SCRATCHER, *see* **güiro; scraper.**

SCUOTERE (It), shake.

S. CYM., abbrev. for *suspended cymbal.*

SEC (Fr), dry, short, choked, dampened.

SECCO (It), dry, short, choke.

SECOUÉ (Fr), shaken.

SECOUER (Fr), shake.

SEGA (It), saw.

SEGA CANTATE (It), musical saw.

SEGUNDILLA (Sp), call bell in a convent.

SEHR (Ger), very.

SEHR HOCH (Ger), very high.

SEHR SCHWER (Ger), very hard.

SEHR SCHWERE SCHLÄGEL (Ger), very hard sticks; very hard timpani sticks.

SEHR WEICH (Ger), very soft.

SEHR WEICHE PAUKENSCHLÄGEL (Ger), very soft timpani sticks.

SEIN (old Fr), church bell.

SEISTRON, ancient Egyptian temple rattle (sistrum); Greek bell clapper.

SEKE-SEKE, West African calabash rattle.

SELĀSIL, another name for *salāsil.*

SELSLĪM, *see* **slasal**.

SĒMANTĒRION, *see* **hanging board**.

SEMBE, small Congolese truncated barrel drum.

SENNPO, rattles from the Ivory Coast.

SENZA (It), without.

SENZA CORDE (It), without snares.

SENZA SORDINO (It), muffler off.

SENZA TINTINNIE (It), without jingles.

SER, ancient Egyptian frame drum.

SERRÉ (Fr), tight.

SERRUCHO (Sp), musical saw.

SEVEN-TONE XYLOPHONE, *see* **ratio xylophone**.

SF. (It), abbrev. for *silofono.* (L)

SG. (It), abbrev. for *sega.* (L)

SGUILLA (It), cowbell.

SHAKEN IDIOPHONE, *see* **rattle**.

SHAKER, empty container with objects such as beans, rice, seeds, sand, or salt inside. It is played by shaking it in the hand. *See also* Illus. 34, p. 133.

SHAKER STICKS, various types of bells and bottle caps attached to long sticks or poles. They are used for stamping on the ground.

SHAK-SHAK, Caribbean rattle. Also *chac-chac.*

SHAKUBYOSHI, pair of Japanese clappers about 2 inches by 16 inches by ½ inch, played edge to face. (L/WM)

SHA LO, Chinese gong dating back to at least the sixth century.

SHAQEF (Arabic), tambourine.

SHAQ-SHAQ, North African rattle.

SHEKERE, gourd rattle covered with bead netting originally from Nigeria. *See also* **afuche**; "Latin-American Percussion," p. 227; Illus. 34, p. 133.

SHELL CHIMES, susended pieces of sea shells. (L)

SHIMEDAIKO, *see* **diabyoshi**.

SHIP'S BELL, bronze bell of various sizes with a clapper. It is struck with a metal beater. *See also* Illus. 32, p. 131.

SHIP'S WHISTLE, *see* **fog horn**.

SHOKO, Japanese bronze gong; it has a distinct pitch and is long ringing.

SHUN, Chinese resting bell found in Buddhist temples.

SHU PAN, Chinese clappers.

SI, Burmese drum.

SIAO PO, Chinese cymbals.

SIBILUS (Lat), pipe or whistle.

SIBLET (Lat), whistle, particularly a bird whistle.

SIDE DRUM, British term for snare drum. *See also* "The Rope-tensioned Drum," p. 281.

SIFFLEMENT (Fr), hissing.

SIFFLET (Fr), whistle, pipe.

SIFFLET À COULISSE (Fr), slide whistle, song whistle.

SIFFLET À ROULETTE (Fr), police whistle, penny whistle, pea whistle.

SIFFLET COUCOU (Fr), cuckoo.

SIFFLET D'OISEAU (Fr), bird whistle. (L)

SIFFLET IMITÉ DU ROSSIGNOL (Fr), nightingale. (L)

SIFFLET SIGNAL (Fr), signal whistle. (L)

SIFFLET SIRÈNE (Fr), siren whistle, mouth siren.

SIGNALPEIFE (Ger), signal whistle. (L)

SIGNAL WHISTLES, short whistle flutes approximately 2 to 4 inches long, made of wood, metal, or horn. They come singly, or in twos, or threes, mounted together and blown through a mouthpiece thus having multiple pitches.

SIGNIFIER (Fr), signifies.

SIGNULUM (Lat), small bell.

SIGNUM (Lat), same as campana.

SIL, ancient Persian cymbals.

SILAMBU, leg rattles made of hollow tubular silver rings of South India dancers. The rings contain small pellets.

SILBADOR, whistling pot of South America. Also *silvador*.

SILBATO (Sp), whistle.

SILBATO SIRENA (Sp), mouth whistle.

SILOFONO(E) (It), xylophone(s).

SILOFONO A TASTIERA (It), keyboard xylophone.

SILOFONO BASSO (It), bass xylophone.

SILOMARIMBA (It), xylomarimba.

SILSELIM, *see* **selslīm**.

SIL-SIL, Tibetan cymbals.

SIL-SNYAU (GSILL-SNYAN), quiet Tibetan cymbals used in Buddhist ritual.

SILVADOR, *see* **silbador**.

SIMANDRON, large wooden board that is hit with a mallet. *See also* **hanging board**.

SINETA, South American bell.

SINGENDE SÄGE (Ger), musical saw.

SINGLE TIMPANI, timpano.

SINISTRA(O) (It), left.

SINJ, Persian cymbals, Arab finger cymbals.

SINO (Port), South American bell.

SIREN, hand-cranked or electrically powered siren that produces musical tones through the rapid interruption of air created by a perforated rotating disk. It can be stopped on cue by another hand crank at the bottom. Also *police siren*.

SIRENA (It, Sp), siren.

SIRENA A FIATO (It), mouth siren.

SIRENA A MANO (It), siren.

SIRENA BASSA (It), low siren or fog horn. (L)

SIRENA DA BATTELO (It), warning siren or fog horn. (L)

SIRENE (Ger), siren, police siren.

SIRÈNE (Fr), siren. Also *trompe de brume*.

SIRÈNE À BOUCHE (Fr), mouth siren.

SIRÈNE AIGUE (Fr), high siren, police siren. (L)

SIRÈNE GRAVE (Fr), low siren. (L)

SIRENENPFEIFE (Ger), siren whistle, mouth siren. (L)

SIREN WHISTLE, whistle that produces a siren sound when blown. Also called *cyclone whistle*.

SISSLET (Fr), whistle. (L)

SISTRE (Fr), sistrum.

SISTRO (It), group of small bells set in a frame with a handle; forerunner of keyboard glockenspiel. Italian, Spanish for *sistrum.*

SISTRUM, rattle with a handle and made of metal, gold, silver, wood, or clay, originally from ancient Egypt and Ethiopia; used by the Japanese in folk dances in the temple. In medieval music it was a triangle with jingle rings and a series of small mushroom-shaped bells. In the original score of Gioacchino Rossini's *The Barber of Seville* (1816), the part is written on a single line without a key signature. A set of tambourine jingles mounted on a handle is generally used today. *See also* Illus. 33, p. 132.

SIZZLE CYMBAL, cymbal with jingles or metal rivets attached loosely through holes drilled in it for this purpose. (L)

SKOR, Cambodian goblet drum.

SKOR ARAK, Cambodian frame drum.

SKOR THOM, Cambodian barrel drum.

SLAPSTICK, modern hand clapper made of two pieces of wood hinged together at one end and clicked or slapped together at the other by flicking the wrist. It can also be made of two pieces of wood with separate leather straps on each, using two hands to clap together. The sound produced is that of a cracking whip. Also called *orchestral clappers. See also* Illus. 36, p. 135.

SLASAL, ancient Israeli cymbals. Also *seslīm.*

SLED GONGS, metal disks used as snow sleds for children; when struck they have a bending or boinging sound. Also known as *boing gongs.*

SLEIGH BELLS, small non-pitched bells mounted on a strap or handle. They are most commonly affixed to the harness of a horse drawing a sleigh. As a percussion instrument they are mounted to a handle and shaken. Commonly known as *jingle bells. See* Illus. 33, p. 132.

SLIDE WHISTLE, tubular whistle with a plunger unit in its column, approximately 12 inches long. The pitch is changed by moving the slide plunger in and out, producing ascending and descending glisses. Also known as a *piston flute, swanee piccolo, swanee whistle. See also* Illus. 33, p. 132.

SLIT DRUM, percussion instrument with a resonating chamber tube; in its earliest form it was a hollowed-out tree trunk placed over a pit and stamped. The larger forms of slit drums are called log drums.

SMALL DRUM, *see* **snare drum.**

SMORZARE (It), damp(en).

SNAIL SHELL RATTLES, from New Guinea, these rattles, known as arbu, are made of snail shells and worn by dancers.

SNAKE CHARMER'S HORN, horn originally from India with a mouthpiece over a double reed connecting to a gourd-like body at one end and a pair of pipes at the other. There is no definite pitch.

SNAKE-DANCE RATTLE, *see* **Chinese hand drums.**

SNARE, gut or synthetic string stretched over the head of a drum that is not struck. The tension can be regulated, with the tighter tension giving a crisper sound. *See also* "The Rope-Tensioned Drum," p. 281.

SNARE DRUM, small double-headed cylindrical drum with a metal shell; the upper head is hit with two drumsticks and is known as the "batter head"; the lower, the "snare head," has snares. Originally a military instrument, it is also called the *side drum* in Britain. *Caisse claire, petit tambour, tambour d'ordonnance,* and *tambour militaire* in French; *kleine*

Trommel in German; *cassa, tamburo militare* in Italian; *caja milita, tambor* in Spanish; *field (snare) drum, parade drum, small drum, tenor drum* in the United States. *See also* "The Rope-Tensioned Drum," p. 281; "The Snare Drum," p. 295; Illus. 26, 44, 45, p. 128, p. 140.

SNARE HEAD, bottom head of a snare drum. When a snare drum is struck, the snares vibrate against the snare head. (L)

SOALHA (Port), jingles of a tambourine.

SOBAN, large Japanese bronze bell gong, about 12 by 3 inches, played with a horn hammer. (L/WM)

SOCK CYMBALS, *see* **hi-hat.**

SODOKU, *see* **daiko.**

SOFFICE (It), soft.

SOFFOCATO (It), choke, muffle.

SONAGLI (It), sleigh bells, harness bells, jingles.

SONAGLIA (It), pellet bell.

SONAGLI A MANO (It), hand bells or harness bells.

SONAGLIERI (It), jingles, sleigh bells, or chocalho.

SONAGLIO (It), small bell, rattle.

SONAILLES DE TROUPEAU (Fr), Alpine herd bells.

SONAJA (Sp), Mexican-Indian term for maracas.

SONAJAS (Sp), maracas, sleigh bells.

SONAJERO (Sp), rattle.

SONATORE (It), player.

SONERIA DI CAMPANE (It), chimes or tubular bells. (L)

SONG BELLS, metal bar keyboard percussion instrument that sounds one octave lower than orchestra bells and has the range and quality of a celesta. Each bar, in the shape of piano keys, has a resonator for sustaining quality.

SONG BIRD CALL, instrument made of birchwood pewter covered with rosin that produces wild songbird sounds when it is twisted.

SONG WHISTLE, *see* **slide whistle.**

SONNAILLE(S) (Fr), bell(s) made of sheet metal hung around the neck of a domestic or herd animal. *See also* **cowbell.**

SONNAILLES SUR BÂTON (Fr), stick rattle.

SONNEAU (Fr), sixteenth-century small bell or pellet bell worn for ornamental purposes.

SONNENT À L'8VA SUPÉRIEURE (Fr), sounding an octave higher.

SONNETTE (Fr), pellet bell or hand bell of Renaissance France.

SONNETTE DE TABLE (Fr), dinner bell, small bell.

SON RÉEL (Fr), real pitch.

SONS VOILÉS (Fr), muffled.

SOPRANO METALLOPHONE, same as the alto metallophone, except that the range is middle c^1 up an octave and a half to f^2, or sometimes a^2. It sounds one octave higher than written and is struck with hard felt beaters.

SOPRANO XYLOPHONE, xylophone with a range of c^1–f^2, or a^2, sounding an octave higher than written and played with small wooden-headed sticks.

SORDINO (It), mute.

SORDINO INTERNO (It), internal tone control.

SOSP. (It), abbrev. for *sospeso.* (L)

SOSPESO (It), suspended.

SOTTILE (It), thin.

SOUND EFFECTS, *see* **effects.**

SOURDINE (Fr), mute.

SOURDINE INTERNE (Fr), internal tone control.

SPANISH TAMBOURINE, tambourine with rippled, shaped jingles.

SPANNREIFEN (Ger), tension hoop (rim). (L)

SPANNVORRICHTUNG (Ger), tension. (L)

SPAZZOLE DI JAZZ (Ger), wire brushes. (L)

SPEGNERE (It), dampen quickly.

SPENTO (It), without.

SPERONI (It), spurs.

SPESSO (It), thick.

SPIELER (Ger), players.

SPIELHOLZPLATTE (Ger), wood drum.

SPIELSÄGE (Ger), musical saw.

SPIKE LUTE, *see* **ektara.**

SPOONS, tablespoons used in minstrel or vaudeville by percussionists and dancers. Two spoons are held back to back and slapped in between the hand and leg.

SPOREN (Ger), spurs.

SPRING GÜIRO, South American metal tube with a bell-shaped opening mounted with three tunable springs. Sounds are created when the springs are scraped. (L)

SPRONI (It), spurs.

SPUGNA (It), sponge.

SPURS, set of tambourine jingles or small metal disks mounted on an ornamental rod or handle shaken to simulate the sound of horseback riders. (L)

SQU, *see* **Vietnamese fiddle.**

SQUARE CYMBALS, pair of square cymbals (6 to 8 inches) mounted on tongs.

SRN., abbrev. for *siren.* (L)

ŚRUTI-PEṬṬI, *see* **hand harmonium.**

ST., abbrev. for *stick.* (L)

STABGLOCKENSPIEL (Ger), orchestra bells. (L)

STABPANDERETA (Ger), single stick, pandereta brasileño.

STABRASSEL (Ger), stick rattle.

STABSPIEL (Ger), bar chime metallophone.

STAHL (Ger), steel.

STAHLKLAVIER (Ger), keyboard metallophone.

STAHLLÖFFEL (Ger), steel spoons. (L)

STAHLSCHLÄGEL (Ger), steel sticks.

STAHLSPIEL (Ger), orchestra bells, bell lyre.

STAHLSTÄBE (Ger), steel bar (L); glockenspiel.

STAHLTROMMEL (Ger), steel drum.

STAINLESS STEEL MUSIC BOWLS, stainless steel salad or mixing bowls that can be struck upright or on their bottoms. They either produce a bell-like sound or a "boing" sound when struck.

STAMPFROHR (Ger), stamping tube.

STAMPFTROMMEL (Ger), stamping tube.

STAMPING TUBE, tuned wooden or bamboo tube that is played by beating it rhythmically on the ground.

STANDGLOCKE (Ger), resting or temple bell.

STAPPARE LA BOTTIGLIA (It), pop gun.

STARTER'S PISTOL, pistol used to create sounds of pistol shots, using blanks.

STARTING GUN, *see* **blank gun.**

STEAMBOAT WHISTLE, whistle made of three wooden or metal pipes, each having a different pitch. The pipes are attached to each other and blown through one mouthpiece. *See also* **fog horn**.

STEAMTABLE, a metallophone used at one time in place of tuned gongs at the Metropolitan Opera for performances of Giacomo Puccini's *Turandot* (1926). *See also* **vibraphone**. (L)

STEEL BAND, group of idiophones played and developed in Trinidad and Tobago. *See also* "Steel Band/Pan," p. 297.

STEEL DISCS, round steel plates of various sizes that are suspended or mounted and struck with metal beaters. They are also known as metal disks or steel plates. (L)

STEEL DRUM, oil or gas drum used as a musical instrument. The chromatic steel drum, originating in Trinidad, has different pitches determined by punched and hammered grooves of different sizes and shapes. The diatonic steel drum is flat to a diatonic pitch and played with rubber mallets. Also called *melody steel drum, oil drum*. *See also* "Steel Band/Pan," p. 297; Illus. 31, p. 130.

STEEL MARIMBA, *see* **marimbaphone**.

STEEL PLATES, *see* **steel discs**.

STEEPLE BELL, *see* **church bell**.

STEGEREIF (Ger), triangle.

STEIL-HANDGRIFF (Ger), handle.

STEILKASTAGNETTEN (Ger), finger cymbals, mounted castanets. (L)

STEINHARMONIKA (Ger), lithophone.

STEINPLATTEN (Ger), stone disks, lithophone. (L)

STEINSPIEL (Ger), stone disks, lithophone. (L)

STEMPELFLÖTE (Ger), slide whistle, swanee whistle.

STICCADA (It), xylophone. (L)

STICCADO PASTORALE, crystallophone popular in the eighteenth century in England; it is similar to the xylophone but has glass bars. Also known as *keyboard orchestra bells*.

STICCATO (It), xylophone.

STICCATO PASTORALE (It), keyboard glockenspiel. (L)

STICK EKTARA, *see* **kingira**.

STICK RATTLE, rattle in which objects are strung on a bar or ring.

STICKS, *see* **mallets**.

STIEL-HANDGRIFF (Ger), handle.

STIERHORN (Ger), cow horn.

STONE CHIMES, keyboard instrument in which the bars are made of stone disks and hit with hard mallets or hammers. *See also* **ch'ing**.

STONE DISKS, *see* **lithophone; stone chimes**.

STONES, two flat stones that produce sound by striking the edge of one to the surface of the other.

STORM BELL, any size cast bronze bell with a metal clapper. *See also* **ship's bell**. (L)

STOSSTROMMEL (Ger), stamping tube.

STRAW FIDDLE, xylophone whose bars rest on a bed of straw. *See also* **straw xylophone**.

STRAW XYLOPHONE, xylophone whose bars are separated by straw.

STRICKNADEL(N) (Ger), knitting needle(s).

STRIKE NOTE, first tone of a struck bell that is prominently heard.

STRING DRUM, cylindrical drum made of wood or metal with a skin head. In the center of the skin is a hole in which a gut string protrudes. Sound is made by pulling a moistened piece of leather or canvas along the string away from the drum, producing a roaring sound. *Tambourin à cordes* in French. *See also* **jackdaw**; **lion's roar**; Illus. 35, p. 134.

STRING-FRICTION DRUM, *see* **string drum**.

STRISCIANDO (It), rubbing.

STRISCIARE (It), rub, brush.

STROHFIEDEL (Ger), straw fiddle.

STROMENTI DI PERCOSSA (It), percussion instruments.

STROSCIANDO (It), swishing.

STRUCK IDIOPHONE, instrument constructed so as to vibrate when it is struck.

STRUMENTO D'ACCIAIO (It), bell lyre.

STRUNG CLAPPER, series of small boards strung together at each end; it is played with a whip motion to simulate the sound of a row of dominoes falling over. *See also* **bin-sasara**.

STRUNG RATTLE, rattle consisting of small objects that are strung on cords or tied in bundles.

STURMGLOCKE (Ger), storm bell.

SUDSU, *see* **suzu**.

SUGHERO (It), cork.

SU KU, Chinese frame drum with two nailed heads.

SUL BORDO (It), at, near, on the edge.

SULLA CASSA (It), on the shell (frame).

SULLA CASSA DEL TAMBURO (It), on the shell (frame) of the drum.

SULLA CON BACCHETTE SOTTILE (It), on the skin with thin sticks.

SULLA CUPOLA (It), on the bell or cup (of a cymbal).

SULLA MEMBRANA (It), on the skin, on the drumhead.

SUL LATO (It), laid on its side.

SULLE CORDE (It), on the snares.

SUL MEZZO (It), in (on) the center, middle; on the bell or cup of a cymbal or gong.

SUNG CHUNG, *see* **po chung**.

SUNŪJ (Arabic) cymbals, finger cymbals; *sanj* is the singular.

SUONO DI BOTTIGLIA (It), tuned bottles.

SUONO DI OSSO (It), bones, slapstick.

SUONO REALE (It), real pitch.

SURAIGU (Fr), very short, high.

SURDO, large Latin-American tom-tom.

SURDO MARACANÃ, large Brazilian two-headed drum (about 26 inches by 18 to 26 inches), played with a stick. *See also* "Brazil: Percussion Instruments," p. 153.

SURDO PEQUENO, two-headed Brazilian drum (16 inches by 14 inches), played with one stick. *See also* "Brazil: Percussion Instruments," p. 153.

SURF EFFECT, sand pan, swishing effect, brushed cymbal. (L)

SURIGANE, small Japanese gong.

SURIZASARA, Japanese slit bamboo tube, about 1 inch in diameter, 18 inches long, scraped against a notched stick. (L/WM)

SUR LA CADRE DU TAMBOUR (Fr), on the shell of the drum.

SUR LA CAISSE (Fr), on the shell (frame).

SUR LA PEAU (Fr), on the skin.

SUR LA PEAU DES BAGUETTES MINCES (Fr), on the skin with thin sticks.

SUR LA PROTUBÉRANCE (Fr), on the bell or cup of a cymbal or gong.

SUR LA SCÈNE (Fr), onstage.

SUR LA TÊTE (Fr), on the bell or cup of a cymbal or gong.

SUR LE BOIS (Fr), literally, on the wood; on the shell of the drum.

SUR LE BORD (Fr), at (near) the edge.

SUR LE REBORD (Fr), at the edge.

SUR LES TIMBRES (Fr), on the snares.

SURROGATE KITHARA, original instrument built by composer Harry Partch that has two redwood resonators with eight strings each. One set of strings is in major tonality and the other is in minor. A glass rod is used for muting.

SURRSCHEIBE (Ger), disc buzzer.

SUR UNE CYMBALE (Fr), on one cymbal.

SUS. CYM., abbrev. for *suspended cymbal.* (L)

SUSP. CYM., abbrev. for *suspended cymbal.* (L)

SUSPENDED CYMBAL, single cymbal of any size suspended on a stand or held by hand that can be struck with any kind of beater. *See also* Illus. 22, p. 127.

SUSPENDU(E) (Fr), suspended.

SUSPENSION RATTLE, idiophones such as jingles that are mounted together to strike against each other when shaken.

SUWUKAN, *see* **gong suwukan**.

SUZU, small Japanese sleigh bells. (L/WM)

SVISTULKA (Russ), clay whistle with two finger holes.

SWANEE PICCOLO, *see* **slide whistle**. (L)

SWANEE WHISTLE, *see* **slide whistle**. (L)

SWISS BELLS, modern percussion clapper bell used in rhythm bands.

SWISS DRUM, early name of the snare drum.

SWITCH, bunch of twigs attached to a handle and played on the shell of a bass drum, now replaced by wire brush. *Verge* in French, *Rute (Ruthe)* in German, *verghe* in Italian. Also called *twig brush.*

TABALLI (It), timpani.

TABALLO, early Italian word for timballo (kettledrum).

TABALU, generic name for drums in ancient Mesopotamia.

TABBĀL (Arabic), kettledrum.

TABELLA (It), slapstick, board clappers, hanging board.

TABIR, TABIRA, ancient Persian hourglass drum.

ṬABL, plural of tubul; generic Arabic name for cylindrical drum.

TABLĀ, hand drum of India, with a body of metal, wood, or clay in the shape of two truncated cones joined at the widest part. Also the pair of drums called the tablā and the bāmyā that are played by one performer. The bāmyā, on the left (also called *duggī*), is the lower-sounding drum, and the tablā (also known as the *dāhinā*), on the right, is the higher drum, most commonly made of a wood shell. The head has two skins with a circular black paste in the center, which gives it its characteristic tone. The drums are tuned with small wooden blocks placed between the shell and leather straps that hold the skin head in place. The blocks are moved up and down and can produce up to sixteen pitches. The playing technique has the fingers and hand striking various surfaces of the drum and requires highly developed finger execution. Also called *timbales orientales, timpani orientali. See also* "Percussion and Dance," p. 265; Illus. 39, p. 137.

TABLA-TROMMELN (Ger), tablās.

TABLE DE BOIS (Fr), a wooden board. (L)

TABLETTES, medieval French clappers. *See also* **bones**; **slapstick**.

TABLILLA, obsolete Spanish term for a clapper.

TABL MUKHANNATH, *see* **kūba**.

TABOR, twelfth-century English ancestor of the snare drum, originally round and shallow and with or without snares. Also *taborel, tabour, tabourin, tabouret* in French. *See also* **tambourin**; **tambourin provençal**.

TABOR AU FLAHUTEL (Fr), drum in ensembles of pipes and tabors.

TABOREL (Fr), small tabor of the thirteenth and fourteenth centuries.

TABORET (Fr), tambourin provençal.

TABOUR (Fr), drum from the eleventh to the fifteenth century. *See also* **tabor**.

TABOURET (Fr), tambourin provençal, tabor.

TABOURIN, small fifteenth-century tabour from France, later known as a tambourin.

TABOURIN DE BASQUE (Fr), frame drum tambourine with small bells and jingles.

TABRET (Fr), small fifteenth-century tabor.

TABUR (old Fr), drum first used in the eleventh century.

TABURN (medieval Eng), drum.

T. À CORD. (Fr), abbrev. for *tambour à cordes.* (L)

TAIERZE (Polish), cymbal.

TAIKO, shallow Japanese barrel drum with a wooden shell and horseskin or cowhide head. It is played with two sticks and makes a cracking sound. *See also* **odaiko**; "Percussion and Dance," p. 265.

TAILLE (Fr), size.

TA-KU, Chinese barrel drum.

TALANCGÂ (Romanian), cowbell.

TALETTA (It), cog rattle used during Easter week; bones; slapstick.

TALKING DRUM, African hourglass-shaped drum held under one arm and used for transmitting messages. The pitch is changed by squeezing the rope tension to imitate actual words. Also known as the *bend drum* in West Africa. *See also* Illus. 39, p. 137.

TALYIKA (Sanskrit), cymbals.

TAMBAL (Romanian), dulcimer.

TAMBAQUE, variation of the atabaque.

TAMBATTAM (Tamil), large, round frame drum from South India.

TAMBINO. (It), abbrev. for *tamborino.* (L)

TAMBI-TAMBU, Brazilian bamboo tubes used by Heitor Villa-Lobos. Also known as *tambor de crioulo.*

TAMB. MIL., TAMB. MILIT. (Fr), abbrev. for *tambour militaire.* (L)

TAMBOR, in Portugal and Spain, a kettledrum; in Latin America and most other areas, a snare drum.

TAMBORA, in South America, a two-headed drum with no snares that is played on the rim, shell, and head; in Spain, a bass drum.

TAMBOR DE CRIOULO (Port), *see* **tambi-tambu**.

TAMBOR DE FRICCIÓN (Sp), friction drum, lion's roar.

TAMBOR DE MADERO (Sp), slit drum.

TAMBOR DE MARCO (Sp), frame drum.

TAMBOR DE TRONCO (Sp), a tree-trunk drum; in Latin America, the name for a yuka.

TAMBOR DE TRONCO HENDIDO (Sp), slit drum, log drum.

TAMBORETO (Sp), piccolo snare drum. (L)

TAMBORI, *see* **tamboril.**

TAMBORIL (Sp, Basque, Catalan), small snare drum with two laced heads that accompanies the pipe (pito), tambourin provençal. Also *tambori. See also* **tabor**.

TAMBORILETE (Sp), tambourine. (L)

TAMBORIM (Port), small one-headed drum with a wooden frame and a tacked-on skin head; it is held under the left arm and played with the right. *See also* "Brazil: Percussion Instruments," p. 153; Illus. 34, p. 133.

TAMBORÍN (Sp), tabor.

TAMBOR INDIO (Sp), (American) Indian drum.

TAMBORINO (Sp), tenor drum.

TAMBOR MILITAR (Sp), military drum.

TAMBORÓN (Sp), bass drum. (L)

TAMBOR-ONÇA, cuíca (friction drum) in Brazil.

TAMBOR PROVENZAL (Sp), tambourin provençal.

TAMBOR TERRERO (Sp), ground drum.

TAMBOUR (Fr), generic word for a drum. Since the fourteenth century denotes a snare drum, kettledrum, or tambourine. Most commonly it means a snare drum.

TAMBOUR À CORDES (Fr), string drum, lion's roar.

TAMBOUR À FENTE (Fr), slit drum.

TAMBOUR AFRICANO, tambourine without jingles in South America.

TAMBOUR À FRICTION (Fr), friction drum, pasteboard rattle.

TAMBOUR ARABE (Fr), darabucca, Arabian hand drum.

TAMBOUR AVEC TIMBRES (Fr), snare drum.

TAMBOUR CON CUERDES (Sp), lion's roar.

TAMBOUR D'ACIER (Fr), steel drum.

TAMBOUR D'EAU (Fr), water gourd.

TAMBOUR DE BASQUE (Fr), tambourine.

TAMBOUR DE BISCAYE (Fr), synonym for tambour de Basque.

TAMBOUR DE BOIS (Fr), slit drum, log drum, woodblock.

TAMBOUR DE BOIS AFRICAIN (Fr), log drum.

TAMBOUR DE FREIN (Fr), brake drum.

TAMBOUR D'EMPIRE (Fr), parade drum.

TAMBOUR DE PERSE (Fr), obsolete term for kettledrum.

TAMBOUR DE PROVENCE (Fr), tambourin provençal.

TAMBOUR EN CÔNE (Fr), conical drum.

TAMBOUR EN CYLINDRE (Fr), cylindrical drum.

TAMBOUR EN DOUBLE CÔNE (Fr), double conical drum.

TAMBOUR EN GOBLET (Fr), goblet drum.

TAMBOUR EN PEAU DE BOIS (Fr), wood-plate drum or wooden tom-tom. (L)

TAMBOUR EN SABLIER (Fr), hourglass drum.

TAMBOUR EN TERRE (Fr), ground drum.

TAMBOUR EN TONNEAU (Fr), barrel drum.

TAMBOUR-HOCHET (Fr), rattle drum.

TAMBOURIN (Fr), two-headed tabor of Provence, meaning *tambourin provençal* in French scores. It originally had a long cylindrical body and was played together with the galoubet (wooden recorder); used in Bizet's *L'Arlésienne* (1872). *See also* **tabor**; **tambourin provençal**; **tenor drum**; "Tambourin Provençal," p. 335.

TAMBOURIN À CORDES (Fr), string drum.

TAMBOURIN À MAIN (Fr), hand drum. (L)

TAMBOURIN DE CAMPAGNE, in South America, a tambourine; in Portuguese, a military or field drum with snares. (L/JG)

TAMBOURIN DE PROVENCE, *see* **tambourin.**

TAMBOURIN DE SUISSE (Fr), fifteenth- and sixteenth-century name for the snare drum.

TAMBOUR INDIEN AMÉRICAIN (Fr), American Indian drum.

TAMBOURINE, descendant of the hand frame drum of Eastern Mediterranean cultures; it is the modern name of a timbrel. Mentioned in the Old Testament of the Bible, it was introduced to pop and folk culture by the Gypsies. The modern tambourine, usually circular in shape, has a single head nailed over a hoop with jingles inserted in rods attached in the hoop. It is played with the fingers, knuckles, or sticks, and it is shaken. *See also* "The Tambourine," p. 333; Illus. 36, p. 135.

TAMBOURINE DE SAMBA, South American tambourine with jingles.

TAMBOURINET (Fr), tambourin provençal.

TAMBOURIN PROVENÇAL, large double-headed drum of Provence, often called *tambourin* or *tambourin de Provence. See also* **tambourin**; "Tambourin Provençal," p. 335.

TAMBOUR MILITAIRE (Fr), side drum, military drum. (L)

TAMBOUR MILITAIRE SANS TIMBRES (Fr), military drum without snares.

TAMBOUR PAR PINCEMENT (Fr), plucked drum.

TAMBOUR PETITE (Fr), piccolo snare drum.

TAMBOUR PROVENÇAL (Fr), tambourin provençal.

TAMBOUR ROULANT (Fr), tenor drum, snare drum, field drum.

TAMBOUR ROULANT SANS CORDES, SANS TIMBRES (Fr), tenor drum without snares.

TAMBOUR SUR CADRE (Fr), frame drum, hand drum, tambourine without jingles.

TAMBOUR SUR PIED (Fr), footed drum.

TAMB. PICCO. (It), abbrev. for *tamburo piccolo.* (L)

TAMBR., abbrev. for *tambourine.* (L)

TAMBU, large hollowed-out tree trunk with a leather or parchment membrane, found in Brazil.

TAMBUE, Congolese friction drum with a decorated round body and a sound like that of a lion's roar.

TAMBULA (Lat), kettledrum, Latin-American drum. *See also* **tambu.**

TAMBURA (Lat), kettledrum.

TAMBURELLO (It), tambourine.

TAMBURELLO BASCO (It), tambourine. (L)

TAMBURI (It), timpani. (L)

TAMBURI BASCHI (It), timbrels, tambourines. (L)

TAMBURI MILITARI SENZA CORDE (It), military drums without snares.

TAMBURIN (Ger, Russ), tambourine.

TAMBURIÑA (Sp), string drum in Basque areas.

TAMBURINO (It), tambourine; used, for example, in W.A. Mozart's *German Dances* K. 571 (1789). (L). Also *snare drum.*

TAMBURINO BASCO (It), tambourine. (L)

TAMBURIN OHNE SCHELLEN (Ger), tambourine without jingles, hand drum, frame drum.

TAMBURINO PROVENZALE (It), tambourine. (L)

TAMBURINO SENZA CIMBALI (It), tambourine without jingles, frame drum.

TAMBURI SENZA CORDE (It), drums without snares.

TAMBURO (It), drum.

TAMBURO A CORDA (It), string drum.

TAMBURO ACUTO (It), high sharp drum, small snare. (L)

TAMBURO ALTO (It), snare drum. (L)

TAMBURO A MANO (It), hand drum.

TAMBURO ARABO (It), darabucca, African hand drum. (L)

TAMBURO BASCO (It), tambourine. (L)

TAMBURO BASSO (It), field drum, long drum with snares. (L)

TAMBURO CHIARO (It), snare drum. (L)

TAMBURO CON CORDE (It), snare drum.

TAMBURO CON SORDINO (It), muted snare drum.

TAMBURO D'ACCIAIO (It), steel drum.

TAMBURO DI BASILEA (It), parade drum.

TAMBURO DI FRENO (It), brake drum.

TAMBURO DI FRIZIONE (It), friction drum.

TAMBURO DI LATTA (It), steel drum. (L)

TAMBURO DI LEGNO (It), woodblock, log drum. (L)

TAMBURO DI LEGNO A FESSURA (It), slit drum.

TAMBURO DI LEGNO AFRICANO (It), log drum. (L)

TAMBURO DI LEGNO PELLE (It), wooden tom-tom, wood-plate drum, plate drum.

TAMBURO DI PROVENZA (It), tambourin provençal.

TAMBURO GRANDE (It), bass drum.

TAMBURO GRANDE CON CORDE (It), large snare drum.

TAMBURO GROSSO (It), bass drum.

TAMBURO INDIANO (D'AMERICA) (It), American Indian tom-tom.

TAMBURO MILITARE (It), military drum.

TAMBURONE (It), bass drum.

TAMBURO ORIENTALE (It), Chinese drum. (L)

TAMBURO PICCOLO (It), snare drum, small snare drum, piccolo snare drum.

TAMBURO PROVENZALE (It), tambourin provençal.

TAMBURO RULLANTE (It), tenor drum or field drum.

TAMBURO RULLANTE CON CORDE (It), tenor drum with snares, field drum.

TAMBURO RULLANTE SENZA CORDE (It), tenor drum.

TAMBURO SENZA CORDE (It), drum without snares.

TAMBURO SORDO, South American snare drum with no snares that is muted.

TAMBURO SURDO (Port), (1) drum without snares; (2) family of drums used in the Brazilian Carnaval, without snares, and played with one hand and one stick. (L/JG)

TAMBURO TAROLE (It), tarole drum.

TAMMITTAM, generic term for African drum, used in many different languages.

TAMPON, obsolete double-headed bass drumstick in English, used for playing rolls. Bass drumstick in French. Also *mailloche double.*

TAM-T., abbrev. for *tam-tam.* (L)

TAM-TAM, flat-surfaced, indefinitely pitched circular gong in the United States and Europe. Made of hammered metal such as bronze, it comes in many different sizes and has an ornamental surface and curved rim. *Tam-tam* is also the name given to some African slit drums. *See also* Illus. 20, p. 126.

TAM-TAM GRAVE (It), low or deep tam-tam. (L)

TAM-TAM TIEF (Ger), low-sounding tam-tam.

TAMUKKU, *see* **tarshā**.

TANBORETE (Sp), a small drum.

TANBORÍN, Basque tabor.

TANGALA, Congolese conical drum played with sticks and hands.

T'ANG KU, Chinese barrel drum with calfskin heads.

TANG LO, Chinese brass gong.

TANG TSE, Chinese flat gong.

TANTĀ, Latin-American and Brazilian term for a gong.

TAN-TAN (Sp), tom-tom. (L)

T'AO, small Chinese cylindrical drum.

T'AO KU, small ancient Chinese rattle drum attached to a handle made from two snakeskin heads. There are one or two cords, ending in a knot, attached to the rim of the drum. When the drum is moved, the ends of the cords strike the skin. *See also* **Chinese hand drum**.

TAPAN, two-headed rope-tensioned drum, either a small bass drum or a large tenor drum. It is played vertically. *See also* **tupan**.

TAP BELL, small bell that produces a single tone. Also *finger bell*.

TAP BOX, woodblock. (L)

TAPHŌN, Thai barrel drum. Also *daphon*, *tapone*. *See also* **samphor.**

TAPONE, another spelling of *taphōn*.

TAP SHOES, tap shoes nailed loosely onto two boards, one held in each hand and beaten on a wood floor to simulate tap-dancing sounds.

TA PU, Chinese name for daf.

TA PU LA, Chinese name for the tabl.

TAQUARÁ, Brazilian stamping tube.

TĀR, Middle-Eastern frame drum with jingles, played with the fingers; *tīran* in plural.

TARBOURKA, goblet-shaped handheld drum made out of clay or metal with sheepskin heads that are tightened by strings or tension rods. It is played with the fingers or the open palm in the center and on the edge of the head; used in Hector Berlioz's *Les Troyens* (1863). *See also* **darabucca**.

TARÉLKI (Russ), cymbals.

TA'RIYA, North African cylindrical clay drum played in pairs.

TARÓ, TAROL, Brazilian snare drum 13 or 14 inches in diameter, with a 3½-inch metal shell. *See also* "Brazil: Percussion Instruments," p. 153.

TAROLA (Sp), Mexican timbales.

TAROLE, small snare drum made by Grégoire of Nantes in 1861. Now a piccolo snare drum.

TAROLE-TROMMEL (Ger), tarole drum.

TARR, *see* **tār**.

TARREÑA, TARRAÑUELA (Sp), castanets, flat clappers, bones.

TARSA, *see* **tarshā**.

TARSHĀ, small clay kettledrum of North India, with a thin skin head that is glued on; it is played with sticks.

TARTARIE (Fr), rattle; sometimes used to mean *crécelle*.

TARTARUGA, Brazilian friction instrument made from a tortoise shell treated with oil and rubbed with the hands; used by Heitor Villa-Lobos. *See also* "Brazil: Percussion Instruments," p. 153.

TĀSĀ, kettledrum of ancient Persia, modern North India.

TĀSHA, *see* **tarshā.**

TASSA, drumming tradition of Trinidad that originated in India. The tassa ensemble has two bowl-shaped *tassa* drums, a *dhol* drum, and a pair of cymbals, the *jhanj*. *See also* "Steel Band/ Pan," p. 297.

TASTENXYLOPHON (Ger), keyboard xylophone. *See also* "The Xylophone," p. 347.

TAVOLA DA LAVARE (It), washboard.

TAVOLA DI LEGNO (It), wooden board. (L)

TAVOLETTE (It), horse hooves.

TAXI HORNS, *see* **auto horn.**

T.B., abbrev. for *temple blocks*. (L)

TBILAT, *see* **African clay bongos.**

TCHANCHIKI, small Japanese gong in the shape of a pot, with a grooved outer edge. The beater is made out of a horn.

T.D.B. (Fr), abbrev. for *tambour de Basque*. (L)

T. DE B. (Fr), abbrev. for *tambour de Basque*. (L)

T'E CH'ING, Chinese musical stone, suspended and struck with a mallet. Also *tse king*.

T'E CHUNG, Chinese flat bell.

TELA, South American and African membrane in the resonator of a marimba (known as a *buzz marimba*) that buzzes or hums on notes of the lower register. (L)

TELLER (Ger), plates; refers to cymbals.

TELLERN, MIT (Ger), (with) crash cymbals. (L)

TEMPELBLÖCKE (Ger), temple blocks.

TEMPELBLOKI (Polish), temple blocks.

TEMPELGLOCKE (Ger), dobači, Japanese temple bell. (L)

TEMPLE BELLS, *see* **temple cup bells.**

TEMPLE BLOCKS, hollowed-out blocks of wood that are round or square and come in sets of three, five, or seven. They are non-pitched, with large resonating chambers, and are played with mallets. Modern temple blocks can be made out of plastic for durability. *See also* Illus. 23, p. 127.

TEMPLE-BLOCS (Fr), temple blocks.

TEMPLE CUP BELLS, bells coming in a variety of sizes. They are set on a cushion or soft surface and struck with a leather mallet. Most commonly they are used in Buddhist rites. Also known as *temple cup gongs*, *temple bells*. *See also* Illus. 37, p. 136; Illus. 40, p. 138.

TEMPLE CUP GONGS, *see* **temple cup bells.**

TEMPLES., abbrev. for *temple blocks*. (L)

TENABARI, pellet bells made out of butterfly cocoons.

TEN. DR., abbrev. for *tenor drum*. (L)

TENOR DRUM, deep two-headed cylindrical drum larger than a snare drum, originating from the military drum. The shell is usually wooden but can be metal or plastic. It has no snares. *Caisse roulante*, *caisse sourde* in French, *Rührtrommel*, *Tenortrommel*, *Wirbeltrommel* in German, *cassa rullante* in Italian, *redoblante* in Spanish. *See* Illus. 27, p. 128.

TENORTROMMEL (Ger), tenor drum.

TEPANAHUASTE, Guatemalan Indian drum. Also, in Latin America, a *slit drum.*

TEPONAZTLI, Mexican log drum or tuned log. Also *teponaxte, teponaxtle, toponhaztle.*

TERBANG, Javanese and Sundanese frame drum.

TERKOTKA (Polish), rattle.

TESCHIO CINESE (It), Chinese woodblock. (L)

TESTA (It), head.

TÊTE (Fr), the head, cup, bell of a cymbal, the head of a stick. (L)

TÊTE EN FEUTRE DUR (Fr), head of hard felt. (L)

THAILAND GAMELAN, *see* **thōn**.

THAILAND GAMELAN GONGS, *see* **kong wong yai**.

THAILAND TREE BELLS, series of cup-shaped bells in graduating sizes mounted on a single rod, played with a brass mallet in a glissando fashion. Most are a series of thirty-seven bells collected in Thailand. *See also* **bell tree**.

THAILAND VIOLIN, *see* **Vietnamese fiddle**.

THAMBATTI, Indian tambourine. *See also* **tambattam**

THICK PLATES, crash cymbals, antique cymbals. If a pitch is indicated, the part should be played on antique cymbals; if no pitch is indicated, it should be played on crash cymbals.

THIRTY-ONE TONE BELLS, bells tuned microtonally with thirty-one tones in a one-octave range.

THŌN, Thai goblet drum made of a highly lacquered clay and plaster shell. Also called *Thailand gamelan, ton.*

THUMB PIANO, series of tuned metal tongues that are attached to a wooden box over a sound hole. It is played by plucking the tongues. *See also* **marimbula**.

THUNDER SHEET, any large piece of thin metal suspended and shaken to produce the sound of thunder. *See also* Illus. 6, p. 119. (L)

THUNDER STICK, *see* **bull roarer**.

TIBETANISCHE GEBETSTEINE (Ger), Tibetan prayer stones.

TIBETAN PRAYER STONES, *see* **prayer stones**.

TIBETAN RATTLE DRUM, small drum that is mounted on a wooden handle. Attached to the shell are two leather straps with beads or knotted ends. The ends of the straps alternately strike the heads when the drum is twirled in the hand. *See also* **Chinese hand drum**; **Chinese paper drum**. *See* Illus. 37, p. 136.

TIEF (Ger), low (pitch or sound), deep.

TIEFE GLOCKE (Ger), steeple bell. A chime or church bell can be substituted.

TIEFE GLOCKEN VON UNBESTIMMTEM KLANG (Ger), low bells of indefinite pitch.

TIEFES GLOCKENGELAÜTE (Ger), low tolling of bells or chimes. (L)

TIMB. (It), abbrev. for *timbales.* (L)

TIMBAL (Sp), kettledrum; *timbales* in plural.

TIMBALAO, Latin-American tenor drum.

TIMBALE (Fr, Port), kettledrum.

TIMBALE À LEVIER (Fr), pedal timpani.

TIMBALE À PÉDALE (Fr), pedal drum.

TIMBALES (Fr, Port, Sp), timpani; introduced in the early fourteenth century. In English they are single-headed drums with the open end on the bottom, with a Latin association. They have metal shells that are played with thin sticks.

See also "Latin-American Percussion," p. 227; Illus. 28, p. 129.

TIMBALES-CHROMATIQUES (Fr), group of kettledrums in which open frames replace the shells; devised by Adolphe Sax in 1857. The drums were tuned to the diatonic scale. Also known as *pedal timpani.*

TIMBALES CUBAINES (Fr), timbales.

TIMBALES CUBANIS (It), timbales.

TIMBALES CUBANOS (Sp), timbales.

TIMBALES LATINO-AMERICANO (It), timbales.

TIMBALES ORIENTALES (Fr), Arabian tablās.

TIMBALE-TROMPETTE, *see* **trompette-timbale.**

TIMBALLE (Fr), *see* **timbale.**

TIMBALLI(O) (It), timpani, kettledrums.

TIMBALOU(N) (Provençal), kettledrum.

TIMBANA, Sudanese drum.

TIMBANO (Lat), timbrel.

TIMBILA, Mozambique xylophone with ten slabs of wood on a horizontal frame with dried fruit resonators.

TIMBREL, frame drum with jingles introduced during the Crusades and played by women. *See also* **tof.**

TIMBRES (Fr), jingles, snares (when referring to a snare drum), bells (as in Maurice Ravel's *Tzigane,* 1924). (L)

TIMP., abbrev. for *timpano.* (L)

TIMPAN, medieval kettledrum.

TIMPANETTI (It), timbales. (L)

TIMPANI, the plural of *timpano,* from the Italian, also known as *kettledrums.* They have vessel-shaped bodies made mostly of metal. Some shells or bowls are made of fiberglass. The bowls act as resonators for the distribution of vibrations of definite pitch. A single head made of calfskin or plastic is attached to the bowl by a rim and tension keys. The pitch is determined by means of tuning with the tension keys or a pedal mechanism. Timpani come in different sizes depending on the manufacturer and are played with many different types of mallets. *See also* "The Kettledrum," p. 201; Illus. 2, p. 117, and Illus. 13, p. 123.

TIMPANI A PEDALI (It), pedal drums.

TIMPANI ORIENTALI, Arabian tablās.

TIMPANO (It), kettledrum. Also singular of *timpani.*

TIMPANO PICCOLO (It), small timpani.

TIMPANO SENZA PEDALE (It), timpano without a pedal.

TIMPLIPITO (Russ), pair of non-pitched, small kettledrums that are throng-tensioned.

TINBUK (TIMBUK, TIMBUL), Melanesian xylophone. *See also* "The Xylophone," p. 347.

TIN HORN, *see* **metal rattle.** (L)

TINNIOLUM (Lat), small bell. *See also* **tintinnabulum.**

TIN RATTLE, *see* **metal rattle.**

TINTINNABULUM, (1) ancient Roman bell; (2) herd animal bell in late antiquity; (3) in early medieval times, the hammer with which the bells were struck from the outside. *See also* **cymbalum.**

TIN WHISTLE, *see* **penny whistle.**

TIOMPAN, modern Irish drum.

TĪRĀN, *see* **tār.**

TIRANT (Fr), pulling, tension.

TIRRAGIO (It), tension.

TIRYĀL (Arabic), tambourine.

TISCHGLOCKE (Ger), dinner bell.

TIUMBELECK (Bulgarian), kettledrum.

TJING, *see* **gongs of Korea.**

TLAPANHUEHUETL, Mexican-Indian war drum used mainly by the Aztecs, it is a large ornately covered, single-headed wooden drum either in the shape of a barrel or cylinder. Now a cylindrical footed drum.

TMB., abbrev. for *tamburo* (It), *tambour* (Fr), *timbales.*

TMB.B. (Fr), abbrev. for *tambour de Basque.*

TMBL., TMBLO. (It), abbrev. for *tamburello.*

TMBL.B. (It), abbrev. for *tamburello basco.* (L)

TMP., abbrev. for *timpani.* (L)

TM-T., abbrev. for *tam-tam.*

TOBÂ (Romanian), drum.

TOBA MARE (Romanian), bass drum.

TOBOINHA SONANTE, Brazilian thunder stick.

TOCSIN (Fr), alarm bell dating from medieval times.

TOF (Hebrew), biblical frame drum with a wooden hoop, two membranes, and no jingles. It was played by women. Also *toph. Tupim* in the plural. *Timbrel* in English.

TOGHA (Sanskrit), cymbals.

TÔLE (Fr), thunder sheet. (L)

TÔLE POUR IMITER LE TONNERRE (Fr), thunder sheet. (L)

TOLOMBAS (Albanian, Polish), kettledrums.

TOMBAK, *see* **zarb.**

TOMS., abbrev. for *tom-toms.* (L)

TOMS À UNE PEAU (Fr), single-headed tom-toms. (L)

TOM-T., abbrev. for *tom-tom.* (L)

TOM-TOM AIGU (Fr), small tom-tom.

TOM-TOM A UNA PELLE (It), single-headed tom-tom. (L)

TOM-TOM CHINOIS (Fr), Chinese tom-tom. (L)

TOM-TOM CINESE (It), Chinese tom-tom. (L)

TOM-TOM GRAVE (Fr), large tom-tom.

TOM-TOMS, cylindrical drums with no snares, with one or two heads, and usually in a set of varying sizes. They have modern tension rods, heads, and rims and are usually made of wood. In the West they are tunable drums used to imitate the sounds of, for example, Indian, African, and Chinese drums. *See also* Illus. 8, p. 120; Illus. 38, p. 137.

TOM-TOM SPIEL (Ger), roto toms.

TOM TOMY (Polish), tom-toms.

TON (1) (Ger), sound; (2) another name for thōn.

TONABULUM (medieval Lat), small bell.

TONE MODULATOR, a device that can be attached to any musical instrument or the human voice to change the tone. It has two oscillators that modulate in opposite directions.

TONGGON (Dutch), kentongan.

TONG PAL, Korean copper cymbal that comes in many different sizes.

TONHÖHE (Ger), pitch.

TONNERE À POIGNÉE (Fr), thunder sheet.

TOPAN, *see* **tupan.**

TOPFTROMMEL (Ger), pot drum.

TOPH, *see* **tof.**

TOPONHAZTLE, see **teponaztli.**

TOQUASSEN, medieval French spelling of tocsin. Also *toquesing.*

TOUETTE, hollowed-out section of a tree with a horizontal slit that is played with two sticks. Also known as *Polynesian slit drum.*

TOUPIE BOURDONNANTE (Fr), humming top.

TOURNER (Fr), turn.

TOY DRUM, child's snare drum. *See* Illus. 31, p. 130.

TOY MUSICAL HOSE, actual hose that is held at the end in a player's hand and revolved around the player's head, producing bugle-like intervals.

TOY TRUMPET, child's instrument used to produce sound by a blown reed.

TP., abbrev. for *timpani.* (L)

TP.BL., abbrev. for *temple block.* (L)

TRAIN WHISTLE, whistle made out of three wooden or metal pipes, each having a different pitch. The pipes are attached to each other and blown through one mouthpiece.

TRANCHE (Fr), slice, edge.

TRAPS, old term for drum set. *See also* "The Drum Set: A History," p. 173. (L)

TRAP SET, standard set of drums including the snare, tom-toms (mounted and floor), pedaled bass drum, hi-hat, and cymbals played by one person. *See also* "The Drum Set: A History," p. 173.

TREE BELLS, *see* **mission bell tree.**

TREE CYMBALS, *see* **cymbal tree.**

TREM.M.D. SCHWAMMSCHL. (Ger), abbrev. for *Tremolo mit dem Schwammschlägel.* (L)

TREMOLO MIT DEM SCHWAMM SCHLÄGEL (Ger), roll with soft sticks.

TREPEI (Fr), triangle.

TREPPIEDE (It), triangle.

TRESCHOTKA (Russ), ratchet.

TRÈS DOUCE (Fr), very soft.

TRÈS DUR (Fr), very hard.

TRÈS MOLLE (Fr), very soft.

TRES PALOS (Sp), Dominican Republic drum, like the yuka.

TRÈS SERRÉ ET RÉGULIER (Fr), very tight and regular.

TREUGOL'NIK (Russ), triangle.

TRG., abbrev. for *triangle.* (L)

TRI., abbrev. for *triangle.* (L)

TRIA., abbrev. for *triangle.* (L)

TRIANGEL (Ger), triangle.

TRIANGELSCHLÄGEL (Ger), triangle beater. (L)

TRIANGELSCHLÄGEL GESTRICHEN (MIT) (Ger), scraped with triangle beater.

TRIANGELSTAB (Ger), triangle beater. (L)

TRIANGLE, piece of a steel rod bent in the shape of a triangle struck with a metal beater. It has many high inharmonic overtones and indeterminate pitch. There is an opening at one corner end, and the triangle is suspended on a thin chord and attached to a clamp. Up to the nineteenth century jingling rings were attached. It entered the orchestra in the eighteenth century. *See also* "The Triangle," p. 337; Illus. 46, p. 141.

TRIANGOLO(I) (It), triangle(s).

TRÍANGULO (Sp), triangle.

TRIANGULUM (Lat), triangle.

TRIGONO (Greek), triangle.

TRILL COLLE MONETE (It), roll, trill with coins.

TRILLER (ZU 2) (Ger), (two) cymbals rubbed together. (L)

TRILLER AVEC DES PIÈCES DE MONNAIE (Fr), roll with coins. (L)

TRILLERPFEIFE (Ger), pea whistle.

TRILLO (A 2) (It), rub (two) cymbals together.

TRINIDAD-GONGTROMMEL (Ger), Trinidad steel drum.

TRI-NOME, electric metronome able to play three different rhythms against each other at different speeds; it also has three different pitch pulses.

TRIP GONG, bowl-shaped brass bell played with a hammer hitting its side.

TRIPHON (Ger), a form of xylosistron. *See also* "The Xylophone," p. 347.

TR-LO., abbrev. for *triangle.* (L)

TR.M.B. VON EINEM GESCHLAGEN (Ger), abbrev. for *Trommel mit Becken von einem geschlagen.* (L)

TROCANO, large Brazilian log drum; used by Heitor Villa-Lobos. *See also* "Brazil: Percussion Instruments," p. 153.

TROCKEN (Ger), dry, hard.

TROGXYLOPHON (Ger), trough xylophone.

TROM (Dutch), drum.

TROMMEL (Ger, Dutch), drum. (L)

TROMMELFELL (Ger), drum skin.

TROMMEL MIT BECKEN VON EINEM GESCHLAGEN (Ger), bass drum and cymbals played by one person.

TROMMEL OHNE SAITEN (Ger), drum without snares.

TROMMELSCHLEGEL (Ger), drumstick(s).

TROMMELSTOCKEN (Ger), drumsticks.

TROMPE D'AUTO (Fr), auto or taxi horn. (L)

TROMPE DE BÉARN (Fr), *see* **guimbarde.**

TROMPE DE BRUME (Fr), fog horn. Also *sirène.*

TROMPETTE-TIMBALE (Fr), kettledrum invented by Adolphe Sax in 1855, where the pitch is changed by a series of pedal-operated valves, slides, or keys that are manipulated by air volume. Also called *timbale-trompette.*

TROMPO SILBADOR (Sp), humming top.

TRONCA (Sp), cut off. (L)

TRONCS D'ARBRES (Fr), log drum, switch. (L)

TRONG, Cambodian goblet drum.

TRONG COM, Vietnamese barrel drum. Also *cai trong com.*

TR.O.S. (Ger), abbrev. for *Trommel ohne Saiten.* (L)

TROTTOLA (It), humming top.

TROUGH XYLOPHONE, xylophone with trough resonators, common in Asia; used by Carl Orff in *Antigonae* (1949) and *Oedipus* (1959).

TRÚBCHATYE KOLOKOLÁ (Russ), chimes.

TRUMM (Estonian), drum.

TRUMMA (Swedish), drum.

TRYPHONE, nineteenth-century French xylophone designed by Charles de Try. *See also* "The Xylophone," p. 347.

TSANATSEL, sacred Ethiopian sistrum.

TSANG, Burmese drum. Also *tsong.*

TSCHINELLEN (Ger), Austrian term for cymbals.

TSE KING, *see* **t'e ch'ing.**

TSÉPI (Russ), iron chains.

TSILINDRICHESKII BARABÁN (Russ), tenor drum.

TSONG, *see* **tsang.**

TSURIDAIKO, wooden Japanese barrel drum suspended in an elaborate circular frame. The body and heads are both painted. At the center of the top head is a patch of deerskin, which is played with knobbed sticks. Also known as a *hanging drum.*

TSURIGANE, Japanese hanging gong.

TSUZOMI, Japanese hourglass drums.

T.T., abbrev. for *tam-tam, tom-tom* (L).

T. TAM., abbrev. for *tam-tam.* (L)

TUBALCAIN, keyboard glockenspiel. (L)

TUBAPHON (Ger), tubaphone.

TUBAPHONE, set of brass or steel tubes arranged in keyboard fashion and played with spoon-like wooden mallets.

TUBES, JEU DE (Fr), chimes. (L)

TUBES DE BAMBOU (Fr), bamboo wind chimes. (L)

TUBES DE CLOCHES (Fr), chimes. (L)

TUBI DI BAMBÙ (It), bamboo wind chimes. (L)

TUBO, South American metal tube shaker of varying sizes. *See also* **chocalho.**

TUBOFONO (It), tubaphone.

TUBOLARI (It), chimes. (L)

TUBOLO, *see* **chocalho.**

TUBO SONORO (It), shaker. (L)

TUBUL, plural of tabl.

TUBULAR BELLS, modern tuned metal tubes suspended vertically in a frame and struck with mallets. They are usually one-and-a-half octaves and have varying lengths. Damping is accomplished by hand or with a dampening pedal. A rawhide mallet is usually used to play them. Also called *tubular chimes. See also* **chimes**; Illus. 30, p. 130.

TUBULAR CHIMES, chimes, tubular bells.

TUBULAR WOODBLOCK, two-toned woodblock. *See also* **cylindrical woodblock.**

TUBUSCAMPANOPHON (Ger), tubaphone. (L)

TULUMBAZ (TULUMBAS), Russian metal kettledrum.

TUMBA, Afro-Cuban single-headed drum that is vertical and comes in a variety of shapes. Also *goblet drum* of Zaire. *See also* **conga.** (L)

TUMBADORA, largest of the conga drums.

TUMBAK, *see* **tunbūk.**

TÚMBANO (modern Greek), drum.

TUMBELEK, *see* **dümbelek.**

TUMBELEKI, modern Greek clay goblet drum.

TUMBUK, goblet-shaped Middle Eastern drum made of clay shells and played with the fingers of one hand and the open palm of the other. *See also* **darabucca.**

TUMBUKIN (Sanskrit), drum.

TUN, Central American tuned log.

TUNBAK, *see* **tunbūk.**

TUNBŪK, old Persian goblet drum. *See also* **darabucca.**

TUNED BONGOS, *see* **boobams.**

TUNED BOTTLES, series of glass bottles suspended by their necks from a rack and played with hard-covered mallets. The bottles are chosen for their specific pitch and arranged to produce a chromatic scale. Inexactness in pitch may be corrected by adding water to the bottle. This instrument was popular in the vaudeville orchestras in the first third of the twentieth century. Scoring for tuned bottles may be found in Erik Satie's *Parade* (1917), Arthur Honegger's *Le dit des jeux du monde* (1918), and Bo Nilsson's *Reaktionen* (1960). *Bouteillophone* in French.

TUNED BOWLS, *see* **jaltarang.**

TUNED GLASSES, *see* **musical glasses.** (P)

TUNED LOG, *see* **log drum.**

TUNED PICCOLO WOODBLOCK, woodblocks cut and tuned to the two highest octaves of the xylophone. They are laid out in keyboard fashion and played with rubber or wooden mallets.

TUNED PIPES, aluminum pipes tuned diatonically, mounted on foam, and placed over a plastic timpani head, which is then placed over a hollow barrel to act as a resonator. *See* Illus. 31, p. 136.

TUNOUL, Mayan tuned log.

TUNTINA, *see* **ektara.**

TUNZU, Latin-American slit drum.

TUONI (It), thunder sheet.

TUONO A PUGNO (It), thunder sheet.

TUPAN, Balkan two-headed cylindrical drum that is similar to a bass drum. It is played vertically and struck with a cloth or felt beater. The drum is suspended by a strap over the left shoulder. Sometimes the left hand uses a switch in the Turkish manner of the davul. Also *topan.*

TUPIM, *see* **tof.**

TURÁ-MARACÁ (Port), Brazilian stamping tube with a maraca tied to it.

TÜRKISCHE BECKEN (Ger), Turkish cymbals or crash cymbals.

TÜRKISCHE MUSIK (Ger), Janissary music.

TURKISH CRESCENT, pole with a metal top shaped like a crescent, from which are suspended bells and jingles. The pole is shaken or struck on the ground. Also known as *hat, pavilion. See also* **Jingling Johnnie.**

TURKISH DRUM, name of the bass drum up to the nineteenth century. It was laid on the side and played with a beater or hands on the head or the shell. Sometimes a switch was used on the shell.

TURMGLOCKENSPIEL (Ger), chimes. (L)

TURTLE RATTLE, form of an American Indian rattle.

TU-TI, castanets from Santo Domingo.

TUYAU DE FER (Fr), iron pipe.

TWENTY-TWO TONE TRANSCELEST, keyboard percussion instrument made from square brass tubing that has a long sustaining quality. It is known for the unearthly quality of its glissandos.

TWENTY-TWO TONE VIBES, keyboard percussion instrument similar to the vibraphone but divided into twenty-two notes per octave. The divided parts are not equal. It was invented by Erving Wilson.

TWENTY-TWO TONE XYLOPHONE, keyboard percussion instrument similar to the xylophone but divided into twenty-two notes per octave. The divided parts are not equal in a system similar to the theoretical Indian scale of twenty-two S'rutis. This instrument is suited to playing the Greek modes. It was invented by Erving Wilson.

TWIG BRUSH, *see* **switch.**

TYMBALON, small tambourine of Provence; formerly the tymbalon was one of a pair of small copper kettledrums suspended from the player's neck and beaten with two sticks.

TYMBRIS (Lat), clapperless bell.

TYMPALI (Ger), kettledrums, as used in the J.S. Bach's *Magnificat* (1723).

TYMPAN, twelfth- and thirteenth-century French drum.

TYMPANA, Latin-American timpani, plural of tympanum.

TYMPANE (Old and Middle Eng), kettledrum.

TYMPANI, modern misspelling of timpani.

TYMPANON, frame drum of ancient Greece played with the hands; like the tof.

TYMPANUM, hand-beaten frame drum of ancient Rome, developed from the tympanon; later came to mean copper kettledrums, i.e., timpani. Tympana in plural.

TYMPANY, misspelling of timpani. (L)

TYMPELLES (Ger), kettledrums, used in J.S. Bach's Cantata No. 100 (1735).

TYPEWRITER, office typewriter machine used as a percussion instrument.

TYPOPHONE, dulcitone. (L)

TZICAHUAZTLI, Mexican Indian güiro.

UCCELLI (It), bird whistle.

UCHIWADAIKO, single-headed Japanese drum, about 6 inches in diameter, mounted on a paddle-like frame. *See also* **kabuki drum** (L/WM).

UDÁRNYE INSTRUMÉNTY (Russ), percussion.

U.GR.TR. (Ger), abbrev. for *und grosse Trommel.* (L)

UKKĀLI, Bengalese drum.

'ULĪ'ULĪ, Hawaiian vessel rattle.

UMFANG (Ger), extent, range.

UNAFON, keyboard instrument with rows of tubes sounded by electrically powered mallets. (L)

UNBESTIMMTER KLANG (Ger), indefinite pitch.

UND GROSSE TROMMEL (Ger), and bass drum. (L)

UNE CONTRE L'AUTRE (L') (Fr), one against the other.

UNGHIA (It), fingernails.

UPBEAT ROLLS, *see* **press rolls.**

URUCUNGO, *see* **berimbau.**

USIGNUOLO (It), nightingale; a recording of "canto dell' usignuolo" is used in performances of Ottorino Resphighi's *Pines of Rome* (1924). (L)

UTA DAIKO, *see* **diabyoshi.**

VALIMBA (VARIMBA), xylophone of lower southeastern Africa. Also *mambira. See also* "The Xylophone," p. 347.

VBF., abbrev. for *vibraphone.* (L)

VENEZUELAN FRICTION DRUM, barrel drum that makes a sound when a rosined cord is pulled through an opening in the drumhead.

VERGA (It), switch.

VERGE(S) (Fr), switch(es), wire brush(es) (in twentieth-century music). (L)

VERGHE(I) (It), switch(es), wire brush(es) (in twentieth-century music). (L)

VERKLINGEN LASSEN (Ger), let ring, let the sound die away.

VERRES CHOQUÉS (Fr), glass harmonica. Also *glass harp.* (L)

VERRILLON (Fr), musical glasses.

VERSTIMMT (Ger), not tuned (L); out of tune.

VESSEL RATTLE, gourd or calabash held by its neck containing small objects that make a rattling noise when shaken. This gourd or vessel can be made of fruit shells, clay, basketry, wood, metal, and most often, calabashes. It contains seeds, shells, rocks, pebbles, or small bells that strike against the inner vessel walls. *See also* **gourd rattle**.

VETRATA (It), sandpaper blocks.

VIBE, vibes, *see* **vibraphone**.

VIBES, *see* **vibraphone**. (L)

VIBR., abbrev. for *vibraphone, vibrato.* (L)

VIBRAFÓN (Russ), vibraphone.

VIBRAFONI (It), vibraphone.

VIBRAFONO (It), vibraphone.

VIBRAHARP, trade name, along with vibraphone, for the vibe. Instrument manufacturers decided to use phone or harp as part of their brand names for vibe. *See also* "The Vibraphone, Vibraharp, and Vibes," p. 339.

VIBRAPH., abbrev. for *vibraphone.* (L)

VIBRAPHON (Ger, Russ), vibraphone.

VIBRAPHONE, the trade name of *vibes*, an instrument constructed in the United States in 1922. It has metal alloy or aluminum bars arranged in keyboard fashion over metal resonators on a wheeled frame. A damper pedal enables a note to be sustained when struck with a mallet or dampened similar to a piano damper pedal. It is the first metal bar capable of producing a tremolo by means of agitating the air with motor-driven propellers inside the resonators. These propellers are circular metal disks that, when driven by the electric motor, create the vibrato effect. The speed of the tremolo is determined by how fast the disks are circling. The usual range is three octaves, f to f^3. *See also* "The Vibraphone, Vibraharp, and Vibes," p. 339; Illus. 9, p. 121.

VIBRAPHONSCHLÄGEL (Ger), vibraphone mallet.

VIBRASLAP, modern adaptation of the sound produced by the jawbone or quijada; it makes a long sustained rattling noise by striking a ball with the hand or fist. The ball's vibration causes small pegs to vibrate inside a wooden sound chamber. The ball and sound chamber are attached by the same piece of thin metal. *See also* Illus. 34, p. 133.

VIBRATOPHONE, vibraphone. (L)

VIBRIEREN LASSEN DURCH LEICHT BERÜHREN (Ger), let vibrate gently by barely touching.

VIEHSCHELLE(N) (Ger), cowbell(s).

VIERER-TEMPELBLÖCKE (Ger), (use) four temple blocks. (L)

VIETNAMESE BELL, *see* **chung**.

VIETNAMESE FIDDLE, two-stringed instrument with a seashell bridge and a coconut shell resonater; used in the Pi Phat Ensemble. Also *squ.*

VILLĀDIVĀDYAM, four-part idiophone of south India.

VITESSE VARIABLE (Fr), variable speed (motor).

VOÉNNYI BARABÁN (Russ), military snare drum.

VOGEL-LOCKRUF (Ger), bird call. (L)

VOGELPFEIFE (Ger), bird whistle.

VOILÉ(E) (Fr), covered, muffled.

VON EINEM GESCHLAGEN (Ger), played by one person.

WACHTEL (Ger), quail call; used in Leopold Mozart's *Toy Symphony* (1786). (L)

WACHTELPFEIFE (Ger), quail whistle.

WADA, Chilean maracas.

WALDTEUFEL (Ger), friction drum whose sound is produced by a rosined cord or horsehair passing through a parchment membrane and being rotated. Waldteufel also sometimes refers to a pasteboard rattle. *Bourdon* in French. *See also* Illus. 37, p. 136.

WALZENTROMMEL (Ger), cylindrical drum.

WARBLER, *see* **bird whistle**.

WARNING SIREN, hand or electric perforated rotating disk that interrupts the flow of air, creating a glissando effect.

WASAMBA (Fr, It), wasamba rattle.

WASAMBA-RASSEL (Ger), wasamba rattle.

WASAMBA RATTLE, African gourd rattle consisting of disks strung loosely on a handle that, when played (usually in pairs or in choirs), create a light clatter sound. The disks are made from fruit husks, and the handle is usually taken from a tree branch. *See also* **African gourd sistrum**.

WASCHBRETT (Ger), washboard.

WASHBOARD, actual household washboard used in music consisting of a wooden frame surrounding a metal serrated surface. The sound is produced by scraping a thimble or metal object across the surface.

WATER CHIMES, four mounted brass clock disks on a pipe frame activated by a foot pedal. After the chimes are struck, the pedal lowers the disks into a metal container filled with water. The pitch is lowered and amplified by an underwater microphone. The device was invented by Emil Richards. Similar to the water gong.

WATER DRUM, *see* **water gourd**.

WATER GONG, name given by John Cage to a tam-tam or gong that, upon being struck, should be immediately immersed in water halfway down. The water causes the pitch to slide down and create a glissando effect. The glissando can be ascending or descending depending upon which direction the gong is going, up or down. *See also* "Percussion and Dance," p. 265.

WATER GOURD, made from half a gourd or calabash, floating in a pan of water and played with a stick. It is of African and Central and South American origin, and it is mainly played at funereal rites. The gourds are placed in the water with the open ends facing down and can be of different sizes. They are struck with a small gourd or calabash that has a handle. The sound is similar to a cupped hand beating the surface of the water.

WATER-PHONE, instrument created by Dick Waters of California, consisting of two cooking pots welded together. Different sized brass rods are also welded to its inner and outer rims. Water placed in the pots is activated after the rods have been struck with a rubber mallet. The rods can also be bowed to produce other tones. Also known as a *cooking pot*. *See also* **roasting pan**.

WATTIERT (Ger), padded.

WATTIERTERSCHLÄGEL (Ger), padded sticks.

WA-WA CYMBALS, Thai hand cymbals that can create either a cymbal crash or an air cup suction that produces a "wa-wa" effect. Also called *chap*.

W.B., abbrev. for *woodblock*. (L)

W.BLK., abbrev. for *woodblock.* (L)

WEICH (Ger), soft.

WEICHENFILZ PAUKENSCHLÄGEL (Ger), soft felt timpani sticks.

WEICHENFILZ SCHLÄGEL (Ger), soft felt sticks.

WEICHE PAUKENSCHLÄGEL (Ger), soft timpani sticks.

WEICHER FILZ (Ger), soft felt.

WEICHE SCHLÄGEL (Ger), soft sticks.

WELLENSIRENE (Ger), siren.

WERBEL (Polish), drum.

WEWETL, Mexican Indian large wooden one-headed drum that is very ornate.

WHALE SKIN RATTLES, Eskimo rattles.

WHIP, *see* **slapstick**. *See* Illus. 36, p. 135.

WHIRLED FRICTION DRUM, friction drum with a notched stick that is held and whirled.

WHISTLE, instrument that has one tone produced by air blown through it. It has no fingerholes and sometimes contains a pellet or ball. *See also* **police whistle**.

WHIZZER, *see* **bull roarer**.

WIE AUS DER FERNE (Ger), as from a distance; used in Alban Berg's *Wozzeck* (1925). (L)

WIE AUS WEITER FERNE (Ger), as if from a great distance; used in Gustav Mahler's Symphony No. 3 (1896). (L)

WIE VORHER (Ger), as before; used in Gustav Mahler's Symphony No. 1 (1888). (L)

WILMURRA, North Australian bull roarer that comes in two sizes.

WIND CHIMES, objects such as metal, wood, bamboo, brass, rock salt, keys, shell, and glass hung from a string and agitated. They can be played in any key.

WIND MACHINE, a cylinder with a canvas loosely draped over it that produces a whirring sound when turned by a crank.

WINDMASCHINE (Ger), wind machine.

WINDSCHLEUDER (Ger), wind machine.

WINE GLASS, a crystal, resonant glass whose vibration is started by rubbing a moistened finger along the top edge; can be pitched by adding water. (L) *See also* **bowls**.

WIRBEL (Ger), roll.

WIRBEL MIT DEN FINGERN (Ger), finger roll.

WIRBELTROMMEL (Ger), tenor drum.

WIRE BRUSH, brush of thin flexible steel wires gathered in a handle, used instead of a switch. *See also* Illus. 42, p. 139.

WIRE COILS, *see* **coil spring**.

WIRKLICHER KLANG (Ger), real pitch.

W/O, abbrev. for *without.* (L)

WOBBLE BOARD, piece of masonite board cut to the player's arm length, held horizontally at the ends, and shaken to produce the sounds of water bubbling.

WODA, Latin-American maracas.

WOLLE (Ger), wool, yarn.

WOLLE UMWICKELT (Ger), yarn-wound.

WOLLSCHLÄGEL, wool-headed stick(s). (L)

WO MÖGLICH (Ger), when possible, where possible.

WO MÖGLICH MEHRFACH BESETZT (Ger), wherever possible use several players; used in Gustav Mahler's Symphony No. 2 (1895). (L)

WOOD BELL, woodblock shaped like a maraca and sometimes mounted when shaken, it makes a sound produced by a beater on each side or in the middle of the block.

WOODBLOCK, rectangular piece of wood with a slit down the side creating a sound chamber. It is played with mallets or sticks. *See also* Illus. 35, p. 134.

WOOD(EN) DRUM, *see* **log drum; woodblock; wooden tom-tom.**

WOODEN AGOGÔ, two pitched tubular blocks of hardwood hollowed out at the ends. Slits are cut at both openings. *See also* **agogô.**

WOODEN BARREL, *see* **barrel.**

WOODEN BOARDS, any boards played with round wooden sticks that when struck create a light, clapping sound.

WOODEN CLAPPER, *see* **slapstick.**

WOODEN FISH, five blocks of wood that are either round or square and are traditionally tuned to a pentatonic scale. The pieces are hollowed out; when hit with a fairly soft mallet, they create a resonate wood sound. *See also* **Chinese temple blocks.**

WOODEN GONG, hollowed-out log or wooden rectangular box with tongues cut into the lids. The tongues produce certain pitches to imitate an African slit drum.

WOODEN SCRAPER, hollowed-out piece of wood with notches. Sound is produced by scraping a stick across the notches. Also *wooden scratcher. See also* **reco-reco.**

WOODEN SCRATCHER, *see* **wooden scraper.**

WOODEN SHAKER, wooden object containing seeds or other small objects. *See also* **shaker.**

WOODEN SPOONS, actual hardwood spoons, both held in the hand and played by opening and closing the fingers.

WOODEN TOM-TOM, single-headed tomtom with a thin wooden head. (L)

WOODEN WIND CHIMES, *see* **bamboo wind chimes.**

WOOD-PLATE DRUM, single-headed drum with a wood head.

WOOD TABLE, device created by Emil Richards with nine slabs of Brazilian rosewood, two Chinese woodblocks, six Japanese small temple blocks, five Korean small temple blocks, one African wood bell, and one Turkish cymbal. The table is played with rubber mallets and has many high indefinite pitches.

XAQÚE-XAQUE, two Afro-Brazilian rattles mounted on a stick; or a general term for various types of rattles.

XERE, general term for an Afro-Brazilian metal rattle.

XF., abbrev. for *xilofono* (It). (L)

XIAOGU, *see* **hsiao-ku.**

XILOFÓNO (Sp), xylophone.

XILOFONO (It), xylophone.

XILOFONO A TASTIERA (It), keyboard xylophone.

XILOFONO BASSO (It), bass xylophone.

XILOFONO IN CASSETTA DI RISONANZA (It), trough xylophone.

XILOMARIMBA (It), xylomarimba.

XILORGANO (Sp), xylophone.

XUCALHO DE METAL, Brazilian metal shaker. *See also* **chocalho.** (L)

XUCHA, South American rattle. (L)

XYL., abbrev. for *xylophone.* (L)

XYLEUPHONE, keyboard xylophone invented by Culmbach. *See also* "The Xylophone," p. 347.

XYLHARMONICON, keyed *xylosistron. See also* "The Xylophone," p. 347.

XYLO., abbrev. for *xylophone.* (L)

XYLOFONE (Port), xylophone.

XYLOMARIMBA, keyboard instrument that is suspended over resonators mounted on a sturdy frame and played with mallets. It is a combination of a marimba and xylophone in timbre and range and was made in the 1930s for use in rhythm bands. Also called *marimba-xylophone, xylorimba. See also* "Range of Mallet Instruments," p. 367.

XYLOPH., abbrev. for *xylophone.* (L)

XYLOPHON (Ger), xylophone.

XYLOPHONE, percussion instrument with wooden or synthetic bars arranged in keyboard fashion. It is played with hard rubber, wood, or plastic mallets. The keys are suspended over resonators mounted on a wheeled frame. The normal range is three or three-and-a-half octaves, and the written range is from c to c^4 or f (g) to c^4. It sounds one octave higher. *Xylophone, claquebois* in French, *Xylophon, Holzfiedel, Holzharmonika* in German, *silofono, xilofono* in Italian, *xilofóno* in Spanish. *See also* "Range of Mallet Instruments," p. 367; "The Xylophone," p. 347; Illus. 11, p. 122; Illus. 43, p. 139.

XYLOPHONE, ALTO, *see* **alto xylophone**.

XYLOPHONE, ALTO-SOPRANO, *see* **alto-soprano xylophone**.

XYLOPHONE, SOPRANO, *see* **soprano xylophone**.

XYLOPHONE À CASSETTE-RÉSONANCE (Fr), trough xylophone.

XYLOPHONE À CLAVIER (Fr), keyboard xylophone.

XYLOPHONE BASSE (Fr), bass xylophone.

XYLOPHONSCHLÄGEL (Ger), xylophone sticks.

XYLORGANUM, seventeenth- and eighteenth-century term for xylophone. *See also* "The Xylophone," p. 347.

XYLORIMBA, *see* **xylomarimba**.

XYLOSISTRON (Ger), friction xylophone consisting of wooden bars touched by the performer's rosin-coated gloves.

YAK BELLS, bronze bells with a clapper that were originally placed on the backs of animals. They are mounted on a horseshoe-shaped frame. When struck, each bell produces a primary tone and a secondary tone a minor third below. *See also* **hin**.

YING KU, Chinese barrel drum that is suspended on a very ornamental frame and played with two sticks. In the past it was known to be associated with the Confucian temple and was called *chien ku. See also* **Chinese tom-tom**.

YOTSUDAKE, Japanese bamboo clappers (about 2 inches by 6 inches by ½ inch) played face to face. (L/WM)

YUKA, Afro-Cuban cylindrical single-headed dance drum that is hollowed out; it usually comes in three sizes. Also called *fumabata ngoma. Tambor de tronco* in Spanish.

YUN-LÖ, Chinese gong chime.

YUNQUE (Sp), anvil.

ZABUMBA, (1) Brazilian bombo; (2) Brazilian and El Salvador friction drums. *See also* "Brazil: Percussion Instruments," p. 153; "Latin-American Percussion," p. 227.

ZACAPA, Andean jingle rattle, also used by the Taino Indians of Central America, made of dried shells and sometimes referred to as ankle shakers. *See also* **pod rattle**.

ZACATÁN, very large vertical Mayan wooden drum with a single head and ornately decorated.

ZAMBOMBA, Spanish friction drum having one end covered with membrane and utilizing a friction stick. The drum is usually made of tin or clay. *See also* **zabumba**.

ZANZA, *see* **sansa**.

ZAPOTECANO, Mexican Indian buzz marimba, in which a membrane covers the aperture close to the base of the resonators.

ZARB, Iranian goblet-shaped clay drum. Also called *dombak, tombak*. *See also* **darabucca.**

ZARGE (Ger), shell.

ZEBRA HAIR SKIN DRUM, *see* **rukinzo**.

ZICCHIGNOLA (It), rattle.

ZICHIREI, *see* **kajirei**.

ZIEHPFEIFE (Ger), slide whistle, swanee whistle.

ZIEMLICH HART (Ger), medium hard.

ZIEMLICH SCHWERE SCHLÄGEL (Ger), medium hard sticks.

ZIEMLICH WEICH (Ger), medium soft.

ZILAFONO (It), xylophone. (L)

ZILS, ancient Arabic or Turkish cymbals similar to finger cymbals; still used by Turks for cymbals. *See also* "Janissary Music," p. 195.

ZIMBEL(N) (Ger), cymbal(s), antique cymbal(s), cratale(s), small medieval bell.

ZIMBELRAD (Ger), bell wheel or cymbal wheel.

ZIMBELSTERN (Ger), bell wheel.

ZISCHEND (Ger), literally, hissing; used in Richard Strauss's *Ein Heldenleben* (1898) played by pulling a file or threaded rod across the edge of a cymbal. (L)

ZUBUMBA (Port), lion's roar.

ZUMBA (Basque), large cowbell, bull roarer in Spain and Latin America.

ZUMBADOR (Sp), bull roarer.

ZUMBIDOR (Port), Brazilian bull roarer or thunder stick.

ZUPFTROMMEL (Ger), plucked drum.

ZǓRGALAǓ (Romanian), pellet bell.

ZURRIAGO (Sp), slapstick.

ZURÜCK (Ger), back.

ZURÜCKSTIMMEN (Ger), retune.

ZURÜCKTRETEN (Ger), step back, diminuendo.

ZUSAMMEN (Ger), literally, together; in music, crash cymbals.

ZU 2 (Ger), with 2 (players, instruments).

ZUZÁ, Brazilian metal tube shaker.

ZU-ZU, folk dance bell rattle used in a religious temple. *See also* **sistrum**.

ZWEIERSATZ (Ger), two sizes.

ZWEIKÖPFIGE SCHLÄGEL (Ger), two-headed stick (double stick).

ZWEI SPIELER (Ger), two players.

ZYLINDERTROMMELN (Ger), cylindrical drums.

ZYMBEL (Ger), Paul Hindemith's own term for use in his opera *Cardillac* (1926) to indicate a small cymbal with a clear, metallic sound.

II.
Illustrations of Percussion Instruments

Illustrations of Percussion Instruments

Laurie Beck Tarver
Photographer

1. Multiple percussion setup

2. Dresden timpani

3. Tunable bass drum made by William L. Cahn

4. Concert bass drum

5. Concert bass drum with attached cymbal

6. Thunder sheet

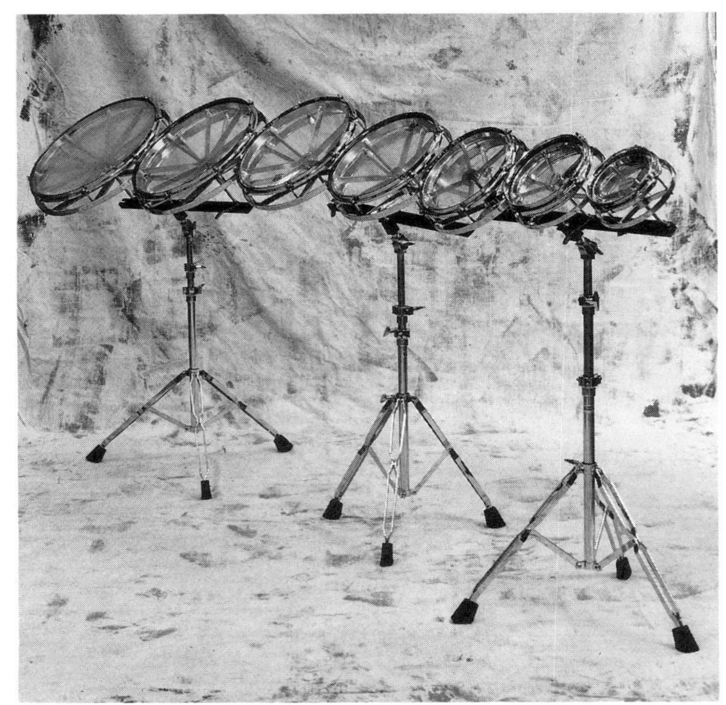

7. Roto toms

8. Concert tom-toms

9. Vibraphone

10. Marimba

11. Xylophone

12. Concert cymbals

13. Timpani

14. Concert bells

15. Crotales

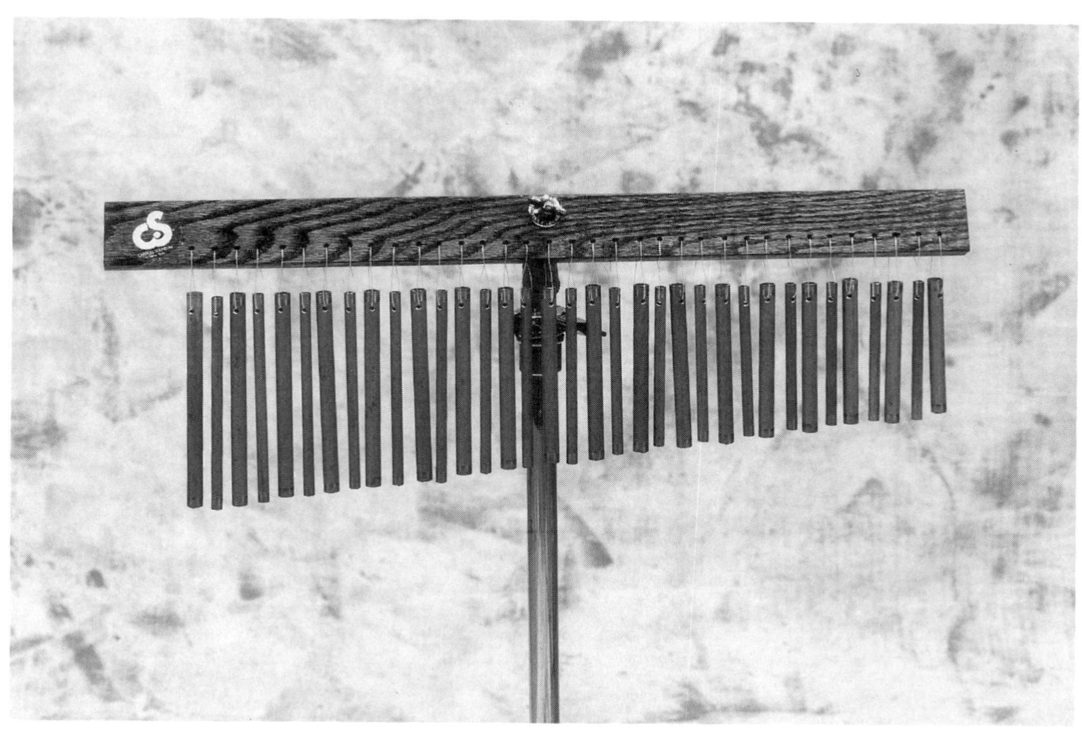

16. Mark tree

17. Octave-set of tuned gongs

18. Two-octave set of Almglocken (Alpine herd bells)

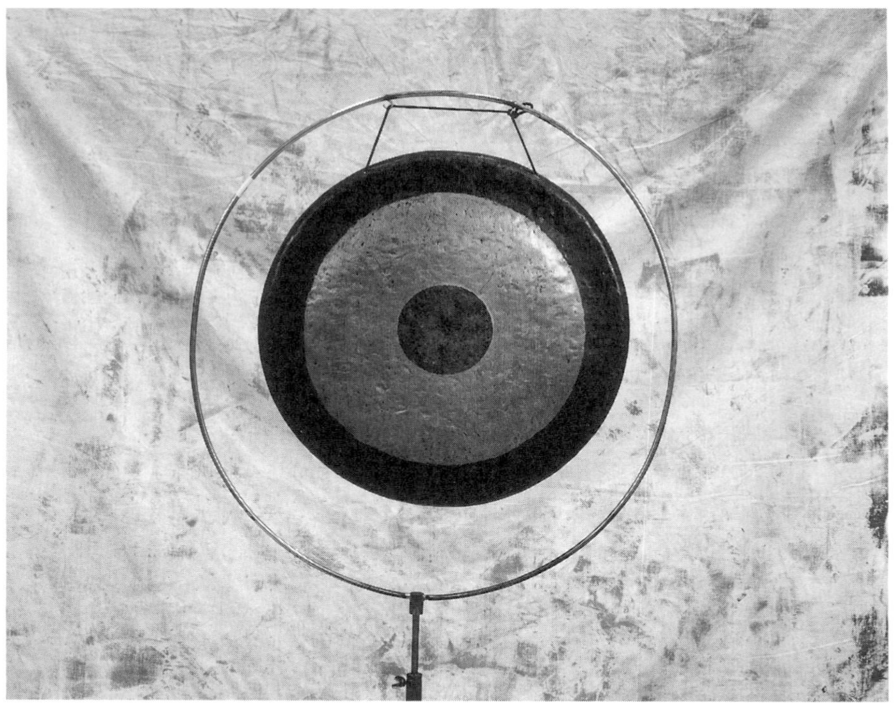

19. Chinese gong

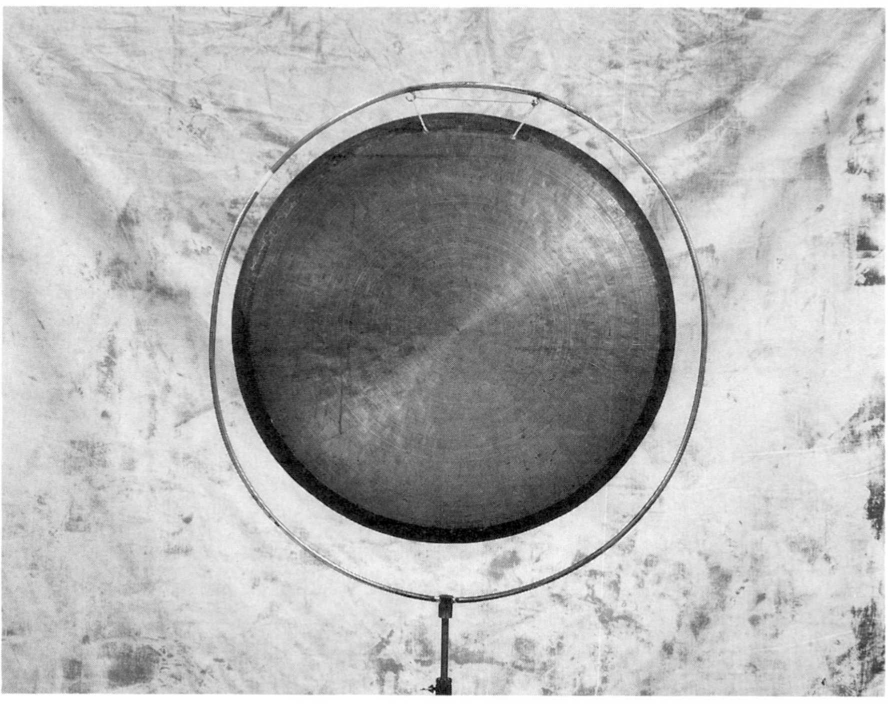

20. Tam-tam

21. Chinese cymbal

22. Suspended cymbal

23. Temple blocks

24. Bongos

25. Field drum

26. Snare drum

27. Tenor drum

28. Timbales

29. Conga drums

30. Chimes

31. Back row left to right: galvanized electric tubes, toy snare drum, manufactured log drum. Middle: steel drum. Front: chimta, pū'ili

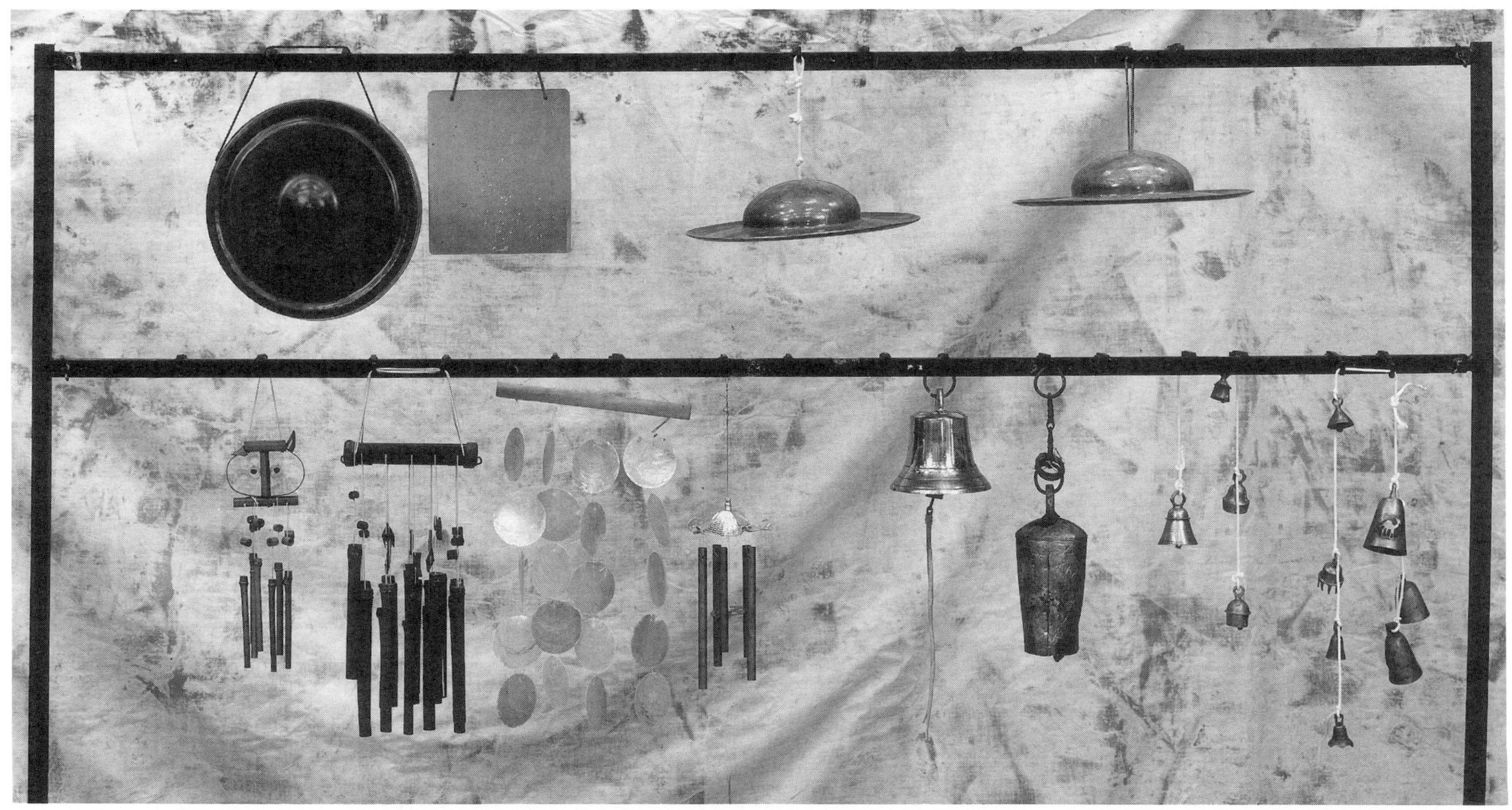

32. Top row left to right: button gong, metal plate, Tibetan cymbals.
Bottom row: bamboo fish scales and metal wind chimes, ship's bell, camel bell, sarna bells

33. Center rear: plastic hose, wine bottle

Back row left to right: clock chime, boat whistle, ratchet, sistrum (3), sleigh bells

Front row: taxi horn, bicycle horn (2), coconut shells and marble slab (horse's hoof effect), bones, cricket effect, ocarina, slide whistle, pop gun

34. Back row left to right: African rattle, afuche, cabasa, Bolivian drum, maracas, caxixi, ganzá, metal shaker, güiro with scraper
Front row: wooden shaker, vibraslap, pandeiro, tamborim, wooden scraper, agogô

35. Back row left to right: woodblocks, lion's roar, bell tree, brake drums
Front row: "Flexatone," pod rattles, machine castanets, various paddle castanets

36. Back row left to right: slapstick (whip), tambourine, large ratchet, large slapstick

Middle row: claves

Front row: duck call, police whistle, bird whistle, finger cymbals, samba whistle, mouth siren

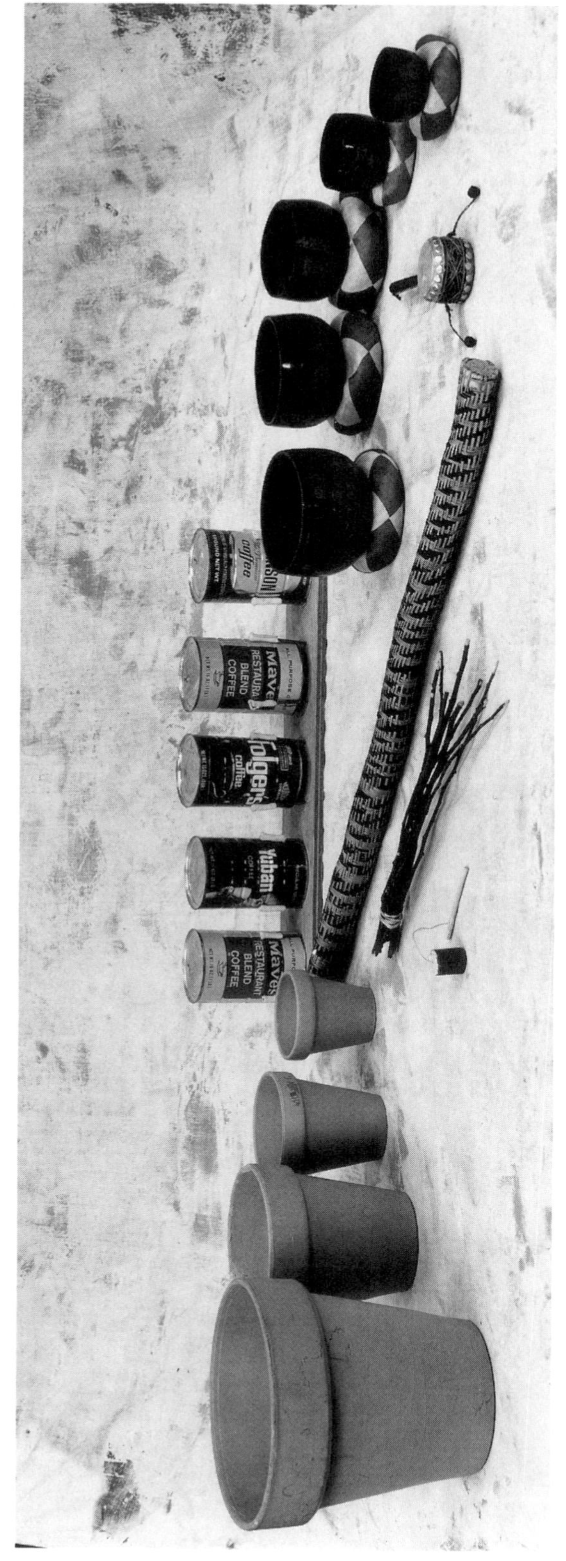

37. Back row left to right: flowerpots, coffee cans, temple bells
Front row: Waldteufel (friction drum), switch (rute), rain stick, Chinese paper (hand) drum

38. *American Indian Drums*

Back row left to right: birchbark tom-tom, Taos tom-toms (3),

Front row: frame drum (Western Canada), Taos frame drums (2), Taos tom-tom, Seneca Indian drum

39. *Asian-African-Caribbean Drums*

Back row left to right: dono talking drum (Ghana), dholki (India), darabucca-dümbek (Syria), carved wood drum (Haiti), merengue drum (Dominican Republic)

Middle row: tacked drum (China), tablā (India), bāmyā (India), cuícas (Brazil)

Front row: carved-log drum (Bali)

40. Top row left to right: temple bell (Japan), temple bell (China)
Bottom row: wooden water buffalo bell (Thailand), bronze artillery-shell casing (United States), prize bell Almglocken (Switzerland)

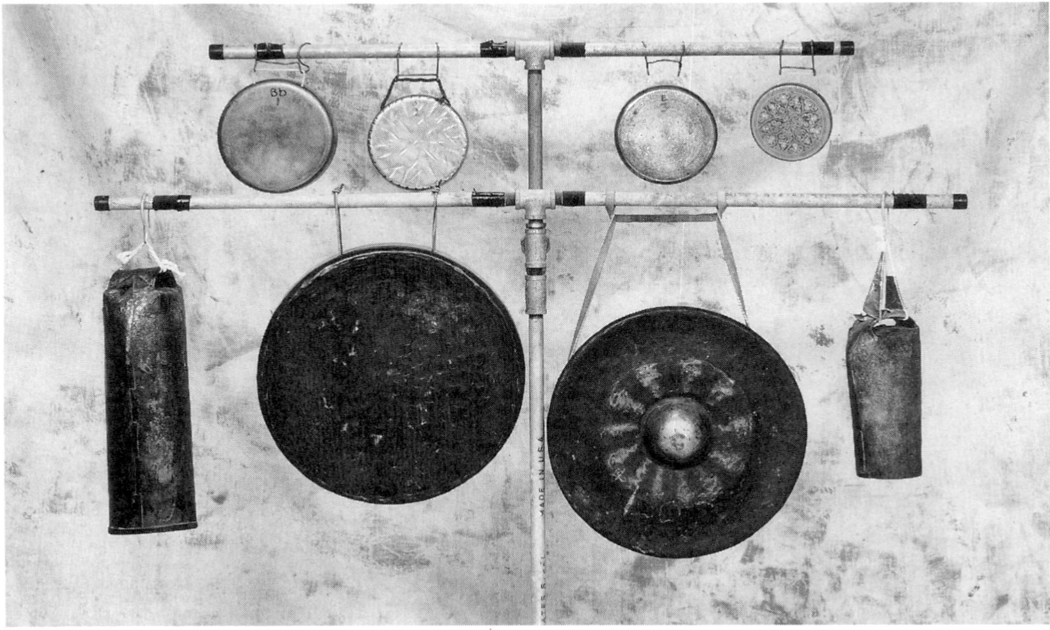

41. Top row left to right: gong (Southeast Asia), gong (Burma), gong (Southeast Asia), gong (India)
Bottom row: iron bell (Pakistan), cylinder gong (Singapore), button gong (Indonesia), iron bell (Pakistan)

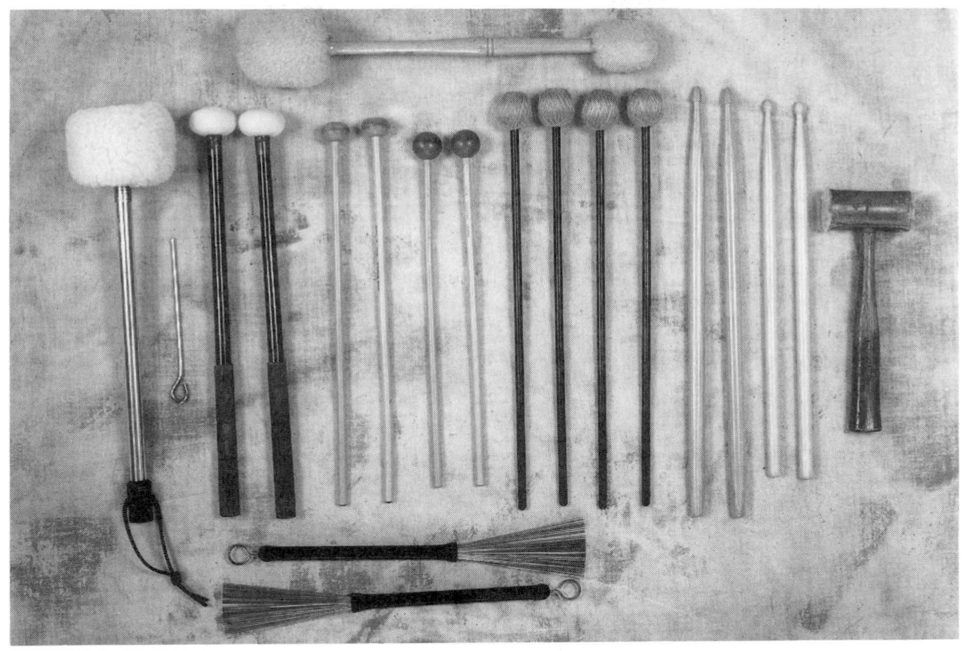

42. Top row: double-headed bass drum beater

Middle row: gong mallet, triangle beater, timpani mallets, rubber marimba mallets, xylophone mallets, yarn marimba mallets, concert snare drumsticks, drum set snare drumsticks, chime mallet

Bottom row: wire brushes

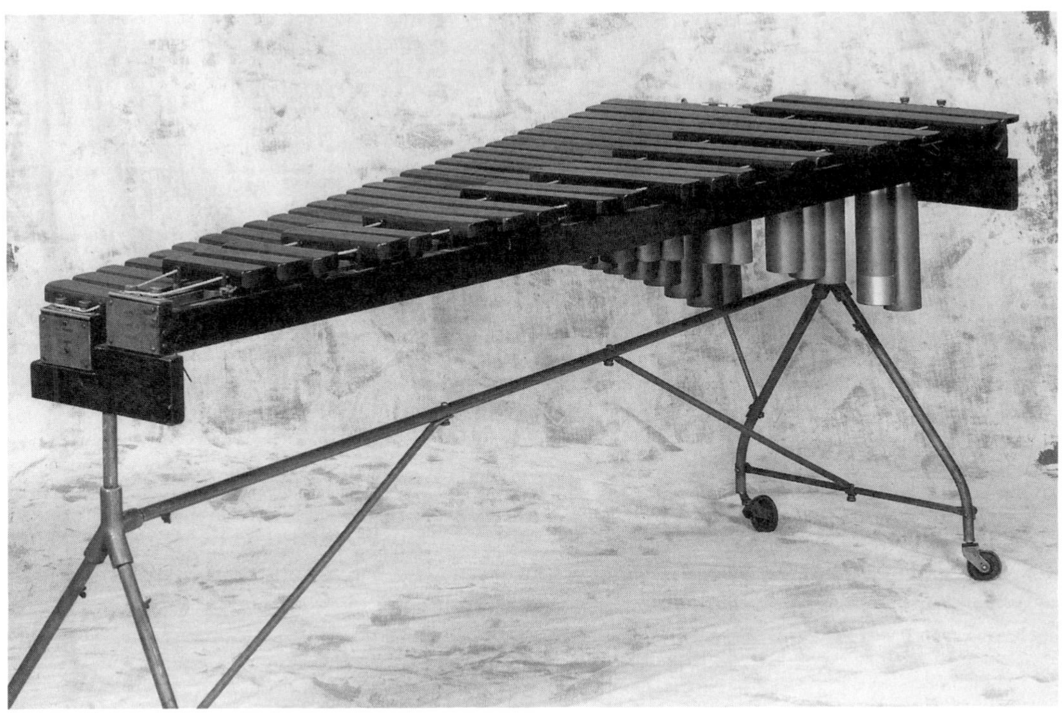

43. Artist special Deagan xylophone (c. 1920)

44. Three examples of rope-tensioned snare drum

45. Various types of single- and double-tensioned snare drums

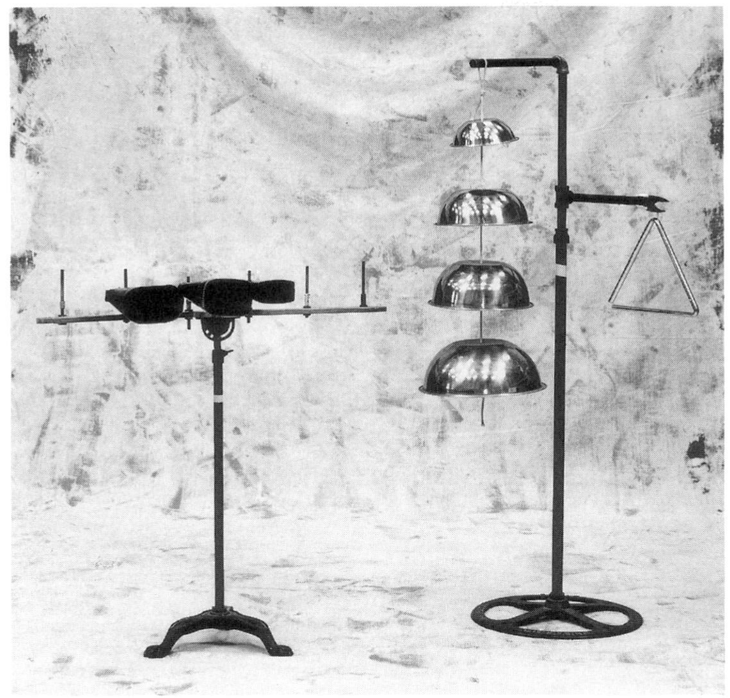

46. Left to right: cowbells (3), stainless steel bowls (4), triangle

47. Drum set

Courtesy of Ludwig/Musser Industries.

III.
Articles

The Basel Drum

The standard *Basel drum* of today is a descendant of the typical *side* or *snare drum* of the Middle Ages but differs in size, proportion, construction, and method of tensioning. Its name derives from the Swiss city of Basel, where, for several reasons, drumming became very popular and where about three thousand drummers cultivate the highly developed technique of Basel drumming. The Basel drums are rope-tensioned field drums measuring about 16 inches in diameter and 16 inches in depth. The shell is usually made of chromium-plated brass, although some fancy versions are made of wood, as they were in earlier days. The drum is roped with hemp or nylon cording passing through holes in the wooden counter hoops that are on both the batter head and the snare head. To strain or tension the drum, twelve leather braces or leather "ears" are pushed toward the bottom of the drum. This pulls two strands of the rope together, causing more tension to be applied to the counter hoops. The wooden counter hoops are painted in alternating stripes of black and white, the colors of the city of Basel. As these drums are often used outdoors and under extreme weather conditions, the standard Basel drum is usually equipped with two plastic heads. However, whenever possible the drummers prefer to use calfskin heads mounted on flesh hoops. The top head is the thicker of the two and is called the batter head. The bottom head is called the snare head, because eight or more snares of gut, nylon, electrical wire, or wire-covered silk are stretched across it, which add to the brilliance and give a timbre to the vibration, impossible to obtain in any other way. A snare strainer mounted on the shell makes it possible to regulate the amount of tension on the snares by screws or wing nuts, thereby achieving the proper sound. Today the instrument is usually fitted with an internal damper for controlling the resonance of the batter head.

The Basel drum is supported by a shoulder strap or leather sling, suspended in front of the player at an angle of about forty-five degrees. It is played with two wooden sticks that are about 16 inches in length, with round or olive-shaped heads. Side drums from the thirteenth to the seventeenth century varied considerably in size; some were deeper and others smaller than today's standard drum. The shells were fabricated from wood or made of different metals, such as brass, copper, or alloys, usually nicely decorated with ornaments or engravings. A very fine collection of old side drums is on display at the Musikinstrumenten Sammlung in Basel. The oldest Basel drum, dated 1571 and in the Historisches Museum of Basel, has a shell 5 inches deeper than its 20-inch diameter.

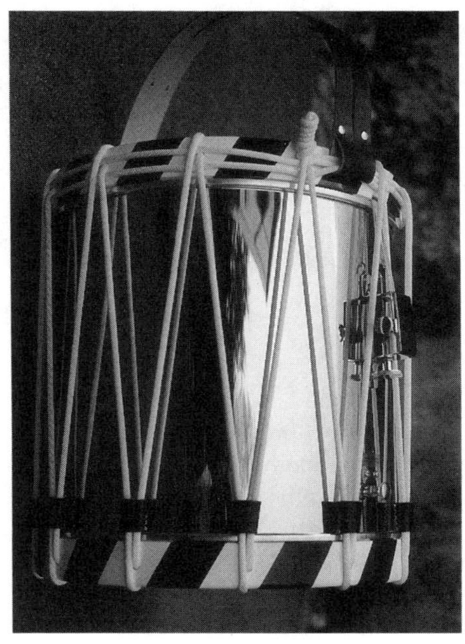

Fig. 1. Basel drum with chromium-plated brass shell.

Fig. 2. Basel drum with wooden shell.

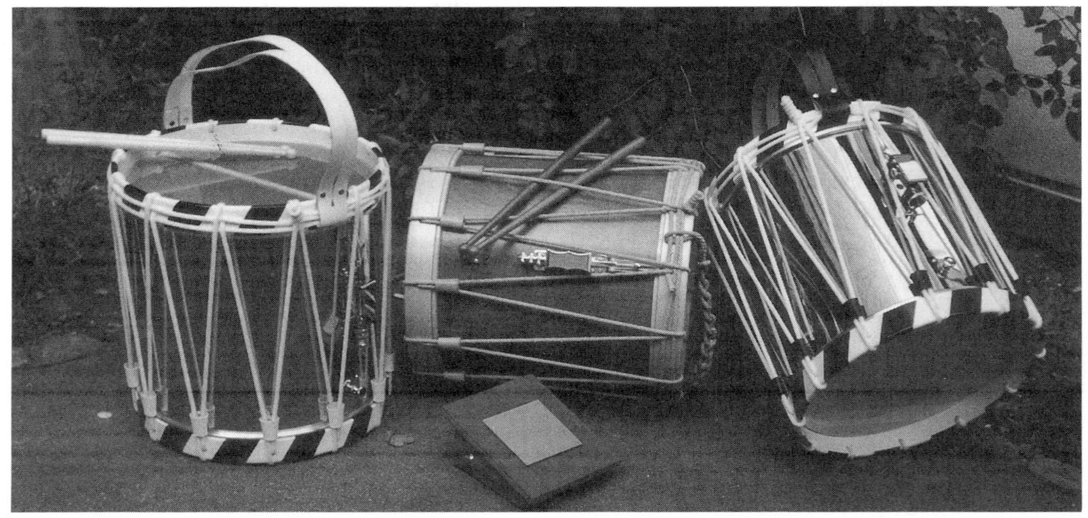

Fig. 3. Chromium-plated brass shell and wooden-shell Basel drums, with practice pad and snare drum sticks.

Even more important than the instrument is the drum style of the Swiss city, known as Basel drumming. Its peculiarities, its differences from other drumming styles, and the probable reasons for its development and persistence in Basel are described below.

Basel was founded more than two thousand years ago and soon became an important port of transshipment because of its ideal location on the Rhine River, which is Switzerland's only maritime gateway. Basel today is a modern and dynamic commercial town. It is the home of many pharmaceutical firms and a famous university, which is more than six hundred years old. Although Basel has had to keep pace with the development of modern life, its people care greatly for numerous old customs and pass these traditions down to the next generation.

One of these customs, and without a doubt the most significant annual event in the city's social life, is the "Fasnacht," the traditional carnival which begins at four o'clock in the morning of Shrove Monday. To the music of drums and fifes march the so-called "cliques" ("guard" groups or corps) through the darkened streets of the town carrying colorfully painted lanterns. The drummers and fifers participating in the parade wear original costumes and masks that more often than not serve as caricatures of important people in the news of the world. The music of the drums and fifes is an indispensable part of carnival time in Basel. The drums play a leading role, and the carnival would be unimaginable without them. It is thus understandable that through an evolution of hundreds of years, the Basel drummers have developed their own unique style, perhaps one of the most perfect rudimental drumming styles and techniques in the world today.

Fig. 4. Two drummers in Fasnacht.

In Basel there are about three thousand drummers and fifers in a population of nearly three hundred thousand citizens. Each drummer belongs to one of the numerous cliques. A clique consists of fifteen to forty fifers, fifteen to thirty-two drummers, and a drum major, who marches behind the fifers and in front of the drummers. To be a good drummer or fifer is a significant honor and, therefore, the cliques usually have their own drum and fife schools. Although membership in a drum and fife band or corps is voluntary (there are no professional drummers or school bands), there is no problem in finding enough young aspirants from the new generation. This is due to the fact that fifes and drums are so popular, primarily because the carnival (Fasnacht) is an old established tradition, and to be active in it is exciting and rewarding. The cliques also offer an attractive social life throughout the year. The drummers and fifers of a clique are people in all vocations and professions, and anybody with a good sense of rhythm, tradition, and wit is welcome to join.

The first use of fifes and drums by Swiss army units is confirmed in a chronicle of the battle of Sempach in 1386. The Swiss soldiers of this time were very brave and famous fighters, but in addition, their field music, including their way of using drums and fifes in military campaigns, was extraordinary. Between the fifteenth and nineteenth centuries, some 2.5 million Swiss mercenaries had the particular privilege of using their own military signals and drum ordinances. In this way they introduced their drum and fife marches into other European countries. The Swiss drummers and fifers and their marches were often praised in many old documents. But it was not until 1589 that a clergyman in Dijon, Thoinot Arbeau, noted the "Swiss stroke" and the "Swiss storm stroke" (known as the "coup de charge") in music notation. Some two hundred years later, we find the same strokes and several Swiss marches in military drum books of Bern and Biel. The first complete collection of marches and signals was compiled in 1819 by J. Buehler, a Basel musician, who created a new ordinance for drummers and fifers of the Swiss army.

Although Basel itself had no regiments serving under foreign flags, the officers of the merchant guilds, in whose hands lay the defense of the city's territory, acquired military experience in Swiss regiments abroad and brought back with them their drum and fife marches. Some of the marches are still played by the cliques of Basel. The guilds were also the center of the city's social life, so that the playing of drums and fifes gradually lost its military significance and became a popular custom to such an extent that it enabled Erasmus of Rotterdam to write the following to his friend Valerius on September 26, 1529: "In Basel the drums are heard not only in war but at weddings and on holidays too, indeed even in the churches, and the children run in the streets and the young brides dance to their sound."[1]

Basel remained the "drum city" of Switzerland, and it is to the credit of Basel's drummers that they have preserved the old rhythms and melodies of the past right up to the present time. As in everything else, of course, the drumming style and technique underwent a normal development and modernization before it reached today's high level. The mercenaries did not only introduce the rudiments and marches into foreign countries, but they also learned from, and were influenced by, their colleagues abroad. They often brought back to Switzerland their new knowledge, including some of the very elegant and vivacious drum beats of France. The development and enrichment of Basel drumming under the influence and the inclusion of French strokes began around 1870, but it was E. Krug, especially, who was finally successful in modernizing the drumming style when he published several marches in the 1890s with some of the French strokes (*maermelli, walliser, buren*).

In addition to some French rudiments, namely *pataflafla*, *ra saute*, *coup anglais*, *moulin strokes*, *ratafla*, and *coup de charge*, some new rudiments were created by the Basel drummers, the *Millwheel stroke*, the *flammed coup de charge*, several *end stroke combinations*, and several *reveille stroke combinations*. This amalgamation of the more ponderous Swiss beats with those of the French elegance was a very fortuitous one and, together with the dynamic expression, gave Basel drumming its proper character. The official drum schools of the cliques began at this point to systematically teach their pupils these new rudiments, and they presently constitute the basis of Basel drumming.

Regarding the notation of Basel drumming, in the past, it was the custom to indicate the drum beats with words or make use of onomatopoeia. This system sufficed for a long period of time, since the rhythms then were relatively simple and the drummers did not care about making a difference in the playing of right- and left-hand beats. As the rudiments became more complicated, the drummers arrived first at a combination of words and letters and finally at several systems of signs and letters. Thus evolved the technical fundamentals of drumming. These rather primitive remedies however, were never satisfactory, although some of these systems are still in use. It is obvious that no one can play a drum march written in one of these systems without having heard the score previously, because the signs and letters express the technical aspects only and do not have any rhythmical value whatsoever. It was a big step forward, therefore, when in 1928, Dr. Fritz R. Berger created a monolinear notational system that represented the exact rhythms, dynamics, and techniques. This highly developed notation enabled drummers at last to read, to learn, and to correctly interpret their drum marches. There are many drummers all over the world who have learned this drumming style through self-instruction by us-

Fig. 5. Chart illustrating the evolution of music used for Basel drumming.

ing Berger's drum books, and some of them have composed even remarkably good original compositions in the Basel drumming style. Figure 5, from *Das Basler Trommeln, Werden und Wesen* by F.R. Berger, gives an idea of the development of the notational system.

Thus far we have learned quite a lot about the history and development of Basel drumming and its organization in the cliques. The reader might ask, with justification, what is it that makes Basel drumming so special? What does it sound like? What is the technique? Drumming is generally spoken of as a kind of marching music by means of which the drummer attempts to keep the marchers in the same step. So it is with Basel drumming. All drum and fife marchers are in two-step measures and the main accent is usually on the left foot. However, and this is one of the characteristics of Basel drumming, the main accent is often on the right foot or in counter or contrary time. Usually the marches are divided into verses of eight two-step measures (sixteen steps), although this is not a specified rule. If the drums and fifes play together, they often play different rhythms; the drummers play, so to speak, their own melody but without disturbing the rhythmic pattern of the fife score. Many times the drum introduces a rhythmic theme, which will be taken over by the fife. On the other hand, the fife can introduce the rhythmic theme but the drummers never beat just the rhythm of the melody of the fifes.

Another characteristic of Basel drumming is the well-emphasized dynamic expression. The drums may swell in a crescendo of sound and diminish in a seemingly irregular pattern; the tone rises and falls and the accelerations and decelerations are interrupted by well-placed single accents. Besides the marches and pieces for drums and fifes together, in which the drum score should not be overloaded with technical difficulties in order to avoid interference in the teamwork of the two instruments, there are more and more compositions for the drums alone. Here the drummer may dynamically unfold his whole spectrum of technical ability and express his personal feelings by his own interpretation of the score.

The construction of a Basel drum march is usually made up in pairs of verses. The rhythmic motif is introduced in the first verse. The same theme along with a new motif is taken over and conjugated in many ways in the second verse. This will appear again in the third verse, etc. This pattern of construction gives rhythmical coherence to a composition and makes it possible to increase the technical difficulties continuously from its beginning to its end. However, and this should be emphasized, it is not so much the technical difficulty by which a Basel drum march should be judged, but rather its rhythmic originality.

Note

1. Fritz R. Berger, *Das Basler Trommeln, Werden und Wesen* (Basel: Trommel Verlag, 1928).

Bibliography

Adams, A., and C. Collison. "Interview with Alfons Grieder, Swiss Rudimental Drummer." *Percussive Notes* 30, no. 5 (1992), part 1; no. 6, part 2.

Berger, Fritz R. *Das Basler Trommeln, Werden und Wesen*. Basel: Trommel Verlag, 1928.

———. *Instructor for Basel Drumming*. Basel: Trommel Verlag, 1964.

———. *Trommelmärsche*. Vols. 1–3. Basel: Trommel Verlag, 1959–1965.

Duthaler, Georg. *Trommeln und Pfeifen in Basel*. Basel: Christoph Merian Verlag, 1985.

———. "Zum Trommeln und zum Pfeifen." *Unsere Fasnacht*. Basel: Verlag Peter Herman, 1971.

Grieder, Alfons. *Das Basler Trommeln*. Basel: Musik Hug, 1971.

———. "Introduction to Swiss Basel Drumming." *Ludwig Drummer* 8, no. 1 (1968).

Alfons Grieder

The Bass Drum

Fr: *grosse caisse*; Ger: *Grosse Trommel*; It: *gran cassa*; Sp: *bombo*

The bass drum was introduced into the western orchestra through the influence of the Turkish Janissary bands of the seventeenth and eighteenth centuries. In these bands, the bass drummer used both hands to strike the instrument. One hand held a felt-covered wooden mallet and primarily kept the pulse of the music. The other carried a switch that produced a higher pitched sound and played accompanying rhythmic patterns. This style of playing was used until the rise of the French rescue and grand operas in the late eighteenth and early nineteenth centuries.

The orchestral bass drum of the middle eighteenth and early nineteenth centuries seems to have had two main influences: the Turkish drums mentioned above, and the *long drum*. The long drum was an instrument in which the depth of the shell was greater than the diameter of the heads, hence its name. Indeed, it may have been the long drum that was used by Mozart and Beethoven in their Turkish-inspired music.

The Parisian opera composers often scored the bass drum and cymbal parts to be played by one performer. This was achieved by attaching one cymbal to the shell of the bass drum. The other cymbal was held by one hand of the percussionist, while the other hand held the bass drum mallet. This allowed the percussionist to play both instruments simultaneously. Eventually, the two instruments were played by two performers, since the sound of both instruments suffered when played by a single percussionist. However, the frequent use of the bass drum in opera scores led to its inclusion in the western orchestra of Romantic and twentieth-century orchestras.

In the late nineteenth and early twentieth centuries, orchestras for vaudeville shows and silent movies often employed only one percussionist. This required that the percussionist have the ability to play the snare drum and bass drum at the same time. Therefore, various forms of pedals were invented to play the bass drum. The number of various devices used to facilitate bass drum performance by the foot is rather astounding. However, William F. Ludwig's invention in 1909 of a toe-operated pedal that featured a short beater rod supported by a brace, which attached easily to the rim of the bass drum, became the prototype of most modern bass drum pedals.

The modern orchestral bass drum ranges in diameter from 32 to 40 inches. The depth of the shell is between 18 and 22 inches. It almost always is a double-headed drum employing either calfskin or synthetic vellums (the former generally acknowledged to produce a preferable sound). In the earlier part of the twentieth century a shallow, single-headed drum of great diameter (up to 60 inches) become quite popular in England. However, the *gong drum*, as it was known, lost its popularity as the century progressed.

The most frequently desired tone from the bass drum is one of a low, undefined pitch. Most performers avoid tuning the drum to a specific pitch, as it may clash with the tonality of the work being performed. The bass drum is played with a wide variety of mallets. The most common are large felt-covered wooden mallets, which produce a deep, rich tone from the drum. However, composers often call for other mallets including snare drum sticks, brushes, switches, and wooden mallets.

The bass drum is often mounted on a stand that allows the instrument to be placed at any angle. This lets the performer position the bass drum at the most comfortable playing angle. Earlier stands were simple cradles that supported the drum in one position with the heads perpendicular to the floor. These cradles are still in use today.

A list of works that make prominent use of the bass drum includes:

Mozart, Wolfgang Amadeus
Overture to *Die Entführung aus dem Serail* (1782)

Spontini, Gasparo
Overture to *La Vestale* (1807)

Beethoven, Ludwig van
Symphony No. 9 (1824)

Berlioz, Hector
Symphonie fantastique (1830)

Tchaikovsky, Piotr Ilyich
Symphony No. 4 (1878)

Mahler, Gustav
Symphony No. 3 (1897)

Mahler, Gustav
Symphony No. 5 (1902)

Stravinsky, Igor
Le Sacre du printemps (1913)

With attached cymbal:

Mahler, Gustav
Symphony No. 1 (1888)

Stravinsky, Igor
Petrouchka (1911)

See also "Janissary Music," p. 195; and Illus. 3–5, pp. 118–119.

Bibliography

Blades, James. *Percussion Instruments and Their History*. 2nd ed. London: Faber and Faber, 1974.

Brown, Theodore D. "The Bass Drum Pedal: In the Beginning." *Percussive Notes* 21, no. 2 (1983): 28–32.

———. "Double Drumming." *Percussive Notes* 20, no. 1 (1981): 32–34.

DePonte, Neil. "Janissary Music and Its Influence on the Use of Percussion in the Classical Orchestra." *Woodwind World, Brass and Percussion* 15, no. 4 (1976): 44f.

Peinkofer, Karl, and Fritz Tannigel. *Handbook of Percussion Instruments*. London: Schott, 1976. Originally published in German (Mainz: B. Schott's Söhne, 1969).

Peters, Gordon. *The Drummer: Man, a Treatise on Percussion*. Rev. ed. Wilmette, Ill.: Kemper-Peters, 1975.

Schneider, Walter C. "Percussion Instruments of the Middle Ages." *Percussionist* 15, no. 3 (1978): 106–117.

Andrew Spencer

Brazil: Percussion Instruments

The percussion instruments of Brazil reflect a unique blend and adaptation of the three important strands of Brazilian music: Brazilian Indian, West African, and Euro-Portuguese. The various rattles, shakers, drums, and imitations of animals, such as the *cuíca* and *ganzá*, are derived from the Brazilian Indians. The enslaved West Africans modified the instruments they remembered from their cultures, such as musical bows, drums, and bells, into the *berimbau, atabaque, afoxê,* and *agogô*. The folk percussion instruments, such as military drums, tambourines, and triangles, which were derived from the Euro-Portuguese cultures, were modified into the *surdo*, *caixa*, and *pandeiro*. The use and performance styles of these instruments all contribute to the identity and variety of Brazilian music.

Samba Batucada

The street *samba* used for the large parades during the Carnival in Brazil is called the *samba batucada*. It is performed by a *bateria* of fifty to five hundred players who dance and entertain as well as play handheld or attached instruments made of light metal and/or membranes of plastic or animal skin.

Technique

The techniques reflect the requirements for the street *samba*, i.e., to be loud, to play continuously for an hour or more, and to keep the dancing and singing vibrant. Most of the techniques require minimal facility as long as the *samba* "feel" is present. All membranophones are played with one stick or one hand (except for the *tarol*) with the other hand holding and muffling or changing the tension of the head. The idiophones are all played by one stick or shaken.

Use in Ensemble

In general, the larger the drum, the simpler the repetitive pattern. Most of the patterns are fixed, while some instruments are allowed to improvise. Also the timbre of each of the instruments is unique and can be distinguished within the ensemble. Select groups of instruments within the *bateria* will play alone to change the texture. All of the changes of timbre and/or rhythmic patterns are signaled by the *apito* whistle by the *mestre da bateria* (percussion master).

Instruments

Surdo maracanã. This is a large two-headed drum about 26 inches in length and 18 to 26 inches in diameter. It is played by a stick 13 inches long and 3/4 inch in diameter, the playing end being a wooden ball covered with leather. The sound is loud and is intended to echo the sound of Maracanã Stadium, which holds 200,000 people for Sunday soccer matches. The full stroke is played on the downbeat while the left hand muffles the drum on the upbeat.

Surdo pequeno. A two-headed drum, 16 inches in length and 14 inches in diameter. It is played with one stick 11 inches long and 3/4 inch in diameter. The performance technique is to play a stroke with both stick and hand together, stick alone, or muffle alone. The *surdos* play an interlocking pattern with the highest pitched *surdos* and the lowest pitched *surdos* outlining the important beats and the middle pitched *surdos* playing in between these beats. The effect is a multi-timbral pattern with the *surdo maracanã.*

Repique. This two-headed drum is played in an improvisational style. It is usually 12 inches in length and diameter. It is played with one stick, the size of a model 7A snare drumstick. The *repique* is tuned tightly and uses techniques of rimshots, left-hand muffles, one stick buzz rolls, single-hand stick tremolos, and open and stopped sounds.

Tarol. This is a piccolo snare drum, 13 to 14 inches in diameter, with a 3½-inch metal shell. It has four coiled wire snares and is often held by the left arm. Two snare drumsticks are used with the right hand playing the accents and the left hand adding alternating buzz rolls.

Tamborim. This is a one-headed drum, 5½ inches in diameter, with a 2-inch metal shell. It is played with a ¼-inch wood stick about 10 inches in length. Today, the *tamborim* is often played with prefabricated plastic rods held together on a handle. The technique used consists of holding the *tamborim* in the left hand and muffling the underside with the middle finger. The right stick plays a combination of stopped strokes, rimshots, muffled strokes, and open strokes.

Pandeiro. This tambourine-like instrument has a diameter of 10 to 14 inches, with 6 to 10 pairs of jingles fixed so that there is a very short ring sound. The shell is usually wooden. The *pandeiro* is held in the left hand, with the middle finger muffling the head on the underside. The right hand plays a combination of palm slaps, finger, thumb, and heel of the hand, as well as thumb and finger rolls. Also, the left wrist rotates to play certain strokes. This instrument is also used to perform acrobatic feats of spinning, passing the *pandeiro* around various parts of the body and throwing it up to 20 feet in the air.

Cuíca. This is a friction drum played by rubbing a thin stick with a cloth. The drum has one head, 10 inches in diameter, and a 12-inch metal shell (formerly wooden). The thin bamboo stick is mounted on the inside of the drum in the center of the head. The stick is about 8 inches long and is rubbed with a damp cloth to produce the sounds of the harmonic series. The left hand holds the *cuíca* (if it is not carried on a strap) and changes the tension of the head by pressing with the thumb and/or fingers. Usually, the *cuíca* can produce over an octave in pitch range. This instrument is used by the Indians of Brazil to imitate the sound of a marsupial called a *goiacuíca*.

Agogô. A double bell attached to a "u-shaped" metal rod. The bells are conical in shape, with an opening 2½ to 3 inches long and 1½ to 1¾ inches wide. The total length of the bells varies from 6 to 8 inches. The interval is usually a whole step between the bells. Sometimes as many as five bells are added to the holder. The right hand plays the *agogô* on the side of the bell with a metal rod or a wooden stick ⅜ inch in diameter and about 7 inches long. The left hand holds the *agogô* and squeezes the bells together to produce an interlocking pattern with the right hand.

Frigideira. This metal instrument is a one-egg frying pan played with a metal rod about 3/16 inches thick and 6 inches long. The *frigideira* has a diameter of about 5 inches. The left hand holds the instrument and muffles the "inside" with the middle finger. The right hand plays the rod on the "fire-side" of the *frigideira* with stopped strokes, edge strokes, and strokes in the middle, performing a rapid tremolo as the left wrist rotates. As this instrument is chromed, it catches the spotlights in a dazzling display.

Afoxê. This instrument, sometimes called a *cabaça,* is about 5 inches in diameter and consists of a coconut shell with about 50 indented ridges. A wooden handle, 4½ inches long and ¾ inch thick is attached to the end of the shell. A netting of seeds called a *lagrima da nossa senhora* (Holy Mother's tears) covers the coconut shell in about 1½-inch squares. The technique is to hold the seeds against the shell with the left hand and twist the handle with the right hand to produce a raspy sound. The speed and length of the twist controls the articulation of the *afoxê.*

Chocalho. This is a metal tube shaker, 12 to 14 inches in length and 2 to 3 inches in diameter. It is filled with stones or pellets. Often two or more tubes are connected together for louder sounds. The technique consists of moving the *chocalho* back and forth parallel to the ground. Accents are produced by a more rapid stroke.

Ganzá. Another form of *chocalho,* it is a metal shaker. The *ganzá* has a 9-inch-long handle with a 2-inch diameter, which is attached to the shaker in a cylinder that is 3 inches wide and 7½ inches in diameter. On the top and bottom of the cylinder are conical caps, 3 to 4 inches in length. The technique is to play one *ganzá* in each hand like Cuban maracas. Another form of *ganzá* is a metal frame with two or more rows of jingles. This is shaken like the *chocalho.*

Reco-reco. This instrument is a notched hollow bamboo stick 10 to 12 inches in length and 2 inches in diameter. It is played with a bamboo scraper, which has 4 or 5 cuts extending from the handle to the end. The length of the handle is about 10 to 12 inches. The gentle rubbing of the notches creates the sound of the instrument, *reco-reco.* Another version of the *reco-reco* is made of a metal tube 10 to 14 inches in length and 2½ inches in diameter. A slot is open under a spring attached to each end of the *reco-reco,* and the right hand rubs the spring with a thin metal rod, 3/16 inch thick. Other *reco-recos* have three or more springs for a louder sound.

Apito de samba. This whistle was originally made of wood but today is constructed of metal. It is a chamber with a hole on each side and a ball or small dowel rod inside. These holes are covered with the fingers and thumb to allow the player to sound three pitches to imitate the sound of the *agogô, surdos,* etc., for signaling a change in timbre or rhythmic pattern in the *bateria.* It is played by the *mestre da bateria.*

Brazilian Instruments Used in the Scores of Heitor Villa-Lobos

Trocano. A large log drum used in *Descobrimento do Brasil* (1937). It is 2 to 3 yards long and 4½ feet in diameter. The center is hollowed out by fire, and it is played with large wooden sticks wrapped with rubber strips.

Tartaruga. A giant sea turtle shell used in the *Choros No. 9* (1929). This is played on the underside of the shell with two wooden sticks, similar to a drum.

Caxambo. A large one-headed drum used in *Dansas africanas* (1914). It is a closed barrel with the head attached by stakes hammered into the shell.

Xucalho, caracaxà. Other indications for *chocalho* used in various works by Villa-Lobos.

Coco. This is an instrument constructed by cutting a coconut shell into two halves. The insides are held in the palms of the hands, and the outsides of the shells are struck together. This instrument is used in the *Fantasy in Three Movements* (1922). In orchestral performance, Chinese temple blocks are usually substituted.

Matraca. Two wooden blocks about 4 to 6 inches long and 3 inches wide that are held in the hands and clapped together. They are used in the *Bumba-meu-boi* pageants in northeastern Brazil. These are commonly utilized in *Bachianas Brasileiras No. 2* (1930).

Prato de louca. This is a dinner plate with fluted edges that is rubbed by a knife blade. It is used in the *Noneto* (1923).

Pio. An imitation birdcall produced by rubbing two pieces of wood together. Villa-Lobos preferred a conductor's baton and a cigar box. The *pio* is used in *Descobrimento do Brasil* (1937).

Camisão. A large one-headed frame drum played traditionally with a leather strap or whip. Two sizes, high and low, are used in the *Choros No. 6* (1926). Two tom-toms can be substituted.

Tambi and *tambu.* Two bamboo tubes, 2 and 3 feet in length and 3 to 4 inches in diameter, are held in the hands and played on a piece of wood. They are used in the opening of *Choros No. 6.*

Capoeira Music

Instrument Description

Capoeira uses the *berimbau* as the principal instrument, sometimes in groups of twos and threes. Also, the *pandeiro, agogô, atabaque,* and the *reco-reco* may be added.

Technique

The *berimbau* sets the tone for the *capoeira* dancers with the tempo, style, and quality of the music. The player is usually the lead singer as well. The other players borrow rhythms from samba or *candomblé* to fit the *capoeira* music.

Instruments Used in the Ensemble

Berimbau. A musical bow with a gourd attached (called *cabaça*). The string is struck with a stick and the pitch changes are made by pressing a coin (*moeda*) or stone (*dobrão*) along the string. A basket rattle, *caxixi,* is shaken at the same time. Other names indicating *berimbau* are *urucungo, orucungo, goba, bucumbumba, macungo,* and the *berimbau de barriga* (*berimbau* of the belly). The wood of the bow is made from a vine called *berba* or *mucuje.* It is usually 50 to 54 inches long and about 3/4 inch in diameter. The string is a metal cord, usually from a radial tire. The size and construction vary, as each player traditionally makes his own instrument. The coin (*moeda*) was formerly a *dobrao,* a Portuguese copper coin from the Brazilian colonial period about the size of a United States silver dollar. The *cabaça* is 4 to 7 inches long and 5 to 8 inches in diameter, with an opening cut from the lower 1/3 of the gourd to be held against the player's belly. The *caxixi* is a wicker reed with a piece of gourd at the bottom filled with seashells or *ticum* seeds. It is about 6 inches long and 3 inches in diameter, with a loop in the top for placing the middle fingers of the right hand. The *baqueta* or *vareta* is a stick of *candeia, jandia,* or *braruna* wood, or thin bamboo about 16 inches long and 1/4 inch in diameter. A newer technique utilizes two *baquetas.*[1]

The traditional technique is to hold the *berimbau* in the left hand and the *moeda* with the first finger and thumb pressing against the string. The right hand holds the *baqueta* and loops the *caxixi* through the middle fingers. The gourd is held against the belly or lifted away for another timbral change. Basically, as in many Brazilian instruments, the right hand creates the sound and the left hand modifies the quality. If more than one *berimbau* is used, they are tuned in three registers.

The bass is *berimbau gungo,* the middle is *berimbau de centro,* and the high register is *berimbau viola.* The *berimbaus* play an interlocking pattern with the *berimbau de centro,* leading and improvising. The *pandeiro* is played with *batucada* techniques but with a simpler pattern following the *atabaque* pattern. More accents are played with the slap of the palm of the right hand. The *agogô* is played more in the style of *candomblé,* with more emphasis on the single bell.

The *atabaque* is usually one drum instead of the set of three used in *candomblé.* It is usually played with hands in a simple dance pattern for the *capoeiristas.*

The *reco-reco* is usually bamboo and is played with the *batucada* techniques following the rhythmic patterns of the *atabaque.*

Candomblé Music

Instrument Description

The usual *candomblé* ensemble has three *atabaques* and an *agogô.* Often a shaker, bell, and/or *afoxê* is played by dancers or the celebrant.

Technique

The function of the *atabaques* is to summon the *orixás* (spirits or deities) during the *candomblé, umbanda,* or *macumba* ceremonies. Each *atabaque* summons a specific *orixa* with a traditional rhythmic pattern, and the three *atabaque* patterns interlock with the *agogô* pattern of a length of 5- to 7-beat cycle. The basic function of the music is to produce a trance state in the participants.

Instruments and Techniques

The *atabaques* are named in size and importance, with the *rum atabaque* being the largest and most important. The *rum* has the same configuration of all *atabaques*, with its conical barrel about 40 inches in length, a head diameter of 11 inches, and the opening at the opposite end tapering down to 5 inches.

The middle *atabaque* is called the *rompi* and has a length of 33 inches, a head diameter of 9 inches, and an opening of 4½ inches. The smallest *atabaque* is called the *le* and has a length of 23 inches, a head diameter of 8 inches, and an opening of 4 inches. The *atabaques* are tensioned by an interlaced rope system and are played with two hands, one stick and one hand, or two sticks according to the particular traditions of the *candomblé*. The players are seated with the opening of the *atabaques* facing away from the players toward the dancer/participants. The *agogô*, sometimes called *ngonge*, is the same instrument used in *samba batucada*. In *candomblé*, usually one bell is played, maintaining a continuous rhythmic pattern.

The *afoxê* is the same instrument as found in the *samba batucada* and is played with the same techniques according to the style of the *candomblé*.

Zabumba Music

Instrument Description

The *zabumba* is a Brazilian dance derived from the military tradition of Europe. The percussion of the *zabumba* is a bass drum called *bombo* or *zabumba*, *pratos* (crash cymbals), and a snare drum, *taro* or *tarol*. These instruments play with a pair of flutes called *pifes* or *pifanos*. Other ensembles from the northeast of Brazil use an accordion to replace the *pifes* and the *pandeiro* and *ferro*, or *ferrinho* (triangle), to replace the *tarol* and the *pratos*. The *zabumba* plays in both ensembles. Music such as *baião*, *forro*, *desafio*, and *embolada*, as well as others, use this latter instrumentation.

Technique

Since the *zabumba* is more danceable than the usual military bass drum style, the *bombo* plays more timbres.

Use in Ensemble

In general, the *pratos* play on the beat while the *tarol* keeps a constant rolling rhythmic pattern. The *bumbo* imitates a melodic bass part of tonic/dominant by muffling techniques. The effect is a march style with a bouncy, off-beat flavor like the *frevo*.

Instruments and Techniques

The *zabumba* or *bumbo* is a bass drum about 22 inches in diameter having a wooden shell of 10 to 15 inches. It is played with a leather covered stick in the right hand and a thin stick played on the rim in the left hand. By playing a stopped stroke(s) and then an open stroke(s), the player can effect a simulated melodic bass pitch of alternating tonic and dominant. The stick on the rim plays an interlocking pattern to create a multitimbral effect.

The *taro* or *tarol* is the same type that is used in the *samba batucada*. The techniques are the same, with a strong right-hand accent and the left hand playing buzz rolls. The *pratos* are crash cymbals different from the usual in that they are two different sizes. The lead *prato* is 12 inches in diameter and the second *prato* is only 10 inches. The effects used in addition to the usual crashes are stopped sounds and tremolos from rattling the two *pratos* together. The *pandeiro* employed is very similar to the one used in the *samba batucada*, without the acrobatic, showy style.

The *ferro*, or *ferrinho*, is an 8- to 10-inch iron triangle. It is held in the left hand so that the mute can be made in an open and closed manner. The right hand plays an iron beater against the two sides in a constant repetition.

Samba-Afro

This is music for the *bloco-afro* (African block) groups that parade throughout the streets of Salvador, Bahia, during Carnival.

Instrument Description

It employs the *surdo*, *repique*, and *caixa* (*tarol*) from the *batucada*. Cuban *timbales* have been introduced more recently.[2]

Technique

Although the instruments come from the *batucada*, the techniques are quite different. In the *batucada*, the *surdo* and the *repique* each play using one stick (or covered mallet) and one hand, while in *samba-afro* a majority of the *surdos* play with two covered mallets (*surdos* that only "mark the beat" use the traditional technique), and the *repiques* play with two thin sticks called *aguidavi*. This *repique* technique is borrowed from the *Ketu* nation (or style) of *candomblé*, which primarily uses *aguidavi* on the *atabaques* as opposed to open hands. The *caixa* (or *tarol*) uses standard snare drumsticks and is played with a similar technique to the *batucada*.

Use in Ensemble

In a five-*surdo* ensemble (which is quite small, considering that hundreds parade in the streets during Carnival), the *surdos* combine to form a four-beat pattern. Players 1 and 2 "mark the beat" alternating high-low-high-low. Player 3 plays primarily on the "second eighth note of beat two," creating high-low-*higher*-high-low. In addition, Player 2 also improvises on a minimal basis, adding occasional notes on "eighth-note offbeats." Players 4 and 5 play four successive sixteenth notes on beat four of the pattern, resolving on beat one, creating a reverberating "Boom Boom Boom Boom Boom!" In addition, surdos 4 and 5 create "arm choreography" when they do not play.

The *repique* uses two *aguidavi*, heavily accenting with one hand, and lightly "filling in" with the other, creating the feeling of a quarter-note triplet, which is resolved by the *surdo* response. Some variations utilize accents similar to a reggae rhythm guitar, accenting the "eighth-note offbeats."

The *caixa* (or *tarol*) plays in a manner similar to a reggae rhythm guitar as well, accenting the "eighth note off-beats," and adding a slight buzz on the first of the two "off-beats." Recent additions include a "master drummer," who improvises on Cuban *timbales*, using *aguidavi* as opposed to *timbale* sticks.

Afoxê. It has the same spelling as the instrument *afoxê* and is the secular version of the *candomblé*, which parades during Carnival in Salvador, Bahia. It features *atabaques*, *agogôs*, and *afoxês*, playing the slow trance-like rhythm called "ijexá."[3] Technique and style are the same as instruments of the *candomblé*.

Pagode. A form of "partido alto" (which, literally, means music that comes from the "top of the hill"), it is a style of samba that is one of the elements that helped shape the *Escolas de samba*. It uses styles of instruments of the *batucada* (*pandeiro*, *tamborim*, *chocalho*, *reco-reco*, etc.). Larger drums have been replaced by smaller, more easily portable drums. The *surdo* has been replaced by the *tan-tan*, a long cylindrical single-head drum, and the *repique* by the *repique de mão*, a short version of the tan-tan. Other instruments include metal bar chairs and beer bottles.[4]

Technique

Techniques are basically the same for the instruments that are used in the *batucada*. However, the *pandeiro* is played with a more aggressive style, accenting more "sixteenth note off-beats," emphasizing a more erratic style. Also, the style of the *reco-reco* has been modified to a crisper, more percussive sound. Instead of the traditional back and forth rubbed motion of the stick, the instrument is played with short, quick accented strokes (more like a tapping than a rubbing).

The basic technique of the *tan-tan* and the *repique de mão* is virtually the same. The drum is laid across the player's lap (sitting position), and the head is played with the right hand while the shell is played with the left hand.

Use in Ensemble

Overall, the formula concept used is as in the *batucada*. However, the phrasing follows the lead singer, with formulaic rhythmic "turnarounds" on the refrains. The *tan-tan* follows the same conceptual pattern of the *surdo* (and when two or more *tan-tans* are combined, the high-low call and response function of the *surdo* is implied), and although the *tan-tan* is much lighter than the *surdo*, it is more rhythmically complex.

The *repique de mão* functions similarly to the phrasing of the *repique* in the *batucada*, improvising and superimposing rhythmic phrases over two or more measures.

See also Illus. 34, p. 133.

Notes

1. Luiz Almeida da Anunciação, *A percussão dos ritmos brasileiros,* vol. 1, *Berimbau* (Rio de Janeiro: Edição Europa, 1990), 9.

2. Antonio Riseiro, *Carnaval Ijexá* (Salvador, Brazil: Corrupio, 1981), 27.

3. Ibid., 23.

4. Ricardo Ohtake, *Instrumentos musicals brasileiros* (São Paulo: Rhodia, 1988), 14.

Bibliography

Adato, Joseph, and Judy George. *The Percussionist's Dictionary*. Melville, N.Y.: Belwin-Mills, 1984.

Almeida, Bira. *Capoeira: A Brazilian Art Form*. Berkeley, Calif.: North Atlantic Press, 1981.

Almeida, Laurindo. *Latin Percussion Instruments and Rhythms*. Sherman Oaks, Calif.: Gwyn Publishing, 1972.

Almeida da Anunciação, Luiz. *A percussão dos ritmos brasileiros*. Vol. 1, *Berimbau*. Rio de Janeiro: Edição Europa, 1990.

Appleby, David. *The Music of Brazil*. Austin: University of Texas Press, 1983.

Byrne, David, and Charles Perrone. *Brasil Classics*. Vol. 2, *O samba*. Liner notes. Los Angeles: Luaka Bop/Sire Records #26019-1 (1988).

Da Camara Cascudo, Luis. *Dicionário do folclore brasileiro*. 3rd ed. Rio de Janeiro: Instituto Nacional do Livro, 1972.

Fink, Siegfried. *Percussion Brasil*. Mainz: B. Schott's Söhne, 1983.

Funarte, Zabumba. Liner notes. Rio de Janeiro: MEC-CDBF 001 (1972).

Galm, John. "Batucada—Percussion Music of the *Escola de Samba*." *NACWPJ* (*National Association of Wind Percussion*) 21, nos. 1 and 2 (1973): 17–23; 42–48.

———. "The Use of Brazilian Instruments in the Music of Villa-Lobos." *Musicology at the University of Colorado*. Boulder: University of Colorado Press, 1977.

Henrique, Jorge. *Brazilian Rhythm Instruments and How to Play Them*. Santa Cruz: Brazilian Imports, 1972.

Jucata (José Diaferia). *Ritmos Brasileiros: A Tutor for Latin-American Instruments and Rhythms*. São Paulo: Fermato do Brasil, 1957.

McGowan, Chris, and Ricardo Pessanha. *The Brazilian Sound: Samba, Bossa Nova, and the Popular Music of Brazil*. New York: Billboard Music, 1991.

Marcal, Milton. *A incrivel bateria do mestre Marcal*. Liner notes translated by Regina Wernyk. Rio de Janeiro: Polygram Discos #835123-1 (1987).

Moreira, Airto. *The Spirit of Percussion*. Wayne, N.J.: 21st Century Productions, 1988.

Ohtake, Ricardo. *Instrumentos musicals brasileiros*. São Paulo: Rhodia, 1988.

Paulinho (Paulo Fernando Magalhães). *Rhythms and Instruments of Brazil*. Hollywood, Calif.: D.C. Publishing, 1965.

Peixe, Guerra César. "Zabumba; orquestra nordestina." *Revista brasileira de folclore* 10, no. 26 (1970): 15–38.

Perrone, Charles. *Masters of Contemporary Brazilian Song*. Austin: University of Texas Press, 1989.

Ribeiro de Souza, José. *Cerimonias da umbanda e do candomblé*. São Paulo: Livraria Cultura Editora, 1973.

Riseiro, Antonio. *Carnaval Ijexá*. Salvador, Brazil: Corrupio, 1981.

Eric A. Galm
John K. Galm

Calfskin Heads: Their History and Manufacture

The origin of the skin drumhead predates recorded history. Indeed, the first "skin drum" may well have been discovered, as James Blades suggests, upon testing the condition of a fresh hide, which had been stretched over a hole in the earth for drying.[1] The earliest skin drumheads were made from a variety of water animals—lizards, fish, snakes, and other reptiles—and were stretched over drums carved from wood and fashioned of clay. Skin-headed drums existed in almost every known primitive and ancient civilization. Larger animal skins were utilized as the sizes of drums increased and included every imaginable variety of hide, from deer and elephant to the present commonly used goat- and calfskins. A variety of drums appeared during the Middle Ages: nakers, calvary timpani, and the tabor, which led to the orchestral timpani and military drum, respectively, and later the modern orchestral snare drum and drum set. The heads of these precursor instruments were thick and crudely processed and produced tones that were "tubby" by modern standards. The making of skin drumheads was originally part of the art of early drum-making. As the demand for skin drumheads increased, the supply of heads became part of the business of expert tanners in Europe and later in America.

Every drum set and orchestral percussion membranophone recorded before the "invention" of plastic heads around 1957 (and for many years after) carried the unmistakable skin head sound that many artists still prefer and play exclusively today. Gerry Carlyss, former timpanist with the Philadelphia Orchestra and professor of percussion at Indiana University, who played calfskin heads prior to his retirement from the Philadelphia Orchestra in 1987, remarked that "young players would hear him play and they would say, 'Wow, where can I get some of that stuff?' yet they had no idea what goes into playing skin."[2] Carlyss played calfskin heads much to his own taste and at the request of conductor Ricardo Muti, who insisted "at all costs" that Carlyss play them. (In Vienna percussionists play goatskin heads, according to Bruno Hartel and Roland Altmann of the Vienna Philharmonic.)

Recent History and Manufacturers

Contrary to some beliefs, although "invented" in 1957 concurrently by Chick Evans and Remo Belli, the plastic drumhead in no way quickly replaced calfskin heads. M.L. "Chick" Evans started developing a mylar drumhead in Santa Fe, New Mexico, around 1956, and his early experiments eventually led to the founding of the Evans Drum Head Co. in Dodge City, Kansas, which is still going strong today.[3] During this time, Evans claimed that "a former customer had started manufacturing drumheads under his own name."[4] Belli recounted the origin of Remo, Inc., in a 1980 interview, in which he stated, "In 1957, while working to create a display at Drum City, in Hollywood, which I owned with Roy Hart, we . . . bought some plastic material . . . and stapled it to a (wooden) hoop and put it on the drum."[5] The Du Pont company had introduced mylar at this time to Bud Slingerland and William Ludwig, Sr., of the Slingerland and Ludwig companies, but Belli pursued the idea to claim eventually that he developed "the first successful (plastic) drumhead" and opened Remo, Inc., on June 1, 1957.[6]

As stated earlier, the manufacture of skin drumheads became a part of the business of expert tanners in Europe and then in America. One of the oldest European companies that only recently went out of business was the H. Band & Co. Ltd., Light Leather Tanners and Dressers, Parchment and Vellum, of Brentford, England. This company was established in 1845 as contractors to the H.M. Stationery Office, Ministry of Supply, Commonwealth Government Offices. In 1984 it sold out to the William Cowley Parchment Works Company of Bucks, England. These companies manufactured drumheads in addition to their main products, which were sheepskin parchment and calfskin vellum for writing, printing, and bookbinding. Today the Cowley firm continues to supply fine quality calfskin heads to percussionists around the world.

Perhaps the oldest manufacturer of calfskin heads in Europe is the firm of Vellum & Parchment Works Ltd., successor to N. Elzas & Zonen Ltd., now located in Celbridge, Ireland. The firm got its start in Borculo, Holland, when Nathan Elzas, a devout Jew and trader in skins, began his quest for manufacturing prime white parchment of calf- or goatskin for the purpose of recording the Talmud, the sacred oral law and rabbinical commentary of the Jews. Nathan founded the company in 1830 as N. Elzas & Zonen (Zonen meaning "sons" in Dutch). The business was carried on by his son Abraham who, in turn, left it to his two sons, Nathan and Moses.[7] Under their partnership the business prospered greatly throughout the world and expanded to include, in addition to parchment and vellum, drumheads, lampshades, wallcoverings, bookbindings, coverings for artificial limbs, and sporting goods. In May of 1989 the factory was purchased by Joseph Katz and renamed Vellum & Parchment Works Ltd.

Skin drumheads are manufactured around the world by other firms with varying degrees of quality. Water buffalo and goat heads are available from the Sultan Parchment Agency and M.H. Geoffrey & Co. of Pakistan, and also from India. Calf heads can be obtained from Phillips of Hong Kong, and calfskin heads are used throughout Europe on all but the finest timpani made by the firm of Altenburg of Leipzig. Leo White, owner and proprietor of Leo F. White Mfg. of Botany, Australia, also has supplied excellent quality calf heads to the percussion world. One American maker even claims to have tried processing kangaroo heads but finds it problematical to obtain the kangaroo hides and especially ones large enough to make into timpani heads.

Calfskin drumhead making in America was and remains a profession carried on by European craftsmen who immigrated to the United States and opened leather tanneries for the production of drumheads in addition to primarily making furniture, clothing, orthopedic supplies (artificial limbs), and shoes. Indeed, cities such as Philadelphia were tanning capitals of the world until the advent of synthetic shoes (sneakers), which put all but a few of these leather tanneries out of business in the mid-1900s. Steve Weiss, owner of a drum specialty shop in Philadelphia, recalls drumheads made for him by his Ukrainian ex-father-in-law. He ran the Huchman tannery in Philadelphia until the advent of sneakers and made drumheads on the side in his basement and outside, because of the smell of the chemicals.

As for the calfskin head market, a survey of calfskin timpani heads, obtained from old drum manufacturer's catalogs, reveals a slow rise in prices until the 1960s, when the plastic heads were introduced. The 1936 *Leedy Catalog No. 41* (Leedy was founded in 1895) listed Leedy "Kafette" timpani heads costing from $7.80 for a 30-inch untucked head to $10.45 for a 36-inch head.[8] The tucking fee was $1, and any size metal flesh hoop was $2. Leedy had its own skin head department and boasted of its "secret formulas and processes" developed by department supervisor John Gyukas.[9] In the 1965 *Leedy Catalog No. 70* (eight years after the invention of plastic heads), the price of a 29-inch untucked calfskin head had increased to $28.50, with a 36-inch head costing $37.50.[10] The tucking fee was $3, and metal flesh hoops were $10.

In 1968, the *Slingerland Catalog No. 69* (the Slingerland Drum Company was founded in 1916) listed its line of calfskin timpani heads, manufactured by the United Rawhide Company, costing from $33 for an untucked 29-inch head to $43.40 for a 36-inch head.[11] The cost of Slingerland's plastic timpani heads was less than half that of calfskin in the 1973 catalog: $20 for a 23-inch plastic drumhead and $27 for a 32-inch plastic drumhead.[12] It is not hard to understand why the next catalog discontinued calfskin heads.

Similarly, in 1969, over a decade since the introduction of plastic heads, the *Ludwig Catalog No. 71* (Ludwig Industries was founded in 1909) listed "Wm. F. Ludwig selected timpani heads" costing from $43 for a 29-inch untucked head to $58 for a 36-inch head.[13] The tucking fee was $7.50, and metal flesh hoops were $9. The 1970 *Ludwig Catalog No. 71-1* listed the same heads at $47.25 for a 29-inch untucked head and $63.75 for a 36-inch head.[14] The tucking fee increased to $7.90, and metal flesh hoops to $9.50. These prices increased in the 1972 *Ludwig Price List 71.1* to $49 for a 29-inch head, $66.50 for a 36-inch head, $8.20 for tucking, and $11.20 for flesh hoops.[15] By comparison, the cost of Ludwig plastic timpani heads remained unchanged from the 1970 prices: $20 and $29 for comparable plastic heads. The *Ludwig Catalog No. 73* (copyrighted 1972) contained the following statement:

> Due to the popularity of plastic drum and timpani heads, we no longer list calf heads in our catalog. We will continue to supply calf heads on special orders for all drums listed in our catalog. Price and delivery information available on request.[16]

In addition to the major percussion manufacturers, skin heads were made in America by the firms of AMRAWCO (American Rawhide Manufacturing Company), National, and White Eagle. Today the United Rawhide Company of Chicago is the only manufacturer of skin drumheads remaining in America. Founded around 1950 by its current owner, Steve Palansky, who is a third or fourth generation Czech tanner, the United Rawhide Company used to supply heads to Ludwig, Gretch, and Slingerland as well as independent jobbers.[17] The company operates only three days a week at present, as Palansky is semi-retired. He cites the difficulty in obtaining high-quality, carefully skinned raw hides as the only reason he is not able to produce more fine calfskin drumheads. He blames the inferior raw materials on the lack of training, poor attitudes, and lack of pride in the piecework production incentives of the skinners. When available, United's heads still offer a quality product to the discriminating percussionist.

The Manufacturing Process

The manufacturing process of a calfskin head involves first the selection of the raw hides. Many variables here affect the final product: the diet, sex, and age of the animal; the country, climate, and season in which the hide was obtained; and the general quality, color, and texture of the hide. Vellum & Parchment Works Ltd., successor to N. Elzas & Zonen Ltd., select their hides from around Europe, and many are bought from dealers in the Netherlands who have been supplying hides to the Elzas firm for hundreds of years. The United Rawhide Company of Chicago obtains its hides from the midwestern United States, and Leo White obtains his raw hides from New Zealand. After selection, the hides are lightly salted and limed for short storage at the plant before processing.

Next, the hides are soaked in secret chemical solutions in large tubs to loosen the hair and specially prepare the skins. Then they are flushed with fresh water, sometimes for days, in revolving horizontal cylinder-like vats to wash away all chemicals and further loosen the remaining hair and prepare the skins.

The hides are then dehaired and defleshed either by hand with a tool that is called in the profession an "unhairing knife" or by machine.[18] At Vellum & Parchment

Works Ltd. a special planing machine is used for this; it consists of a roller onto which the wet hides are draped and a series of moving knife blades that evenly shave the hides. This machine is capable of adjustments to one-hundredth of a millimeter.

After this, the skins are stretched by hand for slow, careful drying by either tacking the edges of the skins onto large boards or by stretching the skins across a wooden frame by lacing the skin to turnpegs. This drying process is one of the most crucial stages in production and takes place both in shaded outdoor areas and in humidity-controlled rooms containing complex fans and vents. This slow drying ensures good head color, evenness, and durability.

After the skins are evenly dried (their thickness measures about .8 to .88 inches [20–22 millimeters] at this point in production), they are polished by machine and hand to specifications averaging from between .24 to .4 inches (6–10 millimeters) in thickness depending on the head size and order specifications. This polishing process is a guarded secret in the production of most manufacturers' heads.

Finally, after many inspections along the way, the finished skins are sized with backbones centered (for timpani) and cut into circular heads. They are then carefully packaged and shipped.

The Present Situation

While many professional American and English percussionists and especially timpanists have opted for the stability of plastic heads over skin, many "established timpanists" still prefer skin, and a great number of "emerging timpanists" have chosen to use skin heads in spite of increasing costs and difficulties in obtaining them. American artists such as Tele Lesbines, Salvatore Rabbio, and Gerry Carlyss have been joined by a network of calfskin head players including Paul Yancich of Cleveland, Jessie Kregiel of Buffalo, David Kent of Toronto, Rick Holmes of St. Louis, Dave Gross of Grand Rapids, and Jonathan Haas of New York, to name but a few. In addition, many established and emerging timpanists in major European and radio orchestras clearly prefer natural skin timpani heads (including goat heads as used in the Vienna Philharmonic). It is said that Reiner Seegers, timpanist of the Berlin Philharmonic, has never even played plastic timpani heads. One has only to listen to any past or recent Berlin Philharmonic recording (especially on compact disc) with Herbert von Karajan to hear this.

The Future

At the present time the manufacture of fine quality calfskin heads is indeed an endangered art. Whereas some thirty years ago there were four manufacturers in the United States alone producing calf heads, there remains only one today, United Rawhide of Chicago. Many European firms that were founded in the 1800s for the production of vellum, parchment, drumheads, and the like have since folded due to lack of demand for their products. H. Band & Co. sold out to the William Cowley firm in 1984 for these reasons. The European percussion manufacturers who still supply instruments with skin heads rely on only a handful of producers for heads. Of these, only a few are capable of producing quality calfskin heads suitable for the most discriminating performers. The various calfskin head manufacturers around the world are striving to find consistent raw materials and maintain the highest quality control in processing. With increasing demands for quality calfskin heads by players and conductors, the prospects for a competitive world market in calf heads is again reappearing. It is the hope of many percussionists and especially timpanists (not to mention conductors, students, instructors, and music lovers in general), who favor natural animalskin heads over synthetics, that reasonably priced, high-quality heads will be continually available to those who prefer them.

Notes

1. James Blades, *Percussion Instruments and Their History,* rev. ed. (London: Faber and Faber, 1984), 49.

2. Telephone interview with Gerry Carlyss, April 1989.

3. K.C. Compton, "Better Drumming Through Chemistry," *The New Mexican* (Santa Fe), January 1, 1988, sec. C, p. 2.

4. Ibid.

5. Dave Levine, "Inside Remo," *Modern Drummer Magazine* 4, No. 2 (April/May 1980): 26.

6. Ibid.

7. Denis Kelleher, "N. Elzas & Zonen Makers of True Parchment," a booklet distributed at the factory, originally an article published in the American trade magazine *The Paper Maker* on the occasion of the 125th anniversary of N. Elzas & Zonen (Celbridge, Ireland: N. Elzas & Zonen, 1955), 22.

8. *Leedy Catalog No. 41* (Elkhart, Ind.: Leedy Mfg. Co., 1936), 64.

9. Ibid.

10. *Leedy Catalog No. 70* (Chicago: Leedy Drum Co., 1965), 37.

11. *Slingerland Catalog No. 69* (Niles, Ill.: Slingerland Drum Co., 1968), 72.

12. *1973 Slingerland Catalog* (Niles, Ill.: Slingerland Drum Co., 1973), 79.

13. *Ludwig Catalog No. 71* (Chicago: Ludwig Industries, 1969), 98.

14. *Ludwig Catalog No. 71-1* (Chicago: Ludwig Industries, 1970), 98.

15. *Ludwig Price List 71-1* (Chicago: Ludwig Industries, 1972), 9.

16. *Ludwig Catalog No. 73* (Chicago: Ludwig Industries, 1972), 98.

17. Telephone interview with Steve Palansky, April 1989.

18. Henry W. Taylor, *The Art and Science of the Timpani* (London: J. Baker, 1964), 33.

Gary Cook

Castanets

Fr: *castagnettes;* Ger: *Kastagnetten;* It: *castagnette;* Sp: *castañuelas*

Castanets date from the ancient civilizations of the Orient as well as Egypt. It is assumed that the Moors on the Iberian peninsula brought the instrument to Spain. It is probable that in the Spanish castanets the metal shells of the Egyptian instruments were replaced by chestnut (*castañuelas* in Spanish) hulls. Ever since the Renaissance, castanets have been associated with the music and dance of Spain. While castanets are most commonly used to evoke the image of Spain or Spanish-flavored music, in the present century the instrument can be found in a variety of settings that have no relationship to Spanish music or locales.

Castanets are comprised of two shells of hard wood (ebony or rosewood). The shells are strung together so that their concave sides face one another. As the shells strike one another, a sharp, crisp, high-pitched sound is produced. Traditionally, the castanets are played by passing the thumb through the string loop, which creates enough tension to force the castanets apart. The remaining four fingers then strike one castanet against the other. This technique requires considerable practice to master. The orchestral percussionist will generally use either paddle or machine castanets.

There are two types of paddle (or handle) castanets. The first consists of a handle upon which the two castanets are mounted and a thin board that passes between the wooden shells. This instrument is rather awkward for use in reproducing intricate rhythms but is very successful in producing loud, raucous rolls. The other type of handle castanet is similar in construction to the first except that there is no board between the two shells. This greatly facilitates the execution of intricate rhythms while still allowing the instrument to retain its capability to produce louder sounds.

The machine (mounted) castanets are capable of playing intricate rhythms and can produce these rhythms in very soft dynamic ranges. However, they are somewhat at a disadvantage when trying to produce louder sound. The mounting system makes it possible for the percussionist to play the castanets with the fingers or a pair of soft mallets. One technique which produces a tremendously loud roll is to strike the machine castanets with a pair of paddle castanets.

A sampling of works that make use of the castanets includes:

Wagner, Richard
Tannhäuser, Bacchanale Scene (Scene 1) (1845)

Bizet, Georges
Carmen (1875)

Ravel, Maurice
Rapsodie espagnole (1905)

Debussy, Claude
Iberia Suite (1906)

Ravel, Maurice
Alborada del gracioso (1907)

Falla, Manuel de
The Three-Cornered Hat (1917)

Prokofiev, Sergei
Piano Concerto No. 3 (1921)

Varèse, Edgard
Ionisation (1931)

Orff, Carl
Carmina burana (1937)

Nono, Luigi
The Red Cape (1954)

Malec, Ivo
Miniatures pour Lewis Carroll (1964)

See also Illus. 35, p. 134.

Bibliography

Blades, James. *Percussion Instruments and Their History*. 2nd ed. London, Faber and Faber, 1974.

Peinkofer, Karl, and Fritz Tannigel. *Handbook of Percussion Instruments*. London: Schott, 1976. Originally published in German (Mainz: B. Schott's Söhne, 1969).

Peters, Gordon. *The Drummer: Man, a Treatise on Percussion*. Rev. ed. Wilmette, Ill.: Kemper-Peters, 1975.

Andrew Spencer

Cymbals

Fr: *cymbales;* Ger: *Becken*; It: *cinelli, piatti;* Lat: *cymbala;* Sp: *címbalos*

Cymbals are one of the most ancient of all percussion instruments. Their ancestry can be found in the most primitive, idiophonic order of instruments, one that includes rattles, clappers, sticks, and castanets. Cymbals were in use in Israel by about 1100 B.C., but did not appear in Egypt until approximately 800 B.C.; there they had large central bosses and flat rims. In Europe cymbals appear intermittently from the thirteenth century on, although they had been imported earlier.

The evolution of cymbals occurred in the Bronze Age. In early Roman civilization, bronze cups used initially to hold vinegar and spices were among the first devices adapted for use on the fingers, thus becoming the finger cymbals known today.

As the metalworking artisans of the Bronze Age improved their techniques of making discs, the cymbals became larger and more resonant. Better methods of casting and the expansion of the market in western Asia prompted the cymbal makers to expand their craft. Armies incorporated cymbals accompanied by large, heavy kettledrums. What the bugle was to American Civil War soldiers, the cymbals were to Near East warriors.

By the dawn of Christianity, most of Asia Minor employed cymbals in its religious ceremonies. Cymbals reached the Western world by a slow process of development. Romans were great users of cymbals. Among the ruins of Pompeii was discovered a complete collection of cymbals ranging from finger cymbals up to some which were 16 inches in diameter. These are now housed in the museum of Pompeii in Naples.

It was during the Middle Ages that the development of bells, descendants of the cymbals, became a symbol of the church. Bells were made in a similar fashion. They have the same copper, tin, and bronze alloy of a cymbal, and it seems logical to surmise that the early castings of a bell were an offshoot of a cymbal casting. Metalworkers found that the thicker the instrument, the more definite the pitch, and the pitch could be varied by the size and thickness of the metal casting.

Sixteenth-century Armenia was known all over Asia and Europe as the place to visit if one were interested in vessels and containers made of fine-quality bronze. It was also the world center for cymbals and cymbal making.

Only one artisan, however, was known for cymbals of unparalled beauty and richness of sound, and his name was Avedis Zildjian. "Zildjian" means "cymbal maker," i.e., in Turkish, *zil* means cymbal, *dj* means "maker," and *ian* means "son of." Today, 368 years later, Zildjian Company is still producing cymbals of beauty and of superior tone and durability.

Following the development of cymbals, one of the first uses of these instruments in an orchestral composition was by the German composer N.A. Strungk in his opera *Esther,* in 1680. In 1779 Christoph Willibald Gluck scored his "Oriental" chorus of Scythians in *Iphegenia en Tauride* for cymbals.

Cymbal Manufacturing

European cymbals, generally imported from China or Turkey, are made from an alloy of copper and tin. Chinese cymbals, from thin metal, have bent rims and bosses in the center. Their more expensive Turkish counterparts, constructed from thicker metal, are considered to be of better quality. The standard orchestral cymbal today is of the heavier kind and is from 14 to 18 inches in diameter. Rhythm bands tend to use lighter cymbals.

The most difficult quality to achieve in cymbal making is the individualized consistency, i.e., the ability to produce cymbals that are consistent within their model classification but individualized in sound and character, cymbal to cymbal. That is where the art of rolling, shaping, hammering, and lathing bring each cymbal model into sharp focus. Combine this with the beauty of the cast alloy and its natural, warm, and inherent musical quality that blesses each cymbal with its own individual sound, and one has a one-of-a-kind masterpiece. In fact, it is even possible to get a beautiful tone out of a raw, unrolled casting.

Cymbal Types

Cymbals perform many functions in music depending on many variables, thus the reason for so many models of different weights, sizes, and shapes. If one examines the earlier question of why cymbals have survived in music for centuries, one might have to go beyond examining just the obvious applications of cymbals as timekeeping instruments.

The theory that cymbals are not heard as much as they are felt does help to explain the impressive longevity that cymbal sounds have had in music. If one thinks of a cymbal as just an abstract sound within a musical background, one begins to understand why the cymbal is so much more than a timekeeper. The *ride cymbal,* for instance, actually does carry the pulse, but looking at it strictly from a standpoint of sound (the way a recording engineer might), the pitch, attack, and decay all combine at once and find their musical "place" along with the other instruments in the ensemble.

The ability to excite the high frequencies to support and smooth out the entire sound scope as well as adding excitement to the music by nature of their volume potential gives cymbals a chameleon-like magical quality that has kept them an important part of all music, a sound that never goes out of style.

Cymbal companies now manufacture many types. As an example, the Zildjian Company in Norwell, Massachusetts, produces five different series of cymbals. They include the *A Zildjian, K Zildjian, Z Zildjian, Scimitar,* and *Scimitar Bronze.* To understand the differences among these various lines clearly, it is important to know the two basic classifications. Most cymbals fall into cast and non-cast categories. *A Zildjian, K Zildjian,* and *Z Zildjian* are included in the cast series, while *Scimitar* and *Scimitar Bronze* are in the non-cast series.

There are differences between the two categories, as stated earlier. An *A Zildjian* cast cymbal is a musically highly individualized wide-frequency cymbal. These are all desirable characteristics for most players. Some drummers, however, require a tighter, more focused sound with less variance. For these players, the non-cast series is available.

Besides the sound of these different series, another way of understanding the basic differences between these two types of cymbals is a knowledge of how they are made. An *A Zildjian* cast cymbal, whether it is an *A, K,* or *Z* line, is made from raw material at the Zildjian factory. Pure blocks of copper and tin are melted in the Zildjian foundry, blended together in a way that has been a Zildjian family secret for almost four centuries, and poured into ingot-shaped molds, where they cool and harden.

From here, the ingots are reheated and rolled several times until the desired thickness is reached. At this point, the round-shaped alloy sheets are tempered, cut to a near-perfect circle, then pressed into basic shapes including different cup sizes. They are then hammered, lathed, and sometimes buffed and plated, and finally given a logo and trademark.

The important thing to remember here is that the Zildjian cast alloy including the secret process starts out as virgin metal and is individually poured into separate ingot-shaped castings (or discs). This means that every Zildjian cut cymbal is a separate and highly individualized instrument from its birth to the final product. This will help to explain the subtle and not so subtle differences among Zildjian cast cymbals. Even from within the category of cast cymbals, there is an almost infinite number of different sounds and feels available. Another characteristic of the Zildjian cast alloy is its sensitivity to changes in shape, size, weight, hammering techniques, and lathing and buffing processes. The slightest variance in any of these procedures will cause a dramatic change in sound. Fortunately, Zildjian's many years of experience have set forth very strict specifications and quality control for all these areas. So, while specific models have a high level of consistency, the Zildjian secret cast alloy will bring forth the individual voice that is a Zildjian cast cymbal.

Zildjian's non-cast lines, *Scimitar* and *Scimitar Bronze,* are made with the same rigid specifications and quality-control standards that all Zildjian cymbals must pass. These two non-cast lines are also made on special Zildjian-designed equipment and are formed, hammered, and lathed in a similar way to the cast lines.

The difference between the two is mostly the metal itself and how it is made. The bronze blanks that are used to make the *Scimitar* lines are created for Zildjian by one of the largest and most advanced metal suppliers in the world, made exactly to Zildjian specifications and checked regularly for consistency and quality. The bronze blanks, which are made of copper and tin, are shaped, hammered, and lathed into the final product, which is then tested for sound and appearance several times, a standard procedure for all cymbals that leave the factory.

This system for producing non-cast cymbals therefore is obviously different, starting at the beginning of the process, from the way cast cymbals are produced. For a non-cast cymbal, the alloy itself is different and starts out as a sheet of metal that at one point was part of a larger sheet. This explains a non-cast cymbal's extraordinary consistency, cymbal to cymbal. The non-cast alloys sound characteristics have less spread, a tighter feel, a faster decay, and a more compressed frequency range, desirable qualities for many players.

Regardless of the period or the style, cymbals have always been an integral part of music. From 1623, in the city of Constantinople, when an alchemist discovered the secret process to produce cymbals, to the present day, cymbal manufacturers have strived to improve the product and meet the demands of the current musical genres.

See also Illus. 12, p. 122.

Leonard DiMuzio

The Drum Set: A History

Pre-Dixieland

The origin of the modern drum set is generally traced to a period when one drummer began to serve the function that two or three drummers had in the past: the snare drum, bass drum, and accessory/sound effect instruments were all manipulated by one musician.

Following the Civil War, many black musicians began to form groups, first serving as funeral bands in New Orleans and other large metropolitan areas. These ensembles included instruments such as cornets, trombones, and clarinets, which were often left from the war and became indigenous with later "Dixieland" styles. Banjos and guitars were also incorporated into these groups. The marching units of this time featured at least two drummers, with one playing the snare drum and the other the bass drum, often with a cymbal attachment. The instruments, implements, and playing techniques ("traditional" snare stick grip, etc.) was the style of these marching units. Bass drums were 20 to 30 inches in diameter, and the snare drums were of the rope-tensioned "barrel" type typical of regimental marching bands. Musical selections consisted of an interesting mix of blues, spirituals, and folk songs.

During the late nineteenth century, these marching units began to perform indoors, providing entertainment for dances, parties, and various social gatherings. As certain ensembles began to exist solely for indoor entertainment, the need for two or more drummers diminished, both through economic pressures and ingenious inventions of these early drummers. Snare drums that had been used on a sling were replaced by smaller, orchestral-type drums that were either placed on a chair or cradled in a stand. Drummers developed a curious method of playing both a snare drum part and the bass drum, called *double drumming*. This method involved coordinating the hands to play both parts, accomplished through clever positioning of the snare drum (at an angle), the bass drum (to the right of the drummer), the small Turkish cymbal (mounted on the bass drum), and through various double-sticking patterns, a technique that became a hallmark of jazz drumming in future generations. Many players found the double drumming approach limiting and concentrated their efforts on developing methods to free the hands to play patterns on the snare drum while playing the bass drum with the foot.

Early attempts at developing the bass drum pedal included a device that would strike a small cymbal attached to the bass drum rim simultaneously with the striking of the bass drum, emulating the sound of the traditional marching bass drum/hand cymbal function. Other early efforts at bass drum pedal design included crude, though ingenious inventions by George Olney and H.A. Bower (Fig. 1) and a revolutionary design by a young Chicago percussionist, William F. Ludwig (Fig. 2), who later became one of the world's foremost drum manufacturers.

The early sit-down drum set also included a variety of sound-effect instruments and percussion instruments from other cultures. The sound-effect instruments, referred to as "contraptions" or "traps," consisted of various whistles, slapsticks, washboards, and other devices used by drummers for minstrel shows, vaudeville shows, and in silent movie houses in the 1930s. Instruments such as woodblocks, temple blocks, tom-toms, camel bells, and Chinese cymbals were introduced to the American drummer through immigrants or through the popular world's fairs of the late 1800s

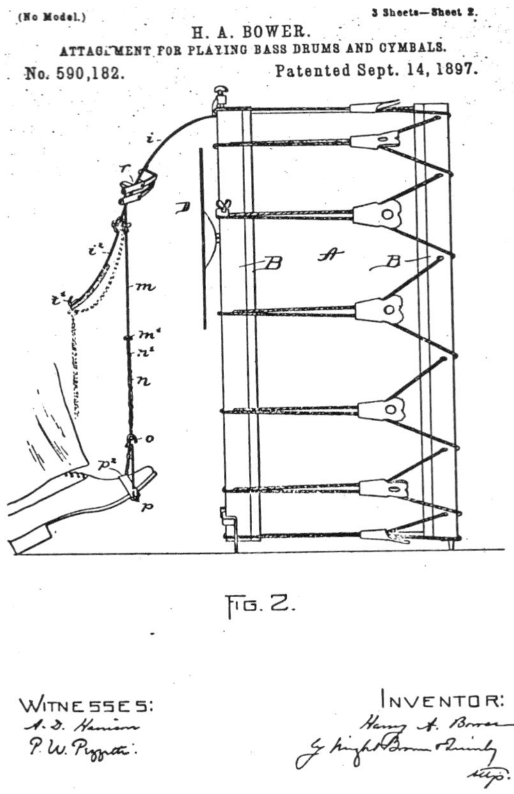

Fig. 1. Early example of bass drum/cymbal attachment.

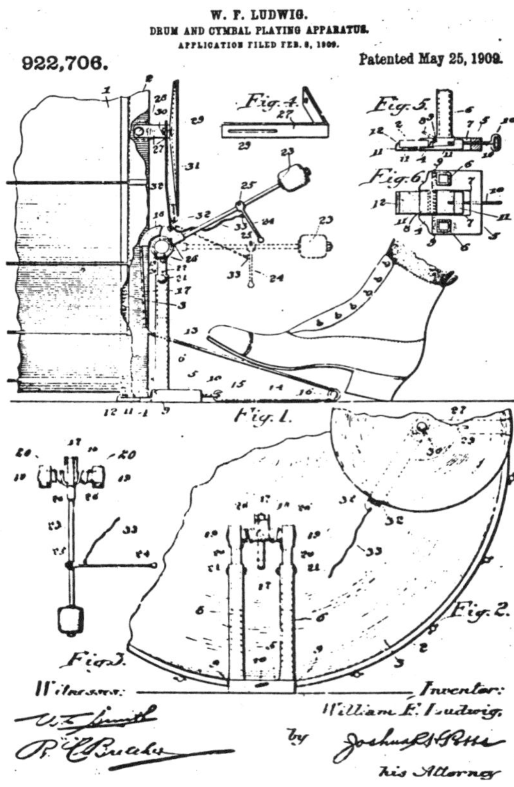

Fig. 2. First Ludwig pedal patent.

and early 1900s. By 1920 the standard instrumentation of the drum set included bass drum with pedal and cymbal attachment, concert snare drum, Turkish cymbal, Chinese cymbal, woodblock and/or temple blocks, camel bell/cowbell, small and/or large Chinese tom-toms, and assorted sound-effect instruments.

Performance—Pre-Dixieland

Early drum set players were influenced by the regimental music of the Civil War, as well as the African-influenced dance music, which remained a part of the black heritage of New Orleans and other cities. Ragtime's syncopated feel was infectious and became a part of the repertoire of New Orleans brass bands, as well as the popular John Philip Sousa Concert Band. The ability to improvise and/or augment drum parts within a particular style was a necessity. Many drummers created a "syncopated" quality to both the march-style music and ragtime by emphasizing the "weak" or "upbeat" (2 and 4), often accomplished through the use of a closed or "crush" roll on those beats or by mirroring the melodies on the drum set (primarily in ragtime).

Dixieland

By 1910, improvised music based on the blues, ragtime, and other influences was being performed by many groups in New Orleans and in other cities. All-black ensembles were gaining popularity throughout America and Europe, and the drummer was the focal point of much of the excitement, due to the array of instruments that was often a part of the drummer's setup. Drummers began to mix dotted rhythms and triplets with syncopated eighth-note patterns when playing solo. Tony Spargo (1897–1969) (also known by his real name, Tony Sbarbaro) was the drummer for a group called the Original Dixieland Jazz Band (ODJB). This was an ensemble of young white musicians who emulated the improvised music they had heard black bands perform in the cafes of New Orleans's Storyville district, the red-light district that spawned much of the early examples of the music that became known as "jazz." Spargo, generally considered to be the strongest musician in the ODJB, was known for his flamboyant style of playing, much of it based on a syncopated ragtime style.

Warren "Baby" Dodds (1898–1959) is considered by many to be the first "jazz" drummer, because of his ability to support the improvising soloist as well as to improvise himself. Dodds's musical foundation was deep, having been born to a family whose ancestors were African drummers and whose brother, Johnny Dodds (1892–1940), was a noted clarinetist. The younger Dodds grew up in New Orleans, influenced by street drummers as well as ragtime players. His playing with the "King" Oliver band and with Louis Armstrong in the early and mid-1920s reveals the typical "New Orleans" Dixieland style, more controlled than ragtime, often in a "four" feel rather than in "two," as was often the case with both ragtime and the later "Chicago-style" Dixieland. Dodds's improvisatory efforts are best documented with the Oliver band when playing woodblock, where he effectively mixed rolls, triplets, and dotted rhythms as background to the horn solos, rather than to simply play a series of ostinato patterns or to elaborate on a melody in the manner of the ragtime drummers. This characteristic set Dodds apart from drummers before him and depicts the primary role of the drum set drummer to the present day: to support and in turn become influenced by the musicians whom the drummer is accompanying.

Dodds and other drummers of the 1920s such as "Zutty" Singleton (1898–1975), Paul Barbarin (1899–1969), Ben Pollack (1903–1971), and Chauncey Morehouse (1902–1980) were to continue the development of the timekeeping nature of the instrument through New Orleans Dixieland, as well as a more rollicking version, called "Chicago-style" Dixieland. The Chicago style often featured the "two-feel," in which the down-beats were accentuated. The "backbeat" feel developed in the Chicago style, as drummers stressed the "weak" beats with snare drum rolls or accented patterns. The cymbal was often choked for accent effects as well as being used as a timekeeping instrument, the performer applying wood-block rhythms directly to the cymbal and alternating between open and choked sounds; this predated the open/close hi-hat rhythms of the 1930s. Some drummers placed coins under the cymbal, producing a "shimmering" effect, which must have been in the thoughts of players of the period, such as Jo Jones (1911–1985), when they began to "ride" the new instrument added to the standard drum set in the 1930s, the hi-hat.

The *hi-hat*, also called the *high-hat*, did not begin in its modern form but started as the *snowshoe cymbal beater*, a device that featured two small cymbals attached to wood planks and operated by the foot. The snowshoe, as well as the predecessor of the modern hi-hat, called the *low-boy*, appeared as a part of drum sets beginning in the mid-1920s. The low-boy, which was 10 to 12 inches high, was operated by means of a foot pedal attached to a metal rod holding a cymbal that, when the foot was depressed, moved toward the other cymbal. The cymbals used on both the low-boy and early hi-hat were called *charleston cymbals*. These small, rather thick brass cymbals had an exaggerated bell designed to provide the impact needed for the backbeat, or "sock," function of this early device. The low-boy was popular, since it could produce the backbeat without being in the way of other instruments, a distinct advantage for the performer who required a large amount of equipment, such as a vaudeville percussionist. The hi-hat first appeared in the late 1920s and soon became part of the standard drum set.

Drummers began to use brushes (which were fly-swatters before being mass-produced by the drum companies) in Dixieland music, emulating the sound of sandpaper blocks rubbed together, a popular dance effect used by minstrel show and vaudeville show drummers. The legato effect of the brushes was created by moving the brush in a rotating motion on the drum head. Both hands could move in this fashion, creating a very smooth sound, or one hand could drag the brush in an oval, while the other hand played a rhythmic pattern. Drummers such as "Zutty" Singleton and later William "Chick" Webb (1909–1939) and Jo Jones made an art out of manipulating the brushes.

By the end of the 1920s the drum set had not changed dramatically, with the exception of the addition of the low-boy (or hi-hat) and brushes. Recording techniques were improving, allowing the drummer to bring the battery of instruments into the recording or radio studio rather than compromising the performance by playing drum parts on instruments such as the woodblock. This was a common practice of the early 1920s and makes the study of drum set development more difficult, since early recordings often do not represent the actual performance practice of the period.

Swing

The beginning of the "swing" sound is difficult to pinpoint, but a variety of developments in jazz of the late 1920s led to this new form. During the mid- to late 1920s, large ensembles began to form in New York, featuring written arrangements and led by musicians such as Don Redman (1900–1964), Fletcher Henderson (1898–1952), and Duke Ellington (1899–1974). Employment for these groups came from large ballrooms, where a large ensemble was appropriate and organized arrangements featuring both improvisation and ensemble playing were used. While "two-beat" styles remained popular, especially with the white dance bands (called "sweet" bands), black and white audiences began to listen and dance to a new style of jazz that featured a more restrained, "flat-four" feel (more equal emphasis to each note) to the music. The development of this style had a profound effect on the drummer and the entire rhythm section, which by the early 1930s included piano, drums, string bass (double bass), and guitar.

Drummers of the period supported the new style by incorporating connected legato rolls, sustained cymbal crashes, and ostinato patterns onto various instruments (especially the hi-hat cymbals), creating a timekeeping effect on a lighter sound. Timekeeping on an instrument with a lighter texture had the effect of relaxing the feel as well as enhancing the efforts of the strong bass players, such as Jimmy Blanton (1918–1942) with Duke Ellington, and Walter Paige with Count Basie (1904–1984). The drummer and the bass player became a cohesive timekeeping team. The ostinato patterns were often quarter notes or a combination of quarter notes and triplet figures, a carryover from the woodblock beats of the Dixieland style, which were to become known as "ride" patterns as they were applied to the cymbal (see Ex. 1).

Ex. 1. "Ride" patterns.

Since the right hand was usually the limb that played the cymbal ostinato, the left hand was free to begin occasionally to punctuate on the snare drum, in support of the musical arrangement, the melody or the improvisations of the soloists. Drummers such as Walter Johnson (1904–1977) and Kaiser Marshall (1899–1948) were the pioneers of these early examples of "independence," with Count Basie's drummer Jo Jones being the primary exponent of this style. Jones, coupled with bassist Paige, guitarist Freddie Greene (1911–1987), and Basie on piano, redefined the role of the rhythm section in jazz through the development of the flat-four feel and Basie's sparse chordal backgrounds. Jo Jones's reputation was built on his uncanny abilities as an accompanist, through the use of brushes and his development of three distinct hi-hat sounds: the closed hi-hat (with the backbeat played on the hi-hat stand), open/closed combinations and the half-open hi-hat, all being descendants of the hand-held cymbal techniques of the previous decade.

The 1930s brought recognition to the drummer as a soloist. Gene Krupa (1909–1973), a Chicago drummer, made an international reputation for himself as a "Swing Era" musician playing a drumming style much more associated with ragtime and Dixieland. Krupa was a dynamic soloist and became a star as a member of the Benny Goodman group before forming his own band. Krupa was known for his relentless bass drum beats, as well as his boundless energy and hand-to-hand technique. His extended solos became a trademark, and the accented tom-tom patterns seemed to be borrowed from the Dixieland drum solo style which "Baby" Dodds called "spooky drums." Krupa's ability to structure a drum solo captured the imagination of audiences of the era and set a style that drummers continue to use in the present day. Chick Webb was the only major jazz drummer to lead his own band in the 1930s, allowing him to experiment with his playing style within the context of a big band. Webb's playing was very influential for drummers of the 1930s. His playing technique was exceptional, utilizing rhythmic groupings and double-stroke techniques containing elements of both Dixieland and swing drumming but accompanying ensembles and soloists with a tasteful, unabrasive style.

The drum set of the late 1930s was generally devoid of many of the traps of earlier sets, reflecting instead the demands of drummers of the period. All sets included the typical bass drum, but the Chinese tom-toms had begun to be replaced by single- and later double-tensioned tom-toms produced by the drum companies. Ride cymbals were expanded to 18 to 22 inches in diameter and reached sizes as large as 25 to 26 inches during the 1940s and 1950s. Chinese cymbals (often 14 to 16 inches in diameter) were included in many sets. The crash cymbal came into vogue as the ride cymbal became a single-function instrument, with the crash cymbals ranging from 12 to 16 inches in diameter and the hi-hats generally from 12 to 15 inches in diameter. The snare drum had become the trademark of many players and companies, utilizing the latest in features, such as separate tensioning of the heads, a variety of snare adjustment mechanisms, and a wide choice of shell materials and designs.

Bebop

The early 1940s saw revolutionary changes in the way jazz musicians viewed themselves and their music. Many musicians began to recognize jazz as an expressive art form, capable of bold rhythmic and harmonic experimentations. Small groups of musicians were leading a movement away from the dance halls and into small venues, where the purpose of the band was for listening rather than frivolous amusement. The art of improvisation was the focal point of this new music, called "bebop." Bebop featured disjunct melodies, extended harmonies, alternate chord changes, and a variety of musical concepts and materials that provided the basis for the study and application of jazz improvisation to the present day. Since the purpose of the music was to showcase the talents of the improvising musician, tempos became faster as well as slower for ballad playing, the result of not being driven by the demands of the dance band.

Kenny Clarke (1914–1985) was the pivotal drummer between swing and bebop styles. While drummers such as Jo Jones and "Dave Tough" (David Jarvis, 1908–1948) began to move ostinato "ride" patterns onto the cymbal in the late 1930s, it was Clarke who officially broke the "barrier." He began to use the bass drum as a punctuating and independent voice on the drum set around 1940, first in Teddy Hill's (1909–1978) band and most notably with pianist Thelonius Monk (1920–1982) at Minton's Playhouse, an after-hours club in Harlem managed by Hill. It was at Minton's that bebop, a cult following for the music and the corresponding drumming style was born. Clarke's playing was a departure from what had come before. By the end of the 1930s, drummers had begun to use the bass drum as an independent voice in solos and fills, but it was Clarke who incorporated this independent playing, sometimes called "dropping bombs," into the timekeeping and accompanying function. Clarke was also responsible for playing the majority of his cymbal ostinatos on a large cymbal, soon to become known as the *ride*, or *bop* cymbal. He also began to fill with the left hand on the snare drum, or in combination with the snare drum and bass drum, in odd groupings rather than in phrases. The mature bop drumming style, heard in the playing of Sid Catlett (1910–1951), Shelly Manne (1920–1984), and especially Max Roach (b. 1924), is a combination of technique and communication between drummer and soloist.

Max Roach was considered to be a part of the mainstream of the bop movement by the time he had reached his early twenties, working with the major purveyors of the art, saxophonist Charlie Parker (1920–1955), trumpeter Dizzy Gillespie (1917–1993), and Thelonious Monk. Roach, unlike Clarke, did not alter an existing swing style but developed his own approach to the music, thriving on the challenge of the breakneck tempos and free-flowing rhythmic ideas between drummer and soloist. The technique of passing ideas between the *limbs* was referred to as "coordinated independence," a term invented by teacher and author Jim Chapin (b. 1919) in the late 1940s, as he began to analyze and codify the techniques that drummers such as Clarke, Catlett, Roach, Manne, Tiny Kahn (1924–1953), Stan Levey (b. 1925), and others were using in the new style. Bebop offered the drummer the opportunity to be considered an integral and equal member of the ensemble, not just as a soloist but as an improvising member of the group. Roach was a dynamic, articulate soloist, generally using hand-to-hand patterns in his improvisations and tuning his drums considerably higher than drummers of previous styles, so as to enhance the clarity of his ideas.

Cool

The development of an art form is often marked by individuals or groups who create a new artistic style as a reaction to a previous style. Such was the case with a new style of jazz, called "cool." Cool jazz generally featured moderate tempos, vibrato-less playing, and a much more restrained approach. Musicians such as pianist/composer Lennie Tristano (1919–1978), saxophonists Lee Konitz (b. 1927) and Gerry Mulligan (b. 1927), and trumpeter Miles Davis (1926–1993) were among the major exponents of this style, which met with relative commercial success and paved the way for the "West Coast" jazz sound that developed in the 1950s. Drummers often accompanied this style with brushes. The limited equipment demands of this style helped to "downsize" the standard drum set: the bass drum was often 20 to 22 inches in diameter, and the tom-toms were 12 to 13 inches and 14 to 16 inches in diameter. Tom-toms were affixed to the bass drum by sturdy mounts, and by the late 1940s floor toms had removable legs. Bass drums began to appear with a revolutionary concept, "retractable" spurs. Many of these equipment changes reflected the less obtrusive role of the drummer in the cool style as well as accommodating the increased popularity of the small "club-date" combo rather than the big band.

Professional drummers, especially those who were living in New York or touring by car were demanding more portability in their equipment.

Hard-Bop

Many jazz musicians found the "cool school" limiting and lacking emotion. During the mid-1950s a growing number of young disciples of the bebop style began to form groups that featured improvisation and an increased emphasis on composition within a jazz context. These groups were to also feature the drummer as a soloist, often improvising as an introduction or over the entire form of the tune rather than in an "open solo" style. Max Roach, a notable bandleader in the hard-bop style, was a major exponent of these techniques, as was Art Blakey (1919–1990), a young bandleader whose Jazz Messengers included some of this music's greatest stars early in their careers. Blakey typified the hard-bop style with a forceful backbeat on the hi-hat, as well as the energetic and liberal use of polyrhythm and independence techniques. Blakey, as well as other major performers such as "Philly Joe" Jones (1923–1985) and Roy Haynes (b. 1926), began to use the bass drum freely as a melodic voice during solo improvisations. Other major bandleaders of the period included Miles Davis, Horace Silver (b. 1928), and "Sonny" Rollins (b. 1929).

West Coast, Third Stream

The growing population and public infatuation with California in the mid-1950s was mirrored in a new and popular outgrowth of cool jazz called "West Coast." Most of the musicians who made this music popular were alumni of the Stan Kenton (1911–1979), Woody Herman (1913–1987), and Les Brown (b. 1912) big bands who moved to California to become a part of the growing recording industry in Los Angeles and Hollywood. West Coast jazz was primarily consumed by white audiences who were listening to a more restrained jazz product than the hard-bop groups were producing in New York at the time. The West Coast drumming style was generally very smooth, utilizing brushes and other implements such as mallets and fingers to produce new effects. Drummers including Shelly Manne, who were excellent bebop players in their own right, seemed to adapt well to this style and became an integral part of the West Coast movement. Although West Coast jazz was generally known to feature small groups, such as those led by Barney Kessel (b. 1923) and André Previn (b. 1929), the big bands of Shorty Rodgers (b. 1924) and especially Terry Gibbs (b. 1929), featured outstanding drumming by Mel Lewis (1929–1990). Lewis's interpretation of big band "charts" was a curious mixture of the relaxed West Coast small-group style and the bebop approach.

A nontraditional facet of the music, called "third stream," developed toward the end of the 1950s and featured nontraditional groups, instrumentation, and musical materials. Musicians such as Gil Evans (1912–1988) and the members of the Modern Jazz Quartet (with Kenny Clarke as the original drummer in the group) had met with success in mixing "classical" instrumentation (Gil Evans's orchestra with Miles Davis) and musical forms. Composer/pianist Dave Brubeck (b. 1920) (a pupil of Darius Milhaud) gained an international following for his music, which featured "odd" meters of 3/4, 5/4, 7/4, 11/4, and others, popularizing a technique that Max Roach's groups had been featuring for some time. Brubeck's drummer, Joe Morello (b. 1928), became a sensation in drumming circles due to his uncanny fluidity in these meters as well as for his displays of technical skill, such as the one-handed "roll." Chico Hamilton (b. 1921) was noted for his unique approach to the drum set, utilizing mallets, and accessory instruments, as well as a 16-inch bass drum. The four-piece drum set remained standard through the 1950s, with the cowbell and woodblock still considered a part of the standard set-up for commercial Latin-American rhythms such as the cha-cha and mambo.

Latin-American

During the late 1940s bandleaders such as Dizzy Gillespie and Stan Kenton began to incorporate elements of Latin music as well as Latin percussion instruments and instrumentalists in their bands. Gillespie hired Cuban hand drummer Machito as a member of his band, recording stylized but exciting music. Kenton began to tour with a Latin percussionist at this time, and his band was to become identified with Latin-influenced arrangements and compositions. Drummers of the time learned to play "commercial" beats such as the samba and the mambo on the full set, but when coupled with an entire Latin percussion section, as was the case with some of the Gillespie recordings, the drummer merely kept time, delegating most of the work to the Latin percussionists. The interest of jazz musicians in Latin and Latin-influenced music continued, becoming a part of the hard-bop repertoire as well as gaining mass appeal around 1960 with the emergence of the Brazilian "bossa-nova." Part of the lure and the challenge for the jazz drummer playing Latin music was the fact that he had to perform a "new" style of music in which the rhythmic emphasis fell on the "downbeat" rather than the "upbeat," as was the case in most jazz styles to this point. The influence of Latin music in jazz has remained strong, providing a major element in the eclectic or "fusion" styles of jazz.

Four-Way Independence/Neo-Bop

By the beginning of the 1960s, drummers had learned to utilize all four limbs for soloing, with a few pioneering efforts to use all limbs for timekeeping as well. Elvin Jones (b. 1927) made a reputation for himself as the drummer for the quartet of saxophonist John Coltrane (1926–1967), a part of what some observers have called the "neo-bop" movement. Jones's playing generally had an underlying triplet feel, with each part of the triplet distributed to a different limb. Many observers have felt that Jones intentionally created "polyrhythmic" patterns between the limbs in his solos and during his accompanying. However, careful listening will often reveal that the note distribution, coupled with his unique ability to displace accents and stress points, gives the music a polyrhythmic or polymetric "feel" rather than changing the meter. Roy Haynes helped break the hi-hat "barrier" in much the same manner that Kenny Clarke freed the bass drum around 1940, by using the hi-hat for various fills and anticipations during the course of timekeeping. Haynes seldom left the ride cymbal and became known as a master of the ride rhythm; the ride patterns had a "duple" quality and varied with the music rather than remain in a stagnant ostinato pattern. Haynes's drum set of this period (as well as the set that Tony Williams was to play) included an 18-inch bass drum, a 12-inch diameter mounted tom-tom, a 14-inch diameter floor tom-tom, and a standard or piccolo snare drum. Cymbals included a 20- to 24-inch ride, a 16- to 20-inch crash, and 14-inch hi-hats.

Tony Williams (b. 1945) was a young prodigy when he joined Miles Davis's group in 1963, having been a student of the master teacher Alan Dawson (b. 1929) and a veteran of saxophonist Jackie McClean's group. Williams was to gain fame as a part of a spectacular young rhythm section in Davis's band, which also included bassist Ron Carter (b. 1937) and pianist Herbie Hancock (b. 1940). Williams's work with the Davis group was so notable that performers still consider an accurate transcription of a Tony Williams accompaniment or solo to be a formidable accomplishment. The elements of four-way control were so complete in his playing that Williams was able to keep time with ride cymbal patterns, drum patterns, or through his seemingly limitless hand-to-foot coordination. These techniques predate and serve as the impetus for the development of "linear" drumming concepts, a term depicting the use of a single line or sticking pattern that is distributed among the limbs to create interesting patterns. Williams's popularity and notoriety with the Miles Davis group seemed to underline the fact that, since the 1920s, drum set playing had advanced from a truly "dependent" two-way system (snare drum and bass drum) to an advanced method of playing, incorporating all limbs. The next logical advancement in drum set playing was its use in music, where boundaries of form and structure were either liberal or non-existent.

Free Jazz

The term "free jazz" defines a style in which adherence to musical structure is eschewed, with the result being a product that many choose not to define as "music," due to its disjunct quality. Musicians such as Ornette Coleman (b. 1930) rarely employ standard forms, chord changes, and the like to construct their compositions. Coleman will often use a "head" or melody as a basis for the song but does not adhere to a particular melodic, harmonic, or rhythmic structure for soloing. Free jazz musicians found a loyal audience of artists, intellectuals, and human rights activists because of the "freedom" that many feel the music depicts. Drummers such as Ed Blackwell (b. 1929) and Billy Higgins (b. 1936) were active in this movement, making significant contributions with Ornette Coleman and others but not playing with the total improvisatory freedom of players such as Rashied Ali (b. 1935), Andrew Cyrille (b. 1939) (with pianist Cecil Taylor, b. 1933), and Sonny Murray (b. 1937). Complete freedom in this music permits the drummer to respond to the music in any manner, either by providing a time line that may or may not be adhered to by the other musicians, or by improvising freely on the drums and accessories without regard for providing a particular pulse. Free jazz drummers would often supplement the standard "four-piece," or four drum set, with a variety of accessory and ethnic percussion instruments.

Rock Drumming

Early rock, or "rock and roll" drumming was a combination of two drumming styles: country and western and rhythm and blues. These drummers borrowed techniques and set design from the jazz drummers of the day, but the music had its own distinct rhythmic feel by the beginning of the 1960s.

The triplet or 12/8 feel was prevalent in early rhythm and blues and rock styles. Drummers outlined this feel by using the ride cymbal, with pioneering rock drummers such as Fred Below playing fills reminiscent of jazz styles. Strong emphasis on the backbeat, often played on the snare drum, was a part of this style. Evidence suggests that the backbeat, which became a part of early rock drumming, was the drummer's version of "slap bass," a technique used by string bass players in which the downbeats were played and the string was slapped against the fingerboard on the upbeats (beats two and four). Some early rock recordings also suggest Latin/Cajun influences upon drummers, as well as examples that incorporated only drums and cymbals. Drummers also began to incorporate straight eighth-note ride patterns and to construct various beats that used the bass drum as a facet of the pattern.

By the early 1960s rock and roll had taken on a life of its own, complete with electric guitars, basses, and a growing youth population to support it. Rock drumming's notable advances during this period came in the form of the sheer popularity of the music and the drums, led by drummers and groups such as Cozy Cole ("Topsy, Part II"), Sandy Nelson ("Teen Beat"), and The Surfaris ("Wipe Out"). With the exception of "Wipe Out," these drum features and many that followed (including the enormously successful "In-A-Gadda-Da-Vida," by Iron Butterfly, and "Toad" highlighting Ginger Baker with Cream) used drumming techniques and patterns made popular by Gene Krupa twenty years earlier. Krupa remained popular through the 1960s and served as an inspiration to many young players, who found him to be more accessible as a person and as a drummer than many of the modern jazz players.

Prior to the early 1960s the drum set was essentially the same instrument for all musical styles: a four-piece set. Drummers began to add a second tom-tom, mounted on the bass drum, during this period, possibly to allow for a descending "melodic" line from snare drum to floor tom during the course of a four-beat fill. Hal Blaine (b. 1929), one of the most recorded drummers of all time, expanded the drum set to a multi-tom setup. This change in the instrument was a significant departure from the standard outfit and helped to signal a change in the development and marketing of the major drum manufacturers. Following the arrival of the Beatles in the United States in 1964, the market for "combo" instruments exploded, with changes in rock music setting the trends for drum set design. The music and drumming were less subtle than jazz, with each drum and cymbal becoming one-dimensional in their function within the drum set. Larger, lower-pitched drums were used in rock music, both for increased projection and for visual impact. Hi-hat cymbals were made thicker to accommodate the heavier playing and the fact that the cymbal ostinato, which had been played on the ride cymbal in the past, was now being played on the closed hi-hat. Single-headed tom-toms were popular, producing a direct sound that could project through amplified music easier than other tom-toms. Fiberglass became a popular shell material because of its brilliant sound. Drum companies were marketing hardware based on strength and durability rather than portability. Drumheads and sticks became thicker. Multi-tom and double-bass drum outfits became prominent in drum catalogs, with the five-piece drum set replacing the four-piece set as the standard configuration by 1970. Cowbells, woodblocks, and brushes no longer came as standard equipment with the purchase of a drum set. Rock music had become the popular music of the era as well as the driving force of the musical instrument market.

During the mid- to late 1960s, black drummers such as Benny Benjamin and Bernard Purdie (b. 1939) had developed a more syncopated form of rock drumming within "soul" or "Motown" music. These styles required great facility and independence between the limbs, especially the snare drum and bass drum. By this time there was a clear distinction between fundamental rock and jazz drumming: basic rock patterns arose from the right foot and left hand (bass drum and snare drum), while in most jazz styles of the day the basic swing pattern arose from the opposite limbs. These differences, along with attitude, caused some players to view rock drumming as a "simple" form. The efforts of Benjamin and Purdie with Motown, James Brown (b. 1928), and others offered a challenge to many drummers and spawned interest in black music of the 1960s. Drummers like David Garibaldi, with groups like Tower of Power, gave rise to "funk" styles, which provided many of the technical influences for the "fusion" groups of the 1970s and 1980s.

Jazz-Rock/Fusion

The late 1960s featured a myriad of musical influences, with an audience for nearly every effort. No one group or sound dominated the popular music scene as had the Beatles, just a few years earlier. Instead, many different facets of the contemporary musical culture were heard, with an expanding market for "intellectual" rock, which mixed elements of other music, such as jazz and Eastern music, with rock and roll.

Groups such as Blood, Sweat and Tears (featuring the drumming of Bobby Colomby, b. 1944), Chicago (Danny Seraphine, b. 1948), and Dreams (Billy Cobham, b. 1944) introduced horn sections into the rock context and in turn, were responsible for a music called "jazz-rock." These bands were not the first to employ horn sections; James

Brown's group and other rhythm and blues artists had been using horn sections for quite some time. However, these bands integrated the horns into arrangements of tunes rather than using them for "riffs" and backgrounds, as was the case earlier. The drummers and the rhythm sections were forced to be flexible and literate in both styles. Rock drumming was also affected by the emergence of two outstanding British drummers, Mitch Mitchell (b. 1946) (with Jimi Hendrix) and John Bonham (1947–1979) (with Led Zepplin). Mitchell and Bonham stand out from a multitude of drummers playing "hard" rock during the late 1960s. They possessed fine technique, boundless energy, and the ability to incorporate techniques such as "linear" sticking and rhythmic displacement into their playing. The application of these techniques was important for the advancement of rock drumming, as well as for the "fusion" music that developed around 1970.

Tony Williams was already considered the "boy wonder" of contemporary jazz during the 1960s, making himself a legend in music by the time he had reached his early twenties. However, as he began to listen and become influenced by rock music, Williams chose to leave Miles Davis—who also had begun to experiment with rock elements (the "Bitches Brew" sessions, which included the fine playing of Jack DeJohnette [b. 1942]) in his own group—and form a highly influential band called Lifetime, which included organist Larry Young (1940–1978) and guitarist John McLaughlin (b. 1924), who was to later form the Mahvishnu Orchestra. Many consider this effort to be an example of the true "fusion" of jazz and rock styles rather than a music that incorporated elements of either style. Williams was spectacular in this medium, redefining the possibilities of drumming within a rock-related context with his mastery of four-limb independence. Late in 1970, the Mahvishnu Orchestra, featuring Billy Cobham on drums, was formed. This band featured music that used changing meters and seemed to be influenced by Eastern melodic and harmonic materials, perhaps a reflection of John McLaughlin's interest in Eastern culture at the time. Cobham's dominance of the music was staggering, utilizing his impressive hand-to-hand technique on a drum set that evolved to enormous proportions (including as many as three bass drums at one point) during his tenure with the band. Cobham was also an exponent of an "ambidextrous" approach to the drum set, playing the ride cymbal and hi-hat with either right or left hands and feet. Due to this "balanced" approach, Cobham used "matched" grip nearly all the time, an unusual technique for a player outside the rock arena at the time.

English drummer Bill Bruford (b. 1949) proved to be influential, serving as a member of the groups Yes and King Crimson, as well as leading his own recording dates. Bruford's fluid control of sticking patterns while executing the intricate meter changes of King Crimson's music made him a joy to watch. Bruford was also one of the pioneers of the electronic percussion movement.

An important element of the fusion style during the 1980s was Latin-based music. Pianist Chick Corea (b. 1941) has continued to incorporate Latin influences into his music, beginning with the inclusion of Brazilian drummer and percussionist Airto Moreira in the classic Return to Forever band of the early 1970s. The work of Alex Acuna (b. 1944) with Weather Report in the mid-1970s was an early example of Latin-influenced drumming in a mature fusion context. This playing required the drummer to approach the instrument differently; intricate sticking patterns were often distributed between the limbs while the bass drum and/or hi-hat played an ostinato pattern, an unusual but infectious sound that created a great deal of excitement. Drummers such as Steve Gadd (b. 1945), Peter Erskine (b. 1954), and Vinnie Colaiuta are important exponents of these influences.

Electronic Drums and Accessories

Electronic devices have been associated with rock music since the 1950s, but not until the 1970s did electronics have a lasting impact on drums and drumming. Early efforts at "electrifying" drums (Hollywood brand drums in the 1960s) were not successful and were merely designed to be a self-contained electronic drum set with pickups, based on the principle of the electric guitar. The acoustics of the drums and the lack of technology did not permit those efforts to succeed. Internally and externally mounted microphone systems, which were more successful, were developed in the 1980s. Drummers began to become aware of microphones and sound reinforcement techniques during the 1970s, as it became evident that a sound system could not only enhance but drastically alter the sound of the drum set.

Electronic drums began to appear in the 1970s as single-drum units containing a pickup that channeled the electronic signal through filters and was amplified by a guitar amplifier or sound system. These devices (the most popular being the Synare and Syndrum) had limited diversity of sounds and became stylized as a popular sound in "disco" music. The Simmons company developed the widely available electronic drum set, a five-piece set of "pads," each containing a pickup, or transducer. Each signal had a separate channel on a mixing board. These sounds became very popular in music of the early 1980s but were still analog sounds, much like those generated from early synthesizers.

The most dramatic changes in electronic percussion came with the developments of the *drum machine* and the *Musical Instrument Digital Interface* (MIDI). The drum machine had the ability to play "per-

Fig. 3. Electronic drum set.

Courtesy of the Yamaha Corporation of America.

fect" time and be programmed to play standard patterns and song forms or to create new patterns that might be impossible for a drummer to play. Many drummers felt this device, which was programmed through the use of buttons, was a threat. The drum machine did, in fact, replace musicians in some production-related facets of the music business, where creativity and "human" feel were not as critical as the cost-effectiveness of the electronic device. Many other musicians felt threatened by the advances in MIDI technology, in which drum machines, synthesizers, computers, and sequencers could "talk" to each other through digital (computer-based) signals and information. This technology permits the performer to "trigger" a variety of sounds through one instrument. In other words, one instrument, or computer, becomes the controller, or "master," while the other instruments become "slaves." The excitement or "silver lining" to this process is that percussionists can use the controller concept to access an unlimited number of sounds. During the late 1980s it became apparent that electronics were here not to make the acoustic drum set or the drummer obsolete but to enhance the sound possibilities of the drummer, something drummers had attempted to do since the beginning of the century.

Through increased literacy drummers found new life in the electronic music world, while other musicians were generally unable to realize and program drum "parts" on the electronic drum machines and computers in the same manner that a drummer could. This reality supports the case for continued study of "standard" practices in drumming and the teaching of various drumming styles on the acoustic drum set. The drummer of the future will need to be well-versed in fundamental technique and style as well as the technology that will shape the future.

See also Illus. 47, p. 141.

Bibliography

Blades, James. *Percussion Instruments and Their History*. New York: Praeger, 1970.

Brown, Theodore Dennis. *A History and Analysis of Jazz Drumming to 1942*. Ann Arbor, Mich.: University Microfilms International, 1976.

Collier, James Lincoln. *The Making of Jazz*. New York: Delta, 1978.

Jones, LeRoi. *Blues People*. New York: Putnam, 1974.

Ludwig, William F., Sr. *My Life at the Drums*. Chicago: Ludwig Drum Co., 1972.

Schuller, Gunther. *Early Jazz: Its Roots and Musical Development*. London: Oxford University Press, 1968.

Williams, Martin T. *The Jazz Tradition*. New York: New American Library, 1970.

Robert B. Breithaupt

Drum Set Players

The following is a list of the most influential drum set players of the twentieth century. Birth and death dates are included when known. For more information, see the works cited below.

Acuna, Alex (b. 1944)
Aldridge, Tommy
Alexander, Mousey (b. 1922)
Ali, Rashied (b. 1935)
Allen, Pistol
Allison, Jerry
Altschul, Barry (b. 1943)
Appice, Carmine
Arnold, Horacee (b. 1937)
Aronoff, Kenny (b. 1953)
Avory, Mick (b. 1944)
Baird, Mike
Baker, Ginger (b. 1940)
Barbarin, Paul (b. 1901)
Barrett, Carlton
Bauduc, Ray (1909–1988)
Bayers, Eddie
Bellson, Louis (b. 1924)
Below, Fred
Benjamin, Benny
Berton, Vic (1896–1951)
Best, Denzil (1917–1965)
Bissonette, Greg
Black, Dave (b. 1928)
Blackwell, Ed (b. 1929)
Blaine, Hal (b. 1929)
Blakey, Art (1919–1990)
Bonham, Jason
Bonham, John (1947–1979)
Bozzio, Terry
Brechtlein, Tom
Bruford, Bill (b. 1949)
Bunker, Clive
Burns, Roy (b. 1935)
Calhoun, Will
Capp, Frank (b. 1931)
Carmassi, Denny
Carrington, Terri Lynn
Castillo, Randy
Castronovo, Deen
Catlett, Sid (1910–1951)
Chaffee, Gary
Chambers, Dennis
Chambers, Joe (b. 1942)
Chancler, Ndugu (b. 1952)
Chapin, Jim (b. 1919)
Chester, Gary
Christensen, Jon (b. 1943)
Clarke, Kenny (1914–1985)
Clarke, Mike
Clarke, Terry
Cobb, Jimmy (b. 1929)
Cobham, Billy (b. 1944)
Colaiuta, Vinnie
Cole, Cozy (1909–1981)
Collins, Phil (b. 1951)
Colomby, Bobby (b. 1944)
Copeland, Stewart (b. 1952)
Cottler, Irv
Craney, Mark
Crawford, Jimmy (1910–1980)
Cyrille, Andrew (b. 1939)
Danelli, Dino (b. 1944)
Dawson, Alan (b. 1929)
DeJohnette, Jack (b. 1942)
Demms, Barrett (b. 1913)
De Vito, Liberty
Dodds, Warren "Baby" (1898–1959)
Dunbar, Aynsley
Dunlop, Frankie
Emory, Sonny
Erskine, Peter (b. 1954)

Fatool, Nick (b. 1915)
Ferrone, Steve
Fig, Anton
Fontana, D.J.
Foster, Al (b. 1944)
Franco, Joe
Gadd, Steve (b. 1945)
Garibaldi, Dave (David)
Goodwin, Bill (b. 1942)
Gordon, Jim (b. 1946)
Gottlieb, Danny (b. 1953)
Graves, Milford (b. 1941)
Greer, Sonny (1895–1982)
Guerin, John (b. 1939)
Gurtu, Trilok (b. 1951)
Hakim, Omar (b. 1959)
Hall, Tubby (1895–1946)
Hamilton, Chico (b. 1921)
Hamilton, Jeff (b. 1953)
Harris, William "Beaver" (b. 1936)
Hart, Billy (b. 1940)
Hart, Mickey (b. 1943)
Hayes, Louis (b. 1937)
Haynes, Roy (b. 1926)
Heard, J.C. (1917–1988)
Heath, Albert "Tootie" (b. 1935)
Helm, Levon (b. 1942)
Higgins, Billy (b. 1936)
Hooper, Stix (b. 1938)
Houghton, Steve (b. 1954)
Humair, Daniel (b. 1938)
Humphrey, Ralph (b. 1944)
Humphries, Roger (b. 1944)
Igo, Sonny (b. 1923)
Imboden, Teis
Jackson, Al (b. 1935)
Jackson, Duffy (b. 1953)
James, Clifton
Johnson, Walter (1904–1977)
Jones, Elvin (b. 1927)
Jones, Harold (b. 1940)
Jones, Jo (1911–1985)
Jones, Kenny (b. 1948)
Jones, "Philly Joe" (1923–1985)
Jones, Rufus (b. 1936)
Kahn, Tiny (1924–1953)
Katche, Manu
Kay, Connie (b. 1927)
Kay, Stanley
Keltner, Jim (b. 1942)
Kennedy, Will
King, Stan (1900–1949)
Krupa, Gene (1909–1973)
Kunkel, Russ
Laine, Papa Jack
Lamond, Don (b. 1920)
Lee, Tommy (b. 1963)
Leeman, Cliff (1913–1986)
Levey, Stan (b. 1925)
Lewis, Mel (1929–1990)
Lewis, Victor
Londin, Larrie
McCracken, Chet
McCurdy, Roy (b. 1936)
McKinley, Ray (b. 1910)
Manne, Shelly (1920–1984)
Marotta, Rick
Marshall, Kaiser
Mason, Harvey (b. 1947)
Miles, Buddy
Miles, Butch (b. 1944)
Mitchell, Mitch (b. 1946)
Modelist, Joseph "Zigaboo"
Mohammed, Idris
Moon, Keith (1947–1978)
Morales, Richie
Morehouse, Chauncey
Moreira, Airto
Morell, Marty (b. 1944)
Morello, Joe (b. 1928)
Morgenstein, Rod
Morris, Chuck
Mortian, Paul (b. 1931)
Moses, Bob (b. 1948)
Mouzon, Alphonse
Moye, Don

Murray, Sonny (b. 1937)
Nash, Lewis
Nelson, Sandy (b. 1938)
Newmark, Andy
Nussbaum, Adam (b. 1955)
Paice, Ian
Palmer, Earl, Sr. (b. 1924)
Parker, Chris
Payne, Odie
Payne, Sonny (1926–1979)
Peart, Neal (b. 1952)
Persip, Charli (b. 1929)
Phillips, Simon
Pollack, Ben (1903–1971)
Porcaro, Jeff (1954–1992)
Porcaro, Joe (b. 1930)
Powell, Cozy
Purdie, Bernard (b. 1939)
Rich, Buddy (1917–1987)
Richmond, Dannie (1935–1988)
Riley, Ben (b. 1933)
Roach, Max (b. 1924)
Robinson, John
Rock, Bobby
Rockenfield, Scott
Roker, Mickey (b. 1932)
Rosengarden, Bob (b. 1924)
Sbarbaro (Spargo), Tony
Scheuerell, Casey
Seraphine, Danny (b. 1948)
Shaughnessy, Ed (b. 1929)
Singleton, "Zutty" (1898–1975)
Smith, Jimmie (b. 1938)
Smith, Steve (b. 1954)
Soph, Ed (b. 1945)
Sorum, Matt
Spencer, O'Neil (1909–1944)
Stafford, George (1898–1936)
Starr, Ringo (b. 1940)
Stevens, Mark
Stoller, Alvin (b. 1925)
Stubblefield, Clyde
Tate, Grady (b. 1932)
Taylor, Art (b. 1929)
Thigpen, Ed (b. 1930)
Thompson, Chester (b. 1926)
Tough, Dave (David Jarvis) (1908–1948)
Van Eaton, James
Van Halen, Alex (b. 1955)
Von Ohlen, John (b. 1941)
Wackerman, Chad
Walden, Narada Michael
Washington, Kenny (b. 1958)
Watts, Charlie (b. 1941)
Watts, Jeff "Tain"
Webb, William "Chick" (1909–1939)
Weckl, Dave (b. 1960)
Wettling, George
White, Lenny (b. 1949)
White, Maurice (b. 1941)
Williams, Tony (b. 1945)
Woodyard, Sam (1925–1988)

Bibliography

Feather, Leonard, and Ira Gitler. *Encyclopedia of Jazz in the 70's*. New York: Horizon Press, 1976.

Kernfeld, Barry, ed. *The New Grove Dictionary of Jazz*. 2 vols. New York: Stockton Press, Groves Dictionaries of Music [Macmillan], 1988.

Korall, Burt. *Drummin' Men*. New York: Schirmer Books, 1990.

Larrick, Geary. *Biographical Essays on Twentieth-Century Percussionists*. Lewiston, N.Y.: The Edwin Mellen Press, 1992.

Spagnardi, Ronald. *The Great Jazz Drummers*. Edited by William F. Miller. Cedar Grove, N.J.: Modern Drummer Publications, 1992.

Robert B. Breithaupt

Electronic Percussion

Electronic percussion instruments differ from their acoustic counterparts in that their sound is produced by passing organized electrical current through an amplification system, rather than a portion of the instrument actually vibrating the surrounding air. The first electronic percussion instruments were introduced in the mid-1970s with the release of the *Syndrum* and the *Synare.* These two devices were natural extensions of the increasing popularity of modular synthesizers of the time, such as those made by Moog, Buchla, ARP, and others. Both instruments produced a distinctive falling sound that became a trademark of the early disco music style. By 1982 complete electronic drum kits were available. These consisted of multiple pads integrated into a single configuration that emulated the traditional setup.

Along with the introduction of electronic percussion instruments, which were designed to be played "live" by hitting drumlike pads with sticks, another type of instrument was in the developmental stage. The first production model *drum machine* was manufactured by Roger Linn in 1981. Called the LM-1 (termed a "drum computer" at the time), this drum machine was programmed by the performer to play drum and percussion parts on its own.

Early electronic percussion instruments offered the performer/programmer few options. Sounds were low quality (by today's standards), and control of musical parameters such as dynamics, tuning, and tempo were minimal.

Today, electronic percussion instruments have been fully integrated into the world of keyboard synthesizers by offering the percussionist a new palette of sound, control, flexibility, and creativity. With the advent of MIDI (Musical Instrument Digital Interface) in 1983, it became possible for a percussionist to trigger and play sounds from a wide variety of electronic instruments.

MIDI actually translates the physical gestures of a musical performance into a digital language. Since the MIDI language is a standard interface to which most electronic instrument manufacturers adhere, all instruments are capable of understanding and reacting to each other. Using this technology, percussionists have access to all performance commands of synthesizers, digital samplers, digital effect processors, and even multitrack tape decks. At this time, electronic percussion instruments fall into three main categories: electronic drum kits, drum machines, and alternate controllers.

Electronic drum kits, although they look quite different, can be positioned in a physically similar layout to acoustic drums. Each electronic pad might be shaped like a circle, triangle, octagon, polygon, or almost any other shape. Pads create their sounds by sensing vibration with a piezo transducer or sensing pressure with a force-sensing resistor mounted under the striking surface. Once the vibration is recognized, an electrical spike (called a trigger) is sent through an attached cable to the electronic drum kit's "brain."

The "brain" of the electronic kit is actually a sophisticated computer (microprocessor) that reads the voltage signals from the pads and produces the sound. These sounds can be synthesized imitations of percussion timbres or digital recordings (called samples) of actual drum sounds that were recorded in a studio under ideal conditions.

Depending on the features included in the microprocessor, sounds can be controlled in terms of their dynamics, touch sensitivity, pitch (sometimes a ten-octave range), length of decay, tonal qualities, etc. Many electronic drum kits offer additional features such as layering (a single pad might produce two to five sounds at once), velocity switching (soft playing activates one sound while playing with a harder stroke activates a different sound), and velocity cross-fading (smooth transition of sound from one timbre to another as the performer changes velocity). Once the desired sounds and effects are programmed into the brain, the settings can be memorized into locations called programs, patches, presets, or kits. It is then possible for a performer to change from one group of sounds to another by pressing a button, hitting a pad, or operating a foot switch.

Drum machines operate in a different manner from electronic kits. The drum machine programmer builds a musical performance by instructing the microprocessor inside the unit to play various drum and/or percussion sounds at specific points within a measure. Short groupings of two to four measures are programmed into patterns. Complete compositions (called songs) are created by instructing the drum machine to play one series of patterns after another.

The two main techniques of programming patterns on a drum machine are called "real-time" entry and "step-time" entry. When programming patterns in real-time, the operator tells the drum machine the minimum note value to be performed, puts the drum machine into a recording mode, and instructs the machine to begin playing the pattern. As the pattern repeats, the programmer builds the pattern (usually one voice or instrument at a time) by striking buttons on the front panel that trigger selected sounds at the actual time the button is pushed. In step-time programming, the operator determines the durational value of the step (usually anywhere from a quarter-note to a thirty-second triplet, although some machines support a resolution as fine as 192 divisions per quarter) and moves the machine to a particular step within the pattern. Once at the desired step, the programmer instructs the machine to play one or more of the sounds at that particular step. This process is continued until the pattern is completed "one step at a time."

A number of controls are available to help customize the sampled sounds included with the drum machine to the programmer's preference. Often, the programmer can choose the tuning, decay, and tonal qualities of the sounds. Additional controls help the programmer enter patterns and construct songs. Some of these controls include copying patterns, erasing patterns, adding flams or rolls, multi-pitch or multi-level options, adjusting the tempo, and adjusting the relative balance and stereo placement of each instrument.

Alternate controllers are types of input devices that do not correspond to the traditional drum kit layout. Most often, alternate controllers do not actually produce any musical sounds of their own. Instead, they rely upon their sophisticated internal microprocessors to translate certain physical gestures into MIDI data. These MIDI messages and commands are relayed to a MIDI-compatible sound generator that then plays the desired timbre.

The most popular style of alternate controller is the multi-pad. A multi-pad is a small, box-like device that contains eight or more electronic drum surfaces. The *Octopad* (manufactured by Roland) was the most popular multi-pad. This instrument had eight surfaces, each of which could be programmed to send a single MIDI pitch message over a single MIDI channel (making it possible to send discrete messages to several MIDI sound generators). The second generation of multi-pads, such as the *DrumKat* by Kat (now the most popular multi-pad), the *PortaKit* by Simmons Electronics, and even Roland's *Octopad II*, have made multi-pad systems even more popular by offering the percussionist more control, flexibility, and surfaces to play.

Alternate controllers run the gamut from instruments that emulate the vibraphone (in design and performance technique) by Kat and Simmons to those that require entirely new physical techniques and musical approaches. An example of this type of controller is the *Air Drums* by Palmtree Instruments. These devices are two clave-like tubes that respond to changes in movement along twelve different directional planes. By shaking the tubes along the different planes (not actually striking anything), various types of MIDI messages are created and sent to external sound generators.

While not exactly alternate controllers, devices are available that will read signals from acoustic drums and translate these signals into MIDI messages. It is even possible to create input devices by placing vibration-sensing triggers on literally any surface. Thus, one can control MIDI sound generators, synthesizers, and other electronic equipment from a variety of acoustic percussion instruments.

For the first time, electronic percussion instruments have given the contemporary percussionist total control of an entire musical performance. A percussionist equipped with MIDI-compatible electronic percussion interfaced to a computer can now perform all the individual parts of a composition, edit, or correct any aspect of the performance, orchestrate the work using any tone color imaginable, and record the result in a multitrack digital environment for state-of-the-art sonic quality.

Bibliography

Grigger, David. *The MIDI Drummer.* Newbury Park, Calif.: Alexander Publications, 1987.

Vilardi, Frank, and Steve Tarshis. *Electronic Drums.* New York: Amsco Publications, 1985.

Weinberg, Norman. *The Electronic Drummer.* Cedar Grove, N.J.: Modern Drummer Publications, 1989.

Norman Weinberg

Janissary Music (Turkish Music)

Fr: *musique turque*; Ger: *Janitscharenmusik, türkische Musik*; It: *banda turca, banda dei giannizzeri*; Sp: *música turca*

During the eighteenth century, European composers imitated and mimicked the exotic sound of the Turkish military band (*mehter* or *mehterhan*) belonging to the sultan's elite troops. The *mehter* served official and military functions in the Ottoman Empire and consisted of double-reed shawms (*zurna*), trumpets (*boru*), double-headed drum (*davul* or *tabl*), kettledrums (*naqqārah* or *kös*), and cymbals (*zils*).

The term Janissary is a corruption of the Turkish *yeñi-ceri*, meaning the "new troops." In a footnote to Pietro delle Valle's *Travels in Persia* (1658), John Pinkerton, editor of *A General Collection of the Best and Most Interesting Voyages and Travels in All Parts of the World* (London, 1811, p. 90), writes,

> This word [Janissary] is constantly written thus; it should be *Yeni cheri*, as pronounced in Turkey, the meaning is "a new soldier." The Germans not having in their language the sound of *ch*, substitute an *s*, and pronounce it *Yeniseri* or *sari*, spelling it with a J, sounded by them [as] a Y with us. Retaining the German spelling, the word is consequently but improperly pronounced by us [as] *Janissary*.

The Janissaries were created as an elite corps during the reign of the Ottoman Sultan Orkhan (1326–1359). They were originally young male prisoners, who, after several years of working at menial tasks and learning Turkish, were brought back to the sultan's court as his loyal slaves, the *yeñi-ceri*.

In the late fourteenth and early fifteenth centuries, the Turks began to levy tribute upon conquered peoples in the Balkan region. Part of the forced tribute (later known as *devshirme*) consisted of Christian boys to fill the ranks of the Janissaries. Christian parents often viewed this system as a privilege, since it provided a means for their children to rise to power and influence in the Ottoman government. Freeborn Moslems were excluded to prevent family dynasties. Consequently, the court slaves (converted Christians), including the Janissaries, actually ruled the empire. The system worked well, especially during the reign of a strong sultan, e.g., Suleiman I (1520–1566). It broke down during the seventeenth century, however, when freeborn Moslem Turks entered the state service. Nepotism flourished as the vitality of the empire languished from the concessions of weak sultans more interested in the harem than the battlefield.

The Janissary corps also became so inbred that even the sultan feared their unity of purpose and military power. The corps revolted frequently under the pretext of claiming an accession gift that, on their enthronement, the sultans used to distribute to their troops. Symbolic of their revolt was the overturning of the large bronze cauldron (*kazan*) around which they assembled not only for meals but also to take counsel. The "kettles" became symbols of military pride, and their loss in battle was a disgrace. Legend records that they beat on them with wooden spoons as one would drums.

The second unsuccessful siege of Vienna by the Turks during the summer of 1683 (Suleiman I led the first siege in 1529) marked the end of Turkish domination and freed Europe from the constant fear of invasion. Throughout the eighteenth century the Turks suffered military defeats because their military system was outdated and inefficient against the newly trained armies of Europe. The wars against Russia at the end of the century finally persuaded Sultan Selim III (1789–1807) to reform the military. Reforms were begun in 1791, but, opposing modernization, the Janissaries revolted. Finally, in 1826 when Sultan Mahud II ordered the creation of a modern army, more than 15,000 revolting Janissaries were killed by loyal troops; over 20,000 were banished by royal decree, thus ending the corps.

Because the Janissary organization was thoroughly destroyed, little of its military music survives. Attempts at reconstruction, based mainly on late nineteenth-century models, may be seen and heard at the Military Museum and the Rumeli Hisar Fortress in Istanbul. Gunther Joppig (1989, p. 299) informs us that the oft-repeated illustration of a *mehter* performance from c. 1825 (e.g., see Peter Panoff, *Militärmusik*, 1938, pl. 56, and Karl Signell, 1967, pl. 3) is probably a reflection of military musical practices from the mid-nineteenth century rather than the 1820s, since the undated illustration was first printed in Arif-Pascha, *Les Anciens costumes de l'empire ottoman*, published in 1863. The nineteenth-century military reforms included adopting western musical styles that incorporated the traditional Turkish idioms. Assisting in the early stages of these musical reforms was military bandmaster Giuseppe Donizetti (1788–1856), brother of the famous composer.

Turkish military music has been described with varying degrees of accuracy by western observers since the Crusades in the twelfth century. A miniature in a 1237 manuscript (Paris, Bibliothèque nationale, MS arabe 5847, fol. 19r) depicts two long trumpets and a pair of mounted kettledrums along with battle flags and standards (Joppig, 1989, p. 297). The year 1289, however, is the traditional date given for an organized *mehter* when, according to Signell, the first *mehter* (evidently made up of only doubled-headed drums [*davul*] and kettledrums [*naqqārah*]) was sent as a present to Osman Ghazi. Accounts of Turkish military music are often sketchy and inaccurate, because most of the writers were not musicians, nor were they schooled in the cultures they were describing. The early accounts from the sixteenth and seventeenth centuries, however, are not colored by the eighteenth-century European imitations of Turkish military music. The earliest such account mentioning the size of the Turkish *mehter* is found in Benedetto Ramberto's *Libri tre delle cose de Turchi* (1539). He describes a *mehter* of two hundred mounted and walking trumpeters and drummers led by the bearer of the sultan's standard.

In 1553 Pierre Belon, in his *Les Observations de plusieurs singularitez et choses mémorables, trouvées en Grèce, Asie, Iudée, Egypte, Arabie, et autres pays estranges* (Paris), gives a rather complete account of a *mehter* comprised of two types of drums (pairs of kettledrums made of brass [*naqqārah*] and a large drum [*davul*]) and oboes (*zurna*). He seems to be the first to describe the manner of playing the *davul*: the right hand, holding a curved stick, plays accented beats while the left, holding "une vergette deliée" (a thin switch or bundle of rods), plays more rapidly. He also mentions the mounted performance of the *naqqārah*.

Michael Praetorius, in his *Syntagma musicum: De organographia* (1619), was not impressed by what he described as the noisy and shabby military music of the Turks. Most accounts echo this view for the next two hundred years:

> Henry Blount (1636): a mounted band of about a dozen musicians who "noise along" playing "brass dishes" (*zils*), "ugly" drums, and wind instruments; d'Arvieux (c. 1660s [printed 1735]): a warlike mounted band of fifty-one musicians (15 large drums, 15 shawms, 15 trumpets, 3 pairs of kettledrums, and 3 pairs of cymbals); G.B. Donado (1668): a loud military band of thirty-six who play on drums, kettledrums, and various-sized shawms; Luigi Marsigli (c. 1660s [printed 1732]): an inventory of military instruments and an accompanying illustration of a mounted Turkish military band (7 *zurna*, 7 *davul*, 2 *naqqārah*, 5 *boru*, and 2

zils, reproduced in Henry George Farmer's translation of Ewilyā Chelebī (*Turkish Instruments of Music in the Seventeenth Century*); John Covel (1670–1679): loud trumpets, shawms, large drums beaten on both ends, pairs of little kettledrums, and cymbals "about a foot wide," and a mounted band he saw in 1675 in Adrianople of thirty-four musicians (12 shawms, 12 large drums, 6 trumpets, and 4 pairs of cymbals); Daniel Speer (1683): the sound of the Turkish instruments "should not be called music"; Aaron Hill (1709): "warlike thunder" and a "wild, extravagant, and artless fancy"; Thomas Shaw (c. 1720s [printed 1758]): "a shrill and jarring, but martial sound"; Jean-Antoine Guer (1747): the loud, piercing sound of a mounted band (9 drums, 9 shawms, 7 trumpets, and 4 pairs of cymbals); Carsten Niebuhr (1772): "an unpleasant, jarring noise"; and Giambatista Toderini (1787): a rather complete listing of instruments.

While these accounts cover a wide span of time, they are consistent with regard to instrument types and general musical style.

As the political influence of the Ottoman Empire diminished after the second unsuccessful siege of Vienna in 1683, the image of the Turk in the eighteenth century changed for Europeans. No longer a political or military threat, the Turks became symbols of the exotic East and the Enlightenment. Some authors have described a veritable "Turkomania" sweeping from the East, through Poland and Russia, across Austria and Prussia, to France, Italy, and finally to England. Turkish candy, coffee, and costumes were much in vogue, especially in Vienna. "Turkish music" (implying the European imitation of the *mehter*) "invaded" opera houses and European military bands. Yet, even as early as 1670 at the court of Louis XIV, the exotic Turkish elements in the Mamamouchi scene of Molière's *Le Bourgeois gentilhomme* (with incidental music by Jean-Baptiste Lully) confirm a sophisticated knowledge of the Turkish culture by both poet and musician.

The accounts of the adoption of certain elements of the *mehter* into European music found in encyclopedias and histories of military music seem to be based on the pioneering work of Henry George Farmer. Yet, he seems to draw heavily on the first major study of military music, Jean-Georges Kastner's *Manuel général de musique militaire* (1848). Kastner's discussion of the adoption of Turkish musical elements in the eighteenth century (pp. 129–130) derives from an article in J.A. Hiller's 1770 music periodical *Musikalische Nachrichten und Anmerkungen*. This account of music in Russia by Jacob von Stählin seems to be the earliest document that refers specifically to European imitations of the *mehter*. Stählin states that he had heard a genuine Turkish military band given to Augustus II [reigned as king of Poland 1697–1733] and the imitation of "Turkish music" at the Russian court of Empress Anna [reigned 1730–1740] at the "occasion of the Turkish peace celebration of 1739." He then describes in some detail the "Janissary music" during the reign of Empress Elizabeth (1741–1762). He mentions a chamber musician and violinist Schnurpfeil who had been with the imperial Russian embassy in Constantinople. This musician organized, probably in the 1740s, a "complete choir of 'Turkish music' with twelve to fifteen well-rehearsed musicians." In addition to five or six Turkish shawms (*zurna*), a pair of kettledrums, the large double-headed drum (*davul*), beaten on the upper head with a large stick, the lower with a twig cluster, two pairs of cymbals, he mentions a "shrill transverse fife" and two triangles "which they beat with an iron rod, causing the dancing rings of steel on the base of the triangle to produce a multiplicity of sounds." It is indeed probable that the Russian adaptations of Turkish music blended the sounds of the *mehter* with traditional Turkish art music instruments (e.g., small bell trees and tambourines) to make a more palatable sound for indoor entertainments (Stählin often had his ensemble, small by Turkish standards, perform indoors at banquets).

Another oft-quoted writer on eighteenth-century manners and culture is C.F.D. Schubart. Writing in the early 1780s he mentions the bands of Turkish musicians maintained by Frederick the Great in Berlin and Maria Theresa in Vienna. Christoph Willibald Gluck (1714–1787) used some of these musicians to augment the orchestra for his "Turkish" operas of the 1760s performed in Vienna (see below). Schubart dates the introduction of the "Turkish music" in German military regiments to the 1740s and seems to be able to distinguish between the original and the European imitations. He seems unclear, though, when he includes among the Turkish instruments the triangle, tambourine, and "Glockenspiese." The inclusion of the triangle, an instrument never mentioned in the accounts of the *mehter*, probably indicates that Schubart was describing the European imitation.

The tambourine and the "Glockenspiese" are also not discussed in accounts of Turkish military music, but they do exist in the art music tradition. Indeed, the "Glockenspiese" seems to be a form of the Turkish crescent or *Schellenbaum* (bell tree) more often associated with nineteenth-century European military bands. Chelebī, writing in the mid-seventeenth century, mentions a small crescent-shaped, jingling stick-rattle with bells, the *cewhan*, and the tambourine (*daf*). As the name Janissary is a corruption of the Turkish *yeñi-ceri*, so is the English *Jingling Johnnie* a corruption of *cewhan*, or as it is sometimes transliterated, *chaghāna*. The name "Turkish crescent" is also used in English. The French, however, call it the *châpeau chinois* or *pavillon chinois*, reflecting its foreign, exotic nature, making no attempt to associate the instrument with Turkey but rather with the East.

The *cewhan* and *daf* are not specifically associated with the *mehter*. Confusion among European writers stems perhaps from the military standards with horsetails (*tug*) that often preceded the *mehter*. The crescent that was hung with small bells atop a pole seems to be a European adaptation of several Turkish elements, melded together to form a conducting stick or baton coupled with an exotic, near-eastern shape and sound. Few, if any, examples of Turkish crescents made before the early nineteenth century exist, and all extant instruments are of European origin.

Franz Joseph Sulzer's book, *Geschichte des transalpinischen Daciens* (1781–1782), gives the most detailed account of both "Turkish music" and the *mehter*. He describes performance practices in detail and discusses accurately the various instruments used in each. A German-Turkish work with a piccolo, horns, bassoons, oboes, strings, and percussion (field drum, bass drum, cymbals, and tambourine) is compared to the noisy Turkish *mehter* of twenty large drums and a like number of shawms with nine or ten untuned trumpets.

Although "Turkish music" and other exoticisms were most popular in European art music during the second half of the eighteenth century, French operatic works beginning with Lully (1633–1687) display many imported charms. Turkish scenes are also found in operas by André Campra (1670–1774) and Jean-Philippe Rameau (1683–1764). Gluck's *Le Cadi dupé* (1761) and *La Rencontre imprévue* (1764) are typical of a popular genre of exotic operas emerging in the third quarter of the eighteenth century. Franz Joseph Haydn explored the Turkish setting in his *L'incontro improvviso* (1775), using cymbals, triangle, and tambourine. Wolfgang Amadeus Mozart's *Die Entführung aus dem Serail* (1782) is still in the repertory of major opera companies throughout the world. Both his Violin Concerto in A Major, K. 219, and Piano Sonata in A Major, K. 331, exhibit elements of the "Turkish" style. Selected studies on Mozart's exotic style are listed in the bibliography. Ludwig van Beethoven effectively uses "Turkish music" in his incidental music to *The Ruins of Athens*, Op. 113 (1812), *Wellington's Victory*, Op. 91 (1813), and in the last movement of Symphony No. 9, Op. 125 (1824). The use of "Turkish music" in battle symphonies was very popular several decades before Beethoven's work. Compositions by Georg Druschetzky (1745–1819) and Franz Christoph Neubauer (c. 1760–1795) date from the 1780s and 1790s. Also very fashionable were works by Muzio Clementi (1752–1832) and Daniel Steibelt (1765–1823) for piano solo with added percussion instruments. So well did the fad catch on that many continental pianos built in the early nineteenth century were fitted with attachments to make realistic battle sounds, the so-called *Janissary stops*.

Bibliography

Altar, Cevad Memduh. "Wolfgang Amadeus Mozart im Lichte osmanisch-österreichischer Beziehungen." *Revue belge de musicologie* 10 (1956): 138–148.

Arbatsky, Yury. *Beating the Tupan in the Central Balkans*. Chicago: Newberry Library, 1953.

Arvieux, Laurent d'. *Mémoires du chevalier d'Arvieux*. Vol. 4, edited by L. B. Labat. Paris: C. J. B. Delespine, 1735.

Baines, Anthony. *European and American Musical Instruments*. New York: Viking Press, 1966.

Belon, Pierre. *Les Observations de plusieurs, singularitez et choses mémorables, trouvées en Grèce, Asie, Iudée, Egypte, Arabie, et autres pays estranges*. Paris: G. Corrozet, 1553.

Bessaraboff, Nicholas. *Ancient European Musical Instruments*. Cambridge: Harvard University Press, 1941.

Blades, James. *Percussion Instruments and Their History*. New York: Praeger, 1970.

Blount, Henry. *A Voyage into the Levant*. London: J[ohn] L[egate] for Andrew Crooke, 1636. Reprint, Amsterdam: Theatrum Orbis Terrarum, 1977.

Brenet, Michel [Marie Bobillier]. *La Musique militaire*. Paris: Henri Laurens, 1917.

Chelebī, Ewilyā. *Turkish Instruments of Music in the Seventeenth Century*. Translated and edited with notes by Henry George Farmer. Glasgow: Civic Press, 1937.

Covel, John. "Diary, 1670–1679." In *Early Voyages and Travels in the Levant*, edited by James Theodore Bent. London: Hakluyt Society, 1893.

Donado, Giovanni Battista. *Della litteratura de' turchi*. Venice: Andrea Polletti, 1688.

Farmer, Henry George. *Handel's Kettledrums and Other Papers on Military Music*. London: Hinrichsen, 1950.

———. "Janitscharenmusik." In *Die Musik in Geschichte und Gegenwart*, edited by Friedrich Blume. Vol. 6, cols. 1706–1709. Kassel: Bärenreiter, 1957.

———. *Military Music*. New York: Chanticleer Press, 1950.

———. "Oriental Influences on Occidental Military Music." *Islamic Culture* 15 (1941): 235–242.

———. *The Rise and Development of Military Music*. London: W. Reeves, 1912. Reprint, Freeport, N.Y.: Books for Libraries Press, 1970.

Farmer, Henry George, and James Blades. "Janissary Music." In *The New Grove Dictionary of Music and Musicians*. Vol. 9, pp. 496–498. London: Macmillan, 1980.

Feldman, W. "Mehter." In *Encyclopedia of Islam*, edited by C.E. Bosworth, E. van Donzel, W.P. Heinrichs, and Ch. Pettat. Vol. 6, cols. 10007–10009. New ed. Leiden: E. J. Brill, 1991.

Guer, Jean-Antoine. *Moeurs et usages des Turcs*. 2 vols. Paris: Cousetelier, 1746–1747.

Hill, Aaron. *A Full and Just Account of the Present State of the Ottoman in All Its Branches with the Government, and Policy, Religion, Customs, and Way of Living of the Turks*. London: n.p., 1709.

Hunt, C. L. "Janissaries." In *Encyclopedia of Islam*, edited by M. Th. Houtsma, A.J. Wensinck, T. W. Arnold, W. Heffening, and E. Levi-Provençal, Vol. 4, pp. 572–575. Leiden: E. J. Brill, 1927. Reprint, Leiden: E. J. Brill, 1987.

Joppig, Gunther. "Alla turca: Orientalismen in der europäischen Kunstmusik vom 17. bis 19. Jahrhundert." In *Europa und der*

Orient, 800–1900, edited by Gereon Sievernich and Hendrik Budde, 295–304. Berlin: Bertelsmann Lexikon Verlag, 1989.

Kappey, Jacob A. *Military Music: A History of Wind-Instrumental Bands*. London: Boosey & Co., 1894.

Kastner, Jean-Georges. *Manuel général de musique militaire à l'usage des armées françaises*. Paris: Didot Frères, 1848.

Koch, Heinrich Christoph. "Janitscharenmusik." In *Musikalisches Lexikon*. Frankfurt am Main: A. Hermann dem Jungern, 1802. Reprint, Hildesheim: G. Olms, 1985.

Mahling, Christoph Helmut. "Die Gestalt des Osmin in Mozarts *Entführung*." *Archiv für Musikwissenschaft* 30 (1973): 96–108.

Marsigli, Luigi Ferdinando. *Stato militare dell' imperio ottomano*. 2 vols. The Hague: D. Grosse & J. Neaulme, 1732.

Meyer, Eve R. "Turquerie and Eighteenth-Century Music." *Eighteenth-Century Studies* 7 (1974): 474–488.

Niebuhr, Carsten. *Reisebeschreibung nach Arabien und andern umliegenden Ländern*. Copenhagen: N. Moeller, 1772; Travels through Arabia and Other Countries in the East. Vol. 1. Translated by Robert Heron. Edinburgh: R. Morison & Son, 1792.

Palmer, J.A.B. "The Origin of the Janissaries." *Bulletin of the John Ryland Library* 35 (1953): 448–481.

Panoff, Peter. "Das musikalische Erbe der Janitscharen." *Atlantis* 11 (1938): 634.

———. *Militärmusik in Geschichte und Gegenwart*. Berlin: Karl Siegismund, 1938.

Pirker, Michael. "Bilddokumente zum Einfluss der Janitscharenmusik auf die österreichische Militärmusik." Ph.D. Diss., University of Vienna, 1986.

———. "Die türkische Musik und Mozarts *Entführung aus dem Serial*." In *Die Klangwelt Mozarts*, edited by Gerhard Stradner, 133–148. Vienna: Kunsthistorisches Museum [1991].

Praetorius, Michael. *Syntagma musicum*. Vol. 2, *De organographia*. Wolfenbüttel: Elias Holwein, 1619. Reprint, Kassel: Bärenreiter, 1929.

Obelkevich, Mary Rowen. "Turkish Affect in the Land of the Sun King." *Musical Quarterly* 63 (1977): 367–389.

Ramberto, Benedetto. *Libri tre delle cose de Turchi. Nel primo si descrive il viaggio da Venetia a Constantinopoli*. Venice: In Casa de' Figliuoli di Aldo, 1539.

Rycaut, Paul. *The History of the Present State of the Ottoman Empire*. 4th ed. London: J. Starkey, 1675.

Sachs, Curt. *The History of Musical Instruments*. New York: Norton, 1940.

Schubart, Christian Friedrich Daniel. *Ideen zu einer Ästhetik der Tonkunst*. Vienna: J. V. Degan, 1806.

Shaw, Thomas. *Travels or Observations Relating to Several Parts of Barbary and the Levant*. Oxford: At the Theater, 1758.

Signell, Karl. "Mozart and the Mehter." *Consort*, no. 24 (1967): 310–322.

Speer, Daniel. *Türckischer Vagant; oder, Umschweiffend-türckischer Handelsmann*. N.p., 1683.

Stählin, Jacob von. "Nachricht von der Musik in Rußland." *Musikalische Nachrichten und Anmerkungen*, edited by J. A. Hiller, nos. 18–30 (April 30–July 23, 1770): 135–232.

Sulzer, Franz Joseph. *Geschichte des transalpinischen Daciens, das ist der Walachey, Moldau, und Bessarabiens*. 3 vols. Vienna: Rudolph Graffer, 1781–1782.

Szabolczi, Bence. "Exoticisms in Mozart." *Music and Letters* 37 (1956): 323–332.

Toderini, Giambatista. *Letteratura turchesca*. Venice: G. Storti, 1787.

Valle, Pietro delle. *Travels in Persia* (1658). In *A General Collection of the Best and Most Interesting Voyages and Travels in All Parts of the World*, edited by John Pinkerton. Vol. 11, p. 90. London: Longmann, Hurst, Rees, Orme, & Brown, 1811.

Yönetken, Halil Bedi. "Mozart und die türkische Musik." In *Internationale Konferenz über das Leben und Werke W. A. Mozarts*, edited by Pavel Eckstein, 118–120. Prague: Verband Tschechoslowakischer Komponisten, 1958.

Harrison Powley

The Kettledrum

Fr: *timbale(s)*; Ger: *Pauken*; It: *timpano(i)*; Sp: *timbals, atabul*

Kettledrums (often called *timpani*, from the Italian, and played in pairs) are the most important percussion instruments of the orchestra. They are the only member of the drum family in western art music that can produce notes of definite pitch and thus take part in the harmonic fabric of the music. Each drum in the orchestra is tuned to a given note according to the directions in the musical score. During the performance of a work their pitches can be changed as required by tightening or slackening the drumhead, either by means of screws placed equidistantly around its circumference or by other mechanical means such as a lever or pedal.

The kettledrum consists of a large hemispherical shell (the resonating chamber) usually of copper (and more recently, fiberglass), across the open top of which is stretched a head, ordinarily of calfskin or plastic, mounted (lapped) on a hoop that is secured by an overriding metal ring, or counterhoop, through which pass threaded screws or rods that allow the skin's tension to be varied. Kettledrums are available in standard sizes from 20 to 32 inches in diameter, with an approximate pitch range from high b-flat to low D. Typically, a set of four instruments will be found in the modern orchestra.

Kettledrums (as opposed to the small-sized nakers) came to western Europe in the fifteenth century as cavalry instruments; they were played on horseback by Muslims, Ottoman Turks, and Mongols. In 1457 a magnificently equipped embassy representing King Ladislas V of Hungary left Prague for Paris to seek the hand of the French king's daughter in marriage. In the huge procession of over 500 people, 700 horses, and 26 baggage-wagons were mounted drums; the entry into France created a sensation, one eyewitness observing that such instruments on horseback, like large cauldrons, had never been seen before. To make the impression even more spectacular, the horses bearing these drums pranced to their rhythm. It was mainly via the courts in German-speaking lands that these large, mounted kettledrums spread throughout Europe (see Fig. 1). Following eastern custom, they were paired with the trumpet and were soon appropriated as exclusive insignia of rank at court and an essential element in image-building so important to the elite. Taking their cue again from the east, the nobility made possessing timpani an exclusive right, jealously restricted.

During the fifteenth and sixteenth centuries, therefore, the employment of both trumpeters and kettledrummers was restricted to emperors, kings, electors, dukes,

Fig. 1. Michael Praetorius, *Syntagma Musicum*, II, Plate XXIII (*De Organographia*) (Wolfenbüttel, 1615).

princes, counts, lords, and others of high rank, as well as to a few imperial cities granted the right by charter to employ these musicians. Along with trumpeters, the timpanist belonged to an exclusive guild, a step achieved only after up to seven years of apprenticeship. Taking an oath to keep their skilled art secret, the members all held the rank of officers, could wear the ostrich feathers associated with nobility in their hats, and were furnished with both horses and a groom. They were forbidden from associating with other instrumentalists, who were considered mere household employees of inferior rank.

In the seventeenth century kettledrums found their way indoors, joining the orchestra along with the trumpets, horns, and oboes. Improvisation and conspicuous display associated with outdoor parades and entertainments gave way to more formalized playing, ultimately from written music. The true introduction of timpani took place around 1670 by way of an orchestral score into the court orchestral and operatic ensembles, as well as in large liturgical pieces.

For several centuries, construction of the kettledrum remained virtually unchanged except for the gradual introduction of instruments of larger diameter (see Fig. 2). While on some early examples the skins were affixed by means of rope tensioning, the requirements of maintaining constant tension on these large heads, plus the growing use of precise notes in addition to the traditional rhythmic function, brought about a tuning system based upon screws. These were distributed around the drum's rim and attached to a hoop, or ring, which bore down upon the skin, thus controlling the skin's tension (see Fig. 3). At first the tension was adjusted by means of a dozen or so bolts or screws threaded into receptacles fastened to the sides of the drum, turned by means of a key that fitted over the square end of each bolt. About 1790 the T-handle was introduced to facilitate faster changes of pitch, used to this day on hand-tuned kettledrums.

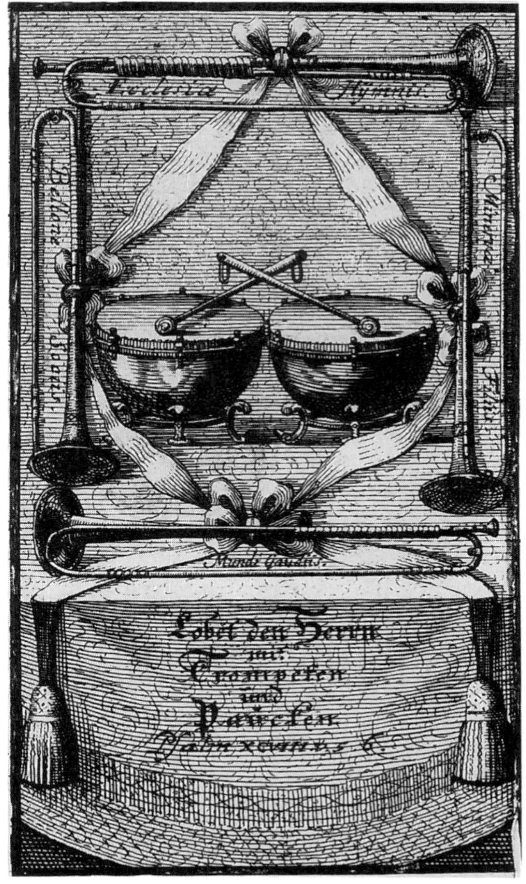

Fig. 2. Friedrich Friese, *Ceremoniel und Privilegia derer Trompeter und Pauker.* Frontispiece (Dresden, 1650).

During the first half of the nineteenth century a number of composers of both orchestral and operatic music variously wrote for three or four drums or required rapid changes of pitch that, with only hand-tuned drums available, demanded extra instruments pretuned to the additional notes. As a result, radical alterations took place in both the use and construction of the timpani. Composers, teachers, and performers alike began calling for the addition of one or two drums to the orchestra, and technicians began speculating on just how to facilitate more rapid tuning.

Indeed, this period was an era of vitality, innovation, and change in the design and manufacture of musical instruments

Fig. 3. Timpani (German, eighteenth century). Presented by the Butchers' Guild to the Kremnitz Lutheran Church on successive Easter Sundays, 1736 and 1737. Magyar Nemzeti Museum, Budapest (Inv. No. 1916.56a and b).

generally, corresponding somewhat belatedly to the Industrial Revolution. Numerous inventors, working hand in hand with mechanics and metalworkers, developed various means for rapidly changing the pitch of a kettledrum, in so doing both speeding up and simplifying the tuning so that only a single tension screw, the kettle itself, or a foot pedal had to be manipulated. Some of these so-called *machine drums* had their tuning mechanisms on the exterior, like an armature, while others contained the device inside the kettle. All of these improvements were handmade in unique examples or small quantities in what might be called a cottage industry. The most successful of these machine drums were tuned either with a single master screw or lever, by rotating the kettle itself, or by using the foot to manipulate a gear wheel or pedal. Other approaches, soon abandoned, included tuning by means of a cable and turnbuckle or via concentric rings that pressed up from underneath the head.

The first major step that allowed for rapid tuning changes on the timpani was taken in 1812, when Gerhard Cramer, the Königliche Hofpauker (Royal Court Timpanist) in the Munich court orchestra (formerly quartered at Mannheim) invented the first rapid tuning device (see Fig. 4). Taking advantage of the mechanical technology, which flourished in that enlightened center, such as automata, clocks, stage machinery, and the like, as well as the availability of cast iron, Cramer worked in the electoral metalworking shop with the court armorer and locksmith on the design and fabrication of his machine drums. According to contemporary references, tuning was accomplished "in a flash," and the new timpani "stood to ordinary drums as the pedal harp to the diatonic model" ("Neue Erfindung," 1812).

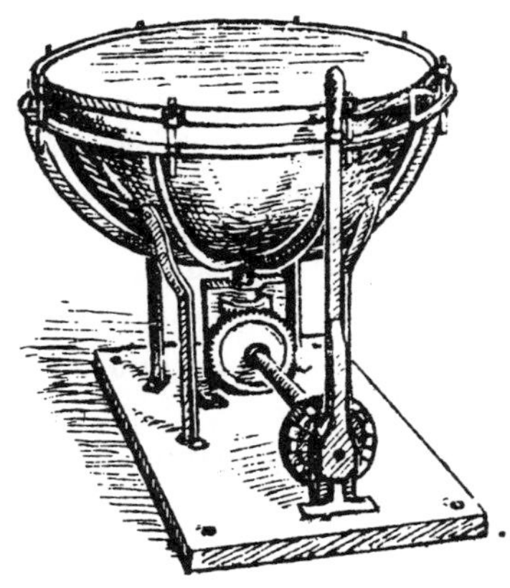

Fig. 4. Drawing of a machine drum, probably that of Gerhard Cramer (Munich, 1812).

The kettle itself was firmly attached to a wooden base by means of metal struts bolted to the device. The metal hoop, or rim, was equipped with tuning screws that, in turn, were affixed to a parallel ring immediately below. This ring was supported by an armature circling the bowl and terminating at a central screw. Tuning was accomplished by moving a vertical lever operating a horizontal axle, which turned a crown gear, thus raising or lowering the central screw and with it the attached armature and hoop around which the drum's skin was lapped. With its massive gear mechanism and long lever, Cramer's instrument represented a rather primitive approach to the problem of rapid tuning, an almost mechanical overkill, but it was a quantum leap from the primitive hand screws. For whatever reason, the inventor sold his two sets of kettledrums to Georg Joseph Vogler (1749–1814), a theorist, organist, and composer. Vogler had them shipped to Darmstadt for the court orchestra of Archduke Ludwig; they have since vanished without a trace.

The Amsterdam musician-inventor Johann Stumpff introduced a rotating type of machine drum around 1815 (patented in 1821) (see Fig. 5). In his novel system, a large screw attached perpendicularly to a wooden base penetrated the bottom of the kettle through a large nut. Inside, it was attached to an internal armature of four iron struts terminating at a metal ring just below the drum head. When the kettle was rotated, the whole instrument raised or lowered itself on the central screw (much like a desk chair), thereby altering the pressure on the hoop and tension of the skin. In the words of Jean-Georges Kastner, composer, author, and fellow timpanist, the pitch of Stumpff's drums could be accomplished "in less than a second" (?1845).

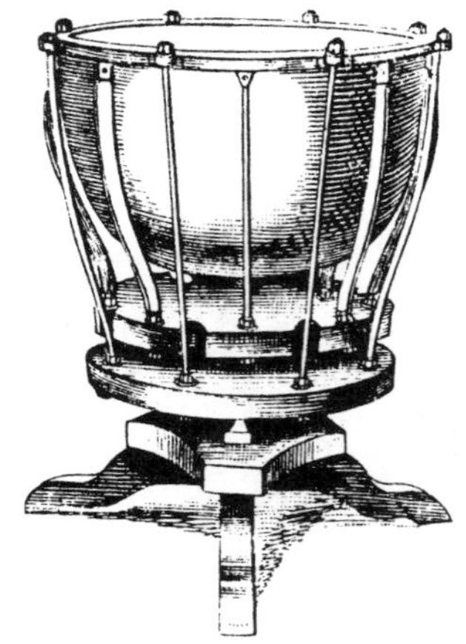

Fig. 5. Rotating machine drum of the Stumpff type.

The main disadvantages of Stumpff's system were that both hands of the player had to be used to turn the drum, thus interrupting the performance and requiring that both sticks be set aside temporarily; and since rotation of the entire drum altered the beating spot, the best points on the skin were not necessarily in front of the player. However, because they were cheap to manufacture, lightweight, and easily transported, Stumpff's timpani were ideal for the city musician who had to perform in different locations. Before being superseded by other models, they were popular in the Netherlands and Germany; the timpanist-inventor Ernst Pfundt (1806–1871) saw a pair in Karlsruhe in 1844.

Vienna reflected the same kind of environment as Munich, a sophisticated court that depended upon a high degree of technical skill on the part of artisans of all sorts. A tuning mechanism was first mentioned in 1831 by the timpanist Georg Hudler, who stated that he had invented a machine drum. The prototype may well have been constructed by his father, the well-known timpanist of the Viennese court, Anton Hudler. Very little is known about the precise construction of this instrument. According to its inventor, adjusting all tension screws simultaneously was achieved "by a single motion" up or down. Other sources confirm that Hudler "invented" a workable arrangement to turn the screws "with one motion." However, the instruments were apparently never mass-produced, and after local use were soon forgotten.

Johann Kaspar Einbigler of Frankfurt invented an important prototype mechanism for rapid tuning in 1836 and supervised the manufacture by a Leipzig artisan named Glanert as well (see Fig. 6). Einbigler suspended the bowl from its upper portion by means of metal struts terminating in short iron legs below. The hoop over which the skin was lapped was attached to eight vertical supporting rods functioning in addition as individual tuning screws, all of which terminated at a thin, weblike base plate directly below the kettle. Action by a threaded, vertical tuning crank pressing against a pivoted lever, or rocker arm, below the plate raised or lowered the entire base assembly (rods and hoop), thus lessening or increasing the skin's tension.

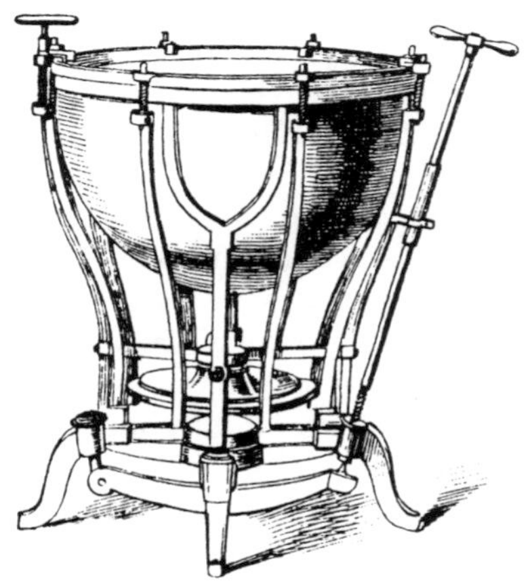

Fig. 6. Einbigler type of machine drum.

The tone of Einbigler's drums was rounder and fuller than previous models, owing to the fact that the kettles were both suspended and free of any internal mechanisms, thus able to vibrate freely without any impediment to the sound waves. Moreover, the use of a threaded screw acting upon a rocker arm—transmitting horizontal cranking motion into vertical lift—represented a far more efficient solution to the problem of rapid tuning than Cramer's lever and gears, for example. Einbigler's instruments were so impressive that several composers, including Felix Mendelssohn, signed a joint statement in the *Allgemeine musikalische Zeitung* (1836) describing them to the musical community at large. Indeed, contemporaries described the drums' operation variously as "amazing" and offering "a thousand advantages never dreamed of before" (Gustav Schilling, 1835). Pfundt reported having seen them in opera houses in Munich, Frankfurt, Paris, and Cologne.

In December 1837 a British patent was issued to Cornelius Ward of London, a maker of flutes, bassoons, and drums, for his invention of two types of unique tuning mechanisms (see Fig. 7). In the first, the head was tensioned by means of an endless cord or wire cable passing over pulleys from the exterior to the kettle's inside, where it passed through pairs of pulleys attached to two threaded T-bars. These bars approached or receded from each other by means of a long, horizontal double turnbuckle, with right- and left-handed threads at each end, respectively. This turnbuckle formed a rod running through the interior of the drum and terminating at one end in a wooden handle outside the kettle. When the timpanist turned this handle to the right or left, the cable was pulled tighter or loosened as the two T-bars moved closer together or farther apart. The pitch was thus raised or lowered accordingly. There were two principal disadvantages to this first design of Ward's (that owed more to naval hardware than to scientific instrument-building). The lack of tensioning screws made it impossible to compensate for uneven pressure on, or thickness of, the skin, because tension on the cable itself was least at the point farthest away from the turnbuckle. In addition, tuning changes had to be made by turning the small handle with the player's wrist, a weak spot in human anatomy. When the skin was under high tension, the torque made twisting the rod very difficult. However, in spite of these drawbacks, Ward's early machine drums continued to be manufactured, principally by George Potter in Aldershot, in various versions until the late nineteenth century.

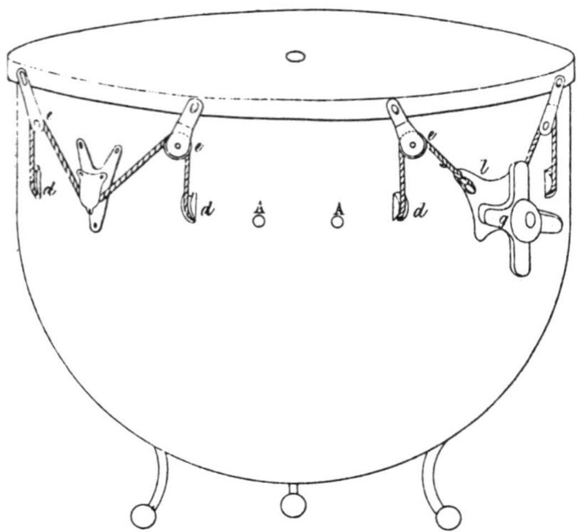

Fig. 7. First turnbuckle-type machine drum invented by Cornelius Ward (1837).

Ward's second and far superior device employed a mechanism typical of the locksmith's art. A number of levers was connected to the hoop over which the head was lapped. These levers were divided into two pairs, one of which was bent to the right and the other to the left. The lower ends of each pair were engaged in a movable horizontal bar and each overlapped the other at their movable ends. They were racked (toothed), with one set pointing upward and the other downward. By turning a notched pinion inserted between these two racks, or bars, a corresponding motion was given to each set of levers connected to the rim, thus tightening or relaxing the skin according to which direction the pinion's handle was turned. Ward's new machine drums were tried out in the 1836–1837 season at Covent Garden and in the Philharmonic concerts and found immediate acceptance in several other English and continental orchestras as well. Indeed, Richard Wagner thought that timpani from London (Ward's?) were the best ones being made and noted especially the superiority of British materials and metalworking (Wagner, 1910).

The next important tuning mechanism was invented by August Knocke, a Munich gunsmith, around 1840 (see Fig. 8). He conceived of a rather elaborate system of gears allowing the timpanist to alter the pitch of his drums. Vertical rods attached to the counterhoop terminated in a large wheel placed directly beneath the kettle. At the center of this supporting disc was a threaded hole through which ran a screw. This in turn was connected below to a gear meshing with a series of cogwheels operated by a small control wheel near the base of the drum. When rotated by the player's feet, the horizontal motion was translated into a vertical thrust that either raised or lowered the wheel with its rods connected to the rim, thus altering the tension of the head. A hand crank also interlocked with the series of gears for fine-tuning. Knocke's device offered for the first time a tuning mechanism that left the player's hands completely free for performing while changing the pitch of his instruments. However, the gear-train was awkward and the foot device clumsy and hard to move; Pfundt, Mendelssohn's favorite timpanist, reports in his little book on kettledrums, of having had difficulty in rotating the device with his foot. Despite this, Knocke's drums, manufactured by the firm J. Kaltenecker, were used in a number of German orchestras, such as those at the Munich and Berlin operas. One of the two pairs in Munich was used until 1963 by the Bavarian State Opera for rehearsals.

In 1842 Carlo Antonio Boracchi, timpanist of the Royal Opera Orchestra in Milan (La Scala), authored an instruction manual for his instrument describing his own invention of a machine drum on which he had been working for some fourteen years (see Fig. 9). Consisting of an armature fitting over a conventional hand-tuned drum, eight vertical rods were attached to the skin's counterhoop, their lower ends bolted to the projecting arms of a base plate underneath the instrument. This, in turn, moved up and down on a large, threaded central screw, to the bottom of which was attached a long, horizontal tuning lever jutting out just above the floor. When moved to the right or left, this lever turned the screw, raising or lowering the entire base plate and assembly of struts, and thus altering the tension of the head.

Fig. 8. Foot-activated machine drum by August Knocke, Deutsches Museum (Munich, c. 1840) (Inv. No. 79220).

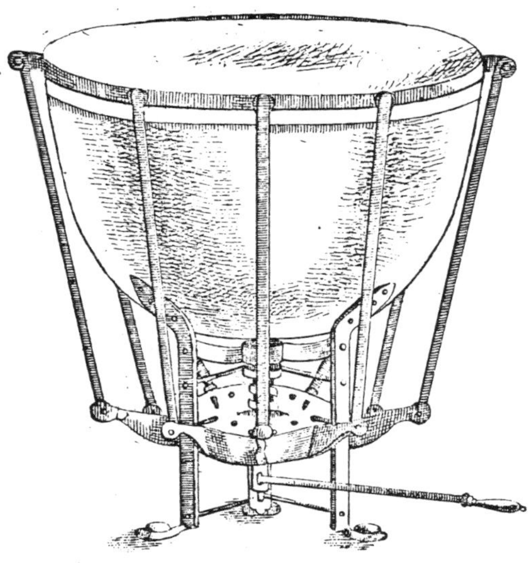

Fig. 9. Carlo Boracchi, *Manuale pel Timpanista*, Plate V (Milan, 1842)

Boracchi's instrument had several drawbacks, judging by the illustration provided in the author's timpani manual: the performer had either to bend way down in order to move the tuning lever by hand or push it from side to side with his foot. The supporting metal tripod bolted to the kettle not only limited the horizontal movement of the tuning lever but restricted the drum's free vibration as well, thus adversely affecting its tone quality. As far as is known, aside from a pair of prototype models, Boracchi's kettledrums were never manufactured; and his invention could be ignored except for the tantalizing possibility that Verdi might have been familiar with it through Pietro Pieranzovini, his favorite timpanist and Boracchi's successor in the La Scala Orchestra. Quite likely, the drums were used by them during their tenures.

Ernst Pfundt, Germany's most famous timpanist and member of the Leipzig Gewandhaus Orchestra, not only wrote one of the first tutorials for the instrument but was an inventor as well. He had obtained firsthand knowledge of machine drums from viewing and trying out various models in Paris, London, Vienna, Berlin, Munich, and Prague. By the 1840s he was using three Einbigler timpani in his own orchestra, so it was only natural that, in the process of developing his own attempts to advance the state of the art, he sought out the mechanic and artisan Glanert, who was turning out these instruments. Pfundt made suggestions for improving the tuning mechanism that were incorporated into the manufacturing process; but what exactly these changes were can only be surmised from examining the technological improvements that took place during the next step in the machine drum's evolution: the so-called Pfundt/Hoffmann model.

Friedrich Hentschel, celebrated timpanist of the Royal Opera Orchestra in Berlin, made further improvements on the pair of Einbigler/Pfundt drums he used between 1853 and the 1880s. Manufactured in Leipzig by an engineer named Carl Hoffmann, the kettles were made larger and thicker and the entire iron assembly much heavier. To support the instrument better, the framework, in the form of forked braces, was attached at the very rim of the bowl rather than on its side. Reinforced crosspieces were added below, connecting opposite supports. The thin, perforated base plate was replaced by a massive disk. In place of a small pin projecting from the bottom of this plate (to which the pivoting lever was connected), a thick, vertical axle pierced the disk and connected the rocker arm.

Just how much Pfundt and Hentschel each contributed to the overall design of the improved machine drum remains a matter of some speculation; both men made claims of their own, and since Pfundt wrote that he had "improved" Einbigler's model, it is probably fair to say that he conceived certain modifications (such as a stronger supporting mechanism) that were realized and no doubt refined by Glanert. Hentschel, too, claimed to have "designed" an improved version of this drum (manufactured by Hoffmann), but again, just what these alterations were is impossible to tell; and Hentschel must surely have to share credit with his engineer/maker as well.

Be this as it may, the Pfundt/Hoffmann design and its refinements made by their successors represented important innovations in a traditional design that solved the dual problems of inertia and lack of speed found in the earlier screw and gear-type mechanisms. The contribution was a single, threaded crank acting upon a pivoted lever, or rocker arm, that controlled the armature to which the tuning rods were attached. More significant was the fact that this simple device multiplied the force transmitted to the base plate by the crank, making for a far more efficient and powerful mechanism. Significantly, both Mendelssohn and Robert Schumann (distantly related by marriage to Pfundt) wrote parts requiring rapid pitch changes and made use, albeit sparingly, of three drums. And the Pfundt/Hoffmann model was subsequently acquired by orchestras in many of the major European cities; the 80th pair was honored at the Dresden Trade Show in 1875.

A machine drum with an interior tuning device was invented and manufactured by Louis Jena in Reudnitz (a Leipzig suburb) beginning in 1877 (see Fig. 10). The kettle itself was suspended in a semicircular, curved, cast-iron frame that, in turn, was mounted on a large central shaft with a screw thread attached to the metal base. Thus, for the first time, a drum could be raised or lowered much like a modern desk chair and tilted as well to suit the performer. Conventional tuning bolts were provided. The inner mechanism consisted of two levers working against each other on which wedges were fastened, all activated by a horizontal screw with an exterior handle. By means, then, of lever, wedge, and screw, a ring just inside the top of the kettle was pushed up against the skin to alter the tensions and, hence, the pitch. The timpani were portable, weighing about 130 pounds per pair. Jena's important contribution was the notion of a tuning mechanism that could be added to an existing hand-tuned drum. The Leipzig manufacturer Glanert, who also made Stumpff rotary timpani on order, refitted old kettles with Jena's new device.

Heinrich Max Puschmann, a mechanical engineer from Chemnitz, patented a novel type of machine drum in 1880 (see Fig. 11). Following other German models, the kettle was supported by external rods, like an armature, connected to a hollow base assembly. The head or counterhoop was attached to six equidistantly placed screw-threaded vertical rods that passed through the top of the base and terminated in small gear wheels. These, in turn, meshed with a similar gear at the end of an external tuning rod, or lever. By turning the handle, the smaller gears were activated, thus turning the large gear wheel and pulling down or pushing up the external supporting rods and hoop. In spite of the fact that the torque on this device was considerable, making cranking hard, Puschmann's timpani were manufactured for a decade or more, as attested to by his firm's catalogs.

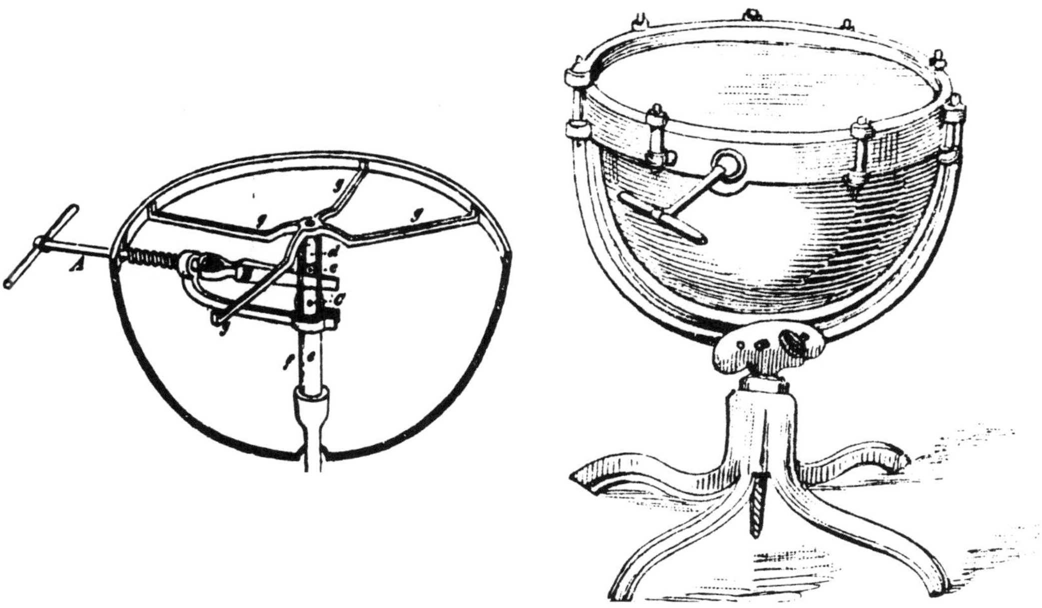

Fig. 10 a and b. Jena machine drum.

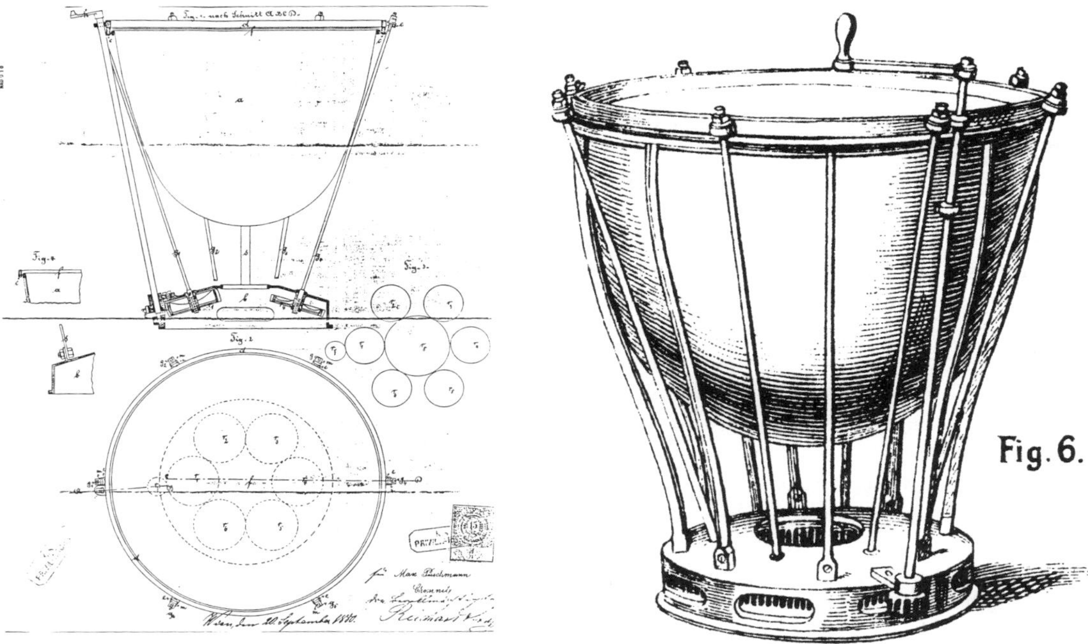

Fig. 11 a and b. Machine drum invented by Max Puschmann (1880).

The final stage in the evolution of machine drums during the nineteenth century was the so-called Dresden model patented in 1881 by Carl Pittrich, Kapelldiener in the Royal Saxonian Orchestra (see Fig. 12). What he actually developed was a tuning device, or "Stimmvorrichtung," first manufactured as a separate mechanism to be attached to existing drums. Produced by the firm of Ernst Queisser Nachfolger, it was only later sold as a complete drum assembly by Paul Focke in Dresden. Pittrich's invention, however, differed from its predecessors in employing a foot pedal, ratchet, and mechanical couplings to effect rapid tuning, using the newly available high-quality steel, both greater in tensile strength and much lighter than iron. Essentially, the semicircular motion of the pedal was converted into the reciprocating motion of the base plate to which the struts connecting the counterhoop were attached, a concept used widely in steam engines, punch presses, and machines controlled by treadle linkages such as the common mangle used in commercial laundries. The pedal itself was attached to a lever, at the upper end of which (in the complete drum model) was a heavy club or ball acting as a counterweight. At its other end the lever was attached to a shaft that conveyed motion to the actual tuning device by means of various mechanical couplings (see Fig. 13). Specifically, an eccentric activated a horizontal lever pivoting from the base plate. By means of a bolt flexibly attached at the center of this lever, the heavy plate was moved up or down, and with it the rods or struts connected to the metal counterhoop, thus raising or lowering the drum's pitch accordingly. To accomplish this change, the player's heel was pressed outward against a spring, disengaging it from a saw-toothed clutch and releasing the pedal. After moving it up or down to find the desired pitch, the heel was slid back to its normal posture, re-engaging the ratchet and locking the pedal into its new position. However, in spite of the relative ease of operation, the foot pressure required was considerable, and in the early models without counterweights the player's chair had to be fastened to the floor so that it would not slide back as he worked the pedals. A tuning gauge controlled by a linkage to the pedal indicated the correct pitch by means of a pointer and adjustable markers. The single master screw was used for fine-tuning made necessary by momentary changes in temperature and humidity or the pressure of heavy beating.

From a musical point of view Pittrich's device was truly a giant step forward that ended forever the limitations placed upon composers and performers alike. From the standpoint of design it represented the ultimate refinement in substituting a foot pedal for the old-fashioned screw mechanism, along with a ratchet and eccentric capable of converting and multiplying the pedal's force sufficiently to overcome the resistance of the base plate and move with ease the counterhoop with its supporting struts. Thus, the so-called Dresden model achieved ultimate success by substituting a far more rapid and powerful tuning mechanism for its predecessors. Moreover, it was the first machine drum the pitch of which could be changed reliably by the foot while the performer continued to play with both hands, and it solved the problem of how to correct an out-of-tune note without interruption. Finally and most importantly, the wholesale adoption of the Pittrich model was made easier by the fact that the pedal mechanism had been designed specifically to be installed on existing drums of the Pfundt/Hoffmann type. Consequently, those many orchestras owning these older instruments could easily convert them to pedal timpani. The way was led by Otto Lange, timpanist of the court orchestra in Dresden, who, with the encouragement of its conductor, Ernst von Schuch, had his drums outfitted with Pittrich's new pedal tuning device. Much later, these drums found their way to the rehearsal stage of the State Opera, where they miraculously escaped damage during the bombing of

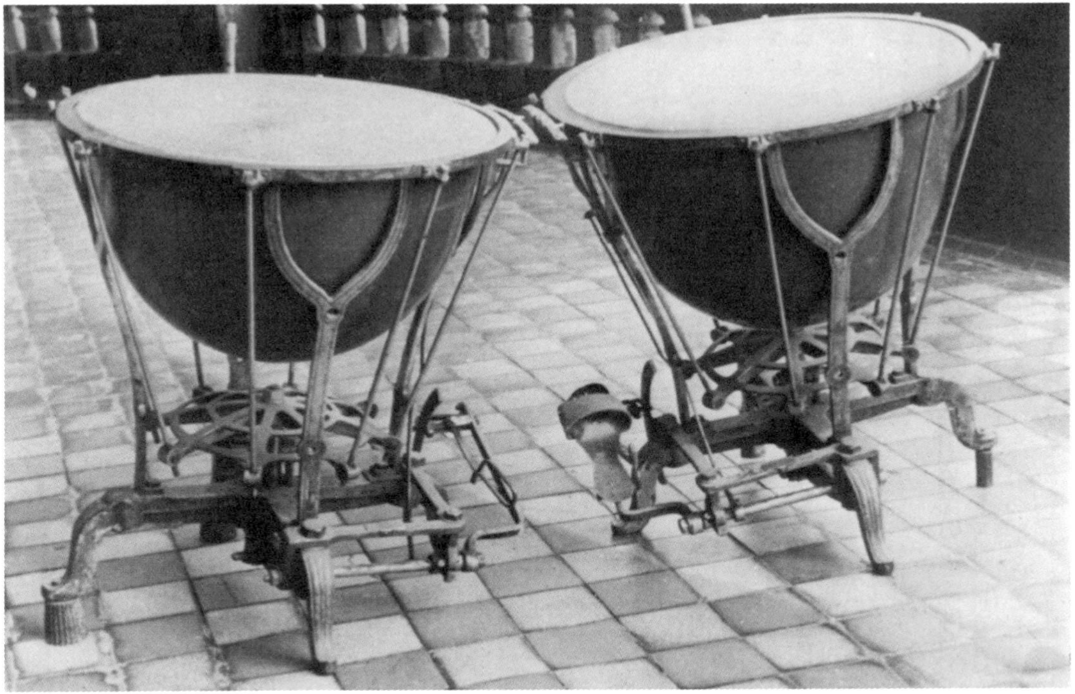

Fig. 12. Original pair of machine drums outfitted with Pittrich's mechanism by Ernst Queisser (1881).
Courtesy of Peter Sondermann, Dresden.

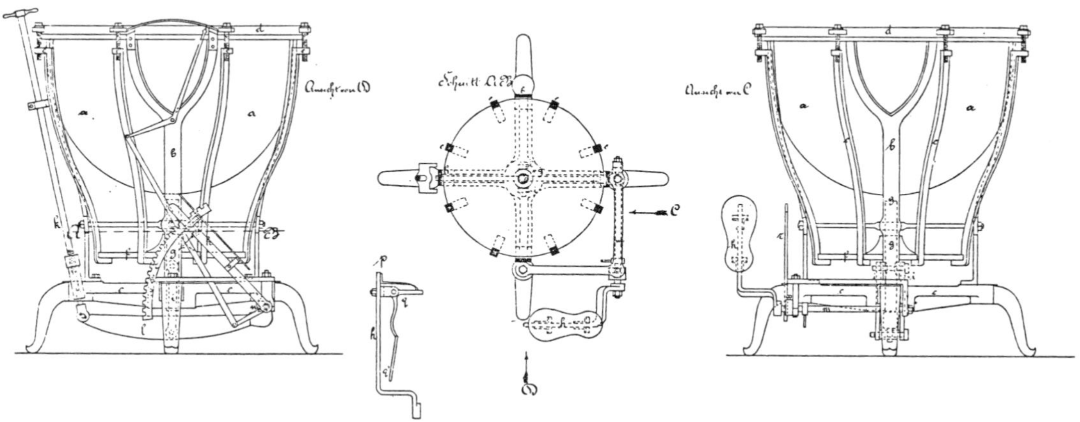

Fig. 13. Pittrich pedal timpani (sketch).

Fig. 14. Improved Pittrich pedal timpani with counter-weight and solid, thick baseplate (c. 1885). Staatliches Institut für Musikforschung, Musikinstrumenten Museum, Berlin.

Dresden in World War II. A set of three was purchased by the Leipzig Gewandhaus Orchestra in the early 1880s (see Fig. 15).

While other methods of mechanical tuning continued to be used, it is the Pittrich model that, with minor changes and improvements, has remained in widespread use to this day (see Fig. 14). In 1900, when the Focke firm was taken over by Jähne and Baruvka, the kettles were made both larger and lighter in weight. (Currently, these drums, virtually unchanged mechanically, are being manufactured by the Dresdner Apparatenbau.) A pair was imported to London by Sir Henry Wood in 1905 and used in the Queen's Hall Orchestra; around 1930 the BBC Orchestra acquired a similar pair.

There was an immediate symbiosis between composers and the new pedal timpani, especially in Germany and Austria; and many compositions by Gustav Mahler and Richard Strauss, for example, particularly the latter's operas, could not be played easily or at all without them. Thus, not surprisingly, it was in the opera house where Pittrich's pedal drums were ubiquitous. Timpanists could now easily correct those countless passages in French and Italian operas (Rossini, Bellini, and Donizetti, for example) where, owing to the lack of time for quick changes, the composer left the drums tuned to their original key in spite of a change in the rest of the orchestra, thus causing painful dissonances. The symphony orchestras were slower to adapt to the new drums, both because it took longer for composers of symphonic works to require many quick changes of pitch, and also owing to an innate conservatism, particularly in England and the United States. The London Philharmonic, Opéra Comique in Paris, and New York Symphony, for example, all employed hand-tuned drums, the first two until after World War II. Even orchestras such as the Boston and Chicago Symphonies used a hand-tuned drum (usually a

Fig. 15. Timpanist Otto Seele of the Leipzig Gewandhaus Orchestra (1905).

large one for the low notes) to supplement their sets of pedal timpani.

An early twentieth-century European drum requiring mention was developed by Hans Schnellar, timpanist of the Vienna Philharmonic and State Opera for almost forty years. He produced several successively improved models of lever timpani, beginning in the early 1900s. While based largely upon the Einbigler/Pfundt/Hoffmann concept of a screw operating on an eccentric to raise or lower an armature connected to the hoop (Viennese timpani have no counterhoop), there were several important differences. The kettles were all approximately the same depth, whatever their diameters, reaching down to the base (see Fig. 16). This shape gave Schnellar-type drums their unique "tubby" sound. Unlike the German models with their suspended kettles, however, the Viennese versions incorporated the drum and its stand, thus cutting down on the instrument's natural vibration. The vertical tuning lever, with its very large T-handle, was easy to grasp; and only a fraction of a turn was required to change the pitch. For rapid chromatic passages, a second operator is called for while the first timpanist continues to play. An improved model by Richard Hochrainer, late timpanist of the Vienna Philharmonic, is manufactured by the Wiener Schlaginstrumentenbau under the supervision of Wolfgang Schuster (see Fig. 17).

During the present century, technological improvements in the construction of the timpani have taken place largely in the United States, where, with fewer operatic ensembles and orchestras in their own halls—or, until after World War II even owning their instruments (especially true with community and institutional ensembles)—the timpanists themselves were often forced to supply their own instruments. Few of the extremely heavy German machine drums were available and portability as a basic requirement made hand-tuned drums an unfortunate necessity. Recognizing the need for an inexpen-

Fig. 16. Modified Schnellar-type machine drums by Richard Hochrainer (Vienna, 1960).

Fig. 17. Schnellar-type lever timpani manufactured by the Wiener Schlaginstrumentenbau. Courtesy of Wolfgang Schuster.

sive, lightweight machine drum, William F. Ludwig, Sr., together with his brother-in-law, the engineer Robert C. Danly, designed the first American pedal timpani (see Fig. 18). This first version, invented in 1911 and patented two years later, featured a hydraulic foot pump and expandable rubber tube that pressed a hoop up against the vellum head from inside the kettle. A pressure gauge attached to the line was calibrated to indicate pitches (see Fig. 19). The first pair was acquired by the St. Paul Symphony Orchestra. However, the tendency of the material to disintegrate and burst under pressure prompted Ludwig and Danly to abandon this approach early on, replacing it with an improved model designed in 1917 and patented three years later.

In their second version, flexible cables were connected to the mountings of six tensioning screws around the counterhoop (see Fig. 20). These cables penetrated the kettle and joined together at the drum's center, where they were attached to a vertical mechanism controlled by a foot pedal with a self-locking device to hold the cables in position and thus fix the desired pitch. Sets of three (25, 28, and 30 inches in diameter) were purchased by the Chicago, Detroit, and Philadelphia Orchestras; word soon got around and a number of other major American symphony orchestras acquired these instruments in pairs or trios.

Three years later Ludwig's Chicago firm announced the "Natural Way Balanced Action" machine drums, utilizing a compression spring for tension balance to hold the pedal in position, and a stiff rod linkage to the pivoting mountings of eight tuning screws on each drum (see Fig. 21). The copper bowls in standard sizes were spun on a lathe, shaped over a hemispherical spindle. Until the widespread importation of the Dresden model following World War

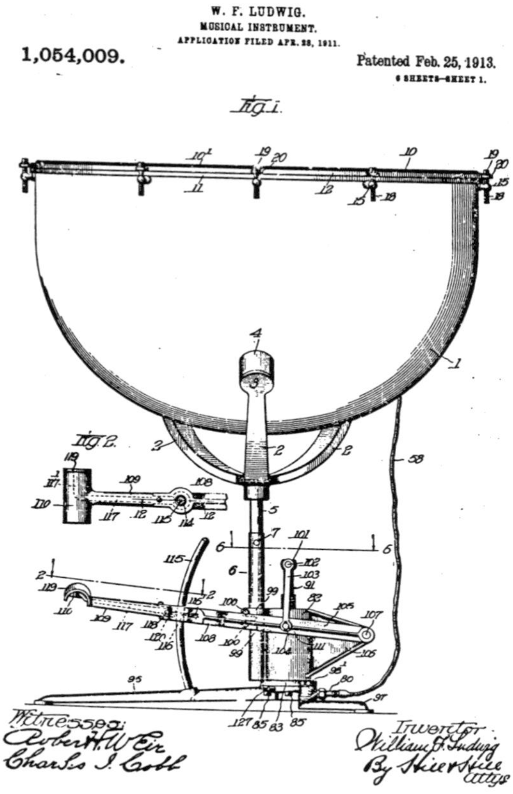

W. F. LUDWIG.
MUSICAL INSTRUMENT.
APPLICATION FILED APR. 28, 1911.
1,054,009.
Patented Feb. 25, 1913.
6 SHEETS-SHEET 1.
Witnesses:
Inventor:
William F. Ludwig
By Hill & Hill Attys

Fig. 18. Ludwig hydraulic model pedal timpani.

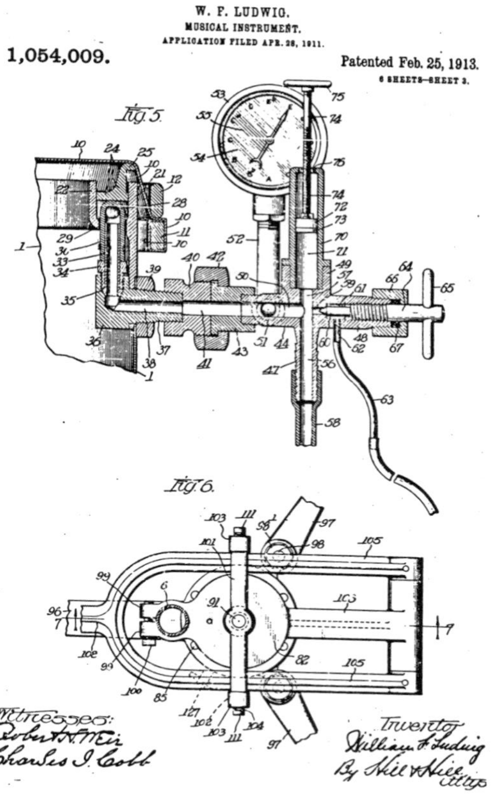

W. F. LUDWIG.
MUSICAL INSTRUMENT.
APPLICATION FILED APR. 28, 1911.
1,054,009.
Patented Feb. 25, 1913.
6 SHEETS-SHEET 3.
Witnesses:
Inventor
William F. Ludwig
By Hill & Hill Attys

Fig. 19. Ludwig pressure gauge.

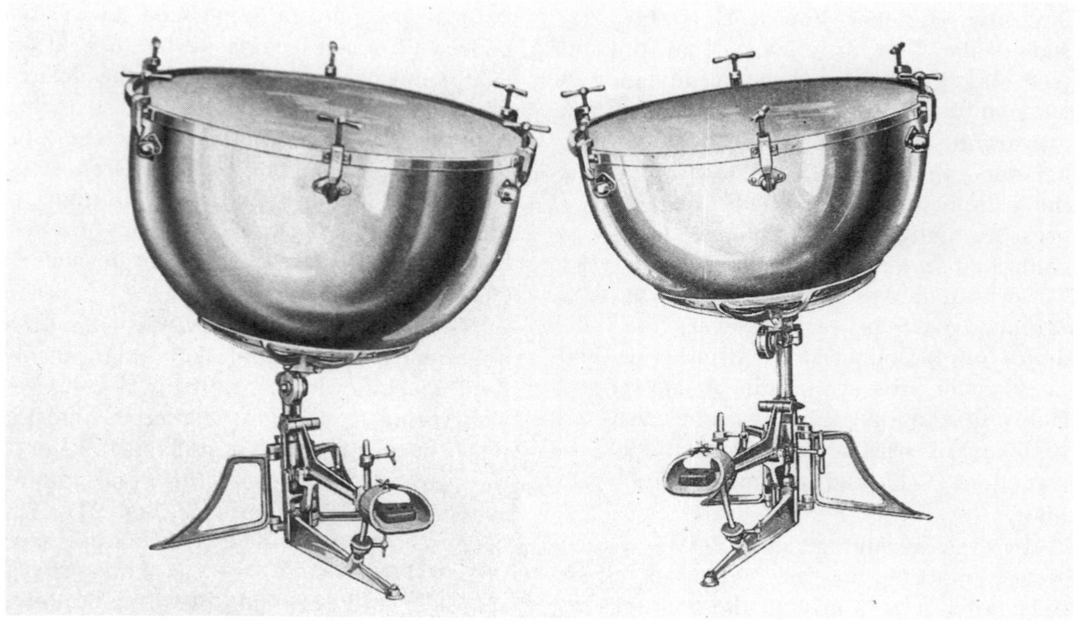

Fig. 20. Robert C. Danly, cable pedal timpani. Manufactured by W.F. Ludwig (c. 1919).

II and the introduction of a modified American version, the Ludwig balanced action model was ubiquitous, finding its way into all sorts of orchestras from the major ensembles to school bands. The Ludwig & Ludwig Company itself went through several transformations and mergers: with C.G. Conn in 1930; as the W.F.L. Drum Company in 1936; as the Ludwig Drum Co. in 1955; as part of Ludwig Industries in 1966; and as a division of Selmer, a North American Philips subsidiary, in 1982. A number of different models were or are still offered, the top of the line being the Dresden-style pedal timpani designed and licensed by Günter Ringer, featuring hand-hammered, camber-shaped kettles and finely crafted mechanical construction of an unusually high order. They are to be found in major orchestras all over the United States. (Other companies, such as the American Drum Manufacturing Company, sell similar models of their own design.)

Another lightweight, portable pedal timpani was patented in 1923 by Cecil Strupe, factory superintendent of the Leedy Manufacturing Company in Indianapolis (see Fig. 22). His design featured a ratchet and pawl clutch for locking the foot pedal in position and rods connected to the tensioning screw mechanisms around the drum's rim. The copper bowls were formed in a specially designed hydraulic press, rather than hammered over wooden molds. Leedy drums were exported to England during the 1920s, serving as the model for the first English machine drums manufactured by the Premier Drum Company. However, owing to the stiff import duties, soon only the parts were shipped by Leedy and the instruments themselves assembled by the Hawkes firm using locally produced kettles. Leedy was purchased by the C.G. Conn Company in 1927 and its production combined with that of Ludwig & Ludwig, acquired two years later. The Leedy/Ludwig Division con-

Fig. 21. "Natural way balanced action machine drums."

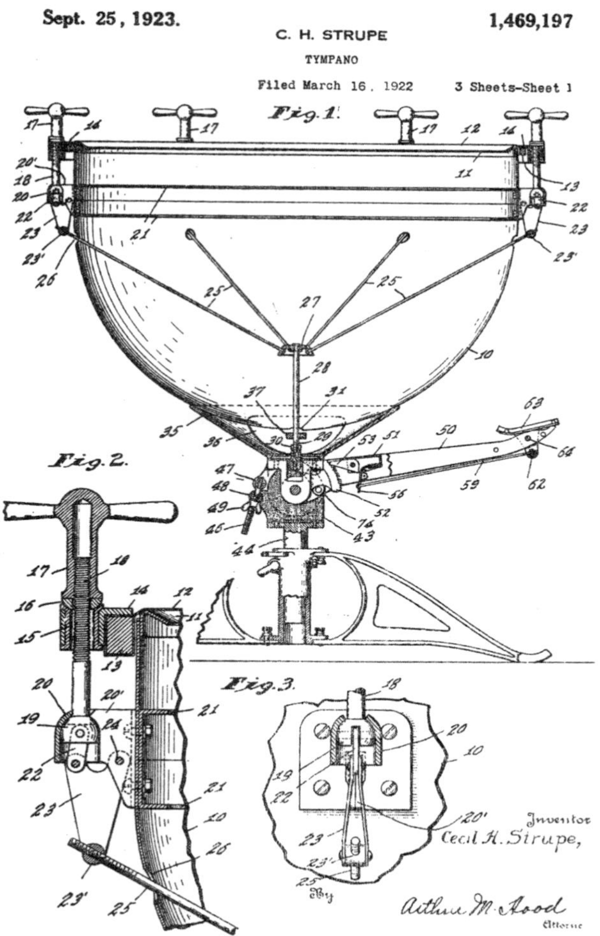

Fig. 22. Strupe portable pedal drum.

tinued to operate as a unit until its sale to the Slingerland and Ludwig family, respectively, in 1955; production of the Strupe/Leedy model ceased in 1958.

The so-called cable drum represents a separate development outside the technological mainstream described above. Curiously, perhaps, the principle of attaching a chain around the rim of the kettle engaging the tensioning screws by means of tiny gear wheels thereon, and thus turning them all simultaneously by means of a pair of opposing handles did not appear at the time of the invention of the bicycle's chain-and-sprocket mechanism. An early attempt (in 1924) by Hans Anheier, a German, consisted of substituting small, flexible cable reels for the tuning handles. A special key, employed singly or in pairs, was inserted into the flat, top surface of the spool in order to rotate the tuning screws simultaneously. The obvious disadvantage, of course, was that all screws turned an equal distance, meaning that the player could not tune each one individually in order to adjust the skin around its circumference for uneven thickness. In addition, the smooth cable could slip under high tension.

It is Saul Goodman, longtime timpanist of the New York Philharmonic, who is credited with introducing the first domestically produced chain-tuned drum, patented in 1952. His version, while similar to the

Anheier model, represented a distinct improvement in that, by means of a jockey wheel, the cable could be disengaged temporarily from any cog, thus permitting fine-tuning. By substituting a chain-and-sprocket mechanism for the cable and spool, Goodman eliminated the bulky spools and the possibility of slippage. A further refinement was made by the English timpanist Henry Taylor, who retained the T-handled tensioning screws and added cog or sprocket wheels halfway down their length, thus placing the chain well below the playing area. By loosening a pair of locking nuts above and below each wheel, the respective tuning screws could be fine-tuned individually. The main drawbacks to this approach were two: the massive, often crude hardware around the instrument's rim was awkward, the cables often placed above the level of the drumhead, intruding into the playing area; and the kettle's natural vibrations were somewhat impeded by its many attachments.

Both cable and chain drums were never intended to replace pedal timpani but merely to augment them. They are extremely lightweight and portable; and many symphony and opera orchestras employ them as adjuncts to a pair of pedal drums, placing them typically to either side in order to provide for the lowest and highest notes called for with less frequency, and using the center pair of machine drums for the major duties.

During the entire span of this technical revolution, the sizes of timpani changed as well. In the seventeenth and early eighteenth centuries, influenced by the tradition of small, lightweight cavalry instruments, the kettles were considerably smaller and shallower than today's instruments; Praetorius (*De Organographia*, 1619) gives the diameters of a pair as 17½ and 20½ inches (see Fig. 1), and an early eighteenth century pair in the Vienna Musikinstrumenten-Sammlung (see J. Schlosser, *Die Sammlung alte Musikinstrumente*, Vienna, 1920, p. 94) measures approximately 22½ and 24⅜ inches in diameter, respectively. Producing less resonance and volume of sound, they were ideally suited to the much smaller ensembles of the period, when the drummer was required to play indoors with a lower level of dynamics and with more articulation. Indeed, there are many references to players having to transpose the lower note up an octave so as to be within the drum's natural compass, an entirely acceptable step well into the nineteenth century.

Some confusion still exists ever since Charles Burney, in describing a performance of Handel's *Messiah* in Westminster Abbey (1784), referred to "common," "double," and "double-base" [*sic*] drums. The former were the so-called *cavalry timpani*; double-drums were comparable to a standard pair; while double-bass drums were substantially larger than those now being manufactured; the pair from the Tower of London, now lost, measured 38 and 39 inches in diameter. John Marsh wrote in 1807 that double-drums had replaced the common cavalry timpani, owing to their "more mellow" tones and greater sonority.

By the mid-nineteenth century, the sizes of a pair of kettledrums in the orchestra had increased to around 24 and 26 inches in diameter, although this varied slightly from maker to maker and from country to country. The Paris Opéra had larger drums, apparently, and English timpani tended to be larger still. A visiting Felix Mendelssohn complained in his letters from 1830 to 1832 about their booming sound. As time went on, influenced by the demands of the late Romantic and early modern composers, the dimensions of timpani increased at the lower end of the scale and increased at the upper end in order to accommodate these new musical requirements. For example, Mahler's Symphony No. 7 (1906) required a low D-flat, while in Strauss's *Die Frau ohne Schatten* (1918) three large drums are required for the syncopated Keikobad *Leitmotiv* A-flat, F-flat, and E-flat. At the upper end of the scale, Stravinsky's *Le Sacre du printemps* (1913) calls for a piccolo timpano among the three used by the second player. In Leoš Janáček's *Sinfonietta* (1926) three drums are tuned to high g-flat, a-flat, and b-flat. Today, the average orchestral timpanist is outfitted with four or five drums, ranging in size from 20 to 32 inches in diameter, and thus not only can meet the demands by any composer but can also assign each note required to the ideal compass of the appropriate drum.

Both the depth and contour of the kettledrum have been altered over time as well. In the earlier periods, the choice was largely empirical, producers settling ultimately on an approximate hemisphere. The modern science of acoustics has demonstrated that whatever the shape, the sound waves should be "bounced" from the beating spot into the kettle, deflecting in such a way as to be directed back out at a point exactly opposite that position. Experiments with lycopodium powder have demonstrated this phenomenon. As to the drum's depth, shallow instruments tend to emphasize the fundamental over its harmonic overtones, while deeper shells create more resonance. Whatever the shape, hemispherical, parabolic, or sloping, the usual rule of thumb today is that the kettle's depth should be one-half its diameter.

The supports for kettledrums show an interesting evolution. The earliest forms consisted of a squat, metal base that set the instrument close to the floor. In point of fact, this was but a way of adapting the mounted, cavalry-type drums to indoor performance while providing some sort of stability. This type of appendage sufficed during the era when most music for kettledrums was improvised, since the performer, bent way over his instruments, had nothing to read. But when confronted by a *Kapellmeister* leading his ensemble and a written part, the timpanist had to raise himself to a more upright position so that he could read his music while keeping an eye on the leader's beat. The obvious solution was to elevate the drums by means of legs so that they could be played from a standing or sitting position, thus facilitating a closer interaction between the performer, the director, and the music. With the introduction of the machine drum, the heavy base assembly precluded such an arrangement; and to raise or tilt the instruments, small blocks of wood were used under the feet; now threaded bolts serve the same purpose.

In earlier days, skins for the drums were fashioned by the parchment-maker, who as a rule used goat- or calfskin. The skin was much thicker than those of more modern times, and being hand scraped, far less uniform in thickness, with a surface like coarse sandpaper. According to the authors of the period, the best skins were half-tanned. In any case, the sound produced was dull and thick, owing in part to the preponderance of overtones that tended to obscure the fundamental. Wirdung (in 1511) called the drums "rumbling barrels," while Praetorius a century later called them "great rattletraps." The refinement of timpani heads began over a century ago. Opaque, white skins (*"Kalkfell"* in German) had been produced by treating them with a lime solution, smoothing them with chalk, and scraping them with a pumice stone, after which they were shaved and then dried, or "cured," in the sun, making them hard and stiff, and finally rubbed with brandy and garlic. By the 1850s, much thinner, translucent skins (*"Glasfell"*), treated with alum and subjected to mechanical processing, were produced just for timpani. Salted on the flesh side to preserve the skin, the heads were first bathed in a tub of slaked lime and water, loosening the hair. Then, after a thorough rinse, the skin's protein was "fixed" with a vegetable tanning material or metallic salt. Next, the skin was carefully stretched on a frame, neck at the top (12 to 6 o'clock: the line of the backbone). So as to minimize stretching along this line, the principal points of tension were maintained at 8, 9, and 10 o'clock and at 2, 3, and 4 o'clock. It was generally agreed that these thin, translucent skins produced a far better tone than their predecessors.

The ubiquitous plastic heads (polyethylene terephthalate) of today, introduced in the 1950s, have a different tone quality, with less resonance and elasticity. Their sonority is dryer and thinner, more brittle, and the tone itself shorter in duration. The chief physical differences are that notes produced on plastic heads have a faster decay and produce more sound, or noise, at low frequencies, thus providing uneven dynamics. They are favored particularly because of their imperviousness to atmospheric changes, making them ideal for outdoor performances or environments with constantly changing humidity. Being completely uniform in thickness, there is, of course, no necessity for finding the ideal beating spot or avoiding the backbone area as with skin heads.

Early drumsticks were short, fabricated out of wood or occasionally ivory, terminating in tiny knobs. Producing a loud, dry sonority, they were ideal for the open-air ceremonial music of mounted kettledrummers. Felt, of course, was unknown, and for funeral processions the players covered the ends of their sticks with woolen cloth or chamois; Eisel (1738) speaks of woolen cloth, chamois, or leather. Even when the timpani moved indoors and joined the court and operatic ensembles, these wooden sticks continued to be used. However, their sound proved too loud and unvarying; and by the end of the eighteenth century, they were usually covered with different types of material. For example, between 1775 and 1795 ten French operas needed covered sticks; and Koch (1802) mentions that this strategy was an absolute requirement when playing orchestral music. Chamois or flannel, a soft woolen cloth, was wrapped around the knob, its soft texture producing a more musical sound. In a new departure, thin, donut-shaped discs wrapped in flannel were inserted on the stick and held in place with a screw. Various-sized discs and varying thicknesses were used in order to provide sticks of differing tone quality. Both Kastner (*Méthode complète*) and Berlioz (*Grand traité d'instrumentation et d'orchestration*), writing in the 1840s, noted that the timpanist should have three pairs of sticks: wooden-ended for a hard, dry, and brilliant sound; leather-covered for a softer and less percussive sound (deerskin or buffalo hide, which came in different thicknesses); and sponge-headed (introduced by the French timpanist Jean Schneitzhoeffer in the 1820s and popularized by the German Pfundt), producing a very clear tone (Berlioz called it "velvety") and providing a faster rebound owing to the material's porous elasticity. Called "elephant's ear" (*Spongia agaricina*), it was introduced from the French colonies surrounding the Mediterranean for many applications. The final step was the appropriation of piano felt, which could be applied in various thicknesses to give the timpanist several sets of sticks suitable for producing any effect the music required, covering its entire dynamic range. (This material had first been applied to the hammerheads of pianos by the maker Henri Pope in 1826.) The drummer Carl Gollmick seems to have been the first to have mentioned in print the use of felt sticks (1846); two years later, in his book on the kettledrums, Christian Reinhardt wrote that felt sticks were being used by "some timpanists." Thus, with the abandonment of wooden and leather-covered sticks as the mainstay, and the advent of softer material such as flannel, sponge, and felt, the sound produced by the kettledrums became mellower and less dry, "full-bodied," according to the English timpanist Victor de Pontigny, writing in the *Proceedings of the Royal Musical Association* (1875–1876) and no longer "hard, stiff and banging" as Pfundt recollected in his treatise on the instrument. By the twentieth century, sticks of all sorts were being commonly fabricated with wood, bamboo, or slightly flexible cane for the shafts. Aluminum is favored by some timpanists today. American drummers especially prefer harder sticks, owing both to the penchant for louder sounds and to the lack of "bounce" of plastic heads; the softer the material, the less the rebound.

Representative Milestones in the Music for Kettledrums

Date Composer
Work
Description

c. 1656 Nicolaus Hasse
Auffzüge 2 Clarinde [und] Heerpauken
The first extant written fragment of music for kettledrums.

1667 Johann Schmelzer
Arie per il balletto a cavallo
Music for an equestrian ballet, commissioned for the wedding celebrations of Emperor Leopold I of Austria and Margarita Teresa of Spain.

1675 Jean-Baptiste Lully
Thésée
The first published opera featuring a part for timpani; for example, Act I, Scene 9 (march and entry).

c. 1682 Heinrich Biber or Andreas Hofer
Salzburger Festmesse
The first major composition for two pairs of kettledrums and two players.

1685 André Philidor
Pièces de trompettes et timbales
The first collection of outdoor court festival music including written parts for kettledrums.

1692 Henry Purcell
The Faerie Queene
Includes the first solo passage for drums in an opera.

c. 1692 Giuseppe Torelli
Sinfonia for Oboes, Trumpets, and Timpani
Probably the first composition featuring three timpani.

1733 Johann Sebastian Bach
Cantata No. 214 ("Tönet ihr Pauken! Erschallet Trompeten!")
Features an opening kettledrum solo in the first movement; used again in the *Christmas Oratorio.*

1743 Francesco Barsanti
Concerto grosso
Drums tuned to three different keys in three successive movements.

1749 Christoph Graupner
Sinfonia a 2 corni, 6 timpani, 2 violini, viola e cembalo
One of the first in a series of *pièces d'occasion* written for multiple timpani.

1773 Wolfgang Amadeus Mozart
Divertimento for 2 Flutes, 5 Horns, and 4 Timpani (K. 188)
Features four drums throughout (G, A, C, D).

1785 Antonio Salieri
La grotta di Trofonio
Requires a drum to be retuned during a tacet period; asks for an unusual tuning of a diminished fifth (C- and G-flat).

c. 1785 Johann Carl Fischer
Concerto for 8 Timpani Obbligato
The first piece written for one solo performer and eight drums spanning an entire octave.

1786 Antonio Sacchini
Oedipe à Colone
An early example of an opera calling for four drums, tuned to B-flat, b-flat, F, and f (an early use of octaves).

1787 Antonio Salieri
Tarare
Calls for the musical tuning of d- and B-flat

1789 Jean-Baptiste Lemoyne
Nephté
Requires rapid retuning in a number of passages; for example, from e-flat and B-flat to c and G in only nine bars of allegro.

1791 Nicolas-Jean Le Froid de Mereaux
Jocaste
A very early use of a piccolo timpano; specifies a *petite timbale* tuned to high a-flat.

1794 Franz Josef Haydn
Symphony No. 102 in B-flat
Prescribed muffled drums (*con sordini*) to go along with muted trumpets.

1794 Johann Paul Martini
Overture to *Sappho*
First use of chords and double rolls played on two drums simultaneously.

1795 Franz Josef Haydn
Symphony No. 103 in E-flat
The timpani solo opening the first movement gave this symphony its nickname: *Paukenwirbel* or *Drumroll.*

1800 François-Adrien Boieldieu
Overture to *Le Calife de Bagdad*
Features a rapid change of pitch from d to e and back again.

1803 Georg Joseph Vogler
Overture to *Samori*
The use of three timpani throughout influenced numerous composers, including Vogler's pupil Carl Maria von Weber.

1805 Ludwig van Beethoven
Fidelio
Features a timpani solo in the prison scene (Act II), tuned a diminished fifth apart (E-flat and A).

1807 Nicholas-Marie Dalayrac
Lina, ou Le Mystère
First known reference in opera to types of sticks called for; in this case, *baguettes garnies* (covered timpani mallets).

c. 1810 Ferdinand Kauer
Six Variations for Strings, Winds, Timpani, and Percussion
Requires six drums in a variation featuring solo timpani, requiring considerable virtuosity.

c. 1815 Antonín Reicha
Die Harmonie der Sphären
Calls for four timpanists, each playing a pair of drums, as well as for the use of rolled chords to support the chorus, serving as a model for Hector Berlioz.

1824 Ludwig van Beethoven
Symphony No. 9 in D minor
Features drums tuned in octaves (f, F) as well as two drums hit simultaneously (B-flat, f).

1830 Hector Berlioz
Symphonie fantastique
Calls for two players, each with a pair of drums; for wooden sticks; for a quick change of pitch by the second timpanist at two places in the fourth movement.

1831 Giacomo Meyerbeer
Robert le Diable
Probably the first grand opera requiring four drums, featuring a melodic solo (Act IV, No. 17).

1833 Ludwig Spohr
Calvary
Requires two timpanists executing rolls variously on three drums each, during a section depicting an earthquake at the moment of crucifixion.

1839 Hector Berlioz
Requiem Mass
The "Tuba mirum" was written originally for thirty-two drums played by twenty players; the composer compromised in the printed score by calling for only sixteen drums and ten players.

1841, rev. 1851 Robert Schumann
Symphony No. 4, in D Minor
Influenced by the Einbigler machine drums in the Leipzig Gewandhaus orchestra, the composer required that the pair of timpani be rapidly retuned at three places in the first movement.

1883 Léo Delibes
Lakmé
Calls for a pair of *petites timbales* an octave above the normal range.

1890 Nicholas Rimsky-Korsakov
Mlada
Requires two sets of drums and two players, as well as a *piccolo timpano* in Act IV; influenced the composer's pupil Igor Stravinsky.

1895 Gustav Mahler
Symphony No. 2 ("Resurrection")
The first major symphony requiring two performers, each playing on three drums; a third timpanist also joins them briefly in one movement.

1895 Richard Strauss
Till Eulenspiegels lustige Streiche
The first major orchestral piece requiring pedal timpani.

1899 Edward Elgar
Enigma Variations
Specifies a timpani roll using snare drumsticks; often performed with two coins instead, since Charles Henderson of the London Symphony demonstrated this substitution to the composer.

1900 Gustav Mahler
Symphony No. 4 in G major
Two sticks together hit three drums in playing the principal motif of the first movement.

1902 Ermanno Wolf-Ferrari
La vita nuova
Written for seven drums divided between two players.

1903 Vincent d'Indy
Symphony No. 2, in B-flat
Possibly the first symphony written specifically for *timbales chromatiques* and unplayable without them.

1903 Richard Strauss
Sinfonia Domestica
With the composer's approval, the Viennese timpanist Hans Schnellar improvised an upward stepwise progression in the last movement (3 mm. after #142), a virtuoso solo used in performances to this day.

1905 Richard Strauss
Salome
The most demanding opera of this period, requiring rapid executions of chromatic passages, simultaneous playing, and tuning, etc.

1906 Gustav Mahler
Symphony No. 7 in E minor
Requires a large drum tuned to low D-flat, as well as "very good mechanical pedal drums" for rapid retuning.

1910 Charles Stanford
Songs of the Fleet
Requires a roll, or tremolo, to be played with the fingertips.

1914 Walford Davies
Conversations for Piano and Orchestra
The first known use of a glissando on the timpani.

1916 Carl Nielsen
Symphony No. 4 ("Inextinguishable")
Features a duet in the fourth movement for two drummers, who execute parallel chromatic stepwise passages upwards, a minor third apart.

1923 Gustav Holst
The Perfect Fool
Requires the use of one felt and one wooden stick alternating notes in the "Dance of the Spirits of Fire."

1927 Havergal Brian
Symphony No. 1 ("Gothic")
A massive work Berlioz would have loved; its second part ("Te Deum") calls for six timpani in the orchestra (two drummers) and four brass choirs, each with three drums (one timpanist each), arranged spatially.

1933 William Russell
Fugue for Eight Percussion Instruments and Piano
Calls for unusual effects: sweeping a wire brush across the timpani head near the rim; striking the kettle itself with a triangle-beater.

1935 William Walton
Symphony No. 1
Features a duet for two timpanists in the last movement.

1953 Franco Donatoni
Concertino for Strings, Brass, and Timpani
Features playing two drums at once, double-sticking, hitting the center of the head, glissandos.

1954 Werner Thärichen
Concerto for Timpani and Orchestra
One of the first truly virtuoso pieces in the solo literature, requiring pedal timpani and great technical skill.

1958 Arthur Bliss
Meditations on a Theme by John Blow
Calls for unusual effects: two cymbals placed on the timpani heads and struck with glockenspiel beaters.

1959 Benjamin Frankel
Symphony No. 1
Requires the timpanist to play with his or her hands on the drumheads in place of sticks.

1960 Elliott Carter
Eight Pieces for Kettledrums
Requires split-second dampening of drums ("controlled resonance") in the Recitative and Improvisation.

1962 Harold Faberman
Concerto for Timpani and Orchestra
Requires five timpani and the use of several different kinds of sticks, often together.

1973 Benjamin Britten
Death in Venice
Specifies at certain points in the opera that the drumhead is to be hit with a bundle of twigs (*Ruthen*).

1983 William Kraft
Concerto for Timpani and Orchestra
Requires the timpanist to play with several types of timpani mallets, gloved fingers, and natural fingers, and needs much pedaling and technical skill.

1984 Christopher Rouse
Gorgon
Extensive timpani part throughout—soloistic in nature.

1986 Joan Tower
Fanfare for the Uncommon Woman
Several soloist sections of technical display.

Bibliography

Avgerinos, Gerassimos. *Lexikon der Pauke*. Frankfurt am Main: Musikinstrument, 1964.

Benvenga, Nancy. *Timpani and the Timpanist's Art: Musical and Technical Development in the 19th and 20th Centuries*. Göteborg: University of Göteborg, 1979.

Berlioz, Hector. *Grand traité d' instrumentation et d'orchestration modernes,* new ed. Paris, 1870, 262, or the English translation of M.S. Clarke. *A Treatise on Modern Instrumentation and Orchestration*. Rev. ed. London: J. Bennett, 1882, 214.

Blades, James. *Percussion Instruments and Their History*. 3rd ed. London: Faber & Faber, 1984. Rev. ed. Westport, Conn.: Bold Strummer, 1992.

Bowles, Edmund A. "The Double, Double, Double Beat of the Thundering Drum: The Timpani in Early Music." *Early Music* 19 (1991): 419–435.

———. "Nineteenth-Century Innovations in the Use and Construction of the Timpani." *Journal of the American Musical Instrument Society* 5–6 (1979–80): 74–113.

———. *The Timpani: A History in Pictures and Documents*. Buren, The Netherlands: Frits Knuf, in press.

Browne, P.A. "The Orchestral Treatment of the Timpani." *Music & Letters* 4 (1923): 334–339.

Burney, Charles. *An Account of the Musical Performances in Westminster Abbey*. London, 1785, 7f.

Eisel, J.P. *Musicus autodidaktos. Der selbst informierende Musicus*. Erfurt, 1738, 67f.

Farmer, Henry George. *Handel's Kettledrums and Other Papers on Military Music*. London: Hinrichsen, 1950.

Fechner, Georg. *Die Pauken und Trommeln in ihren neueren und vorzüglichen Konstruktionen*. Weimar: B.F. Voigt, 1862.

Gollmick, Karl. *Autobiographie von Carl Gollmick nebst einigen Momenten aus der Geschichte des Frankfurter Theaters.* Frankfurt am Main, 1846, 119.

Kastner, Jean-Georges. *Methode complète et raisonné de timbales.* Paris: Schlesinger, ?1845.

Kirby, Percival R. *The Kettle-Drums.* London: Oxford University Press, 1930.

Koch, Heinrich. *Musikalisches Lexikon.* Frankfurt am Main, 1802, col. 1143.

Marsh, John. *Hints to Young Composers of Instrumental Music.* London, 1807, *passim.*

"Neue Erfindung." *Allgemeine musikalische Zeitung* 14, no. 61 (October 1812): n.p.

Pfundt, Ernst G.B. *Die Pauken: Eine Anleitung dieses Instrument zu erlernen.* Leipzig: Breitkopf und Härtel, 1849.

Pontigny, Victor de. "On Kettledrums." *Proceedings of the Royal Music Association* 2 (1875–76): 53.

Praetorius, Michael. *Syntagma Musicum.* Vol. II, *De Organographia.* Wolfenbüttel, 1619). Facsimile edition by Wilibald Gurlitt. Kassel, 1958, 77.

Reinhardt, Christian. *Der Paukenschlag.* Mehlis, 1848, 114.

Schilling, Gustav. *Encyclopädie der gesammten musikalischen Wissenschaften.* III. Stuttgart, 1835, V, 397.

Schlosser, J. *Die Sammlung alte Musikinstruments.* Vienna, 1920, 94.

Taylor, Henry W. *The Art and Science of the Timpani.* London: J. Baker, 1964.

Titcomb, Caldwell. "Baroque Court and Military Trumpets and Kettledrums: Technique and Music." *Galpin Society Journal* 9 (1956): 56–81.

Tobischek, Herbert. *Die Pauke: Ihre spiel- und bautechnische Entwicklung in der Neuzeit.* Tutzing: Schneider, 1977.

Wagner, Richard, ed. "Die Königliche Kapelle betreffend." In *Der junge Wagner: Dichtungen, Aufsätze, Entwürfe (1832–1849).* Berlin/Leipzig, 1910, 390f.

Wirdung, Sebastian. *Musica Getutscht.* Basel, 1511, cited by Curt Sachs, *The History of Musical Instruments.* New York: W.W. Norton, 1940, 329.

Edmund A. Bowles

Latin-American Percussion

Latin-American percussion instruments provide a reflection of the different cultural influences prevalent in each region. The primary influence for most of the instruments and rhythms is undoubtedly African. Elements of European culture, particularly Spanish, are also present.

Although there are numerous percussion instruments in each country, most of the instruments discussed in the following section are of Afro-Cuban origin. Afro-Cuban rhythms, such as the mambo, cha-cha, and *son montuno*, have become popular throughout the world, subsequently bringing attention to the instruments. Although the description of the instruments is designed to give an overview, the hundreds of years of tradition and the rich heritage associated with the music should not be overlooked.

Batá Drums

The *batá* drums represent one of the closest links to African culture in the Western world. Culturally, they are direct descendants of the Nigerian Yoruba people brought to Cuba during the slave trade. Used primarily for religious purposes, the *batá* drums and their playing techniques have been kept closely guarded but have also been combined with other Afro-Cuban musical styles.

The *batá* are double-headed drums similar in shape to an hourglass; each head is a different size and pitch. Usually made of wood, they are tuned by adjusting the tension on leather straps attached to the skins and wrapped around the drum. A modern version, made of fiberglass and tuned by screw tensioning, also exists.

Fig. 1. Batá drums.

Traditionally played in sets of three, each *batá* is a different size and has a specific function within the ensemble. The smallest drum, called *okónkolo*, usually maintains a basic rhythm, while the mid-sized *itótele* and the large drum, *iyá*, communicate in a complex rhythmical language that takes years to master. The *iyá* is the "master drum" and has the most important function within the trio. Always played by the most advanced player, seated in the middle, the *iyá* patterns and subsequent improvisations are connected to a specific deity of African origin. The *iyá* also has bells attached to the heads, adding a metallic texture to its sound.

Batá drums are placed on the thighs of the seated player; a strap provides added support. The higher-pitched half of each drum is played with the left hand; the right plays the larger head. The drums are struck using an upward, glancing motion. Different pitches and overtones can be produced by striking with various finger combinations; slaps and muted tones are also used. When combined, the rhythms of the *batá* trio contain rhythmic, tonal and harmonic elements to which supernatural powers are ascribed.

Bombo

The *bombo* is one of the most common South American percussion instruments. In the countries bordering the Andes mountain range, such as Argentina, Chile, and Bolivia, it is primarily a folk instrument used in the indigenous music of this region.

The *bombo* is a large wooden drum similar in size to a floor tom-tom and typically made from a tree trunk that is hollowed out with burning coals and then chiseled inside. It has cowhide or lambskin heads, often with some of the animal's fur still remaining, somewhat muffling the drum's sound. Similar to field drums of European origin, the *bombo* is tuned by adjusting a movable hoop through leather thongs interconnecting both rims.

It is held under the left arm and supported by a leather strap slung around the shoulder. The left hand strikes the rim with a short dowel, producing a wooden clicking sound. The right hand holds a leather-tipped beater that strikes on the middle of the drum and also on the rim. Many of the rhythms played on the *bombo* are in 6/8 meter and combine both drum and rim sounds.

✕ = L.H. rim click

• = R.H. drum

Ex. 1.

Bongos

One of the more versatile instruments in the Latin percussion family, the *bongos* have been used in a variety of musical settings. Their distinctive sound is heard in many different types of Latin rhythms.

The *bongos* are a pair of tapered single-headed drums connected by a block of wood. Head sizes range in diameter from about 7 inches for the small drum to approximately 9 inches for the large. Typically, rawhide heads are used and tuned by screw tensioning. The drums are generally made out of wood, although a fiberglass version is also produced.

Interestingly, the drums are given male and female connotations. The high bongo, called *macho* (male), is tightly tuned, yielding high-pitched popping sounds as well as sharp slaps used for accents. The low drum is called *hembra*, meaning female, and produces a deeper, mellower sound for tonal contrast.

The bongos are held between the legs of the seated player, slightly above the knees. Tilted downward, they are played with the fingers near the edge of the drums. For right-handed players, the bongos are

Fig. 2. Bongos.

placed with the high drum on the left. The playing technique includes a rocking motion between the thumb and fingers of the left hand on the high bongo. The right hand alternates between the high and low bongo, playing both muted and open tones.

The bongo player (*bongosero*) switches to a handheld cowbell (see p. 232), particularly during choruses or ensemble sections within a typical *salsa* arrangement. For the cha-cha rhythm, the *bongosero* usually plays the *güiro* (see p. 233). The bongos have the most rhythmic freedom in the Latin percussion section. In addition to a basic timekeeping pattern called *martillo* (hammer), the bongo player improvises accents and figures within the melodic line.

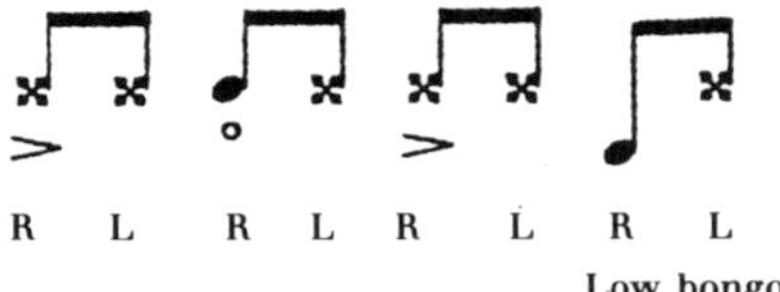

Ex. 2. Martillo

Claves

Claves are a pair of wooden dowels that play an integral part in Afro-Cuban music, maintaining a pattern appropriately called the "clave," meaning the key.

Claves are made of resonant hardwoods, such as rosewood or grenadilla, and range from 6 to 10 inches in length and about 1 inch in diameter. Playing technique involves holding one *clave* lightly with the fingers, creating a sound chamber underneath, and striking on the middle with the other *clave*, producing a rich, resonant sound.

The *clave* pattern acts as a timekeeper and sets the rhythmic direction of the music. The *son clave*, named after a popular Cuban rhythm, consists of two measures: three strokes in the first and two in the second. A variation of the *son clave*, the *reverse clave* begins, as the name implies, with the two-stroke measure and is also referred to as *2/3 clave*. The *rumba clave*, used in folkloric Afro-Cuban rhythms such as the *guaguanco*, stems from the African bell pattern (Ex. 3) and can be played in 6/8 or 4/4 time, depending on the particular rhythm.

Ex. 3. African bell pattern.

Ex. 4. Son clave.

Ex. 5. Reverse clave.

Ex. 6. Rumba clave.

Ex. 7. 6/8 clave.

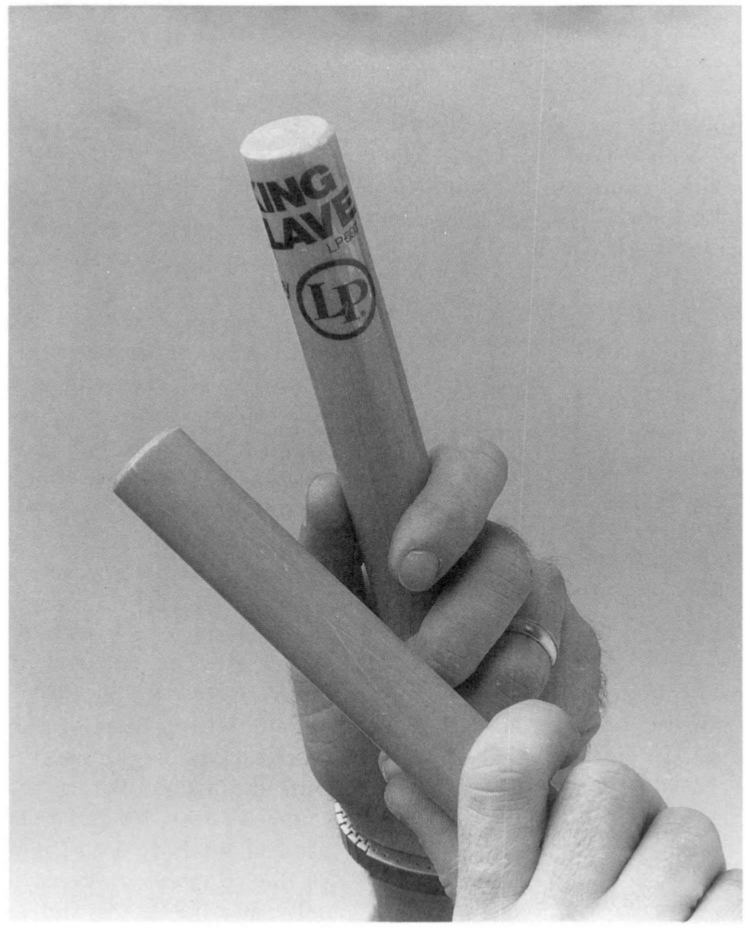

Fig. 3. Claves.

Conga Drums

Perhaps the most important instrument in Afro-Cuban music, the conga drum is a direct descendant of African barrel-shaped, wooden drums having animal hides stretched over the top opening. Often present during religious rites or social functions of the African-influenced cultures in the Americas, the conga drums' initial entrance into popular music is credited to the Cuban bands of the 1930s. As the popularity of Latin music and dancing spread worldwide during the 1950s, congas began to appear in other contexts, particularly Latin jazz. The Cuban tradition was continued by Puerto Rican *salsa* bands, whose conga drummers adapted and expanded the playing techniques. Currently, congas are an integral part of a percussionist's arsenal and a common fixture in a wide variety of musical styles.

The basic design of the conga has not changed much from its African ancestor. The barrel-making technique of joining wooden slats is still used in making the body of the conga, although now modernized for mass production and consistency. Use of fiberglass shells is a modern innovation resulting in increased durability and louder projection. The Cuban method of tacking the heads to the shell and "heat-tuning" has been replaced by mechanical tuning devices that control head tension and pitch; mule or buffalo rawhide heads are still used for an authentic sound. Congas are available in a variety of sizes and are classified accordingly. The Cuban word *tumbadora*, although referring to conga drums as a whole, generally specifies the largest and deepest-sounding drum, with a head diameter of 12½ inches. The conga is generally around 11¾ inches and the *quinto* 11 inches. The height of the drums ranges from 28 to 30 inches to accommodate a seated player.

Conga drumming technique involves the mastery of different handstrokes in order

Fig. 4. Congas.

to produce the open tones, sharp slaps, muted sounds, and resonant bass tones characteristic of the instrument. When two drums are used, the lower drum is placed to the right of a right-handed player and tuned a fourth or fifth lower. The main conga pattern in Latin music is called the *tumbao* (Ex. 8) and combines a slap with muffled and open tones in an eighth-note sequence.

Ex. 8. Tumbao.

Cowbell, Cencerro, and Campana

The modern *cowbell* has not changed much from its rural predecessor. Made from metal that is shaped into a flattened bell and then welded at the seams, the cowbell is one of the most widely used Latin-American percussion instruments.

Latin music employs a variety of cowbells each with its own specific function and distinct sound. The *timbale* player (see below) generally uses two cowbells in his setup. The smaller cha-cha bell is approximately 5 inches in length; the larger mambo bell ranges around 9 inches. The cha-cha bell is used primarily for the slower cha-cha (Ex. 9) and the moderate *charanga* rhythms. The lower-pitched mambo bell (Ex. 10) is played in the faster tempos such as mambo and *son montuno*.

The *bongo* player (see below) plays a large handheld bell by striking it with a thick beater, such as a small hammer handle. The *bongo* bell (Ex. 11) is played during the louder sections of the song; its deep, dry sound and basic pattern help to anchor the rhythm.

A variety of sounds is used when playing the cowbell. The mouth or opening of the bell is struck for a loud, resonant tone. The center or edge is played for a thinner, higher-pitched sound. Typically, both sounds are incorporated within the patterns and are used for phrasing and accents.

Ex. 9. Cha-cha.

Ex. 10. Mambo.

Ex. 11. Bongo bell.

> = mouth

• = center

for 2-3 clave

Fig. 5. Cowbell.

Güira

The *güira* is a metal scraper used to accompany the merengue, Santo Domingo's national dance. It is made from a sheet of metal punched with small holes and rolled into a cylinder open at both ends. The *güira* is held by a small handle and played with a fork-like scraper.

The *güira* adds a metallic sound and propels the exciting merengue rhythm. Its pattern is a mixture of long and short sounds created by varying the length of the strokes. In the hands of a skilled player, the *güira* can produce elaborate syncopations that complement the rest of the merengue percussion section, composed of *tambora* and conga drum.

Similar to the *güiro* in concept, the Dominican *güira* employs an opposite motion of the hands to facilitate playing at faster tempos.

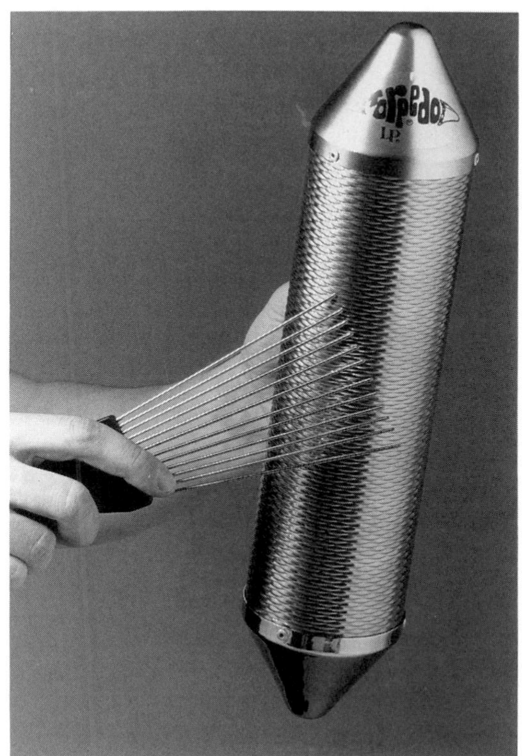

Fig. 6. Güira.

Güiro

One of the instruments most closely associated with Latin music, the *güiro* is made from a long gourd that is dried, hollowed out, and then cut on one side with horizontal grooves. It is held in the left hand, for right-handed players, and grasped with the thumb and middle finger inserted into two holes cut on the underside of the gourd. Sound is produced by rubbing a small scraper over the surface. The typical *güiro* pattern includes short and long sounds created by varying the length and duration of the strokes.

The playing technique for the *güiro* involves using a contrary motion of the hands in which the hand holding the instrument moves downward as the stroke moves up and vice versa. This is particularly important for maintaining faster tempos, since it reduces the hand movements. The *güiro* pattern remains basically the same for fast and slow tempos.

Ex. 12.

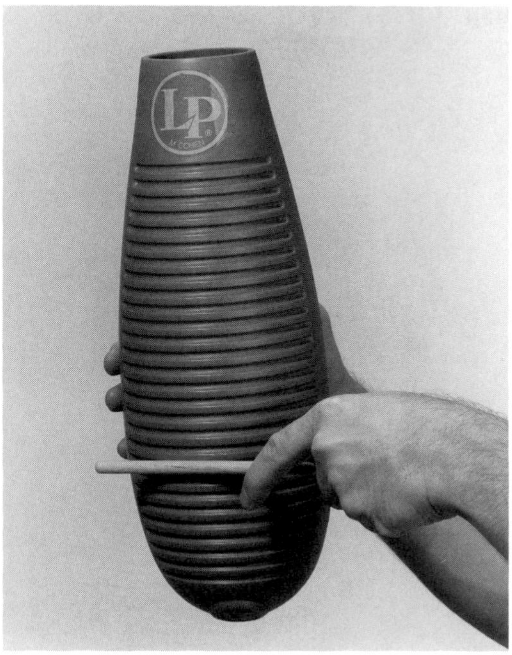

Fig. 7. Güiro.

Maracas

The *maracas* are a pair of handheld rattles or shakers. Essentially small gourds filled with pellets and mounted on handles, the maracas provide a continuous timekeeping pattern for a variety of Latin-American rhythms and tempos. Although rattles of different types are present in many cultures, the maracas are a versatile instrument that can be used as the sole percussion instrument in a small group setting or can add a crisp edge to a large *salsa* band.

Depending on their origin, maracas can be made of various materials, such as small coconut shells, gourds, and stitched rawhide. They can be filled with beads, dried beans, and various types of hard pellets, according to the sound desired. Sound is created as the pellets strike the inside of the gourd.

Although playing styles vary, the maracas are generally held horizontally and played with an up-and-down wrist movement, as if striking a drum. This technique is particularly suited for soft playing and staccato passages. For a louder sound and faster tempos, the maracas are held vertically and played with a forward arm motion. A sustained sound or roll, sometimes called for in contemporary music, can be achieved by holding the maraca upside down and playing with a stirring motion. The basic pattern for Latin music involves steady eighth notes enhanced by accents and short rolls (see Ex. 13).

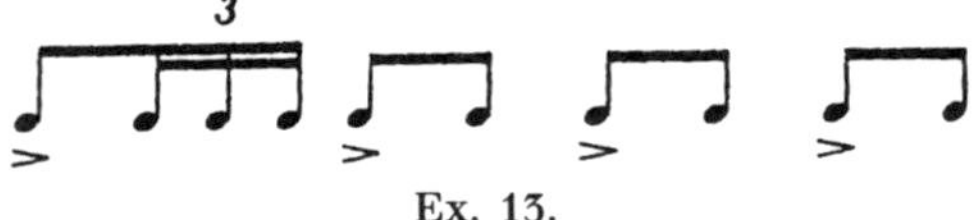

Ex. 13.

Quijada and Vibraslap

The *quijada*, made from the jawbone of an ass, was used as a sound effect in Latin music. The jawbone, with the teeth still attached, created a long rattling sound when struck. Because of the fragile nature of the instrument, the *quijada* was replaced by a modern version, the *vibraslap*, which simulates the sound by means of metal rivets vibrating inside a wooden sound chamber.

The vibraslap is played by striking a wooden ball attached to a bent metal rod connected to the sound chamber. The resulting sound is considerably louder and longer than the *quijada* and has been used as an effect in many different types of music.

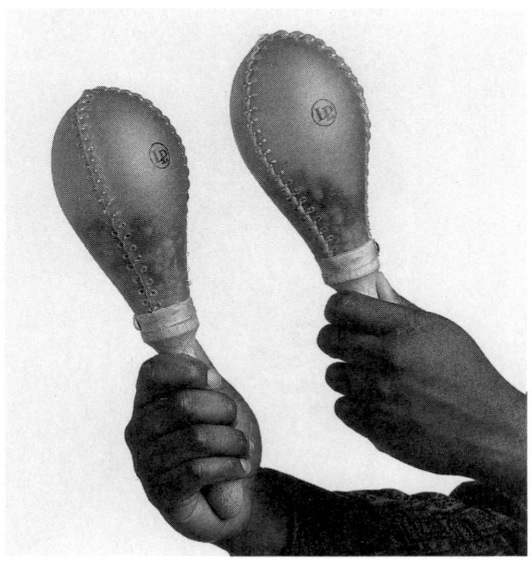

Fig. 8. Maracas.

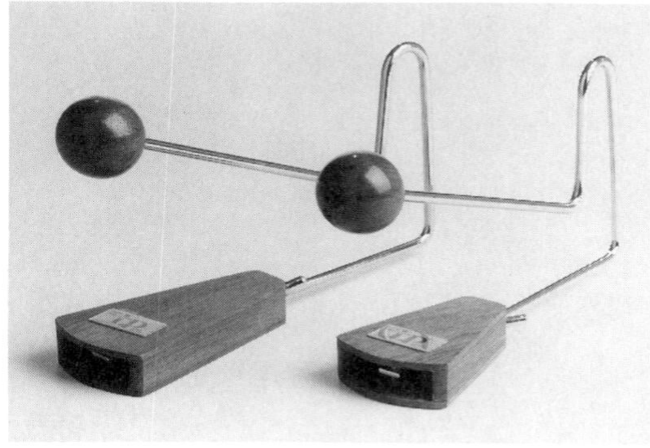

Fig. 9. Vibraslap.

Shekere

The *shekere* was originally an African instrument brought to Cuba during the slave trade. Like the *batá* drums, the *shekere*, also called by its African name, *agbe*, is primarily used for the ceremonies of Santería, a religion based on African deities. It is also used as a shaker in nontraditional contexts where a loud, piercing sound is desired.

Made from a large gourd or calabash, the *shekere* is cut open at the top, hollowed out, and dried. A net of beads strung around the gourd produces a sharp, rattling sound as it strikes against the sides.

Playing technique involves rhythmically moving the *shekere* between the hands using a sideways motion. The right hand cradles the bottom of the gourd, while the left holds it around the top or neck. Accents within the pattern are played by striking the bottom of the *shekere* with the palm of the hand, producing a rich resonant tone.

Traditionally, *shekeres* are played in groups of three—high, middle, and low—and are accompanied by a bell player and a conga drummer who improvises over the steady pattern. As with most Afro-Cuban rhythms, each player maintains a repetitive pattern that interlocks with the others in polyrhythmic counterpoint.

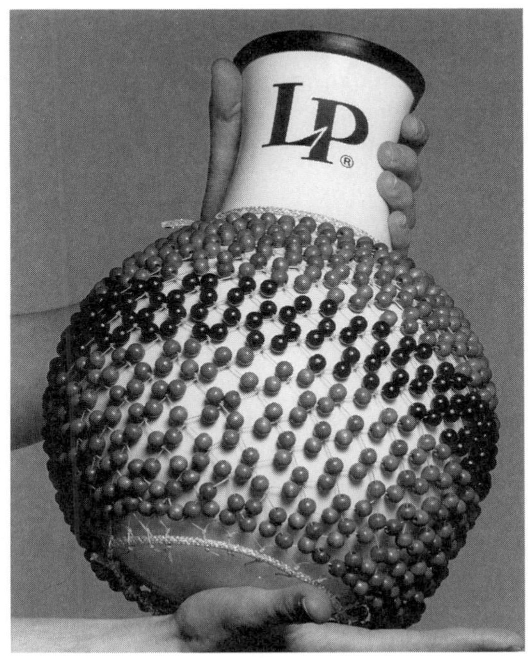

Fig. 10. Shekere.

Tambora

Originating in the Dominican Republic, the *tambora* is the main percussion instrument used to accompany the merengue, one of the most popular Latin-American rhythms. It is a wooden, two-headed drum ranging about 2 feet in length, with head diameters of 12 to 14 inches. The traditional *tambora* is tuned by adjusting leather straps that interconnect both rawhide heads. Mechanically tuned versions are also produced, sometimes made out of fiberglass.

R.H. = on rim

L.H. = slap

Ex. 14. Merengue.

Fig. 11. Tambora.

Placed on the laps of a seated player and supported by a neck strap, the *tambora* is played with a thick beater in the right hand that alternately strikes the upper rim and the head. The left hand plays open tones and slaps on the other side of the drum. The typical merengue rhythm includes a combination of wooden clicking sounds, slaps marking the beat, and open tones.

Timbales

The *timbales* are descendants of the European orchestral timpani that were used in the Cuban *danzón* bands of the early 1900s. Retaining their French name, the *timbales*, greatly reduced in size and with an attached cowbell, provided the rhythmic foundation for the *charanga* orchestras of the 1920s. By the 1940s the *timbales* had become an integral part of the Latin percussion section and Afro-Cuban music as a whole.

Modern *timbales* consist of a pair of single-headed drums mounted on a stand with shells made of brass, stainless steel, and sometimes wood. The heads are either calfskin or plastic and are tuned by screw tensioning. Head sizes range from 13 to 15 inches; the smaller *timbalitos* range from 9¼ to 10¼ inches.

Fig. 12. Timbales.

The typical *timbale* setup consists of two cowbells mounted on an attachment set between the drums. The large mambo bell is on the right, while the smaller cha-cha bell, positioned slightly higher, is on the left. A suspended cymbal is used to complement the setup. The small *timbal (macho)* is set in front of the player, or *timbalero*; the larger drum (*hembra*) is to the left, a holdover from the timpani.

Timbale technique includes matching the appropriate sound with a particular section in the music. For softer passages, such as an introduction or piano solo, the shells of the drum (*cáscara*) are used. During choruses or ensemble sections, the *timbalero* generally plays the cowbells or cymbal. Timekeeping patterns are based on the *clave* and often include a muffled and open sound played on the large *timbale* with the fingers.

A trademark of the *timbales* is a figure called the *abanico*. Played on the small *timbale*, the *abanico* is used as a cue to signal different sections within an arrangement. Although many variations exist, it basically consists of a short roll leading to a rimshot on the downbeat (see Ex. 15).

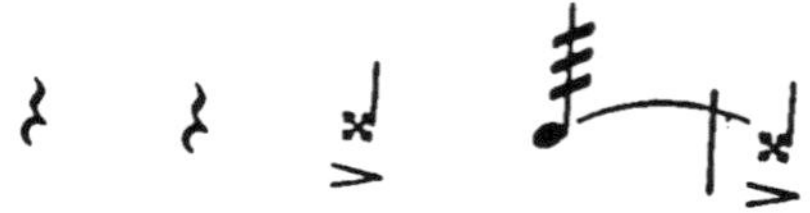

= rim shot

Ex. 15. Abanico.

Norbert Goldberg

Photographs courtesy of Martin Cohen, Latin Percussion, Inc., Garfield, N.J.

Latin Percussionists

The following is a list of the most influential Latin percussion players of the twentieth century. Birth and death dates are included when known. For more information, see *The New Grove Dictionary of Jazz*, edited by Barry Kernfeld (New York: Stockton Press, Groves Dictionaries of Music [Macmillan], 1988).

Acuna, Alex (b. 1944)
Barretto, Ray
Candido (b. 1921)
Conte, Luis (b. 1954)
Goldberg, Norbert (b. 1953)
Hidalgo, Giovanni (b. 1963)
Malabe, Frankie (b. 1940)
Mangual, José (b. 1924)
Marrero, Nicky (b. 1950)
Mendoza, Victor
Montalvo, Eddie (b. 1952)
Oguendo, Manny (b. 1931)
Peraza, Armando (b. 1924)
Pozo, Chino (1915–1980)
Puente, Tito (b. 1923)
Quinones, Mark (b. 1963)
Sánchez, Poncho
Stinholtz, Jerry
Valdez, Carlos "Patato" (b. 1926)
Vilato, Orestes

Norbert Goldberg

The Marimba in Mexico and Related Areas

At the close of the twentieth century, Mexico's marimba tradition continues to be concentrated in, but not limited to, the southernmost state of Chiapas. The marimba is also heard in the neighboring states of Veracruz, Oaxaca, and Tabasco, as well as in the nation's capital. Although marimba groups are scattered throughout the rest of the country, Mexico City and Chiapas display the most vibrant traditions. In Mexico multiple players on one or two marimbas are more common than solo players, the dominant performance style in the United States, Europe, and Japan.

Today in Mexico the music of the marimba is widely viewed as a regional phenomenon. Identified with the southern part of the nation, this music is often placed in the same context as other popular music genres such as the *jarocho* (the state of Veracruz), *mariachi* (the state of Jalisco), or *norteño* (northern Mexico). The Chiapan marimba tradition will serve as the point of departure for this article, although aspects of the marimba's history, classification, and performance practice throughout Central America and parts of South America will also be addressed.

Introduction

The Chiapan marimba is a type of xylophone that is table-like in design. The two most basic types are the diatonic instrument, often called the *marimba sencilla* (simple marimba), and the *marimba doble* (double marimba), a chromatic instrument of two keyboards that are similar in configuration to those of a piano. On the top there are wooden slabs, commonly referred to as *teclas* (keys or bars). The suspension of the bars is made possible by drilling through each bar at two nodal points that do not vibrate. A long rope is then placed through each hole, thereby connecting each bar consecutively, which in turn is strung through a suspension peg. Each suspension peg is fastened at its base to the instrument's frame, permitting maximum freedom of vibration to enhance the tone. The teclas are graduated in size and suspended over open rectangular resonating chambers called *cajones,* which are quadrangular and hollow, open at the top and closed at the bottom in a pyramidal shape. The length of each *cajón,* along with its air volume, is carefully calibrated to precisely amplify acoustically each *tecla*'s fundamental pitch, thus producing the optimum enhancement of tone. Directly over the closed bottom is a protruding piece of wax fastened over an aperture. Stretched over this opening is a thin sheath of pig intestine. This membrane vibrates sympathetically when the bars are struck, creating a buzzing effect. The number of keys and corresponding resonators are determined by the range of each particular instrument. From maker to maker the sizes and ranges of instruments vary; however, the full-sized chromatic instrument is usually six-and-a-half octaves (C to f^5), while smaller chromatic instruments (called *requinta)* are usually less than five octaves but do not go below the second C on the full-sized instrument. In total the large instrument would have upwards of seventy-eight keys while the smaller marimba would have less than sixty.

In Mexico the word marimba is used in two distinct contexts. If speaking of an ensemble it can denote a group of individuals who often play on multiple instruments. It may also be spoken of as a single instrument.

Classification

The *Diccionario de la música labor* has two entries for the term marimba.[1] The first states that the instrument is originally from the Congo and arrived in the Americas by way of black Africans. It also says that the original instrument had sixteen gourds of different tones. The next entry is for the marimba *mejicana*, which is described as a type of xylophone with twenty-one wooden slabs suspended over wooden tubes that are closed at the bottom. The *Diccionario de la lengua española* of the Spanish Royal Academy defines marimba as a percussion instrument "similar to a xylophone with strips of wood."[2] It states that the word marimba is from an African language.

The New Grove Dictionary of Musical Instruments splits marimba into three parts or types of instruments: (1) the marimbas of Africa and Latin America; (2) the modern orchestral marimba; and (3) the marimbas of Harry Partch. The term is defined as "a group of idiophones, some of which are plucked (lamellaphones) and some of which are struck (xylophones)." It also states that the Latin-American instrument came from Africa.[3]

Since the marimba is generally accepted to be a type of xylophone, that term also deserves further scrutiny. The xylophone article in the *New Grove Dictionary* was written by Lois Ann Anderson, James Blades, George List, and Linda O'Brien. There is much more detail in it regarding the marimba than in the marimba entry (in the same compendium) by Gerhard Kubik, Blades, and Rosemary Roberts. Anderson states that the first recorded oral reference to the instrument in Africa was made in thirteenth-century Mali; it was mentioned in a written document in the following century. Her account includes information on many types of xylophones seen and heard in Africa and Southeast Asia. George List and Linda O'Brien go on to describe the origins of the Latin-American xylophone, which is called marimba. They endorse the concept that the African xylophone was the model upon which the Guatemalan marimba *de tecomates* was developed. Basing this premise on the fact that the word marimba is derived from an African language, they cite the lack of archaeological evidence of any pre-Columbian marimba. This theory regarding African origins (vis-à-vis language) has long been shared by several scholars. Kubik puts this forth in his *New Grove Dictionary* article about the marimba, as does Robert Garfias[4] and Fernando Ortiz.[5]

In the first volume of his classic series, *Los instrumentos de la música afro-cubana*, Ortiz discusses the etymological origins of the marimba. This discourse reveals that the word marimba is derived from the Bantu language and that the suffix "-imba" means to sing. Kubik goes one step further and shows that "-rimba" in Bantu can define a single-note xylophone in Malawi or Mozambique and that "ma-" is a plural prefix. Therefore, marimba can mean a complete instrument made up of numerous individual keys.

A crucial link between the African and Latin-American marimbas/xylophones seems to be the vibrating membranes attached to the resonators, be they gourd or wood. Roger Blench states that an important aspect of all African xylophones is the use of "mirlitons or kazoo membranes."[6] These vibrating tissues near the bottoms of the resonators are also found on virtually all Central and some South American marimbas. The African instruments used spider cocoons (or cigarette paper in modern times). In Latin America there almost always has been a piece of pig or sheep intestine stretched across an opening in the resonator to create a buzzing sound.

It has already been stated that the marimba is a type of xylophone. But we may conclude that its meanings are slightly different in Latin America and Africa. In Africa, it refers to many types of xylophones with or without resonators, as well as types of lamellaphones. In Latin America, marimba refers to a xylophone with resonators and a type of lamellaphone.

The Origins and Development of the Marimba in Chiapas

In Mexico, several books have been written on the origins of the marimba. In addition to the Montiel anthology,[7] Jaime Rodas and Amador Hernández C. have published books on this subject, *La marimba* (1971) and *El origen de la marimba* (1975), respectively. Rodas subtitles his book *Its Origins and Modifications Until the Present with a Brief Anthology of Chiapan Poems.* He presents several viewpoints, including those of Ortiz and Curt Sachs (*The History of Musical Instruments,* 1940), as well as several interesting hypotheses. Among these is an account by Mexican historian Flavio Guíllen stating that a "black African" came with Father Las Casas and introduced the instrument in the area that is now known as San Cristóbal de las Casas. Even more noteworthy is Rodas's citation of Mexican historian Manuel Trens (*Historia de Chiapas,* 1957), a scholar well respected for his exhaustive writings on the histories of Veracruz and Chiapas. Trens upholds the African theory by citing the fact that black slaves were brought to the Fraylesca region of Chiapas by Dominican friars, most specifically the plantations of San Lucas and San José. He also reported that these slaves introduced a highly primitive and rudimentary instrument that was the actual forerunner of the traditional Chiapan marimba. Rodas notes that in 1870 there was a rudimentary marimba in Fraylesca played by three individuals of African origin.[8]

Amador Hernández C. cites numerous scholarly journals, books, periodicals, and compendiums for his research on the origins of the marimba and devotes a chapter to oral histories. A central focus of his work is the exposure of a mysterious document, dated 1545, that refers to an instrument with eight wooden slabs. The document is titled "The Christianization of the Indians of Santa Lucia, 1545." The title is followed by the name Pedro Gentil de Bustamente. The name of this instrument, *yolotli,* is claimed to be of Mexican origin. This word is obviously not Spanish, but probably from an Indian language of the "Santa Lucia" estate, which today is in the *municipio* Jiquipilas. Hernández writes that this document was given to his father, along with a copy of the Royal Academy's *Diccionario de la lengua española* in 1914 to save them from being burned in the revolutionary fighting in that area. Hernández laments that academics he has contacted have not accepted the validity of this document. Montiel (*Investigando la historia,* 1985) devotes a chapter of his anthology to this work of Hernández. He is correct to approach the document with caution, but it should not be dismissed.

Guatemalan author David Vela devotes a section of his book, *Information on the Marimba* (1958), to the Chiapan marimba tradition. After several anecdotal and folkloric accounts of the marimba in southern Mexico, he cites some serious scholarship from Eduardo J. Selvas (1957) and Henrietta Yurchenco (1943). He also goes on to cite Selvas who stated that the marimba was brought to Chiapas from Africa and was composed of sixteen to twenty-one sonorous planks that were suspended in some manner. Selvas identifies the original scale as diatonic, broadening in time to the chromatic scale. Before the chromatic pitches were added to the instrument, however, semitones were obtained by attaching small balls of beeswax to the bottom of the bars. The instrument was situated on three legs and played by two to four individuals.[9]

The Chromatic Marimba in Mexico

The introduction of the chromatic marimba allowed the assimilation of other musics from outside Mexico, while expanding the means of expression for Chiapans to interpret their own traditional and popular musics. Morales Avendaño[10] says that the traditional marimbas (diatonic instruments) prior to this invention were three octaves and that this new chromatic instrument was five octaves. Yet there is disagreement about exactly when the new instrument was developed and who deserves the credit for it. Claim to the invention, for example, is also made by Guatemalans. Corazón de Jesús Borraz Moreno (1877–1960) of San Bartolomé de los Llanos (today Venustiano Carranza) is generally credited with having made the chromatic additions to the instrument during the last decade of the nineteenth century.

In *La marimba*, Rodas describes a scenario in which an uncle of Borraz, Mariano Ruperto Moreno, drew a pencil design of a marimba with two keyboards on the wall of the carpenter's shop of Jesús's father. From that sketch Corazón de Jesús Borraz Moreno, with his father's assistance, finished the instrument and completed modifications in February 1896. "The first people to play this marimba were Manuel Trinidad Santiago, Corazón de Jesús Borraz Moreno, José and Angel Domingo, the last three were brothers."[11]

Morales Avendaño cites 1897 as the year that the second keyboard was added, and he too describes the same scenario as Rodas. In a history of the town where the invention took place, Avendaño gives a more detailed account of the background of the new instrument's designer, Mariano Ruperto Moreno, saying that he was an organist and violinist as well as an uncle of Borraz.[12]

Exactly where the chromatic marimba was invented—Chiapas or Guatemala—may be a lesser consideration. Perhaps the larger issue is to view southern Chiapas and northern Guatemala as an area of people who share a common cultural heritage that reflects the boundaries of the sixteenth through the eighteenth centuries, when Mexico's border ended north of Spanish Chiapa. Perhaps Alan Riding sums it up best when he recognizes that the Chiapan people have more in common with Guatemalans than the neighboring Oaxacans to the west.[13]

Aspects of Performance Practice

According to Theodore Solís, "*las muñecas de chiapaneco*" (the wrists of a Chiapan) is a commonly used phrase that succinctly summarizes the widely held view that Chiapans are superior marimbists by birthright. Of course, the assumption is taken for granted in Chiapas, but even in Mexico City there is a generally held notion that a "true" marimbist must be a Chiapan.[14]

Part of the reason for this mystique is that many Chiapans have played the marimba since their earliest years. This has allowed them, in time, to develop rapid alternation of the mallets by use of extremely powerful and developed wrist muscles. This, in turn, allows them to sustain (or roll) notes in a smooth and expressive manner. It is the most challenging technical (and expressive) aspect of marimba playing, which generally takes many years to develop fully. It would be extremely difficult for anyone to acquire this skill in a short time.

Most Chiapan marimbists perform with two or three mallets. Only a few use four. Several variables determine what combination the player will employ. The hardness of the mallets is graded according to the register for which it is used. Contrary to the North American solo technique, in which a player covers the entire range of an instrument, Chiapans generally play in groups, and most of the time they stand within a certain area or register of the marimba. These positions are called *puestos* (stands). The low register players use mallets that are large and heavy, so as to best activate the low voice. The uppermost keys are struck with small hard rubber mallets. And in turn, the individual combinations will determine a group's sound.

Two-mallet technique involves holding a single mallet in each hand. Guatemalan players usually extend the index finger in a straight position that points toward the mallet head. In most of Chiapas (as well as the United States) players generally wrap the index finger around the mallet shaft.

The use of three or four mallets depends on two variables: (1) the individual player's technique; and (2) the arrangement system used by the group. The group's leader, who is almost always the arranger, determines the number of voices in an arrangement according to the number of mallets his players are able to use. The most common combination of mallets in Chiapas is two mallets for the outer voices (the melody and bass lines) and three or four mallets for inner parts. Only the most talented players use four mallets. But even highly skilled players have difficulty projecting in the upper register of the instrument while holding four mallets. The reason for this is that the keys narrow considerably in the higher range of the instrument. A smaller bar needs both a harder mallet and more energy behind the stroke in order to balance with the other voices. Zeferino Nandayapa of Mexico City is one of the few players who has both the technique and physical strength to use four mallets in the upper register and achieve a balance with the other players.

Marimba Repertoire in Chiapas

The Chiapan marimba repertoire is almost exclusively derived from other musical traditions. There is very little original music for the marimba in Chiapas. That is why the group leader/arranger is such an important figure. Yet the Chiapan marimba repertoire is diverse. The arrangers adapt music from a wide range of popular and classical sources.

In his detailed anthology about the marimba tradition in Chiapas, César Pineda del Valle, formerly of the state government's Office of Cultural Investigation, lists the following instrumental musical types under the distinct heading, "Música popular chiapaneca": "*Sones, Zapateados, Marcha, Valses, Polkas, Danzones, Boleros, Corridos, Guajiras, Baladas, Guarachas, Jarabes, Pasos Dobles, Chotis, Tropical, Ranchero, Himnos,* etc."[15] All of these different styles have been and continue to be interpreted on the marimba. E. Thomas Stanford says that the word *son* is a generic term for rural or peasant music, *zapateado* is the movement of a dancer's feet against the ground, usually during an interlude in the *son,* that the *vals, polka,* and *chotis* are nineteenth-century dance forms aligned with Mexican *música norteña*, and that the *paso doble* and *corrido* are twentieth-century forms. He goes on to define *jarabe* as another *son* type with additional properties.[16]

The diversity of the Chiapan marimba repertoire contrasts sharply with other Mexican regional repertoires, which are significantly more narrow. Solís illustrates this point by citing the "static" nature of repertoires found in other regional music styles in Mexico (i.e., *jarocho, huastecan* guitar, *mariachi*, or *ranchero*) and writes that marimbists blend many styles in a repertoire that leans toward tropical, rock, and other musics. He goes on to hypothesize that marimbists look for the acquisition of a higher degree of musical complexity within the parameters of their specific musical setting. These comments certainly put the adaptive nature of the marimba in a true light.[17]

The Chiapan marimba tradition, as a type of regional music, contrasts significantly with the *son jarocho,* a regional musical style of Veracruz. The repertoire of the neighboring Veracruz *jarocho* musicians, in fact, is quite small. David Stiberg laments the loss of standard repertoire in Veracruz. He says that while the older professional musicians of the *son jarocho* tradition know the standard repertoire of the region, their patrons do not recognize this type of music.[18] Therefore, only several *sones* are commonly known, and few are requested for performance with any regularity. And there seems to be little inclination on the part of these musicians of Veracruz to widen their repertoire as the marimbists of Chiapas have done.

The Distribution of the Marimba in Mexico, Central, and South America

Contemporary Instruments with Wood Resonators

Marimba Doble (double or chromatic marimba)

Marimba Grande

Chiapas: $6\frac{1}{2}$ octaves (C to f^5)
Guatemala: 6+ octaves (G to b^5)
Belize: 6+ octaves
Costa Rica: 6+ octaves
Honduras and El Salvador (instruments that were fabricated in Guatemala)

Requinta

Chiapas: $4\frac{1}{2}$ octaves (f–c^4). Also called *tiple, chica, requinto, tenor*
Guatemala: 3+ octaves f^1–e^4. Also called *cuache, requinto, tenor, piccolo, fife*
Belize: 4+ octaves
Honduras and El Salvador (instruments that were fabricated in Guatemala)

Marimba Sencilla (diatonic instrument)

Chiapas: no contemporary performance practice, but some instruments survive. One with 42 keys was sighted in San Cristóbal de las Casas in 1985.
Guatemala: according to Chenoweth, at the time of her research a marimba maker in Antigua was still making these instruments. Those had 45 keys. She identifies several other types that were still in use in the 1950s.[19]
Costa Rica: 24 keys
Nicaragua: 22 keys
Southern Colombia: 24 keys (bamboo resonators)
Northern Ecuador: 21–26 keys (bamboo resonators)

Marimbas with Gourd Resonators

Chiapas: these were last used in the nineteenth century
Guatemala: Garfias shows a 30-key *marimba de tecomates*. These diatonic instruments are also called *marimba de arco* when they have a wooden arc frame behind the keyboard. (The Nicaraguans still use the arcs but have wooden resonators on their instruments instead of gourds.)

The Marimba in Other Mexican States

Bordering Chiapas are the states of Oaxaca, Veracruz, and Tabasco, and they have marimba traditions that have survived to the present. Oaxaca has two distinct areas of marimba activity: the rural Isthmus of Tehuantepec and the capital city, Oaxaca. The tradition of the Isthmus of Tehuantepec has been the subject of study by North American ethnomusicologist Robert Garfias, who recorded and issued two recordings titled *Marimba Music of Tehuantepec* (1972). The accompanying liner notes are rich in detail and highly informative.

Perhaps the most visible marimba tradition in all of Mexico is that of the *ambulantes (*street musicians) of Veracruz. These players perform (and compete for business) nearly twenty-four hours a day in the colorful *zocalo* of white buildings and green palm trees, which is only blocks away from the Atlantic Ocean and a major seaport. The sharp-edged, heavily syncopated playing of Veracruz is indicative of the Afro-Cuban influence that is apparent in the music and culture of this seaport city.

Usually only one marimba is used in performance with two to four players. In addition there is almost always a rasp player. He scrapes a hollow gourd that has ridges on the side with a small stick and solicits funds from the audience.

Marimba virtuoso Fernando Morales Matus (b. 1945) resides in Jalapa, the state capital of Veracruz. Having fled the political upheaval of Guatemala in 1981, Morales Matus performs as a concert artist on a limited basis. Well known for his outstanding recordings of traditional Guatemalan marimba music, he has appeared as a concerto soloist with the Guatemalan National and Jalapa Symphony orchestras.

Probably the least visible marimba tradition of the states that surround Chiapas is that of Tabasco. The marimba of Tabasco was introduced near the region of Balancan, *municipio* of Los Rios. Black slaves fled from the Spaniards to this area, and their descendants still live there. In the village of Mactum the Mayans and blacks built marimbas. When Tabasco's border was with Guatemala, Chiapan and Tabascan traditions mixed with those of Guatemala. The marimba tradition still exists in the region of Los Rios. In the eighteenth and nineteenth centuries marimba groups were created and their tradition grew with that of military bands.

The marimba groups in Mexico City with the greatest acceptance are led by individuals from the state of Chiapas. Solís gives an excellent accounting of their marimba activity in his dissertation.[20]

Important Performers/Leaders and Their Groups

There is very little information on individual marimbists who lived before 1890. The earliest player mentioned by Rodas, Hernández, and Pineda del Valle is Manuel Bolán (c. 1810–1863). Rodas describes him as both a marimbist and composer of renown.[21] He was especially well known for composing outstanding *sones*. Pineda del Valle calls Bolán the father of the Chiapan marimba,[22] but, more precisely, he was one of the first marimbists to gain public attention. Bolán, born in Buena Vista, Chiapas, is said to have toured the state of Chiapas and Guatemala playing the marimba. According to Hernández,[23] Fermín Trujillo (a 105-year-old marimbist) said in an interview that the most famous marimbist of the mid-1800s was indeed Manuel Bolán, and the specific type of marimba he used employed three musicians, the other two being Juan Zárate and José Martínez. Bolán also influenced other marimbists, among whom was Benjamin Roque, who in 1885 attempted unsuccessfully to add a second keyboard to the marimba. Roque was also from Buena Vista, Chiapas.

Corazón de Jesús Borraz Moreno (1877–1960) of Venustiano Carranza, cited earlier for having invented the second keyboard of the marimba, was another outstanding marimbist of the nineteenth century. Regarding Borraz Moreno's invention of the chromatic keyboard, Avendaño reports that the old, single keyboard instruments (diatonic) were only three octaves and that the instrument Borraz Moreno constructed was five octaves, "permitting the execution of classical pieces."[24] Both Morales Avendaño and Armando Alfonzo A.[25] attribute Borraz Moreno's innovation to the desire to perform classical music on the marimba.

Identifying prominent performers other than Borraz Moreno during the first several decades of the twentieth century is difficult. The next generations of marimbists, however, born between 1890 and 1940, are much more accessible through recordings, personal interviews, and newspaper articles.

David Gómez, Sr., and David Gómez, Jr., are both important individuals in the history of the marimba in Chiapas. David Gómez, Sr., was born in Tuxtla Gutiérrez in 1867 and died there in 1945. Based on existing recordings, the Gómez group of the 1950s represented a high standard of marimba performance of Western classical music. The lead playing by Gómez was inspired and highly original. He made excellent use of roll speed[26] to effect timbral nuance. He also possessed a wide dynamic range in the highest octave without striking the bars too hard (as was the custom with many players).

Solís lists five marimbists as outstanding "formally trained marimbists." They are Abel Domínguez, Aristo López, Rafael de Paz, Zeferino Nandayapa, and Abraham Cuesta Grajales. According to Solís, they were all born in Chiapas, all were sons of musicians, and all performed in professional groups in the outlying regions before coming to Mexico City.[27]

Zeferino Nandayapa is perhaps one of the most famous marimba artists of all time. Nandayapa was born on August 26, 1931, in Chiapa de Corzo, Chiapas. He is undeniably the most visible marimba artist in Mexico, having recorded over two hundred long-playing records, cassettes, as well as three compact discs. He makes many concert appearances weekly (as well as playing many of the most fashionable social and civic gatherings in Mexico City, Guadalajara, and other locations). His television documentaries on the marimba are shown many times each year on Mexico City television. Furthermore, he regularly appears overseas representing Mexico at cultural events and other venues. He is one of the most active international touring artists from Mexico and is seen as a representative of Mexican culture.

Nandayapa's sons joined his group during the 1970s. Several of them attended the National Conservatory of Music. The Nandayapas project a high level of marimba performance in Mexico in the 1990s. They represent the rare type of marimba group that combines artistic and commercial aspirations.

Another one of the great contemporary marimba artists and leaders is Límbano Vidal Mazariegos of Comitán. His outstanding group, "Las Aguilas de Chiapas," has recorded twenty-two albums. Another out-

Fig. 1. Marimba Nandayapa. Led by Chiapan-born virtuoso Zeferino Nandayapa, this ensemble has been based in Mexico City since the mid-1950s. This photo was taken in 1992, at which time the ensemble included his four sons: Javier, Norberto, Mario, and Oscar.

Fig. 2. A Mexican marimba made by Alejandrino Nandayapa Ralda, in Chiapa de Corzo, Chiapas, 1992.

standing player is Manuel Vleeschower Borraz (b. 1923) of Venustiano Carranza.

Recordings of the Gómez group of the 1950s reveal second marimbist Daniel García Blanco to be a gifted player. His place in the marimba history of Chiapas, however, may best be defined as a chronicler and arranger of the popular music of Chiapas. He has long been a champion of the tradition of *marimba pura* (marimba without other instruments).

The late Hermisendo Paniagua Pérez is another Chiapan marimbist who migrated to Mexico City. Along with Zeferino Nandayapa he represented Mexico overseas as both a commercial marimbist and a cultural ambassador. Other notable marimbists in late-twentieth-century Chiapas are Mario Penagos Rojas and Ricardo Sánchez Solís.

Regarding *indigenous* performers in Chiapas, Henrietta Yurchenco observed in 1943 that although the marimbas were heard in most villages, they exercised no influence on the Indians' traditional music.[28]

Dennis Breedlove, a specialist in the flora and fauna of Chiapas, has reported hearing Indian marimbists performing on a weekly basis at the Sunday morning markets in the pueblos of Las Margaritas and La Independéncia, which are located near Comitán. He too found that most of the contemporary marimba tradition is carried on by the mestizo (ethnically mixed individuals) and that these musicians were not playing any sort of music that could be associated with Mayan antecedents.[29]

The Marimba outside Mexico

Marimba activity and tradition can be found throughout much of Latin America. Abraham Cáceres divides the Latin-American marimba tradition into two parts: (1)

Central America, which extends from Mexico through Costa Rica and; (2) the Colombo-Ecuadorian region, which runs from the Buenaventura River, Colombia, to the Province of Pichincha, Ecuador.[30] Garfias basically agrees with Cáceres's Mexican to Costa Rican division. In a highly informative article in the *Latin-American Music Review*, he describes and shows in pictures marimba activity in Mexico, Belize, Nicaragua, Costa Rica, El Salvador, Honduras, and Guatemala.[31]

Regarding the Caribbean, John Storm Roberts cites an account of a marimba heard in the Barbados Islands in 1673. This description is not unlike that of the early marimba called *yolotli*, which was first described in Chiapas a century earlier.[32]

There exists an active marimba tradition in the South American areas described by Cáceres.[33] The blacks of southern Colombia and northern Ecuador share a border and a tradition of playing a single keyboard marimba. These diatonic instruments employ tuned bamboo resonators and, unlike Chiapan marimbas, do not have any vibrating membrane. Aside from the investigation conducted by Cáceres, Norman Whitten (1970) has written descriptively of the marimba in Colombia and Ecuador within its social and cultural contexts and includes a photograph of this instrument being played.[34] As far as other South American countries are concerned, Robert Stevenson cites a publication from 1791 as naming the marimba as an instrument played by blacks in Colonial Peru.[35]

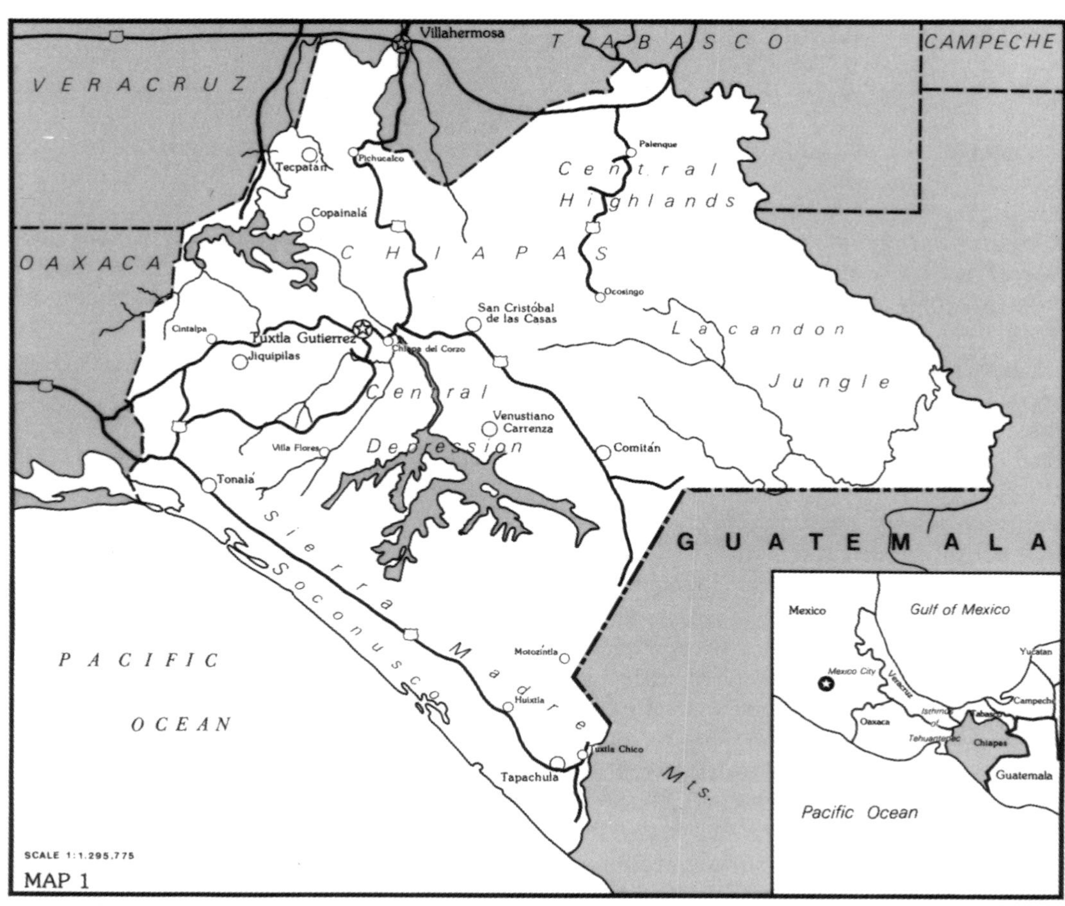

Fig. 3. Map of Chiapas.

Plate 12 in Rolando Mellafe's *Negro Slavery in Latin America* (1975) carries a caption that reads, "Musical entertainment of blacks and black mestizos in Peru, late eighteenth century." This painting shows two individuals playing a marimba-like instrument with one stick or beater in each hand.

Though several sources suggest that in Brazil the marimba is currently in disuse, there is evidence that, though it is no longer played as a solo instrument, it is employed in an accompanimental role. George List and Linda O'Brien state that the marimba is still used in Brazil, not as a solo instrument but to accompany dramatic dances called *congadas*.[36]

This author witnessed the use of the marimba in a similar role in Nicaragua in 1981. In the village of Masaya near Monimbo, diatonic instruments are played by a single player and usually used to accompany dance. In Nicaragua the marimba is played solo as well. A recording by Nicaraguan marimbist Elías Palazzio, titled "Marimba típica" (traditional marimba), uses a small diatonic marimba with guitar accompaniment. Robert Garfias has a picture of this combination in his article that appeared in the 1983 Fall/Winter issue of the *Latin-American Music Review*.

One of his photos illustrates a Belizian group of six marimbists from San José Soccotz playing on two chromatic instruments. Garfias also includes a photograph of a Costa Rican marimbist from Cacao playing a twenty-four-key diatonic marimba with metal resonators, as well as a trio of players performing on a large chromatic instrument in Guanacaste, Costa Rica (plates 11 and 12, n.p.)

Outside Chiapas the most active and visible marimba tradition is in Guatemala, where the marimba is the national instrument. Much information has been written about the Guatemalan marimba. The types of marimbas described in the aforementioned accounts are generally chromatic instruments with two keyboards. The urban performance practice of Guatemala remains that of an ensemble usually consisting of two chromatic instruments, with several marimbists playing on each instrument (usually six to seven total marimbists). This ensemble is often augmented by other instruments. This author witnessed many live performances of *marimba doble* (chromatic marimbas) and *marimba sencilla* (diatonic marimba with resonators made out of wood), and a trio from a village near Guatemala City on a *marimba de tecomates* (diatonic marimba with gourd or calabash resonators). There are daily live radio broadcasts of marimba music broadcast by station TGW in Guatemala City.

Touring Ensembles

Tours by many Mexican and Central American marimba ensembles in the early 1900s directly contributed to the rise of the marimba in the United States. Among these were the Hurtado Brothers Royal Marimba Band, the Imperial Marimba Band, Cárdenas Marimba Band, and the Blue and White Marimba Band, all of Guatemala. They made acoustic recordings for RCA Victor, the Edison Company, and the Columbia record labels between 1916 and 1919.

One of the most prominent early family marimba ensembles, "Lira de San Cristóbal," was made up of the internationally famous Domínguez brothers. This group was one of the first to use their performance opportunities as a means not only of migrating to Mexico City but of expanding their musical activities into composition. Brothers Abel and Alberto especially excelled in the latter area. Alberto's compositions *Frenesí* and *Perfidia* are certainly familiar to any North American who followed the big-band era of the 1940s (and they were recorded by pop music star Linda Ronstadt in 1992). In 1921 the Domínguez brothers went to Mexico City, and in 1937 they toured Europe, South America, and the United States. During their career they even appeared in the Hollywood musical comedy *Tropic Holiday*.

Numerous other Chiapan groups also toured the United States. Amador Hernández reports that a group from Chiapas called "Cuarteto Ovando" toured the United States extensively in 1911, making appearances in Texas, Georgia, and Kansas, as well as Washington, Chicago, and New York. Near the end of the 1925 tour by the "Cuarteto Hermanos Gómez," Hernández writes that they returned to Chiapas with their own reworking of the "Charleston," and that they played it at every fiesta and social occasion in which they performed.[37] North American marimba scholar Solís writes that a group of his ancestors toured the United States during the first three decades of this century and used the following names: "Solís Brothers," "Solís Quartet," "Four Solís," and the "Solís Marimba Band."[38] The Solís brothers later changed the name of their group to "La Poli de Tuxtla," where they were identified with the state police. This group is still extant into the 1990s and is still subsidized by the government of Chiapas.

Clair Omar Musser is generally credited with introducing the North American marimba to audiences in the United States. His own discovery of the marimba came after his father had taken him to hear a touring Honduran marimba ensemble at the 1915 World's Fair in San Francisco.

In January 1991 the presidents of all Central American nations and Mexico traveled to Tuxtla Gutiérrez, Chiapas, for an historic summit meeting. After spending several days discussing cultural practices shared by these Latin-American nations, the group identified two common threads connecting the nations from Panama through northern Mexico: poetry and the marimba. Clearly the marimba permeates much of Latin America. Aside from its role as a replicator and sustainer of many diverse musical genres, it serves as a cultural icon woven into the fabric of everyday life. The marimba is often described as having human qualities in both conversation and in literature, and the people of Chiapas often refer to the marimba as *las maderas que cantan* (the wood that sings).

Notes

1. "Marimba," *Diccionario de la música labor*, vol. 2 (Barcelona: Labor, 1954), 1476.

2. "Marimba," *Diccionario de la lengua española* (Madrid: Real Academia Española, 1984), 878.

3. Lois A. Anderson, James Blades, George List, and Linda O'Brien, "Xylophone," in *The New Grove Dictionary of Musical Instruments*, vol. 3 (London: Macmillan, 1984), 614–615.

4. Robert Garfias, "The Marimba of Mexico and Central America," *Revista de música latino americana/Latin-American Music Review* 4, no. 2 (1983): 203–212.

5. Fernando Ortiz, *Los instrumentos de la música afro-cubana,* vol. 1 (Havana: Publicaciones de la Dirección de Cultura del Ministerio de Educación, 1952), 268.

6. Roger Blench, "Evidence for the Indonesian Origins of Certain Elements of African Culture," *African Music Society Journal* 6, no. 2 (1982): 84.

7. Gustavo Montiel, *Investigando la historia de la marimba* (Mexico City: Gustavo Montiel, 1985).

8. Jaime Rodas, *La marimba* (Mexico City: Secretaria de Educación Pública y Subsecretaria de Asuntos Culturales, 1971), 22.

9. Eduardo Selvas, "La musica valiviana," *Revista Ateno* (Tuxtla Gutiérrez, Chiapas) 4 (1957): 32, as cited in David Vela's *Information on the Marimba,* trans. and ed. Vida Chenoweth (Auckland, New Zealand: The Institute Press, 1957).

10. Juan María Morales Avendaño, *San Bartolomé de Los Llanos* (Tuxtla Gutiérrez, Chiapas: Universidad Autonoma de Chiapas, 1985), 260.

11. Rodas, 35–36.

12. Morales Avendaño, 261–262.

13. Alan Riding, *Distant Neighbors* (New York: Vintage Books, 1986), 424.

14. Theodore Solís, "Muñecas de chiapaneco: The Economic Importance of Self-Image in the World of the Mexican *Marimba*," *Revista de música latino americana/Latin-American Music Review* 1, no. 1 (1980): 34.

15. César Pineda del Valle, "Música popular chiapaneca," unpublished manuscript, n.d., p. 1.

16. E. Thomas Stanford, "The Mexican Son," *Yearbook of the International Folk Music Council* 4 (1972): 68.

17. Solís, "Muñecas de Chiapaneco," 34.

18. David K. Stiberg, "Jarocho, Tropical and "Pop": Aspects of Musical Life in Veracruz, 1971–72," in *Eight Urban Musical Cultures,* ed. Bruno Nettl (Urbana: The University of Illinois Press, 1978), 269.

19. Vida Chenoweth, *The Marimbas of Guatemala* (Lexington: The University of Kentucky Press, 1964), 40–51, passim.

20. Theodore Solís, "The Marimba in Mexico City: Contemporary Contexts of a Traditional Regional Ensemble," Ph.D. diss. (University of Illinois, 1983), passim.

21. Rodas, 24.

22. César Pineda del Valle, "Program Notes" for *1er Concurso Estatal de Marimba* (Tuxtla Gutiérrez, Chiapas, 1984), 9.

23. Amador Hernández C. *El origen de la marimba*. Mexico City: n.p., 1975, 48.

24. Morales Avendaño, 261.

25. Armando Alfonzo A. *Comitán: 1940* (Mexico City: Litográfica Kamesa Rómulo, n.d.), 120.

26. Rapid alternation of mallets to sustain a pitch.

27. Solís, "The Marimba in Mexico City," 194.

28. Henrietta Yurchenco, "La música indígena en Chiapas, México," *América Indígena* 3, no. 4 (1943): 306.

29. Personal communication, March 12, 1988.

30. Abraham Cáceres, "The Marimba in the Americas," in *Discourse in Ethnomusicology: Essays in Honor of George List* (Bloomington: Ethnomusicology Publications Group of Indiana University, 1978), 225.

31. Robert Garfias, 203.

32. John Storm Roberts, *Black Music of Two Worlds* (New York: Praeger, 1972), 23.

33. Cáceres, 230.

34. Norman E. Whitten, "Personal Networks and Musical Contexts in the Pacific Lowlands of Colombia and Ecuador," in *Afro-American Anthropology,* ed. Norman E. Whitten and John F. Szwed (New York: Collier-Macmillan, 1970), 23 (photo).

35. Robert Stevenson, *Music in Mexico* (New York: Thomas Y. Crowell, 1952), 303–304.

36. Anderson, Blades, List, and O'Brien, 877.

37. Hernández C., 69–70.

38. Solís, "The Marimba in Mexico City," 7–8.

Bibliography

Alfonzo A., Armando. *Comitán: 1940.* Mexico City: Litográfica Kamesa Rómulo, n.d.

"The Americas." *Musical Instruments of the World.* New York: Facts on File, 1976.

Anderson, Lois Ann. "The African Xylophone." *African Arts* 1, no. 1 (1967–68): 46–49, 66, 68–69.

Anderson, Lois A., James Blades, George List, and Linda O'Brien. "Xylophone." In *The New Grove Dictionary of Musical Instruments.* Vol. 3. London: Macmillan, 1984.

Anleu Díaz, Enrique. *Esbozo histórico social de la música en Guatemala.* Guatemala: Departamento de Actividades Literarias de la Dirección General de Cultura y Bellas Artes en Guatemala, n.d.

Armas Lara, Marcial. *Origen de la marimba, su desenvolvimiento y otros instrumentos músicos.* Guatemala: Folklore Guatemalteco, 1970.

Baines, Anthony, ed. *Musical Instruments Through the Ages.* New York: Walker and Co., 1961.

Béhague, Gerard. "Folk and Traditional Music of Latin America: General Prospects and Research Problems." *The World of Music* 25, no. 2 (1982): 3–18.

———. "Latin-American Music: II. Folk Music, III. Afro-American Music (4, Folk Music), IV. Popular Music." In *The New Grove Dictionary of Music and Musicians.* Vol. 10, pp. 516–522, 526–528, 529–534. London: Macmillan, 1980.

Beltrán, Gonzalo. "La marimba es el genuino instrumento musical de México." *Mujeres-Suplemento Cultural* (January 1980): 20–21.

Blades, James. *Percussion Instruments and Their History.* 2nd ed. London: Faber and Faber, 1974.

Blench, Roger. "Evidence for the Indonesian Origins of Certain Elements of African Culture." *African Music Society Journal* 6, no. 2 (1982): 81–93.

Boone, Olga. "Les Xylophones du Congo Belge." In *Annales du Musée du Congo Belge* (Ethnographie—Série III). Vol. 3, no. 2, 69–144, plates X–XIV. Belgium: Tervueren, 1936.

Bowles, Paul. "On Mexico's Popular Music." *Modern Music* 18, no. 4 (1941): 225–230.

Cáceres, Abraham. "The Marimba in the Americas." In *Discourse in Ethnomusicology: Essays in Honor of George List,* pp. 225–250. Bloomington: Ethnomusicology Publications Group of Indiana University, 1978.

Cahn, William. "The Xylophone in Acoustic Recordings (1877–1929)." *The Percussionist* 16, no. 2 (1979): 133–152.

Calzada, Romulo. "Historia de un árbol." *Mujeres-Suplemento Cultural* (January 1980): 24–25.

Castañeda Paganini, Jorge. "La marimba, su origen y evolución." *Diario Imparcial* (Guatemala) 30, no. 10046–10047 (October 27–29, 1951): 3.

Castillo, Jesús. *La música Maya-Quiché.* Quezaltenango, Guatemala, 1941. Reprint, Guatemala City: Editorial Piedra Santa, n.d.

Chamorro, Arturo. *Los instrumentos de percusión en México.* Zamora: El Colegio de Michoacán, 1984.

Chase, Gilbert. *A Guide to the Music of Latin America.* 2nd rev. ed. Washington, D.C.: The Pan American Union and the Library of Congress, 1962.

———. "Carlos Chávez." In *The New Grove Dictionary of Music and Musicians.* Vol. 4, pp. 185–188. London: Macmillan, 1980.

Chenoweth, Vida. *The Marimbas of Guatemala.* Lexington: The University of Kentucky Press, 1964.

Coleman, Satis N. *The Marimba Book.* Rev. ed. New York: The John Day Company, 1930.

Covarrubias, Miguel. *El sur de México.* Mexico City: Instituto Nacional Indigenista, 1980.

Curtin, Philip D. *The Atlantic Slave Trade.* Madison: The University of Wisconsin Press, 1969.

"Discurso sobre la música." *Diario de México* (Mexico City) (October 24, 1807): 245.

Dietz, Betty Warner, and Michael Babatunde Olatunji. *Musical Instruments of Africa.* New York: The John Day Company, 1965.

Enciclopédico Chiapas. 101st ed. Mexico City: Fernández Editores, S.A. de C.V., 1984.

Estrada, Julio, ed. *La música de México.* Mexico City: Universidad Nacional Autónoma de México, 1984.

Eyler, David Paul. "The History and Development of the Marimba Ensemble in the United States and Its Current Status in College and University Percussion Programs." Monograph. The Louisiana State University and Agricultural and Mechanical College, Baton Rouge, 1985.

Fernández Troncoso, Raul. *La marimba, su origen y leyenda.* Mexico City: Talleres Gráficos Nacionales, 1957.

"Francisco Santiago Borraz, inovador de la marimba." *Mujeres-Suplemento Cultural* (January 1980): 23.

Galindo Arce, Marcelina. "Artifice en la creación de marimbas." *Mujeres-Suplemento Cultural* (January 1980): 30–33.

———. "Mas datos para la historia de la marimba." *Mujeres-Suplemento Cultural* (January 1980): 22.

García Blanco, Daniel. "Algunas consideraciones sobre la marimba." In *Investigando el origen de la* marimba, edited by Gustavo Montiel, pp. 157–168. Mexico City: Gustavo Montiel, 1985.

———. *Cuadernos del la casa de la música Mexicana.* Vols. 1 and 2. Mexico City: Casa de la Música Mexicana, 1992.

———. *Danzas y bailes regionales de México.* Vol. 1, 4th ed. Mexico City: Daniel García Blanco, 1984.

———. *Danzas y bailes regionales de México.* Vol. 2. Mexico City: Daniel García Blanco, 1982.

———. "La música en Chiapas." *Nueva Revista Chiapas* 1, no. 4 (1986): 28–29.

García Riera, Emilio. *México visto por el cine extranjero, 2, 1906/1940.* Guadalajara: Ediciones Era, 1987.

Garfias, Robert. *Marimba Music of Tehuantepec.* Liner notes. University of Washington Press, UWP1002 (1972).

———. "The Marimba of Mexico and Central America." *Revista de música latino americana/Latin-American Music Review* 4, no. 2 (1983): 203–212.

Garrido, Juan S. *Historia de la música popular en México.* 2nd ed. Mexico City: Editorial Extemporáneo, 1981.

Geijerstam, Claes. *Popular Music in Mexico.* Albuquerque: University of New Mexico Press, 1976.

Gerhard, Peter. *The Southeast Frontier of New Spain.* Princeton, N.J.: Princeton University Press, 1979.

González Hernández, Guillermo. "Chujes y jacaltecos: Música de la frontera sur." Record liner notes. Mexico City: Cenzontle, n.d.

Gordillo y Ortiz, Octavio. *Diccionario biográfico de Chiapas.* Mexico City: B. Costa-Amic Editor, 1977.

Hernández C., Amador. *El origen de la marimba.* Mexico City: n.p., 1975.

Hornbostel, Erich M., and Curt Sachs. "Instruments, Classification of. Appendix A." In *The New Grove Dictionary of Music and Musicians.* Vol. 9, pp. 241–245. London: Macmillan, 1980.

Hurtado Aquilar, Gerardo. "La marimba de Guatemala." 21 articles. *Prensa Libre* (Guatemala City) (November–December 1975).

"Idiophones." *Musical Instruments of the World.* New York: Facts on File, 1976.

Jones, A.M. *Africa and Indonesia—The Evidence of the Xylophone and Other Musical and Cultural Factors.* Leiden, Netherlands: E.J. Brill, 1964.

Juárez Toledo, J. Manuel. "Aportes para el estudio de la etnomusicología guatemalteca." *Tradiciones de Guatemala* 8 (1977): 141–183.

Kaptain, Laurence D. "Chiapas and Its Unusual Marimba Tradition." *Percussive Notes* 26, no. 5 (1989), 28–31.

———. "Focus on Performance: Interview with Zeferino Nandayapa." *Percussive Notes* 28, no. 2 (1990): 48–50.

———. "Heart of Wood Song." *Mexico Journal* 2, no. 25 (1989): 25–26.

———. *Maderas que cantan.* Tuxtla Gutiérrez, Chiapas: Instituto Chiapaneco de Cultura, 1991.

———. *The Wood That Sings: The Marimba in Chiapas, Mexico.* Everett, Pa.: HoneyRock Publications, 1992.

Kubik, Gerhard. "Angolan Traits in Black Music, Games and Dances of Brazil." *Estudos de Antropología Cultural* 10 (1979): 36–41.

———. "Lamellaphone." In *The New Grove Dictionary of Music and Musicians.* Vol. 10, pp. 401–407. London: Macmillan, 1980.

———. "Stability and Change in African Musical Traditions." *The World of Music* 28, no. 1 (1986): 44–68.

Liberman, Baruj, Eduardo Llerenas, and Enrique Ramírez. *Anthology of Sounds.* Record liner notes. Mexico City: Fonart, 1985.

List, George. "Colombia: II. Folk Music (2. The Pacific Coast Region)." In *The New Grove Dictionary of Music and Musicians.* Vol. 4, pp. 574–577. London: Macmillan, 1980.

———. "The Musical Bow at Palenque." *Journal of the International Folk Music Council* 18 (1966): 36–50.

Lopez Mayorical, Mariano. *Momentos estelares de la historia de la marimba en Guatemala.* Guatemala: Editorial "José de Pineda Ibarra," 1982.

Loza, Steve. "The Origins of the Son." *Aztlan* 15, no. 1 (1984): 105–121.

Lydia Trejo, Blanca. "La marimba." *Mujeres-Suplemento Cultural* (January 1980): 25–28.

MacCallum, Frank. *The Book of the Marimba.* New York: Carlton Press, 1969.

Malmström, Dan. "Introduction to Twentieth Century Mexican Music." Ph.D. diss., Uppsala University, Sweden, 1974.

Marcuse, Sybil. *Musical Instruments: A Comprehensive Dictionary.* New York: Norton, 1975.

———. *A Survey of Musical Instruments.* New York: Harper and Row, 1975.

"Marimba." In *Diccionario de la música labor.* Barcelona: Labor, 1954.

"Marimba." In *Diccionario general etimológico de la lengua española,* edited by Roque Barcia. Madrid: Alvarez Hermanos Impresores, 1889.

"Marimba." *Diccionario de la lengua española.* Madrid: Real Academia Española, 1984.

Mellafe, Rolando. *Negro Slavery in Latin America.* Translated by J.W.S. Judge. Berkeley: University of California Press, 1975.

Mendoza, Vincente. *Panorama de la música tradicional de México.* Mexico City: Imprenta Universitaria, 1956.

Monsanto, Carlos. *La Marimba.* Guatemala: Piedra Santa, n.d.

———. "Guatemala a través de su marimba." *Revista de música latino americana/Latin-American Music Review* 3, no. 1 (1982): 60–71.

Montiel, Gustavo. *Investigando el origin de la marimba.* Mexico City: Gustavo Montiel, 1985.

———. *Tuxtla de mis recuerdos.* Mexico City: Gustavo Montiel, 1972.

Morales, Salvador. *La música mexicana.* Mexico City: Editorial Universo México, 1981.

Morales Avendaño, Juan Maria. *San Bartolomé de Los Llanos.* Tuxtla Gutiérrez, Chiapas: Universidad Autónoma de Chiapas, 1985.

Nettl, Bruno. *The Western Impact on World Music.* New York: Schirmer Books, 1985.

O'Brien, Linda. "Guatemala: II. Folk Music." In *The New Grove Dictionary of Music and Musicians.* Vol 7, pp. 776–780. London: Macmillan, 1980.

———. "Marimbas of Guatemala: The African Connection." *The World of Music* 25, no. 2 (1982): 99–103.

———. "Música folklórica de Guatemala." *Tradiciones de Guatemala* 5 (1976) 7–19.

———. "Son Guatemalteco." In *The New Grove Dictionary of Music and Musicians.* Vol. 17, pp. 24. London: Macmillan, 1980.

Oddo, Louis G. "Searching for Marimbas in Guatemala." *Modern Percussionist* 1, no. 4 (1985): 22–25, 52–53.

Orta Velázquez, Guillermo. *Breve historia de la música en México.* Mexico City: Joaquin Porrua, S.A. de C.V., 1970.

Ortiz, Fernando. "La marimba afroamericana." *Guatemala Indígena* 6, no. 4 (1971): 9–43.

———. *Los instrumentos de la música afrocubana.* Vol 1. Havana: Publicaciones de la Dirección de Cultura del Ministerio de Educación, 1952.

Palmer, Colin A. *Slaves of the White God: Blacks in Mexico, 1570–1650.* Cambridge: Harvard University Press, 1976.

Pérez Villatoro, Camilo G. "Corazón de madera." *Bonampak* 2, no. 2 (1985): 31–33.

———. "La marimba, auténtica expresión del pueblo chiapaneco." *Integración,* no. 9 (n.d.): 16–18.

Peters, Gordon B. *The Drummer: Man, A Treatise on Percussion.* Rev. ed. Wilmette, Ill.: Kemper-Peters, 1975.

Pineda del Valle, César. *Fogarada: Antología de la marimba.* Tuxtla Gutiérrez, Chiapas: Instituto Chiapaneco de Cultura, 1990.

———. "Música popular chiapaneca." Unpublished manuscript, n.d.

———. "Program Notes" for *1er Concurso Estatal de Marimba.* Tuxtla Gutiérrez, Chiapas, 1984.

———. "Program Notes" for *2o Concurso Estatal de Marimba.* Tuxtla Gutiérrez Chiapas, 1985.

———. "Program Notes," *3er Concurso Estatal de Marimba.* Tuxtla Gutiérrez, Chiapas, 1986. n.a.

———. "Program Notes" for *4o Concurso Estatal de Marimba.* Tuxtla Gutiérrez, Chiapas, 1987.

"Requinto." In *The New Grove Dictionary of Musical Instruments.* Vol. 2, p. 240. London: Macmillan, 1984.

Reuter, Jas. *La música popular de México.* 4th ed. Mexico City: Panorama Editorial, 1985.

Riding, Alan. *Distant Neighbors.* New York: Vintage Books, 1986.

Roberts, John Storm. *Black Music of Two Worlds.* New York: Praeger, 1972.

———. *The Latin Tinge.* New York: Oxford University Press, 1979.

Robledo Santiago, Edgar. "Verdadera fiesta para el espíritu." *Mujeres-Suplemento Cultural* (January 1980): 29–30.

Rodas, Jaime. *La marimba.* Mexico City: Secretaria de Educación Pública y Subsecretaria de Asuntos Culturales, 1971.

Rundall, W.H. "A Curious Musical Instrument." *The Musical Times* (May 1, 1901): 310–312.

Sachs, Curt. *Real-Lexikon der Musikinstrumente.* New York: Dover, 1929.

———. *The History of Musical Instruments.* New York: Norton, 1940.

Salazar Salvatierra, Rodrigo. *La marimba: empleo, diseño y construcción.* San José: Editorial de la Universidad de Costa Rica, 1988.

Saldivar, Gabriel. *Historia de la música en México.* Mexico City: Biblioteca Enciclopedia del Estado de México, 1980.

Sandí, Luís, and Francisco Domínguez. "Informe sobre la investigación folklórico-musical realizada en el estado de Chiapas en Abril de 1934." In *Investigación folklórica en México,* pp. 262–317. Mexico City: Secretaria de Educación Pública Instituto Nacional de Bellas Artes, 1934.

Santamaría, Francisco J. *Antología folklórica y musical de Tabasco.* Villahermosa, Tabasco: Gobierno del Estado de Tabasco, 1985.

Scruggs, T.M. *Nicaraguan Folk Music from Masaya.* Liner notes. Flying Fish Records 474 (1988).

———. Review of *Nicaragua . . . Presente!,* by John McCutcheon, Paul Riesler, and Bill Nowlind; and *Patria: Music from Honduras and Nicaragua,* by David Blair Stiffler. *Revista de música latino americana/Latin-American Music Review* 12, no. 1 (1991): 84–96.

———. "Whose baby? El baile de la marimba in and outside of Masaya. 'The cradle of Nicaraguan folklore.'" Austin, Texas: Papers on Latin America, no. 91–106, Institute of Latin-American Studies, 1991.

Selvas, Eduardo J. "La musica valiviana." *Revista Ateno* (Tuxtla Gutiérrez, Chiapas) 4 (1957): 32, as cited in David Vela, *Information on the Marimba,* translated and edited by Vida Chenoweth. Auckland, New Zealand: The Institute Press, 1957.

Shiloah, Amnon. "The Traditional Artist in the Limelight of the Modern City." *The World of Music* 28, no. 1 (1986): 87–98.

Solís, Theodore. "The Marimba in Mexico City: Contemporary Contexts of a Traditional Regional Ensemble." Ph.D. diss., University of Illinois, 1983.

———. "Muñecas de chiapaneco: The Economic Importance of Self-Image in the World of the Mexican Marimba." *Revista de música latino americana/Latin-American Music Review* 1, no. 1 (1980): 34–46.

Stanford, E. Thomas. "The Mexican Son." *Yearbook of the International Folk Music Council* 4 (1972): 66–86.

———. "Mexico: II. Folk Music." In *The New Grove Dictionary of Music and Musicians.* Vol. 12, pp. 229–240. London: Macmillan, 1980.

———. "Sandunga." In *The New Grove Dictionary of Music and Musicians.* Vol. 16, pp. 469. London: Macmillan, 1980.

Stevens, Claire. "La marimba." *Heterofonia* 5 (1969): 27–30.

Stevenson, Robert. "Latin-American Music: III. Afro-American Music (1. Colonial Period, 2. Independence to c. 1900, 3. 20th Century)." In *The New Grove Dictionary of Music and Musicians.* Vol. 10, pp. 522–526. London: Macmillan, 1980.

———."Mexico City." In *The New Grove Dictionary of Music and Musicians.* Vol. 12, pp. 240–242. London: Macmillan, 1980.

———. *Music in Aztec and Inca Territory.* Berkeley: University of California Press, 1968.

———. *Music in Mexico.* New York: Thomas Y. Crowell, 1952.

Stiberg, David K. "Jarocho, Tropical, and Pop: Aspects of Musical Life in Veracruz, 1971–72." In *Eight Urban Musical Cultures,* edited by Bruno Nettl. Urbana: The University of Illinois Press, 1978.

Taracena Arriola, Jorge Arturo. "La marimba: ¿un instrumento nacional?" *Tradiciones de Guatemala* 13 (1980): 1–26.

Tompkins, William David. "Musical Traditions of the Blacks of Coastal Peru." Ph.D. diss., University of California, Los Angeles, 1981.

Trens, Manuel. *Historia de Chiapas.* Mexico City: Talleres Gráficos, 1957.

Vela, David. *Information on the Marimba.* Translated and edited by Vida Chenoweth. Auckland, New Zealand: The Institute Press, 1957–1958.

Velasco Palacios, Antonio. *Geografía de Chiapas.* San Cristóbal de las Casas, Chiapas: Impresiones Santiago, 1984.

———. *Historia de Chiapas.* Tuxtla Gutiérrez: Tallers Gráficos del Estado, 1987.

Wasserstrom, Robert. *Class and Society in Central Chiapas.* Berkeley: University of California Press, 1983.

Whitten, Norman E. "Personal Networks and Musical Contexts in the Pacific Lowlands of Colombia and Ecuador." In *Afro-American Anthropology,* edited by Norman E. Whitten and John F. Szwed, pp. 203–215. New York: Collier-Macmillan, 1970.

"Xylophones." *Musical Instruments of the World.* New York: Facts on File, 1976.

Yurchenco, Henrietta. "La música indígena en Chiapas, México." *América Indígena* 3, no. 4 (1943): 305–311.

Laurence D. Kaptain

Multiple Percussion

Multiple percussion as a force to be reckoned with in contemporary music began about the same time that tonality became less dominant. Throughout the course of the late eighteenth and nineteenth centuries, percussion instruments served essentially a single purpose, that of giving dramatic and coloristic emphasis to structural harmonic movement. The nature of the tonal language practiced by classical and romantic European composers meant that percussion sounds had to be folded into the limited timbral, rhythmic, and melodic rhetoric of the orchestra.

The dissolution of tonal harmony as a means of engineering large-scale musical architecture meant the liberation of percussion from a merely supportive role. Free of the constraints present in tonal music, composers of the twentieth century began a period of almost manic exploration of the "inherent" qualities of percussion sounds. The sound of the tam-tam, for example, once tied to the harmonic cadences of Modest Mussorgsky's "Great Gate of Kiev" from his *Pictures at an Exhibition* (1874, orch. 1922), could be explored for its own sake in Karlheinz Stockhausen's *Mikrophonie* (1964).

Released from its limited role in the orchestra, percussion became fertile ground for the passionate experimentalism of the early twentieth century. Among many other things, composers were fascinated by the "timbral efficiency" of percussion—by the ability of percussion instruments to produce an enormous number of sounds in the hands of relatively few players. This vitality led logically to the idea of multiple percussion, where sonic diversity could be multiplied by asking a single player to perform on two or more percussion instruments.

A quick look at works for multiple percussion by European and American composers between 1917 and 1945 reveals that it was rarely more than an art of convenience. The instruments normally played by an entire section of percussionists were combined and played by one player for the sake of efficiency (see Illus. 1, p. 117).

In Igor Stravinsky's *L'Histoire du soldat* (1918), a single performer is asked to play all of the percussion instruments that might be typically assigned to an entire section in a band or orchestra. Specifically, Stravinsky scored the percussion part of *L'Histoire du soldat* for a combination of drums of various sizes, cymbal, tambourine, and triangle—a model clearly based on the rapidly developing American drum set.

Like *L'Histoire du soldat,* the percussion writing in Béla Bartók's Sonata for Two Pianos and Percussion (1937) consolidates the instruments of an entire section for a single player. The percussion part consists of practically all of the standard instruments of the orchestral percussion section: xylophone, snare drum, bass drum, triangle, cymbals, and tam-tam. The timpani part, owing perhaps to the prestige of timpanists in the orchestra, is relatively free of this kind of heretical combination.

The Bartók Sonata for Two Pianos and Percussion is unquestionably a work of abiding quality. And, in its time, it was of unequaled importance for bringing percussion instruments out of the netherworld of the orchestra and putting them on equal footing with the piano. We should not underestimate the symbolic importance of thematic parity among the four players in the ensemble and Bartók's unprecedented gesture of both beginning and ending a major work with solo percussion writing.

The ubiquitous multiple instrument of the 1920s and 1930s was the drum set. Its use in the American jazz idiom served as a model not only for Stravinsky's *L'Histoire du soldat,* for example, but also for Darius

Milhaud's *La Création du monde* (1923) and William Walton's *Façade* (1922), to name three important pieces. The drum set also has its genesis in the reduction of a percussion section to a single player. It clearly owes much to polyphonic West African percussion music, but its most immediate ancestor is the percussion section of brass bands popular in the United States in the late nineteenth and early twentieth centuries.

The drum set gradually became a fixed set of instruments in a particular physical setup—a rare standardized multiple percussion setup among generally ad hoc arrangements. The increasing availability of this standard drum set, both as an instrument to be studied and as a model for composers, exerted a stabilizing effect on the development of multiple percussion.

Nevertheless, multiple percussion as a discipline lacked an intrinsic performance practice in these early days. Multiple percussion parts continued as simple combinations of several individual percussion instruments. Each individual instrument in a setup may have had a performance practice and history, but multiple percussion as a separate art remained a vague notion. There were few performers with expertise on several instruments and little music that demanded the skills of a multiple percussionist.

The first attempts to weld unity out of multiple percussion came from the percussion ensemble compositions of avant-garde American composers John Cage (1912–1992) and Lou Harrison (b. 1917). In the late 1930s and early 1940s, both Cage and Harrison redefined traditional ideas of percussion sounds and opened the door to uses of junk and noise-producing instruments. Their infatuation with novel timbres and their willingness to explore eclectic combinations of instruments led them to treat arrays of multiple percussion as the norm and not the exception for percussionists. They had the distinct advantage of being largely ignored by the traditional percussion community at the time, and, as a result, their music was performed by idealistic, young players who considered multiple percussion perfectly normal practice.

Two works of John Cage illustrate different directions in the fledgling art of multiple percussion. *Third Construction* (1941) is essentially an orchestral work written for percussion instruments. Each of the four players has a large arrangement of percussion instruments that can be separated into choirs of wood, skin, and metal instruments. Additionally, Cage combines instruments of widely different heritage, so that one player might play instruments of a half-dozen different musical cultures. Little attempt is made to retain indigenous performance practices. The work features a relentless kind of polyrhythmic energy in which the colors of the instruments serve to delineate the various strands of rhythmic activity.

The result is something that to this day is shocking and vital—a kind of Jackson Pollock painting brought to sound. Every time a sonic saturation level seems to be reached, Cage assaults the listener with a new sonority or a bewildering maze of rhythms. *Third Construction* careens through the percussive landscape in a way that would be impossible to achieve if the composer were limited to a single instrument for each performer.

Amores (1943), for percussion trio and prepared piano, uses multiple percussion for very different effect. Perhaps because the gamelan-like prepared piano presents such a rich source of tone colors, Cage feels comfortable with a much more restrained aesthetic in the percussion writing. The percussion movements of *Amores* are essentially monochromatic: the second movement features nine tom-toms and a pod rattle, and the third movement uses only woodblocks. By neutralizing the issue of timbre, he forces percussion into a melodic arena. Slight variations of tone color, by playing at the center and edge of the skin, for example, then have thematic ramifications. Cage succeeds in fashioning a symbiosis between the realm of timbre and that of melody that is still perhaps the most successful realization of Schoenberg's idea of "Klangfarbenmelodie"—tone-color melody.

By the 1960s multiple percussion had developed sufficiently to interest serious composers in it as a solo medium. When Christoph Caskel (b. 1932) treated the setup of instruments in *Zyklus* (1959) by Karlheinz Stockhausen (b. 1928) as an instrument, a single instrumental entity, it marked the beginning of multiple percussion having a history and performance practice separate from its constituent instruments.

The idea of multiple percussion as a unique discipline among the percussive arts allowed the creation of a set of issues and questions that addressed its complex performance problems and aesthetics. To a large extent the multiple percussion compositions of the 1960s and early 1970s, principally by European composers, defined the central concerns of multiple percussion. Among these ideas were: (1) the recognition of the visual aesthetic in multiple percussion and the exploration of its inherent choreographic and sculptural parameters; (2) the unification of percussive sounds with spoken or sung text; (3) percussion as theater; and (4) the meaningful exploration of new sonorities.

Zyklus was among the first major solo works to explore the fertile new ground of multiple percussion. In a real way *Zyklus* is a development of the orchestral ideas Cage used in *Third Construction*. However, where Cage was carefree and almost irreverent in combining instruments of different cultures, Stockhausen treats timbre with a serious constructivist philosophy. In *Zyklus* the physical arrangement of the instruments themselves and, by extension, the movements of the percussionist within the setup are tied intimately to the structure of the work.

The word *Zyklus* itself means cycle, and in the work each instrument is assigned a position in the circular setup. The truly experimental aspect of *Zyklus* is found in the combination of a thorough exploration of tone colors with the acrobatic virtuosity required of a single performer who must negotiate whiplash spins around an array of instruments, each with specific and different technical performance problems. This produces an inevitable and inherent visual and physical quality in performance.

Therefore, the structure of *Zyklus* is revealed almost as much by how the performer moves as by how the piece sounds. Stockhausen extends this natural physicality of multiple percussion into the formal conception of the piece by constructing a form of overlapping acceleration/deceleration cycles among the instruments. At any given point, one instrument is at a peak density of activity while all of the other instruments are either approaching their peak density or receding from it. By linking each instrument to a physical location on the circular setup of instruments, these cycles dictate the way in which the performer's movements are focussed and directed around the setup. Multiple percussion almost always implies dance.

In this light, *Zyklus* becomes a microcosmic precursor to spatial multiple percussion works on a grander scale. In *Persephassa* (1969) by Iannis Xenakis (b. 1922), for example, six percussionists are stationed around the audience in a kind of exploded version of a multiple percussion setup with the audience taking the central position at the instrument normally reserved for the player.

Luciano Berio (b. 1925) uses two huge percussion setups for his work *Circles* (1960) for voice, harp, and two percussionists. Berio pairs largeness of physical gesture, implicit in the enormous array of instruments, with intimate connections of percussion, voice, and text. The poems of e.e. cummings, which Berio sets, are tantalizing in the richness of their sonorities and invite many connections with percussive sounds. From a gesture as simple as doubling the "sh" sound in the voice with sandpaper blocks, to much larger sections where the percussion constructs rhythms and shapes into words and sentences, Berio repeatedly evokes the ancient connection between chanting and drumming.

This lesson is not lost on the generation of young composers. In *To the Earth* (1985) Frederic Rzewski (b. 1938) sets a Homeric hymn in honor of the earth on earthen flowerpots. A single percussionist speaks the texts while playing the flower-pots. The powerful *Toucher* (1973) of Vinko Globokar (b. 1934) sets a text of Bertolt Brecht in French translation. The percussionist chooses seven instruments that can imitate the sounds of the French language, and while speaking, the text accompanies him or herself on these instruments. By associating a specific sound in the language with a percussive sound that imitates it, the percussion instruments can be made to "speak" the text.

The reunion of text with percussion sound combined easily with the growing awareness of percussion's choreographic side. Indeed many composers in the 1970s and 1980s began to think of multiple percussion as primarily a theatrical medium. Mauricio Kagel (b. 1931), in his *Dressur* (1977), for three percussionists, provides one of the best examples of European music in this genre. In addition to the musical notation in the score, Kagel gives the percussionists detailed instructions for their positioning and movements on the stage.

Kagel treats percussion as theater, not by asking the percussionists to enact the emotional import of their musical gestures, but by composing a carefully controlled visual scenario in addition to the acoustical score. This last point is important because it demonstrates that multiple percussion is an inherently theatrical art. Kagel did not invent a theatrical scenario to add to *Dressur*; he discovered the natural physical theater of multiple percussion.

As revolutionary as the theatricality in multiple percussion works by Kagel, Globokar, and the Greek-French composer Georges Aphergis (b. 1945) might have seemed, they were by no means the first such experiments in this area. American composers had long been aware of the theater in multiple percussion. One could argue that early jazz and blues could not be separated from the natural drama in the lives of the musicians and listeners. Therefore, drum set playing in this idiom constituted a kind of folk theater. Both in and outside the jazz idiom, American composers showed an unwillingness to abstract percussion sounds from the physical acts required to play them.

The American iconoclast Harry Partch (1901–1974) referred to this physical quality in his music as "corporeality." And, although his earliest works were scored largely for voice and string instruments, from the 1940s until his death, percussion became the principal voice of corporeality in his music. Partch spent much of his life inventing and constructing new instruments to suit the demands of his microtonal system of harmony. An unexpected side effect of these new instruments was that ideas of movement that were common to ordinary percussion instruments, such as the marimba or timpani, did not work on Partch's instruments. The cloud chamber bowls, resonant glass instruments that Partch made by cutting and then suspending large glass jugs, are instruments that demand great skill in moving both vertically as well as laterally, a kind of motion not found in most conventional percussion instruments. Performance on these instruments therefore produces a unique visual as well as an acoustical experience. Again, theater is implicit in multiple percussion. In the case of Partch, his unconventional musical vocabulary produced similarly unconventional physical theater.

The current understanding of experimentalism in the world of multiple percussion still retains at its core the idea of the expanding universe of sonority. To many, the lesson of Edgard Varèse, Cage, and even Stockhausen was one of incorporating ever larger and more exotic sonic resources into the compositional rhetoric. Multiple percussion becomes a logical outlet for these expansionist instincts in part because a multiple percussionist can negotiate a very large number of different instruments and, by using different mallets, can produce an enormous diversity of sound. Percussion was attractive also because its sounds, often coming from musical cultures outside the European/American mainstream, were not already "used up" by older music. Many twentieth-century composers have been intoxicated by the same love of the exotic that led Claude Debussy to borrow Asian harmonies and orchestral colors. Composers for percussion often have replaced the "tired" sound of the ordinary orchestral tam-tam, for example, with the "nouvelle sonorité" of a Javanese gong or Japanese temple bell.

The problem is not simply that, with overuse, these new sounds will also seem as limp as the ones they replaced. Worse is that often a percussion work for a large number of "non-Western" instruments will seem like an American Express package tour of musical cultures. Sounds wedded inextricably to certain musical, aesthetic, and religious traditions are mingled in a kind of superficial *chinoiserie*. It is true that issues of orchestration are often questions of taste and the difference between a defensible use of a Javanese gong, say, and one that smacks of a cheap effect is often difficult to define. Furthermore, practically all of the instruments available to composers of music for multiple percussion came originally from outside the European/American musical tradition. One can hardly argue against the use of African drums as a kind of cultural imperialism while accepting the use of cymbals from Turkey or the marimba from Latin America.

Fortunately for us these questions will generally sort themselves out with time. It has become clear, for example, that the percussion writing of George Crumb (b. 1929), which often swims in the heavy perfume of exotic sounds, undeniably beautiful as these sounds might be, seems by the early 1990s to have run its course as a style. The English composer James Wood (b. 1953), on the other hand, uses large numbers of percussion instruments from around the world in a way that assimilates them into a comprehensible compositional vocabulary. In *Stoichiea* (1988), Wood's massive work for 16 percussionists playing more than 600 instruments, the rhythmic and formal ideas seem to grow organically from the nature of the instrumental timbres.

There are numerous occasions where, for one reason or another, composers have chosen not to deal with the problem of orchestrating their works by leaving the choice of the instruments open to the performer. One great advantage to such a plan is that it leaves the question of cultural compatibility of percussion sounds open to changing perceptions as time passes.

Three important works for solo percussion fall into this category of open instrumentation. Each composer had different—and honorable—reasons for leaving this important decision unfixed.

Morton Feldman (1926–1987), in his *King of Denmark* (1964), instructs the performer to play very softly using only his or her hands and fingers. The player is encouraged to cultivate a personalized palette of sounds which might change from performance to performance. This underscores Feldman's ethereal musical language as a kind of whispered riposte to the unabashed certainty of Stockhausen's *Zyklus*.

Feldman also seems to be aware of the difficulty of dictating specific percussive sounds. A composer who asks for a violin is reasonably sure of getting roughly the same sound from different performers. However, calling for a gong, even when specifying the size, a medium gong for example, can produce wildly different results from player to player. In *King of Denmark* Feldman chooses to allow each player to describe a coherent sonic universe for him or herself. The alternative to this path might easily lead to an obsessively detailed description of instruments and sounds that would only serve to make this highly personal piece sound generic.

Xenakis seems at first to be taking some risk in deciding to leave open the choice of instruments for his percussion solo *Psappha* (1975). After all, a performer who chooses overly sweet or weak sounds could undermine the strength and pungency of Xenakis's rhythmic language. Perhaps his confidence in allowing choice of instruments is based on the knowledge that inappropriate choices could never weather the storminess of his music.

Briefly, *Psappha* is scored for sixteen instruments organized into five groups of three instruments and a single instrument standing alone. Xenakis gives the performer some indications about how to divide the instrumentarium into wood, skin, and metal instruments, but otherwise leaves the choice of specific instruments free.

A performer soon discovers that certain practical considerations dominate the decision-making process. For one, there are many sections where several instruments sound simultaneously, making mallet choice a serious consideration. One must choose instruments that require no more than four types of mallets at a given time. A further consideration lies in the polyphonic rhythmic writing. Groups of instruments must be separated enough from one another to give each group a recognizable identity and to keep the polyphony from becoming a one-dimensional composite. At the same time, instrumental choices that are radically different from one another resist the linkage among sonorities necessary to project linear connections among different groups. Often the question boils down to one of envelope, dynamic, and durational similarities. Two instruments of different materials played with very different sticks can be heard as a linear phenomenon if their durations and envelope characteristics are roughly similar and if they respond with a similar dynamic to strokes of equal force.

Xenakis himself frequently has raised the question of incorporating "non-Western" instruments into his percussion compositions. He is quite fond of the strong and beautiful percussion sounds found in African and Asian musical cultures. A cursory look at the middle sections of *Persephassa* reveals his love for Thai gongs and the extraordinary sounds of wooden and metal simantras. At the same time he warns against treating his percussion music as an extension of the non-European/American ethnic traditions. If there is an ideal choice of instruments for *Psappha*, it would certainly exclude instruments whose associations with traditional musical cultures make it impossible to mix well with the other instruments of the setup. Caskel's idea of the multiple percussion setup being a single instrument is once again valid.

Bone Alphabet (1991) by Brian Ferneyhough (b. 1943) is a work composed for seven instruments of the performer's choice. Instruments on adjacent lines in the score must be of different materials, which makes it possible to project very tightly woven contrapuntal structures. Like the rest of Ferneyhough's music, *Bone Alphabet* is a rigorous working out of demanding rhythmic structures. It is not uncommon to see four separate polyphonic lines proceeding simultaneously in different rhythmic values. The initial problem of how to execute 7:4, 9:8, 11:3, and 21:12 at the same time, for example, is made doubly difficult by the necessity of finding instruments whose sonorities can project the complexity of such structures.

The problem is in fact similar to that of *Psappha*—how to find instruments that can delineate a polyphonic structure without being so different from one another as to make monophonic writing impossible to execute. Again, it seems that compatibility of envelope and dynamic range are essential. Additionally, in the case of Ferneyhough, instruments with rich harmonic spectra, able to be activated with different mallets, make projecting multiple polyphonic lines easier by assigning each line to a different mallet.

The difficulty in trying to make encyclopedic statements about multiple percussion lies in its very brief history as an art form.

As with other instruments, the expertise required to play multiple percussion is defined by problems posed by composers in various pieces and by the solutions found by performers over a period of time. Dilemmas of substance posed by composers and the experiences of performers in solving them allows the small level of generalization in this essay. The most fruitful form of speculation in the area of multiple percussion performance practice remains the active commissioning and performance of new works.

Steven Schick

Percussion and Dance

The stars twinkle as they dance about
the summer sky.

The leaves in the giant oak gently
rustle in the evening breeze.

An elder rubs a piece of sharkskin on
the wood of the drum finishing the
surface to doeskin smoothness.

My heart beats, I am one—with the
earth.

I composed this poem as a gesture of a context from which the following entry in this percussion encyclopedia would emerge. That is, dance (movement) and percussion (sound) have occurred separately and together in virtually every social group throughout the world. It is most interesting to this author to present, in the broadest terms, conceptual impressions of how and why dance and percussion have been interwoven in hopes of inspiring further creative interaction among dancers and percussionists. For specific factual information on, for instance, the first documented use of clapping sticks, I would respectfully refer you to books like the remarkably authoritative *Percussion Instruments and Their History* by James Blades.[1]

The probability seems high that one brisk, foggy morning in ancient times, an evolutionary precursor to you and me emerged out of a protective cave shelter only to look up at the sky and observe with utter horror that the sun was slowly disappearing; day was turning back to night. Australopithecine (as it had done to ward off marauding neighbors), with adrenalin forcing the heart to pound wildly, let out a chilling yell while beating on its chest and jumping up and (due to gravity) *down*. This reaction could have been the visceral response that set in motion a ritual that, for generations to come, celebrated what was then unexplainable but is now known as a solar eclipse. Ancient societies created a mythology in order to explain the unexplainable. Along with that mythology, rituals were created and expanded upon to psychologically deal with those things that were recognizable yet unexplainable in scientific terms. Perhaps the solar eclipse ritual evolved into a circle dance in which the members of the society, accompanied by rattles and drums, also sang while pounding rhythms on their chests.

Rites of passage—the birth of a child, the coming of age, and death—have incorporated percussion and dance to mark and note a special event. Music and dance, percussion and movement, have been an integral part of rituals and rites from around the world—whether it's the Olympia Brass Band playing for a New Orleans funeral with family and friends dancing with their umbrellas to the drummers' street beat as they march up St. Charles Avenue, or a lone individual high on a mesa chanting and playing a deep tom-tom while turning to the North, the South, the East, and the West, honoring the "four grandfathers" and reflecting on the life of a recently deceased relative. A 1939 Nazi rally in Berlin orchestrated with divisions of soldiers standing at attention while a military band plays the ending of Liszt's *Les Préludes* (1848) with thundering timpani, bass drums, and cymbals; a *Scola de samba* marching, dancing, and playing in Rio de Janeiro during Carnival; and a drum line feature with the band members dancing in a Saturday afternoon football halftime show are also examples of ritual events incorporating percussion and movement. The above examples indicate a *functional relationship* integrating music and dance into events in a society.

Drumming is physical; it often requires a high degree of dexterity and stamina. The actuation of the drum with hands, fingers, and/or beaters is generated through a gesture or series of gestures. The mental and physical preparation in advance of playing a tone on a large Japanese *ō-daiko* is as significant as the tone itself; and the "ma," the silence after the decay of the tone, is equally significant. When observing the *ō-daiko* player or a *taiko* ensemble, one is taken with the importance of the physical gesture as well as the depth of the fundamental tone and the richness of the full blossom of the overtones. Korean percussionists playing membranophones and metallophones dance and swirl long tassels attached to their hats, thus incorporating movement as an integral part of their percussion performance. An Ewe master drummer from West Africa playing a *talking drum* or participating in signal drumming moves his body in a way that reinforces the timbral inflection of these communication drumming modes, and though not intended to be dance- or percussion-linked, is welcomed by this observer as such. Even the drum set player who places the cymbals way up high for the visual impact of the performer's motion at the expense of efficiency is keenly aware of the direct tie between movement/gesture and the resultant sound. An orchestral percussionist's greatest concern is producing quality sounds with exacting precision; however, many performers are also acutely aware of their visual deportment on stage.

Indian Kathak and Kathakali dancers use a syllabic "notation" system somewhat similar to that of *tablā* or *mirdangam* players. The rhythmic and timbral inflections of the drummer are highly integrated with the rhythmic and gestural nuances of the dancer(s), thus creating a wonderful interplay of interaction. The 12/8–6/4 cross-rhythmic syncopations of the Ghanaian dance form, *adbajia*, create a constant textural weaving of the rhythms that are then enhanced by the master drummer. The earthbound and skybound gestures of the dancers create an inseparable link with that of the percussion ensemble. This link extends far beyond that of inter-arts; as pointed out to this author by master drummer Professor William Amawaku, plants cannot grow without rain and sun. Many cultures, including the Native Americans of North America, weave an inseparable matrix fusing music (that often utilizes drums and rattles) with dance in relation to planting, harvesting, and other social events within the community. In these contexts, the relationship between the sound and the movement to each other as well as to nature is symbiotic. The gamelan of each village in Indonesia performs traditional and recently composed music. The gamelan also accompanies dance and shadow puppet shows in which a master puppeteer manipulates ornate paper stick figures who actively "dance" behind a backlit screen portraying ancient mythological stories to the delight of all people in the village, both young and old. These all-night puppet shows, wayangs, have a festival atmosphere in which the audience members are free to roam about, leave the area to take part in refreshments, and then to return to the puppet show.

Another type of festival event, John Cage's Music Circus, "happened" at the University of Illinois in the fall of 1967. This festival event occurred in the stock pavilion normally used to show animals. Multiple stages were set up such that Morton Feldman's solo percussion work *King of Denmark* (1965) was juxtaposed with Salvatore Martirano's *L'sGA* (1968). Ben Johnston's percussion/piano-destruction *Knocking Piece* (1962) was integrated with a computer light realization of the same score, while dancers from the Merce Cunningham Company improvised, and members of the participating audience built pipe sculptures in the center of the dirt floor pavilion. Percussion (the "all sound music of the future" as described in Cage's *Silence*[2]) and dance occurred simultaneously with electronic sounds and pedestrian movement in the ultimate breakdown of "haute culture."

The boundaries of melding music, with dance coming out of the European court music traditions and further established within the Ballet Russe, were still the norm as exemplified in the collaborations of composers Louis Horst and Aaron Copland with choreographer Martha Graham. The discussions and ultimate collaborations in the late 1950s of John Cage, Merce Cunningham, poet Robert Bly, and visual artist Robert Rauschenberg sprang forth and broke down the assumed, one-to-one, cause-and-effect relationship between music, dance, and the visual arts. The mere coexistence of music occurring in the same place at the same time with dance in a performance context produced its own validity. The random coincidence of these simultaneous multisensory events proved quite stimulating and most interesting.

When this author thinks of John Cage, percussion, and movement, two important stories come to mind. When Cage was the music director for the University of California–Los Angeles women's synchronized swimming team, he was perplexed when the swimmers were not able to hear the beat of the music. In desperation he grabbed a gong, and, while playing the basic beat, he placed the gong in the water. To the delight of the swimmers, they could hear the music. To the delight of Cage, percussionists, and audiences everywhere, the water gong was invented! While Cage was accompanying the dance classes and composing for choreographer Bonnie Byrd at the Cornish Institute in Seattle, Washington, he felt limited by the physical space, as the piano he was playing took up all of the room provided for him to make music. He was interested in having a greater variety of multiple and diverse timbres integrated with the sound of the piano, and so he devised the *prepared piano*, thereby creating an entire percussion orchestra at his fingertips.

There have been many Western composers, choreographers, and improvisers who, with dancers and percussionists, have collaborated in pairs or in larger ensembles, composing, choreographing, improvising, and performing interesting works.

Notes

1. James Blades, *Percussion Instruments and Their History,* 2nd ed. (London: Faber and Faber, 1974).

2. John Cage, "Credo," *Silence* (Cambridge: MIT Press, 1967), 5.

Michael W. Udow

Percussion Ensembles

A percussion ensemble is the assemblage of percussionists and percussion instruments to perform music written for them. The percussion ensemble had its beginning in the United States on March 6, 1933, in New York City, with a performance of *Ionisation* (1931) by Edgard Varèse (1883–1965), conducted by Nicolas Slonimsky. *Ionisation* requires thirteen performers playing thirty-nine different percussion instruments.

The number of percussionists may range from three to perform *Percussion Music for Three Players* (1935) by Gerald Strang to twenty-two to perform *Estudio en forma de preludio y fuga, para 37 instruments de percussión, fricción y silbido* (1933) by José Ardévol. The number of percussion instruments may range from one instrument per player, as in *Toccata* (1942) by Carlos Chávez, to any number able to be performed by one player, as in *Los dioses aztecas* (1959) by Gardner Read. Each composition requires a specific number of performers and a specific number of percussion instruments.

Prior to the 1930s, significant developments were taking place in the world of music that had an influence on percussion music. A futurist movement in Italy in 1914 begun by Luigi Russolo using *intonarumori* (noise organs) and *Ballet mécanique* (1923) by George Antheil, which employs airplane motors, are two examples of music that was using nonmusical sounds as part of the composition. Other compositions around this time employed extensive use of traditional percussion instruments: Igor Stravinsky's *Petrouchka* (1911), *Le Sacre du printemps* (1913), and *Les Noces* (1923). Chamber music of this period included Stravinsky's *L'Histoire du soldat* (1918), Paul Hindemith's *Kammermusik No. 3* (1925), and Henry Cowell's *Ensemble* (1925).

During the 1930s, American composers employed elements alien to Western music in their works. The use of Eastern materials, newly created scales, experiments with microtones, Latin-American music, jazz music, and a reaction against Romanticism and Impressionism all created an atmosphere conducive to experimentation. Between 1930 and 1945, the percussion ensemble emerged through the efforts made by composers in the Western Hemisphere.

The earliest examples of extant works written for the percussion ensemble are *Rítmica No. 5* and *Rítmica No. 6* (1930) by Amadeo Roldán. The following is a list of percussion ensemble music written between 1931 and 1939:

Varèse, Edgard
Ionisation (1931)

Russell, William
Three Dance Movements (1933)

Cowell, Henry
Ostinato Pianissimo (1934)

Beyer, Johanna M.
Auto Accident (1935)

Green, Ray
Three Inventories of Casey Jones (1936)

Becker, John
A Dance (1938)

Cowell, Henry
Pulse (1939)

Ionisation, like most of the early 1930s' compositions, was a mixture of many influences: Latin-American music, jazz music, many players using one percussion instrument per player, noisemakers (sirens), uneven rhythmic patterns against each other, meter changes, and piano used to create noise rather than melody. Henry Cowell's (1897–1965) compositions had a strong Oriental influence, with their use of gongs, rice bowls, and tom-toms. The music of William Russell (b. 1905) and Gerald Strang (1908–1983) took full advantage of the linear aspect of percussion composition. These composers created moving rhythmic lines through the complex interplay of each player's part. Johanna Beyer (1888–1944), Ray Green (b. 1909), and John Becker (1886–1961) all created what might be called programmatic music for percussion. Although all these compositions are different from each other, they all employ the element of experimentation and help to create an understanding of the potential of percussion instruments.

Henry Cowell became the leader of a Pacific coast group of composers who wrote forty percussion ensemble compositions between 1938 and 1942. Two of the members of this group, Lou Harrison (b. 1917) and John Cage (1912–1992), became well known for their percussion compositions as well as for works for other instrumental groups. Harrison emerged as the most prolific and is known for such works as *Fifth Simfony* (1939), *Canticle No. 3* (1941), *Double Music* (1941) (Harrison and Cage), *Fugue* (1941), *Labyrinth No. 3* (1941), and *Song of Quetzalcoatl* (1940). Cage is known for such works as *First Construction in Metal* (1939), *Imaginary Landscape* (1939), and *Amores* (1943). Carlos Chávez stood out in this period and is best known for his *Toccata* (1942), which is the percussion piece performed most often from this era. *October Mountain* (1942) is a well-known percussion piece of Alan Hovhaness (b. 1911).

Chávez's *Toccata* and Hovhaness's *October Mountain* were among the last ensemble pieces that were added to the gradually increasing repertoire of early percussion works. A hiatus during and following World War II brought the early period of the percussion ensemble to a close. What followed was an interest in the rudimental ensemble consisting of marching percussion: snare drums, bass drums, and cymbals. This led to the drum corps concept, which is still a vital part of percussion performing.

In the 1950s, after a lapse of several years, composers, percussionists, educators, and manufacturers participated in a revival of interest in percussion. Hundreds of compositions employing a wide range of percussion instruments and encompassing many areas have since been written. Several publishing houses dealing exclusively in percussion music have been formed. A vital step forward was made when the percussion ensemble was accepted into the curriculum of colleges and universities. The first institution to make this commitment was the University of Illinois in 1950. Paul Price was the percussion instructor and was responsible for initiating the program. Now most colleges and universities and many high schools have the percussion ensemble in their curriculum. It is also becoming popular to employ percussion ensembles in orchestral works as well as in drum corps.

The following list of composers and their compositions is a good representation of percussion ensemble music written between 1950 and 1991:

Colgrass, Michael
Three Brothers (1951)

Miller, Malloy
Prelude for Percussion (1956)

Ginastera, Alberto
Cantata para América mágica (1960)

Kabeláč, Miloslav
Eight Inventions (1962)

Benson, Warren
Streams (1964)

Beck, John
Jazz Variants (1969)

Gauger, Thomas
Gainsborough (1974)

Trythall, Richard
Bolero (1979)

Leonard, Stanley
Fanfare, Meditation and Dance (1982)

Gauger, Thomas
Portico (1983)

Hoffer, Bernard
The River (1984)

Whettam, Graham
Percussion Partita (1985)

Hennagin, Michael
Duo Chopinesque (1986)

Vayo, David
Border Crossing (1987)

Riley, Steve
Declarative Stances (1988)

Alfieri, John
Fanfare for Tambourines (1989)

Galvic, James M.
The Three Furies (1990)

Gauger, Thomas
Past Midnight (1991)

The following list of percussion ensembles is an overview of significant contributions to the percussion ensemble literature from its inception until the late twentieth century.

1930 Roldán, Amadeo
Rítmicas No. 5 and No. 6

1931 Varèse, Edgard
Ionisation

1933 Ardévol, José
Estudio en forma de preludio y fuga

1933 Becker, John
The Abongo

1933 Russell, William
March Suite

1933 Russell, William
Three Dance Movements

1934 Cowell, Henry
Ostinato Pianissimo

1935 Beyer, Johanna M.
Auto Accident

1935 Beyer, Johanna M.
IV

1935 Cage, John
Quartet

1935 Strang, Gerald
Percussion Music for Three Players

1936 Green, Ray
Three Inventories of Casey Jones

1938 Becker, John
Vigilante

1939 Beyer, Johanna M.
March

1939 Beyer, Johanna M.
Three Movements for Percussion

1939 Cage, John
First Construction in Metal

1939 Cage, John
Imaginary Landscape

1939 Cowell, Henry
Pulse

1939 Harrison, Lou
Fifth Simfony

1939 Russell, William
Three Cuban Pieces

1940 Cage, John
Living Room Music

1940 Harrison, Lou
Canticle No. 1

1940 Harrison, Lou
Song of Quetzalcoatl

1941 Cage, John
Third Construction

1941 Cage/Harrison
Double Music

1941 Harrison, Lou
Canticle No. 3

1941 Harrison, Lou
Fugue

1941 Harrison, Lou
Labyrinth No. 3

1942 Cage, John
Credo in Us

1942 Cage, John
Imaginary Landscape No. 2

1942 Cage, John
Imaginary Landscape No. 3

1942 Chávez, Carlos
Toccata

1942 Harrison, Lou
Concerto for Violin and Percussion Orchestra (revised 1959)

1942 Harrison, Lou
Suite

1942 Hovhaness, Alan
October Mountain

1943 Cage, John
Amores

1943 Partch, Harry
US Highball

1951 Colgrass, Michael
Three Brothers

1952 Brant, Henry
Symphony for Percussion

1952 Johnston, Ben
Concerto for Percussion

1956 Miller, Malloy
Prelude for Percussion

1958 Kraft, William
Suite for Weather Kings

1959 Kelly, Robert
Toccata

1959 Read, Gardner
Los dioses aztecas

1960 Ginastera, Alberto
Cantata para América mágica

1962 Kabeláč, Miloslav
Eight Inventions

1962 Johnston, Ben
Knocking Piece

1964 Benson, Warren
Streams

1965–66 Serocki, Kazimierz
Continuum

1969 Beck, John
Jazz Variants

1969 Ishii, Maki
Marimbastücke

1969 Wuorinen, Charles
Ringing Changes

1969 Xenakis, Iannis
Persephassa

1971 Reich, Steve
Drumming

1973 Reich, Steve
Music for Pieces of Wood

1974 Brün, Herbert
At Loose Ends

1976 Cage, John
Branches

1977 Kagel, Mauricio
Dressur

1982 Leonard, Stanley
Fanfare, Meditation and Dance

1983 Gauger, Thomas
Portico

1983 Takemitsu, Toru
Rain Tree

1984 Cage, John
Music for (variable instruments)

1984 Hoffer, Bernard
The River

1984 Miki, Minoru
Marimba Spiritual

1985 Cage, John
But What About the Sound of...

1985 Whettam, Graham
Percussion Partita

1986 Hennagin, Michael
Duo Chopinesque

1987 Vayo, David
Border Crossing

1988 Riley, Steve
Declarative Stances

1989 Alfieri, John
Fanfare for Tambourines

1990 Galvic, James M.
The Three Furies

1991 Gauger, Thomas
Past Midnight

Bibliography

Blades, James. *Percussion Instruments and Their History*. New York: Praeger, 1970.

Peters, Gordon B. *The Drummer: Man, a Treatise on Percussion*. Rev. ed. Wilmette, Ill.: Kemper-Peters, 1975.

Price, Paul. "Percussion Up-To-Date." *Music Journal* 22, no. 48 (December 1964): 32.

Vanlandingham, Larry Dean. "The Percussion Ensemble: 1930–1945." Ph.D. Diss., The Florida State University School of Music, 1971.

John H. Beck

The Percussive Arts Society: An Historical Perspective

The international organization known as the Percussive Arts Society (usually referred to as PAS) traces its origins to the 1950s, evolving from casual discussions among percussionists and music educators who attended the annual Midwest Band Clinic (later the Midwest International Band and Orchestra Clinic) in Chicago. The impetus for creating a bona fide organization was given by percussion manufacturer Remo Belli in December 1960, when he sponsored an informal dinner meeting at the Clinic. As a consequence, in the spring of 1961 the Percussive Arts Society was established through the efforts of California percussionist and teacher Robert Winslow, with resources provided by Belli's North Hollywood company. The Society's goals, stated in a letter written in early 1961, were:

1. To stimulate a greater interest in percussion performance and teaching.
2. To promote better teaching of percussion instruments.
3. To establish standard criteria of adjudication for percussion performance in light of today's demands on the percussion player.

Membership was "open to anyone interested in (the) stated purposes." The PAS newsletter, *Percussive Arts Society Bulletin*, first published in September 1961, listed fourteen founding members.

The resultant workload of increasing membership, along with Belli's desire to prevent the Society from becoming identified with a single commercial entity, led Winslow to relinquish his duties in 1963 to Donald Canedy at Southern Illinois University who, with Neal Fluegel, established *The Percussionist*, a professional journal, as the main educational and informational vehicle. Music industry funds were solicited to support the project. In December of that year, the Midwest Band Clinic provided a convenient framework for the first of many annual membership meetings. The 1964 meeting established a constitution and elected officers (including Gordon Peters as president, Jack McKenzie as vice president, and Canedy as executive secretary) and a board of directors consisting of prominent percussionists, educators, and members of the music industry. Meetings in Chicago over the next few years resulted in various committee projects, largely related to percussion education. Neal Fluegel of Indiana State University in Terre Haute gradually took over the daily administrative duties of the Society (including publication of *The Percussionist*) from Canedy, succeeding him as executive secretary and editor in 1966. In 1967 the PAS assumed publication of James L. Moore's popular magazine *Percussive Notes*, retaining Moore as editor. *Percussive Notes* disseminated news and dealt with general percussion matters, while *The Percussionist* specialized in more scholarly articles. The PAS was formally incorporated as a nonprofit organization in 1969.

Beginning with the "Day of Percussion," held at DePaul University in Chicago on December 18, 1971, the annual meetings included performances, clinics, and lectures, and, by 1976, had expanded into "Percussive Arts Society International Conventions" (PASIC) lasting several days. The first such PASIC was held at The Eastman School of Music in Rochester, New York, on October 15–17, 1976, with subsequent conventions taking place in various cities in the United States. Pre-conference programs of specialized topics were instituted at the 1986 PASIC in Washington, D.C.

In the fall of 1980, the title of *The Percussionist* was changed to *Percussive Notes: Research Edition*, the name it retained until its last issue in 1986, when its functions were integrated into *Percussive Notes*. The PAS was able to establish an independent office with a professional staff in 1981, when it moved from Terre Haute to Urbana, Illinois. In 1982, the office staff started *Percussion News*, a monthly newsletter consisting of brief news items. The Society was incorporated in Illinois in 1985.

Although the most visible aspects of the Percussive Arts Society are its journals and conventions, much of its work has been concerned with other projects. Its committees have dealt with topics as diverse as percussion notation, revision of the American snare drum rudiments, education, and acoustics. Publications have included extensive solo and ensemble booklets, a pamphlet on notation, a research bulletin, and the publication *The Percussive Arts Society International Drum Rudiments*. Its Hall of Fame awards, honoring outstanding contributors to the percussive arts, have been given annually since 1972, when the first recipients were William F. Ludwig, Sr., Haskell W. Harr, Saul Goodman, John Noonan, and Roy C. Knapp. The annual percussion composition contest, established in 1974, has encouraged the writing of hundreds of works. Student competitions have included the mock orchestra auditions, marching percussion contests, and percussion ensemble competitions. The establishment over the years of an extensive network of "chapters" in many countries and in the United States and Canada has been important in carrying out the Society's activities. Many chapters have published their own newsletters, sponsored events similar to the early "Days of Percussion," organized contests, and even commissioned new works.

In 1992 the Percussive Arts Society established permanent headquarters in Lawton, Oklahoma.[1] With a grant from The McMahon Foundation and a gift of land from the city of Lawton, PAS, through the architectural firm of Howard and Porch, designed an international headquarters and museum. From these headquarters and the establishment of a computer network called "World Percussion Network," PAS is capable of communicating percussion education throughout the world. The PAS Museum houses representative percussion equipment from all corners of the world, as well as older equipment donated by retired members.

Note

1. The address of the Percussive Arts Society's International Headquarters and Museum is 701 NW Ferris, Lawton, Okla. 73507.

Bibliography

Fairchild, Frederick. "A Brief History of the Founding of the Percussive Arts Society." *Percussive Notes* 24, no. 2 (January 1986): 7–9.

———. "A Brief History of Percussive Arts Society Conventions." *Percussive Notes* 25, no. 6 (Fall 1986): 71–72.

Fluegel, Neal. "The Percussive Arts Society in the Golden Age of Percussion." *Percussive Notes* 9, no. 1 (Fall 1970): 6, 12.

The Percussive Arts Society International Drum Rudiments. Sherman Oaks, Calif.: Alfred Publishing, 1985.

Fred Fairchild

The Plastic Drumhead: Its History and Development

The earliest recorded attempt to patent a synthetic drumhead occurred in the late nineteenth century. The head was made from cloth saturated with cellulose acetate and was designed to solve the inherent problems of susceptibility to the weather conditions of humidity and dryness.

Polyester film was invented in England by the Imperial Chemical Company (I.C.I.) in the 1940s. John Rex Winfield, of Aurington, England, and James Tennant Dickerson, of East Lothian, Scotland, were listed on the application of September 24, 1945 (serial number 613,398), in Great Britain, and credited with the first patent. After World War II, E.I. Du Pont De Nemours and Company bought the patent rights to manufacture it.[1] E.I. Du Pont applied for its own patent under serial number 476004, filed February 13, 1943, which was later abandoned. On March 22, 1949, the U.S. Patent Office, however, did issue patent rights to Du Pont, which expired on July 29, 1961,[2] patent No. 2,465,319 "Polymeric linear terephthalic esters." This patent (#2465319) was a continuation in part of the 1943 application by Du Pont, serial # 476004.

There seems to be no doubt that I.C.I. and E.I. Du Pont were the leading companies perfecting polyester film. This new film lent itself to drumhead use in the 1950s since it could be produced within .002 inches of the desired thickness in great widths up to 84 inches in diameter, to accommodate any size drumhead of a single-ply film. This film could also be seamed to accommodate larger size drumheads, if necessary. Polyester film has great tensile strength in the .0075 and .010 thicknesses, which can withstand the impact of the drumsticks, extending the life expectancy more than the calfskin drumhead. The polyester drumhead resists moisture absorption, thus holding its tension and thereby correcting one of the biggest problems of the animal skin drumhead. Unlike animal skin, polyester has very little reaction to sunlight and heat and is not affected by commonly used chemicals. Eventually, it was produced more economically than animal skin and can now be produced in various thicknesses from .002 to .014 mil. (with a tolerance of .0005 mil. for drumhead application).

Polyester film is formed by the transesterification of dimethylterphalate (DMT) and ethylene glycol, a petroleum derivative, and is used in producing Mylar, Dacron, rynite, cronar, and other polyester films. The three processes used to produce this film are (1) continuous melt, (2) batch process, and (3) solid phase. Du Pont Mylar utilizes the continuous-melt process. ICI melenex utilizes the batch process.

The continuous-melt process puts the two main ingredients, DMT and ethylene glycol, through a polymerization process subjecting it to high temperatures, high vacuum, and filtration to casting a solid film. The transverse direction stretches to more than 84 inches; however, the excess edges on both sides of the film are waste. The stretching process is used to reduce thickness and increase tensile strength and stiffness.

The batch process is used by I.C.I. to produce melenix. DMT in powder form and ethylene glycole in liquid form are mixed together to produce a solid ingot, which is stored until ready for use. The continuous-melt and batch processes are the most successful processes used for drumheads.

Du Pont classifies this film by letter "A," "B," "C," etc., for identification and control. Du Pont "A" film has proven to be most stable and suitable for drumhead use and is the most widely used film for drumheads to date. "A" film is also used in other industries for release liners, carbon ribbon, control tape, and plain/metalized labels (see Fig. 1).

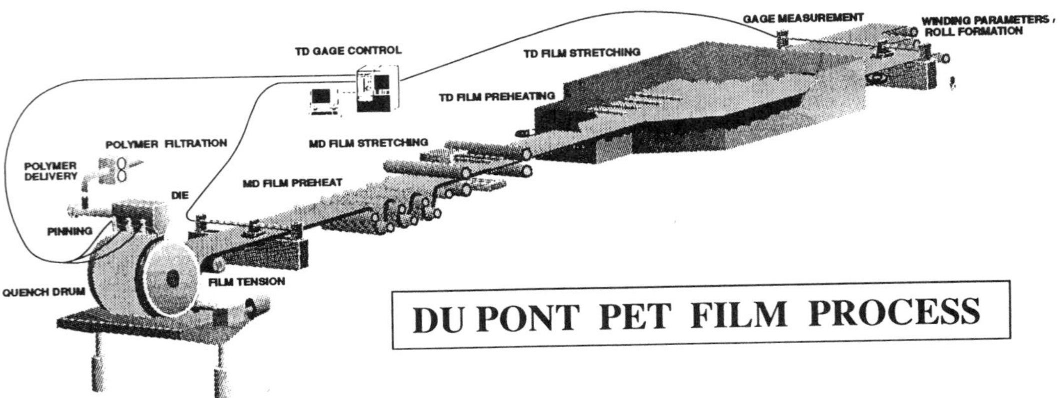

Fig. 1. *Courtesy of E.I. Du Pont De Nemours & Co.*

The first attempt to use polyester film for a drumhead was made in 1953 by Jim Irwin, a chemical engineer for the 3M Company in St. Paul, Minnesota. Irwin had been working with polyester film at 3M for several years and had the idea that this polyester film might work as a drumhead. He made up sample heads by serrating the edge of a circular piece of polyester film so it could be bent around and attached to a wooden drumhead flesh hoop. According to Irwin, Sonny Greer, Duke Ellington's drummer, was the first drummer to approve the use of polyester film as a drumhead. Irwin applied for a patent on his Mylar head in 1953, and it was granted in 1955.

During the same period, Joe Grolimund, employed by the Ludwig Drum Company in Chicago, was also working with Du Pont Mylar by tacking the film to a wooden flesh hoop. Grolimund said he suggested to the Ludwig Drum Company that they develop a drumhead from Mylar, but like Jim Irwin, he found that the drum companies were not interested in pursuing it at that time. Around 1957, the Ludwig Drum Company recalls receiving orders for wooden flesh hoops from Marion L. "Chick" Evans, of Santa Fe, New Mexico, who indicated to the Ludwig Company that he was making a new kind of drumhead and sent a sample to them. It was a circular piece of Mylar tacked or stapled to the wooden drumhead flesh hoop.

Evans became familiar with Mylar in 1954, by seeing it on television. He ordered material and made sample drumheads. The results were very good; however, there were two main weaknesses. First, the forming of the polyester film created folds and creases at the radius, and second, the mounting system of tacking the film on the wooden hoops failed under performance tension.

Heat-forming the Mylar was very difficult, and the folds and creases were created as the polyester film went around the wooden hoop to be stapled. This was corrected by scalloping the circumference of the circular film, removing material to prevent folds and creases, much in the same manner as a seamless ball timpani stick cover is applied to timpani sticks. The second weakness remained, however.

Meanwhile, Evans attempted to interest professional players, band directors, and retail drum shops throughout the United States in his drumheads. Evans, being a drummer himself, understood the potential use of Mylar as a synthetic drumhead. Bennett Shacklette, band director of the Santa Fe High School, also realized the potential of a polyester drumhead for use in inclement weather. Remo Belli and Roy Hart, co-owners of Drum City of Hollywood, also could see the potential of a polyester drumhead. In April 1957, Belli visited Evans in Santa Fe to see his operation and discuss his becoming a distributor of the Evans drumhead. Belli returned to Hollywood disenchanted, however, and started producing drumheads himself.

Up to this time, the mounting systems used in Evans and Belli drumheads were of the same style of tacking a skin head to a tambourine or bongo drum. Tacks and staples still failed under tension when the heads were tuned up to playing tension. Meanwhile, both Evans and Belli continued to perfect their drumheads and to look for a better mounting system. It was well established that Mylar was a fine substitute for animal skin; however, the mounting system needed to be improved.

Evans turned to using reinforced fiberglass hoops instead of the tacked wooden hoops. He made a die with a circular trough cutout of a hoop configuration, then inserted the perforated edge of the head into the polyester resin and removed the resin hoop from the trough after it had hardened. Thus, the Evans head had a flexible resin hoop reinforced internally with butcher twine.

Belli continued to refine his mounting system. Sid Gerwin, Belli's accountant, introduced his friend Sam Munchnik to Belli. Munchnik, a chemist specializing in adhesives from the aviation industry, came up with the idea of forming the circle of Mylar under heat and pressure into a hat shape and inserting it into a U-shaped aluminum hoop, filling the hoop with a liquid epoxy adhesive. Holes were punched around the circumference of the vertical leg of the membrane to allow the liquid adhesive to flow through the holes, completely embedding the Mylar in the epoxy in the U-shaped aluminum hoop. This led to the Remo, Inc., patent that bears the names of Munchnik and Belli as the inventors.[5] (Fig. 2).

Evans soon learned of Belli's attempt to make Mylar drumheads and filed a quarter-million-dollar lawsuit charging Remo, Inc., with illegally appropriating his idea. Belli's defense was that Jim Irwin held the

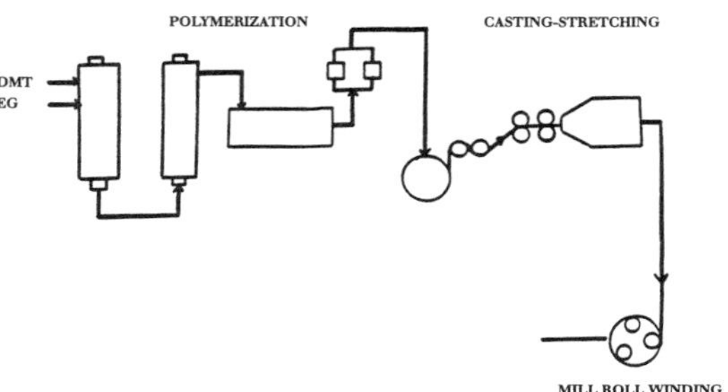

Fig. 2. *Courtesy of E.I. Du Pont De Nemours & Co.*

patent rights to a polyester head, not Evans. Further, the use of polyester film as a drumhead was probably not patentable. Munchnik's mounting system was, since it was Remo, Inc.'s own design.

The Ludwig Drum Company was a large user of drumheads and stood to gain most with a new synthetic drumhead. It was now experimenting with making Mylar drumheads using the same method of tacking Mylar to wooden flesh hoops. Ludwig experienced the failure of the mounting system and started to buy Belli's drumheads, since the Munchnik mounting system seemed to be the best available.

These early synthetic drumheads were fine for many different uses, such as for the bottom-side drumhead. However, the batter-side heads continued to fail in styles of music that required high tension, such as the Highland pipe drummers, drum and bugle corps, and competing marching bands. For styles of music such as orchestral, society bands, and student use, the synthetic drumhead had useful applications. Since the Ludwig Drum Company was a large user of drumheads, it had difficulty receiving enough of them from Remo, Inc., and it continued to research and develop a synthetic drumhead of its own, in the style of the Munchnik-Belli mounting system. A complaint from Remo, Inc., of an infringement on their patent soon stopped the Ludwig production; however, the research continued.

Meanwhile, in Basel, Switzerland, there was also a need for a good synthetic drumhead. The Basel style of drumming requires very high tension and just such a synthetic head to avoid all the ills of skin heads. Prominent leaders in this Basel style were also conducting research to find a successful synthetic drumhead.

By this time, the aluminum hoop was found to be superior to wooden hoops. With all this research going on around the world, a new mounting system was developed that involved placing the Mylar film into an aluminum hoop, inserting a solid metal hoop on top of the Mylar film in the aluminum channel, and crimping the outside leg of the aluminum channel, pressing the metal hoop insert further into the aluminum hoop, thus locking the Mylar film into it. This proved to be another acceptable mounting system. When it is used, the counterhoop under tension further presses the crimped edge of the hoop downward, thus locking the film further onto the flesh hoop. The more tension is applied, the firmer the lock on the film. The Ludwig Drum Company patented this crimped, dry mounting system in the United States (patent number 2,979,981) in 1961.

The Slingerland Drum Company, a rival of the Ludwig Drum Company, also stood to gain from a synthetic drumhead and began manufacturing Mylar drumheads in the crimped, dry mounting system, copying the Ludwig system. Ludwig sued Slingerland and lost, as the court ruled that the Ludwig patent was invalid because of prior art. This meant the Ludwig mounting system had been used before in other applications and was therefore not patentable. Ludwig appealed to a higher court; however, the lower court decision was upheld. As of 1992 there was no exclusive patent on a mounting system of polyester film applied to drumheads. All past patents have run out and are in the public domain. There are, however, trademarks on different styles of drumheads such as PinStripe, FiberSkyn, and Controlled Sound.

See also "The Basel Drum," p. 145.

Notes

1. Charles "Woody" Thompson, "The Mylar Drum Head," *Modern Drummer* (August 1989): 34.

2. United States Patent Office, dated March 22, 1949, #2,465,319, "Polymeric Linear Terephthalic Esters."

3. United States Patent Office, dated May 3, 1960, #2,934,989, application August 15, 1957, #678,339.

Bibliography

Levine, David. "Inside Remo." *Modern Drummer* (April/May 1980): 24.

Majeski, Brian. "Remo at 25." *Music Trades* (February 1982): 50–56.

———. "Remo Drums—Another Revolution in the Making." *Music Trades* (December 1985): 64–68.

Miller, William F. "Inside Evans." *Modern Drummer* (March 1989): 32.

Suggs, Michelle S. Electronic Department, Sales Division, Du Pont, Wilmington, Del.

Van Horn, Rick. "Industry Insights." *Modern Drummer* (December 1986): 30.

———. "Inside Ludwig/Musser." *Modern Drummer* (April 1990): 32.

Lloyd S. McCausland

The Rope-Tensioned Drum in America

Rope-tensioning was the only method of tensioning employed for the earliest drums until after the American Civil War, when rod-tensioning became common.

The Snare Drum

In Switzerland and Germany, the snare drum was known as a *Trommel*[1]; in France, *le tambour militaire* or *tambour d'ordonnance*[2]; and in England, the *side drum*.[3] (When the drum was first brought to England in 1492, at the time of Henry VII, it was known as the *Sweche*, and in Scotland by 1533 it was called the *Swasche Talburn*, attesting to its Swiss derivation.)[4] In the United States, it has been known as the *field snare drum, parade drum, tenor drum, small drum*, or sometimes *kettle* (*kittle*, colloquially) *drum*, or, in early records, simply *drum*.

The current British name, side drum, attests to the fact that these instruments of the sixteenth and seventeenth centuries were so large (a shell depth of 20 inches by 20 inches was not unusual) that they had to be carried on the side, well up under the left arm. This indicates why the traditional left-hand grip was invented, it being impossible to wield the left drumstick otherwise without colliding with the counterhoop.

As new weapons were invented and tactics changed, the tempo at which soldiers marched gradually increased and the size of the drum gradually decreased from the huge, square-proportioned side drums of medieval days to a more manageable average size of 16 inches by 16 inches by the eighteenth century. During the Civil War a 16-inch-wide by 12- or 13-inch-deep drum was called for in regulations,[5] and by the turn of the twentieth century, the drum had grown even smaller to a shell depth of 9 or 10 inches with a 16-inch diameter. The Sears, Roebuck Acme professional snare or tenor drum of 1902 was advertised at 14 inches by 8 inches, with 7 braces. It is interesting to see the terminology "snare" and "tenor" meaning the same instrument at this late date, either for a concert rod tension "Prussian pattern" (16 or 14 inches by 6 inches) or for the deeper field drums. Changes in the popularity of differing size drums had a reverse effect in the United States of the 1930s. Sanford E. "Gus" Moeller and others manufactured very deep field drums, some as large as 17 inches by 21 inches. Although these were accepted until quite recently as the "ancient" style snare drum, they did not accurately reflect the reality of researched United States instruments, or those in museums and collections, for that matter, being more reminiscent of the *Landsknechtstrommel* drums of Germany. Drums designed by Moeller nevertheless have had their own history since the 1930s, being used by the United States Army Band, the Old Guard, and numerous other "ancient" fife and drum corps of the northeast. Some venerable fife and drum corps of Connecticut, such as Moodus, Chester, and Mattatuck Drum Band, of Waterbury, still use very large "square" dimension snare and bass drums made by Eli Brown at the beginning of the nineteenth century. They are played in a very open style at moderate tension at a slow tempo that results in a very powerful, impressive American drum style that has its roots possibly with the beginning of snare drumming in the Europe of the Middle Ages.

It is predominantly the fullness of tone and projection available from a larger shell depth and diameter that characterize the rope-tensioned drum. Built in the light but strong manner of the old manufacturers, without the weight and muffling imposed by heavy hardware, and with synthetic heads for easy maintenance, the rope snare and bass drums are now an eminently practical and useful addition to every serious percussionist's inventory. For drum parts written before 1865, when rod drums came into vogue, rope drums are indispensable if the part is to have the correct historical timbre.

Fig. 1. Example of an early rope-tensioned drum.

Bass Drums

The bass drum advertisement in the 1905 Sears catalog lists the following options for sizes: 30 by 12 inches, 28 by 12 inches, 26 by 11 inches, and 24 by 10 inches, with the "Prussian" models all 9½ inches deep.[6] Prior to 1905, the bass drum had also undergone changes in style and size, with a few drums actually made with separate tension, being roped with two sets of ears.

In the eighteenth century, when the Janissary craze brought the bass drum into bands and the orchestra, the instrument was usually wider than its head diameter, hence the term "long drum." Some existing examples are: 23.4-inch diameter and 30.4-inch hoops and shell (Dorset Military Museum Dorchester, England)[7]; 22-inch diameter and 26 5/16-inch hoops and shell (Glen Collection, used at the Battle of Waterloo)[8]; 25-inch diameter and 25-inch hoops and shell (New-York Historical Society, New York City).[9]

Construction

The principal part of any drum is called the body, better known as the barrel or shell. Except when it was made of brass, it was constructed by heating a long, thin sheet of wood, sometimes veneered, in a steam box or with boiling water until it became pliable. According to Elias Howe, in the mid-nineteenth century, rock maple, ash, oak, beech, spruce, and black walnut were used, but other woods were also employed.[10] After steaming, it was wrapped around a form the size of the inside of the shell and clamped until it cooled. In the twentieth century, a special bending machine with heated rollers does the same job. Traditionally, the shell was overlapped, glued (not pasted) with hide glue, and nailed with iron or ornamental brass tacks in a design that was often quite complex. This tack design personalized the instrument and, in some cases, became a sort of trademark of the maker. Inside the shell were glued and nailed narrow reinforcing bands called stay-hoops or glue rings, which reinforced the extremities and helped keep the shell round. These were usually tapered in a scarf joint that was glued and nailed together. Counterhoops, batter on the top and snare on the bottom, were constructed of hardwood and, in the eighteenth century, were overlapped into a scarf joint.

Occasionally, a drum is found with the stay-hoops made outside the shell with similar workmanship to that used on canteens, pails, and kegs; the hoops are notched and interlocked to form a bulky and primitive, yet strong joint. The shell has two indentations on the snare side to receive the snare as it turns from the vertical to the horizontal while wrapping around the bottom of the shell. Called the "bed," it allows the snares to contact the snare head properly to insure that all dynamics can be played. Heads are made from pig, goat, calf, or other animal skins and are not tanned as

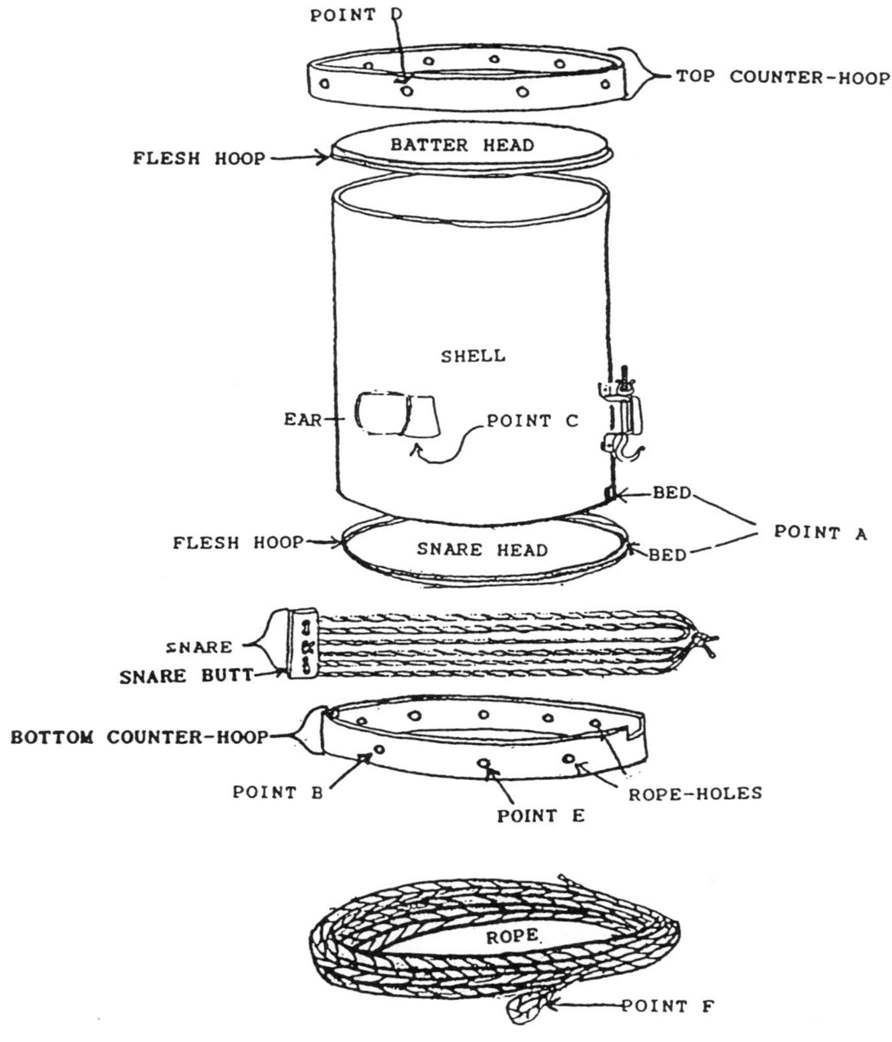

Fig. 2. Diagrams from Bruce and Emmett.

Courtesy of George Carroll.

for leather. They are processed from "green" hide by soaking and scraping. After preparation, they are soaked in water and lapped or tucked on a small flesh hoop, where the natural glue in the skin is sufficient to form a permanent bond. After drying, the rope is overhauled.[11]

Overhauling and Bracing

Before the drum is played, it must be "overhauled" and "braced." Overhauling in this case is the old dictionary term "haul over," meaning to haul the rope taut before the drum is braced for playing. Because the rope is one piece embracing the entire shell, it is necessary to vary the tension applied on the rope, starting with little and increasing the amount as the shell is encircled in order not to apply too much tension to the hoops and heads at one spot, thus warping the heads and hoops from the shell.[12] The beginning portion of the rope is where the loop is made and where the roping returns as the shell is encircled, with the tail of the rope going through the loop. A temporary knot is tied at this point to get the drum ready for the next round of the overhaul, of which six to twelve or more turns must be taken to bring the instrument to the desired tension, slack or taut according to the player's taste.[13]

After the unique "pig-tail" knot is tied, the ears, which have been mounted during the assembly of the drum, are then pressed to the bottom of the shell to achieve playing tension. In the words of Bruce and Emmett,

> care should be taken that the braces (ears) are not driven down with a jerk; new beginners are liable to this fault, thus causing something to give way, either cord, hoop or head, but generally the latter. Commence by tightening every other brace moderately, so that the remaining ones, when braced down, can draw with the same power, thereby giving the performer a chance to tune his drum to suit himself, by making it either flat or sharp in tone.[14]

Snares and Strainers

Snares are historically made from rawhide or catgut; wire and hemp have been tried but were not popular due to their mismatch with the slightly heavier heads required on a deeper rope-tensioned drum. According to Elias Howe, "the size of the snares used should depend upon the thickness of the snare heads as very thick heads require thick snares and thin heads, smaller ones."[15] Bruce and Emmett stated, "some performers prefer catgut, others rawhide; both are good, but for general use, the rawhide is preferable, as in damp weather, the catgut is the most affected by the dampness, which causes a contraction, and prevents the proper vibration."[16]

On early American and some European drums, snares were simply jammed between the snare head and the bottom counterhoop. The ears had to be released each time the snares were to be tuned. It worked well but was time-consuming. Howe was also the first in America to mention the snare strainer ("fastener," he called it).[17] Although it was a feature on many European drums from the earliest ones known, some British and very few American drums that have survived have this device. It frequently took the form of a hook working vertically through an iron or brass bracket mounted vertically on the shell, with a leather butt on the outside of the counterhoop or a post or hoop to secure the opposite end of the snare. The gut was tied or singed to keep it from pulling through. Another popular type worked horizontally much as would a small hinge with a clamp and thumbscrew on the outside leaf to secure and adjust snare tension. After the Civil War, a post-type strainer was invented with a snare clamp that worked vertically on a thumbscrew rod. This turned in a small cup mounted on the snare hoop.

Fig. 3. Early brass snare strainer from drum used in the Dorr Rebellion, c. 1841.

Blazons

The emblazonment of the shell with heraldic devices and regimental badges is almost as old as the snare drum. That of Sir Francis Drake, for instance, was painted brightly with his complete family coat of arms.[18] It was not until the Royal Warrant of 1768 that British colonels were prohibited from having their family coats of arms painted on their drums; it took that long for the last vestiges of feudalism to subside. In their place, the front portion of the drums had to be painted in a similar fashion to the regimental color (flag), with the king's royal cypher, crown and the rank, or number of the regiment in Roman numerals. All of this was to be executed on a background of the regiment's facing color, which was the shade used on the soldiers' lapels, collars, and cuffs to identify their specific regiment. This color was also used on the fife cases, tents for storing muskets (bells of arms), and as the main color of the fifers and drummers' uniforms. The musicians wore the colors opposite to the men in the ranks, so if the regimental color was green, for instance, the men wore red coats with green trim, while the fifers and drummers were dressed in green coats with red trim and unique regimental worsted "lace" on the seams. In some regiments, engraved brass drum shells were substituted for the painted wood shells.[19]

This European tradition held over into the Continental Army of the American Revolution, where the musicians were dressed in the colors opposite to the soldiers, whose uniforms differed according to the states in which they were raised.[20] In the present day, U.S. Marine Corps documents portray a green uniform with white facings. On the drums are painted, on a white background, the rattlesnake motto "Don't Tread On Me"

Fig. 4. Artillery side drum, 1862, Elias Howe.

Fig. 5. Eagle drum.

all from the Continental cruisers' ensigns or flags.[21] By the War of 1812, the drums had to be painted with the eagle on a blue ground color for the infantry and red for the artillery, 22 inches around the front of the shell. A surprisingly large number of well-painted, and not a few very crude, examples of "Eagle" bass and snare drums exist from the late eighteenth century. By the time of the Civil War, Eagle drums were already a solid American tradition used by both the North and South by the thousands. Many others exist with state or regimental numbers and symbols. The beautifully painted Eagle rope drums made for the U.S. Army Band by "Gus" Moeller and "Buck" Soistman were retained despite the suggestion made to go with British "heraldic regalia" rod drums, when the band turned to the British drum major staff, herald trumpets, and Hussar Guards-type uniforms in the 1960s. At least part of the venerable American martial drum tradition was thereby preserved. After the Civil War fifes and drums had been rendered obsolete as a component of the seventeenth- and eighteenth-century lineal tactics so wasteful of manpower during the war, and were gradually replaced by the bugle in the regular infantry and the Marine Corps, holding on a little longer in the U.S. militia known as the National Guard. Only the shield and "U.S." fit between the rods on the new military field drums, and by World Wars I and II, the shield was dropped, leaving only the letters "U.S." in blue, outlined in gold.

Civil and Military Usage

The advent of military usage of fifes and drums is claimed by the Swiss, who first recorded this phenomenon in the thirteenth century. By the fifteenth and sixteenth centuries the drums themselves were known as "the Swiss," because of their wide usage by these European mercenary soldiers.[22]

In Switzerland there is a depiction of the 200-man Swiss Papal Guard entering Rome by beat of drum in the reign of Pope Julius II in 1513. The tradition of the Swiss Guard still exists there, where the Vatican continues to employ Swiss fifers and drummers with rope drums.

By 1627 the drum had migrated to the New World. It was noted in New Plymouth, Massachusetts, that "they assemble by beat of drum, each with his musket or firelock, in front of the captain's door."[23] In 1636 at Cambridge, Massachusetts, Edward Johnson said, [they] "had as yet no bell to call men to meeting and therefore made use of a drum."[24]

In Boston in 1637, the first drummer of the Ancient and Honorable Artillery, Arthur Perry, was required to beat the call for worship on Sundays, lectures on Thursdays, give notice of town meetings, auction sales, the departure of vessels, advertise for rooms for rent, for children lost and found, and the importations of goods. He operated in much the same way as the tower musicians of Continental Europe or the Waits of England of the Middle Ages. The Farmington, Connecticut, drum, used for town crier purposes, is now in the Connecticut Historical Society and may be the oldest existing American drum. It is of the same proportions and construction as medieval European drums.

This nonmilitary use of the rope drum is still being employed today in areas such as the Andes Mountains of South America, where a town crier with a rope drum beats a long roll to announce the latest gold prices acquired daily from London by Telstar (satellite), or in Switzerland, where every male citizen is sent off from his hometown with a drummer marching him to his girlfriend's house for a last formal party before entering the army for the first time. The fife and drum have long been on the scene in New England towns, and there the tradition still exists, where it has waxed and waned for over two hundred years. It has been taken up in many other parts of the country, particularly the east, from the northeastern influence, and in some foreign countries.

Drummer's Instruction

The *field drum,* being a direct descendant of the *tabor drum,* presented some obvious technical problems for the first generation of players because two sticks now had to be manipulated. Although coordinating a wind instrument with one hand while playing rhythms with the other on a drum must have been quite a challenge, the new task was to make intelligible sounds with the two sticks. Thoinot Arbeau, in 1588, in his *Orchésographie,* notated (for the first time) strokes in various combinations but did not indicate which hand (sticking) was to play. Spinney interpreted the figure as the present day flam, a close double stroke.[25] By 1636 Marin Mersenne mentions the drummer's loud blow like the discharge of an arquebus, fast beats coming down like hail, and the clear, soft sound achieved by using the edge of the head. He refers to the *"bâton rond"*—single beating, *"bâton rompu"*—double beats, and *"bâton mesle"*—single and double beats.[26]

Rudiments

This realization of single, double, and combination beats of the drum, in differing strengths and variations of simple or complex rhythms, is still with us today and is known as the "rudiments" (meaning the fundamentals) of drumming or, as a genre, "rudimental drumming" (published and widely recognized systems of technique taught to be memorized and practiced until they become reflexes, playable accurately at a high rate of speed).

As far as the sometimes fragmentary records show, the term "rudiment" was first used by Charles Stewart Ashworth, who was the leader of what was to become the world renowned U.S. Marine Band, to classify a group of drum figures. During his tenure, the Marine Band was a small group of musicians and a field music school for the fleet, and the drum major's principal responsibility at that time was the training of his regiment's field musicians. Drum Major Ashworth came from England, where he was a drummer. He joined the U.S. Marines in Boston in 1802 and was promoted to drum major two years later at the Washington Barracks. On January 15, 1812, he deposited a copy of his *A New Useful and Complete System of Drum Beating . . . Particularly for the Use of the United States Army and Navy* with the clerk of the District of Columbia, thus establishing himself as the father of rudimental drumming. When compared to Drum Major Samuel Potter's *Art of Beating the Drum,* published in London in 1815, very few differences can be found in the rudimental content, although Potter's work goes into very valuable explanations of technique absent from Ashworth's.[27] The latter work notates in detail all of the Camp Duty calls mentioned in *Of the Drum,* Chapter 21, by Baron von Steuben, thereby preserving the Revolutionary War Camp Duty.[28] The bible of American rudimental drumming, Bruce and Emmett's *The Drummers' and Fifers' Guide* (1862), was the first work in America to succinctly notate the rudiments, the Camp Duty, and a large body of fife and drum material in readable notation. It included "Army 2/4" ("Biddy Oats"), "Army 6/8" ("The Corconian"), "The Downfall of Paris," "Three Camps," and many other staples of the rudimental repertoire. Until its publication in 1862, all drum tutors in the United States were notated in phonetics, coded notation, or were merely guides to the technical manner in which the beats were to be played. George B. Bruce, its coauthor and principal instructor at the School of Practice, the U.S. Army's music school in the nineteenth century, thought very highly of Ashworth's work. He stated, "After carefully examining all the Drum books that have been published during the past twenty-five years, the author finds none to compare with 'Ashworth's Rudimental School,' which has, however, long been out of print." (It had actually been fifty years since the Ashworth book was published.) Bruce continues,

> He has therefore adopted Ashworth's system, which he has himself taught, adding to it the results of his own knowledge and experience, and rendering it better adapted to the modern style of Drum Music. The "Duty," as laid down in this book, is in strict conformity with that officially authorized for use in garrisons and camps of the United States Army. After acquiring a thorough knowledge of the rudiments as laid down in this work the student will have no difficulty in making himself perfect in the "Duty."[29]

The Bruce and Emmett work was not the only book to incorporate Ashworth's material, as the Howe book in 1861 and Nevins in 1864[30] were both to use the exact Ashworth notation without giving credit to the author. The Howe book handled it this way:

> The Old Style of Drum Instructions, Used in 1812. It is called the Drummer's Notation and is in the Old English style. It will be seen the Half, Quarter and 16th notes are used simply to express the force of the beats, and without any regard to their relative value as to their length.[31]

Although the United States saw an unusually high number of drum tutors published in its early years, the significant works were by Ashworth, Bruce and Emmett, and Hart. Col. H. C. Hart's work incorporated a unique notation (as did most) and had some rudiments otherwise unknown to us that deserve to be incorporated into current listings. Some figures that were to become common in ragtime and jazz are found in the Hart.[32] Another important tutor was that of Gardiner Strube.[33] For a chronology of rudimental publications, see "Published Writings on Methods for Percussion," p. 385.

Head Drum Major Samuel Potter of the Coldstream Regiment of Foot Guards stipulated proper instructions starting with the stance of the drummer. His requirements were, "The first thing previous to a (Drummer) Boy practising is to place him perfectly upright and place his left Heel in the hollow of his right Foot. . . . Let the Boys drum be slung on the neck being careful the Drum Carriage is of a moderate length."[34] The U.S. Regulations of 1812 called for the drum carriage to be 1¼ yards long or 45 inches, "the Drum bearing on the left Thigh, so that when the Knee is bent, the Drum balances on it, if the Carriage is too long, it will prevent the Boy's striking the Drum with that force required."[35]

The slinging of the drum carriage on the drummer's neck allowed the drum to move outward from his body more than would a shoulder carriage, thus making the center of the head, where the desirable tone was produced, to be more easily accessible. Bennett Cuthbertson's direction was as follows: "a carriage slung from the neck, places the drum more convenient for the performance of the beatings, than hanging it from the shoulder. . . . Very few excel upon the drum who sling it otherwise."[36]

The shoulder slings were used in some regiments however, particularly on the Continent. French buff leather shoulder slings were sent to America along with their drums at the end of the Revolutionary War. In the United States, both methods were utilized, with the tutors, until the end of the nineteenth century, generally stipulating the neck sling, or carriage. This custom died very hard. The author of this essay was required to sling a Moeller drum from the neck in the U.S. Army Band in the late 1950s.

Grip and Form

Ashworth (1812) taught the grip as follows: "the left stick must be firmly held between the thumb and two middle fingers, to rest on the third finger a little above the middle joint. The . . . right hand stick must be held fast by the little finger, and be allowed to play with ease through the others, as a man may use a stick in fencing."[37]

Potter (1815) and other tutors stated basically the same grips; by the time of Hart (1862) other ideas on grasping the drumsticks were forthcoming. Hart said:

> the right stick was to be held with all of the fingers closed around it, the stick balancing between the ball of the thumb and the joint of the first finger. The left stick rested in the hollow of the thumb with the first joint of the first finger curled around the stick and the ball of the thumb on the first joint. It was to balance on the second joint of the third finger with the hand slightly open.[38]

Drumsticks, until about the turn of the twentieth century, were conical in shape with a slight thickening toward the butt. Field sticks were quite short and heavy at first but, by the eighteenth century, were becoming longer and slimmer, approximating a modern 3S model in length and weight, if not a little heavier. They were usually of dark imported hardwood and sometimes had ferrules on the butt. Fifers were often drummers who were taught to fife as an added responsibility. Fifes were frequently made in Europe, so that they could be utilized as drumsticks in a pinch; they carry a vestige of that shape to this day. As the playing of a field drum frequently required the use of the upper and lower arms as well as the wrists, Potter, in his book of 1815, taught that,

> all rudiments were to begin very slowly. If any mistakes were made, the drummer was to begin again. In this manner he would avoid bad

> habits that would cause his body unnecessary labor and appear awkward.[39]

The drummers were enjoined never to play with stiff wrists or arms. The drummers were started very young because their wrists were thought to be more supple. Said Potter, "Pay attention to his Arms so that the Elbows and Wrists move in Good form and not touch the sides, and the Drum to be struck as near the centre as possible. In so doing the Boy will never fail having a Good even Roll."[40]

This concept was reinforced by Rumrille and Holton (1817) in Albany, New York, who added, "The arms must be habituated to move with the greatest of ease, while joints of the shoulders and wrists are exercised in performing the principal parts."[41]

The old teachers knew well that if a rudiment was not properly assimilated, the reflexes the drummer had to rely upon when the rudiment was closed would be flawed and not serve him well. He was taught (1) accuracy; (2) evenness and uniformity; and (3) speed.

> The drummer was to strike his double strokes for the long roll as evenly and uniformly as possible, while keeping the sticks as far away from the head between strokes as the speed of the roll would allow. He was to take pride in making it look easy and to beat his duty with spirit.[42]

This "waterfall" style of drumming became a legend in New England and can be seen in practice by a Civil War drummer who was captured on sound film at the beginning of sound movies in the 1930s. Although he was obviously very old by that time, he could still execute "Army 2/4" to the fifing of "Turkey in the Straw" with his sticks coming up as high as his hat brim.

By the 1860s some authors had modified this older style, for Hart (1862) taught that drawing or sideway strokes were absolutely to be avoided and the drumhead was to be struck squarely. Although a slight up-and-down motion of the forearms was permitted, as well as outward movement of the elbows, movements of the upper arms and shoulders were not. The rolling or turning of the wrists was to be the principal action of drumming, despite what professional teachers were then advocating.[43]

Bruce and Emmett (1862) still taught the old style 7: "The arms must be habituated to move with the greatest ease, while the shoulder joints and wrists are exercised in performing the principal part."[44]

The principal utilization of the martial rope-tensioned field drum and its initial reason for existence was for and by the military.

Camp Duty—The Principal Function of Field Musicians

In the preface of the monumental *The Drummers' and Fifers' Guide*, Bruce observed that the old style of thorough rudimental teaching was becoming obsolete with the standard of drumming and fifing deteriorating. Indifferent players, ignorant of the nature of their instrument, would therefore be the result. He personally saw numerous instances of incompetent militia field musicians unable to perform the Camp Duty at the beginning of the Civil War in Washington.[45]

"Camp and garrison duties" was more commonly referred to as "Camp Duty" (more rarely "Camp Duties") or just "the Duty." The phrase held a special meaning for the field musicians of the seventeenth, eighteenth, and nineteenth centuries. It neatly and succinctly spelled out the part of their work that regulated the soldiers of their regiment in camp or garrison or the sailors and marines on bases and shipboard.

As early as 1717, Will Breton expounded in his "Military Discipline," that after the British soldiers had learned their manual of arms, it was necessary for them to know all of the several drumbeats, because, with the noise and confusion of battle, the commanders' verbal orders could not otherwise be heard.[46]

In all instruction books for the fife and drum, the basic rudiments were considered as components which, when combined, made up the next section—the calls of the camp.

The great emphasis placed upon learning the Camp Duty in these works attested to the importance of the usage of musical instruments to convey the wishes of the commanders. In the days before the radio, written field orders were dispatched by mounted and foot messengers, oral commands, signal cannon, visual signal flags, and lamps as well as the routine and tactical use of field music.

The Camp Duty can be divided into three categories:

1. Regulatory Calls

Those that set in motion a specific act immediately upon hearing a call. They included, but were not confined to, "The Reveille" (to arouse the men in the morning), "The Assembly" (to signal the forming of a company), and "The Tattoo" (to call the men back to their quarters). Such calls were heard daily at the same time and were soon to become part of the normal routine.

2. Tactical Signals

During field maneuvers the commander could save his voice by having his orders conveyed by drum. This was also done on the many long tactical marches, when the drum was reserved for such work and not used to beat a cadence. Von Steuben's *Regulation* included

> For the front to advance quicker—the long march.
>
> to march slower—the taps
>
> front halt—two flams from right to left, and a full drag with the right, a left hand flam and a right hand full drag.[47]

Nineteenth-century regulations called for a more extensive use of the drum or bugle for such work.

3. Ceremonies

Some of the more colorful and enjoyable duties were to "troop the line" on dress parade at the slow cadence and quickstep, march through the streets of a friendly town or city, or perform the ruffles and "cheers" (fife trills) to salute a dignitary or general.[48] On the somber side the field musicians were responsible for the wielding of the cat-o'-nine-tails for corporal punishment. They also were involved in military executions, playing the death march to and from the scene, and, as in all funerals, a lively quickstep back from the cemetery to leave the sorrow at the grave.

The importance of music not only for functional purposes but also for the morale of the regiments was not lost on the leaders of America's first army, for General George Washington wrote the following order shortly after taking over command of the Continental Army:

> The music of the army being very bad, it is expected that the drum and fife majors exert themselves to improve it, or they will be reduced, and their extraordinary pay taken from them.... Hours are to be assigned for all the drums and fifes of each regiment, and they are to attend them [the drum and fife majors] and practice. Nothing is more agreeable, and ornamental, than good music. Every officer, for the credit of his corps, should take care to provide it.[49]

A Captain John Hiwell of Crain's Artillery was subsequently appointed as inspector of music for the Continental Army, and he was to ascertain that all of the calls were "performed agreeable to the 21st chapter of the regulation" (von Steuben's), "exact uniformity in the different beats prevail through the army" for which mostly British music was used, and that "the signals of the drum are . . . continually made use of and pointedly attended to."[50]

That the music was much appreciated and remembered in later years with great fondness is evident from the Revolutionary War journal of Dr. James Thacher, who participated in the Battle of Yorktown. He wrote,

> A splendid world is open to our view, all nature is in animation—the fields and meadows display the beauties of spring, a pleasing variety of vegetables and flowers perfume the air, and the charming music of the feathered tribe delight the ears. But there is a contrast in music. What can compare with that martial band, the fife and drum, the bugle horn and shrill trumpet, which set the warhorse in motion, thrill through every fibre of the human frame, still the groan of the dying soldier and stimulate the living to the noblest deeds of glory? The full roll of the drum, which salutes the commander-in-chief, the animating beat which calls To Arms for a battle, The Reveille, which breaks our slumber at dawn of day, with "come, strike your tents, and march away," and the evening tattoo, which commands to retirement and repose; these form incomparably the most enchanting music that has ever reverberated on my ear.[51]

Notes

1. Peinkofer and Tannigel, 11.
2. Goute, 3.
3. Blades, 210.
4. Farmer, 11.
5. Howe, 2
6. Sears, Roebuck, 213.
7. Baines, 156, no. 817.
8. *European Musical Instruments Catalog*, 65, no. 466.
9. Spinney, vol. 2, 8.
10. Howe, 2.
11. *Field Musicians Journal,* 13.
12. Bruce and Emmett, 4.
13. Ibid.
14. Ibid.
15. Howe, 2.
16. Bruce and Emmett, 4.
17. Howe, 2.
18. Blades, pl. 104.
19. Strachan, 159.
20. Copeland, Fall 1966, 73.
21. McBarron, Jan. 1949, 2.
22. Peinkofer and Tannigel, 91.
23. Colonial Society of Massachusetts, 75.
24. Ibid.
25. Spinney, Vol. 1, 9.
26. Blades, 212.
27. Potter, 1–18.
28. *Drummers Assistant*, July 1962, 5.
29. Bruce and Emmett, 1.
30. Nevins, 4.
31. Howe, 72.
32. Hart, 46.
33. Strube, 1–13.
34. Potter, 2.
35. Ibid.
36. Strachan, 160.
37. Ashworth, 1.
38. Hart, 3.
39. Potter, 3.
40. Ibid, 4.
41. Rumrille and Holton, 3.
42. Potter, 3.
43. Hart, 3.
44. Bruce and Emmett, 5.

45. Ibid, 1.
46. Barty-King, 13.
47. Stevens, 84.
48. Miller, 24.
49. *Drummers Assistant*, Spring 1966, 21.
50. Ibid., 23.
51. Thacher, 59.

Bibliography

The Ancient Times (Ivoryton, Conn.). The Company of Fifers and Drummers.

Ashworth, Charles Stewart. *A New Useful and Complete System of Drum Beating.* Washington, D.C., 1812. Reprint, Street, Md.: Cousin Sally Ann, 1990.

Baines, Anthony. *European and American Musical Instruments.* New York: Viking, 1966.

Barty-King, Hugh. *The Drum.* London: Keyline, Dunstable, 1988.

Bittel, Josef. *Tambouren und Pfeifer im Dienste der Heimat.* Visp, Switzerland: Offset Mengis, 1970.

Blades, James. *Percussion Instruments and Their History.* New York: Praeger, 1970.

Blades, James, and Jeremy Montagu. *Early Percussion Instruments.* London: Oxford University Press, 1976.

Bruce, George B. and Dan Emmett. *The Drummer's and Fifer's Guide.* New York: Firth, Pond & Co., 1862. Reprint, Street, Md.: Cousin Sally Ann, 1990.

Clark, Benjamin. *Benjamin Clark's Drum Book.* Boston: Massachusetts Historical Society, 1797.

Colby, J.B. *Chart Showing Origin of Rudiments.* Chicago: W.F.L. Drum Co., 1936.

Copeland, Peter. *Military Collector & Historian* (Fall 1966): 73.

The Colonial Society of Massachusetts. *Music in Colonial Massachusetts.* Charlottesville: University Press of Virginia, 1980.

Cuthbertson, Bennett. *A System for the Compleat Interior Management and Economy of a Battalion of Infantry.* Dublin, 1768.

"Drum Beating." Unpublished manuscript, Sir Samuel Hellier Collection, England, eighteenth century. Reprint, Street, Md.: Cousin Sally Ann, 1992.

The Drummers Assistant. Williamsburg, Va., 1812.

The Drummers Assistant (Spring 1966): 21, 23.

The Drummers Assistant (July 1962): 5.

European Musical Instruments Catalog. Edinburgh International Festival 1968. Edinburgh: Reid School of Music, Edinburgh University, 1968.

Farmer, Henry George. *Handel's Kettledrums and Other Papers on Military Music.* 2nd ed. London: Hinrichsen Edition, 1960.

Field Musicians Journal. Quarterly periodical of the International Association of Field Musicians. Street, Md.

Fife, David. *Manuscript Collection of Fife Duty & Tunes.* Ottawa, Ontario, Canada: Public Archives of Canada, c. 1790.

Finke, Detmar, and H. Charles McBarron. "Uniforms of the Continental Army." *Military Collector & Historian* (Washington, D.C., 1960).

Goute, Robert. *Le Tambour d'ordonnance.* Domont, France: Author, 1970.

Hart, H.C. *New and Improved Instructor for the Drum.* New York: Author, 1862. Reprint, Street, Md.: Cousin Sally Ann, 1992.

Hazeltine, David. *Instructor in Martial Music.* Exeter, N.H.: C. Norris and Co., 1810. Reprint, Street, Md.: Cousin Sally Ann, 1990.

Howe, Elias. *Howe's United States Regulation Drum and Fife Instructor.* Boston: Author, 1861. Reprint, Street, Md.: Cousin Sally Ann, 1992.

Ludwig, William F. *The Thirteen Essential Rudiments. . . .* Chicago: Ludwig Drum Co., n.d.

McBarron, H. Charles. *Military Collector & Historian* (January 1949): 2.

Manual for Drummers, Trumpeters and Fifers, U.S. Marine Corps. 2nd rev. ed. Washington, D.C.: U.S. Marine Corps, 1942.

Miller, Delavan. *Drum Taps in Dixie.* Watertown, N.Y.: Hungerford-Holbrook, 1909. Reprint, Street, Md.: Cousin Sally Ann, 1992.

Musical Instruments of the World. New York: Diagram Visual Information, Ltd., Bantam ed., 1978.

Nevins, William. *Army Regulations for the Drum, Fife and Bugle.* Chicago: Root & Cady, 1864.

Peinkofer, Karl, and Fritz Tannigel. *Handbook of Percussion Instruments.* London: Schott, 1976. Originally published in German (Mainz: B. Schott's Söhne, 1969).

Père, Marguery. *Instruction pour les tambours.* Carroll Collection. Paris, c. 1775. Originally titled *Fife and Drum Routine of Louis XVI.* Translated by Irving Block.

Potter, Samuel. *The Art of Beating the Drum.* London: Samuel Potter, 1815. Reprint, Street, Md.: Cousin Sally Ann, 1990.

Robinson, Alvan, Jr. *Massachusetts Collection of Martial Musick.* Hallowell, Maine: Goodale, 1818. Reprint, Street, Md.: Cousin Sally Ann, 1990.

———. *Massachusetts Collection of Martial Musick.* 2nd ed. Exeter, N.H.: Alvan Robinson, 1820. Reprint, Street, Md.: Cousin Sally Ann, 1990.

———. *Massachusetts Collection of Martial Musick.* 3rd ed. Hallowell, Maine: Glazier and Co., 1826. Reprint, Street, Md.: Cousin Sally Ann, 1990.

Rumrille, J. L, and H. Holton. *The Drummer's Instructor; or Martial Musician.* Albany, N.Y.: Packard & Van Benthuysen, 1817. Reprint, Street, Md.: Cousin Sally Ann, 1990.

Rutherfoord, Dayd. *The Complete Tutor for the Fife.* London, c. 1756. Reprint. Street, Md.: Cousin Sally Ann, 1990.

The Sears, Roebuck Catalog. 1905. Reprint, New York: Crown, 1969.

Sousa, John Philip. *A Book of Instruction for the Field-Trumpet and Drum.* Washington D.C., 1886. Reprint, Cleveland, Ohio: Ludwig Music Co. Inc., 1985.

Spencer, R. *The Drummer's Instructor.* London: Author, c. 1760.

Spinney, Bradley. *Encyclopedia of Percussion Instruments and Drumming.* Vol. 1, Book A, and Vol. 2, Book B. Kew Gardens, N.Y.: Author, 1959.

Steuben, Baron Friedrich von. *Regulations.* Valley Forge, Pa.: Continental Congress, 1778. Reprint, Philadelphia: Ray Riling Arms Books, 1966.

Stevens, William. *A System for the Discipline of the Artillery of the United States of America.* New York: W.A. Davis, 1797.

Strachan, Hew. *British Military Uniforms 1768–1796.* London: Arms and Armour Press, Lionel Leventhal, 1975.

Strube, Gardiner A. *Strube's Drum and Fife Instructor.* Washington, D.C.: Adjutant General's Office, 1869. Reprint, Street, Md.: Cousin Sally Ann, 1990.

Thacher, James. *Military Journal . . . 1823.* Reprint, Hartford, Conn.: Hurlbut, Williams & Co, 1862.

Wanamaker, Jay, and Rob Carson. *International Drum Rudiments.* Sherman Oaks, Calif.: Alfred Publishing, 1984.

Winter, George. *Kurze Anweisung das Trommel-Spielen. . . .* Berlin: G.L. Winters Witwe, 1777. Carroll Collection.

The Young Drummers Assistant. London: Longman & Broderip, 1760. Sir Samuel Hellier Collection, eighteenth century. Reprint, Street, Md.: Cousin Sally Ann, 1992.

George Carroll

The Snare Drum

Fr: *caisse claire, tambour*; Ger: *kleine Trommel*; It: *cassa chiara, tamburo alto*; Sp: *tambor, caja*

The snare drum can be traced back 250 years to the *tabor* and *side drum*. These earlier instruments were generally much larger and used exclusively for military purposes. In the eighteenth and nineteenth centuries the side drum was incorporated into opera orchestras for military scenes. During the middle and latter part of the nineteenth century, the instrument gradually made its way from the opera pit to the concert stage.

The principal difference between the modern instrument and the older ones is the use of tension rods for the heads as opposed to rope tensioning or simple tacked-on heads. This change was first introduced in 1837 by Cornelius Ward. His drum used screw tensioning instead of rope, had a brass shell, and was considerably smaller than earlier drums. The size of the drum was reduced to accommodate its use in nonmilitary events.

The modern snare-drum shell is made from metal (steel, aluminum, brass), wood (maple, rosewood), or a synthetic material. The most common dimensions range from 13 to 15 inches in diameter and from 4 to 8 inches in depth. The heads are either synthetic material or calfskin. The bottom, or snare head, is generally thinner than the top, or batter head. In addition, the snare head has stretched across it a number of snares that rattle against the membrane when the drum is struck. These snares are generally composed of wire, cable, or cat gut.

Striking implements for the snare drum are most generally a pair of wooden sticks, which have been turned in such a fashion as to produce a tip at the end of the stick that strikes the head. Other striking implements include wire brushes and, on occasion, a timpani mallet.

The technique used for the snare drum is one of the most demanding and exact of all the percussion instruments. For that reason, it is often the first instrument studied by the young percussionist. The fine degree of muscle control for performance on the snare drum, especially at extremely soft dynamics, requires many years of study. The player must be able to control a variety of strokes including the single, double, and multiple bounce. In addition, a great variety of sticking patterns is used to achieve various effects and musical shadings. The sustained sound of the snare drum is known as the "roll." This effect is achieved through a variety of means. The most common is either the double-stroke or multiple-bounce roll. In the former, the hands alternate in an even rhythm, each striking the drumhead twice. The result is a clean and open sound of very rapidly played double strokes. The multiple-bounce roll, favored in most orchestral situations, has the same rhythmic alternation of the hands, but the tip of the stick strikes the head at least three or more times. The relative density of the multiple-bounce strokes as opposed to the double stroke gives the illusion of an even, sustained sound.

The snare drum has a distinctively high-pitched, dry, and crisp sound when the snares are engaged across the bottom head. When the snares are not in contact with the bottom head, the drum has a hollow sound much like a high-pitched tom-tom. Béla Bartók uses this effect in his Concerto for Orchestra (1943). Other effects are possible on the snare drum. The *rim shot* is produced by placing the tip of one stick on the drumhead with the shaft of the same stick on the rim, while the other stick strikes it across the shoulder. The resulting sound is much like a gunshot. An example may be heard in Aaron Copland's Symphony No. 3 (1946). Striking the shell of the drum with the stick produces a dry sound, similar to a woodblock. Maurice Ravel makes use of this in his orchestration of Modest Mussorgsky's

Pictures at an Exhibition (1922). A sound very similar to the claves is produced by placing the tip of one stick near the center of the head while striking it across the rim. Jazz drummers make frequent use of this technique.

On the marching field the snare drum fills a role much different from its function on the concert stage. The marching snare drum serves as the soprano voice in the percussion section and, as such, often provides the most prominent rhythmic voice in the marching ensemble. The modern marching snare drum differs in several other ways from its concert hall counterpart. The marching snare drum is deeper, with most lengths measuring 15 inches. The tensioning of the heads is much tighter than on the concert snare drums. This high tensioning creates a much stronger rebound of the stick, which is necessary when executing the complex sticking patterns used on the marching field.

The sticking patterns used by modern marching snare drums are referred to as rudiments. They have descended from antique calls of the military drums in the seventeenth and eighteenth centuries. In general these rudiments are various rhythmic patterns that incorporate alternating and repeating stickings with a variety of embellishments. These embellishments include the *flam* (one primary note with a single grace note), the *ruff* (one primary note with two grace notes), and the *open double-stroke roll,* as described above.

Representative works in the orchestral literature using the snare drum include:

Rimsky-Korsakov, Nikolai
Scheherazade (1888)

Nielsen, Carl
Symphony No. 5 (1922)

Nielsen, Carl
Symphony No. 6 (1925)

Ravel, Maurice
Boléro (1927)

Nielsen, Carl
Concerto for Clarinet and Orchestra (1928)

Prokofiev, Sergei
Lieutenant Kijé Suite (1934)

Shostakovich, Dmitri
Symphony No. 7 (1941)

Schuman, William
Symphony No. 3 (1941)

Bartók, Béla
Concerto for Orchestra (1943)

Prokofiev, Sergei
Symphony No. 5 (1944)

Creston, Paul
Invocation and Dance (1953)

Barber, Samuel
Medea's Meditation and Dance of Vengeance (1956)

Bernstein, Leonard
Overture to *Candide* (1956)

Bresgen, Cesar
Intrada (1964)

Niehaus, Manfred
Pop & Art (1968)

See also "The Rope-Tensioned Drum in America," p. 281; and Illus. 26, p. 128.

Bibliography

Ashworth, Charles Stewart. *A New Useful and Complete System of Drum Beating.* Washington, D.C., 1812. Reprint, Williamsburg, Va.: Drummer's Assistant, 1966.

Blades, James. *Percussion Instruments and Their History*. 2nd ed. London: Faber and Faber, 1974.

Brown, Theodore D. "Double Drumming." *Percussive Notes* 20, no. 1 (1981): 32–34.

Peinkofer, Karl, and Fritz Tannigel. *Handbook of Percussion Instruments*. London, Schott, 1976. Originally published in German (Mainz: B. Schott's Söhne, 1969).

Peters, Gordon. *The Drummer: Man, a Treatise on Percussion.* Rev. ed. Wilmette, Ill.: Kemper-Peters, 1975.

Schneider, Walter C. "Percussion Instruments of the Middle Ages." *Percussionist* 15, no. 3 (1978): 106–117.

Andrew Spencer

*Steel Band/Pan**

Fr: *tambour d'acier;* Ger: *Calypsotrommel, Stahltrommel, Trinidad-Gongtrommel;* It: *tambour d'acciaio*; Trin: *pan*

Pan[1] and the steel band[2] were created and developed by predominantly Afro-Trinidadian[3] lower-class urban dwellers on the islands of Trinidad and Tobago during the early to mid-1930s. Since that time this ensemble and its primary instrument have achieved international recognition. However, pan and the steel band are only the most recent in a lengthy succession of similarly associated instruments and ensemble types with roots extending back over time and distance (from Trinidad and other New World territories) to portions of West and Central Africa. Although detailed historical and cultural analysis is beyond the scope of this article, it is essential to present an overview of Trinidad Carnival and profile pan's most immediate precursors before proceeding to the current tradition and tuning techniques.

I. Historical Background

Trinidad was first sighted by *Christopher Columbus* during his third voyage to the New World, on July 31, 1498. Columbus claimed the island as a colony of the Spanish crown, thus setting the stage for the decimation of the indigenous Amerindian population and the eventual influx of foreigners from around the world.

Despite Columbus's claim, the most profound early European cultural influence was not Spanish but French. In the late 1700s French-speaking planters with sizable retinues of African slaves began emigrating from neighboring Caribbean islands such as Martinique, Guadeloupe, St. Lucia, Santo Domingo, St. Vincent, Dominica, and Grenada. These settlers were fleeing regional turmoil stirred by upheavals in Europe (the French Revolution and hostilities between Great Britain and France) and were eager to take advantage of liberal land, tax, and trading concessions that were being offered by the king of Spain in order to develop a thriving planter-slave economy in Trinidad.

The dominant social, cultural, and political force in Trinidad from roughly 1783, then, was the French Caribbean planter elite. Their most festive holidays were Christmas and a celebration known as "Masquerade" (later "Carnival"), a season that began after Christmas and culminated on the Sunday, Monday, and Tuesday preceding Ash Wednesday. Slaves were officially barred from Carnival, but they were given considerable freedoms and were encouraged to participate in the spirit of the season by holding their own dances, dinners, and gatherings. The slaves began to adopt and interpret aspects of both these seasonal customs to suit their own needs.

In 1797 the Spanish governor of Trinidad capitulated to a large British naval force, and British rule over the island began. Immigration increased and diversified to include former residents of the British Isles, some Chinese, Venezuelans, many more slaves from Africa, and freed slaves from the United States who had served with the British during the War of 1812. After twenty-five years the free colored population outnumbered whites by four to one, while the ratio between slaves and whites was seven to one.

Christmas and Carnival remained largely the domain of the white upper class and free colored middle class until the emancipation of the slaves was fully effected, a process lasting from 1834 to 1838. Following this, the distribution of the Afro-Caribbean population throughout the island began to shift, and within the next few years, a large number of these people began to take up residence in and around urban centers, principally Trinidad's capital, Port of Spain. The drain on the plantation work force necessitated fresh immigrant labor to keep the estates functioning. The migration to Trinidad of Chinese, Portuguese, free African Americans from the United States, and residents of neighboring Caribbean islands and Central and South American nations all began to increase beginning around the 1840s. The largest single labor force, of East Indian indentured workers, began emigration a few years later, in 1845.

The majority of the developing urban underprivileged working class made their homes in various makeshift shantytowns or within the confines of what were known as barrack yards, built behind the frontages of city streets. These barrack yards were centers of neighborhood activity: informal social gatherings including drinking, gambling, gaming, recreational song, dance, and music. These gatherings gradually began to assume the proportions of well-structured and formalized neighborhood masquerade bands that participated in a pre-Carnival, midnight torchlit procession called Canboulay,[4] sought out rival bands during Carnival to challenge as a group or in individual Kalinda[5] competitions, and generally carried on in a manner that the white, upper-class citizenry considered lewd, disgraceful, and dangerous.

As the respectable and well-to-do withdrew from the streets, recoiling in horror and disbelief at the increasingly disreputable condition into which they felt Carnival had fallen, the underclass continued to raise its collective voice and make its presence felt. The criminal element mixed with the lower-class working folk in the barrack yards and on the streets. To many of these people Carnival represented a rare opportunity to release pent-up tension, anxiety, and aggression caused by the pressures of struggling to survive under a repressive and racist colonial system and in an often harsh and hostile urban environment. It was an affirmation of cultural identity, a tribute to emancipation, and a much-needed forum for the airing and working out of class antagonisms. It was also an invitation to some to defy the laws of the colony by creating public disturbances, flaunting obscenity (by the upper-class standards of the day), disrupting the peace, and inciting crime.

By the 1860s the residents of the barrack yards began to be referred to as the *jamette*[6] class, and their pre-Lenten street revelry as Jamette Carnival. The jamette class *masquerade bands* organized themselves into what amounted to tiny barrack yard "kingdoms," presided over by a "king" and "queen" with attendant courtiers, singers, dancers, musicians, and a strong army of bodyguards, each typically carrying a lighted torch and a hardwood Kalinda stick. These were the "king's" champion stick fighters, who would march ahead of their bands issuing boastful challenges to rivals.

The dancing, singing, masquerading, parading, and stick fighting all demanded musical accompaniment. Drums and chacchacs[7] were essential, joined possibly by cowhorn and conch-shell trumpets, banjars,[8] and any other object with a sound deemed suitable for inclusion (e.g., salt boxes, tin kettles, glass bottles, cooking-oil tins, metal scraps). All this plus a chorus of vocalists was led by the *chantwel*,[9] whose function it was to direct the group in performing composed and extemporized praisesongs for the mask band's "king," sing songs of derision aimed at competing bands' "monarchs," taunt and insult hecklers from opposing bands, and provide song accompaniment to inspire courage, instill confidence, and direct the movements of the band's stick fighting experts during a confrontation.

Slave songs, dances, and recreational assemblies had long been associated with violence and rebellion by colonial government administrators and law enforcement officials on Caribbean islands. Now, as the scope and influence of Jamette Carnival increased, the middle and upper classes supported the government's moves to contain and eventually suppress it. High on the list of the elements of Jamette Carnival to be targeted was its music. It was, after all, the music that stirred the revelers, provided momentum as the Canboulay procession surged through the streets at midnight, inspired the singing, dancing, and masked street parading on Carnival days that the colonial authorities considered so indecent and immoral, and incited, urged on, and accompanied the often violent street band clashes.

During the Carnivals of 1877, 1878, and 1879 measures were successfully implemented to control and begin to neutralize the bands. In 1880 the complete suppression of Canboulay was attempted by calling upon participants to lay down their drums, sticks, and torches. On this occasion the revelers conceded, but by the following year they had banded together in a show of organized, unified resistance against the authorities that resulted in a Carnival marred by riots, disturbances, and injuries to police and revelers alike.

The "Cannes Brûlées Riot," as it came to be known, prompted a series of investigations into the Carnival "problem." Recommendations were submitted suggesting severe restrictions on Carnival celebrations, in particular, Canboulay. Concurrently, suggestions were made to regulate the major East Indian festival, Hosay.[10] This celebration had begun to attract a large number of working-class Afro-Trinidadians as both observers and participants, and it was becoming a rather disorderly affair, with its parades, floats, songs, dances, games, and *tassa* drumming.[11] The government feared another Canboulay on its hands.

Preventive legislation came, in anticipation of the 1884 Carnival, in the form of the Peace Preservation Ordinance. This ordinance provided the legal leverage necessary to outlaw certain offensive aspects of Carnival/Canboulay, including music. It gave the governor the power to restrict or prohibit, among other things, "the beating of any drum, the blowing of any horn, or the use of any other noisy instrument" (*The Law of Trinidad and Tobago*, 341). Also, that year regulations were issued preventing Indians celebrating Hosay from entering Port of Spain or from traveling on any public highway in procession.

With the suppression of Canboulay and the government's increased supervision, the way was cleared for a renewed participation by middle- and upper-class members of society. This significantly altered the context within which the mask bands were now obliged to function. Among other things, certain members of the elite, predominantly white, ruling class began to frequent practice sessions of the mask bands and patronize the various *chantwels*. This prompted a reassessment of the chantwel's role, his eventual disassociation from the masquerade bands, and metamorphosis to full-time singer, and eventually, calypsonian.

Many of the early chantwel/calypsonians turned, for their accompaniment, to music provided by "string bands." The instruments used in these groups included guitars, banjos, mandolins, *quatros*, *chac-chacs*, flutes, and violins. Then later, during the jazz vogue of the 1920s, instruments such as the trombone, clarinet, cornet, and saxophone were utilized.

The lower class and jamettes were faced with a dilemma following the 1884 enforcement of the Peace Preservation Ordinance. Drumming was not abandoned, but it was forced underground, or out into the country districts, where the influence of the law was not so strongly felt. This challenged the urban barrack-yard bands to find some other suitable musical accompaniment for both their Carnival revelries and day-to-day recreation, something to inspire raucous street processions and accompany the illegal, yet still practiced kalinda. Soon ensembles began to develop that would be called *tamboo bamboo* bands.

The evolving calypsonian, with his string-band accompaniment, may well have been enjoyed by members of the lower class, but it was not the kind of music their Carnival revelries demanded. The old style chantwel/chorus with tamboo bamboo remained the most relevant and popular music among the underprivileged.

II. The Development of Pan

The term *tamboo bamboo* (also *tambour bamboo, tambou bamboo, bamboo tamboo*) results from the creolization of the French word for drum (*tambour*), combined with the name for the predominant material used to make instruments for tamboo bamboo bands.

Bamboo stamping tubes are known in parts of Africa, Oceania, Asia, Central and South America, and the Caribbean islands, serving various functions within their respective cultures.[12] On Trinidad the idea of using bamboo stamping tubes may have come with immigrants from Africa, South America, and/or other Caribbean islands. Tamboo bamboo bands, though, did not exist prior to the suppressive legislation of 1884, and they appear to have been developed specifically to fill the need for a strong, rhythmic Carnival music that would not be restricted by any of the existing ordinances.

Tamboo bamboo bands began to emerge sometime during the 1890s. By the early 1900s they had developed, become (more or less) standardized, and assumed the identity of a recognizable type of ensemble.

Like the mask bands for which they provided music, the tamboo bamboo bands were associated with the districts from which they originated. The greater Port of Spain area contained the largest concentration of tamboo bamboo. The downtown areas around Charlotte Street and George Street, Corbeaux Town near the docks, the eastern neighborhoods of Belmont, Gonzales, Laventille, John John, Clifton Hill, La Cou Harpe, the central and more westerly sections of Newtown (and other parts of St. Clair), Woodbrook, and St. James, and Maraval to the north all supported tamboo bamboo bands.

Tamboo bamboo, much like the drumming that had preceded it, was participated in by members of the lower class in their barrack yard communities, in small, informal, spontaneous situations throughout the year, at wakes, at Christmas, and, most of all, during Carnival, in larger organized groups, "beating on the road" to accompany the revelries of large masquerade bands.

A full tamboo bamboo band was a more sophisticated and expanded version of a simple stamping-tube ensemble. The different-sized instruments were fashioned from bamboo stalks or stems that were readily available throughout the islands. Ritual often accompanied the cutting, curing, and fashioning of the stalks into musical instruments. The ceremonies were frequently nocturnal affairs, preferably illuminated by a full moon. A week or more of drying and curing might follow before the tubes would be prepared and ready for playing.

The bass *boom*[13] was the largest, lowest-sounding type of bamboo tube. It was cut from a stalk usually measuring about 5.2 inches (13 cm) in diameter, to a length of about 64 inches (1.6 m) to 72 inches (1.8 m). Holes were punctured through every joint except the bottom one. The bamboo was cut about 3.2 inches (8 cm) below the bottom joint. This extra length was beaten until it softened, frayed, and split out. Only then could the boom produce the desired deep, round tone. Each bass-boom player (of which there could be many) was responsible for a single stamping tube (or, on occasion, two, if they were of a manageable size and weight). To be played, the tubes were held upright and pounded at a slight angle on a dirt or paved surface or on a large flat stone.

A second type of bamboo instrument was known as the *cutter* (called the *chandler* by some bands, the term "cutter" then being applied to very thin stalks of bamboo that would be beaten together). This was considered the lead instrument of the ensemble. The cutter was approximately 3.6 inches (9 cm) in diameter and 28 inches (70 cm) to 43 inches (1.1 m) in length, with two joints. It was cut about 3.2 inches (8 cm) above the upper joint, through which a hole was punctured; and, like the boom, about 3.2 inches (8 cm) below the lower joint. Each cutter was played by a single musician by being held across one shoulder and beaten on the shaft with a hardwood stick, or by simultaneously stamping the bottom on the ground and striking the side.

In support of the cutter was the *foulé* (also called *fuller*, or *buller*). The foulé consisted of a pair of bamboo tubes, each about 3.2 inches (8 cm) in diameter. They were both nearly 12 inches (30 cm) in length. Both pieces were cut about 2 inches (5 cm) below the lower joint, though one piece was cut about 1 inch (2.5 cm) above the second joint, through which a hole was punctured. The other piece was cut about 1 inch (2.5 cm) below the second joint. The playing techniques for the foulé were as follows: one tube was held in each hand and struck end to end, or both tubes were pounded (together or alternately) on the ground or some other appropriate surface.

A wide variety of instruments was employed along with the bamboo, including *chac-chacs,* bugles, saxophones (plus other brass and wind instruments), and (cautiously and/or surreptitiously) skin drums. The tradition of incorporating other, non-musical (from an upper-middle-class Eurocentric perspective) objects continued with the tamboo bamboo bands. Participants would contribute music played upon pieces of scrap metal, discarded containers of various types and materials, abandoned motor-driven vehicle and/or other machine parts, graters, kitchen utensils, jars, dustbins, and glass bottles. The gin flask (typically struck with a spoon) in scholarly and historical reports, local press accounts, and informants' descriptions is the most often mentioned non-bamboo instrument associated with tamboo bamboo bands.

Complete Carnival-size tamboo bamboo bands comprised more than one of each of the bamboo instruments. A band's primary function was to accompany the maskers' dancing, singing, and parading rhythmically. Because of this, large numbers of each bamboo type (along with gin flasks and other instruments) might be employed, interlocking their basic individual patterns into a complex rhythmic tapestry.

Tamboo bamboo beating, though relative-pitched and timbrally varied, was essentially rhythmic accompaniment. Playing was very often spontaneous, with parts improvised on the spot. Previously employed drumming patterns would almost certainly have found their way into the music of tamboo bamboo. However, the lack of dependable observation and documentation during the nineteenth and early twentieth centuries would make any attempt at detailed musical analysis problematic.

While the tamboo bamboo and masquerade bands roamed the streets, European and North-American-influenced music groups were more frequently featured at large Carnival competitions. By the mid-1930s jazz groups and string bands were firmly rooted in the Carnival tradition and became the standard accompaniment for calypsonians. They entered popular competitions held at large venues and also paraded during Carnival days. The revels and music of the underprivileged classes were increasingly more accepted and viewed with a greater degree of tolerance (if not understanding). Indeed, tamboo bamboo became the music expected to be heard accompanying J'Ouvert (Monday morning) Carnival festivities.

Accounts of the origin of the steel band frequently attribute the demise of tamboo bamboo to police intervention and subsequent legal suppression because of clashes between the bands and the use of bamboo instruments as lethal weapons. This writer could find no evidence that tamboo bamboo was ever legally suppressed, as drumming had been before it.[14] Instead, it finally outlived its usefulness and was discarded willingly by its own creators, but not in favor of the more respectable, refined, and "civilized" jazz ensembles or string bands. It gradually succumbed to the lower-class Carnival musicians' inventiveness, resourcefulness, and imagination. Within restrictions imposed by their ethnic, social, and economic status, they began to create a Carnival music reflective of more modern times and the revelers' desires for a louder, more exciting, more inspiring accompaniment.

The transition from tamboo bamboo bands to metal pan bands and the subsequent developments leading to the sophisticated steel bands of the late twentieth century are controversial and hotly debated topics in Trinidad and Tobago. Seemingly countless personal narratives exist detailing the first introduction of pans into bamboo bands and the first recognizable melody to be beaten on a pan.[15] Elements of these accounts may be true, and it is a difficult task indeed to distinguish the subtle shadings of individual observation, history, legend, myth, folklore, and fiction. Finally, it must be recognized that the evolution of the steel pan in Trinidad cannot be clearly understood by adhering to any one personal account, and that it is unlikely that any single individual could claim to be the first to tune a pan or play a melody on a pan, or that a first all pan or all-steel band could be identified. Rather, evidence suggests that there was similarly directed activity throughout Port of Spain as young men experimented with pans of different types, and that these innovations were the results of a gradual process nurtured by a shared body of knowledge. Although a comparative analysis is called for, the scope of this article suggests a composite picture may be more practical and beneficial for gaining a deeper understanding of the transition from bamboo tubes to steel bands.

As was noted above, African and Afro-Trinidadian musicians of both pre- and post-emancipation days maintained a tradition of using metal percussion instruments and found objects in music ensembles. Beginning in the early nineteenth century, there is frequent mention in both local press and historical accounts of gongs, triangles, tin kettles, graters, and pans and cans of various types being incorporated into musical bands. The *jab molassi*,[16] a familiar Carnival character from the late nineteenth century, danced through the streets typically accompanied by one or two boys beating on empty metal pots and/or tins; and *bobolee bands*,[17] organized for both Good Friday and Carnival, featured the beating of effigies of Judas Iscariot to rhythms played upon assorted oil tins, zinc pans, and the like. Even tamboo bamboo bands were known to have utilized metal idiophones, including containers of various types. The uniqueness of the early pan bands, then, lay not so much in their use of metal pans, containers, household utensils, and metal scraps, but rather in the fact that almost the entire ensemble consisted of these instruments, and that the playing surface of each pan had the potential to yield a number of recognizably pitched areas.

From the mid-1930s pans began to replace bamboo in bands all over greater Port of Spain and territories to the east, west, and south. Yet, like the bamboo, these pans were valued primarily for the loud and energetic rhythmic accompaniment they provided revelers. The vast musical potential of these instruments was only beginning to be realized, and there was as yet no systematic experimentation or concerted effort toward improvement. Early innovations were more likely a coincidence of the many idle hours of pan beating in which the semi- or unemployed men of the urban underclass indulged. Within a few years, however, the nature of pan changed, its role expanded, and its playing technique demanded more skill. As the older bamboo players retired, a new, younger group of musicians emerged who took the development of pan to its next stage.

The categorization of sound in the early pan bands was influenced by the tamboo bamboo bands. Different sizes and types of pans (zinc [used as a base ingredient in paint] pans, pitch-oil [kerosene] tins, biscuit drums [from the Sunrise and Bermudez biscuit factories in Port of Spain], cement drums [obtained from Port of Spain's deepwater harbor construction], caustic-soda drums [from two soap factories in the John John section of east Port of Spain], various types of metal tins used at the abattoir near John John, dustbins, and buckets), held under one arm or hung around a neck or shoulder and beaten with open hands, fists, or sticks, produced sounds that were different from one another timbrally and in their relative pitch (low/high). These instruments initially substituted for equivalent bamboo instruments; for example, the foulé was replaced by a zinc pan, the cutter by a caustic-soda drum, and the boom by a biscuit tin.

The early pan bands were also, to varying degrees, modeled upon and influenced by previously extant musical ensemble types in Trinidad. These included Orisha (Shango) and Rada-cult drumming groups,[18] the Indo-Trinidadian tassa ensembles, bobolee bands, the jab molassi Carnival character, the all-about or knockabout sailor Carnival character,[19] and the police and military marching bands that were a by-product of British colonial rule. The most immediate, closely related, and influential precursor, though, was the tamboo bamboo band. It was this type of ensemble that metamorphosed into the pan (or iron) band, itself having already absorbed elements from the influences cited above.

Repeated beating of pans began to reveal the distinctly different sounds of dented and non-dented areas on the playing surfaces, and the exploitation of those differences soon followed. By the late 1930s pans began to be categorized by tuners and players as loosely defined types within a musical family and identified with names such as *dudup* and *ping pong*. These pans, as suggested by their having been named onomatopoeically, were of a type that could produce two or more relatively pitched sounds.

The most sophisticated of these early pans were tuned to play specific melodies or familiar pitch sequences. They were first prepared by beating the playing surface outward into a shallow, convex dome onto which dented areas would be fashioned. A simple melodic motif containing a limited number of pitches was then chosen from a current calypso, a Christian hymn, or other popular or folk song, and the dented areas tuned to those pitches. In performance these pans were usually played to support and accompany the singing of a tune rather than as a lead or solo instrument.

In early 1940 the legendary pioneering pan man and tuner, Winston "Spree" Simon, is said to have created a "melody pan," boasting a gamut of eight pitches and capable of playing some nursery rhymes, simple calypsoes, and popular movie themes. Some other notable innovators in ping-pong tuning during the early to mid-1940s include Ellie Mannette (from the Woodbrook band Oval Boys [later called Invaders]), Carlton "Zigilee" Constantine (from the band Bar 20), Neville Jules and Rudolph "Fish Eye" Ollivierra (both from Port of Spain's Hell Yard area), and Andrew De Labastide (from the band Hill 60).

In January 1942 Trinidad's colonial governor proclaimed the suspension of Carnival and other large public gatherings in order that more of the island's resources and energies could be devoted to assisting Great Britain's war effort and to eliminate the opportunity, during a traditionally chaotic and unruly time, for acts of war-related terrorism. By this time pan or iron bands (the term "steel band" having yet to be recognized) had clearly come into their own all over Port of Spain. During the suspension (1942–1945) calypso tents were allowed to open during their usual season, and pan bands did take to the road at Christmas, Carnival, and on Discovery Day (the first Monday in August, marking Christopher Columbus's first sighting of Trinidad), though these excursions were small in scale and usually cut short by the authorities.

Although public pan band activities were curtailed, pan beaters, at this time still working with various oil tins, caustic-soda drums, and biscuit tins, continued on their own to improve the quality of the instruments and to organize themselves within their communities. In the first half of the decade, the thriving pan scene, in greater

Port of Spain alone, produced such well-known bands as Alexander's Ragtime Band, Bar 20, Cairo, Casablanca, Cross of Lorraine (later to become Trinidad All Stars), Crusaders, John John/Destination Tokyo (later to become Tokyo), Gay Desperadoes, Hill 60, Nobhill, Ohio Boys (later to become Renegades), Oval Boys, Red Army, Spellbound, Swaney River, and Tripoli. San Fernando, Trinidad's second largest city, to the south of Port of Spain, spawned steel bands such as Bataan, Free French, Pearl Harbour, and Rising Sun. During the war years pans were first introduced to Tobago by inter-island workers; by the mid-1940s Tobago steel bands included Black Swan, Casbah, Elite Stars, Lucky Jordan, and Rhythm Tigers.

During the early to mid-1940s the overall appearance, sound, and playing methods of pans continued to evolve. The common method of holding a ping pong with one hand and playing it with a single bare wooden stick in the other began to be replaced. Innovations introduced by such pan pioneers as the above-mentioned Carlton "Zigilee" Constantine, Sonny Roach, and Chick "McGrew" Springer featured strapping the pan across the shoulder or around the neck, thereby freeing both hands to play (in imitation of another contemporary pan type, the *tenor kittle*, itself influenced at least in part by military side drums and/or tassa drums). Ellie Mannette is generally recognized as the first person to introduce the wrapping of the wooden sticks used to beat pans with strips of rubber, thereby softening the sharp attack and helping to draw more of the fundamental pitch from the instrument. Mannette states that this occurred in 1943. The "Behind the Bridge"[20] style of tuning a pan (attributed by many to Simon), in which the playing surface of the pan was given a slightly bulging, convex shape, was replaced. Again, Mannette is the acknowledged innovator, claiming that sometime after the war he was the first tuner to "sink" the surface of a pan into a shallow, concave shape before tapping the pitched areas up and into configuration.

On V.E. Day (May 8, 1945) restrictions were lifted and bands, by now referred to in the press and known to the public as steel bands, once again freely took to the streets. This marked the beginning of a prolonged period, lasting well into the 1950s, of escalating tensions between the bands and the upper-class establishment. Increasingly frequent clashes between members and supporters of rival steel bands prompted efforts to curtail steel band activities through legislation. However, by this time the steel band movement had captured the interest of a handful of concerned citizens and public officials, who were beginning to note its progress. These individuals recognized the steel band as a unique expression of Trinidadian culture and believed that pan players, if given a fair opportunity, could make a valuable and lasting contribution to society.

The first Carnival after the war, 1946, featured the oft-noted event of "Spree" Simon and the John John/Destination Tokyo steel band demonstrating to a masquerade-judging committee, comprised of Trinidad's colonial governor, selected members of the government, and the upper class, the ability of a pan (and pan player) to render recognizable melodies in different musical styles and from a variety of musical periods and genres. By this time Simon's refined version of the "melody pan" was capable of producing fourteen pitches. He treated the governor and his party to a repertoire including "Ave Maria" and "God Save the King," popular calypsoes "Lai Fung Lee" and "Tie Tongue Mopsy," and the Christian hymns "Rock of Ages," "Cleft for Me," and "I Am a Warrior." Later that same year, during an island-wide steel band competition at Mucurapo Stadium, near downtown Port of Spain, other bands exhibited their abilities to perform a wide variety of repertoire and arrangement styles. Casablanca, for example, rendered "The Bells of St. Mary's" (from a film of the same name, starring Bing Crosby), while Sun Valley, the eventual winners, presented "Home, Sweet Home" and "La Paloma."

Between late 1945 and the Carnival of 1947, one of the most significant developments in the history of pan occurred. It was during this period that the larger, heavier types of oil drums (55 U.S. gallon [209 liter], 45 imperial gallon [204 liter], or 44 imperial gallon [200 liter]), which in later years would become commonly associated with pan, were first used to fashion and tune the instruments and were first incorporated into steel bands. As with every other major development noted thus far, there are numerous accounts relating specific incidents and making claims of responsibility; and, again, any number of them may be true. One of the acknowledged claimants to introducing full-sized oil drums into steel bands is renowned steel band leader, arranger, tuner, and visionary Anthony Williams. Williams, a native of the St. James district of Port of Spain, relates that when the masquerade/steel band Sufferers was preparing for Carnival 1946, its members were in need of pans. Williams had noticed discarded oil drums on the beach near the U.S. Army Airforce base at Mucurapo and suggested using those. Although the band rejected his idea, Williams went ahead and tuned pans from two of the oil drums himself, with great success.

Whether this development was the result of simultaneous discoveries or a single idea that spread, by 1947 Carnival oil drums began to take their place in steel bands throughout the city. The steel bands' use of 209-, 204-, 200-liter oil drums made possible previously undreamed-of innovations. The drums were larger in diameter, constructed of a higher quality and more durable metal, and (thanks in part to the U.S. military bases in Mucurapo and Chaguaramas) more abundant and readily available than any of the containers used previously. They enhanced the sound, hastened the progress, and expanded the musical possibilities of the steel bands.

The transition to the exclusive use of oil drums, however, was not immediate. For years they were still used in combination with other pan types. During this period of experimentation and development, many styles of pans were introduced. These have all since been discontinued or radically revised, and there is little reliable information pertaining to their original designs. The difficulty of establishing a clear picture of the early pan styles is compounded by the fact that, while the long process of standardization was getting under way, instrument names and designs were frequently altered and/or exchanged. For instance, a tuner might borrow another band's pan name for an instrument that served much the same function as one he had just introduced into his band; or a fairly common pan design might be slightly revised, but then given an entirely new name to credit its revisor. The myriad of pan names that appeared during the 1940s and 1950s include the *balay, chufak, grumbler, grundig, dudup, ping pong, piano pan, slap bass, boom, bass boom, tune boom, tenor kittle, kittle boom, alto pong, guitar pan, cuatro pan, cello pan, bass pan, second pan, double second pan,* and *double strumming pan.*

Early emphasis was upon development of the ping pong, the pan capable of playing melodies. Oil drums were first used to tune ping pongs because they made possible a louder, clearer, longer sustaining tone, and their larger diameter expanded the available pitch range.

After success was achieved with the ping pong attention began to turn to the inner voices and the bass. By the early 1950s commonly used pans (still categorized as melody, harmony, bass, and rhythm) included the following:

Melody: ping pong (sometimes called a piano pan), and variations such as the tenor ping pong and the soprano ping pong.

Harmony: second pan (also called alto pan, alto pong), tenor kittle, tenor boom, tune boom, guitar pan.

Bass: boom.

Rhythm: kittle, kittle boom (non-pan rhythm instruments at this time included *chac-chacs*, triangles, woodblocks, various Afro-Caribbean idiophones and membranophones, and brake drums).

The melody pans were tuned using 209-, 204-, or 200-liter oil drums. The harmony and bass pans were still made using biscuit tins and caustic-soda drums. The various rhythm pans were not tuned to specific pitches and were made from biscuit tins and other small metal containers.

The formation of the Trinidad All Steel Percussion Orchestra (also frequently referred to by its acronym, TASPO) proved a catalyst for further pan development. TASPO was comprised of ten of the top pan players in Trinidad, guided and conducted by manager/musical director Lieutenant Joseph Griffith, a Barbados-born former member of the Trinidad Police Band and director of music for the St. Lucia Police Band. This ensemble was organized beginning in mid-1950 for the initial purpose of representing Trinidad at the Festival of Britain. This exposition was scheduled to be held in London during the summer of 1951 to mark the centennial of the Great Exhibition of 1851, and it was to feature arts, crafts, cultural events, and exhibitions from all over the United Kingdom and its colonial possessions.

The original plan was to organize a twenty-two-member ensemble, each player chosen from a different steel band belonging to the recently formed Trinidad and Tobago Steel Band Association (TTSBA). However, financial burdens soon halved the number of players, and eventually eleven panmen were chosen to perform as members of TASPO. After one player was forced to turn back en route, because of illness, TASPO arrived in Great Britain as a group of ten pan players and a musical director/conductor.

This group boasted, for the first time, a complete set of pans all tuned to a common concert reference pitch and all possessing a range of at least one chromatic octave. TASPO also featured expanded sets of the tenor- and bass-voiced pans (a set of two tenor booms rather than one tune boom; a set of three bass booms rather than two) and improved quality of construction material (oil drums rather than biscuit drums for the tenor booms, and caustic-soda drums for the bass booms).

The first steel band ever to visit Great Britain, TASPO made its overseas debut in an open-air performance on the Festival's South Band Exhibition Grounds on July 26, 1951. More appearances followed, including a recital at St. Pancras Town Hall, and an engagement at London's prestigious Savoy Hotel. After its final performance in Great Britain, in aid of the Jamaica Hurricane Relief Fund, TASPO embarked upon a brief tour of Paris before returning to Trinidad.

During the 1950s, as the desire to play a broader variety of music grew, tuners began to increase the range of pans. To accomplish this, more surface area was needed, especially for the bass and inner voices. Ping-pongs could be sunk deeper to create more available space for notes, but for other pans, whose individual pitches were lower and therefore needed more surface area, tuners began to experiment with dividing the gamut of pitches up between two or more pans. TASPO had expanded the ranges and numbers of drums for the tenor and bass sections in a stage setting. In August 1952 the first *double second pans* appeared. Conceived by Ernest Ferreira (founding member and leader of the Dixieland steel band) and tuned by Percy Thomas (an early pan virtuoso, skilled tuner, and leader of the Katzenjammers steel band), this pan set consisted of two *single second pans*, welded together and retuned to accommodate twenty-three pitches, rather than the second pan's usual average of twelve. Welding, however, soon proved a less-than-satisfactory solution to joining sets of pans together, and stationary stands were soon being devised to accommodate sets of pans hanging individually next to one another.

With the introduction of a full chromatic range, the ability of oil drums to be sunk deeper to accommodate more pitches, and the techniques of tuning pans in sets of two or more, stylings of note placements on the pans' playing surfaces began to change. Early pan stylings were based upon the placement of pitches necessary to play a particular tune, or refrain. New pitches were added, or a new pan tuned, as needed, to play a new melody. Unless a new pan styling was being tried, there was an effort to keep existing placements intact, except where change was necessary because of space, or to place often used pitch patterns or octaves near to one another.

Tuners began to realize that pans were more playable and more easily tuned when stylings were designed around intervallic formulas. One of the earliest, most innovative, and most influential of these designs was Anthony Williams's *spiderweb pan*, designed in 1953. The range of the spiderweb pan was from B below middle C to the B-flat three octaves above, moving clockwise in a cycle of fourths in three concentric circles. The wedge-like note shape Williams used could accommodate more pitches than the then-current system of circles, and because of the adjacent fourths, fifths, and octaves, the pan was easier to tune and yielded a higher-quality sound. Though the spiderweb design was too radical to be widely accepted in the 1950s, the current popular lead pan, the 4ths/5ths tenor (see Exs. 1, 2, and 3), is modeled almost exactly on Williams's design.

While the number of stylings, range, and quality of pans continued to increase for concert-oriented bands (stagesides) through the mid-1950s, the Carnival bands (roadsides) were still severely limited by the necessity of carrying the pans in their hands or strapped around their necks while "jumping up." Stagesides were using full-sized oil drums to tune bass pans by 1956, when the tune "Puerto Rican Mambo" began to receive radio airplay in Trinidad. It immediately became popular with the steel bands, and many of them wished to add it to their repertoires. However, the song required more pitches for its characteristic bass line than were currently available on the pans. To tune new bass pans was not a problem, but to take those pans on the road to play the tune was difficult. Up to this time roadside bass players used one pan each, tuned from a caustic-soda drum, and strapped across one shoulder. To play

4ths/5ths Tenor

Depth: 8.48 inches (21.2 cm)

Skirt: 5.12 inches (12.8 cm)

Range:

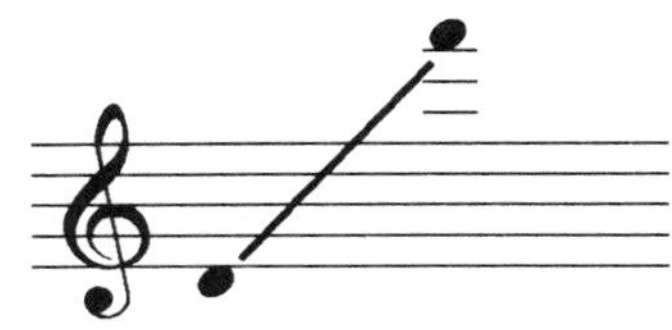

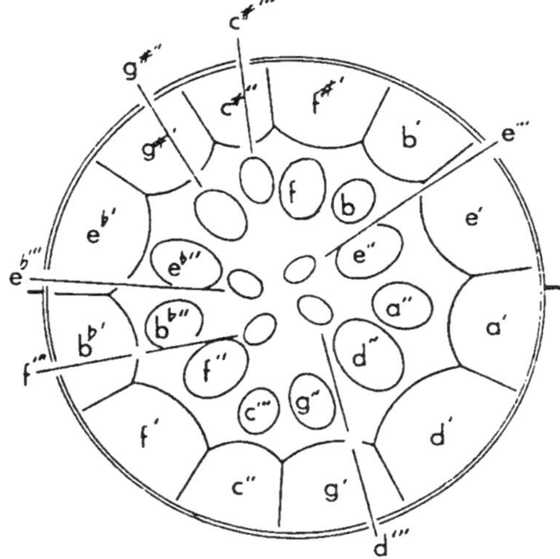

Ex. 1

4ths/5ths Tenor

Depth: 8.72 inches (21.8 cm)
Skirt: 4.84 inches (12.1 cm)
Range:

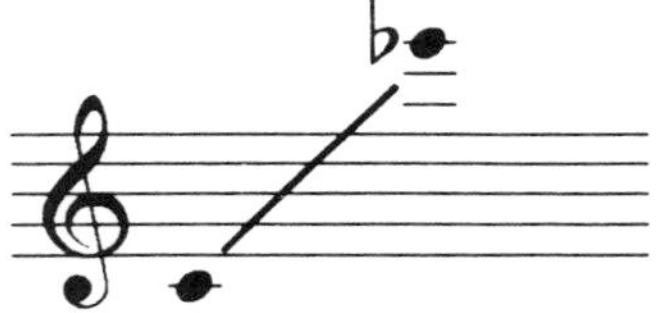

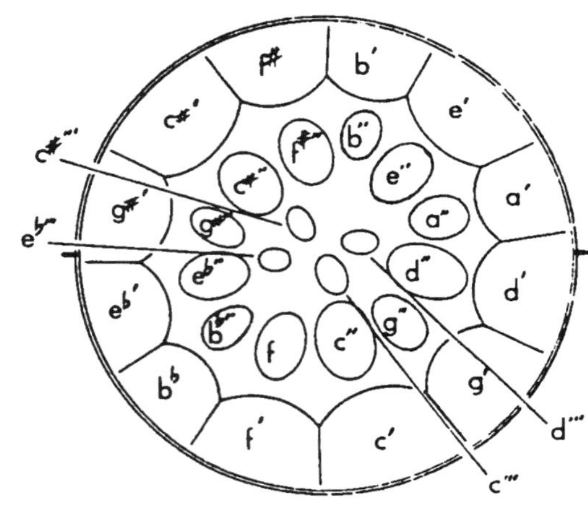

Ex. 2

4ths/5ths Tenor

Depth: 8.16 inches (20.4 cm)
Skirt: 6.2 inches (15.5 cm)
Range:

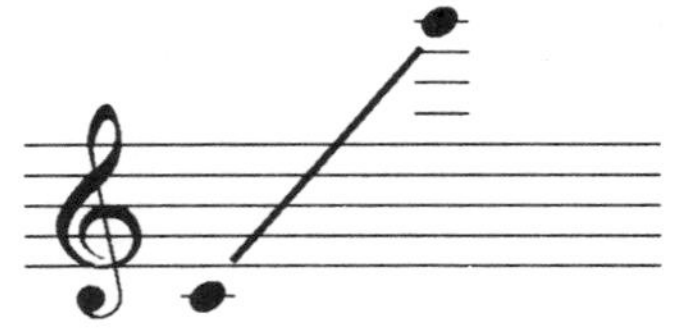

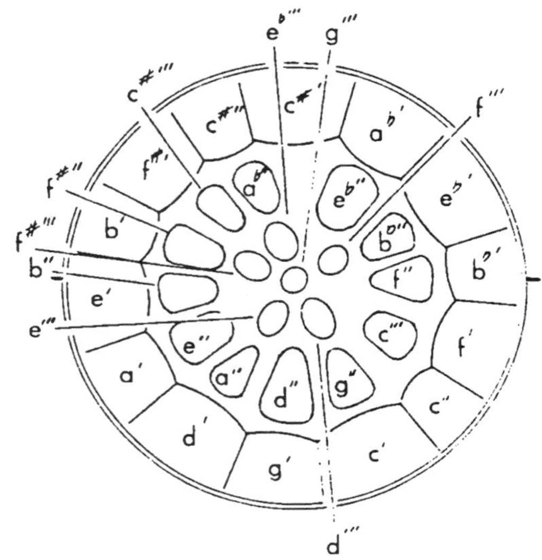

Ex. 3

tunes that were handled on stage by one musician on a set of bass pans, the road-side players would work out a hocket-style arrangement, with each person playing the part of the bass line corresponding to the pitches on the pan he was carrying. To accommodate the greater number of heavier bass pans needed to play "Puerto Rican Mambo" on the road, the leader of the steel band North Stars, Tony Williams, decided to tune his instruments from oil drums and, for the first time, welded wheels to the bottoms of the pans.

This idea rapidly expanded the possibilities for steel bands on the road. By 1957 North Stars and Southern Symphony were performing on the road with sets of two basses on wheels. Pan sets appeared bolted together on wheels or suspended from small carts. In 1958 North Stars expanded to sets of three basses; by 1959 they introduced sets of four basses suspended from a frame on a wheeled cart. That same year Invaders brought out the first double seconds on the road, on wheeled stands. As new pan stylings were introduced, new carts were designed to accommodate them. Band supporters assumed the task of pushing and guiding the carts so the steel band players could devote their full concentration (and both hands) to playing. Eventually the neck straps were discarded altogether, and all road pans were hung on wheeled carts.

By the mid-1960s expert tuner and band leader Bertie Marshall had introduced two more innovations: the *double tenor pans*, and canopies to cover the pans on the road. The double tenors were unique in that they were not a variation or extension of an existing pan styling. Marshall wanted a pan to fit between the tenors and the double seconds, to give the tenors support. Covering pans on the road protected them from the elements, in particular the metal-expanding heat of the sun. Although other bands took some time to adopt the idea, by the mid-1970s most conventional steel bands appeared on the road with canopy-covered pans.

III. The Current Tradition

Sources generally agree that the Red Army steel band, going under the name "Russian Symphony," was the first group of its kind to perform on foreign soil, in British Guiana, sometime in late 1946. Since that time Trinbagonian[21] steel bands (such as Casablanca, Desperadoes, Dixieland, Exodus, Invaders, The National Steel Band, North Stars, Our Boys, Renegades, Silver Stars, Tokyo, Trinidad All Stars, The Trinidad All Steel Percussion Orchestra, and Tripoli) and outstanding pan soloists (including Sterling Bettancourt, Earl Brooks, Robert Greenidge, Annise "Halfers" Hadeed, Sydney Joseph, Othello Molineaux, Ken "Professor" Philmore, Earl Rodney, Len "Boogsie" Sharpe, Rudy "Two Leff" Smith, and Clive "Cokey" Telemaque) have traveled extensively to share their style of pan with other parts of the Caribbean, Canada, the United States, South and Central America, Great Britain, Sweden, Denmark, Norway, Holland, France, Germany, Spain, Italy, Switzerland, Australia, Africa, Dubai, Bahrain, Russia, Japan, China, Indonesia, and Hong Kong.

Many expatriate pan tuners and players have settled in various spots around the globe bringing with them the knowledge of their craft and art. Because of this exposure and the great interest expressed in other countries, this Trinbagonian music form has spread extensively. Currently large and small steel bands, mixed ensembles (i.e., pans combined with the acoustic and electric instruments commonly associated with Western popular music), and featured solo panists[22] can be found in many parts of the world. Large West Indian enclaves exist in cities such as London, New York, Washington, D.C., and Toronto, and these people have imported and successfully developed and integrated into their communities customs such as Carnival and the tradition of the steel band.

In Great Britain, Canada, the United States, parts of Asia, and Trinidad and Tobago, the steel band is being incorporated into the education system. Primary- and secondary-level male and female students in Trinidad and Tobago participate actively in school steel bands throughout the year, during Carnival, and at their own school Panorama steel band competition; and in the U.S., elementary, junior-high, high school, and college-level steel band programs seem to grow yearly in numbers and strength.[23] Jazz, pop, and art-music recordings, film soundtracks, and radio and television advertisements have utilized the sound of pan (although increasingly, sophisticated digital sampling technologies have been used instead to recreate the pan sound).

Let us turn our attention now to the current situation in Trinidad and Tobago, and the events by which it has been shaped. Beginning in the 1950s conventional dance bands, playing the standard European, African American, and Latin-American-influenced repertoire of popular music, found themselves obliged to share, with greater frequency, the numerous pre-Carnival parties (called fetes) with popular stagesides. At that time fetes typically numbered five hundred to one thousand people (as opposed to two thousand or more by the 1980s), and little in the way of electronic amplification was available to the conventional bands. Fetes were frequently held indoors, and it was an easy matter for steel bands to overshadow the conventional bands when vying for the attention and support of revelers. During this period steel band music was without question the dominant popular force at fetes and during Carnival.

In the early 1960s changes in the sound of popular music and the means by which it was reproduced began to manifest themselves on a large scale in Trinidad and Tobago. Electric amplification became more common for conventional bands. This fulfilled the need for more powerful music at fetes, as the increasing commercialization of Carnival created the demand for larger public gatherings. As conventional bands became smaller and louder, steel bands responded by increasing in size. The larger they grew, however, the more difficult it became to accommodate steel bands at fetes, and the more impractical became the logistics and economics of transporting a thirty-piece steel band to nightly engagements. Another factor contributing to the shift in popularity became the conventional bands' ability to recreate or "cover" with far greater accuracy the popular tunes revelers had become accustomed to hearing on the radio and at home on disc recordings. Steel bands were capable of offering arrangements of those tunes, but no matter how brilliantly conceived or executed, pan arrangements were no longer what revelers were coming to expect at pre-Carnival gatherings. The pan's popularity at these events gradually began to wane.

Pre-Carnival fetes are not the only occasions at which a decline in steel band participation may be observed. The streets of Port of Spain (and other urban centers), the birthplace and unquestioned domain of the steel band since the mid-1940s (and its pan or iron band precursors since the mid-1930s), have witnessed a diminishing number of roadsides over the past twenty years.

Trinidad Carnival has undergone increased commodification, broadened in scope, and grown to enormous proportions in recent years. Although the sizes of masquerade bands fluctuate over the years, they continue to be many times what they were in the 1950s or 1960s. As these bands grew, steel bands were obliged to expand with them. However, steel bands reached their manageable size limitations long before costume bands ever began to feel the pressure. The larger the steel band, the more difficult it was to push, pull, and guide their carts, racks, and wheeled stands through the mostly narrow, frequently potholed, and always densely congested streets of Port of Spain during Carnival. Also, the necessity of stretching the groups out along such a long narrow line to pass through the noisy thoroughfares made it difficult at best to maintain the unified, musically complex ensemble standard the bands demanded of themselves. Conventional bands, meanwhile, adapted the available technology to the backs of the trucks on which they rode and played. Generators were added to provide the electricity needed for amplification, and in the present soca bands,[24] tassa groups and disc jockeys are driven slowly through the streets on high flatbed trailers, which place them high above the crowds. Although some steel bands have sought to imitate this approach by placing smaller, amplified ensembles on trailers or modified bus chassis, in general they have relinquished their place as the favored music of large Carnival mask bands.

The two public events presented on the islands of Trinidad and Tobago in which the participation of steel bands is the most prominent are the classical music competition, entitled "Pan is Beautiful," and the annual Carnival competition, Panorama. The roots of these two competitions were planted, as noted earlier, during the 1800s in the barrack yards and on the streets of Port of Spain, by rival jamette bands. More organized public revues and music competitions were one of the results of the gradual upgrading of Carnival following the upheavals of the late 1800s. In the 1920s and 1930s masquerade bands, string bands, jazz orchestras, and (by 1935) even tamboo bamboo bands entered into public competition. The earliest formally organized pan band competition was probably the one held at the Queen's Park Oval (cricket grounds) in 1942. Following the lifting of the wartime restrictions, competitions continued in and out of Carnival season. Steel bands played calypsoes, popular European, North American, and Latin-American tunes (mambos, sambas, rumbas, merengues, waltzes, foxtrots), and arrangements of selections from the European art-music repertoire.

During the 1950s festivals and competitions began to specialize in either European art music or popular music. Thirteen variously sponsored competitions and/or festivals involving steel band and solo pan music were held between 1952 and 1973, and then again beginning in 1980 with "Pan is Beautiful." Since that time this festival has been held biennially at the Jean Pierre Complex, a large outdoor sports facility in Port of Spain. Both steel orchestras, usually between thirty and sixty players strong, and pan soloists participate. The revitalization in the early 1970s of the old-time steel bands, or pan-round-neck bands,[25] has meant the inclusion of a category for these ensembles. The steel orchestras are required to play a test piece, a "classical" composition of their choice, and a calypso/soca of their choice. Soloists perform a piece of their own choosing, and old-time steel bands play a test piece and composition of choice. A panel of five judges the bands on accuracy, tone, rhythm, phrasing, interpretation, and general effect. Pieces chosen in recent years, including Symphony No. 4 in F Minor, Op. 36 (1880) (Tchaikovsky), Symphony No. 40 in G Minor (1788) (Mozart), *Billy the Kid Suite* (1938) (Copland), and *Rhapsody in Blue* (1924) (Gershwin), indicate the degree to which the performance of Western art music had become a firmly rooted tradition within Trinidad and Tobago's steel band movement, and the commitment panists feel to maintain and improve upon the quality of performance within that tradition.

Indigenous popular music is featured in the yearly Panorama. Begun in 1963, this event has expanded into the single most popular attraction during Carnival and the overwhelming focus of steel band activity. The first Panorama comprised ten participant steel bands, and the format required each of them to perform their chosen composition as they paraded, "on the move," past the selected judges. Participation rose to a peak of over ninety bands during the late 1970s, before leveling off to about sixty in recent years. In the early 1970s the decision was made to judge the bands performing in a stationary position. The time allotted to each band has increased from eight to ten minutes; and, because of a steady rise in the number of players in each band, a limit of one hundred was imposed during the mid-1970s. Also, what had originally been a single night of competition has since been divided up into preliminaries, zone (regional) finals, semifinals, and finals.

Each participating band chooses one of a yearly crop of calypsoes and socas that is then treated to a complex and imaginative musical arrangement of up to ten minutes in length. Between Boxing Day[26] and Panorama final night (the Saturday before Carnival) each band embarks upon a rigorous schedule of tuning, repairing, and rehearsing that continues to intensify until either the band is eliminated or they reach the finals. Conventional and old-time steel bands from Trinidad and Tobago are eligible to enter in their respective categories. Early rounds of Panorama are held at outdoor sports venues: Skinner Park in San Fernando, Shaw Park in Tobago, and the Queen's Park Savannah in Port of Spain. By final night the field has been narrowed, and the Savannah plays host to (as of this writing) twelve conventional bands and six old-time steel bands. As with the festival, a panel of five (or occasionally seven) judges scores the bands on arrangement, tone, rhythm, phrasing, and interpretation.

Panorama has become an almost singular focus of the panists' energy and creativity. Year-round employment for steel bands and panists in Trinidad and Tobago is all but unheard of. Stagesides are occasionally engaged to tour outside the country; fetes, business, or promotional functions may require steel bands' services; and the large hotels in Port of Spain may feature weekend steel band poolside entertainment. These, though, do not provide nearly enough employment opportunities to occupy Trinidad's and Tobago's estimated one hundred conventional ongoing steel bands, comprising twenty to forty permanent members each. Fetes and *blockos*[27] feature steel bands during the Carnival season, but with far less frequency or financial gain than in the past. Then there is the steel band participation on Carnival days. Whereas steel bands used to provide the most popular music to accompany revelers from dawn on Monday morning until Tuesday midnight, they now confine themselves mostly to J'Ouvert morning, with a handful of bands appearing on Tuesday to play *a mas'*.[28] It is perhaps understandable, then, that panists devote their greatest energies to Panorama and the steel bands' other featured event, the music festival.[29]

The steel band movement has been represented by a number of governing bodies, beginning in 1950 with the TTSBA and followed by the National Association for Trinidad and Tobago Steelbandsmen (NATTS) in 1962, the Steelband Improvement Committee (SIC) in 1970, and continuing into the 1990s with Pan Trinbago (organized in 1971 out of the SIC). Pan Trinbago's membership comprises over one hundred steel bands in Trinidad and Tobago. Membership is not mandatory, but virtually all steel band activities are initiated, assisted, overseen, or monitored in some manner by Pan Trinbago, and most bands are registered. Also, it is the one recognized representative body for panists and their bands, and their only official forum for the discussion of ideas and the airing of grievances.

Corporate Sponsorship of Steel Bands

Steel band corporate sponsorship can be traced back to at least the late 1940s, when Antigua's first steel band, Hell's Gate, displayed signs for such products as Royal Reserve Barbados Rum, KWV Vermouth, and South African Paarl Tawny, all sold by A. Michael & Sons. In Trinidad, individual corporate sponsorship began in the early 1950s, when Dixieland was sponsored, albeit for only one Carnival, by the Jeffries Beer Company, and Esso Standard Oil S.A. Ltd. occasionally organized small steel bands that would then assume its name. The first instance of a large, established steel band to accept corporate sponsorship appears to have been in 1960, when Invaders became Shell Invaders.

In the mid-1990s in Trinidad and Tobago it is extremely difficult, if not impossible, for a steel band to mount a successful stageside, roadside, or compete effectively in Panorama or the music festival without some form of sponsorship or subsidy. As noted above, there are simply not enough opportunities to generate sufficient income, and for years bands have turned to the business sector, their immediate communities, or small government grants to subsidize their activities and defray the cost of overhead. Expenses include purchase/rent and upkeep of the panyard (rehearsal area), arranger's fee, ongoing tuner's fee, replacement of old pans, maintenance of carts, transportation to and from engagements, uniforms, and miscellaneous material costs. Expenditures for these items can easily exceed $100,000TT (Trinidad and Tobago dollars, in current exchange approximately $23,500) and some of the larger bands maintain budgets of well over $300,000TT (approximately $70,500).

Most of the larger, more popular bands seek sponsorship from a single source, the sponsor's name added to the band title; hence, such bands as Amoco Renegades, Carib (popular Trinidadian beer) Tokyo, Trintoc (Trinidad and Tobago Oil Company) Invaders, or Witco (West Indian Tobacco Company) Desperadoes. Other bands, such as Phase II Pan Groove and Exodus, at present accept sponsorship from a variety of smaller sources and endorse these products in ways other than associating their names directly with products. Still other, usually smaller, less well-known steel bands in Trinidad and Tobago tend to rely more on community support, small business and individual donations, fund-raising events, etc.

Steel Band Arrangement

Steel bands in Trinidad and Tobago come in many shapes and sizes. The standard ensemble averages about thirty players in a year-round stageside, growing to between thirty and sixty for the music festival, and up to one hundred for Panorama. Although many pan designs have been, and continue to be, introduced, a fairly standard arrangement of pan types has come to be adopted by most bands. The chart below lists these types and the number of people playing them in a typical stageside and in a typical Panorama band,[30] while the following page's diagram (Fig. 1) indicates their basic ranges:

	Stageside	Panorama
Tenor	8	30
Double Tenor	3	8
Double Second	3	8
Quadrophonic	2	6
Guitar	3	12
Three/Four Cello	3	6
Tenor Bass	1	8
Six Bass	2	8
Nine Bass	(uncommon)	4
Rhythm	5	10

A steel band's basic rhythm section typically consists of a drum set, cowbell(s), metal scratcher(s) (*giiro*-type idiophones), congas (usually a set of two, played with rubber-tipped pan mallets), tambourine(s), timbales, and brake drum (referred to as "iron"). In the music festival this section may be augmented by percussion instruments called for in the score.

The fashioning of pan sticks/beaters/mallets is the responsibility of the individual player because, as with the pans themselves, there is no mass production or agreed-upon standard. Nevertheless, there are certain generally accepted styles and preferred materials from which to make them. Latex or synthetic-rubber strips are used to wrap the sticks used for pans, from the tenor through the cello. The tenor, double tenor, and double second require a thin material; many panists prefer surgical latex or strips cut from latex gloves. This is wrapped around the tips of various lengths (depending upon the pan) of wooden shafts (or occasionally aluminum or PVC tubing). Surgical tubing is also a

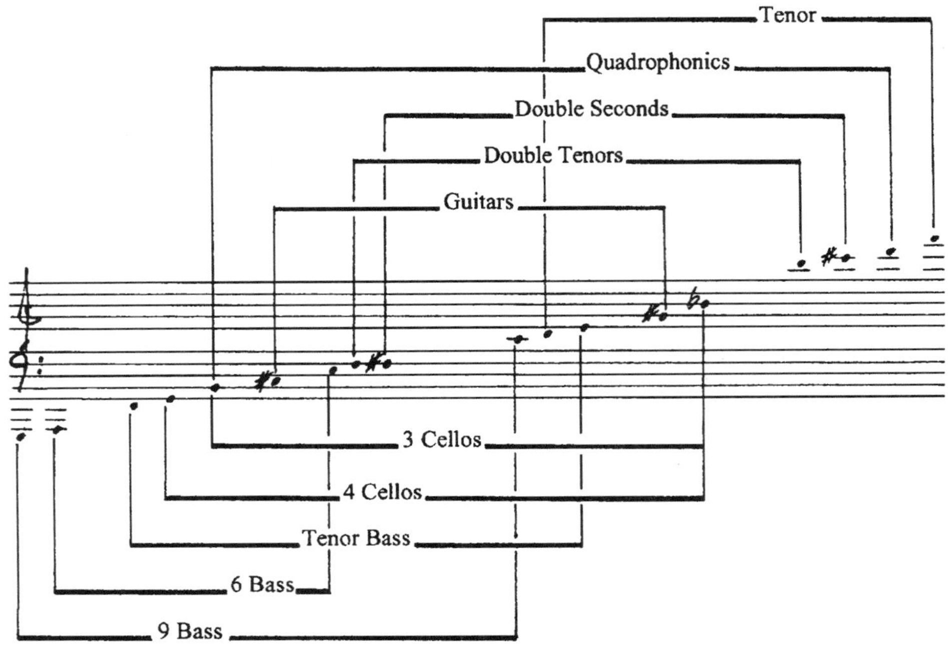

Fig. 1

popular material for tipping tenor sticks, with a short section being stretched over one end of the shaft. The quadrophonic, guitar, and cello require a thicker material. Rubber strips cut from cricket bat handles are a common material. The tenor bass and low bass use various-sized sponge-type balls, which have had the outer coating scraped or sanded off, have been cut to sizes and shapes that best suit the instruments, and have then been attached to the end of a (usually) wooden shaft.

IV. Pan Tuning, Styling, and Standardization

There are seven basic steps involved in fashioning a pan from a steel drum: sinking, grooving, cutting, burning, tuning, touching up, and blending. Although tuning styles are often highly personalized and innovative and new techniques are still being introduced, it is possible to present a general description of this often misunderstood process.

Presently the most common type of steel drum from which pans are made measures 35.4 inches (88.5 cm) in height and 23 inches (57.6 cm) in diameter. The top and bottom are constructed of 18-gauge steel while the shell is 20-gauge. The weight of an empty drum is 38 pounds, and its volume is 209 liters (55 U.S. gallons).

Steel drums come to the tuner in two basic conditions—new and used. If they are available and affordable, the new drums are preferred. No caps or holes of any kind have been cut into these drumshells; hence both ends may be used for tuning.[31] This type of drum is used primarily for tuning tenor, double tenor, double second, and quadrophonic pans, because there is a better chance of obtaining a matching quality of metal on both drumheads, and because the skirts of these pans are shallow enough to accommodate two cuts from one drum.

A hole is first punctured in the side of the drumshell with a large chisel or other sharp tool to allow for the movement of air (this is not necessary if the drum has been tapped at the factory). The initial sinking of the pan—the stretching and molding of the metal of the future playing surface into its characteristic bowl-like, concave shape—is usually accomplished with a large sledgehammer with a sawed-off handle.[32] Each type of pan is sunk to a predetermined, specific depth, and during the sinking process a ruler or other measuring device is used to confirm that the desired depth is being achieved.

After sinking, lines are drawn from edge to edge of the bowl through a center point using a flexible straightedge and an erasable marking device (e.g., chalk, pencil). These lines are then lightly etched into the pan surface with a nail or other sharp metal tool. The lines are calculated by the tuner according to width, length, and angle to generally define the area of placement of pitches on the pan. Pre-cut templates of a flexible material (e.g., plastic, leather, cardboard) are then usually placed inside the pan, used to consistently outline the pitches' correct size and shape. Following the delineation of the pitch areas, the surface of the pan is worked with a small hammer in order to begin to separate the notes from one another and to smooth and even out the pan surface.

The next stage is commonly referred to as grooving. This is the process of indenting the pan surface along the lines that have been marked out to define the pitch areas. This delineates the pitched areas from each other and from the "dead" metal surface area that separates them. The grooving is typically accomplished with a nail punch and hammer. An initial tap is made at the starting point, very quickly, to achieve the correct depth and create a sure beginning mark. Once grooving begins on a line it is not interrupted, in order to attain an evenness of flow both in terms of depth and line.

Next the pan is cut away from the unwanted portion of the drumshell. The pan skirt length is measured and marked, often with a large compass that is scraped along the side of the shell, guided by the top or bottom lip. A hole is punched at one point along the line with a large flat-nosed chisel or other sharp tool to provide a starting place. A hand- or electric saw (or sometimes a chisel and hammer) is then used to cut around the shell, yielding the separated pan (or pans).

The grooved and individually outlined pitch areas are then worked with a hammer to achieve the distinctive, convex, bubble-like shape. The notes around the perimeter of the pan are often shaped from the bottom by wedging a crowbar or piece of wood up into the corner of the overturned pan just between the skirt and the underside of the playing surface, and pulling in toward the center. The inner notes are hammered up from the bottom of the pan.

The fourth step, called burning, involves a rapid heating and cooling of the pan. The pan is placed face down over a fire. The bottom of the pan (now facing up) must reach a desired metallic blue before it is removed. The time needed for this may vary from two to four (or sometimes more) minutes. After it has been burned and cooled down (either naturally or with the aid of water), the face of the pan is left with a sooty black coating, which is partially rubbed off (more will be shaken loose during subsequent tuning).

The detailed tuning work is then begun. Notes are crafted with a small hammer working from both the top and underside of the playing surface, trying to draw out the complex combination of fundamental and overtones necessary to achieve the desired pitch and distinctive timbral quality. Strobe tuners, tuning forks, pitch pipes, portable electronic keyboard instruments, and other pans are commonly used as pitch references at different stages of the tuning process.

When the tuner is generally satisfied, the pan will have holes drilled below the lip for hanging, and then be set aside for chroming or painting. After that it will be returned to the tuner for the final job of touching up and blending. These two final steps involve the fine-tuning of every pitch on the pan to bring the instrument in tune with itself, and adjusting the pitch and timbral quality of the pan to blend with others in the band.

A gradual process of very general standardization of pan tuning and styling (the overall design of notes on the playing surface) has taken place over the years. The types of pans used in steel bands are also fairly standard, though within that standard may be many variations. There are also extremes. Smaller or newer steel bands sometimes do not possess the financial resources necessary to acquire some of the more extravagant pan sets, nor have they yet developed the reputation necessary to attract musicians skilled in playing these instruments. On the other hand, the large, established, influential and financially powerful bands have both the means to experiment with unconventional pan designs and the reputations to attract players adept at mastering them.

The two greatest obstacles preventing widespread standardization of pans are the ongoing independent revising and redesigning of the instruments by tuners and the system of arranging pans within steel bands. The tenor pan is probably the most standardly styled pan among 1990s steel bands. Although earlier popular styles included the old Ellie Mannette design and the high tenor (see Exs. 4 and 5), the cycle of fourths/fifths arrangement has become the overwhelmingly preferred choice for Trinidad and Tobago's bands. Yet even in this pan there are slight variations in range, which alter the styling (see Exs. 1, 2, and 3).

More dramatic design differences become evident upon examining current three and four cello stylings. The old Tripoli steel band styling of three cellos, which can still be found in some bands, is based upon diminished seventh chords (Ex. 6). A more recent popular design (Ex. 7), however, is based upon the sequence of a whole step/perfect fourth/whole step/minor third. Renegades' four cellos (also called four pans) are divided into two types: a wide and a narrow range (Exs. 8 and 9). Their sequencing, based upon major and minor triads, results in a styling quite different from both of the above three cello examples and the four cello styling used by Our Boys (Ex. 10), which is patterned on augmented triads.

A second problem inhibiting standardization is that individual pans, even though they may be identically styled, are frequently grouped and hung differently from band to band. When a new pan or pan set is introduced into a steel band, a decision is made (by the tuner, captain/manager, or the chosen leader of that pan's section) as to how the pans should be arranged. This same scheme is then followed for every one of that kind of pan. However, from band to band there may be significant variances. Not only may the left-to-right, back-to-front sequences of pan sets differ between bands, but each individual pan may be suspended in a manner that reorients its note placement.

Standardization is a popular and controversial topic among panists, tuners, arrangers, administrators, and admirers. Frequent appeals have been made in recent years to embark upon a serious campaign to establish tuning and design standards for pans, yet very little can be agreed upon. Tuners tend to favor their own designs, and many feel that much still needs to be accomplished to improve pans before a standard may be set.

Supporters of standardization claim that it would actually raise the overall quality of pans by setting guidelines and demanding that all tuners conform to a high level of craftsmanship. Another often heard argument in favor of standardization is that it would allow pan players the freedom to perform easily on instruments other than the ones in their own panyards. Ideas could be more rapidly exchanged, music more efficiently taught, and the pan community, both within Trinidad and Tobago and globally, brought closer together.

Old Mannette Tenor

Depth: 3.72 inches (9.3 cm)
Skirt: 6.16 inches (15.4 cm)
Range:

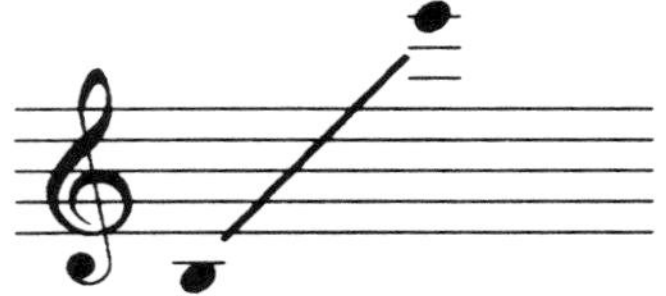

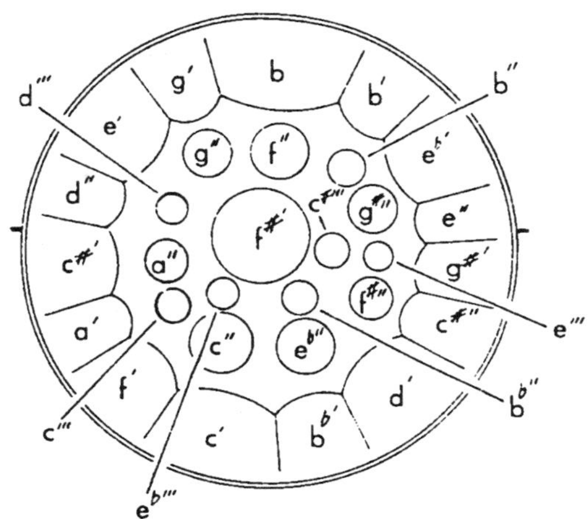

Ex. 4

High Tenor

Depth: 7 inches (17.5 cm)
Skirt: 6.2 inches (15.5 cm)
Range:

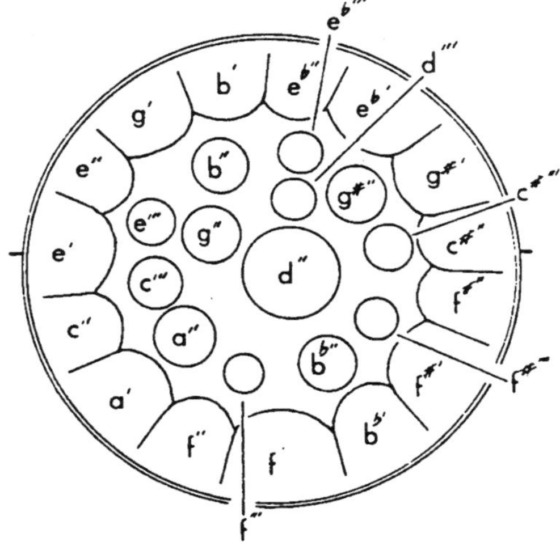

Ex. 5

Tripoli Cellos

(1)

Depth: 4.64 inches (11.6 cm)

Skirt: 31.44 inches (78.8 cm)

Range:

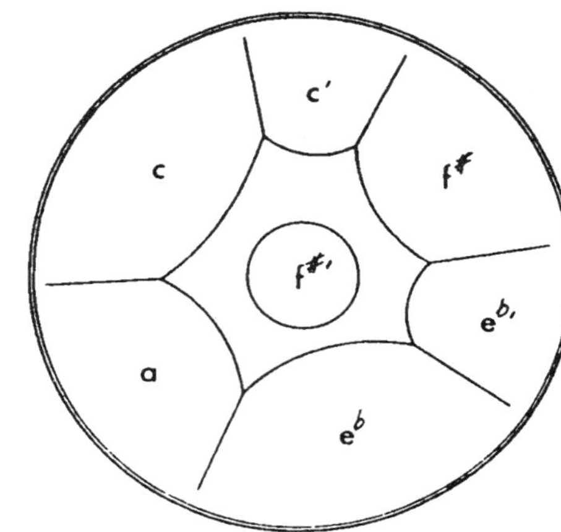

(2)

Depth: 4.8 inches (12 cm)

Skirt: 31.52 (78.3 cm)

Range:

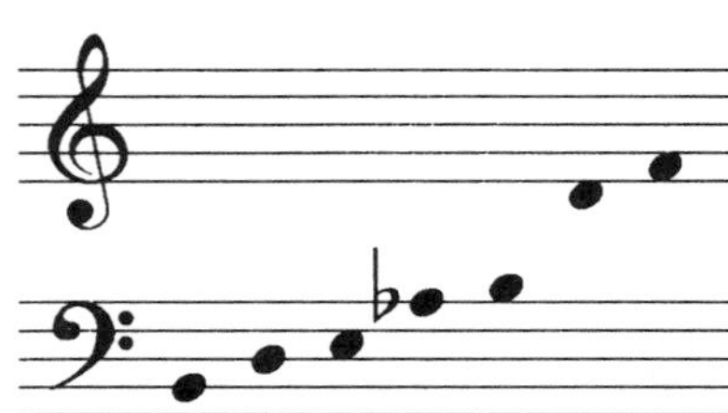

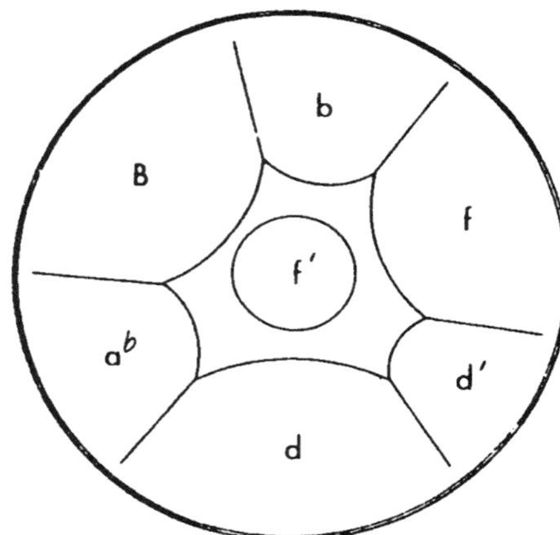

(3)

Depth: 4.56 inches (11.4 cm)

Skirt: 31.52 inches (78.8 cm)

Range:

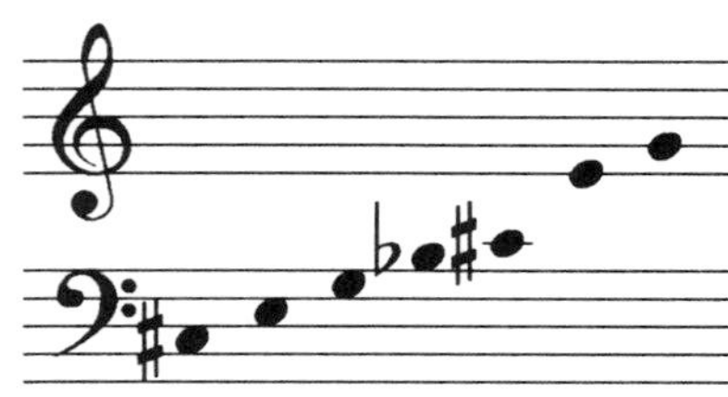

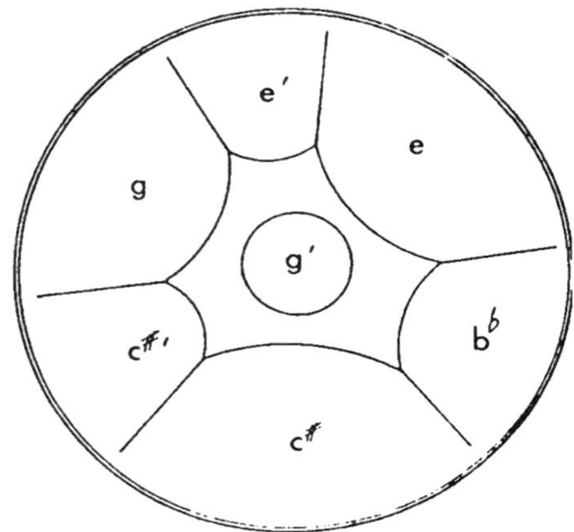

Ex. 6

Cellos

(1)
Depth: 6.28 inches (15.7 cm)
Skirt: 17.6 inches (44 cm)
Range:

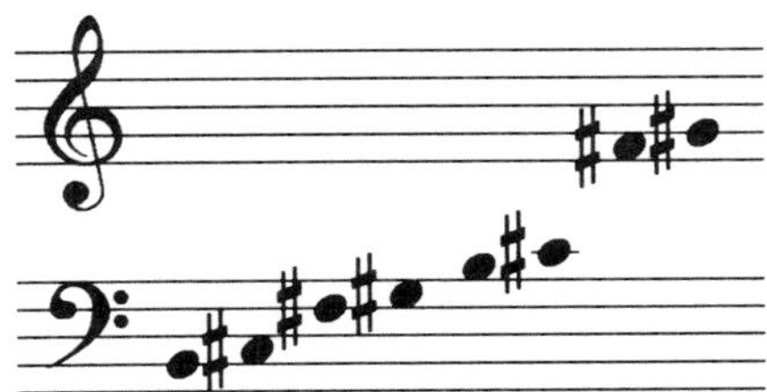

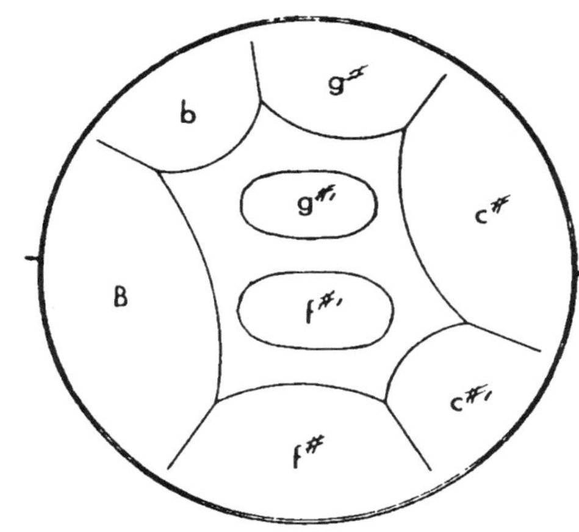

(2)
Depth: 6.28 inches (15.7 cm)
Skirt: 18 inches (45 cm)
Range:

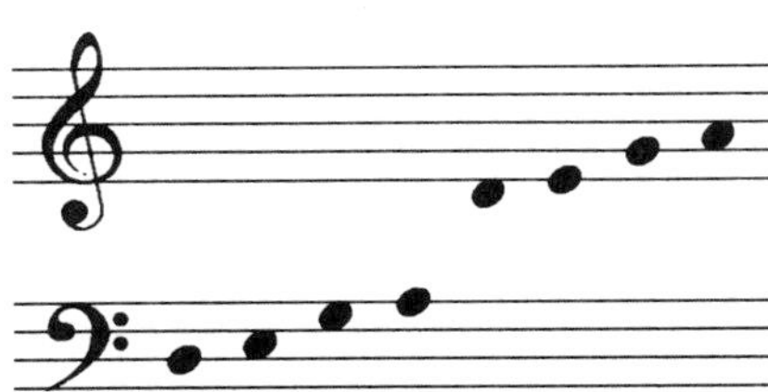

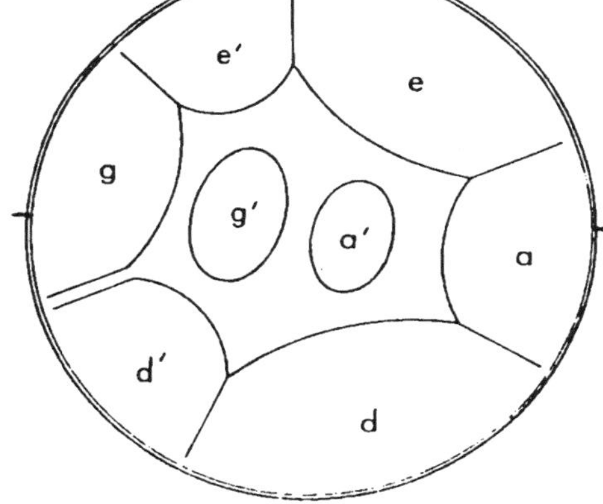

(3)
Depth: 6.44 inches (16.1 cm)
Skirt: 17.76 inches (44.4 cm)
Range:

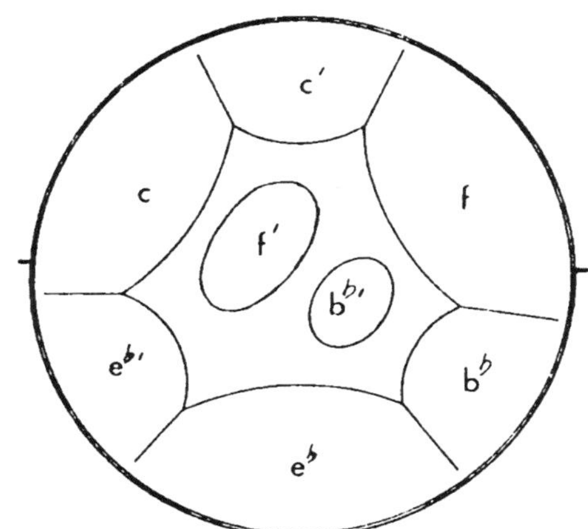

Ex. 7

Renegades' Four Cellos (wide range)

(1)

Depth: 6.08 inches (15.2 cm)

Skirt: 30.44 inches (76.1 cm)

Range:

(2)

Depth: 6.28 inches (15.7 cm)

Skirt: 30.44 inches (76.1 cm)

Range:

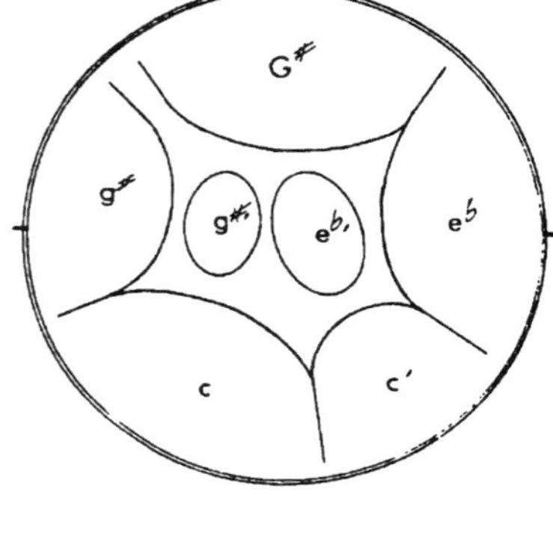

(3)

Depth: 6.16 inches (15.4 cm)

Skirt: 30.52 inches (76.3 cm)

Range:

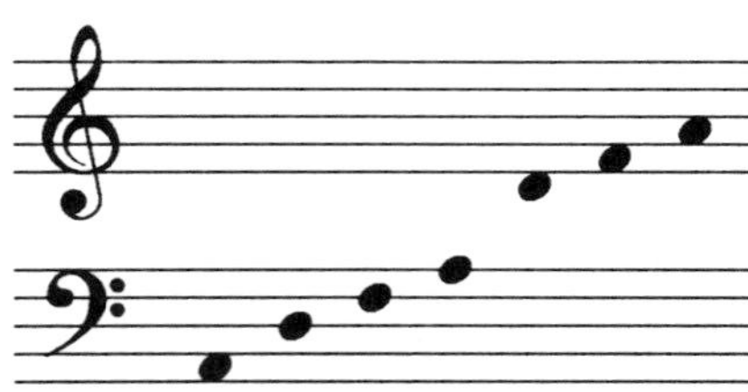

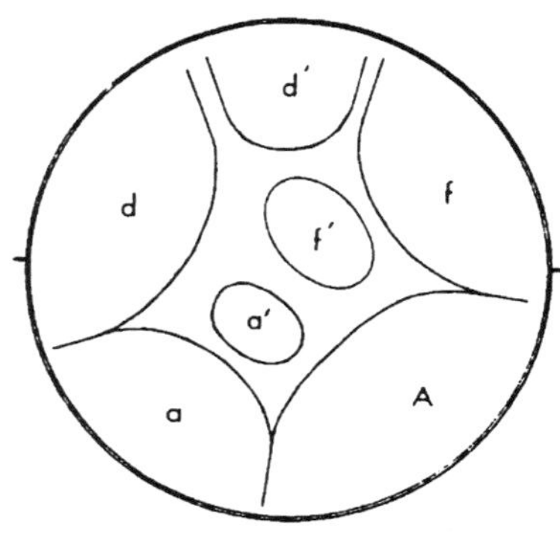

(4)

Depth: 6.16 inches (15.4 cm)

Skirt: 30.6 inches (76.5 cm)

Range:

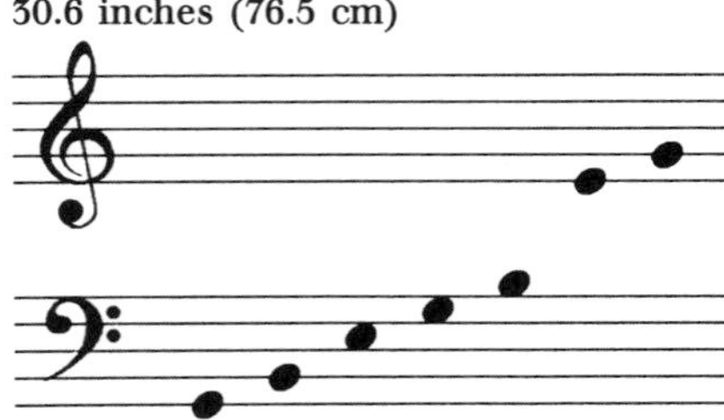

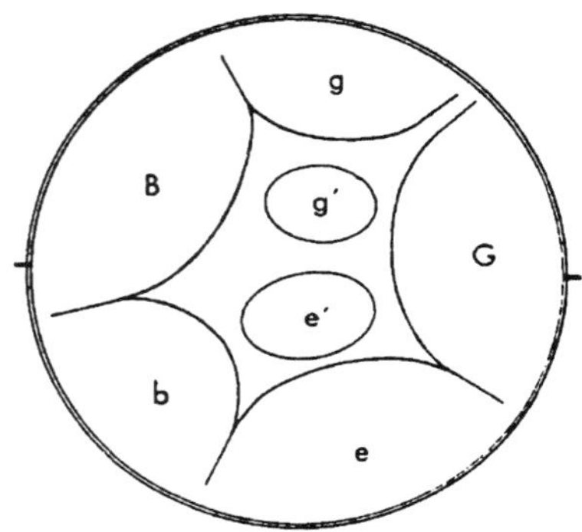

Ex. 8

Renegades' Four Cellos (narrow range)

(1)
Depth: 6.08 inches (15.2 cm)
Skirt: 17.52 inches (43.8 cm)
Range:

(2)
Depth: 6.36 inches (15.9 cm)
Skirt: 17.84 inches (44.6 cm)
Range:

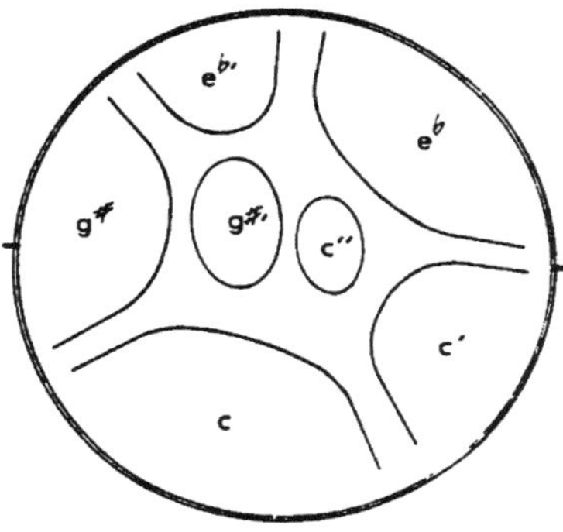

(3)
Depth: 6.16 inches (15.4 cm)
Skirt: 17.92 inches (44.8 cm)
Range:

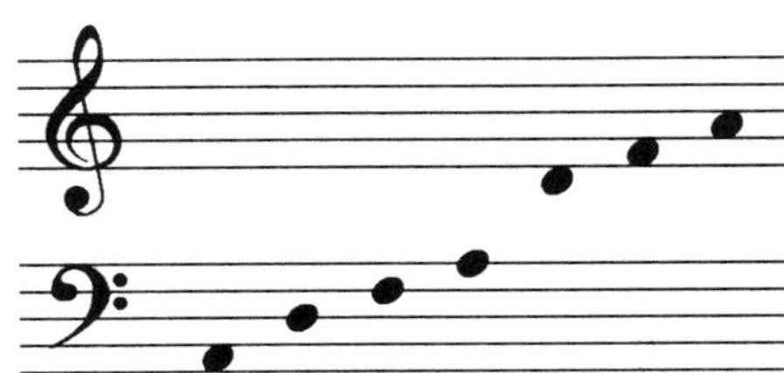

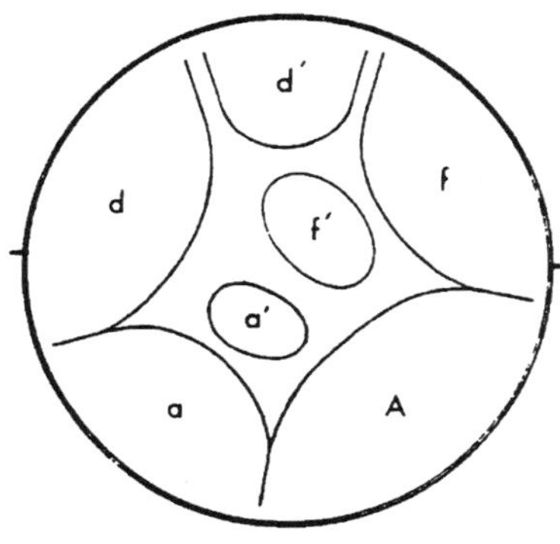

(4)
Depth: 6.2 inches (15.5 cm)
Skirt: 17.32 inches (43.9 cm)
Range:

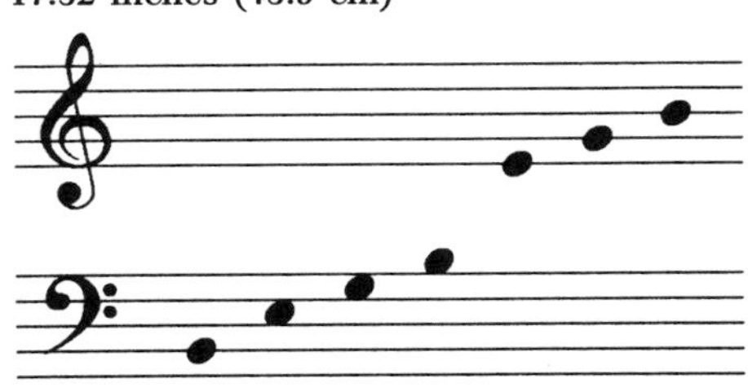

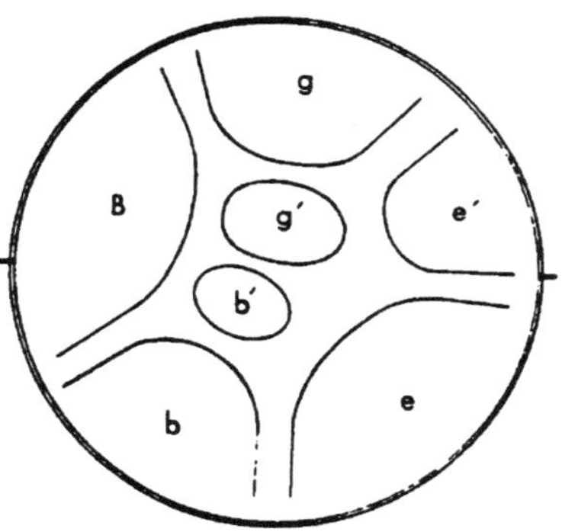

Ex. 9

Our Boys' Four Cellos

(1)

Depth: 5.64 inches (14.1 cm)

Skirt: 31.28 inches (78.2 cm)

Range:

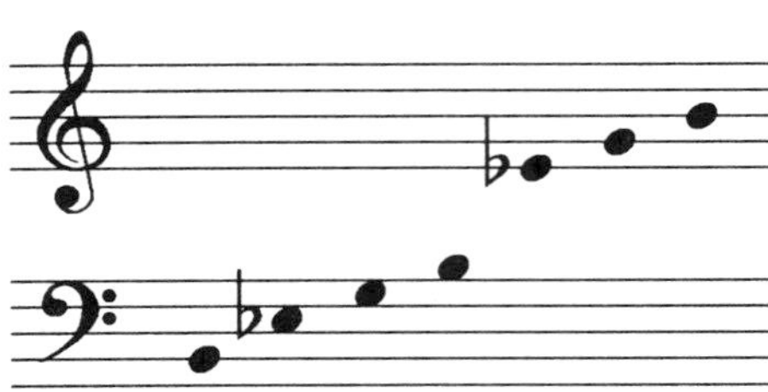

(2)

Depth: 6.08 inches (15.2 cm)

Skirt: 30.88 inches (77.2 cm)

Range:

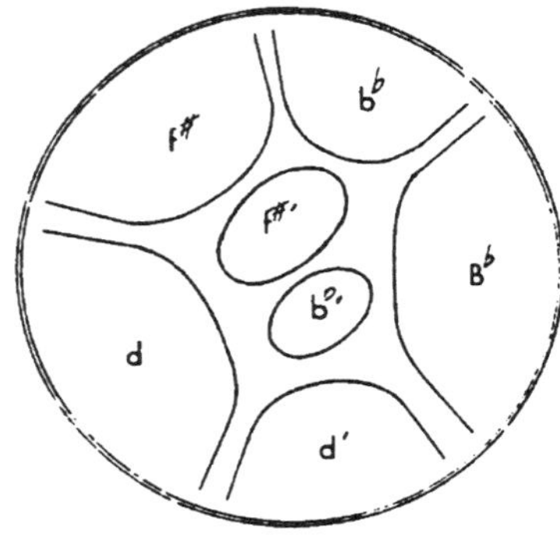

(3)

Depth: 5.72 inches (14.3 cm)

Skirt: 31.08 inches (77.7 cm)

Range:

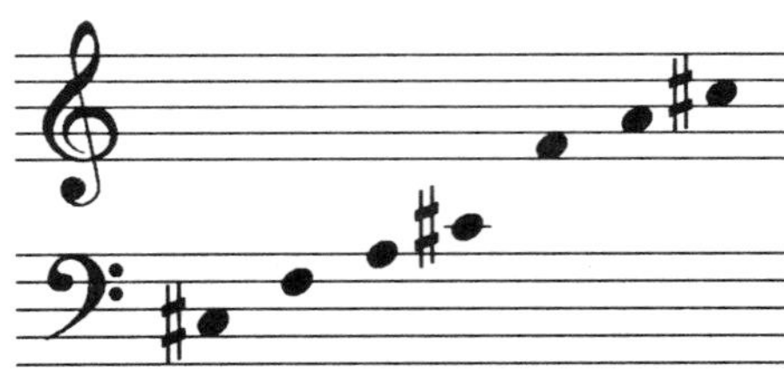

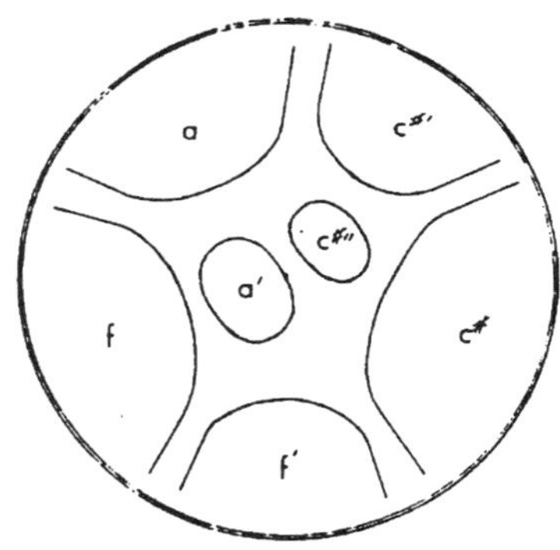

(4)

Depth: 5.6 Inches (14 cm)

Skirt: 31.24 inches (78.1 cm)

Range:

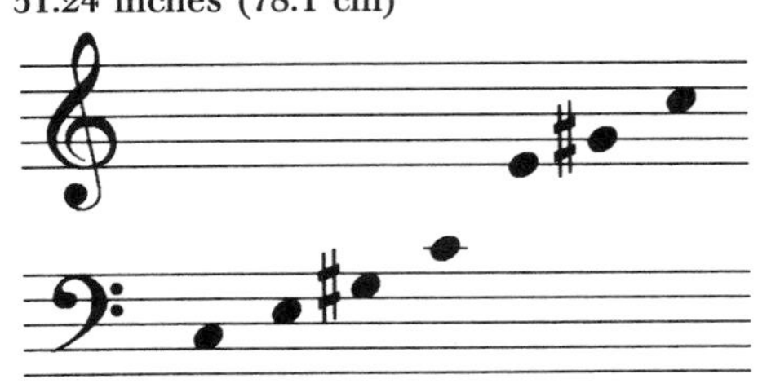

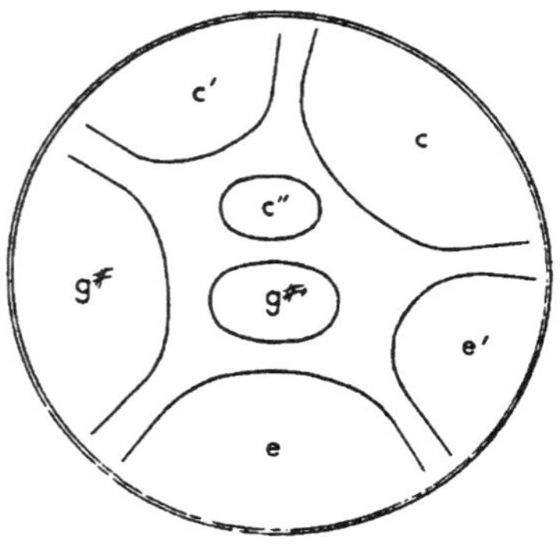

Ex. 10

Selected Art-Music Works

Evans, Vernon
- Concerto for Piano and Steel Orchestra
- Theme and Variations

Haubenstock-Ramati, Roman
- "Vermutungen über ein dunkles Haus," from the opera *Amerika* (1963)

Martirano, Salvatore
- *Underworld* (1965)

Henze, Hans Werner
- *El Cimarrón* (1970)
- *Voices (Stimmen)* (1973)
- *Katharina Blum* (1975)

Bernstein, Leonard
- Mass (1971)

Notes

1. This word has probably been used since at least the mid- to late 1930s in Trinidad to describe the metal idiophones fashioned from tins and other sorts of metal containers and played in *pan bands, iron bands,* and, eventually, *steel bands.* The word "pan" is used to name the sophisticated tuned idiophones made from 209-liter (55-U.S.-gallon), 204-liter (45-imperial-gallon), or 200-liter (44-imperial-gallon) oil drums that comprise steel bands. It is also used to describe all aspects of musical life surrounding the pan instrument and the style of music that is associated with the pan instrument, much as the term "jazz" is associated with a type (or types) of music.

2. Although steel band is frequently spelled as one word, in this article the two-word form of this term is used. There has yet to be a consensus among journalists, authors, scholars, or members of the steel band movement as to a preferred spelling; indeed, some writers have been known to use both forms in different publications. The two-word form is consistent with such related terms as "steel orchestra," "pan band," and "iron band."

3. Various terms are used within this article to identify inhabitants of Trinidad and Tobago. "African" identifies those people born in Africa who found themselves, because of the circumstances of the slave trade, living as prisoners and, later, free persons in the New World. "Afro-Caribbean" refers to people of African descent who were born and raised in the Caribbean. "Afro-Trinidadian" refers to people of African descent who were born and raised in Trinidad. "Indo-Trinidadian" identifies those persons of East Indian ancestry who were born and raised in Trinidad.

4. This procession was one of the events associated with Carnival during the second half of the nineteenth century. The word *Canboulay* is a creolization of the French word *cannes brûlées* or burning cane. This festival, introduced by Africans and Afro-Trinidadians in the years immediately following emancipation, was modelled upon incidents when slaves from various estates were turned out into the sugarcane fields to fight fires, some ignited accidentally, and others started intentionally to burn the sharp outer coverings of the stalks prior to harvesting. Originally held on the first of August to commemorate Emancipation Day, Canboulay had merged with Carnival by the late 1840s.

5. Also *callindar, calendar, kalenda, calienda, calinda.* A term familiar throughout the Caribbean and the southern United States describing various dance and song forms. In Trinidad it represented a highly skilled and often violent African-derived form of martial art, centered around stick fighting with song and instrumental accompaniment.

6. Also spelled *jamet.* The word is a creolization of the French *diametre.* It was applied by the upper class to a person, custom, object, or event associated with

the emerging subculture of the barrack yards, people whose lives often centered around prostitution, petty crime, gambling, fighting, singing, dancing, drumming, and Carnival, and who were considered to be below or beyond the diameter of respectability.

7. Also *shack-shack, schack-schack, shac-shac, shak-shak, shock-shock.* A small rattle, used beginning in the early slave days in Trinidad and other Caribbean islands. It typically consisted of a calabash, dried and hollowed out, filled with seeds or stones, and attached to a handle.

8. Also *banza, banjee, bangee.* A small, four-stringed lute-type aerophone of African origin used in various forms mostly by Afro-Caribbean slaves and their descendants.

9. Also *chantwell, shantwell.* The word is a creolization of the French *chanterelle.*

10. The word *Hosay* (also *Hosse, Hosein, Hussein, Hussey*) is a creolization of *Hosein.* It was originally a commemorative ritual celebrated by the Shiite Moslems on the tenth day of Muharram (or Mohurrum), the first month of the Islamic calendar, in memory of the deaths of both Hassan, the older son of the prophet Mohammed's daughter Fatima and Hasrat Ali, the fourth Caliph (chief ruler) of Islam, and his younger brother, Imam Hosein (sometimes spelled Hussain or Husain). The *Hosay* tradition was brought to colonial Trinidad by indentured Moslem Indian laborers and their families during the mid-1800s. Over time there it became secularized, participated in more by Hindu Indo-Trinidadians and Christian Afro-Trinidadians than by those of the Moslem faith. Today it is the major Indian festival in Trinidad.

11. *Tassa* is an Indo-Trinidadian drumming tradition of East Indian origination, brought to the island with the influx of indentured laborers from India between 1845 and 1917. The basic tassa ensemble consists of four types of instruments: two tassa-type drums, one *dhol* drum, and one pair of hand cymbals, called *jhanj.* The typical tassa drum is bowl-shaped, approximately 14 to 16 inches (35 to 40 cm) in diameter, 12 inches (30 cm) deep, and may be made of clay, metal, or plastic. It is covered with a goatskin membrane, laced to the bowl either with or without a hoop. The head of this drum must be heated (usually by fire) periodically prior to and during performance to maintain the desired tuning and to achieve the distinctive sharp, high-pitched attack. The *tassa* drum is hung from around the neck and played with two very flexible sticks, called *chope,* which are made of strips of pessy vine, mamoo liana, or bamboo, and with balled tips of hardened flour wrapped with tape or cloth. The *dhol* is a cylinder-shaped, double-headed membranophone, approximately 32 inches (80 cm) deep and 24 inches (60 cm) in diameter, and carved from the trunk of a mango (sometimes silk cotton or cedar) tree. Both heads are of thick mulehide, fitted with a hoop on both ends and held tight with rope or leather lacing. The *dhol* is played hung around the neck with a cotton-cloth sling, the left head struck with the player's left hand and the right head struck with a large cloth-wrapped mallet. The *jhanj* consists of a pair of small brass hand cymbals that are held in both hands with cotton-cloth cords and struck together both loosely, so as to be allowed to resonate and vibrate against one another, and tightly, so as to create a staccato, sharply choked effect. *Tassa* ensembles may be heard at Carnival, the Hosay celebration, Indo-Trinidadian weddings, funerals, and various other festivals and public and private functions in Trinidad and Tobago.

12. Examples of bamboo idiophones include the *banzara* (Tanzania); *ambnuda* (Brazil); *dim tenklin* (Malaya); *juk jang go* (Korea); *dendang awi* (West Java); *ch'ung tu* (China); *kā'eke'eke* (Hawaii); *quitiplas* (Venezuela); and *ganbos* (Haiti).

13. Regarding the etymology of this and the other primary tamboo bamboo terms: *Boom* most likely refers to the deep, reso-

nant sound required from that particular category of instrument. *Fouler* is a French word meaning to tread, press, crush, or trample down. This is, in fact, quite descriptive of the various playing techniques of the bamboo foulé. During the early part of the century, and still today, to cut can mean to strike or beat out a rhythm upon a membranophone or idiophone. The term *chandler* seems not to have been as widely accepted as the others. It may have been derived from the French *chandelier*, meaning "candlestick," reflecting the shape of the bamboo tubes used for this particular voice in the ensemble.

14. Based upon the history of band rivalries in Carnival and the popularity of Kalinda, the occurrence of clashes involving bamboo weaponry would seem likely; but there must not have been sufficient reason for the authorities to pass legislation against them.

15. According to sources investigated thus far, the first use of pans in a Carnival band may be attributed to one or more of the following: Alexander's Ragtime Band, bobolee bands, Carlton Forde of Alexander's Ragtime Band, the Gonzales Place Band, "Mando," also known as Victor Wilson, "Mussel Rat," and/or Frederick Wilson. The first pitch and/or melody to be drawn from a pan may be credited to one or more of the following: Alexander's Ragtime Band, Bar 20, Carlton "Zigilee" Constantine, Fred Corbin, Neville Jules, "Totee" Lewis, "Mando" of Alexander's Ragtime Band, Rudolph "Fish Eye" Ollivierra, Winston "Spree" Simon, Aulrick Springer, and/or Hamilton "Big Head" Thomas.

16. "Jab molassi" is a French creole term meaning molasses devil (from the French *diable*). A typical jab molassi was a male of Afro-Caribbean descent, clothed in old swimming trunks or worn out, cutoff trousers. A short wire tail protruded from the back of the trousers, sometimes tipped with a brush of hemp. Chains and locks may have been wrapped around his waist. His head may have been adorned with cowhorns, a wreath of weeds, or an old felt hat. He carried a pitchfork, and his entire body, head, and face were covered with molasses, tar, grease, creosote, or mud.

17. Bobolee bands became popular in Trinidad beginning around the 1860s. Comprised of both males and females of all ages from the underprivileged areas of Port of Spain, these bands were organized for both Good Friday and Carnival celebrations. A bobolee was, in fact, an effigy of Judas Iscariot, which was hung from a tree and beaten with sticks to the shouted refrain, "Beat the bobolee, beat the bobolee."

18. Shango (also *Xango, Chango*) is an African deity of Yoruba origin whose powers are manifested in thunder and lightning. The Shango cult in Trinidad is a syncretic blend of elements of traditional Yoruba religion, Catholicism, and the Baptist faith. Groups of worshipers gather intermittently throughout the year for minor ceremonies and annually for a major four-day ceremony. Drum/percussion groups have always been an integral part of these events. Shango drums are traditionally fashioned from the trunks of breadfruit, avocado, or cedar trees, and the shells are covered on both ends with stretched goatskin. A typical ensemble comprises a set of three drums and rattles. *Bemba*, the largest drum, and *congo*, the middle drum, are each played with one stick and one hand; *oumalay* (or *amalie*), the smallest drum, is played with two sticks. The rattles, called *chac-chacs*, consist of small, round calabashes, which have been dried and hollowed out, filled with seeds, stones, crushed seashells, or a similar material, and fitted with a handle. The Rada tradition in Trinidad, also a syncretic Afro-Christian belief system, derives its name from Allada, a major port and early capital of what was once Dahomey, in West Africa. The percussion instruments used depend upon the particular ceremony. Included are the drums *towonde*, *wyande*, and *hwen'domasu*, *chac-chacs*, and the *gãn*. The wyande and hwen'domasu are supporting drums, single-headed with goatskin

and played with two sticks. The main drum, the towonde, is covered with deerskin and played with one stick and one hand. The gãn is made from a round bar of iron or steel, about thirteen inches in length, which has been beaten flat at both ends to form a sort of "double hoe." It is struck with a thin, round metal rod.

19. Military masques are among the oldest still extant in Trinidad's Carnival, dating back to 1834. The various sailor masques were very popular during the first half of this century. Fancy sailors, sailors ashore, bad-behavior sailors, and all-about or knockabout sailors were all based upon the looks, attitudes, actions, and activities of merchant seamen and sailors who put in to shore in Port of Spain. In 1907 the U.S. Atlantic Fleet visited Trinidad, inspiring the popularity of military sailor masques. During and after World War I, sailors of many nationalities visited Port of Spain, including Americans, Germans, French, and English. Then, during World War II, the U.S. military presence was strong because of the navy and army air force bases established at Chaguaramas and Mucurapo, respectively. Early sailor bands paraded the streets in full uniform, performing drills and accompanied by string bands or military-type brass bands. Later sailor bands, of the bad-behavior and all-about or knockabout variety, sang songs they themselves made up to the accompaniment of rhythms beaten out upon chamber pots and metal tins.

20. "Behind the Bridge" refers to an area of Port of Spain to the east of St. Ann's River (the East Dry River), which includes the Belmont, Clifton Hill, Gonzales, John John, La Cou Harpe, and Laventille districts; an economically depressed area that was the birthplace of some of Trinidad's most renowned jamette, tamboo bamboo, pan, and steel bands.

21. This is a term of relatively recent origin that applies to a citizen of either of the two islands that comprise the Caribbean nation of Trinidad and Tobago.

22. A term of relatively recent origin (c. mid-1980s), a panist is someone who plays a steel pan or set of pans of any type and design. The term evolved as a further step in the continuing efforts by those involved in the steel band movement in Trinidad and Tobago to secure pan's inclusion as an equal among the Western world's established musical instruments. Hence the move to refer to and think of one who plays pan in the same way as one who plays violin (violinist), piano (pianist), percussion (percussionist), etc. Sometimes the term is spelled "pannist," though this spelling is not consistent with the coupling of the suffix "ist" to other instruments' names, as noted above.

23. For a recent index of steel band programs at U.S. academic institutions, as well as independent steel bands, see Jeannine Remy, "Establishing a Steel Band Program in the United States," *Percussive Notes* 28, no. 3 (Spring 1990): 16, 18–19, 22, 24, 26, 28, 30–32.

24. Soca is currently one of Trinidad's and Tobago's, as well as one of the Caribbean's, most recorded, listened to, and performed styles of popular dance music. The most current in a long lineage of African and Afro-Trinidadian song forms preceding or belonging to the calypso genre (slave work songs, praise songs, religious songs, songs of derision, songs of insurrection, kalinda, bongo, *belair*, *cariso*, oratorical calypso, half-tone, single-tone, and double-tone calypso), soca itself began to evolve during the mid-1960s on Trinidad, as local studio musicians and calypsonians began to experiment with fusing musical ideas derived from drumming ensembles used to accompany Afro-Caribbean Orisha (Shango) and Rada ceremonies, elements of tassa and other Indo-Trinidadian styles, music of the Spiritual Baptists, *parang*, reggae, French Caribbean *cadenze*, highlife and other West African popular music styles, and African American music from the United States (disco, funk, r & b, and jazz), with the extant calypso styles. In 1974 calypsonian Lord Shorty (Garfield

Blackman) culminated years of blending these influences (with an emphasis upon East Indian and African American elements) with the release of an album entitled *Endless Vibrations*, a watershed of sorts for the soca style. Also, with this album came the first use of the term "sokah" (spelled to reflect its East Indian influence) to name the developing musical hybrid. The term eventually came to be spelled "soca," an abbreviation/contraction of "soul calypso." Bands playing live soca/calypso are referred to as calypso bands, soca bands, or brass bands. They combine the latest technologies with a high caliber of musicianship. Digital synthesizers and electronic drums blend with electric guitars, horn sections, percussionists, and vocalists to render the season's crop of calypsoes and socas, an occasional reggae from Jamaica or England, and popular African American music from the United States.

25. Old-time steel bands, or pan-round-neck bands, are a recent revitalized and updated version of the early pan bands of the 1930s and 1940s. The popularity of modern-era pan-round-neck bands has grown since its inception in 1971–72, and old-time steel bands in the mid-1990s are sophisticated ensembles, in some cases rivaling, in sound and musical prowess, conventional steel bands.

26. In England, Wales, Northern Ireland, New Zealand, Australia, South Africa, and some former English colonies, a legal holiday occurring on the first weekday following Christmas.

27. Contracted form of *block-o-rama*. A type of steel band held in a panyard and on the adjacent street(s) that has/have been closed to automobile traffic for one or more blocks for that purpose. The host steel band will extend an invitation to (usually) one (but sometimes more) guest band(s) to join them at their panyard for the blocko. Traditionally the host band runs a bar and some sort of concession stand to generate income and provides free transportation and refreshment for the guest band(s). Blockos are more for socializing and listening to pan music than for dancing; crowds of discerning steel band supporters, attracted both from within and without the immediate community, enjoy comparing performances of the informally competing bands. Each band will play several sections in a row, typically encompassing calypsoes, socas, recent Panorama arrangements, American pop tunes, Latin American music, and other popular types of Caribbean music, such as reggae or zouk. Usually a deejay provides the latest in popular recorded music during the interludes between bands. Blockos were first held by steel bands beginning in the late 1960s, and their frequency peaked during the mid-1970s, when they were a popular feature on most weekends. Their numbers began to diminish both because they were all too frequently economically impractical and because of increased exploitation by promoters outside of the steel band community.

28. *Mas'* is a creolization of the French word *masque*. Very simply, playing mas' involves the portrayal of various themes and characters in often elaborate costumes.

29. In recent years other pan competitions have been introduced to extend the interest in pan music, for both listeners and participants, past the Carnival season. Beginning in the late 1980s a sort of mini-Panorama, entitled Pan on the Move, was begun. Held around April/May in the southern town of Point Fortin, this competition requires bands to play one current year's calypso and one that is ten years old. Another popular event is called Pan Ramajay. Begun in 1989 and held biennially at midyear, it is designed to occur between the music festival years and to feature small pan ensemble performances.

30. Other, less common, pan designs include *triple tenors* and *twelve basses*.

31. Caps are typically placed on the top of the container. Occasionally they will be put in the center of the shell. This latter type of drum may also be used for tuning at both ends.

32. Tools commonly used by pan tuners include sledge- and/or ball-peen hammers with sawed-off handles of 6-lb., 4-lb., 40-oz., 32-oz., 16-oz., and 8-oz. weights; nail punches; a flexible ruler; a compass; precut note templates; a tape measure; and a pitch pipe or tuning fork.

Selected Discography

Robert Greenidge/Michael Utley. *Mad Music.* MCA Master Series (1986).

Robert Greenidge/Michael Utley. *Jubilee.* MCA Jazz (1987).

Robert Greenidge/Michael Utley. *Heat.* MCA Master Series (1988).

Andy Narell. *The Hammer.* Windham Hill Jazz (1987).

Othello Molineaux. *It's About Time.* Big World (1993).

Andy Narell. *Little Secrets.* Windham Hill Jazz (1989).

Andy Narell. *Down the Road.* Windham Hill Jazz (1992).

Rudy Smith Trio/Anese Hadeed Quartet. *Jazz 'n' Steel from Trinidad and Tobago.* Delos (1988).

various artists (Fonclaire Steel Band, Harmonites Steel Band, Starlift Steel Band). *The Music of Trinidad.* National Geographic Society (1971).

various artists (Amoco Renegades, Catelli Trinidad All Stars, Len "Boogsie" Sharpe, Phase II Pan Groove, Samroo Jets). *The Steel Bands of Trinidad and Tobago.* Delos (1988).

various artists (Solo Harmonites, Tropical Angel Harps, Valley Harps, WITCO Desperadoes). *Pantastic World of Steel-Music.* Vol. 1—*Classic.* Tropical Music (1989).

various artists (Amoco Renegades, Neal & Massy Trinidad All Stars, Phase II Pan Groove, Solo Harmonites, Valley Harps, WITCO Desperadoes). *Pantastic World of Steel-Music.* Vol. 2—*Calypsoes and Socas.* Tropical Music (1989).

various artists (Amoco Renegades, Carib Tokyo, Phase II Pan Groove, Silver Stars, Solo Harmonites). *Carnival Jump-Up.* Delos (1990).

various artists (Amoco Renegades, Birdsong, Catelli Trinidad All Stars, Mat Securities Merrytones, Pamberi, Samaroo Jets). *The Heart of Steel Featuring Steelbands of Trinidad and Tobago.* Flying Fish Records, Inc. (1990).

various artists (Amoco Renegades, Catelli Trinidad All Stars, Phase II Pan Groove, Solo Harmonites). *Pan Champs.* Vol. 1. Blue Rhythm Records (1990).

various artists (American Stores Exodus, Amoco Renegades, Carib Tokyo, Phase II Pan Groove). *Pan Champs.* Vol. 2. Blue Rhythm Records (1990).

various artists (Amoco Renegades, Phase II Pan Groove, Silver Stars, Solo Harmonites, The Trinidad Cement Limited Skiffle Bunch Steel Orchestra). *Trinidad Carnival—Steelbands of Trinidad and Tobago.* Delos (1990).

various artists (Amoco Renegades, Exodus, Kalomo Kings, Neal & Massy Trinidad All Stars, Pamberi, Phase II Pan Groove, Vat 19 Fonclaire). *Panorama—Steelbands of Trinidad and Tobago.* Delos (1991).

various artists (Exodus, Neal & Massy Trinidad All Stars, Pandigenous, Phase II Pan Groove, Silver Stars, Solo Harmonites, Vat 19 Fonclaire). *Pan Woman—Steelbands of Trinidad and Tobago.* Delos (1991).

various artists (Samaroo Jets, Skiffle Bunch, Solo Harmonites, Sonalal Samaroo, Tropical Angel Harps). *Pan Classics Competition Performances from the World's Finest Steel Bands.* Blue Rhythm Records (1992).

Vat 19 Fonclaire. *Pan Jazz 'n' Calypso.* Delos (1990).

The Westland Steel Band. *The Sound of the Sun.* Nonesuch Explorer Series (1967).

Selected Bibliography

Aho, William R. "Steel Band Music in Trinidad and Tobago: The Creation of a People's Music." *Latin-American Music* 8, no. 1 (1987): 26–58.

Ahyoung, Selwyn Ellore. "The Music of Trinidad." B.A. thesis, Indiana University, 1977.

———. "Soca Fever! Change in the Calypso Music Tradition of Trinidad and Tobago, 1970–1980." M.A. thesis, Indiana University, 1981.

Aldrich, Putnam. "Oil Drums and Steel Bands." *Saturday Review* 29 (September 1956): 35, 62.

"America's First Steel Band." *Music Journal* 26 (September 1958): 42–43.

Bartholomew, John. *The Steel Band.* London: Oxford University Press, 1980.

Bennett, Olivia. "The Story of the Steelband." *Festival! Carnival.* London: Macmillan Education, 1986.

"Boom, Boom, BOOM." *Newsweek* 23 (August 1954): 71.

Borde, Percival. "The Sounds of Trinidad; The Development of the Steel-Drum Bands." *The Black Perspective in Music* 1 (Spring 1973): 45–49.

Brereton, Bridget. *A History of Modern Trinidad, 1783–1962.* Exeter, N.H.: Heinemann Educational Books, 1981.

———. *Race Relations in Colonial Trinidad 1870–1900.* Cambridge: Cambridge University Press, 1979.

———. "The Trinidad Carnival 1870–1900." *Savaco*, nos. 11/12 (September 1975): 46–110.

Burnette, Mackie. "Pan and Caribbean Drum Rhythms." *Jamaica Journal* (March 1978): 14–20.

Bush, Jeffrey E. "Panorama 1981." *Percussive Notes* 19, no. 3 (Spring/Summer 1981): 57.

Callanan, Joe. "Barrels of Music." *The Reader's Digest* 64 (April 1954): 128.

———. "Music from Oil Drums." *Musical Courier* 149 (May 1954): 8–10.

Charles, Wayne E. "Meet the Steelpan." *The Instrumentalist* 34 (August 1979): 86–87.

Courlander, Harold. "Many Islands, Much Music." *Saturday Review* 18 (October 1952): 58–60.

Crahan, Margaret E., and Franklin W. Knight, eds. *Africa and the Caribbean: The Legacies of a Link.* Baltimore: The Johns Hopkins University Press, 1979.

Creed, Ruth. "African Influences on Latin America." M.M. thesis, Northwestern University, 1947.

Dennis, R. A. "A Preliminary Investigation of the Manufacture and Performance of a Tenor Steel Pan." *West Indian Journal of Engineering* 3 (October 1971): 32–71.

deVerteuil, Fr. Anthony. *The Years of Revolt: Trinidad 1881–1888.* Port of Spain: Paria Publishing, 1984.

Dudley, Shannon, ed. "The Most Unique Acoustical Instrument." De Kalb, Ill.: Office of Public Information, Northern Illinois University, 1985.

Elder, Jacob D. "Color, Music, and Conflict: A Study of Aggression in Trinidad with Reference to the Role of Traditional Music." *Ethnomusicology* 8, no. 2 (1964): 128–136.

———. "The Evolution of the Traditional Calypso in Trinidad and Tobago: A Socio-Historical Study." Ph.D. diss., University of Pennsylvania, 1966.

———. *From Congo Drum to Steelband.* St. Augustine, Trinidad: University of the West Indies Press, 1969.

———. "Kalinda—Song of the Battling Troubadours of Trinidad." *Journal of the Folklore Institute* 3, no. 2 (August 1966): 192–203.

Gallaugher, Annemarie, and Pauline Hasslebacher. *Calypso, Pan and Mas' in the Toronto West Indian Community.* Toronto: National Museum of Man, 1987.

George, Kaethe. "Interview with Ellie Mannette." *Percussive Notes* 24, no. 4 (1986): 34, 36, 38.

Gibson, Gary. "Techniques in Advanced and Experimental Arranging and Composing for Steel Bands." *Percussive Notes* 24, no. 4 (1986): 45–49.

Goddard, George. *Forty Years in the Steelbands: 1939–1979.* Trinidad: Karia Press, 1991.

———. "The Steelband." *The Hummingbird.* (Port of Spain) (1964): 5.

Gonzalez, Sylvia. *Steelband Saga. The Story of the Steelband—The First 25 Years.* St. Clair, Port of Spain: Ministry of Education and Culture, 1978.

Hanson, Donald R., and Robert Dash. "The Saga of the Steelband." *The Caribbean* 8, no. 8 (March 1955): 173, 176, 177, 184.

Hebridge, Dick. *Cut 'n' Mix: Culture, Identity and Caribbean Music.* New York: Methuen, 1987.

Herskovits, Melville J., and Frances Herskovits. *Trinidad Village.* New York: Knopf, 1947.

Hill, Errol. "The Trinidad Carnival: Cultural Change and Synthesis." *Cultures* 3, no. 2 (March 1976): 54–86.

———. *The Trinidad Carnival: Mandate for a National Theatre.* Austin: University of Texas Press, 1972.

Holder, Geoffrey. "Drumming on Steel Barrel-Heads." *Music Journal* 13 (May–June 1955): 9, 20, 24.

Horowitz, Michael M. *People and Cultures of the Caribbean.* Garden City, New York: The Natural History Press, 1971.

Howard, Rick. "Is Antiguan Pan Ready to Rebound?" *Pan* 1, no. 1 (Fall 1985): 15–17.

Jones, Anthony Mark. *Steelband: Winston "Spree" Simon Story.* Barataria, Trinidad: Educo Press, 1982.

La Fay, Howard. "Carnival in Trinidad." *National Geographic* 140 (1971): 692–701.

The Laws of Trinidad and Tobago. Summary Convictions Offences, Chapter 25, Section 70, Paragraph 1, p. 341. London: Water-low and Sons Limited, 1925.

MacDonald, Scott B. *Trinidad and Tobago: Democracy and Development in the Caribbean.* New York: Praeger, 1986.

Mahabir, Noorkumar. *The Influence of the Tassa on the Making of the Steelband: The East Indian Contribution to the Trinidad Carnival.* Carapichaima, Trinidad: The Indian Review Committee, Caribbean Institute of Indian Studies and Research, 1984.

Matthews, Basil. "Calypso and Pan America." *The Commonweal* 13 (November 1942): 91–93.

Maxime, Gideon. *History of Steelband Panorama of Trinidad and Tobago 1963–1990.* Barataria, Trinidad: Author, 1991.

———. *Steelband Music Festivals of Trinidad & Tobago 1952–1989.* Barataria, Trinidad: Author, 1990.

Mintz, Sidney W., and Sally Price, eds. *Caribbean Contours.* Baltimore: The Johns Hopkins University Press, 1985.

Moses, Lennard V. "An Annotated Bibliography of the History and Music of Trinidad." *Percussive Notes Research Edition* (March 1984).

O'Connor, G. Allan. "A Brief Survey of Steel Drum Programs in North American Schools." *Percussive Notes* 19, no. 3 (Spring/Summer 1981): 58–59.

———. "A Conversation with Clifford Alexis." *Percussive Notes* 19, no. 3 (Spring/Summer 1981): 56.

———. "Pan: Heartbeat of a Nation." *Percussive Notes* 19, no. 3 (Spring/Summer 1981): 54–55.

———. "So You Want to Start a Steel Band." *Percussive Notes* 19, no. 3: 60.

Parks, Walter Irwin. "Examination of the Role, Value, and Function of Steel Bands in University and College Percussion Programs." Ph.D. diss., University of Houston, 1986.

Pearse, Andrew. "Aspects of Change in Caribbean Folk Music." *International Folk Music Journal* 8 (1955): 29–35.

———. "Carnival in Nineteenth Century Trinidad." *Caribbean Quarterly* 4, nos. 3–4 (1956): 175–193.

Remy, Jeannine. "Establishing a Steel Band Program in the United States." *Percussive Notes* 28, no. 3 (Spring 1990): 16, 18–19, 22, 24, 26, 28, 30–32.

Ross, Paul G. "Feature: Drumset in the Steel Band." *Percussive Notes* 27, no. 1 (1988): 20–26.

Rouff, Anthony E. *Authentic Facts on the Origin of the Steelband.* St. Augustine, Trinidad: Bowen's Printery, 1972.

Sealey, John, and Krister Malm. *Music in the Caribbean.* London: Hodder and Stoughton, 1982.

Seeger, Pete. "Steel Bands Come to the United States." *The Hummingbird* (Port of Spain) (1961): 3–4.

———. *Steel Drums: How to Play and Make Them.* New York: Oak Publications, 1961.

———. *The Steel Drums of Kim Loy Wong.* New York: Oak Publications, 1964.

Seon, Donald "dan." *South Panman.* San Fernando, Trinidad: Author, 1979.

Simmonds, W. Austin. *Pan—The Story of the Steel Band.* Trinidad: R. T. West & Co. Ltd., for BWIA Int'l, n.d.

Slater, John. *The Advent of the Steelband and My Life and Times with It.* New York: n.p., n.d.

Slater, Leslie. "The Music of Carnival (Some Thoughts on the Decline of the Steelband's Role)." The Social and Economic Impact of Carnival: Seminar Held at the University of the West Indies, St. Augustine, Trinidad, on Nov. 24–26, 1983: Seminar Papers with Recommendations. St. Augustine, Trinidad: Institute of Social and Economic Research, University of the West Indies, 1984.

Smith, Louis C. *The First Text Book on "Steel Band."* Port of Spain: Speedo Printery, 1979.

"Sounds from the Caribbean." *Time* 27 (February 1956): 47–48.

"The Steel Band: Musical Tin Pan of Trinidad." *Instrumentalist* (September 1959): n.p.

Stuempfle, Stephen. "The Steelband Movement in Trinidad and Tobago: Music, Politics and National Identity in a New World Society." Ph.D. diss., University of Pennsylvania, 1990.

Thomas, Jeffrey. "The Changing Role of the Steel Band in Trinidad and Tobago: Panorama and the Carnival Tradition." *Studies in Popular Culture* 9, no. 2 (1986): 96–108.

———. *Forty Years of Steel: An Annotated Discography of Steel Band and Pan Recordings 1951–1991.* Westport, Conn.: Greenwood, 1992.

———. *A History of Pan and the Evolution of the Steel Band in Trinidad and Tobago.* Chicago: Author, 1990 (originally an M.A. thesis, Wesleyan University, 1985).

Tracey, Andrew. "New Development in the Trinidadian Steel Drum." *Ethnomusicology* 4, no. 2 (1968): 70.

Wallis, Roger, and Krister Malm. *Big Sounds from Small Peoples.* London: Constable and Company Ltd., 1984.

Waterman, Richard Alan. "African Patterns in Trinidad Negro Music." Ph.D. diss., Northwestern University, 1943.

Weller, Judith Ann. "A Profile of a Trinidadian Steelband." *Phylon: The Atlanta University Review of Race and Culture* 22, no. 1 (1961): 68–77.

White, Landey E. "Steel Bands: A Personal Record." *Caribbean Quarterly* 15, no. 4 (1969): 32–39.

Williams, Dr. Eric. *From Columbus to Castro: The History of the Caribbean 1492–1969.* New York: Harper & Row, 1970.

———. *History of the People of Trinidad and Tobago.* Trinidad: P.N.M. Publishing, 1964.

Yeates, George. "Trinidad's National Instrument." *The Hummingbird* (Port of Spain) (1962): 3, 19.

Jeffrey Thomas

*Portions of this chapter, revised for inclusion in this book, originally appeared in *Forty Years of Steel: An Annotated Discography of Steel Band and Pan Recordings, 1951–1991*, compiled by Jeffrey Thomas. Westport, CT: Greenwood Press, 1992 (an imprint of Greenwood Publishing Group).

The Tambourine

Fr: *tambour de Basque*; Ger: *Schellentrommel, Tamburin*; It: *tamburino, tamburello*; Sp: *pandereta, pandero*

As a member of the frame drum family, the tambourine has a long history that dates from the medieval period back to ancient Balkan and Mid-Eastern civilizations. Generally associated with dance and minstrel music of Europe, it remained a folk instrument until its introduction into the orchestra in the mid-to-late nineteenth century.

The modern orchestral tambourine is a shallow wooden single-headed drum. The shell of the drum contains numerous spaces in which pairs of metal disks, called jingles, are placed. These disks are held in place by metal pins that are driven through holes in the centers of the disks and into the wood of the shell. The diameter of the drum is generally ten inches but may range from six to twelve. There are either one or two rows of jingles. The tambourine's head is most often of animal skin. The head is usually attached by tacks to the shell and the tensioning is produced by drying the skin. The disks may be of a variety of metals including silver, bronze, or steel.

There are a variety of methods employed when playing the tambourine. These include striking the head with the palm, knuckles, and fingertips to achieve various gradations of volume. Rapidly moving the tambourine between the knee and fist produces quick, intricate rhythms at loud dynamics. A sustained sound may be produced by one of two methods. The first is to shake the instrument back and forth using a motion similar to twisting a doorknob. This technique, known as the *shake roll*, produces a sound that can be sustained for an indefinite length of time. However, the smoothness of the roll suffers at softer dynamic levels. The *thumb roll* is a technique that involves moving the thumb along the surface of the skin in such a fashion that the tambourine vibrates, thus producing a sustained sound as long as the thumb is kept in motion. This technique produces excellent smooth rolls at most dynamic levels, especially softer ones. Unfortunately, the thumb roll is generally unable to be sustained indefinitely like the shake roll. Occasionally, the composer will ask that the tambourine be struck with some sort of mallet, generally snare drumsticks.

Representative works from the classical orchestral repertoire using the tambourine include:

Berlioz, Hector
Roman Carnival, overture (1844)

Bizet, Georges
Carmen (1875)

Rimsky-Korsakov, Nikolai
Scheherazade (1888)

Dvořák, Antonín
Carnival, overture (1891)

Stravinsky, Igor
Petrouchka (1911)

Orff, Carl
Carmina burana (1937)

Becker, Günther
Stabil-instabil (1965)

Malec, Ivo
Vocatif (1968)

In popular music the tambourine is often associated with rock and Latin-American music. In rock music the tambourine is generally shaken from side to side in a steady duple division of the beat. Often the second and fourth beats are emphasized by striking the hand. In Latin American music, most notably sambas, the head of the tambourine is struck in a number of areas producing different pitches. The tensioning of the head is looser than that of the orchestral tambourine, which enables the variety of pitches to be produced.

See also Illus. 36, p. 135.

Bibliography

Blades, James. *Percussion Instruments and Their History*. 2nd ed. London: Faber and Faber, 1974.

DePonte, Neil. "Janissary Music and Its Influence on the Use of Percussion in the Classical Orchestra." *Woodwind World, Brass and Percussion* 15, no. 4 (1976): 44ff.

Peinkofer, Karl, and Fritz Tannigel. *Handbook of Percussion Instruments*. London, Schott, 1976. Originally published in German (Mainz: B. Schott's Söhne, 1969).

Peters, Gordon B. *The Drummer: Man, a Treatise on Percussion*. Rev. ed. Wilmette, Ill.: Kemper-Peters, 1975.

Schneider, Walter C. "Percussion Instruments of the Middle Ages." *Percussionist* 15, no. 3 (1978): 106–117.

Andrew Spencer

The Tambourin Provençal

Fr: *taboret, tabouret, tambour de Provence, tambourin, tambourin de Provence, tambourinet, tambourin provençal;* Ger: *provenzalische Röhrentrommel, provenzalische Trommel;* It: *tamburo di Provenza, tamburo provenzale;* Sp: *atabor, tamboril, tambor provenzal, tamburiña*

The *tambourin provençal* is a deep drum that originated in the south of France in the fifteenth century. It has a single snare stretched across the top or batter head. A typical specimen is made out of beech and is 13¾ inches in diameter by 27½ inches deep; it is often ornately carved with bas-relief flowers and has slunk (unborn calfskin) heads. Traditionally, folk musicians hang the drum over the left forearm with a leather strap. At the same time a three-holed wooden recorder-type instrument, called a *glaoubet,* is held with the same hand.

The performer strikes the drum near the center of the snare with a handsomely turned stick held in the right hand. The effect is a rather low buzzing rhythmic ostinato. In the folk idiom drummers will often play in groups and are accompanied by dancers clad in gaily colored costumes. The most typical rhythm played on the drum is a repeated pattern of continuous eighth notes, although there are variations.

There are many drums of this type of various sizes to be found all along the Mediterranean coast from Spain to Italy—with and without snares. The Basques have a drum of the same type that typically measures 12 inches in diameter by 14 inches deep. A similar instrument is found in Mexico under the name of *pito de Veracruz,* most likely brought over with the Spanish explorers of the seventeenth century. Several composers have scored for this drum, including J.B. Lully (1632–1687), as early as 1684, in his opera *Amadis;* Georges Bizet (1838–1875); Jules Massenet (1842–1912); Arthur Honegger (1892–1955); Darius Milhaud (1892–1974); and André Jolivet (1905–1974).

The use of the *tambourin provençal* in an orchestral setting has led to an amount of confusion as to the composer's intention. In the "Farandole" from Georges Bizet's *L'Arlésienne* (1872), for example, the composer indicated the word "tambourin" on the percussion part, which every French percussionist knows is the deep drum discussed above. However, when the music was published by a German music publishing company, a German copyist saw the word "tambourin," which in German means "tambourine," and did not think there was a need to translate it, because to him it already meant "tambourine." The word "tambourin" therefore appears in the score of the German edition. Conductors who were not familiar with the authentic folkloristic origins of this melody incorrectly used a tambourine, assuming that this was Bizet's intent. This is the reason that one finds the tambourine used in this part on some recordings. It should have been translated as *provenzalische Trommel,* or even *Rührtrommel ohne Saiten* (deep tenor drum without snares), which is what it most resembles.

This brings us, finally, to the question of the use of snares. It seems to be the convention in current orchestral performance to use a deep drum without snares, as evidenced by performance practice.

Michael Rosen

The Triangle

Fr: *triangle*; Ger: *Triangel*; It: *triangolo*; Sp: *triángulo*

The triangle is believed to have descended from the ancient Egyptian sistrum. In its earliest form the triangle had as many as three rings, which rode freely on the lower bar. These rings produced a continuous jingle rather than the solitary note achieved by the modern instrument. Indeed, this older version may have been the instrument used through the time of Beethoven's Ninth! Like the sistrum, the triangle was most often associated with religious ceremonies. The Turkish musicians of the late sixteenth and early seventeenth centuries were influential in promoting its use in other contexts.

It is a metallic instrument that derives its name from its shape. Made of hardened steel, the modern orchestral triangle ranges from four to ten inches in the length of one side. Often the instrument is plated with a chrome or silver finish. The beaters are generally made of a metal similar to the triangle itself and are usually chrome-plated. The beaters produce a high-pitched, delicate "ting" from the instrument. In various compositions of the twentieth century, the percussionist is occasionally asked to strike the triangle with a wooden beater, which produces a thinner, mellower sound. An example of this is found in Béla Bartók's Sonata for Two Pianos and Percussion (1937).

The triangle is generally suspended on a thin wire or string (fishing line is quite popular), which, in turn, is strung through a clamp. This allows the triangle to be held with one hand comfortably or suspended from a stand and struck with two beaters for intricate rhythms.

The use of the triangle in the western orchestra dates back to the early eighteenth century. Its influence came from Turkish Janissary (military) bands. The masters of the Viennese school made frequent use of the triangle, as is evidenced by W.A. Mozart's Overture to *Die Entführung aus dem Serail* (1782) and Ludwig van Beethoven's Symphony No. 9 (1824). Throughout the nineteenth century the triangle became more prominent (as did the rest of the percussion section) and reached solo status in the Piano Concerto in E-flat Major (1855) by Franz Liszt. By the middle of the nineteenth century the triangle had become a standard instrument of the symphony orchestra and was included in many prominent works later in the century, and into the twentieth, such as

Brahms, Johannes
Symphony No. 4 (1885)

Rimsky-Korsakov, Nikolai
Scheherazade (1888)

Nielsen, Carl
Symphony No. 6 (1925)

Kodály, Zoltán
Háry János: Suite (1927)

Bernstein, Leonard
Overture to *Candide* (1956)

The triangle is often used in popular music. This use is most notable in the rhythm section of Latin-American bands. In this context, the triangle is held in one hand (without the use of the clamp), which allows the musician to produce both muffled (staccato) and unmuffled (ringing) tones. These two tones are generally alternated in a steady rhythm of quadruple divisions of the beat.

See also "Janissary music (Turkish Music)," p. 195.

Bibliography

Blades, James. *Percussion Instruments and Their History*. 2nd ed. London: Faber and Faber, 1974.

DePonte, Neil. "Janissary Music and Its Influence on the Use of Percussion in the Classical Orchestra." *Woodwind World, Brass and Percussion* 15, no. 4 (1976): 44ff.

Peinkofer, Karl, and Fritz Tannigel. *Handbook of Percussion Instruments.* London: Schott, 1976. Originally published in German (Mainz: B. Schott's Söhne, 1969).

Peters, Gordon B. *The Drummer: Man, a Treatise on Percussion.* Rev. ed. Wilmette, Ill.: Kemper-Peters, 1975.

Schneider, Walter C. "Percussion Instruments of the Middle Ages." *Percussionist* 15, no. 3 (1978): 106–117.

Andrew Spencer

The Vibraphone, Vibraharp, and Vibes

Fr: *le vibraphone*; Ger: *das Vibraphon*; It: *il vibrafono*

The *vibraphone* is the most recently developed mallet percussion instrument, yet it can claim more world-renowned artists, more abundant recordings, and wider recognition by the general public than any other mallet instrument. Of wholly American origin, it evolved in differing designs under the creative influence of two inventive and prolific German instrument designers employed by competing percussion instrument manufacturers. Development in different stages by separate companies gave rise to a duality in names that still persists. Both "vibraphone"[1] and "vibraharp"[2] are trade names coined by the original manufacturers; the generic "vibes"[3] was adopted by a major manufacturer later because of wide currency among players and writers. Variant trade names, subsequently used by other firms such as "vibra-bells," "vibra-celeste," and "harpaphone," were short-lived.

Beginning about 1916, Herman Winterhoff of the Leedy Manufacturing Company in Indianapolis experimented off and on with a variety of motor-mechanical arrangements in his quest for a *vox humana* or tremolo effect from the bars of a three-octave f–f^3 steel marimba, a novelty vaudeville instrument with thin, steel tone bars mounted to the keybed on tapered felt strips. He succeeded in 1922 by mounting a motor on the frame at the narrow end beneath the bars to drive dual shafts fitted with metal discs centered in the tops of each resonator tube. As the

Fig. 1. Deagan vibraharp No. 145 (c. 1922).

Photograph by Louis Ouzer.

discs (pulsators) revolved in the resonator columns under sounding bars, a tonal phase shift was created resembling a vibrato.[4] A vaudeville headliner, Signor Friscoe (Louis Frank Chiha), was intrigued by the unique sound and in 1924 recorded "Aloha 'Oe" and "Gypsy Love Song" on the instrument (then described as a "metal marimba") for the Edison label.[5] The novel recording proved popular on radio, then in its infancy and desperate for musical variety. Interest in the new sound was soon aroused among musicians. George H. Way, Leedy sales and advertising manager, had earlier coined the name "vibraphone," which was adopted in 1924 for the first promotional literature on the instrument. About twenty-five of the original design Leedy vibraphones had been produced (of which several were exported to Europe) when manufacture was halted in the fall of 1927.[6]

The previous April, in Chicago, the "vibraharp" had been introduced by J. C. Deagan, Inc., a firm then in its forty-seventh year of development and manufacturer of mallet instruments and organ percussions and the originator of the steel marimba many years earlier.[7] The Deagan vibraharp was developed by Chief Engineer Henry J. Schluter, who conceived the design as an entirely new mallet instrument, not a modification of an existing design. He drew upon his experience with such earlier Deagan devices as aluminum-bar song bells and the large organ vibratoharp for his first design,[8] which was placed into production as the now-famous Model 145. This model, with its cord-suspended, half-inch-thick, graduated-width, tempered-aluminum tonebars with harmonic tuning, had a pedal-operated damper and adjustable vibrato speed. Introduction of the three-octave f–f^3 Model 145 firmly established the Deagan vibraharp as the significant new musical instrument, which became the basic design concept for all future instruments of this type. Soon after ace Chicago drummer Roy C. Knapp, with the Chicago Little Symphony, demonstrated the expressive potential of the vibraharp in a solo arrangement of "Mother Machree" on radio station WLS in the early fall of 1927,[9] it became a favorite instrumental voice for many bandleaders and featured drummers. Two more compact and portable Deagan vibraharp models were developed and introduced by 1929[10] to satisfy the increasing demand and performer needs of pit drummers and students.

The Leedy Company resumed manufacture of the vibraphone in Indianapolis in 1928, offering a new model incorporating all the design features of the Deagan vibraharp.[11] With virtually identical instruments being offered under two different trade names at that time, a confusion in terms began. Despite the inconsistency, the designation "vibraphone" has gained sufficiently widespread usage among most foreign musicians, many percussion educators, some composers, and younger performers to be accepted as the universal term for the instrument today. Most professionals and many writers, however, recognize only "vibes" for the instrument and "vibist" for the performer.

The standard professional vibraphone range is three octaves, chromatic, f–f^3. Other ranges have been manufactured, chiefly two-and-a-half-octave c–f^3 for pit drummer and student use and f–g^3 for marching. A few instruments have been custom-made in ranges of three-and-a-half-octave c–f^3 and four-octave c–c^4. The standard bar widths on a professional model are graduated from 2 inches to 1½ inches (some manufacturers today offer bars graduated from 2¼ to 1½ inches, and one model has uniform 1¾-inch bars). Several models are usually available from each manufacturer, ranging from "Deluxe" (top-of-the-line professional features and finishes), to "Pro Portable" (large bars, folding frame), to "Semi-Pro" (smaller, narrow-bar, folding portable). Tone bars traditionally have been made from a "half-hard" tempered-aluminum alloy, originally Alcoa 2017/T4 and more recently 2024/T4. (Alloys used in foreign makes differ somewhat.)

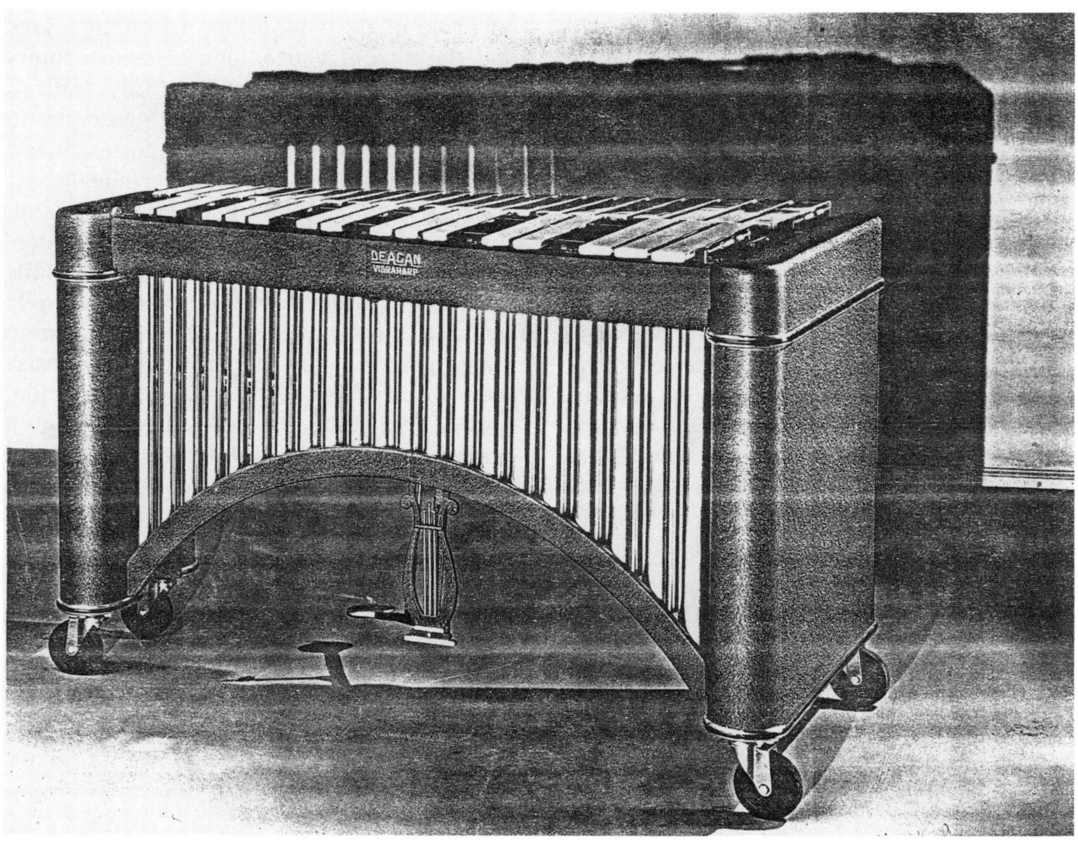

Fig. 2. Deagan vibraharp model 55, "Imperial" (c. 1937).

Various bar finishes have been offered: natural polished aluminum, clear anodize, brass plate and lacquer, and gold anodize. A variety of motors and vibrato controls are employed on different makes. Basic vibraphone structure has changed little since 1927. Changes that have been made have affected appearance and weight reduction and upgraded efficiency of components. Deagan instruments were radically redesigned in 1937 to incorporate new features and to introduce esthetic form to mallet instruments. The now-cherished "Imperial" vibraharp (the name had been revamped, too) and the immensely popular two-and-a-half-octave "Model 30" were among the new entries.[12] More recent innovation has occurred in sound amplification and the electronic manipulation of the tone signal, which is now being developed. The first successful amplifying system ("Magni-Sound") was developed by the Deagan Company in 1962. A small crystal microphone embedded in each resonator gave the vibraphone player pure sound and adjustable volume from his instrument, along with problems of ambient sound amplification, feedback, and delicate components. More advanced systems using attachable strips of magnetic pickups were introduced by both Deagan ("ampli-vibe") and Musser Marimbas, Inc. ("ampli-pickup") in 1969, but the Deagan unit was marketed only briefly with the advent of a far superior transducer pickup developed for the first electronic vibraphone, the three-octave, self-contained, highly portable Deagan "electravibe" introduced in 1970. The new pickup consisted of a tiny piezoelectric chip and a ground bonded to the underside end of the tone bar and wired with a plug-in lead to a terminal strip connected to a coupler and control unit. Pressure on the total mass of the struck bar is converted by the piezochip to an audio-electronic signal and passed to an amplifier for reproduction as audible sound, subject to the user's adjustment of volume, tone balance, and tremolo speed and intensity. Highly efficient and free of the shortcomings of earlier systems, the piezotransducer pickup remains the most reliable means of vibraphone amplification currently in use. A newly engineered magnetic pickup system with sophisticated electronic circuitry was introduced to music dealers at the 1989 summer music tradeshow.[13] These systems can also provide the audio input to digital interface devices that use the vibraphone keyboard as the keying source for various types of electronic sound-generating and computer equipment.

Early manufacturers of vibraphones, in addition to J. C. Deagan, Inc., and Leedy Manufacturing Company, were G.C. Jenkins Company (JenCo), Decatur, Illinois; Ludwig & Ludwig, Chicago, Illinois; and Premier Drum Company and Boosey & Hawkes, Ltd. (Ajax) in England. Manufacturers entering the field after World War II were Musser Division/Ludwig Industries, LaGrange, Illinois; Ross Mallet Instruments, Inc., Chippewa Falls, Wisconsin; Trixon and Studio 49, Germany; Galanti, Italy; Bergerault, Ligueil, France; Kosth Company, Saito Musical Instruments, and Nippon Gakki Company, Ltd. (Yamaha), Hamamatsu, Japan. Only Musser and Ross vibraphones are currently manufactured in the United States. Other major brands now available are Bergerault, Premier, Saito, and Yamaha.

The first vibraphones were used by stage performers as a novelty and by drummers for variation from the customary dry and brittle sound of bells and xylophone. Dance bandleaders soon found the sound appealing to their ballroom clientele and wrote arrangements featuring the vibraphone. Two events in 1930–31 forecast the important role of the vibraphone in modern jazz and the rise of vibraphone artists to international fame. In New York City, Adrian Rollini (1904–1956), a versatile saxophone player whose swinging jazz quartet was a popular draw for a 42nd Street speakeasy, added the 145 vibraharp to his bandstand. His driving improvisation on the new percussion instrument brought jazz musicians from many directions to hear the uniquely original sound and established Rollini as a major jazz innovator of the period. Across the country, in Culver City, California, Lionel Hampton (b. 1909), then a young drummer in the Les Hite Band, was "foolin' around" with a vibraharp when Louis Armstrong (1898–1971), fronting the band at the time, heard the "fascinating" sound.[14] As a result, the first documented jazz vibraphone recording is Hampton's 1931 performance with Armstrong's Sebastian New Cotton Club Orchestra.[15] Five years later, drummer Hampton was doubling on vibraphone with a small jazz group he led in the Paradise Ballroom in Los Angeles, where bandleader Benny Goodman (1909–1986) heard his sound. Joining the Goodman orchestra in 1936, Hampton's distinctive style was regularly featured in the famous Goodman Jazz Quartet. Jazz and the vibraphone made simultaneous debuts in Carnegie Hall with the celebrated Benny Goodman concert of January 16, 1938.[16]

Soon after World War II, the vibraphone reached full maturity when ex-bandleader and creative jazz xylophone artist Red Norvo (b. 1908) joined the Woody Herman Band as a full-time vibraphone player.[17] Two others destined for fame on the instrument were Terry Gibbs (b. 1924) (then with the Benny Goodman Sextet) and Milt Jackson (b. 1923) (then with the Dizzy Gillespie Band), each of whom brought new and distinctive styles of expression to the vibraphone, which soon earned both many followers worldwide. Milt Jackson's sensitive phrasing in the Modern Jazz Quartet contributed to the many honors bestowed on that long-lived and highly respected ensemble. The vibraphone became part of the standard instrumentation in many of the most prominent groups during the heyday of jazz supper clubs in the 1960s, and a number of today's top mallet artists were featured on vibraphone in the ensembles of George Shearing, Herbie Mann, Buddy Rich, and the like. The roster of highly talented jazz vibraphone players grew rapidly to include such names as Peter Appleyard (b. 1928), Roy Ayers (b. 1940), Jack Brokensha (b. 1926), Larry Bunker (b. 1928), Gary Burton (b. 1943), Teddy Charles (b. 1928), Warren Chiasson (b. 1934), Walt Dickerson (b. 1931), Dany Doriz, Victor Feldman (1934–1989), David Friedman (b. 1944), Elmer Gill, Tyree Glenn (1912–1974), Bill Grah (b. 1928), Gunter Hampel, Hagood Hardy, Godfrey Hirsch, Jay Hoggard (b. 1954), Bobby Hutcherson (b. 1941), Margie Hyams (b. 1923), Mike Mainieri (b. 1938), Bill Molenhof, Buddy Charles F. Montgomery (b. 1930), Dave Pike (b. 1938), Tito Puente (b. 1933), John Rae (b. 1934), Emil Richards (b. 1932), Joe Roland (b. 1920), David Samuels (b. 1948), Harry Sheppard, Cal Tjader (1925–1982), Tommy Vig (b. 1938), and Lem Winchester. Gary Burton introduced a unique improvisational structure to his writing and playing, which earned him a large international following. New creative jazz vibraphone artists continue to emerge but are less well-known because of the decline in jazz clubs nationwide and the release of fewer jazz recordings.

The vibraphone reached a peak of public popularity during the 1960s, when three innovative groups from the new state of Hawaii burst on the world music scene with their "exotic sounds." Immensely popular in person and on records, the Martin Denny Group, the Arthur Lyman Group, and the Gene Rains Group were essentially piano-augmented percussion ensembles with the vibraphone basic to the group sound. Each group had numerous hit records over several years, but never had the vibraphone appealed to so large a public as on Arthur Lyman's biggest hits featuring him on vibraphone playing his own arrangements.[18] In the wake of the great popularity of these percussion-oriented groups, interest in percussion ensembles gained momentum in the schools. The vibraphone had already established its value to the jazz ensemble in the stage bands and lab bands rapidly being formed in high schools and colleges. Today, the vibraphone is standard equipment in the inventory of all institutions offering percussion education.

The melodic and harmonic qualities available in vibraphone sound have long endeared the instrument to composers of motion-picture, television, and commercial-advertising music, and made the vibraphone essential equipment in recording studios. Though well-established in jazz, popular, theatrical, and educational music, the vibraphone is less prominent on the symphonic stage than other mallet percussions. Its tone color has been utilized in the Modern Jazz Quartet orchestral experiments with Gunther Schuller's "Third Stream" fusion of jazz and classical music, and in the Stan Kenton Neophonic Orchestra. Given its rich and expressive potential, the role of the vibraphone in classical music is yet to be explored.

For many years, published performance material for vibraphone was limited to practice material in the few general mallet instrument method books then available; for variety, the student was dependent on the teacher to write out parts. In the early 1960s, advanced method material and more challenging performance material began to appear, with Henry Adler Music Company and Kendor Music Publishing among the first to issue new vibraphone material. Today there is an abundance of high-quality teaching material for vibraphone, from beginner to advanced techniques and improvisational theory. Scores of excellent solo and small-to-large ensemble works written by top professionals and teachers are available from many music publishers.

Notes

1. "The Vibraphone," advertising folder (Indianapolis: Leedy Manufacturing Company, 1924), first publication of the "vibraphone" trade name.

2. "A New Sensation in Musical Tone—The New Deagan Vibra-Harp," advertising folder (Chicago: J.C. Deagan, Inc., 1928), first publication of the "vibra-Harp" trade name.

3. Musser Marimbas, Inc., Chicago, adopted "vibes" as a trade name in promotional materials beginning 1948; Ludwig/Musser currently uses "vibraphone." Ross Mallet Instruments, Inc., Chippewa Falls, Wisconsin, adopted the "vibes" trade name with the introduction of its first model in 1986.

4. George H. Way, former sales and advertising manager, Leedy Manufacturing Company, Indianapolis and Elkhart, Indiana. Personal conversations and notes exchanged with writer, 1960 and beyond.

5. Ibid.; Leedy folder, 1924.

6. Ibid.

7. J.C. Deagan, Inc., Chicago. From company archival materials under the custodial care of the writer as Deagan sales and advertising manager, 1950–1982.

8. Henry J. Schluter, sixty-six-year veteran employee of the Deagan Company, in personal statements to writer. (Perceiving the need for a sound different from the long-dominant xylophone for the many mallet-playing drummers in dance bands and the expanding field of radio music, Deagan Sales Manager M.L. "Deacon" Jones had requested development of a mellow-toned, portable, three-octave instrument having piano-like solo and accompaniment qualities and a tremolo capability.)

9. Roy C. Knapp, personal statement to writer, 1976; Henry Schluter statements. First radio broadcast of a professional vibraharp performance. (A prototype Model 145 was demonstrated at radio station WBBM by M.L. Jones in the spring of 1927.)

10. Deagan catalog (Chicago: J.C. Deagan, Inc., 1929).

11. George H. Way, notes and conversations.

12. Deagan catalog 101 (Chicago: J.C. Deagan, Inc., 1938).

13. Developed by Peterson Electro-Musical Products Co., Worth, Illinois, in association with Ross Mallet Instruments.

14. "The Vibe Tribe," *Newsweek* 69, no. 20 (May 15, 1967): 105.

15. From the Lionel Hampton discography compiled in 1985 by Bob Davis, a Chicago jazz authority, collector, and discographer.

16. The vibraphone returned to Carnegie Hall as the featured instrumental voice in June 1979, when Milt Jackson and artists associated with his career presented a retrospective concert entitled "Milt Jackson's 40 Years in Jazz."

17. Whitney Balliett, "Profiles: The Music Is More Important," *The New Yorker* 44, no. 45 (December 28, 1968): 36–47.

18. "Mood Merchants," *Time* 80, no. 7 (August 17, 1962): 62: "One album alone, titled "Taboo," has sold close to 2,000,000 copies, and Lyman fans buy each new effort ("Yellow Bird," "Hawaiian Sunset," "Taboo Vol 2") with the enthusiasm of rare-stamp collectors." Millions of television viewers also became familiar with the vibraphone in this period from frequent Lyman Group appearances written into the story segments of the popular TV series "Hawaiian Eye."

Hal Trommer

Vibraphone Players

The following is a list of the most influential vibe players of the twentieth century. Birth and death dates are included when known. For more information on their lives, see the works cited below.

Ayers, Roy (b. 1940)
Berger, Karl (b. 1935)
Burton, Gary (b. 1943)
Dickerson, Walt (b. 1931)
Feldman, Victor (1934–1989)
Friedman, David (b. 1944)
Gibbs, Terry (b. 1924)
Hampton, Lionel (b. 1909)
Hutcherson, Bobby (b. 1941)
Jackson, Milt (b. 1923)
Mainieri, Mike (b. 1938)
Mendoza, Victor
Norvo, Red (b. 1908)
Pike, Dave (b. 1938)
Piltzecker, Ted (b. 1950)
Richards, Emil (b. 1932)
Rollini, Adrian (1904–1956)
Samuels, David (b. 1948)
Vig, Tommy (b. 1938)

Bibliography

Feather, Leonard, and Ira Gitler. *Encyclopedia of Jazz in the 70's.* New York: Horizon Press, 1976.

Kernfeld, Barry, ed. *The New Grove Dictionary of Jazz.* 2 vols. New York: Stockton Press, Groves Dictionaries of Music (Macmillan Press), 1988.

Larrick, Geary. *Biographical Essays on Twentieth-Century Percussionists.* Lewiston, N.Y.: The Edwin Mellen Press, 1992.

Robert B. Breithaupt

The Xylophone

Fr: *claquebois, xylophone*; Ger: *Holzharmonika, Strohfiedel, Xylophon*; It: *silofono, xilofono*; Sp: *xilofóno*

Definition

The xylophone is a percussion instrument consisting of a series of wooden bars (or logs), increased in length to sound a musical scale, and sounded by being struck with one or more hammers or sticks. Metal-bar instruments (*metallophones*) or stone-bar instruments (*lithophones*), while they may be similar in appearance are not strictly classified as xylophones. In addition, since the mid-1960s, the xylophone may also be defined as a percussion instrument consisting of a graduated series of bars made of synthetic materials (e.g., fiberglass, resins such as kelon or klyperon).

Although technically covering the entire class of wooden-bar instruments (including marimbas, xylorimbas, etc.), the word "xylophone" has come to refer specifically to the standard Euro-American or modern Japanese two-row instrument, with rosewood or synthetic bars, having a range of from two and one-half to four octaves, with c^5 as its highest-pitched bar. Xylophones of North American origin are usually tuned in such a way as to create a predominance of the second upper partial of each bar (a 12th above the fundamental pitch), thus distinguishing them from other instruments in the xylophone class, such as the marimba (which may be tuned in such a way as to create a predominance of the first upper partial of each bar—an octave above the fundamental pitch), the xylorimba (combining first upper partial tuning in the low register with second upper partial tuning in the high register), and all the rest of the wooden-bar instruments. Many xylophones of European origin are tuned with a predominance of the first partial of each bar, thereby making their higher range the primary difference in distinguishing them from marimbas.

General Characteristics

Sound

The sound of each wooden or synthetic bar is determined by several factors.

Timbre

The timbre (and resonance) of a bar is affected by the type of wood (e.g., hardwood or softwood) or by the composition of synthetic materials in the bar. Hardwood bars tend to generate more high partials in the harmonic series (thus sounding "brighter") and to ring slightly longer than softwood bars. Synthetic bars tend to sound even more "bright" or "glassy" and to ring longer than hardwood bars.

In xylophones of North American origin (and in the xylophones of modern Japanese origin), the most desirable wood for the bars is the centerwood (heartwood) of very old rosewood trees. The older the source tree, the more dense will be its heartwood, and the more resonant and durable will be the bars derived from it. Such wood was plentiful until about 1960, when most of the natural stands of mature rosewood trees were completely harvested worldwide. Rosewood has continued to be used by manufacturers in North America and Japan. However, most of the rosewood available since that time is much younger when harvested (from fifteen- to forty-year-old trees), and consequently, the heartwood is less dense, and the newer instruments lack the resonance and durability of older instruments.

Pitch

The pitch of each bar is determined by the length, the thickness, and the density of the bar. The longer, thinner, or denser the bar, the lower its pitch; conversely, the shorter, thicker, or less dense the bar, the higher its pitch.

Any existing bar can be tuned by removing material from the end of the bar (by sanding, filing, etc.) to raise the fundamental pitch or by removing material from the upper or lower center surface of the bar to decrease its thickness and thereby lower its fundamental pitch. In addition, partials (harmonics) may be tuned by removing material from specific locations along the upper or lower center surface of the bar.

The pitch of any existing bar can be temporarily raised by applying a lump of wax (sometimes mixed with lead particles) to the underside of the bar in its center area. This practice is common with Central American instruments.

Resonance

The resonance of each bar is affected by the manner in which the bars are resting. A bar that is supported at its two prime nodal points (nodes) will tend to vibrate more freely and hence have more resonance. The prime nodal points are the points of least vibration. The nodes cross the bar transversely, and they are generally located approximately one-fifth of the length of the bar from each end of the bar.

Bars may be "bedded" by resting loosely at their prime nodal points on supports of soft materials (straw, wool felt, polyfoam, cotton cord, or even the performer's legs), or the bars may be tied together in sets by cords that are either tied around or laced through lateral holes in each bar at its prime nodal points and placed so as to rest on a frame structure that may be covered with strips of soft insulating material.

Strings of bars may be separated by vertical support posts that may also be insulated with soft materials (e.g., rubber) to minimize their dampening effect on the vibration of the bars; the vertical support posts may serve not only to separate the bars but also to maintain the relative position of each bar.

Strings of bars may also be "suspended" by resting the connecting string (or cord) on top of the vertical support posts, so that the bars are not "bedded" or in contact with the frame support, thereby further enhancing the vibration of the bars.

Volume

The loudness of a bar can be affected by its size. Larger bars can produce louder sounds.

Amplification

The resonance of the bars can be enhanced or amplified by placing the bars over a sympathetic vibrating air chamber, or "resonator." There may be a simple resonator for the entire instrument (e.g., a pit in the ground, a box, or a trough), or there may be individual resonators for each bar (e.g., gourds, boxes, open or closed tubing of metal, bamboo, or other materials).

In the case of individual resonators, each one must be tuned to allow its contained air to vibrate at the same frequency (pitch) as the bar that it resonates. In general, the larger the volume of air in a gourd resonator, or the greater the length of a tube resonator, the lower the pitch.

Xylophones of European, North American, or modern Japanese origin will generally have a closed-tube resonator (made of aluminum or brass and plated with nickel or chrome) suspended under each individual bar.

Xylophones of Central American origin will generally have a gourd or carved woodbox resonator suspended under each individual bar.

Xylophones of African origin will generally have a gourd resonator suspended under each individual bar. Examples of instruments having pit, animal-horn, trough resonators, or no resonators are also plentiful.

Xylophones of Southeast Asian origin will generally have trough resonators, though some may have other types of resonators or no resonators at all.

Resonator Timbre

The timbre of a resonator may be affected by the type of material from which it is made, depending on whether or not the material enhances or dampens the vibration of the air that it contains.

The timbre of a resonator may also be altered by the addition of a vibrating membrane (made of spider's egg, pig intestine, plant membrane, wax paper, or cigarette paper, and glued, waxed, or mechanically attached to the resonator) to cover a tone-hole in the wall of the resonator to produce a mirliton-like or buzzing effect. Xylophones having this feature are generally of African or Central American origin, with the notable exception of the "nabimba," manufactured by the J.C. Deagan Company of Chicago in the first half of the twentieth century.

Resonator Volume

The greater the amount of air contained in a resonator, the louder the sound it will produce. In the case of closed-tube resonators, loudness can be increased (without affecting pitch) by enlarging the diameter of the tubing or by placing two resonators of identical size under a bar.

Instrument Support

The entire structure (bars, frame and post supports, and resonators) may have one of several types of support.

It may be placed on the ground, on tree trunks or stems, or on the outstretched legs of sitting performers. This type of support is used for some xylophones of African or Southeast Asian origin.

It may be suspended from the performer's body by means of rope or woven-cloth cord wrapped around the player's waist, neck, or shoulders. Generally, this type of support is used for some xylophones of African or Central American origin. Examples also existed in sixteenth-century Europe.

It may be mounted on structural supporting legs (sometimes having wheels) to bring the instrument within comfortable reach of a standing performer. Generally, this type of support is used for most xylophones of European, Central and North American, or modern Japanese origin.

Xylophones of Southeast Asian origin generally have the top lip of a trough resonator serving as the support frame. The entire unit is generally placed on the ground for performance.

Arrangement of the Bars

The bars may be arranged into various patterns depending on playing technique, the number of players on an instrument, and the musical scales employed. For the most part, bars on xylophones of African or Asian origin are arranged in a single row. Such instruments may be played by one or more performers sitting on either side of the row of bars, with the bars arranged from the performer's left to right.

Bars on xylophones of Eastern European origin may be arranged in four rows, roughly corresponding with the stringing of the Alpine hammer-dulcimer (*Hackbrett*). Such bar arrangements may also be found where there has been East-European cultural influence (e.g., Beijing, China). Such instruments are usually played by a single standing performer, with the four rows running from near to far, the larger bars in each row being nearest to the performer. Generally, the two center rows form a diatonic scale while the two outer rows contain accidentals, some of which are located on each outer row to enable the performer to play them with either hand.

Bars on xylophones of European, American, or modern Japanese origin are usually arranged in two rows, like a piano keyboard. Such instruments are generally played by one or more performers standing on the side of the xylophone corresponding to the white keys of the piano, with the two rows running from the performer's left to right, the larger bars being to the left.

Range

The pitch ranges of xylophones vary greatly due to worldwide usage in differing musical applications. In general, all xylophones will fall within a pitch range from about great C (two octaves below middle C on the piano) to c^5 (the highest C on the piano). Any individual xylophone, however, will generally encompass only a portion of this range, covering from one octave or less to as much as five octaves or more.

The standard pitch range for the two-row Euro-American xylophone (including that of modern Japanese origin) used in present-day symphony orchestras and bands is f^1 (F above middle C on the piano) to c^5, encompassing a range of three and one-half octaves. It is important to note that this instrument is a transposing instrument; its notation is normally written one octave below its actual sound. Many four-octave xylophones (c^1 to c^5) are used in Europe and North America.

Hammers and Mallets

The tone of any xylophone may be affected by the hammers, beaters, mallets, or sticks selected to strike the bars. In general, softer beaters will tend to dampen harmonics and produce a softer (mellower) tone, while harder beaters will tend to accentuate the harmonics to produce a more strident tone.

Xylophone beaters of Euro-American origin (including those of modern Japanese origin) usually consist of sticks (made of wood, bamboo, plastic, or rattan and ranging from about 6 to 14 inches in length) to which a ball is affixed at the striking end. The ball may be ¾ of an inch to 2 inches in diameter and be made of wood, rubber, plastic, wound-yarn, or felt.

A special "Y"-shaped xylophone beater with two heads is used to perform on the *octarimba*, an instrument developed by the J.C. Deagan Company of Chicago in the first half of the twentieth century. This beater is used to play on two bars simultaneously with one stick stroke.

Xylophone beaters of Eastern European origin may also be carved from single pieces of hardwood, approximately 8 inches in length and closely resembling the spoon-like beaters that are used on hammer-dulcimers.

Xylophone beaters of African origin may be simple shaved twigs or carved wooden sticks, and they may be wrapped on the beating-end with rubber or woven cloth or both.

Xylophone beaters of Asian origin may consist of carved hardwood sticks from about 6 inches to 12 inches in length to which a rubber or felt ball or disk (of about 2 to 4 inches in diameter) is affixed at the striking end.

Xylophone beaters may be activated by a keyboard mechanism to enable the performer to use a pianistic technique. In organs, the beaters may be operated by a bellows or by electromagnets to strike the underside of the bars. In a piano-like mechanical system, the beaters are operated directly through levers activated by the keyboard. With any keyboard system, however, it is difficult to achieve differentiation of tone or resonance.

Performance Techniques

Stick Strokes

The manner in which the performer strikes the xylophone bars may also have an effect on the sound produced.

Xylophones of European, American, and modern Japanese origin are usually played by standing performers using one or more ball-on-stick beaters in each hand. Generally, the most desirable stroke is one that rebounds rapidly after striking each bar, in order to prevent dampening of the bar's vibration by the beater.

A "dead" stroke may also be used in which the beater remains on the surface of the bar after striking, in order to dampen the bar's vibration intentionally. This stroke is common to Central American performance practices.

Xylophones of Southeast Asian origin are generally played by sitting performers using one disk-on-stick beater in each hand. Occasionally, one hand will also be used to dampen the bar's vibration.

Xylophones of African origin may be played by sitting or standing performers using one ball-on-stick or shaved-twig beater in one or both hands.

Striking Spot

The place on each bar where the beater strikes will affect the timbre and resonance of the sound.

Generally, the most desirable place to strike a bar is near the center of the top playing surface. Striking the bar in this area enhances the vibration of the fundamental pitch.

A bar may be struck on the top surface at the point that is halfway between a node and the nearest end. Striking the bar at this spot also enhances the vibration of the fundamental pitch, though to a subtle degree less than striking near the center of the bar.

A bar may also be struck on the bottom surface at the point that is halfway between a node and its nearest end. This stroke is commonly employed by performers using two beaters in one hand to produce a tremolo, with one beater striking the top surface on the downstroke and the other beater striking the bottom surface on the upstroke.

A bar may be struck on the top corner of its end. Striking the bar at this spot will enhance the vibration of the fundamental pitch, though to a subtle degree less than striking in the center of the bar. This technique is common on the one-row log xylophones of Africa and Southeast Asia.

A bar may be struck directly over a primary nodal point. Striking a bar at this point enhances the vibration of the partials (overtones) in relation to the fundamental pitch.

Striking a bar on its side also enhances the vibration of the partials while producing almost no fundamental pitch.

Special Effects

Lacing a 2-inch-wide strip of wax paper over and under the bars will produce a sound similar to the sound of a resonator with a buzzing membrane.

A scraping stroke may be employed by the performer in which a stick is held in the manner of holding a pencil, with the pointed end of the stick extending about 2 inches below the performer's fingers and scraped from the node to the center. The resultant sound is a downward-bending (glissando-like), briefly sustained tone.

History

Origins of the Xylophone in Asia

Musicologists have differing opinions on whether the xylophone originated in Africa or Asia. It is generally agreed that the two areas were linked musically, because there are unmistakable parallels in playing techniques, tunings, and even in the music performed. However, most scholars are of the opinion that Asia was the place of the xylophone's origin, and various types can be found on both the Asian mainland and on the archipelago. It is known that around 2000 B.C., there existed in China a wood-harmonicon consisting of sixteen wooden slabs, suspended in two tiers. At about the same period, an instrument resembling the xylophone, called the *ranat,* was used by not only the Chinese, but also by the Siamese and Hindus. However, it is not clear whether the ranat was a wood-bar instrument.

The xylophone's use spread throughout Southeast Asia. Reliefs on the temple of Panataran in Java, carved in the fourteenth century, depict xylophones played by performers (male and female) using "Y"-shaped beaters.

Introduction of the Xylophone into Africa

It is not clear just when the migration of the xylophone from Asia to Africa occurred, but it was at least before the arrival of the Portuguese. Written and oral historical references from the mid-fourteenth century mention xylophones with resonators in the Niger River area (Mali). In the sixteenth century, Portuguese missionaries reported the existence of xylophones with gourd and buzzer resonators in Ethiopia.

The xylophone is not distributed throughout all of Africa. Its use is restricted primarily to an area roughly south of 15° north latitude on the west coast, and of 5° north latitude on the east coast, down to Angola and Mozambique, and the instrument's use has also been mainly associated with African royalty. Virtually all forms of xylophones can be found.

Spread of the Xylophone to Islands of the West Pacific

It is not known when or how xylophones were introduced into the Pacific area, but they probably came from Southeast Asia. The most common xylophones in use are *leg xylophones*, sometimes having pit-hole resonators. Such instruments are common to west Melanesia, and they may be found in New Britain, New Ireland, the Duke of York Islands, Tami Island, and eastern Papua New Guinea.

Appearance of the Xylophone in Europe

Musicologists theorize that the xylophone was probably brought to Europe from Indonesia. However, the possibility of its importation into Europe as a result of the Crusades cannot be dismissed totally. The xylophone's first application in Europe was as an organ stop around 1506. It was mentioned as *hültze glechter* ("wooden sticks") in 1511 by the organist Arnold Schlick, in his *Spiegel der Orgelmacher*.

The first known visual representation of a xylophone in Europe is a woodcut by Hans Holbein the Younger entitled "Dance of Death," dating from about 1523. Curiously, the xylophone shown is a one-row frame instrument carried around the neck, more like certain African xylophones than Southeast Asian instruments, except that the bars do not run from the performer's left to right, but rather from near to far, as in the later four-row xylophones of Eastern Europe. No resonators are depicted. Xylophones of this type were called *Strohfiedel* in German. In Spain they were recorded as *ginebras* in 1628, and in France as *échelette* ("small ladder") in 1636. The "small ladder" xylophone became accepted throughout Eastern Europe (Austria, Germany, Poland, and Russia) as a folk instrument. Also about this time, another form of xylophone, operated by a keyboard, was introduced by the Flemings as a practice instrument for carillonneurs.

Migration of the Xylophone to Central and South America

The xylophone of Central and South America, called marimba, is believed to be of African origin, probably introduced into the New World by slaves in the Colonial period. Evidence for this can be found in the similarities of construction between African and Central American xylophones (e.g., gourd resonators with buzzers), the African derivation of the word "marimba," and the absence of pre-Columbian xylophone references in the Americas.

The earliest written account of a marimba was in Guatemala in 1680. The marimba was found in Mexico, Nicaragua, Costa Rica, El Salvador, Colombia, and Brazil, and it was widely dispersed among the Indians and used mainly for civil and religious occasions.

In the late nineteenth century, woodbox resonators were developed to replace the function of gourds, and in 1894 the two-row chromatic bar arrangement was adopted by Sebastian Hurtado of Guatemala. This arrangement of bars differed, however, from the standard piano keyboard arrangement in that the accidental bars were positioned directly over the ends of the natural bars (e.g., C-sharp placed directly over C), instead of between them (e.g., C-sharp placed between C and D).

Development of the Xylophone in Nineteenth-Century Europe

In 1810 an instrument called the *Triphon* was invented by Wiedner of Fraustadt. It was a xylosistron device consisting of wood bars that were played by stroking them with rosin-coated gloves. This instrument remained a novelty and its use was short-lived. By this time, the "small ladder" one-row xylophone had been altered into a four-row form, possibly influenced by the arrangement of the beating spots on the Eastern European hammer-dulcimer (the beaters also resemble dulcimer hammers).

In the late 1830s a Pole by the name of Michael Josef Guzikov popularized a four-row diatonic xylophone with the bars set on straw supports. He had previously studied a Jewish instrument used in Russia called *Jerova a Salamo*. His virtuosity and his selection of repertoire (including transcriptions of works by Paganini) led to his recognition throughout Europe, and he is credited with making the xylophone an instrument accepted both in the concert hall and in stage and variety shows. Other performers (Eben [c. 1839] and Jakubowsky [c.1866]) followed in Guzikov's path.

Some original music had been composed for the xylophone, including concertante pieces by Ignaz Schweigl (d. 1803). Possibly the earliest orchestral composition to include a xylophone was Ferdinand Kauer's *Sei Varizioni* (c. 1810), which contain solo passages for the instrument.

About 1870 a Frenchman, Charles de Try, who was also a virtuoso on the xylophone, invented the tryphone. It is not known whether this was a two-row or four-row xylophone or whether the instrument was diatonic or chromatic.

In 1886 a xylophone method book by Albert Roth was published by Agence Internationale à Vevey (Switzerland). In this book two systems were presented for arranging the bars: (1) the "Roeser" system—a four-row chromatic system, and (2) the "A. Roth" system—a chromatic two-row piano keyboard system, apparently intended to be played by the performer from the large end instead of from the side, or in other words, with the low bars close to the performer and the high bars away from the performer. Also included in this book are references to published solo pieces for xylophone with piano and orchestra accompaniment.

The Xylophone in North America

Although it might be expected that the xylophone would have been introduced into North America in the same way as in Central and South America, directly through the African slave trade, such was not the case. There seem to have been several parallel influences in the late nineteenth and early twentieth centuries that led to the popularity of xylophones in North America.

First, the migration into North America of highly skilled German and East European musicians at the end of the nineteenth century greatly influenced the course of North American music. Their presence was essential to the creation and development of symphony orchestras, and to concert, theater, and music-hall bands. Xylophonists were among the immigrants, and they not only performed as soloists in concerts but also as entertainers in theater shows.

Second, the development of the phonograph (which brought music into every home) led to the need for high-quality recordings. The xylophone was perhaps the instrument that was best reproduced on the acoustic, wax-cylinder records of the late nineteenth century. Interestingly, many of the earliest recordings featured xylophonists with German names: A.T. Van Winkle (Edison Records, 1889); Charles P. Lowe (Gramophone Records, c. 1890); William Reitz (Victor Records, c. 1909); and Howard Kopp (Columbia Records, c. 1913).

Third, Guatemalan and Mexican marimba players toured North America beginning in the first decade of the twentieth century. They performed at expositions, in vaudeville theaters, and on phonograph recordings. Perhaps the most influential of these was the Hurtado Brothers Royal Marimba Band of Guatemala, featuring Sebastian Hurtado and his sons.

Finally, John Calhoun Deagan, an ex-clarinet player, formed a company bearing his own name, and in 1893 he produced a resonatorless diatonic xylophone. By 1903 he added resonators and a two-row chromatic bar arrangement, and following World War I his company began to manufacture large numbers of high-quality xylophones of various types for vaudeville entertainers, theater orchestras, symphony orchestras, and dance music ensembles throughout North America.

Xylophones in the Industrialized Countries of the Twentieth Century

In the twentieth century many virtuoso performers on the xylophone (including the marimba) achieved widespread recognition. In North America there were Harry Breuer, William Dorn, Lou Chiha "Friscoe," Joseph Green, Sammy Herman, and Red Norvo. Other great virtuosos, such as George Hamilton Green and Clair Omar Musser, not only improved performance techniques but also created a new repertoire for the xylophone and marimba through their many original compositions. More recently the names of Bob Becker, Nexus (the Toronto-based percussion group), Leigh Howard Stevens, and Gordon Stout have achieved distinction.

In England during the first half of the twentieth century Teddy Brown, William Coates (also known as "El Cota"), Harry Robbins, Rudy Starita, and William Whitlock were rated among the greatest of xylophone performers. From Japan, Yoichi Hiroaka (in the 1930s) and Kieko Abe (in the 1980s) exerted much influence worldwide on xylophone and marimba performance.

In addition, manufacturers of xylophones have contributed to refinements in the instrument. The major North American manufacturers include the J.C. Deagan Company, the Leedy Drum Company (no longer active), and the Musser Company (see Illus. 43, p. 139). In England instruments of high quality are manufactured by the Premier Drum Company, in France by Peripole/ Bergerault International, and in Japan by the Korogi (Kori) Company and the Yamaha Corporation.

Twentieth-century symphonic composers have used xylophones extensively in their music. Among the best examples are the following works:

Stravinsky, Igor
Les Noces (1923)

Creston, Paul
Concertino for Marimba and Orchestra (1940)

Lutoslawski, Witold
Concerto for Orchestra (1954)

Messiaen, Olivier
Oiseaux exotiques (1956)

Hovhaness, Alan
Fantasy on Japanese Woodprints (1965)

Pitfield, Thomas
Sonata for Xylophone (1967)

Reich, Steve
Drumming (1971)

Cahn, William
In Ancient Temple Gardens (1976)

Lutoslawski, Witold
Double Concerto for Oboe and Harp (1980)

Names and Distinguishing Features of Various Xylophones

Africa

Abigolo—a large Nigerian xylophone set on banana or plantain stems

Akadinda—a large Ugandan xylophone set on banana stems

Akpaningbo (kponingbo)—a loose-bar xylophone of Zaire

Akuda-omvek—a xylophone of Cameroon

Alimba—a log xylophone of Zaire

Alungba (alungbu)—a log xylophone of Zaire

Amadinda—a large Ugandan one-row xylophone

Ambira—an Ethiopian xylophone with buzzer resonators

Anzang—a xylophone of the Gabon Republic having no resonators

Atranatra (atranatrana)—a loose-bar xylophone of southeastern Madagascar

Bachi—another name for *valimba*

Bala (balo)—a Mali name for xylophone; a log xylophone of Liberia

Balafo—a xylophone of the west Sudan and Congo with gourd and buzzer resonators

Balafon—an alternate word for *balafo*

Balak—a west African marimba

Balangi—a Sierra Leone marimba with gourd and buzzer resonators

Balau—a log xylophone of Liberia

Balingi—a xylophone of the Congo with no resonators and having a banana-tree limb frame

Ballard(s)—a West African xylophone

Bangi—another name for *kweningba*

Banjanga/bandjanga—other names for *manja*

Baza—a xylophone of the Congo

Blande—a log xylophone of Liberia

Bolange (balangi)—a xylophone of Sierra Leone with gourd and buzzer resonators

Carimba—a xylophone of Angola with gourd resonators

Chikonje—a xylophone of Mozambique

Chikulu—another name for *chikonje*

Chikututu—a bass xylophone of Mozambique

Chilanzane—a treble xylophone of Mozambique

Chimhongwana—a treble xylophone of Mozambique

Chinditi—an Angolan xylophone

Chinzumana—a xylophone of Mozambique

Cho—a frame xylophone of Upper Volta

Chohun—a frame xylophone of Ghana

Cikulu—a xylophone of Mozambique

Dibhinda (dibiinda, dibinde)—a bass xylophone of southeastern Africa

Didimbadimba—a xylophone of the Congo similar to the *ambira*

Dimba—an arc marimba of the Congo with gourd resonators

Dimbila—another word for *mangwilo*

Dipela—a South African xylophone similar to the *ambira*

Djan—a log xylophone of Cameroon

Djil—a frame xylophone of Ghana

Dole—a tenor xylophone of southeastern Africa

Dujimba—a xylophone of Zaire having gourd and buzzer resonators

Dzilli—a frame xylophone of Ghana

Ekere-iko—a two-bar xylophone of Nigeria

Elong—a frame xylophone of Upper Volta having gourd and buzzer resonators

Elungu—a log xylophone of Zaire

Embaire—a Ugandan xylophone with fifteen or sixteen keys supported on two banana stems

Enara—a log xylophone of Zaire

Endara—a Ugandan xylophone with sixteen to eighteen keys supported on two banana stems

Endiga—a log xylophone of Uganda

Endum—a xylophone of Cameroon

Entaala—another word for *amadinda*

Entara—a Ugandan xylophone

Gbange—a frame xylophone of Nigeria

Gbingbe—another name for the *kweningba*

Gbo—a log xylophone of the Ivory Coast

Gbwilebo—another name for *bala*

Gil—a xylophone of Ghana and the Ivory Coast

Gombi—a trough xylophone of Zaire

Gubu—a xylophone of Nyasaland

Gulu—("large") another word for *chinzumana*

Gyil (gyilli)—another word for *bala*

Handja—a xylophone of West Africa with gourd and buzzer resonators

Igo—a log xylophone of Nigeria

Ikon eto—a log xylophone of Nigeria

Ikwemgbo—a log xylophone of Nigeria

Ilimba—a xylophone of the Congo with gourd resonators

Imbila—a xylophone of the Transvaal

Itanda—a frame xylophone of Zaire

Jimba—another name in the Congo for the *madimba*

Jinjimba—a two-bar xylophone of northeastern Angola

Kalanba (kalangba)—an arc xylophone of the Congo with gourd and buzzer resonators

Kalangwa—a five-bar arc xylophone of the Congo with gourd and buzzer resonators

Karangba—another name for *kalanba*

Katiboky—another name for *atranatra*

Kende—a xylophone of southern Chad

Kennu—a log xylophone of Benin in West Africa

Kidimba—an arc marimba of the Congo with gourd resonators

Kidimbadimba—a one-bar xylophone of Zaire

Kigogolwa—a log xylophone of Burundi

Kilangay—another name for *atranatra*

Kipelevelegu—another name for *bala*

Kpedimba/kpedimbe/kpendimbe—other names for *kweningba*

Kpenigba/kpeningba—other names for *kweningba*

Kpeninga—another word for *kweningba*

Kpingbi—a loose-bar xylophone of Zaire

Kponimbo/kponingbo—other names for *kweningba*

Kpwenigba/kpweningba/kpweningwa—other names for *kweningba*

Kundi—a xylophone of the Congo

Kundu—(1) a xylophone of central Africa with gourd and buzzer resonators; (2) an arc xylophone of the Central African Republic

Kundung—an arc xylophone of Nigeria with gourd or cowhorn resonators, sometimes with buzzers

Kwengwe—another name in the Congo for *kweningba*

Kweningba—a log xylophone of the Congo without resonators

Ligo—a xylophone of the Congo

Lilimba—a xylophone of the Congo

Lingassio (linga sho)—a four-bar xylophone of the Central African Republic

Linz—another name for *kweningba*

Linzi—another name for *kweningba*

Madimba—an African arc marimba with gourd resonators

Madinda—another name for *amadinda*

Madiumba—a xylophone of Angola with gourd resonators

Madjimba—an African arc marimba with gourd resonators

Madudu—another name for *valimba*

Magogodo—a xylophone of Malawi with gourd resonators

Magondo—a xylophone of the Congo

Majimba—another name in the Congo for *madimba*

Makaji—a xylophone of the Congo

Malimba—a xylophone of the Congo with gourd and buzzer resonators

Malume—a xylophone of the Congo

Mambira—another name for *valimba*

Mambirira—a log xylophone of Malawi

Mandja (mandjanga)—(1) a xylophone of Zaire; (2) another word for *manza*

Mangolongondo—a log xylophone of Malawi

Mangwilo—a log xylophone of southeastern Africa

Manja—another word for *manza*

Manjanga—another name for *manja*

Manza—(1) a ten-bar arc xylophone of the Congo with gourd resonators; (2) another word for *itanda*; (3) another word for *gombi*; (4) a log xylophone of Zaire

Marimba—(1) a xylophone of the Congo with gourd resonators dating back to the seventeenth century; (2) another word for *valimba*; (3) a xylophone having resonators and thus distinguished from a xylophone, defined by some musicologists as an instrument having no resonators.

Maza—a xylophone of the Central African Republic

Mbaire—a xylophone of Uganda

Mbasa—a xylophone of the Congo

Mbila—(1) another name for *ambira*; (2) a xylophone of southern and southeastern Africa having gourd and buzzer resonators

Mbila mtondo (mutondo)—a xylophone of southeastern Africa having gourd and buzzer resonators

Mbingwe (mbingwi)—a xylophone of Mozambique

Medzang—a xylophone of the Gabon Republic with a bamboo frame and bamboo resonators

Medzang m'biang—a log xylophone of southern Cameroon and northern Gabon Republic

Menza—another word for *manza*

Menzagwe—another word for *kalangwa*

Menzan—a west African xylophone

Menzi—a xylophone of the Congo

Midimba—another word in the Congo for *madimba*

Miruli—a log xylophone of Uganda

Morka—a xylophone of Ethiopia

Mozungu—another name for *kweningba*

Muhambi—a South African xylophone

Ndara—a xylophone of Uganda on grass bundles pegged to the ground

Ndjimba—a xylophone of Angola

Ngambi (ngami)—another word for *valimba*

Ngedegwu—another word for *ekere-iko* or *igo*

Ngelenge—a log or trough xylophone of Nigeria

Njaga—a xylophone of the Congo

Njung—a log xylophone of Cameroon

Nsatong—a xylophone of Cameroon

Ntara—a xylophone of Uganda on banana stems

Nyia-mendzang—a xylophone of Cameroon

Odome—another word for *ngelenge*

Okobolo—a two-bar xylophone of Nigeria

Omvek—another word for *akuda-omvek*

Padingbwa/pandingbwa—other names for *kweningba*

Paningba/paningwa/paningwe—other names for *kweningba*

Pendibe/pendimbe—other names for *kweningba*

Penimba—another name for *kweningba*

Queniba—another spelling of *kweningba*

Rongo—a xylophone of the Congo

Sanje (sanzhe, sanzhi)—alto xylophone of southeastern Africa

Shijimba—a xylophone of Zambia with gourd and buzzer resonators

Shinji—a xylophone of Nigeria

Silimba—a xylophone of South Africa having gourd resonators

Timbila—a xylophone of Mozambique with gourd and buzzer resonators

Tshilandzana—another name for *chilanzane*

Tsindza—a xylophone of Nigeria

Ulimba—another word for *valimba*

Valihambalo—another name for *atranatra*

Valimba (varimba)—a xylophone of the lower Zambezi area of southeastern Africa having either a shallow trough resonator or gourd and buzzer resonators

Vilangwi—a xylophone of Tanganyika with bars set on banana-tree trunks

Yo—a xylophone of the Congo

Asia and Pacific

Angramut—a log/pit xylophone of New Britain (Melanesia)

Bakakong—a xylophone of Malaysia

Bas jug—a xylophone of Sulawesi, Indonesia

Bastran—a xylophone of Burma

Boboman—a large pit xylophone of the Mentawai Islands, Indonesia

Bong lang—a xylophone of Thailand

Bulog Tangbut—a leg xylophone of Indonesia

Calon—a bamboo xylophone of northern Sulawesi, Indonesia

Calung renteng—a xylophone of West Java

Canang kayu—("wooden gong") a xylophone of Sumatra

Caruk—a trough xylophone of Bali with suspended bars

Celempung kayu—a xylophone of Sumatra

Cungklik—a trough xylophone of Bali

Dan go—a xylophone of Vietnam

Da'uli-da'uli (doli-doli)—a pit-resonator xylophone played by women in Nias, Indonesia

Do'uda—a xylophone of West Flores, Indonesia

Gabbang—a Balinese or Malaysian trough xylophone with bedded bars

Gagambangam—a West Java xylophone

Galundhang—a log xylophone of Indonesia

Gambang—a trough xylophone of Indonesia

Gambangan—another word for *gambang*

Gambang calung—another term for *calung renteng*

Gambang kayu—a Javanese trough xylophone

Garanktum—a xylophone of Sumatra, Indonesia

Garantung—a xylophone of northern Sumatra, Indonesia

Geko—a xylophone of Flores, Indonesia

Gendang gendang—a leg xylophone of Sulawesi, Indonesia

Gitar bas—a xylophone of northern Sulawesi, Indonesia

Grantang—a bamboo xylophone of Bali

Jatung utang—a xylophone of Indonesia

Jug—another word for *yuk*

Kalondang—a xylophone of northern Sumatra, Indonesia

Kashtha tarang—a xylophone of India

Katongoa kayu—a log xylophone of Indonesia

Kaw law—a xylophone of Thailand

Keka tak—a xylophone of Sumatra, Indonesia

Kelintang—a leg xylophone of Sumatra, Indonesia

Kertok kelapa—a one-bar xylophone of Malaysia with a coconut resonator

Kongkai—a xylophone of Timor, Indonesia

Konkon—a xylophone of Malaysia with bars placed on the legs of two performers

Krotong—a xylophone of Borneo with bars placed on the legs of the performer

Lau lau—another name for *tinbuk*

Ledor (letor)—a xylophone on a banana-stem frame of Flores, Indonesia

Lelega—another word for *tudduglag*

Melodi—a high-pitched xylophone of northern Sulawesi, Indonesia

Mokkin—a trough xylophone of Japan used in traditional Kabuki music

Mon vang—a bamboo xylophone of Burma and Thailand

Muqin—a xylophone of China

Pahu kouhau—an obsolete xylophone of the Marquesas Islands

Paku—a bamboo xylophone of Burma

Patatag—a lap xylophone of the north Philippines

Pattala—a trough xylophone of Burma with bamboo bars

Patti taranga—a xylophone of India or Burma

Preson—a xylophone of Flores, Indonesia

Ranat ek—a trough xylophone of Thailand pitched higher than the *ranat thum*

Ranat thum—a trough xylophone of Thailand pitched lower than the *ranat ek*

Rang nat—a trough xylophone of Laos

Renteng—a bamboo xylophone of West Java

Ridu—another word for *preson*

Rindik—a xylophone of Bali

Roneat ek—a trough xylophone of Cambodia with higher-pitched bamboo bars

Roneat thum—a trough xylophone of Cambodia with lower-pitched bamboo bars

Saron jemblung—a trough xylophone of Java

Selo—a one-row xylophone of northern Sulawesi, Indonesia

Seneh'au—a log xylophone of Timor, Indonesia

Tagading—a two-row xylophone of northern Sumatra, Indonesia

Tambaru dano—a pit xylophone of Nias, Indonesia

Tatung—a xylophone of Vietnam with bamboo bars

Tengkelek kayu—a xylophone of Sumatra, Indonesia

Terkwin—a xylophone of northern Sulawesi, Indonesia

Than-pat-tala—another word for *pattala*

Timboik—another name for *tinbuk*

Tinbuk (timbuk, timbul)—a pit and leg xylophone of Melanesia

Tinglik—another word for *rindik*

Tling tlöör—a log xylophone of central Vietnam

Torung—a one-row xylophone of Vietnam

Trompong misi bruk—a xylophone of Bali

Trúk sinh—a xylophone of Vietnam

Trüng—a suspended xylophone of Vietnam

Tudduglag—a xylophone of the Mentawai Islands, Indonesia

Tudu kat—a xylophone of Indonesia with bars on a tree-trunk trough

Tutupele—another name for *tinbuk*

Udong-udong—a xylophone of Kalimantan, Indonesia

Yuk—a low-pitched xylophone of northern Sulawesi, Indonesia

Europe, North America, and Modern Japan

Carrasquiña—an Andalusian (Spain) xylophone

Claquebois—French for xylophone

Clavitympanum—an obsolete word for xylophone

Échelette (eschelletes)—a seventeenth-century one-row French xylophone

Facimbalon—("wooden dulcimer") a xylophone of Hungary

Gigelira—Italian for xylophone

Gigelyra—Italian for xylophone

Ginebras—Spanish for a single-row xylophone

Hölzernes gelächter—obsolete South German and Austrian word for xylophone

Holzharmonika—German for xylophone

Hültze glechter—sixteenth-century German for "wooden clatter" or xylophone

Legnofono—a xylophone made in Rome by Lasina in 1882

Ligneum psalterium—Latin term for xylophone

Madera y paja—Spanish for a xylophone with bars resting on a straw bed

Marimba—(1) a large two-row xylophone with closed-tube metal resonators generally having a range from C to c^4; (2) a twentieth-century word for a two-row xylophone having each bar made from softer outer wood and tuned with a predominant first upper partial (eighth), thus distinguishing it from a modern Euro-American xylophone, which can be defined as an instrument having bars of hard centerwood and tuned with a predominant second-upper-partial (twelfth) tuning; (3) a xylophone having resonators (see p. 360, Marimba [2])

Nabimba (nadimba)—a two-row xylophone with predominant first-upper-partial tuning and with a buzzing membrane mechanically attached to each resonator. It was manufactured by the J.C. Deagan Company of Chicago between 1910 and 1918

Octarimba—a two-row xylophone with predominant first-upper-partial tuning and with its bars arranged as in a piano keyboard but in side-by-side octave pairings, so that when played with a special "Y"-shaped double-beater, the resulting music sounds in both octaves simultaneously. It was manufactured by the J.C. Deagan Company in the first half of the twentieth century

Patouille—obsolete French term for xylophone

Régale de bois—a sixteenth-century French word for xylophone

Rigols—an eighteenth-century English word for *régale de bois*

Sticcato—Italian word for xylophone

Strohfiedel—German word for straw fiddle or xylophone (with bars bedded on straw bundles)

Tastenxylophon—a German keyboard-operated xylophone

Triphon—a type of xylosistron invented by Wiedner of Fraustadt in 1810

Tryphone—a xylophone designed by Charles de Try in France (c. 1870)

Xyleuphone—a xylophone invented by Culmbach and played from a keyboard that activates a bellows to cause beaters to strike the bars

Xylharmonicon—a keyed *xylosistron*

Xylorganum—a seventeenth- and eighteenth-century term for xylophone

Xylorimba—a twentieth-century word for a two-row xylophone having its lower bars tuned with a predominant first upper partial (eighth), and its upper bars tuned with a predominant second-upper-partial (twelfth) tuning

Xylosistron—a friction xylophone invented by Uthe in 1807 to be played by stroking the bars gently with rosin-coated gloves

Central America

Ginebras—Cuban version of a single-row xylophone

Gog—a Central American Indian word for marimba

Gohon—a Central American Indian word for marimba

H'ajom—a Central American Indian word for marimba

Koj—a Central American Indian word for marimba

Kojom—a Central American Indian word for marimba

K'ojom tepunawa—a Central American Indian word for marimba

Marimba—(1) a xylophone with gourd or box resonators probably derived from xylophones brought to Central America by African slaves in the seventeenth to nineteenth century. There may be one row or two rows of bars; (2) a xylophone having resonators and thus distinguished from a xylophone, which is defined by some musicologists as an instrument having no resonators

Marimba con tecomates—a diatonic marimba with gourd resonators

Marimba cuache—the smaller instrument of the *marimba doble*

Marimba de arco—a marimba with no legs, suspended from the performer's body on an arched bough

Marimba doble (marimba cuache)—a chromatic marimba consisting of two separate instruments—one slightly larger than the other. Hormingo and grenadillo rojo woods are used for bars.

Marimba grande—the larger instrument of the *marimba doble*

Marimba piccolo—another name for *marimba cuache*

Marimba requinta—another name for *marimba cuache*

Marimba sencilla—a chromatic single marimba

Marimba tenor—another name for *marimba cuache*

Oh'on—a Central American Indian word for *marimba*

Pianito—another Cuban word for *ginebras*

Zapotecano—Mexican word for marimba

See also "The Marimba in Mexico and Related Areas," p. 239.

Bibliography

Apel, Willi. *Harvard Dictionary of Music.* Cambridge: Harvard University Press, 1967.

Blades, James. *Percussion Instruments and Their History.* New York: Praeger, 1970.

Cahn, William. *The Xylophone in Acoustic Recordings (1877–1929).* Holcomb, N.Y.: W.L. Cahn Publishing, 1979.

Chenoweth, Vida. *The Marimbas of Guatemala.* Louisville: University of Kentucky Press, 1964.

Holland, James. *Percussion.* London: MacDonald and Jane's, 1978.

Marcuse, Sibyl. *Musical Instruments: A Comprehensive Dictionary.* New York: Norton, 1975.

———. *A Survey of Musical Instruments.* New York: Harper & Row, 1975.

May, Elizabeth, ed. *Musics of Many Cultures.* Berkeley: University of California Press, 1980.

Merriam Webster's New Collegiate Dictionary. Springfield, Mass.: Merriam, 1959.

Musical Instruments of the World by the Diagram Group. New York: Facts on File, 1976.

The New Grove Dictionary of Musical Instruments. 3 vols. Edited by Stanley Sadie. London: Macmillan, 1984.

Nketia, J.H. Kwabena. *The Music of Africa.* New York: Norton, 1974.

Peinkofer, Karl, and Fritz Tannigel. *Handbook of Percussion Instruments.* London: Schott, 1976. Originally published in German (Mainz: B. Schott's Söhne, 1969).

Peters, Gordon. *The Drummer: Man, a Treatise on Percussion.* Rev. ed. Wilmette, Ill.: Kemper-Peters, 1975.

Schneider, Walter C. "Percussion Instruments of the Middle Ages." *The Percussionist* 15, no. 3 (1978): 106–117.

Westrup, J.A., and F.L. Harrison. *The New College Encyclopedia of Music.* New York: Norton, 1960.

William L. Cahn

Appendix A
Selections from Morris Arnold Lang and Larry Spivack, The Dictionary of Percussion Terms

Symbols

+ . . . on Russian cymbal parts; struck with a stick

o . . . on Russian cymbal parts; crash cymbals

+ . . . on some foreign study material; indicates left hand

o . . . on some foreign study material; indicates right hand

• . . . on some foreign study material; indicates left hand

⊕ . . . on cymbal or gong part; stop vibration on sign

* . . . on cymbal or gong part; stop vibration on sign

*Range of the Mallet Instruments**

The exact range of the mallet instruments has not been standardized, although authorities do agree upon the "sounding" qualities of these instruments. [The ranges that follow are written ranges; they sound as written unless otherwise indicated.]

Marimba

The South American marimba is a very large instrument, sometimes extending to seven octaves. The top octaves often have a "buzz" effect built into the resonators to help distinguish the melodic line. Three or more players perform together on the same instrument.

In the United States, instruments of five and six octaves have been built commercially, but a four-octave (c–c^4) range has become accepted as standard in the last years. As of this writing, both the Musser division of Ludwig Industries and J.C. Deagan, Inc., manufacture both a four-octave (c–c^4) and a four-and-a-third-octave (A–c^4) instrument.

A marimba is not merely a lower xylophone or a xylophone with resonators. Although the ranges of the two instruments overlap, the upper register of the marimba is very different in quality from that of the same notes on the xylophone, even if both instruments are struck with the same mallets and both are resonated. The difference in timbre is caused by the fact that the marimba bar is tuned with an octave above the fundamental predominant (frequency ratio of 4:1), while the xylophone bar has a fifth above the fundamental (frequency ratio of 3:1) predominant.

Sounds as Written

Xylophone

In present usage, the xylophone is considered a three-and-a-half-octave (f–c^4) resonated instrument. Some years ago, Deagan manufactured a four-octave (c–c^4) instrument known as the "Grand Xylophone." The Leedy Drum Company sold a five-octave product called a "Marimba-Xylophone" and a four-octave xylophone.

In Europe, not only is the range in question, but there does not seem to be agreement on whether the xylophone should have resonators. The xylophone pictured in a recent German book is an old Deagan instrument.[1] While it is resonated, the bars are narrow and the range is only three octaves (c^1–c^4). A work published as recently as 1969 illustrates a boxed, table-model instrument of three octaves, but without resonators. Stravinsky, in his European period, wrote for a three-octave (c^1–c^4) instrument that, in the author's opinion, was an unresonated instrument; i.e., the xylophone part to *Les Noces*. (When Jean Morel, Stravinsky's percussionist in Paris in the 1920 and 1930s, conducted the Juilliard Orchestra, he requested that the resonators be removed from the xylophone.) Notes above the top C (c^4) must have been available at one time because Bartók wrote for a high D flat (d^4) in the Sonata for Two Pianos and Two Percussion.

There is a great deal of confusion in the use of the terms "xylophone," "xylomarimba," "xylorimba," and "marimba" in the music of Boulez, Messiaen, Stockhausen, etc. In discussing this problem with Pierre Boulez, who was the music director of the New York Philharmonic from 1971 to 1977, he indicated the following: The "xylophone" is an unresonated (c–c^4) instrument, while the "xylorimba" or "xylomarimba" is a resonated instrument of three-and-a-half octaves (f–c^4) or, in some works, four octaves (c–c⁴). The "marimba" is a four-octave resonated instrument.

Sounds One Octave Higher Than Written

Royal Percussion (Studio 49), a German manufacturing firm, shows a "marimbaphone" and a "xylomarimba" in its catalogue. The "marimbaphone" (marimba) is four octaves (c–c⁴), while the "xylomarimba" has an extra octave added to the top register. It is the "same design (construction, bar dimensions, etc.) as the marimba."

Vibraphone (Vibraharp)

The vibraphone is the most recent addition to the mallet family, and the range seems to be rather stable. A three-octave (f–f³) instrument is considered standard, although J.C. Deagan, Inc., is now producing a three-and-a-half-octave (c–f³) instrument. A vibraphone extending below the low F must have been produced in Europe, since a number of composers have written for an extended range, among them Alban Berg in the opera *Lulu*.

Sounds As Written

Orchestra Bells

Here again, the range has not been standardized. Both J.C. Deagan, Inc., and Musser division of Ludwig Industries produce an instrument of two and a half octaves (g–c³). Some years ago, the Leedy Drum Company sold a three-octave (c–c³) set and Deagan produced a full two-and-a-half-octave (f–c³) instrument. Royal Percussion produces an instrument of two-and-a-half octaves (g–c³), while the Lang Percussion Company is producing both an instrument with a full two-and-a-half-octave (f–c³) range and a three-octave (c–c³) instrument. Both the larger Royal Percussion and the Lang Percussion instruments have a foot-activated damper pedal.

It is unfortunate that much of the standard symphonic repertoire cannot be played on the two-and-a-half-octave (g–c³) orchestra bells now being made by the major manufacturers; i.e., Strauss's *Also sprach Zarathustra* and Stravinsky's *Petrouchka*.

Sounds Two Octaves Higher Than Written

Note

* Brackets indicate editorial additions. Octave ranges have been adjusted to agree with system used in this book.

1. Karl Peinkofer and Fritz Tannigel, *Handbook of Percussion Instruments* (London: Schott, 1976; originally published in German [Mainz: B. Schott's Söhne, 1969]), p. 45.

Appendix B
Table of Percussion Instruments and Terms in English, French, German, and Italian

Table of Percussion Instruments

English	French	German	Italian
African wood drum	le tambour de bois (africain)	die Schlitztrommel	il tamburo di legno africano
alarm bell	le tocsin	die Alarmglocke	la campana d'allarme
American Indian tom-tom (drum)	le tambour indien (américain)	die indianische Trommel	il tamburo indiano (d'America)
antique cymbals	les cymbales antiques	die antiken Becken	i cimbali antichi
anvil	l'enclume	der Amboss der Metallblock	l'incudine
Arabian drum	le tambour arabe	die arabische Trommel	il tamburo arabo
auto brake drums	les auto-brake-drums	die Auto-Brake-Drums	gli auto-brake-drums
auto horn (motor horn, taxi horn)	le klaxon la trompe d'auto	die Autohupe	il clacson
bamboo scraper (sapo cubana)	le sapo cubana	die Bambusraspel das Sapo cubana	il sapo cubana
bass drum (big drum)	la grosse caisse	die grosse Trommel	la gran cassa la catuba
bass xylophone	le xylophone basse	das Bassxylophon	il silofono basso lo xilofono basso
bell plate	la cloche en lame de métal	die Plattenglocke	la campana in lastra di metallo
bell tree	le châpeau chinois	der Schellenbaum	l'albero di sonagli la barra di sospensione con i sonagli
bells	les cloches	die Glocken	le campane
bird pipe bird whistle	le sifflet d'oiseau	die Vogelpfeife	gli uccelli
bladder and strings	basse de flandres	der Bumbass	il bumbass
board clappers	la cliquette	die (americanische) Brettchenklapper die Beinklapper	la tabella
bones	la tablette	die Bones	la taletta
bongos	les bongos	die Bongos die Bongo-Trommeln	i bonghi i bongos
boobams	les boo-bams	die Boo-Bams (amerik.)	i boo-bams
Brazilian bamboo shaker	le bambou brésilien	das Tubo	il bambù brasiliano
cannon	le canon	die Kanone	il cannone
castanets	les castagnettes	die Kastagnetten	le castagnette le nacchere
castanets—metal	les castagnettes de fer	die Metallkastagnetten die Gabelbecken	le castagnette di ferro
celesta	la celesta	die Celesta	la celesta
chain	la chaîne	die Kettenrassel	la catena
(bell) chimes	le carillon	das Turmglockenspiel	il gariglione il cariglione la soneria di campane
Chinese block	le bloc de (en) bois	der Holzblock	il blocco di legno la cassettina di legno
Chinese tom-tom	le tom-tom (chinois)	das chinesische Tom-Tom	il tom tom (cinese)

English	French	German	Italian
coconut shells	les coquilles noix	die Kokosnußschalen de coco	le noce di cocco
conga (drum)	la conga	die Conga-Trommel	la conga
cowbell	le bloc de metal	die Almglocke	il campanaccio di metallo
cowbells	le bruit de sonnailles des troupeaux	die Herdenglocken das Geläute	lo scampanellio da gregge le campane da pastore
crotales	les crotales	die Krotalen die Zimbeln	i crotali
Cuban sticks	les claves	die Gegenschlagstäbe	i legnetti
Cuban tom-toms	les bongos	die Bongos	i bonghi
cuckoo call	le coucou	der Kuckucksruf	il cuculo
cymbal—Chinese	la cymbale chinoise	das chinesische Becken	il piatto cinese
cymbals—pair (crash cymbals)	les cymbales (à 2)	die Becken (paarweise)	i cinelli i piatti (a due)
cymbal—suspended	la cymbale (suspendue)	das Becken (freihängend, auf Ständer)	il piatto (sospeso)
dinner bell	la sonnette de table	die Tischglocke	il sonaglio
field drum	la caisse roulante (avec cordes)	die Ruhrtrommel (hoch)	il tamburo rullante con corde
finger cymbals	les crotales	die Fingerbecken die Fingerzimbeln die Krotalen	i crotali i cimbalini
flexatone	le flexatone	das Flexaton	il flessatono
fog horn	la trompa de brume	das Nebelhorn	la sirena bassa
foot cymbal—*see* hi-hat			
frame drum	le tambour sur cadre	die Rahmentrommel	il tamburino senza cimbali
friction drum	le tambour à friction	der Brummtopf	il buttibu la caccavella
glass chimes	les baguettes de verre suspendues	die hängenden Glasstäbe	le bacchette di vetro sospese
glass harmonica	l'harmonica de verre	die Glasharmonika	l'armonica di vetro
glockenspiel	le glockenspiel le jeu de timbres	das Glockenspiel das Stabglockenspiel	i campanelli
gong	le gong	der Gong	il gong
gong drum	la grosse caisse à une seule peau	die einfellige grosse Trommel	la grancassa a una pelle
gourd	le guiro le guitcharo	der Guiro die Kurbisraspel	il guiro
gourd rattle	la cabaza	die Cabaza die Kurbisraspel	la cabasa
Greek cymbals	les cymbales antiques les crotales	die Zimbeln die Krotalen	i cimbali antichi i crotali
hammer	le marteau	der Hammer	il martello
hand bells	les clochettes à mains	das Handglockenspiel	i sonagli a mano
harness bells	les grelots	die Rollschellen	la sonagliera i sonagli
hi-hat (foot cymbal) (high-hat)	la hi-hat les cymbals à pédale	die Charleston Beckenmaschine die Becken mit Fussmaschine die Fußbecken das Hi-hat	il hi-hat i piatti a pedale
horsehooves	les pas de cheval	das Hufgetrappel	
jawbone of an ass	la quijada	die Quijada die Schlagrassel	la quijada la mascella d'asino

English	French	German	Italian
kettledrums	les timbales	die Pauken	i timpani
keyboard glockenspiel	les jeux de timbres à clavier	das Klaviaturglockenspiel	i campanelli a tastiera
	le glockenspiel à clavier		
keyboard xylophone	le xylophone à clavier	das Klaviaturxylophon	lo xilofono a tastiera
			il silofono a tastiera
Korean block	le bloc chinois	der Tempelblock	il blocco di legno coreano
lion's roar	le tambour à corde	die Reibtrommel	il rugghio di leone
lithophone	le lithophone	das Lithophon	il litofono
little bells	le jeu de timbres	das Glöckchenspiel	il sistro
		Vorlaufer der Lyra	
log drum	le log-drum	die Log-drum	il log-drum
long drum	le grand tambour	die Rührtrommel (tief)	il tamburo basso
		die Landsknechtstrommel	il gran tamburo vecchio
			la cassa rullante
lujon (loo-jon)	le loo-jon	das Loo-Jon	il loo-jon
maracas	les maracas	die Maracas	i maracas
		die Rumbakugeln	l'arenaiuolo
marimba	le marimbaphone	das Marimbaphon	la marimba
marimbaphone			il marimbafono
metal disk	la plaque de métal	die Metallplatte	la lastra di metallo
metal foil	le bruit de tôle	die Metallfolie	il foglio di metallo
metallophone	le metallophone	das Metallophon	il metallofono
metal rasp (scraper)	la râpe de métal	die Metallraspel	la raspa di metallo
metal rattle	le maraca de métal	die Metallgefässrassel	il maraca di metallo
military drum (snare drum)	le tambour militaire	die Militärtrommel	il tamburo militare
motor horn—*see* auto horn			
musical glasses	les coupes de verre	das Gläserspiel	i bicchieri di vetro
musical saw	la scie musicale	die (singende) Säge	la sega cantante
		die Spielsäge	
musical tumblers	les verres choqués	die Glasharfe	
nightingale	le sifflet imité du rossignol	der Nachtigallenschlag	i'usignuolo
pandereta brasileño	la pandéréta brésilienne	die Stabpandereta	il pandereta brasiliano
parade drum	le tambour d'empire	die Paradetrommel	il tamburo di basilea
		die Basler Trommel	
pasteboard rattle	le bourdon	der Waldteufel	il diavolo di bosco
	le diable des bois		il tamburo di frizione
	le tambour à friction		
pea whistle	le sifflet à roulette	die Trillerpfeife	il fischietto a pallina
pistol shot	le coup de pistolet	der Pistolenschuss	la pistolettata
plate bell—*see* bell plate			
police siren	la sirène	die Sirene	la sirena
pop bottles	le bouteillophone	das Bouteillophon	il suono di bottiglia
		das Flaschenspiel	
pop gun	le coup de bouchon	der Flaschenkorkenknall	stappare la bottiglia
rain machine	le prisme de pluie	das Regenprisma	l'effetto di pioggia
		die Regenmaschine	
ratchet	la crécelle	die Ratsche	la raganella
rattle	la claquette	die Knarre	il sonaglio
		die Schnarre	
revolver	le revolver	der Revolver	la rivoltella
sake barrel	le baril de sake	das Sakefaß	il barile di sake
Sanctus bells	les clochettes pour la messe	die Messklingeln	le campanelle da messa
sand blocks	le papier de verre	die Sandblöcke	la carta sabbiata

English	French	German	Italian
sandbox	le sablier	die Sandrassel	l'arenaiuolo
sandpaper	le papier de verre	das Sandpapier	la carta vetrata
scraper (scratcher)	la râpe de bois	die Holzraspel	il reco reco
shaker	le tubo	das Tubo	il tubo
ship's bell	le tocsin	die Schiffsglocke	il campanello d'allarme
side drum—*see* military drum			
signal whistle	le sifflet signal	die Signalpfeife	il fischio
siren whistle	le sifflet sirène	die Sirenenpfeife	il fischio sirena
sistrum	le sistre	das Sistrum	il sistro
slapstick (whip)	le fouet	die Peitsche	la frusta
		der Peitschenknall	
		die Klapper	
		die Klappholz	
sleigh bells	les grelots	die Rollschellen	le sonaglieri
		die Schellen	i sonagli
slit drum	le tambour de bois (africain)	die Schlitztrommel	il tamburo di legno africano
small bell	la clochette	das Schallenglöckchen	il sonaglio
small drum	la petit tambour	die kleine Trommel	il tamburo piccolo
snare drum			il tamburo alto
			il tamburo chiaro
			il tamburino
song whistle—*see* slide whistle			
spurs	les éperons	die Sporen	gli speroni
			gli sproni
steeple bell	la grande cloche	die tiefe Glocke	la campana grave
stone disks	le lithophone	das Steinspiel	la lastra di sasso
string drum	le tambour à corde	die Reibtrommel	il rugghio di leone
strings of the piano (struck)	les cordes du piano (frappées)	die Klaviersaiten (geschlagen)	le corde di pianoforte (percosse, battute)
surf effect	le prisme de pluie	das Regenprisma	l'effetto di pioggia
		die Regenmaschine	
slide whistle swanee piccolo swanee whistle	la flûte à coulisse la jazzo-flûte le sifflet à coulisse	die Lotosflöte die Stempelflöte die Ziehpfeife	il flauto a culisse
switch (twig brush)	la verge	die Rute	la verga
tabor-drum of Provence (tambourin provençal)	le tambourin provençal	die provenzalische Trommel	il tamburo provenzale
tambourine	le tambour de basque	die Schellentrommel	il tamburello basco
			il tamburino
			il tamburo basco
tambourine without jingles	le tambour sur cadre	das Tamburin ohne Schellen	il tamburino senza cimbali
tam-tam	le tam-tam	das Tam-Tam	il tam-tam
tarole drum	la tarole	die Tarole-Trommel	il tamburo tarole
		die Tarole	
taxi horn—*see* auto horn			
temple block	le temple-bloc	der Tempelblock	la campana di legno
temple cup bell	dobač i	die Tempelglocke	dobač i
tenor drum	la caisse roulante le tambour roulant	die Wirbeltrommel die Rolltrommel	il tamburo rullante senza corde
		die Tenortrommel	
		die Rührtrommel ohne Saiten	

English	French	German	Italian
thunder sheet	la tôle pour imiter le tonnerre	das Donnerblech	la lastra del tuono i tuoni
timbales	les timbales cubaines	die Timbales	i timbales latino-americani i timpanetti
timpani	les timbales	die Pauken	i timpani
tin horn tin rattle	le maraca de métal	die Metallgefässrassel	il maraca di metallo
tom-tom	le tom-tom	das Tom-Tom	il tom tom
tone block—*see* woodblock			
toy trumpet	le corne d'appel	das Rufhorn	il grido di corno
triangle	le triangle	der Triangel	il triangolo
Trinidad steel drum	le tambour d'acier	die Trinidad-Gongtrommel die Stahltrommel die Blechtrommel die Calypsotrommel	il tamburo d'acciaio
trough xylophone	le xylophone à cassette-résonance	das Trogxylophon das Resonanzkastenxylophon	lo xilofono in cassetta di risonanza
tubaphone	le tubaphone	das Tubaphon das Tubuscampanophon	il tubofono
tubular bells tubular chimes	les tubes de cloches	die Röhrenglocke das Rohrenglockenspiel	le campane tubolari
tumbadora	la tumba	die Tumba	la tumba
Turkish crescent	le châpeau chinois	der Schellenbaum	l'albero di sonagli la barra di sospensione con i sonagli
twig brush—*see* switch			
typewriter	la machine à écrire	die Schreibmaschine	la macchina da scrivere
vibraharp vibraphone	le vibraphone	das Vibraphon	il vibrafono
wasamba rattle	la wasamba	die Wasamba-Rassel	la wasamba
washboard	la râpe de métal	das Waschbrett	la tavola da lavare
whip—*see* slapstick			
wind chimes (glass)	les baguettes de verre suspendues	die hängenden Glasstäbe	le bacchette di vetro sospeso
wind chimes (wood)	le bambou suspendu	die hängenden Bambusrohre	il bambu sospeso
wind machine	la machine à vent l'eoliphone l'aeoline	die Windmaschine die Windschleuder das Aelophon	la macchina dal vento
woodblock	le bloc en bois	der Holzblock	la cassettina di legno
woodblock (cylindrical)	le bloc de bois cylindrique	die Röhrenholztrommel	la cassa di legno
wood drum	le bloc de bois	die Holztrommel	il blocco di legno
wooden barrel	le baril de bois	das Holzfass	il barile di legno
wooden board	la table de bois	das Schlagbrett	la tavola di legno
wood-plate drum	le tambour en peau de bois	die Holzplattentrommel	il tamburo di legno pelle
xylomarimba xylorimba	la xylomarimba la xylorimba	die Xylomarimba	la xilomarimba la silomarimba
xylophone	le xylophone	das Xylophon	lo xilofono

Amy White

Table of Percussion Terms

English	French	German	Italian
attached	fixé	befestigt	fissato
at the center	au centre	auf der Mitte	al centro
		in der Mitte	
at the middle	à demi	halb zur Mitte	alla meta
at the rim	près du rebord	am Rande der Membrane	al margine
	au bord de la membrane	am Rande des Felles	
barely touching	à peine frôlé	leicht, berühren	appena toccata
bass drum beater	mailloche	Schlägel für grosse Trommel	bacchetta di gran cassa
	mailloche de grosse caisse	grosse Trommelstock	mazza della gran cassa
		grosse Trommelschlägel	
batter head	peau de batterie	Schlagfell	pelle battente
brush	brosse	Besen	verghe
(to) brush	frotter	Rute reiben	fregare
	frôler		
cane (out of)	en canne	aus Rohr	di canna
	en jonc		
cane handle	manche en jonc	Rohrstiel	fusto in giunco
cane stick	baguette en canne, en jonc	Rohrschlägel, Rohrstäbchen	bacchetta di canna
choke	étouffé	dämpfen	secco
cotton	de coton	Baumwolle	di cotone
cotton sticks	baguettes de coton	Baumwollschlägel	bacchette di cotone
covered	couvert	bedeckt	coperto
cymbal sticks	baguette de cymbale	Beckenschlägel	bacchette di piatto
damp	étouffé	abdämpfen	spegnere
	étouffez		smorzate
deep	grave	tief	basso
dome, cup, head	tête	Kuppel	campana
drumsticks	baguettes de tambour	Trommelstocken	bachette di tamburo
	mailloches	Klöpper	mazza
	tampons	Schlägel	
felt (out of)	en feutre	aus Filz	di feltro
felt sticks	baguettes en feutre	Filzschlägel	bacchette di feltro
felt timpani sticks	baguettes de timbale en feutre	Filz-Paukenschlägel	bacchette di timpani a feltro
finger roll	roulé avec les doigts	Wirbel mit den Fingern	rullo con il dita
fist (with the)	le poing	mit der Faust	col pugno
great (large)	grande	gross	grande
half-hard	demi-dur	halbharte	mezzoduro
handle	manche	Stiel-Handgriff	manico
hard	dur	hart	duro
hard felt sticks	baguettes en feutre dur	Schlägel mit hartem Filz	bacchette di feltro duro
hard felt timpani mallets	baguettes de timbale tête en feutre dur	Paukenschlägel mit Hartfiltzkopfen	bacchette di timpani con palladine di feltro duro
hard leather sticks	baguettes de cuir dur	Hartlederschlägel	bacchette di ferro
hard sticks	baguettes dures	schwere Schlägel	bachette duro

English	French	German	Italian
head (of a stick)	tête	Schlegelkopf	pallina
head, skin (of a drum)	peau, membrane	Fell	pelle, membrana
heavy	lourd	schwer	pesante
heavy mallet (wood hammer)	marteau	Holzhammer	maglio mazzetta
high	clair	hoch	alto
	aigu		acuto
hissing	sifflement	zischend	cigolio
hoop	cercle	Reifen	cerchio
internal tone control	sourdine interne	Obertonkontrolle	sordino interno
iron	en fer	Eisen	di ferro
iron sticks	baguettes en fer	Eisenschlägel	bacchette di ferro
	morceaux de fil en fer		
kapok	capoc	Kapok	capoc
knife blade	lame d'un canif	Messerklinge	lama di coltello
laid on its side	placé à plat	auf der Seite gedreht	sul lato
leather	en cuir	Leder	di pelle
leather sticks	baguettes en cuir	Lederschlägel	bacchette di pelle
let vibrate gently by barely touching	laissez vibrer doucement en effleurant à peine les deux plateaux	vibrieren lassen durch leicht berühren	lasciare vibrares leggieramente appena toccata
light	légère	leicht	leggiero
light sticks	baguettes légères	leichte Schlägel	bacchette leggiere
long	long	lang	lungo
loosen snares	avec les cordes lâches	ohne Schnarrseiten	lasciare le corde del tamburo
mallets, sticks, beaters	baguettes	Schlegel	bacchette
medium	moyenne	mittel	medio
medium hard	assez dure	ziemlich hart	medio duro
medium hard sticks	baguettes assez dures	ziemlich schwere Schlägel	bacchette medie-dure
medium soft	assez molle	ziemlich weich	medio molle
medium soft sticks	baguettes assez molles	ziemlich weiche Schlegel	bachette medie molle
metal sticks	baguettes en de metal	Metallschlägel	bacchette di metallo (battute metale)
mute	sourdine	Dämpfer	sordino
	sons voilés		
not tuned	mal accordé	verstimmt	scordate
on the dome	sur la tête	auf der Kuppel	alla campana
on the hoop	au rebord	auf dem Reifen	al cerchio
on the skin with thin sticks	sur la peau avec des baguettes minces	auf das Fell mit dünnen Ruten	sulla membrana con bacchette sottile
on the snares	sur les timbres	auf den Saiten	sulle corde
ordinary beaters	baguettes normales	gewöhnliche Klöpper Schlägel	bacchette ordinarie
	baguettes ordinaires		
padded	ouateuse	wattiert	a bambagia
padded sticks	baguettes ouateuses	Wattierterschlägel	bacchette a bambagia
pedal glissando	glissando avec le lever	Glissando mit Pedal	glissando colla pedale
percussion	percussion	Schlagzeug	percussione
	batterie		batteria
pitch	hauteur	Tonhöhe	altezza
played on the shell (of the drum) with handle of the stick	joué sur le cadre du tambour avec le manche de la mailloche	mit einem Holzstäbchen auf dem Holzrand der Trommel geschlagen	esecutato sulla cassa del tamburo col manico della mazza
plush sticks	baguettes de peluche	Plüschschlägel	bacchette felpate

English	French	German	Italian
quarter-hard	quart-dur	viertelhart	quarta-duro
rasped	râpé	gekratzt	raspato
rattan	en rotin	aus Rohr	di canna
rattan sticks	baguettes en rotin	Rohrschlägel	bacchette di canna
rawhide sticks	baguettes en peau (cuir brut)	Naturleder Schlägel	bacchette di pelle cruda
rawhide timpani sticks	baguettes de timbale en peau	Naturleder Paukenschlägel	bacchette di timpani a pella cruda
real pitch	son réel	wirklicher Klang	suono reale
resonators	resonateurs	Resonatoren	risonatori
roll	roulement	Wirbel	rullo
roll on one side with soft sticks	rouler sur un seul coté avec des baguettes molles	mit weichen Schlägel auf einer Seite rollen	rullo sopra uno lato colle bacchette molle
roll on suspended cymbal with sticks	roulement sur une cymbale avec des baguettes	Wirbel auf den Beckenteller mit Schlägel	rullo sopra uno piatto sospeso con bacchette
rubber (covered) sticks	baguettes en caoutchouc	Gummischlägel	bacchette di gomma-elastica
rubber (made of)	en gomme	aus Gummi	di gomma
shake	agiter	schütteln	agitare
	secouer		sbattere
			scoutere
sharp, penetrating	rude	scharf	acuto
shell	fût	Marge	fusto
short	brèf	kurz	breve
			corto
short (small) sticks	petite baguettes	Kleiner Schlägel	piccole bacchette
	petite mailloches		piccole mazzette
single-headed tom-toms	toms à une peau	die Einfell Tom-Toms	tom-tom a una pelle
skin	la peau	das Fell	membrana
small	petite	klein	piccolo
small wood stick	petite baguette en bois	kleiner Holzschlägel	piccola bacchetta di legno
snare drumsticks	baguettes de caisse claire	kleine Trommel-Stocken	bacchette di tambur militare
snare head	peau de timbre	Saitenfell	pelle cordiera
snares	timbres	Schnarrsaiten	corde
snares off	sans timbres	ohne Schnarrsaiten	senza corde
snares on	sur les timbres	mit Schnarrsaiten	con corde
soft	doux, mou, molle	weich	morbido
			soffice
			molle
soft felt sticks	baguettes en feutre	Weichenfilz Schlegel	bacchette di feltro
soft felt timpani sticks	baguettes de timbales en feutre douce	Weichenfilz Paukenschlägel	bacchette di timpani molle a feltro
soft sticks	baguettes douces	weiche Schlägel	bacchette molle
soft timpani sticks	baguettes de timbales douces	Weiche Paukenschlägel	bacchette di timpani molle
sponge	en éponge	aus Schwamm	di spugna
sponge-headed sticks	baguettes d'éponge	Schwammschlägel	bacchette di spugna
	baguettes en éponge		
sponge timpani sticks	baguettes de timbales en éponge	Schwamm-Paukenschlägel	bacchette di timpani a spugna
steel	d'acier	Stahl	d'acciaio
steel sticks	baguettes d'acier	Stahlschlägel	bacchette d'acciaio
stick on cymbal	baguette (mailloche) sur cymbale	Schlägel auf den Becken	piatto colla mazza

English	French	German	Italian
sticks	baguettes	Schlägel	bacchette
	mailloches		
sticks with fiber heads (knobs)	baguettes en capoc	Schlägel mit dem Kopf aus Kapok	bacchette di capoc
strike normally	frapper à la manière ordinaire	gewöhnlich schlagen	colpete al ordinario
strokes	coups	Schläge	colpi
suspended	suspendue	aufgehängt	sospeso
suspended cymbal with stick	cymbale libre avec baguette	Becken frei mit Schlägel	piatti sospeso con bacchetta
swishing	cinglant	peitschend	strosciando
switch (rod)	verge	Rute	verga, verghe
take the other cymbal	prenez l'autre cymbale	anderes Becken nehmen	prendete l'altro piatto
tension	tirant	Spannvorrichtung	tirragio
thick	épais, épaisse	dick	spesso
thick sticks	baguettes épaisses	dicke Schlägel	bacchette grosse
thick timpani sticks	baguettes de timbales épaisses	dicke Paukenschlägel	bacchette di timpani grosse
thin metal sticks	bâtons minces d'acier	Dünne Metallschlägel	piccole bacchette di metallo
thin sticks	baguettes minces	dünne Ruten	bacchette sottile
thin wood sticks	baguettes minces en bois	kleine Holzschlägel	piccole bacchette di legno
timpani sticks	baguettes de timbales	Paukenschlägel	bacchette di timpani
			battute di timpani
triangle beater	baguette de triangle	Triangelstab	battente per il triangolo
	tringle du triangle	Triangelschlägel	bacchetta di triangolo
		Metallstäbchen	ferro del triangolo
trill with coins	triller avec des pièces de monnaie	mit Münzen trillern	trillare colle monete
tuned	accordé	gestimmt	accordato
turn	tourn	kreisformige Bewegung	giro
two-headed stick (double stick)	mailloche double	zweiköpfige Schlägel	bacchetta a due capi
two players	deux éxécutants	zwei Spieler	due esecutori
very hard	très dur	sehr schwer	molto duro
very hard sticks	baguettes très dures	sehr schwere Schlägel	bacchette molto dure
very hard timpani sticks	baguettes de timbales très dures	sehr schwere Schlägel	bacchette di timpani molto dure
very soft	très doux	sehr weich	molto morbido
			molle
very soft timpani sticks	baguettes de timbales très douces	sehr weiche Paukenschlägel	bacchette di timpani molto molle
vibraphone mallets	baguettes de vibraphone	Virbaphonschlägel	battenti di vibrafono
vibrate, to ring	laissez vibrer	klingen lassen	lasciare vibrare
well-tuned	bien accordé	gut gestimmt	ben accordato
(wire) brush	balai métallique	Drahtbürste	scovolo di fil di ferro
	brosse en fil de métal	Jazzbesen	con le spazzole
without jingles	sans tintements	ohne Schellen	senza tintinnie
with the fingernails	avec les ongles	mit den Nagel	colle unghie
with the fingers	avec les doigts	mit den Fingern	con le diti
with the hands	avec les mains	mit den Händen	con le mani
with the knuckles	avec les jointures	mit den Knocheln	colle nocce
with the two sticks on cymbal	avec deux baguettes sur une cymbale	mit zwei Schlägel auf Becken	con due bacchette a piatto
wooden	de bois	aus Holz	di legno
wood(en) sticks	baguettes de (en) bois	Holzschlägel	bacchette di legno

English	French	German	Italian
wood(en) timpani sticks	baguettes de timbales en bois	holze Paukenschlägel	bacchette di timpani a legno
wool	en laine	Wolle	di lana
wool-headed sticks	baguettes en laine	Wollschlägel	bacchette di lana
xylophone sticks	baguettes de xylophone	Xylophonschlägel	bacchette di xilofono

Amy White

Appendix C
Published Writings on Methods for Percussion

Published Writings on Methods for Percussion

The art of drumming and percussion was for many years passed down as an oral tradition, the music for the most part being transferred by rote learning from one generation to the next. As musical notation and printing techniques advanced, the idea of disseminating the musical arts and techniques of playing various instruments through printed means resulted in method books for various disciplines.

The history and evolution of drumming can be traced and partially documented through these printed materials. Therefore, any research in the areas of performance practice, techniques, instrument construction, musical literature, and persons would be incomplete without a careful examination of these materials.

The following list, although far from complete, is intended to offer guidance to anyone attempting to research percussion in its correct historical perspective. It includes printed materials consisting mostly of complete books published before 1960 and currently out of print or not readily available. It also contains works that, while still in print, are historically significant due either to the time period in which they were printed or to the importance of the subject matter contained within them. Collections of solo literature are also included in the lists as an aid to understanding the historical evolution of percussion music.

Some out-of-print books are readily available through the efforts of publishers interested in historical reprints. Others are available in major university libraries and private collections. Entries are organized chronologically by author, title, city of publication, and publisher, when known. A few annotations are included where deemed useful to the historical importance or to aid in the location of a book. The date for each entry has been determined by the copyright date (when known), the inclusion of books in publishers' directory catalogs (approximate date within five years), the listing of a book with date of publication in either a publisher's catalog or other reference book, or the advertisement for first-time sale by the author in periodicals. Where no date is known, a work is entered at the end of each category alphabetically by author.

The books are organized into the following categories:

I. Articles, documents, or encyclopedia entries that discuss some performance, construction, or historical aspect of percussion.

II. Method books relating to timpani.

III. Drum tutors related to marching or military styles.

IV. Schools or methods for snare or side drum, total percussion, drum set, or other popular performance idiom.

V. Schools or methods for mallet or keyboard instruments (bells, chimes, marimba, vibraphone/vibraharp, and/or xylophone).

I. Articles, Documents, or Encyclopedia Entries

1588 Arbeau, Thoinot. *Orchésographie.* Langres, France. Reprint, Paris: Fonta, Viewig, 1888. English translations by C.W. Beaumont, London, 1925, and Mary Stewart Evans, Kamin, New York, 1948.

1621 Pistofilo. *Il Torneo.* Italy.

1623 Emperor Ferdinand II. *Privilege to the Imperial Trumpeters' and*

Kettledrummers' Guild. 12 articles. Saxony. (Confirmed anew in 1630.)

1643 *Warlike Directions or the Soldier's Practice.* 2nd ed. London: Harper.

1653 Emperor Friedrich III. *Privilege to the Imperial Trumpeters' and Kettledrummers' Guild.* 23 articles. Saxony. Translated, with commentary, in Don Smithers, "The Hapsburg Imperial Trompeter and Heerpaucker Privileges of 1653." *Galpin Society Journal* 24 (1971): 84–85.

1684 Mallet, A.M. *Les Travaux de Mars.* Vol. 3. Paris: Thierry.

1687 Speer, Daniel. *Grundrichtiger Unterricht der musikalischen Kunst.* Ulm.

1688? Holme, Randle, III. *Academy of Armoury.* British Museum manuscript, Harl. 2034, folios 75 and 76.

1711 August the Strong. *Mandat wider das unbefügte Trompeten-Blasen* ("Mandate against the Unauthorized Playing of Trumpets and Beating of Military Kettledrums"). Dresden. Reprinted with English introduction by Edward H. Tarr. Tallahassee, Fla.: International Trumpet Guild, 1991. Other mandates were issued in 1650, 1661, 1736, and 1804.

1747 Emperor Franz I. *Privilege to the Imperial Trumpeters' and Kettledrummers' Guild.* 12 articles. Saxony.

1750? *Drum Beatings.* Document from the library of Sir Samuel Hellier.

1759 Walpole, Horace (Earl of Oxford). *Catalogue of Royal and Noble Authors.* 2nd ed. London.

1762 Eisel, J.P. *Musicus autodidaktos.* Erfurt.

1767 Emperor Josef II. *Privilege to the Imperial Trumpeters' and Kettledrummers' Guild.* Saxony.

1775 Pier, Marguarite. *Points of War.*

1779 *French Camp Music.*

1779 Steuben, Baron Friedrich von. *Regulations for the Order and Discipline of the Troops of the United States.* Philadelphia.

1812 Villoteau, G.A. *De l'état actual de l'art en Egypte.* Paris.

1829 Fröhlich, Joseph. *Systematischer Unterricht in den vorzüglichsten Orchester-Instrumenten. . . .* 2 vols. *Paukenschule*, p. 408. Würzburg.

1835 Schilling, G. "Pauke." In *Encyklopädie der gesammten musikalischen Wissenschaften.* Stuttgart: F.H. Köhler.

1836 Cooper, Samuel. *A Concise System of Instructions and Regulations for the Militia and the Volunteers of the United States: Comprehending the Exercises and Movements of the Infantry, Light Infantry, and Riflemen; Cavalry and Artillery; together with the Manner of Doing Duty in Garrison and in Camp, and the Forms of Parades, Reviews, and Inspections, as Established by Authority for the Government of the Regular Army.* Philadelphia: Robert P. Desilver.

1837 Kastner, Jean-Georges. *Traité général d'instrumentation.* Paris.

1848 Kastner, Jean-Georges. *Manuel général de musique militaire*. Paris: Didot Frères.

1854 Scott, Winfield. *Infantry Tactics: or Rules for the Exercise and Manuvres* [sic] *of the United States Infantry*. 3 vols. New York: Harper.

1862 Casey, Silas. *Infantry Tactics, for the Instruction, Exercise, and Maneuvers of the Soldier, a Company, Line of Skirmishes, Battalion, Brigade, or Corps d'Armme*. 3 vols. New York: Van Nostrand.

1867 Upton, Major General Emory. *A New System of Infantry Tactics, Double and Single Rank*. New York: Appleton. Revised in 1880.

1876 Pontigny, Victor de. "On Kettledrums." *Proceedings of the Musical Association*, 2, (London): 48 ff.

1908 Cleather, G. Gordon. "The Timpany, with Special Reference to Their Use with the Organ." London (two lectures for the Galpin Society).

1927 Baggers, J. "Les timbales, le tambour et les instruments à percussion." In *Encyclopédie de la musique et dictionnaire du Conservatoire*. Part II, vol. 3. Paris.

1955 Spinney, Bradley. *Encyclopedia of Percussion*. 2 vols., letters "A" and "B." Hollywood, Calif.: Spinney.

II. Timpani Books

1650 Friese, Friedrich. *Ceremoniel und Privilegia der Trompeter und Pauker*.

1685 Philidor, André. *Pièces de trompettes et timbales à 2, 3 et 4 parties*. Paris: Bellard.

1705 Philidor, André, and Jacques Philidor. *Partition de plusieurs marches*. Paris?: Philidor Frères.

1795 Altenburg, Johann. *Versuch einer Anleitung zur heroisch-musikalischen Trompeter-und Pauker-Kunst*. Halle: Joh. Crist. Hendel. Reprint, Dresden: Bertling, 1911. Translated by Edward H. Tarr, Nashville: The Brass Press, 1974.

1842 Boracchi, Carlo Antonio. *Manuale pel timpanista*. Milan: Luigi di Giacomo Picola.

1845 Kastner, G. *Méthode complète et raisonnée de timbales*. Paris: Schlesinger.

1848 Reinhardt, Fr. *Der Paukenschlag*. Mehlis: Johann Christoph Klett.

1849 Pfundt, Ernst G.B. *Die Pauken*. Leipzig: Breitkopf und Härtel. 2nd ed., rev. and enl. by Friedrich Hentschel, 1880, *Pauken-Schule*. 3rd rev. ed., edited by H. Schmidt, 1894.

1862 Fechner, George *Die Pauken und Trommeln*. Weimar: B.F. Voigt.

1894 Deutsch, Adolph. *Pauken-Schule zum Selbst-Unterricht geeignet* (Tutor for Kettle-drum for Self-Instruction). Leipzig: Carl Merseburger.

1895 Seele, Otto. *Pauken-Schule zum Selbstunterricht*. Leipzig: Breitkopf und Härtel (Zimmermann/C.F. Peters).

1897 Flockton, J.M. *New (Complete) Method for the Side Drum, Xylophone, and Timpani*. Boston: Jean White. Reprint, New York: Carl Fischer, 1908.

1898 Bower, Harry A. *The Imperial Method for the Drums,*

Timpani, Bells, etc. Cincinnati: John Church.

1902 De Ville, Paul. *Universal Method for the Drum (Snare and Bass), Timpanies, Xylophone . . . etc.* New York: Carl Fischer.

1904–08 Eichler, M. *Theoretische-praktische Schule für Pauken, Becken, Triangle.*

1909–13 Knauer, H. *Kleine Paukenschule.* Edited by Gerhard Behsing. Leipzig: Hofmeister. 2nd ed. (C.F. Peters/Zimmermann/AMP).

1909–13 Strauss, Richard. *Orchesterstudien aus seinen Bühnenwerken.*

1911 Bower, Harry A. *The Bower System for Percussion.* Vol. 3, *Timpani.* New York: Carl Fischer.

1912 Wagner, Richard. *Orchesterstudien aus seinen Werken.* In Paul Merkelt, *Pauken-Schule* (see above).

1914–18 Merkelt, Paul. *Pauken-Schule. Praktische Anleitung zur Bedienung sämtlichet Schlaginstrumente.* Hamburg: Domkowsky & Co.

1919 Gardner, Carl E. *Modern Drum Method.* New York: Carl Fischer.

1927 Glassman, Karl. *Art of Timpany Playing, Home Study Course.* 2nd ed. 2 vols. New York: Glassman.

1930 Kristufek, Otto, and Joseph Zettelman. *The Ludwig Timpani Instructor.* Edited by William F. Ludwig. Chicago: Ludwig and Ludwig.

1942 Krüger, Franz. *Pauken und kleine Trommel-Schule mit Orchesterstudien.* Edited by Kurt Schiementz. 2nd ed. Berlin: Arthur Parrhysius, 1951.

1943 Sietz, Frederick. *Modern School of Tympani Playing.* Elkhart, Ind.: Leedy.

1945 Whistler, Harvey S. *Elementary Method for Tympani.* Chicago: Rubank.

1948 Goodman, Saul. *Modern Method for Tympani.* Melville, N.Y.: Belwin-Mills.

1948 Kupinsky, K.M. *Szkola dlia udarnych instrumentor* (School/Tutor for Percussion Instruments). 2 parts. Moscow/Leningrad.

1948? Passerone. *Traits difficiles tires d'oeuvres symphoniquis et dramatiques . . .* Preface by Claude Delvincourt. 2 vols.; and Test, *Éxercices d'epreuves de technique pour 4 timbales.* Paris.

1953 Berg, Sidney. *Belwin Tympani Method.* New York: Belwin-Mills.

1954 Friese, Alfred, and Alexander Lepak. *The Alfred Friese Timpani Method.* New York: Henry Adler (Belwin-Mills).

1954 Torrebruno, Luigi. *Il timpano: Technica dello strumento ad uso dei compositori, del direttori l'orchestra e degli esecutori.* Milan: G. Ricordi.

1957 Ludwig, William F. *Timpani Instructor.* Chicago: W.F.L. Drum Co. (Ludwig Music). 2nd ed., 1964; 3rd ed., 1979.

1957 Pieranzovini, Pietro. *Method for Timpani.* Edited by Luigi Torrebrunno. Milan: G. Ricordi (original edition from late nineteenth century).

1957 Shivas, Andrew. *The Art of Tympanist and Drummer.* London: Dobson.

n.d. Friese: 78 rpm record tutor?.

n.d. Schwar. *Method for Timpani.*

n.d. Sternburg, Simon. *Timpani Method.* Boston?

III. Tutors of Marching and Military Styles

1700 Danish *Fife, Drum, and Bugle Manual.*

1760? *The Drummer's Instructor. . . .* London: R. Spencer.

1769 *Spanish Drum Book Containing the Points of War and Two-Part Fifing.*

1777 Winter, George L. *Kurze Anweisung das Trommel-Spielen.* Berlin: G.L. Winters Wittwe.

1790 *The Young Drummer's Assistant.* London: Longman & Broderip.

1808 Mann, Herman. *The Drummer's Assistant: Instructions for Beating English and Scotch Duties.* Dedham, Mass.

1810 Hazeltine, Daniel. *Instructor in Martial Music, Containing Rules and Direction for the Drum and Fife.* Exeter, N.H.: C. Norris & Co.

1811 Robbins, Charles. *The Drum and Fife Instructor.* Exeter, N.H.: C. Norris & Co.

1812 Ashworth, Charles Stewart. *A New Useful and Complete System of Drum Beating.* Washington, D.C.

1815 Porter, Rufus. *The Martial Musician's Companion.* Porter.

1815 Potter, Samuel. *The Art of Beating the Drum.* London: Samuel Potter.

1815 Weston, Nathan. *The Young Drummer's Assistant.* New York: N. Weston.

1817 Chaine, V.A. *The Drummer's Manual.* London: Lafleur.

1817 Rumrille, J.L., and H. Holton. *The Drummer's Instructor . . . or Martial Musician (Containing Rudiments, Rules, Duties, Instructions for Bass Drum, and Fife Collection).* Albany: Packard & Van Benthuysen.

1818 Lovering, Levi. *The Drummer's Assistant, or the Art of Drumming Made Easy.* Philadelphia: J.G. Klemm (Bacon & Co.?).

1818 Robinson, Alvan, Jr. *Massachusetts Collection of Martial Musick.* Hallowell, Maine: E. Goodale.

1820 Robinson, Alvan, Jr. *Massachusetts Collection of Martial Musick.* 2nd ed. Exeter, N.H.: Author.

1826 Robinson, Alvan, Jr. *Massachusetts Collection of Martial Musick.* 3rd ed. Hallowell, Maine: Glazier.

1850 *Tamplini Drum Major.* Great Britian.

1853 Klinehause, George D. *The Manual of Instruction for Drummers, on an Improved Plan.*

1859 Keach and Burditt. *The Modern School for the Drum.* Boston: Ditson.

1861 Howe, Elias. *United States Regulation Drum and Fife Instructor.* Boston: E. Howe.

1861 Keach, Burditt, and Cassidy. *The Army Drum and Fife Book.* Boston: Ditson.

1862 Bruce, George B. *The Drummer's and Fifer's Guide.* New York: Firth, Pond & Co.

1862 Hart, H.C. *New and Improved Instructor for the Drum.* New York: Author, 1862.

1864 Nevins, William. *Army Regulations for Fife, Drum & Bugle.* Chicago: Root & Cady.

1869 *Ditson Drum and Fife Tutor.* Boston: Ditson.

1869 Strube, Gardiner A. *Strube's Drum and Fife Instructor.* Washington, D.C.: Adjutant Generals' Office. Reprint, Street, Md. Cousin, Sally Ann, 1990.

1880–85 Kling, Heinrick. *Trommel-Schule.*

1886 Sousa, John Philip. *Book of Instruction for the Field-Trumpet and Drum.* Washington, D.C. Reprint, Chicago: Ludwig Drum Co., 1954.

1887 Potter, H. *Drum Major's Manual.* London: H. Potter & Co.

1904 *Simplicity Tutor for the Drums.* London: Hawkes & Sons.

1905 De Ville, Paul. *The Eclipse Self-Instructor for Drums.* New York: Carl Fischer.

1905 Winner, Septimus. *Eureka Method for the Small Drum and Glockenspiel.* Boston: Ditson.

1909 Langey, Otto. *Tutor for Side Drum.* London: Hawkes & Sons.

1916 Safranek, V.F. *Complete Instructive Manual for Field Trumpet and Drum.* New York: Carl Fischer. Revised 1918.

1917 Straight, Edward B. *American Drummer.* Chicago: Frank's Drum Shop.

1918 Gardner, Carl E. *Military Drummer.* New York: Carl Fischer.

1923 Straight, Edward B. *Drum Corps Method.* Oak Park, Ill.: Straight.

1925 Moeller, Sanford A. *The Art of Snare Drumming.* Chicago: Ludwig & Ludwig Drum Co. Reprint, 1939, 1941, 1950.

1929? *Carl Fischer's Drum, Fife, and Bugle Corps Leaflets.* 7 vols., 3 and 6 for snare drum. New York: Carl Fischer.

1931 Stone, G.L. *Military Drum Beats.* Boston: Stone.

1933 Heney, John J. *The Correct Way to Drum.* St. Augustine/Deland, Fla.: Heney.

1935 De Ville, Paul. *Universal Bugle and Drum Manual.* New York: Carl Fischer.

1935 *A Fife, Drum and Bugle Vade Mecum for Teachers.* New York: Carl Fischer.

1935 McKenzie, A.T. *Best Select Album for Fife and Drum Corps.* New York: Carl Fischer.

1935 Martin, William. *Regimental Fife and Drum Album.* New York: Carl Fischer.

1935 *National Fife and Drum Album.* New York: Carl Fischer.

1937 Berger, Fritz R. *Basel Drum Tutor.* Basel: Berger.

1937 Moore, J. Burns. *The Art of Drumming as Taught by J. Burns Moore.* New Haven, Ct.: Gold-Moore. Reprint, Chicago: Ludwig Drum Co., 1954.

1947 Berger, Fritz R. *Das Basler Trommeln, vollständiger Lehrgang nebst einer Sammlung aller Basler Trommelmärsche.* Basel: Berger.

n.d. Berger, Fritz R. *Tambour-Ordonnanz, Lehr- und Marschbüchlein. Uebungstafeln im 6/8 Takt.* Basel: Berger.

n.d. Berger, Fritz R. *Uebungstafeln im 2/4 Takt;*

Werden und Wesen des Basler Trommelns. Basel: Berger.

n.d. Berger, Fritz R. *Vereinfachungstabelle zum Gebrauch der Marschsammlung mit einfachen Grundlagen.* Basel: Berger.

IV. Snare, Side Drum, Total Percussion, and Drum Set

1780? Gehot, Joseph. *Complete Instruction for Every Musical Instrument*. London.

1844? Ernst, J. *Theorie zum Trommel-Unterricht.*

1880 Pepper, J.W. *J.W. Pepper's Self Instructor for the Snare Drum (Side Drum).* Philadelphia: Pepper.

1880 *White's New Method for the Side Drum, Xylophone, Timpani, etc.* Boston: Jean White.

1886–91 Franke. *Trommel-Schule.*

1891 Kietzer. Op. 89, *Trommel-Schule*. Frankfurt am Main: Zimmermann.

1886–91 Kling, H. Op. 402, *Das Gesammtgebiet der Schlaginstrumente*. Hanover: Louis Oertel (Hamburg).

1892–97 Fromann, C. *Schule für Trommel.* Hamburg/Leipzig: Domkowsky & Co.

1892–97 Harnisch, E. *Schule für Wirbel-Trommel.*

1892–97 Wahls, H. *Trommel-Schule.*

1895 Pares, G. *Instruments à Percussion*. Paris: Chez Henry Lemoine et Cie.

1897 Flockton, J.M. *New (Complete) Method for the Side Drum, Xylophone, and Timpani*. Boston: Jean White. Reprint, New York: Carl Fischer, 1908.

1898 Bower, Harry A. *The Imperial Method for the Drums, Timpani, Bells, etc.* Cincinnati; New York; London: John Church.

1898–1903 Berger, Heinrich. *Marsch-Album für Piccolo und Trommel.*

1898–1903 Gottlob, Ph. *Marsch-Album für kleine Flöte und Trommel.*

1898–1903 Helmreich, A. *Trommel-Schule.*

1898–1903 Seele, Otto. *Schule für kleine Trommel*. Leipzig.

1900 Langey, Otto. *Carl Fischer's New and Revised Tutor for Drum, Xylophone, Timpanies, and Castanets*. New York: Carl Fischer. Reprinted in 1948.

1900 Ryan, Sidney. *Ryan's True Drum Instructor.* Cincinnati; New York; London: John Church.

1902? De Ville, Paul. *Universal Method for the Drum (Snare and Bass), Timpanies, Xylophone, Cymbals, Glockenspiel (Bells), Triangle, Tambourine, etc.* New York: Carl Fischer.

1904 *Tutor for the Drums (Timpani, Side Drum, and Bass).* London: Hawkes & Son.

1904–1908 Eichler, M. *Theoretisch-praktische Schule for kleine und grosse Trommel.*

1904–1908 Neuland, E. *Trommelschule* (also album for drum and fife).

1904–1908 Wahls, H. *Neue praktische Trommelschule.*

1904–1908 Zabke, M. *Turner-Flöte und Trommelschule.*

1909 Straight, Edward B. *American School of Double Drumming*. Oak Park, Ill.: Straight.

1909–1913 Berger, H. *Lieder-Märsche für Trommelpfeife und Trommel.*

1909–1913 Bohm, M. *Marsch-Album für Piccoloflöte (Trommelpfeife) und kleine Trommel.* Frankfurt am Main: Zimmermann.

1909–1913 Merkelt, P. *Volkstümlich bearb. Trommelschule.* Hamburg/Leipzig: Domkowsky & Co.

1909–1913 Wassiljew, A. *Praktische Schule für kleine Trommel.*

1909–1913 Zenker, O. *Album für 2 Trommelflöten und 1 Trommel.*

1910 *Orchestral Drummer.* White-Smith Co.

1911 Bower, Harry A. *The Bower System for Percussion* (Vol. 1, *Drums*; Vol. 2, *Bells and Xylophone*; Vol. 3, *Timpani.*) Boston: Bower. Reprinted, New York: Carl Fischer.

1913 Knauer, H. *Kleine Trommelschule.* Leipzig: Hofmeister.

1914? Erdlen, Herm, and Paul Merkelt. *Universal-Schlagzeug-Schule.* Hamburg/Leipzig: Domkowsky & Co.

1914–1918 Merkelt, P. *Schlagzeug-Schule. Praktische Anleitung zur Bedienung sämtlicher Schlaginstrumente.* Hamburg/Leipzig: Domkowsky & Co.

1917 *Drumming Successfully Taught by Mail. Drum Beats Illustrated and Analysed by Means of Actual Moving Picture Photographs.* Boston: International Cornet School, Inc.

1919 Gardner, Carl E. *Gardner Modern Drum Method.* New York: Carl Fischer.

1920 McGeary, Robert E. *The Yankee Doodle Method Simplified Self-Instructor for the Drum.*

1921 Wittman, G. *Méthode élémentaire pour casse claire.* Paris: Evette and Schaeffer.

1921 Wittman, G. *Méthode élémentaire pour casse tambour.* Paris: Evette and Schaeffer.

1921 Wittman, G. *Méthode élémentaire pour grosse claire.* Paris: Evette and Schaeffer.

1922 Rinne, Herman H. *The Herman H. Rinne Correspondence School of Modern Drumming.*

1922 Straight, Edward B. *Straight's Modern Syncopated Rhythms for Drums.* Chicago: Frank's Drum Shop.

1923? Straight, Edward B. *Straight's De-Luxe Drum Solos.* Chicago: Frank's Drum Shop.

1923 Straight, Edward B. *The Straight System of Modern Drumming Analysis 6/8 Time.* Chicago: Frank's Drum Shop.

1923 Straight, Edward B. *The Straight System of Drumming.* Chicago: Frank's Drum Shop.

1923 Straight, Edward B. *The Straight System of Modern Drumming, Lesson File.* Chicago: Frank's Drum Shop.

1923 Thomas, J. *EeasyZ Method, How to Play the Drums, Bells, and Xylophone.*

1924 Foden, William. *Paramount Method for Drums, Bells and Xylophone.* New York: William J. Smith Music Co.

1924 Johnson, Harry. *The Modern Drummer; a Complete and Simplified Self Instructor for the Professional and Amateur*

	Drummer of Today, Not Yesterday. Vol. 1. Chicago: Zipperstein and Johnson.
1925	Gardner, Carl E. *Progressive Studies for Snare Drum*. 5 vols. New York: Carl Fischer.
1925	Clark, Eugene V. *Clark Method of Study for the Drummer* ("with two Victor Records and practical hints for Timpany and Xylophone"). Syracuse, N.Y.: Clark.
1927	Kritzler, C. *Mathima Method of Drumming*. Brooklyn, N.Y.: Kritzler.
1927	*N.A.R.D. Drum Solos*. Chicago: Ludwig Drum Co.
1927	Scott, Andrew V. *Ludwig Elementary Drum Method*. Chicago: Ludwig & Ludwig.
1928	Adkins, H.E. *Boosey & Company's Complete Modern Tutor for Drums, Xylophone, Tubaphone, Glockenspiel, and Accessory Instruments*. London: Boosey & Co.
1928	Dodge, Frank E. *Dodge Drum Chart for Reading Drum Music*. Boston: Stone & Son.
1928	Dodge, Frank E. *Dodge Drum School for Drums, Bells, Xylophone and Tympani*. Edited by G.L. Stone. Boston: Stone & Son.
1928	Snow, Frank A. *The Frank A. Snow Instructions of Rudimental Drumming*. Indianapolis: Leedy.
1929	Lincoln, Eddie. *The Wright Drum Tutor*. Compiled by Eddie Lincoln. London.
1929	Ludwig, William F. *Drum Technique in the Band and Orchestra. The School Drummers' Manual*. Chicago: Ludwig & Ludwig Drum Co.
1930	Scott, Andrew V. *The Leedy Beginner's Drum Method*. Indianapolis: Leedy.
1931	Class, H.C. *The Art of Drumming*. Cleveland: Class.
1931	Lagas, Nic. *Moderne methode voor kleine trom, door Nic Lagas*. New York: Alpha Music.
1931	Rackett, Arthur H. *Fifty Years a Drummer*. Elkhorn, Wis.: Rackett.
1932	Rominger, O.F. *The Rominger Drum Method*. New York: Carl Fischer.
1934	Prescott, G.R. *The Snare Drum*. New York: Carl Fischer; Minneapolis: Paul Schmitt.
1934	Rollinson, T.H. *Rollinson's Modern School for the Drum*. Boston: Ditson (distributed by Presser).
1935	Stone, George Lawrence. *Stick Control for the Snare Drum*. Boston: Stone & Son.
1935	Yoder, Paul. *Rubank Elementary Method*. Chicago: Rubank.
1936?	Bauduc, Ray. *150 Progressive Drum Rhythms*. New York: Bregman, Vocco & Conn.
1937	Bauduc, Ray. *Dixieland Drumming*. Chicago: Ludwig Drum Co.
1937	Prescott, Gerald R. *Prescott Technic System*. 3 vols. New York: Carl Fischer; Minneapolis: Paul Schmitt.
1938	Harr, Haskell W. *Haskell W. Harr Drum Method*. Chicago: M.M. Cole.
1938	Krupa, Gene. *Drum Method*. New York: Big Three.
1939	*Academic Method*. New York: Carl Fischer.
1939	Harr, Haskell W. *Haskell W. Harr's Drum Solos*. Chicago: M.M. Cole.

1939 Knapp, Roy C. *Fundamentals of Modern Drumming.*

1939 Sternburg, Simon. *Modern Drum Studies.* New York: Alfred.

1939 Wersen, Louis G. *Rhythmic Foundation Through Drumming.* New York: Carl Fischer.

1940 Berryman, Grace, and Joe Berryman. (Several method books published during the 1940s and 1950s, exact dates unknown.) *Four Fundamentals of Snare Drumming. Percussion Section Rehearsal* (4 vols.). *Der Schnoopnager Drum Instructor. Easy Street Beats. Rudimental Street Beats. Novel Street Beats.* Itta Bena, Miss.: Band Shed.

1940 Berryman, Joe. *Carl Fischer Basic Method for Drums.* New York: Carl Fischer.

1940 Buggert, Robert. *Rubank Intermediate Method.* Chicago: Rubank.

1940 Clark, Eugene V. *The Legionnaire Drummer.* Chicago: Chart.

1940 Melnik, Henry. *Universal's Fundamental Method.* New York: Universal.

1940 Mitchell, Harland C. *Mitchell's Drum Solos.* Park Ridge, Ill.: Kjos.

1940 Podemski, Benjamin. *Podemski's Standard Drum Method.* New York: Belwin-Mills.

1940–41 Rowland, Sam. *Percussion Technique.* 5 vols. New York: O. Pagani & Bros.

1940 Scott, Andrew V. *Drummology.* New York: William J. Smith.

1940 Scott, Andrew V. *Leedy Beginners Drum Method.* Indianapolis: Leedy.

1940 *Technical Manual 20–250.* Washington D.C.: War Department.

1941 Buggert, Robert W. *Buggert Method for Snare Drum.* 2 vols. New York: Belwin-Mills.

1941 Cole, Cozy. *Cozy Cole Modern Orchestra Drum Techniques.* New York: Belwin-Mills.

1941 Wilcoxon, Charles S. *Modern Rudimental Swing Solos.* Cleveland: Wilcoxon.

1942 Clasgens, George E. *Strokes and Taps.* Utica, N.Y.: Clasgens.

1942 Gardner, Carl E. *Reading Lessons for the First Year Drummer.* New York: Belwin-Mills.

1942 Ludwig, William F. *Elementary Dance Drumming.* Chicago: Ludwig Drum Co.

1942 Ludwig, William F. *Swing Drumming.* Chicago: Ludwig Drum Co.

1942 Ludwig, William F. *Wm. F. Ludwig Collection Drum Solos.* Chicago: Ludwig Drum Co.

1942 Ludwig, William F. *W.F. Ludwig Drum Instructor.* Chicago: Ludwig Drum Co.

1942 Rich, Buddy and Henry Adler. *Modern Interpretation of Snare Drum Rudiments.* New York: Embassy (distributed by Consolidated).

1942 Tallmadge, Irving, and Clifford Lillya. *56 Progressive Duets.* New York: Belwin-Mills.

1944 Donnelly, J.J., and V.L. Mott. *Martial Album.* New York: Carl Fischer.

1944 *Regimental Fife and Drum Album.* New York: Carl Fischer.

1944 Wilcoxon, Charley. *Drum Method.* Cleveland: Wilcoxon.

1945 Wettling, George. *America's Greatest Drum Stylists.* New York: Capital Songs (Criterion).

1945 Wilcoxon, Charley. *The All-American Drummer.* Cleveland: Wilcoxon.

1946 Krupa, Gene. *The Science of Drumming.* 2 vols. Robbins.

1946 Meunier, Herman. *Boosey & Hawkes Instruction Course; Drums.* Edited by Joseph E. Skornicka. London: Boosey & Hawkes.

1946 Ostling, Acton E. *Three R's for Snare Drum.* New York: Belwin-Mills.

1946 Wettling, George, and Brad Spinney. *Professional Drum Studies for Dance, Radio & Stage.* New York: Capital Songs (Criterion).

1946 Whistler, Harvey S. *Rubank Advanced Method.* Chicago: Rubank.

1947 Tough, Dave. *Dave Tough's Advanced Paradiddle Exercises.* New York: Mutual.

1947 Whistler, Harvey S. *Reviewing the Rudiments.* Chicago: Rubank.

1948 Buggert, Robert. *110 Progressive Etudes for Snare Drum.* 2 vols. New York: Belwin-Mills.

1948 Chapin, Jim. *Advanced Techniques for the Modern Drummer.* New York: Chapin.

1948 Kupinsky, K.M. *Szkola dlia udarnych instrumentor* (School for Percussion Instruments). 2 parts. Moscow/Leningrad.

1948–58 Ulano, Sam. *Bass Bops*; *The Drummer's Rudimental Guide*; *Rudi Bops*; *Photo Hand Study Guide*; *Drummers' Roll Study Guide*; *Practical Guide for the Working Drummer*; *ABC Guide to Drumming*; *San Ulano's Solo Guide*; *Foot Development.* New York: Ulano (Lane).

1949 Blanc, Manny, and David Gornston. *Drum Warm-Ups.* Miami: Hansen.

1949 Deems, Barrett. *Drummer's Practice Routine.* Miami: Martin Dixon.

1949 Harr, Haskell W. *Simplified Drum Solos.* Chicago: M.M. Cole.

1949 Harris, Ernest E. *The Solo Drummer.* New York: G. Ricordi.

1949 Marrero, Ernesto. *Drumming the Latin American Way.* New York: Marks.

1949 Morales, Humberto. *Latin-American Rhythm Instruments and How to Play Them.* New York: Adler.

1949 Pace, Ralph C. *Variations of Drumming.* White Plains, N.Y.: Drum Book Music.

1950 Cheyette, Irving, and Edwin M. Salzman. *3-Way Method—Percussion (Bells), Intermediate Band Musicianship.* New York: Leeds Music Corp.

1950 Christian, Bobby. *Bobby Christian Modern Drum Studies for Sight Reading.* Chicago: Christian.

1950 Christian, Bobby. *First Modern School of Percussion.* Chicago: Bobby Christian.

1950 Collins, Myron D. *The Snare Drum at School.* 10 vols. Hollywood, Calif.: Highland Music (Johnson-Hoffman).

1950 Gardner, C.E. *Roll Exercises for the First Year Drummer.* New York: Belwin-Mills.

1950 Grant, Phil. *All American Drummer*. New York: Mercury.

1950 Perrilloux, Eric. *40 Rudimental Drumbeats*. New York: Perrilloux.

1951 Alden, Charles. *The Drum-O-Wheel*. Boston: Alden.

1951 Bellson, Louis. *6 Concert Drum Solos and 4 Duets*. New York: Gornston.

1951 Pace, Ralph C. *Supplementary Drum Study for the Beginner*. White Plains, N.Y.: Drum Book Music.

1951 Wilcoxon, Charley. *Wrist & Finger Control for the Advanced Drummer*. Cleveland: Wilcoxon.

1952 Collins, Myron D. *March and Drum*. San Diego, Calif.: Johnson-Hoffman.

1952 Freiburger, Donald S. *Hide Hits*. FitzSimmons.

1952 Wilcoxon, Charley. *The Junior Drummer*. Cleveland: Wilcoxon.

1953 Schinstine, W. *Futuristic Drum Solos*. San Antonio, Tex.: Southern.

1953 Schinstine, W., and Fred Hoey. *Drum Ensembles for All Occasions*. San Antonio: Southern.

1954 Cole, Cozy. *A Complete Modern Drum Method*. Revised by Cozy Cole and William V. Kessler. Associated Music Publishers.

1954 Price, Paul. *Six Advanced Snare Drum Exercises*. New York: Music for Percussion.

1954 Schinstine, W. *Little Champ Drum Solos*. San Antonio, Tex.: Southern.

1955 Buck, Lawrence. *Buck Elementary Method*. Park Ridge, Ill.: Kjos.

1955 Goldenberg, Morris. *Modern School for Snare Drum*. New York: Chappell.

1955 Harr, Haskell W. *Very Easy Drum Solos*. Chicago: M.M. Cole.

1955 Parnell, Jack. *Drums*. 2 vols. New York: Boosey & Hawkes.

1955 Price, Paul. *Beginning Snare Drum Method*. New York: Morris. Revised ed., New York: Music for Percussion.

1955 Price, Paul. *Triangle, Tambourine and Castanets*. New York: Music for Percussion.

1955 Schinstine, W. *Southern Special Drum Solos*. San Antonio, Tex.: Southern.

1955 Sternburg, Simon. *Drumming in Five Easy Steps*. New York: New Sounds.

1955 Sturtze, Earl S. *The Sturtze Drum Instructor*. New York: Schirmer.

1956 Manne, Shelly. *Shelly Manne Drum Folio No. 1*. New York: Contemporary (Music for Percussion).

1956 Mott, Vincent L. *Evolution of Drumming*. Miami: Charles Hansen. (Reprint, Paterson, NJ: Music Textbook Co., 1957.)

1956 Shanahan, Dick. *Music Book for Drummers Only*. Hollywood, Calif.: Drum City.

1956 Sholle, Emil. *The Big 230 for Snare Drum*. Cleveland Heights, Ohio: Brook.

1956 Sternburg, Simon. *Drumming Made Easy (Easy Steps to Drumming)*. New York: New Sounds.

1956 Ward, Frank E. *Drumcraft*. New York: New Sounds.

1957 Christian, Bobby. *Bop Solos Exposed*. Chicago: Bobby Christian/Frank's Drum Shop.

1957 Colgrass, Michael. *Six Unaccompanied Solos for Snare Drum.* New York: Schirmer.

1957 Hoey, Fred. *A Round of 6/8 Drum Solos.* San Antonio, Tex.: Southern.

1957 Lamond, Don. *Design for the Drum Set.* New York: Adler.

1957 Perry, Charles. *Introduction to the Drum Set.* 2 vols. New York: Adler.

1957 Sholle, Emil. *The Roll for Snare Drum.* Cleveland Heights, Ohio: Brook.

1957 Tourte, Robert. *Méthode de tambour.* Paris: Editions Salabert.

1958 Burns, Roy, and Lewis Malin. *Practical Method of Developing Finger Control.* New York: Adler.

1958 Duetsch, M. *Scheduled Drum Warm-up.* New York: New Sounds.

1958 Fennell, Frederick. *The Drummer's Heritage.* New York: Carl Fischer.

1958 Heim, Alyn J. *Drum Class Method.* 2 vols. New York: Belwin-Mills.

1958 Kinyon, John. *Breeze-Easy Method for Drums.* New York: H. Witmark.

1958 Krupa, Gene, Cozy Cole, and William V. Kessler. *Modern Drum Rhythm.* New York: Belwin-Mills.

1958 Reed, Ted. *Progressive Steps to Syncopation for the Modern Drummer.* Clearwater, Fla.: Reed.

1958 Schinstine, W. *Drumming Together.* San Antonio, Tex.: Southern.

1958 Simons, Charles "Chuck." *Happy Drumming with a Beat.* Robbins.

1958 Spector, Stanley. *Stanley Spector Lessons in Improvisation for the Drummer.* Boston: Spector.

1958 Tiemann, A.G. *Seven Rudiments for the Beginning Drummer.* New York: Pro-Art.

1959 Hall, Rex T. *Twenty Flam Etudes for the Snare Drum.* Detroit: Instrumental Music Center.

1959 Ludwig, William F. *Modern Jazz Drumming* (Swing Method). Chicago: Ludwig Drum Co.

1959 Pratt, John S. *Ancient Rudimental Snare and Bass Drum Solos.* New York: Belwin-Mills.

1959 Pratt, John S. *14 Modern Contest Solos.* New York: Belwin-Mills.

1959 Sholle, Emil. *Here's the Drum.* 2 vols. Cleveland Heights, Ohio: Brook.

1960 Leidig, Vernon F. *Concert Percussion Techniques and Method.* Highland Music.

1960 Pratt, John S. *26 Standard American Drum Rudiments.* New York: Belwin-Mills.

1960 Prentice, Harold F. *Champion Drum Book.* New York: Belwin-Mills.

1960 Schinstine, W., and F. Hoey. *Basic Drum Method (Including Cymbals and Bass Drum).* San Antonio, Tex.: Southern.

n.d. Fischer, Joe. *Rhythmische Übungen und Breaks für verschiedene Schlaginstrumente nebst kurzen Spielanweisungen.* Frankfurt am Main: Zimmermann (C.F. Peters).

n.d. *Kent Drum Method.*

n.d. Little, Eric. *Premier Modern Tutor for Drum, Cymbals and Accessories.* England: Premier Drum Co.

n.d. Mariani, G. *Metodo popolare per tamburo.* Milan: G. Ricordi & Co. (Rome: Edizioni Ricordi).

n.d. Paisner, Ben. *Practical Part Playing for Drums.* New York: Gornston.

n.d. Wenskat, R. *Schule für Jazz-Schlagzeug.* Frankfurt am Main: Zimmermann (C.F. Peters).

V. Mallet or Keyboard Instruments

1695 Paradossi, Giuseppe. *Modo facile di suonare il sistro nomati—il timpano.* Bologna. 2nd ed. of G.B. Ariosti's manual (Bologna, 1686).

1878 Escher, Charles F., Jr. *Popular Melodies and Instructions for Playing Escher's Improved Xylophone or Wood and Straw Instrument.* Philadelphia: Escher.

1880 *White's New Method for the Side Drum, Xylophone, Timpani, etc.* Boston: Jean White.

1880–1885 Lohr. Op. 99, *Neue Schule.*

1885 Roth, Albert. Op. 34, *Neue Schule (Méthode de xylophone).* Vevey, Switzerland: Agence Internationale à Vevey.

1886–91 *Der Xylophonist.*

1886–91 Hertel, Julius. Op. 60, *Xylophone-Schule zum Selbstunterricht.* Leipzig: Hofmeister.

1886–91 Roth, A. *Metodo* (same as 1885?).

1886–91 Steffen. Op. 116, *Xylophone-Schule.*

1892 Langey, Otto. *Method for Xylophone.* Philadelphia: Harry Coleman.

1892–97 Seele, Otto. *Album für Xylophone Solo od. m. Piano.* Frankfurt am Main: Zimmermann (C.F. Peters lists three albums for xylophone and piano, and one for xylophone alone).

1897 Flockton, J.M. *New (Complete) Method for the Side Drum, Xylophone, and Timpani.* Boston: Jean White. Reprint, New York: Carl Fischer, 1908 (contains solos copyrighted in 1886–1898.)

1898 Bower, Harry A. *The Imperial Method for the Drums, Timpani, Bells, etc.* Cincinnati; New York; London: John Church. (Theodore Presser?).

1898 Seele, Otto. *Album für Xylophone allein.* Frankfurt am Main: Zimmermann (C.F. Peters).

1898–1903 Jantzen, M.A. *Xylophone-Schule.* Hamburg/Leipzig: Domkowsky & Co.

1898–1903 Leonhardt, E. *Album für Glockenspiel (Lyraphon, Metallophon).* Frankfurt am Main: Zimmermann.

1898–1903 Rosé, L. *Schule für Tubaphon.*

1898–1903 Rosé, L. *Xylophone-Schule.*

1898–1903 *Solo-Buch.*

1900 De Ville, P. *Universal Method for the Drum (Snare and Bass), Timpanies, Xylophone, Cymbals, Glockenspiel (Bells), Triangle, Tambourine, etc.* New York: Carl Fischer.

1901 *National Self Teacher for Xylophone.* Warner.

1902 *Carl Fischer's New and Revised Tutor for Drum, Xylophone, Timpanies, and Castanets.* New York: Carl Fischer.

1903 Kling, Heinrich. *Leichtfassliche praktische Schule mit vielen Uebungs- und Vortragsstücken.* Hanover: Oertel.

1903 Solobuch Nr. I. *33 Konzert- und Vortragsstücke.* Hanover: Oertel.

1903 Solobuch Nr. II. *30 Konzert- und Vortragsstücke.* Hanover: Oertel.

1904–08 *Der Xylophone Soloist, mit Harmonie-Musik.*

1906 De Ville, Paul. *Universal Method for Xylophone, "The World's Edition."* New York: Carl Fischer.

1906 Rollinson, T.H. *Rollinson's Modern School for the Drum, Timpani, Xylophone, etc.* Boston: Ditson. (Also published in separate volumes.)

1908 De Ville, Paul. *Recreations for Xylophone.* New York: Carl Fischer.

1908 De Ville, Paul. *Xylophone Player's Solo Repertoire.* New York: Carl Fischer.

1908 *Recreations—A Collection of Solos for Xylophone.* (Later editions contain solos copyrighted in 1910 and 1916.) Boston: Cundy-Bettoney; New York: Carl Fischer.

1909 Merckel, A. *Schule für Glockenspiel.* Hamburg/Leipzig: Domkowsky & Co.

1909–13 Eichler, M. *Neue praktische Schule.*

1909–13 Förster, A. *Solisten-Album für Xylophone und Piano.* Frankfurt am Main: Zimmermann (C.F. Peters).

1909–13 Köhler, R. *Schule für Glockenspiel (Lyra, Metallophon, etc.).*

1909–13 Merkel, W.R. *Schule für Glockenspiel (Lyra, Metallophon, Tubaphon, etc.).*

1909–13 Strauss, Richard. *Orchesterstudien aus seinen Bühnenwerken.*

1910 Rollinson, T.H. *Rollinson's Modern School for Orchestra Bells.* Boston: Ditson.

1911 *The Bell Soloist, A Collection of 20 Selected Solos for Orchestra Bells, with Piano.* (Appendix of the Carl Fischer *Tutor for Bells.*) New York: Carl Fischer.

1911 Bower, Harry A. *The Bower System for Percussion.* Vol. 2, *Bells and Xylophone.* Boston: Bower. Reprint, New York: Carl Fischer.

1911 De Ville, Paul, ed. *Carl Fischer's Celebrated Tutor for Bells (Glockenspiel) and Cathedral Chimes with Appendix of 20 Modern Solos for Bells* (*The Bell Soloist*) (reprinted 1950). New York: Carl Fischer.

1912 Fisher, Charles. *Course of Instruction for Bells and Xylophone.* 50 graded lessons. Chicago: Charles Fischer.

1917 Deagan, J.C. *Deagan Musical Dinner Chime Music.* Chicago: Deagan. 2nd ed., 1939.

1918 Rollinson, T.H. *Twelve Bell Solos.* Boston: Ditson.

1919 Gardner, Carl E. *Gardner Modern Drum Method.* Part 2, *Bells, Xylophone, Marimba and Chimes.* New York: Carl Fischer.

1920 Ambrosio, W.F. *Xylophone Instruction and Study.* New York: Carl Fischer.

1922 Green, George H., and Joe Green. *Green Brothers' Beginning Method for Xylophone*. Indianapolis: Leedy.

1922 Jones, M.L. *Special Lesson on Harmony Ragtime*. Lesson 14 of the mail order course from Deagan. Chicago: National School of Vibracussion.

1924 Green, George H., and Joseph Green. *Advanced Instructor*. New York: Green.

1924 Warner. *Warner's Very Easy Method for Xylophone*.

1924–26 Green, George H. *50 Lessons* (Instruction Course for Xylophone). New York: Green.

1925 *Hawkes & Sons Simplicity Instruction Book for the Xylophone*. London: Hawkes & Sons.

1927 *Weidt's Chord System*. How to "Fill in," Improvise, etc. Newark, N.J.: Weidt.

1928 Adkins, H.E. *Boosey & Company's Complete Modern Tutor for Drums, Xylophone, Tubaphone, Glockenspiel, and Accessory Instruments*. London: Boosey & Co.

1929 Green, G.H., arr. *George Hamilton Green's Xylophone Solos of Famous Sam Fox Successes*. Cleveland: Sam Fox.

1931 Thompson, Harry C. *Elementary Instructor for Vibraphone and Vibra-Celeste*. Indianapolis: G.B. Tuthill/ Leedy.

1933 Hampton, Lionel. *Hampton's Folio for Vibes*. Leo Feist (Robbins).

1933 Hampton, Lionel. *Lionel Hampton's Method for Vibraharp*. New York: Robbins.

1933 Hampton, Lionel. *Method for Vibraharp and Xylophone*. New York: Big Three (Robbins).

1933 Norvo, Red. *Feist No. 1 All-Star Series of Modern Rhythm Choruses*. New York: Robbins.

1933 Norvo, Red. *Robbins All-American Modern Rhythm Choruses*. New York: Robbins.

1933 Seele, Otto. *Xylophone, Tubaphon, Vibraphon-Schule, zum Selbstunterricht geeignet*. Frankfurt am Main: Zimmermann (C.F. Peters). Reissued from original with "vibe" section added; see 1898.

1934 Black, Clyde E. *Play Quick Method for Drums (Bells, Chimes, Marimba, and Xylophone)*. Black.

1934 Rollinson, T.H. *Rollinson's Modern School for the Drum*. Boston: Ditson. (Presser). Contains xylophone section.

1936 Breuer, Harry. *Xylophone Technique*. New York: Hansen/Alfred.

1936 Green, George Hamilton. *New Elementary Studies for Xylophone and Marimba*. Elkhart, Ind.: Leedy and Ludwig (Leedy Drums/C.G.)

1936–37 Green, George H. *New Series of Individual Instruction Courses for Xylophone & Marimba, Modern Improvising and Application of Ideas to Melody*. New York: Green.

1937 Greene, Howard A. *Marimba Method*. Kansas City, Missouri: Jenkins.

1937 Jolliff, Art. *Intermediate Method for Marimba, Xylophone, or Vibes*. Chicago: Rubank.

1937 Peterson, H. *Xylophone and Marimba Studies for 3 and 4 Mallets*. Chicago: Rubank.

1938 Farnlund, E. *The Howell-Aretta System of Modern Marimba Study*. 50 lessons. Glendale, Calif.: Howell & Aretta.

1938 Harr, Haskell. *Marimba and Xylophone Method*. Chicago: M.M. Cole.

1938 Herman, Sammy, arr. *Modern Hot Xylophone Solos*. 2 vols. New York: Belwin-Mills.

1938 Musser, C.O., and Paul Yoder. *Modern Marimba Method for Beginners*. Park Ridge, Ill.: Kjos.

1938 Peterson, Howard M. *Rubank Elementary Method for Xylophone or Marimba*. Chicago: Rubank.

1939 Knapp, Roy C. *Fundamental Rudiments of Mallet Technique and Timpani Tuning*. Chicago.

1939 Musser, C.O., and Paul Yoder. *Modern Vibraharp Method for Beginners*. Park Ridge, Ill.: Kjos.

1939 Prescott, Gerald R. *Prescott Technic System*. Vol. 2. *Bells and Xylophone*. New York: Carl Fischer.

1940 Harr, H. *Intermediate Grade Marimba & Vibe Solos*. Chicago: Cole.

1940 Harr, H. *Intermediate Grade Solos for Marimba or Xylophone (2 Hammers) with Piano*. Chicago: Cole.

1940 Luscomb, Cornelia. *Marimba Ensemble Folio*. Chicago: Rubank.

1940 Musser, C.O. *Master Works for the Marimba*. Chicago: Forster.

1940 Musser, C.O. *Master Solo Arrangements for Vibraphone, Vibraharp, and Vibra-Celeste. Four Folios*. Chicago: Gamble Hinged.

1940 Peterson, H. *Keyboard Harmony for Xylophone, Marimba, and Vibes*. Chicago: Rubank.

1940 Quick, J.B. *Soloist Folio for Marimba or Xylophone*. Chicago: Rubank.

1940 Whistler, Harvey S. *Elementary Method for Bell Lyra*. Chicago: Rubank.

1940 Whistler, Harvey S., and Art Jolliff. *Pares Scales for Marimba, Xylophone, or Vibes*. Chicago: Rubank.

1941 Hiraoka, Yoichi. *Xylophone Album*. New York: Marks.

1942 Buggert, Robert W. *Buggert Method for Xylophone and Marimba*. Book 1. New York: Belwin-Mills.

1945 Paisner, Ben. *30 Studies in Swing for Marimba, Vibes, or Xylophone*. New York: Gornston.

1948 Huffnagle, Harry. *Streamlined Etudes for Xylophone and Marimba*. 2 vols. New York: Gornston.

1948 Jolliff, Art. *Music for Marimba*. 3 vols. Chicago: Rubank.

1948 Peterson, Howard M. *Basic Steps in Marimba Study*.

1949 Bower, Bugs. *New Sounds for Vibes*. Colin (Charles H. Hamsen Music).

1949 Jolliff, Art. *78 Marimba Solos*. 2 vols. New York: Belwin-Mills.

1949 Kupinsky, K., arr. *Collection of Pieces from Compositions of Russian and Soviet Composers*. Moscow.

1944–49 Farnlund, Emil. *Lowe Marimba Method.* Series of 20 lessons. Flint, Mich.: Lowe Publishing Co. First published in Los Angeles, Calif.: Marimba Publishing Co.

1950 Goldenberg, Morris. *Modern School for the Xylophone, Marimba and Vibraphone.* New York: Chappell.

1953 Dorn, William. *A Simple and Practical Method for Xylophone, Marimba, and Bells.* New York: Schirmer.

1953 Streslin, William. *New Method of Velocity for Xylophone, Marimba, and Vibraphone.* New York: Carl Fischer.

1956 Kupinsky, K. *Five Pieces Transcribed for Xylophone and Piano.* Moscow/New York: Leeds Music Corporation/MCA.

1957 Huffnagle, Harry/David Gornston. *Melody Way to Syncopation, C Instruments.* New York: Gornston.

1958 Payson, Albert. *Progressive Studies in Double Stops, for Mallet Instruments.* Chicago: Payson.

1958 Schaefer, Florence. *Xylophone and Marimba Method.* Vol. 1. New York: Harms (Adler).

1960 Krauss, Phil. *Mallet Method.* Edited by Doug Allen. 3 vols. New York: Harms.

n.d. Bower, Bugs. *Ad Lib.* Colin.

n.d. Bower, Bugs. *Bop Combo (Vibes).* Colin.

n.d. Bower, Bugs. *Bop for Xylophone & Vibes.* Colin.

n.d. Bower, Bugs. *Chord and Chord Progression.* 2 vols. Colin.

n.d. Cohn, Al. *Jazz Workshop.* Colin.

n.d. Colin, Charles. *Advanced Dance Studies.* Colin.

n.d. Colin, Charles. *35 Original Studies in Modern Rhythm.* Colin.

n.d. Colin, Charles, and Bugs Bower. *Rhythms.* 2 vols. Colin.

n.d. Davis, H. *All Melody Band Folio.* Chicago: Rubank.

n.d. DeLamater. *Utility Collection.* Chicago: Rubank.

n.d. Deven/Hurd. *George Deven's Lesson Plan for Mallet Instruments.* New York: Harms (Adler).

n.d. Gornston, David. *All Chords for Xylophone.* New York: Gornston.

n.d. Gornston, David. *Foundation Studies for Xylophone, Marimba, and Vibes.* New York: Gornston.

n.d. Gornston, David, and Ben Paisner. *Playing with Chords.* New York: Gornston.

n.d. Harr, Haskell. *Marimba and Xylophone Method (Intermediate).* Leedy.

n.d. Hartung, F. *Schule für Vibraphone und Marimba.*

n.d. Herfurth, Paul. *A Tune A Day—Book I.* Boston: Boston Music.

n.d. National School of Vibracussion (J.C. Deagan)—*Home Study Course.* 14 lessons. Chicago: Deagan.

n.d. Pease, Donald J. *Bell Lyra and Orchestra Bell Method.* Chicago: Payson.

n.d. Peterson, Howard M. *Marimba Solo Classics.* Boston: Boston Music.

n.d. Pooles, Carl. *Jazz for Seniors.* (duets).

n.d. Rushford, George. *Miniature Melody Band Method for Xylophone.* 2 vols. Rushford Music.

n.d. Rushford, George. *Rushford Solo & Duet Album*. Rushford Music.

n.d. Stone, G.L. *Mallet Control for the Xylophone (Marimba, Vibraphone/Vibraharp)*. Boston: Stone.

n.d. Van Deusen. *Elementary Band Course*. Chicago: Rubank.

n.d. Wechter and Henry Adler. *Play Vibes*. New York: Harms (Henry Adler).

James Strain

Index